NINTH EDITION

Integrating Music into the Elementary Classroom

William M. Anderson
Joy E. Lawrence

Kent State University

Australia • Brazil • Japan • Korea • Mexico • Singapore • Spain • United Kingdom • United States

Integrating Music into the Elementary Classroom, Ninth Edition
William M. Anderson, Joy E. Lawrence

Publisher: Clark Baxter
Development Editor: Kate Scheinman
Assistant Editor: Elizabeth Newell
Editorial Assistant: Rachael Bailey
Media Editor: Chad Kirchner
Brand Manager: Molly Felz
Market Development Manager: Joshua Adams
Senior Content Project Manager: Lianne Ames
Art Director: Faith Brosnan
Print Buyer: Julio Esperas
Senior Rights Acquisition Specialist: Jess Elias
Production Service: MPS Ltd.
Text Designer: Glenna Collett
Cover Designer: Richard Hannus @ hannusdesign.com
Cover Image: © Ellen Senisi (top), © Ritchie Photographic, F.P. Inc. (middle and bottom)
Compositor: MPS Ltd.

Library of Congress Control Number: 2012943489

ISBN-13: 978-1-133-95797-3

ISBN-10: 1-133-95797-8

Cengage Learning
20 Channel Center Street
Boston, MA 02210
USA

Cengage Learning is a leading provider of customized learning solutions with office locations around the globe, including Singapore, the United Kingdom, Australia, Mexico, Brazil and Japan. Locate your local office at **international.cengage.com/region**

Cengage Learning products are represented in Canada by Nelson Education, Ltd.

For your course and learning solutions, visit **www.cengage.com**

Purchase any of our products at your local college store or at our preferred online store **www.cengagebrain.com**

Instructors: Please visit **login.cengage.com** and log in to access instructor-specific resources.

Printed in the United States of America
1 2 3 4 5 6 7 16 15 14 13

Contents

SONG INDEX

P = Pentatonic

SONG INDEX

On line	Spotify Playlist	Song Title	Grade Level	Key	Range	Meter	Integrative Category	Page
	✔	Five Green and Speckled Frogs	K-3	C	C1-D2	4/4	Nature, Math	43, 417
	✔	Five Little Pumpkins	K-3	F	C1-D2	4/4	Halloween, Nature	27
	✔	Follow the Drinkin' Gourd	4-6	Em	B-D2	2/2	American spiritual, Civil War, Underground Railroad, Astronomy	419
	✔	Frère Jacques	K-3	G	D1-E2	4/4	France	113
✔		Galway Piper	5-6	D	A-D2	4/4	Ireland	315
	✔	Gatatumba	3-6	C	B-A1	2/4	Spain	382
		Go A Tin	1-3	Am	E1-A1	4/4	Taiwan, New Year	408
✔		Go Down, Moses	2-6	Am	E1-E2	4/4	American spiritual	53
✔		Go, Tell It on the Mountain	3-6	F	C1-D2	4/4	American spiritual	107
	✔	Good News	K-2	G	G1-B1	4/4	American spiritual	126
✔		Hahvah Nahgeelah	4-6	Gm	B♭-D2	4/4	Israel	252
		Hanukkah Is Here	K-1	Dm	D1-A1	4/4	Israel, Hanukkah	394
		Hello, There!	K-1	C	C1-B1	2/4	America	76
✔		He's Got the Whole World in His Hands	2-4	D ***P***	D1-B1	4/4	American spiritual	110, 151
	✔	Hickory Dickory Dock	K-2	F	F1-D2	6/8	Early American, Nursery rhyme	46
	✔	Hokey Pokey, The	K-2	G	D1-G1	4/4	America, Movement	372
✔		Home on the Range	2-6	F	C1-C2	6/8	America West	51
	✔	Hot Cross Buns	K-1	G	G1-B1	2/4	England	38
✔		I Wish I Were a Windmill	K-2	F	C1-C2	4/4	Movement	241
✔		If You're Happy	K-1	F	C1-B1	4/4	Action, Movement	374
	✔	I'm Gonna Sing When the Spirit Says Sing	K-6	G	D1-C2	4/4	American spiritual	239
✔		I've Been Working on the Railroad (Dinah)	2-6	G	D1-E2	4/4	Railroad, History	423
✔		Jack-ó-Lantern	1-2	D	D1-D2	3/4	Germany	81
	✔	Jingle Bells	3-6	G	D1-E2	2/4	Early American, Christmas	87
	✔	Joy to the world						46
	✔	Jolly Old Saint Nicholas	K-2	G	D1-B1	2/4	Christmas	136, 398
✔		Keeper, The	4-5	D	C1-D2	4/4	England	108
	✔	Kye, Kye Kule	1-2	B♭ ***P***	B♭-C1	4/4	Africa, Ghana	289

P = Pentatonic

SONG INDEX

On line	Spotify Playlist	Song Title	Grade Level	Key	Range	Meter	Integrative Category	Page
✔		La Cucaracha	4-6	G	D1-E2	3/4	Mexico, Spanish	251
	✔	La Raspa	3-5	G	B-B1	4/4	Mexico, Spanish	325
		Las Posadas Songs	2-4	C	C1-C2	2/4, 3/4	Mexico, Christmas	399
		Let's Make a Jack-o'-Lantern	1-3	F	A-D2	4/4	Halloween	389
	✔	Lift Every Voice and Sing	4-6	G	B-E2	6/8	Kwanzaa	403
	✔	Lightly Row	1-2	G	G1-D2	2/4	Germany	126
		Listen to the Wind	1-2	F ***P***	F-C2	3/4	Germany	76
		Little Marionettes	K-2	G	D1-D2	2/4	France, Movement	240
✔		Little Shoemaker, The	K-3	F	C1-D2	4/4	Movement	230
	✔	Little Tommy Tinker	K-2	D	D1-D2	4/4	Early American, Movement	228
		Lonesome Rider Blues	4-6	D ***P***	D1-A1	4/4	America, Blues	330
✔		Looby Loo	K-1	F	F1-C2	6/8	England, Movement	80
✔		Lullaby	2-3	C	C1-C2	3/4	Germany	36
		Martin Luther King	2-6	D	D1-D2	4/4	African-American, U.S. history	407
	✔	Mary Ann	2-3	C	B-G1	4/4	Trinidad, Calypso	150
	✔	Mary Had a Little Lamb	K-1	G	G1-B1	4/4	Early American, Nursery rhyme	125
✔		Merrily We Roll Along	K-1	C	C1-G1	4/4	Early American	59, 135
	✔	Michael Finnegan	3-4	F	C1-C2	2/4	Children's game song, Movement	89
✔		Michael, Row the Boat Ashore	1-3	C	C1-A1	4/4	American spiritual	126
		Mister Turkey	K-1	G	E1-D2	4/4	Thanksgiving, Movement	391
✔		More We Get Together, The	4-5	D	A-B1	3/4	Germany	57
		Mos', Mos!	1-3	C	C1-G1	2/4	Native American, Hopi	318
✔		Muffin Man	K-2	G	D1-B1	4/4	England	137, 152
	✔	Mulberry Bush, The	K-1	G	D1-D2	6/8	England, Movement	244
✔		My Big Black Dog	K-1	F	C1-D2	4/4	England, Animals	376
✔		My Hat	K-2	C	C1-C2	3/4	Germany	59
	✔	O Come, All Ye Faithful (Adeste, Fideles)	4-6	G	D1-D2	4/4	Christmas, Latin	400
✔		O Hanukkah	3-6	Dm ***P***	C#1-D2	4/4	Israel, Hanukkah	396

P = Pentatonic

SONG INDEX

On line	Spotify Playlist	Song Title	Grade Level	Key	Range	Meter	Integrative Category	Page
✔		O Susanna	3–6	F	F1–D2	2/4	Civil War, Movement	49, 250
	✔	Ode to Joy (Ninth Symphony)	3–6	G	D1–D2	4/4	Twentieth Century	137
	✔	Old Colony Times	3–6	F	C1–B1	4/4	Early American, History	412
	✔	Old MacDonald Had a Farm	K–2	G ***P***	D1–B1	4/4	United States	48, 416
✔		Old Texas	3–6	G	E1–E2	2/4	American West	105
	✔	On Springfield Mountain	4–6	G	D1–C2	3/4	U.S. history, Civil War	414
✔		Over the River and Through the Wood	3–6	C	C1–C2	6/8	Thanksgiving	392
✔		Peddler, The (Korobushka)	3–6	Dm	D1–D2	2/4	Russia	141
	✔	People on the Bus, The	K–2	G	D1–D2	4/4	United States, Movement	227
✔		Piñata Song (Al Quebrar la Piñata)	4–6	C	B–D2	3/4	Mexico, Spanish, Christmas	437
✔		Pop, Goes the Weasel	K–3	C	C1–D2	6/8	England, Movement	248
	✔	Rain, Rain, Go Away	K–1	Em	E1–G1	2/4	Chant	136, 138
	✔	Reveille	1–3	G	D1–B1	2/4	United States	45
✔		Rock-a My Soul	4–6	D	D1–B1	4/4	American spiritual	163
	✔	Roll On, Columbia	4–6	F	C1–C2	3/4	River, Geography	384
✔		Round and Round the Village	K–3	F	C1–C2	2/2	United States, Movement	247
	✔	Row, Row, Row Your Boat	2–4	C	C1–C2	6/8	America	46, 60
	✔	Sakura	3–4	E ***P***	B–C2	2/4	Japan	302
		Salamanca Market	3–5	C	C1–C2	2/4	Australia	106
	✔	Samiotissa	4–6	G	D1–E2	7/8	Greece, Movement	309
✔		Shalom, Chaverim	3–6	Em	B–E2	4/4	Israel	149
✔		Shenandoah	4–6	D	A–D2	4/4	River, Geography, Transportation	386
✔		Shoemaker's Dance	K–2	F	C1–C2	2/4	Denmark, Movement	247
✔		Simple Gifts	4–5	F	C1–C2	2/4	Shaker	65
	✔	Six Little Ducks	K–1	F	C1–D2	4/4	Animals	377
	✔	Skip to My Lou						136
		Somebody Loves Me	K–2	C	C1–C2	4/4	Valentine, Friendship	410

M = Mixolydian *P* = Pentatonic

On line	Spotify Playlist	Song Title	Grade Level	Key	Range	Meter	Integrative Category	Page
✔		Song of the Volga Boatmen	4–6	F#m **Ph**	D1–D2	4/4	Russia	308
✔		Star-Spangled Banner, The	3–6	A♭	A♭–E♭2	3/4	U.S. patriotism	47
	✔	Starlight, Starbright	K–1	Em	E1–A1	2/4	Chant	139
	✔	Steal Away	2–6	F ***P***	F–D2	4/4	American spiritual	55
✔		Sweet Betsy from Pike	2–4	C	C1–C2	3/4	American West	50, 140
✔		Swing Low, Sweet Chariot	3–6	F	C1–D2	4/4	American spiritual	264, 328
	✔	There Are Many Flags	4–6	A♭	C1–C2	4/4	U.S. patriotism	432
✔		There's a Fiesta	4–6	G	B–C2	3/4	Spain	313
✔		This Old Man	K–1	F	F1–D2	2/4	Nursery rhyme	136, 142, 263
	✔	Tideo	2–3	D	D1–D2	2/4	Singing game	98
	✔	Tinga Layo	2–4	C	C1–C2	2/4	West Indies, Calypso	82
	✔	Tue, Tue	3–4	F ***P***	F1–D2	4/4	Africa, Ghana	287
✔		Twelve Days of Christmas, The	3–6	F	C1–D2	4/4	England, Christmas	103
	✔	Twinkle, Twinkle, Little Star	K–1	C	C1–A1	2/4	Nursery rhyme	365
	✔	We Gather Together	4–6	C	C1–D2	3/4	Holland, Thanksgiving	393
	✔	We Shall Overcome	2–6	C	C1–D2	4/4	African-American, U.S. history	406
✔		We Wish You a Merry Christmas	1–6	A	E–E2	3/4	England, Christmas	61
✔		We're America's Children	4–6	C	C1–E2	4/4	U.S. patriotism	279
✔		When Johnny Comes Marching Home	3–6	Em	B–B1	6/8	U.S. history, Civil War	196
✔		Wild Bird (Kagome)	1–3	Am	E1–B1	2/4	Japan, Movement	243
		Witch Rides, The	K–1	Dm	D1–D2	6/8	Halloween	388
✔		Yankee Doodle	2–5	G	B–C2	2/4	U.S. patriotism, Revolutionary War	135, 364
✔		Yankee Doodle Boy	4–6	G	D1–D2	2/4	U.S. patriotism, twentieth century	431
✔		You're a Grand Old Flag	4–6	F	C1–C2	2/4	U.S. patriotism	433
✔		Zum Gali Gali	4–6	Em ***P***	B–B1	2/4	Israel	112

Ph = Phrygian *P* = Pentatonic

Preface

Most elementary schools in the United States require that students receive instruction in music. Although large numbers of schools benefit from music specialists, responsibility for teaching music often falls to the classroom teachers. Even in schools with formally trained music teachers, the amount of time these specialists spend with students is quite small compared with the total time students spend with their classroom teachers.

Most classroom teachers try to teach music (along with other subject areas), but many have a limited understanding of how music can be made to "fit" with the rest of the elementary program. Thus, there continues to be a need for a practically oriented book that illustrates how music can be taught and integrated into other areas of the elementary school curriculum.

Integrating Music into the Elementary Classroom, Ninth Edition, emphasizes the importance of enriching children's lives by making music a central part of the school curriculum. This book provides guidelines for elementary teachers with limited experience as well as for music specialists.

Integrating Music into the Elementary Classroom, Ninth Edition, is comprehensive, covering music fundamentals as well as materials and methods for teaching music in the elementary classroom. The book focuses on how children learn and presents easy-to-use techniques for teaching singing, playing instruments, moving to music, creating music, listening critically, and integrating musical study with the arts and other subject areas.

Integrating Music into the Elementary Classroom, Ninth Edition, provides the following:

- Methods for integrating music across the entire elementary school curriculum
- A contemporary approach with focus on enhancing music teaching and learning through using educational technology
- Updated book layout with photos illustrating students using technology to learn music
- Technology enhancement notes throughout the book
- Designated downloads so that a teacher can easily find materials
- Increased use of Internet resources, especially from major orchestra websites
- Updated focus on helping students meet national and state music standards
- Large number of sample lessons
- Introduction to selected methodologies of Dalcroze, Kodaly, and Orff
- Enhanced listening to music "icon mapping" approach
- Sections for special needs students
- Large number of songs for elementary students, including additional call-and-response songs, which have been added to approximately 125 songs selected from various cultures and historical periods
- Updated references to the current elementary school music series
- Recordings of a number of songs from the book that are available on the book's premium website, as well as listing of downloadable recordings from i-tunes and Spotify.
- Video segments that show students in classroom settings

RESOURCES

Students

Premium Website: Includes a wealth of teaching and learning resources such as chapter-by-chapter online tutorial quizzes, and weblinks for various sites referenced within the text. The *printed access card for the site* provides access to (1) audio files for over sixty of the songs included in the text, (2) classroom videos, and (3) resources for accessing additional music and video selections.

Acknowledgments

I wish to acknowledge the assistance of the following people in the preparation of this manuscript: Grant M. Anderson, Music Technology teacher, Oak Hills Local Schools, Cincinnati, for the technology enhancements and pictures; Lalene DyShere Kay, Director, Cleveland Music Therapy Consortium at Baldwin-Wallace College and the College of Wooster, for the sections on special needs students; Virginia Hoge Mead, Professor Emeritus of music education, Kent State University, for her help with Dalcroze eurhythmics; Dr. Nancy Lineburgh, Nordonia, Ohio City Schools, for assistance with the Kodály lessons; William D. Thomas, former coordinator of vocal music, Cleveland Heights/University Heights schools, for his help with interpretive movement; Kathern Mihelik and Dr. Maria Foustalieraki, for their help with folk dances; Herbert Ascherman Jr. and John Ritchie, photographers, for their assistance with the pictures; Dr. Robert Schneider, vocal music teacher, Shaker Middle School, Cleveland, Chelsey Sweatman, music teacher, Delshire Elementary School, Cincinnati, Kevin Sweatman, band and orchestra director, Rapid Run Middle School, Cincinnati, and Amy Thompson, choir director and general music teacher, Rapid Run Middle School, Cincinnati, for their help in providing students for the photographs; and finally, Steve Rashid, Woodside Avenue Music Productions, Inc., Evanston, Illinois, for the accompanying recorded songs.

I would also like to thank the following reviewers for their comments that helped to shape the ninth edition: Beth Brooks, Indiana University–Purdue University at Indianapolis; James Goodman, Boise State University; and Peggy Wolverton, Northern Kentucky University.

Special thanks to Clark Baxter, publisher; Kate Scheinman, senior development editor; Elizabeth Newell, assistant editor; Rachael Bailey, editorial assistant; Chad Kirchner, media editor; and Lianne Ames, senior content project manager. Their insight, encouragement, and patience throughout the preparation of this book are greatly appreciated.

Finally, a very special tribute to my alma maters, the Eastman School of Music and the University of Michigan School of Music, Theatre, and Dance for the superb education they provided me so many years ago. Special thanks also go to my wife Lee Ann and son Grant for their support through the lengthy endeavor of preparing the ninth edition.

William M. Anderson

Introduction

As a teacher you are about to enter one of the most exciting domains of human experience—sharing with children what you know, cherish, and love so that the quality of their relationships with others will be richer, their perceptions of the world around them deeper, and their own lives more rewarding and fulfilled. This book is for you, the classroom teacher in the elementary school. It is you who will have daily contact with children in grades K through 6 at least 5 hours a day, 25 hours a week, 900 hours a year. The formal education of a child rests in your hands. Your enthusiasm is contagious, your beliefs in life's wonders inspire, your understanding comforts, and your knowledge and skill motivate and mold the intellectual and emotional growth of the children in your classroom.

Classroom teachers have an awesome task, with responsibility in a great many subject areas, including language arts, mathematics, science, social studies, physical education, art, and music. This book is based on the belief that *every* classroom teacher can accumulate knowledge and develop skills that will enable her/him *to lead a child in meaningful experiences with music.* Each of you has particular talents. Some of you sing well; others play instruments; still others may never have sung in a choir or played an instrument but enjoy listening and dancing to music. Some of you have traveled or read a great deal and would like to share with your students music and arts of other countries and peoples. *Whatever your background, this book will help you build on your strengths to teach music and will expand your horizons so that you will be better equipped to integrate musical experiences into the elementary school curriculum.*

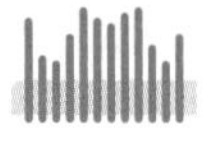

THE IMPORTANCE OF MUSIC AND OTHER ARTS IN THE ELEMENTARY SCHOOL

As you begin your study of music and develop materials for teaching, it will be helpful to ponder several questions that educators and parents often ask about the value of music and other arts in the general education of children: What is art? What is an arts experience? How does it differ from other experiences in life? Why is it important for children to have arts experiences?

At the outset it should be stated that there are many answers to the question "What is art?" When we talk about art, we are usually referring to music, painting, sculpture, dance, poetry, drama, and so on, rather than the sciences, such as physics, biology, and chemistry. Artwork expresses human feelings, such as excitement, awe, or joy. As the artist manipulates and arranges the media unique to a particular art (sounds in music, color and design in painting, and words in poetry), an expressive product emerges that we call a work of art (a musical composition, a painting, or a poem). The result is a projection of the personality and the skill of the artist, a statement of the philosophy of the age in which it is produced, and an expression of a feeling or idea that transcends anything concerned with one individual or single period of time in history.

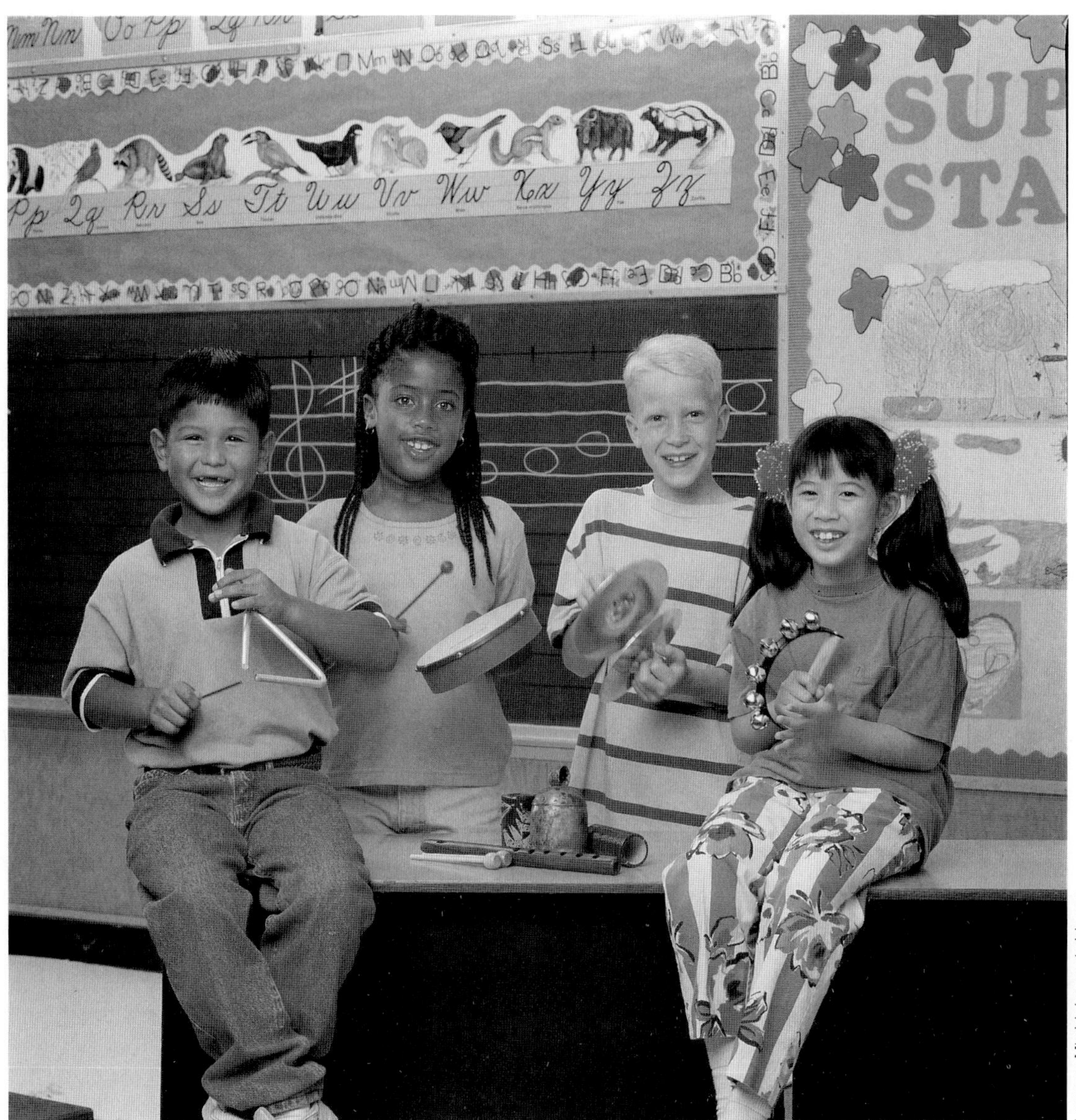

Lawrence Migdale/www.migdale.com

▲ Music can provide a deeply satisfying sense of pleasure.

In studying works of art, we need to focus our attention on some basic criteria. The first of these is *craftsmanship:* How carefully has the artist used materials (sounds, words, paint, or movement)? A second criterion is *creativity* or *imagination:* What has the artist done to create something fresh and new? How is the work *expressive?* Has the artist effectively captured a dimension of human feeling, and does this flow forth to the perceiver? As we select materials to be used in lessons for children, we will learn more about these criteria and how they can help us make decisions regarding our choice of artwork for use in the classroom.

The view taken in this book is that, in an arts experience, a person and a work of art are involved in intense interaction that creates a deeply satisfying sense of pleasure, heightened sensitivity to all dimensions of life, and a powerful feeling of self-worth and fulfillment. For instance, performances of Beethoven's *Symphony No. 9* consistently stir the hearts and minds of audiences. No matter how many times one hears this piece, it always reaches out with fresh and distinctly new meanings. This is the unique quality of a true work of art, and it is precisely here where the arts experience differs from other types of experiences. The uniqueness of artwork is its embodiment of human feeling and the potential it has of sharing that feeling with you and me. Such arts experiences are essential in the general education of every child, for through the arts the child develops his or her own expression of feelings and grows in the ability to understand and appreciate how artists throughout the world have expressed these same feelings, thus enriching the quality and the meaning of life.

WHAT RESEARCH SAYS TO CLASSROOM TEACHERS

A large body of research literature now supports the importance of music in schools by providing evidence that:

- Music is universal in every culture and time period.
- All humans possess musical ability.
- Fostering musical ability to its fullest requires early nurturing of musical potential, particularly during the years of rapid brain development.[1]
- The study of music provides students with an understanding of important aspects of their culture that are unavailable through any other means.
- There are strong links between learning in music and in other areas of the school curriculum—for example, aspects of musical note values and fractions in mathematics, and reading words and reading music.

In essence, increasing evidence supports the centrality of music in the education of all children and the importance of classroom teachers in ensuring that musical study is an integral part of the school curriculum.

Harvard University psychologist Howard Gardner's research has given particular support to the importance of music in the education of children. Gardner contends that intelligence is a broadly based concept actually including various types of intelligences. He states that these multiple intelligences include not only linguistic and logical-mathematical (often emphasized in schools) but also *musical*, spatial, bodily kinesthetic, interpersonal, and intrapersonal, to which he later added naturalistic intelligence. Gardner *encourages teachers to provide a comprehensively balanced school curriculum that assists students in developing the potential of all of their intelligences.*[2]

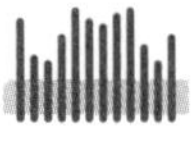

PROMOTING AN INTEGRATED APPROACH TO LEARNING AND TEACHING IN THE CLASSROOM

It is important for elementary school teachers to help students integrate knowledge across subject areas. Specialization is evident in a number of areas of the elementary curriculum, where there are teachers of reading, music, art, and physical education, and the daily schedule is organized around distinct segments such as mathematics and social studies. Although specialization

[1] See "Special Focus: Music and the Brain," in *Music Educators Journal* 87, no. 2 (September 2000), pp. 17–44.
[2] See Howard Gardner, *Multiple Intelligences: New Horizons* (New York: Basic Books, 2006).

has an important place, attention must also be directed toward fostering an integrated structure so that students develop some sense about how knowledge in one area relates to what is studied in another. If students are to learn to identify relationships among subject areas, they will need to learn from an interrelated perspective. We cannot assume that students will somehow assimilate information from various areas and then draw together the necessary integrated relationships on their own. In fact, students often do not see the most basic relationships among subject matter areas and thus must be shown how subjects are related. Teaching from such a perspective need not detract from specialized study, but it does require that classroom teachers go beyond current practices and structure curricula based on relationships within and among subject matter areas.

Integrating music into a child's daily classroom experiences has many advantages. Foremost is that children can be taught to perceive ideas that are related. For example, they can discover that fundamental musical concepts—such as enlargement through repetition, contrast, and balance—are present in many subject areas. Further, as children study music and the visual arts as part of a social studies unit on a historical period or culture, they often develop a much clearer perspective of a particular time and its people. Many children have studied the period of Washington, Jefferson, and Franklin without realizing that several of the world's greatest composers (Haydn, Mozart, and Beethoven) lived during the same time and that the minuet, the third movement in symphonies of the classical period, was also a popular dance of the American colonists. Clearly, the primary focus of this book is to encourage classroom teachers to place music in an integrated learning environment, which we believe will contribute to meaningful and long-lasting educational experiences for children.

Owen Franken/Corbis

▲ Making music part of the classroom experience

THE PLAN FOR THIS BOOK

It is important to design musical learning that focuses on multisensory experiences with music (making music, listening to music, moving to music, and reading music), as research has shown that children differ not only in the rate at which they learn but also in the way in which they learn best.

Chapter 1 focuses on how children learn music, including those students with special needs. It also focuses on the importance of national and state standards in promoting musical learning, and the role of instructional technology in enhancing instruction.

Chapter 2 suggests ways to design learning experiences appropriate to a variety of interests and levels of maturity, and ways for writing lesson plans.

Chapter 3 focuses on fundamentals of music, providing the classroom teacher with knowledge and understanding of the basic elements of music—rhythm, melody, dynamics, tone color, texture and form—on which to base musical study.

Chapters 4 through 8 are designed to provide classroom teachers with the confidence and skills needed in teaching children to sing, play instruments, listen to music, express music through movement, and create music. Included are techniques of Kodály, Orff, and Dalcroze methodologies with suggestions for integrating these approaches into the basic curriculum.

Chapter 9 begins a series of three chapters devoted to distinctive approaches to integrating music with other areas. It focuses on the study of music in a multicultural context focused on greater understanding of peoples, places, and cultures through singing, playing instruments, directed listening, and movement/dance.

Chapter 10 makes suggestions to classroom teachers for relating music and other areas of literary and visual arts, with the intent of helping students understand basic relationships between music and other art forms.

Chapter 11 focuses on thematic and content methodology for assisting classroom teachers in integrating songs with other subjects and activities. This chapter includes suggestions for planning "integrative" programs suitable for open houses or similar events, as well as for creating "resource" units that make use of several arts.

This book can be used both as a methods text for students preparing to be elementary classroom teachers and as a teaching resource in the classroom. Teachers are encouraged to keep this text available for reference and to use the many materials and teaching suggestions as they begin their careers.

© Michael Newman/PhotoEdit

▲ Leading children into the world of music

At the end of each chapter, you will find a link to suggestions for ways in which technology—including software, websites, videos, and music downloads—can be used to integrate music into the elementary classroom. The book concludes with several appendices, including basic fingerings for the recorder as well as guitar chords. A glossary is also provided, along with a song index (placed at the front of the book) that includes grade level, key, range, meter, and integrative category. Indexes of two- and three-chord songs and listening examples in the text are also provided, along with a detailed general index.

It is hoped that as you complete this book, you will have gained a new perspective on integrating music into daily learning experiences and that your students will grow in knowledge, sensitivity, and understanding of themselves and their world.

CHAPTER 1

How Children Learn

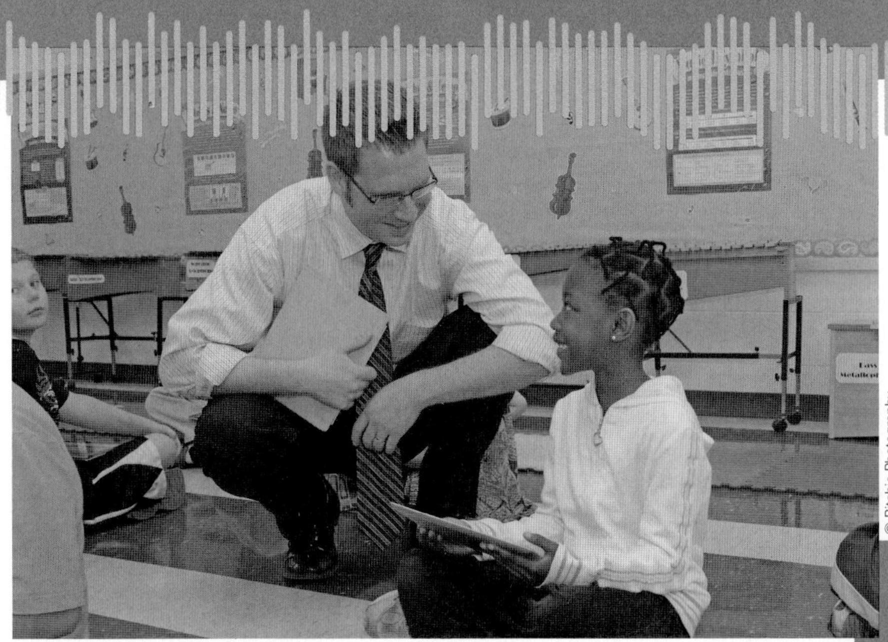
© Ritchie Photography

Objectives

Students will be introduced to fundamental ideas about teaching music:

- Basic types of learning
  - Psychomotor learning
  - Cognitive learning
  - Affective learning
  - Active learning
  - Teacher-centered and child-centered learning
- The structure of musical learning
  - Make what you teach meaningful
  - Organize material sequentially
  - Experience music before labeling it
  - Use a conceptual approach to learning
  - Use a multisensory approach to learning
  - Use a multicultural approach to learning
  - Provide reinforcement
  - Teach for transfer
- Techniques and resources for enhancing musical learning
  - Cooperative learning
  - Interdisciplinary learning opportunities
  - Community and school resources for enhancing musical learning
  - Learning for special needs students
  - The role of national and state standards in enhancing musical learning
- The place of instructional technology in supporting musical learning
  - Learning with a single computer in the classroom
  - Learning in the computer laboratory
  - Learning using tablet computers and other handheld electronics
  - Computer-based assignments extend the learning environment
  - The Internet as a learning tool
  - Downloading quality musical examples for learning

As we begin to think about teaching music to children, we must consider (1) ways children learn, (2) the principles involved in the learning process, and (3) how we apply those principles to musical learning. Although many of the ideas presented in this chapter may apply to any subject area, our interest here is to relate them to the teaching of music and to integrate learning experiences with music.

BASIC TYPES OF LEARNING

Several basic types of learning should be considered when teaching music to children. The first of these may be categorized as *psychomotor learning*—that is, learning involving mental processes that control muscular activity. A second category of learning is *cognitive learning,* which deals with the acquisition of knowledge. A third category of learning is *affective* learning, which concerns itself with a *feeling* response to music.

Psychomotor Learning

Students vary in their psychomotor learning abilities. Some children display considerable ability in singing, playing instruments, and moving to music, whereas others seem less responsive to such psychomotor learning activities. It is important for the teacher to nurture the musical potential of students regardless of their initial level of accomplishment.

Attention to developing psychomotor skills should begin early and continue as an integral part of the training children receive at more advanced levels. For example, an emphasis on movement to music is based on the premise that children should be able to physically feel and respond to musical stimuli before being asked to identify such stimuli on a cognitive level. Such an approach to musical study clearly parallels the pedagogical principle of "sound before sight."

Psychomotor learning is particularly important for training children to listen to music. Directed listening should be approached by having children physically respond to musical sounds; for example, students should learn to follow the beat and indicate changes in tempo through clapping, marching, or other physical movement. They should learn to move in either twos or threes to demonstrate duple and triple meter, and to express high and low sounds with appropriate movements. Only after students have "internalized" sounds through movement and are able to respond accurately to musical stimuli should notation and other information about music be introduced.

An important aspect of psychomotor learning of music is the need for regular practice. Children seem to learn musical skills more effectively if they practice for short periods of time interspersed with intervals of rest. Thus, efforts should be concentrated on a specific task (such as singing, playing an instrument, or listening to music) for a short time each day rather than for a long time once or twice a week.

It is obvious that the classroom teacher is in a better position to help students with skill development because the formal music teacher may see students only once or twice a week. If children are to receive the frequency of training needed for optimum development of musical skills, classroom teachers must allow time in the daily schedule for such skill development.

Cognitive Learning

In terms of music, we ask children to learn about such things as elements of music, composers, style periods, and instruments. One of the most important concerns in cognitive learning is for information about music to be closely linked with actual musical experiences. Children need to have many experiences with sounds to understand musical information. For example, in teaching about 4/4 meter, the teacher may tell students that a quarter note receives one beat, a half note two beats, and a dotted half note three beats. Such information does not take on full meaning, however, until it is placed in an actual musical experience in which students clap or march as they count the beats in various note values.

One of the practical problems teachers must deal with in cognitive learning is that information must be in language that children can easily understand. Teachers must be particularly aware of the *level of language* to be used when presenting information to students at various grade levels. An effective way of dealing with problems of musical terminology is to use diagrams, symbols, or pictures. Often a child can more easily understand rondo form (ABACA; see p. 62) from a diagram, such as ● ■ ● ▲ ●, than from several minutes of words spoken by the teacher.

Affective Learning

If music is to be important in children's lives, the teacher needs to be aware of how music expresses human feeling. Children should experience music in such a way that they are increasingly aware of how composers have used sound to express deep inner feelings, which, like ideas, have transcended the peoples, places, and cultures of many different eras. For example, as students learn to move to the long, flowing melody in Smetana's *The Moldau* [iTunes/Spotify] and learn the folk song on which it is based, they should experience the power and feeling generated by the minor tonality of this melody. In *affective learning* students experience through an art form inseparable mixtures of feelings that words cannot begin to express. This education in the *feeling* expressed in musical artworks becomes a cornerstone on which all musical teaching and learning are based.

Active Learning

All learning needs to be *active:* children need to respond to music by moving, singing, playing instruments, and creating. Linking information about music with actual musical sound encourages children to be actively involved with musical learning. Through such involvement they seem to assimilate and retain information more effectively and to exhibit greater interest and motivation to learn. For example, a teacher wishing to present rondo form to students must go beyond simply diagramming the form with letters (ABACA) on the writing board and telling students to listen for a recurring section of music (A) that alternates with contrasting sections of music (B, C). Children need to sing or play the melodies of various sections, engage in some type of movement to the rhythm (clapping, marching, and so on), and perhaps place letters on a writing board to identify various sections of the form as they hear them.

Teacher-Centered and Child-Centered Learning

In considering various approaches to learning music, you will want to explore both teacher-centered and child-centered methods. The *teacher-centered approach* features the teacher primarily as a lecturer who presents material to the class by *defining* and *explaining*. For example, the teacher who wishes students to learn about *duple meter* approaches the topic by telling them that *duple* means "two," that in duple meter there are, therefore, two beats in a measure, and that the first beat normally receives the greater accent. The teacher may use musical examples to illustrate the definition, but in this approach students assume a rather passive role.

By contrast, the *child-centered approach* to learning actively involves students in the learning process. In this approach the teacher presents students with a problem that needs to be solved. Under the teacher's guidance, students explore possible solutions through trial-and-error examination. The teacher guides students in their exploration, but the ultimate solution to the problem is largely student derived. For example, in presenting duple meter, the teacher first has students sing a song in duple meter, and then has them clap the beat or conduct as they sing the song again. The teacher then asks them if they can feel which beat receives the greater emphasis (first), and finally how the beats seem to group themselves. The teacher guides the students toward their ultimate understanding that the beats are grouped in twos (duple meter).

As you work with students at various age or grade levels, you will undoubtedly use both teacher-centered and child-centered approaches. Because students are more actively involved in the child-centered approach, however, teachers generally favor it, particularly when working with young children.

THE STRUCTURE OF MUSICAL LEARNING

In structuring musical learning for the classroom, you need to (1) make what you teach meaningful, (2) organize material sequentially, (3) experience music before labeling it, (4) use a conceptual approach to learning, (5) use a multisensory approach to learning, (6) use a multicultural approach to learning, (7) provide reinforcement, and (8) teach for transfer.

Make What You Teach Meaningful

You should emphasize activities that closely relate to things children perceive as interesting and meaningful. Some possibilities include capitalizing on children's interest in trains by having them listen to Villa-Lobos's "Little Train of the Caipira" or the bluegrass composition "Orange Blossom Special"; designing a unit of study on electronic music for those with interests in electronics and machines; or having them study nature through such pieces as Beethoven's "The Storm" (Symphony no. 6, fourth movement) or Smetana's *The Moldau* [iTunes/Spotify].

Organize Material Sequentially

One of the most important aspects of structuring musical learning in the classroom is to develop a successful sequence of activities. In developing plans for teaching music, you need to arrange learning experiences into a logical continuum, carefully linking each step with preceding and succeeding steps. Sequence may vary from classroom to classroom; that is, one teacher may develop a sequence of steps that proves successful in teaching certain musical concepts, whereas a second teacher who is teaching other students the same material may develop a different but equally logical sequence.

Often teachers develop several alternative plans for presenting material. In a classroom of twenty-five students, there will usually be children who have a variety of academic and musical abilities and backgrounds. Some students may have had considerable experience with rhythmic activities, for example, whereas others may have had none. In presenting a rhythmic learning experience to such a class, the teacher needs to consider several alternatives in the sequence of events undertaken by the students.

Experience Music before Labeling It

A young child may have many experiences with an apple—such as eating it, feeling that it is round, and seeing that it is green or red—long before being asked to label it with the word *apple.* Music should follow this same pattern of learning; that is, the child should have experiences with sounds by singing, playing instruments, listening to fast and slow tempos, or listening to loud and soft dynamics before being asked to place these labels (*fast* or *slow, loud* or *soft*) on these musical events. Because music is the most abstract of all the arts—that is, it passes through time and exists only in the memory—actual experiences with musical sounds are essential before discussing any specific musical concept.

Use a Conceptual Approach to Learning

Teachers have discovered that one of the most effective ways of helping students assimilate and retain information is through a conceptual approach to learning. Conceptual learning involves "students developing the ability to give a common name or response to a class of stimuli varying in appearance."[1] Teachers using a conceptual approach focus learning on certain fundamental ideas considered basic to understanding music. These include concepts of rhythm, melody, dynamics, timbre, texture, and form (see Chapter 3). For example, melody as a fundamental concept in music involves a succession of pitches that are perceived as belonging together. Melodies may vary greatly with respect to their internal characteristics, such as a differing number of pitches, various scales, movement principally by step or skip, variety of contour directions, and range. It is important, therefore, that in the classroom students experience a wide array of melodies from various historical periods in Western music and from other musical traditions around the world. They should explore characteristics of melodies through singing, playing instruments, and listening. If learning experiences are carefully organized over a period of time, students will indeed develop a concept of melody and the many characteristics it may have.

In addition to strictly musical concepts, analogous concepts are found in visual and literary arts. Among these are repetition and enlargement, contrast and variety, and balance (see Chapter 10). Each of these concepts operates in a similar fashion but through different means in various art forms. Experiencing a concept through several art forms encourages integrated learning.

Use a Multisensory Approach to Learning

Students learn through a combination of their senses. Some learn more quickly through the visual sense, which is highly developed through watching television or playing video games. A chart or musical picture provides these children with something tangible to which to relate the music. The visual image remains even though the sound may end. Others may learn more quickly by moving to the music. For example, a child might perceive triple rhythm more quickly by moving in some fashion, such as tapping his or her thighs or swaying with the beat. Another child might learn just as quickly through the aural sense—that is, by hearing a melody a second time. People have different aptitudes and talents; the skillful teacher recognizes these differences and creates lessons that involve as many of the senses as possible.

Use a Multicultural Approach to Learning

Music and the arts from different cultures contribute to our understanding of both others and ourselves. As the teacher creates lessons that involve singing and playing instruments from many musical traditions, students are encouraged to experience, respect, and appreciate the contributions of peoples, cultures, and eras different from their own. This may be true whether they are sharing music of a popular song, the black gospel tradition, or a Renaissance dance. In the United States, one of the goals of education is to broaden and appreciate our heritage of diversity. Music and other arts provide valuable insights and opportunities for such growth and development.

---

[1] Janice T. Gibson, *Psychology for the Classroom* (Englewood Cliffs, NJ: Prentice Hall, 1976), p. 243. See also "Learning and Teaching about Concepts," in Anita Woolfolk's *Educational Psychology* (Boston: Pearson Education, Inc., 2007), pp. 286–294.

Provide Reinforcement

One of the most important tasks in the learning process is to provide reinforcement for learning. Children seek to be successful at whatever they undertake, and teachers need to construct music lessons that include effective rewards.

The focus of any system of rewards should be on positive reinforcement. Positive-reinforcement techniques should be applied consistently and in a variety of ways in every musical learning experience. The proper use of praise, for example, is a powerful way of encouraging students to repeat something they have done well. Reinforcement can often be as simple as a smile. Teachers often reward by granting privileges to students who successfully complete a task. These privileges may be relatively simple, such as "Carlos, since you sang that part so well, you may now play the xylophone in this piece." Often the most effective types of reinforcement are those selected by the child. Children always have favorite things they like to do. Be sensitive and observant, and use these things as rewards for accomplishments in the classroom.

Use reinforcement techniques during music lessons to reward both musical accomplishments and good behavior. Cooperative student behavior is essential if children are to accomplish musical tasks, so you should design reward techniques to encourage productive student behavior and optimize musical learning.

One of the most important goals for music teaching is to have students learn for intrinsic as well as extrinsic rewards. The real excitement in learning about music occurs when students want to sing, play instruments, or listen to music because of the intrinsic rewards of the musical experience itself. Although you may initially feel a need to use a variety of extrinsic rewards, you should encourage students to study music just because of the pleasure it gives them. Intrinsic rewards are especially important because they stay with students long after formal school experiences have been completed.

Teach for Transfer

An essential goal in structuring musical experiences for children is *transfer*. The teacher needs to make a concerted attempt to encourage students to use what they have previously learned and relate it to what they are currently studying. For example, if in a previous lesson students identified the balance of ABA form in the song "We Wish You a Merry Christmas" (p. 61), we hope that in a succeeding lesson they will be able to transfer the concept of balance through ABA form to another piece of music.

Children should also be encouraged to transfer ideas learned about music to other studies and to settings outside as well as inside the school. For example, they should be able to recognize concepts such as repetition and enlargement, variety and contrast, and balance in the visual and literary arts and in everyday examples at school and at home. They should also have some sense of how music and composers in a particular time period are related to history, geography, and other subject areas. For example, when students listen to a piece by Mozart, they should locate Austria on a map of Europe and learn about Salzburg and Vienna, where he lived and worked. As students identify the dates when Mozart lived (1756–1791), encourage them to associate these dates with famous Americans who lived at the same time (Washington, Jefferson, and Franklin) and with events that took place then (the signing of the Declaration of Independence and the American Revolution).

One of the principal advantages of teaching for transfer is that material will often take on a greater sense of meaning for children if they can see relationships with other learning experiences. Further, if children have learned material by using it in a variety of settings, they are more likely to remember the information.

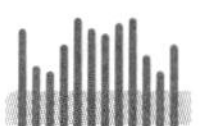

TECHNIQUES AND RESOURCES FOR ENHANCING MUSICAL LEARNING

Cooperative Learning

Cooperative learning involves organizing students into small groups to undertake together a particular learning experience. Students of varying abilities are asked to work with one another to solve problems, to study an issue, or to complete a project. For example, students may be divided into several small groups to investigate the reasons for differences in tone quality among stringed, wind, and percussion instruments. Each group is asked to construct either a stringed, wind, or percussion instrument and create a short composition demonstrating the instrument's distinctive timbre. The small-group projects can then be shared with the entire class.

In cooperative learning it is felt that slower students benefit from the challenge of working with those more advanced and that advanced students profit from helping explain things to others. The teacher in a cooperative learning setting tends not to tell students "how" but rather acts as a resource and guide for each group of students.

▲ Cooperative learning

Research has shown that cooperative learning promotes student learning and academic achievement, increases students' retention of information, enhances students' satisfaction with their learning experiences, provides greater use of higher-level reasoning skills, develops students' collaborative skills, and promotes better self-esteem, more positive heterogeneous relationships, and more on-task behavior.[2]

Interdisciplinary Learning Opportunities

The classroom teacher is in a unique position to promote interdisciplinary learning opportunities in music. Foremost, obviously, is the role of the classroom teacher in working with the special music teacher who may visit the classroom one or two times weekly. It is extremely important for the classroom and music teachers to work together so that in the intervening days when the music teacher is not present, the classroom teacher continues and enhances the musical study presented by the special teacher. Classroom teachers are uniquely positioned to be able to encourage music study done in collaboration with the art teacher, the physical education instructor, and perhaps other elementary school specialists working in such areas as English language arts, foreign languages, social studies, science, and mathematics. These subject-matter specialists are able to bring distinctive perspectives to music study. For example, classroom teachers, working with other

---

[2] See Phyllis R. Kaplan and Sandra L. Stauffer, *Cooperative Learning in Music* (Lanham, MD: Rowman & Littlefield Education, Inc., 1994); and David J. Johnson, Roger T. Johnson, and Edythe Johnson Holubec, *Cooperative Learning in the Classroom* (Alexandria, VA: Association for Supervision and Curriculum Development, 1994); available at www.amazon.com.

teachers, can encourage multi-art (e.g., music, art, dance, poetry) units of study; the examination of music in relation to a particular time period (e.g., American Independence); or the use of music to illustrate a particular science lesson (e.g., pitch related to length of strings) or mathematical concept (e.g., musical notation values). Often, collaborative, interdisciplinary teaching can lead to special school programs throughout the year.

Community and School Resources for Enhancing Musical Learning

The classroom teacher can also substantially enhance musical study by drawing on resources in the greater community. For example, teachers may plan special trips for their students to hear an outstanding orchestra, band, or chorus. Students benefit greatly from hearing and seeing live performances. They can also be taught the basic rules of concert etiquette (the importance of sitting and listening quietly, appropriate times to clap, and so on). On such trips, students also often have opportunities to engage in dialogue with the performers. Sometimes teachers find it easier to invite guest artists to their schools to perform for and talk with their students. For example, students always enjoy having an opportunity to study the bagpipes. Invite a piper (appropriately dressed in full Scottish attire, if possible) to play for the class and introduce some of the ways in which sound is produced by the instrument. Elementary classroom teachers can also take advantage of the musical groups that are already present in their own school systems. For example, high school band, orchestra, and choral directors can have their ensembles play for elementary school classes. Encourage the directors to talk about the music played by the groups and to introduce the instruments to the elementary school students (see Chapter 6).

Learning for Special Needs Students

Classroom teachers must deal with the reality of students in their classrooms who require special adaptations or accommodations because of cognitive, physical, or sensory disorders. In some cases the disorder is identified and a special individualized program is constructed to assist teachers with planning and adaptations. In other situations the child may not have an "identified" disorder but may demonstrate skills significantly below or above the average performance level—enough so that the teacher is challenged to adapt, create, or substitute experiences to maximize the child's participation in classroom learning.

Federal legislation mandates these accommodations by educators for "identified" students, and educators are trained to assist assessment professionals in identifying children who may require special services or adaptations for them to be successful in regular school programs. PL 94-142, the Education for All Handicapped Children Act of 1975, defined IEP (individualized education plan), FAPE (free and public education), and LRE (least restrictive environment) as integral components of services for special needs children. In 1990, PL 101-476, the Individuals with Disabilities Education Act (IDEA), replaced the 1975 federal legislation. It continued many of the concepts from PL 94-142, replaced the word *handicapped* with *disabled,* and outlined more specific and extensive services for special learners. In 1997 IDEA was reauthorized (PL 105-17) and additional modifications were made to the provisions for special needs students. This legislation will continue to be reviewed and amended as increases in research, information, and public awareness require more logical and effective educational methods for all public school students.

Since this legislation first began affecting programs around the country, many teacher training programs and national organizations offering continuing education have responded by adapting and creating workshops, publications, and websites to aid classroom teachers in their

© Bob Rowen, Progressive Image/CORBIS

▲ Special needs students involved in musical learning

never-ending quest to offer appropriate and meaningful learning experiences for *all* of their students. As a teacher plans adaptations for special needs students, a common ethical question often arises—"how will this affect the rest of the students in the class?" In most cases, a deliberate presentation of material, a consistent sequence of presentation and use of language, as well as the repeated practice of the skill will likely benefit (or at least will not hinder) the development of skills for typical learners.

Music is a basic human experience through which many other academic and artistic pursuits may be experienced. Music experiences are vital for *all* students. Music may be experienced at almost every level of consciousness and may provide functional (learning, memory skills), therapeutic (self-awareness, self-expression), and aesthetic (perceptual, affective integrated with cognitive) outcomes regardless of the student's functioning level. Accounts of the benefits of music for children with aural, visual, and cognitive disabilities date back to the early 1800s. Today's classroom may include children who have physical, sensory (hearing and/or visual), emotional, and cognitive disorders—each year new disorders with their respective characteristics and diagnostic criteria are reported and added to the "special needs" list. Though today's methods may be more sophisticated (supported by nearly 200 years of experience and research), there are some basic principles that pervade most of the approaches currently acknowledged as effective for special needs students. Some of these principles are as follows:

- Observe students' reactions carefully. Everyone learns differently—some learn more from visual demonstration, some learn better from explanation, and some learn best by actual physical involvement in the activity.
- A child's identified disorder may not represent his/her capabilities, interests, or current skills.
- Each child, "typical" or not, is unique, and each child's response to and interest in music is affected by much more than the "potential characteristics" of his or her disorder.

Following are some suggested guidelines for enhancing classroom music experiences for special needs students.

Students with Physical Disabilities

- Provide ample space for adaptive equipment (wheelchair, walker, and such) while maintaining the student as part of the group. Larger ambulation equipment (wheelchairs, for example) may require extra space—but avoid allotting this space in the back of the classroom where the separation may hinder the student's participation or interaction with peers.
- Create alternative ways of responding to rhythm other than walking (moving hands or head, tapping fingers, playing classroom instruments).
- Cover percussion handles with heavy carpet tape or sponges to make them bigger and easier to grasp.
- Fasten instruments to wheelchairs with notebook binder rings or Velcro to avoid students' dropping the instrument.
- Place books, charts, and instruments at a comfortable reaching and sight level for students in wheelchairs.
- Allow the student to assist/make suggestions about how to make accommodations in the music class. Often students with physical disabilities have been confronted with similar challenges in other situations and may be able to make suggestions for environmental adaptations.
- If the child is regularly seen by a physical therapist, the PT may be able to make suggestions for appropriate instruments as well as recommend appropriate physical activity.

Students with Visual Impairments

- Determine the extent of the visual impairment.
- If the student uses any aids such as a monocular, a device that the student looks through to enlarge visual material that is at a distance, make sure he or she uses the device in your class.
- Make reading material larger by using the enlarging feature on the photocopy machine.
- Keep the physical setup of the classroom the same (keep instruments, piano, chairs, and so on in the same place).
- Use tactile devices, such as rough and smooth surfaces, to aid in the playing of instruments.
- Develop the student's spatial consciousness (e.g., the location of the black and white keys on the keyboard and the frets on the guitar).
- Adapt movement activities by setting steps to number sequences (such as four steps right, two steps forward, three steps left). Visually challenged students are highly sensitive to such directions and can often learn dance steps before their sighted peers.
- Encourage visually challenged students to lead in ear-training games. Their hearing sense is generally much more acute than that of sighted students.
- Get textbooks in large print when they are available. Often there is a special budget for such aids for special needs children. Many of the music series books are available in both large-print editions and braille from the Library of Congress in Washington, D.C.

Students with Hearing Impairments

- If possible, hold class in a room with a wooden floor so that students can feel the vibrations of the music.
- Have students feel the vibrations of a drumhead and create an inner feeling of beat by following a leader's motions.

- Arrange classroom seating so that students have a full view of the teacher's face (facilitates lip reading and the ability to read facial expressions). Ensure that students are close to the front of the room to give maximum access to sound sources (CD player, piano, and so on).
- The use of earphones may enable students with hearing aids to hear the music, thus opening a world of sound to them. However, be cautioned that the volume of hearing aids and earphones may be inadvertently set too high and can potentially damage the ear. The speech therapist or audiologist should be consulted for the best settings to use for a particular student.

Gifted Students

- They learn quickly and need to be challenged often.
- They have a wide range of interests and a high energy level.
- They display a great curiosity about objects, situations, or events.
- They are persistent and independent.
- They are able to extend learning, demonstrate a broad perspective on the material being taught, and provide multiple solutions to a problem.
- They make unusual associations between remote ideas.
- They often ask provocative questions, challenging teachers and parents.
- The gifted student's broad vocabulary can be acknowledged and reinforced by encouraging lyric rewriting activities. These activities may focus on providing rhyming words, filling in words, or changing certain objects or ideas expressed in the original lyric to represent academic concepts or other themes from classroom learning objectives.
- The gifted child may pick up on "sign language" quickly and enjoy enhancing the singing of songs with this extra language. Some gifted children focus on book work and studious tasks over physical activity. Directed movement and improvised movement may offer them a creative outlet and unique challenges that they do not often encounter in typical classroom activity.

Guidelines for Musical Experiences for the Gifted Student

- **Vocal range:** Wide, usually an octave or more. Build confidence by asking students to sing syllable patterns, such as:
- **Melody:** Choose songs that are longer and are more complex than the grade level attained.

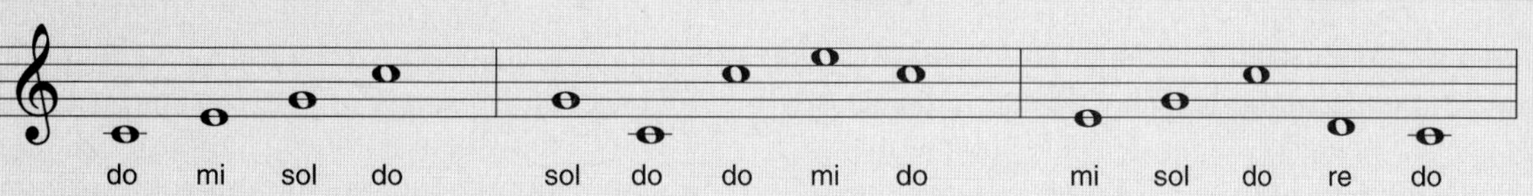

- **Rhythm:** Provide opportunities for experiences with rhythms on a variety of complexity and creativity levels. Give a gifted child extra opportunities for creating patterns.
- **Harmony:** Provide extended opportunities for playing harmony on the Q-Chord, guitar, or even the piano. A gifted student can often remember chord sequences.
- **Word meaning:** The gifted student has a broad vocabulary and can give meaning to words. When possible, choose songs that are above the chronological age of the student; for example, "This Old Man" would be too babyish for a talented first grader. When a song such as "This Old Man" is used with a gifted first grader, consider having the child make up new rhymes for the song as an extended activity.

Students with Cognitive Disorders

- They learn at a slower pace—repetition is essential and "revisiting" similar material at different times during the music class may enhance recall and enjoyment as familiarity increases.
- They often have difficulty with motor coordination.
- They need constant and immediate reinforcement.
- They have short attention spans.
- They require patience and much love and understanding.
- They are often quite affectionate and may need guidance to learn how to appropriately express their affection—especially as they get older.
- Be observant of spontaneous responses to musical presentations. These "natural" behaviors may help the teacher to understand and identify preferred music styles as well as musical skills that might represent a different functioning level (while in the music environment) than what would generally be anticipated.
- Music can be used effectively as a "classroom manager" to cue beginning and ending of activities, lunch, snacks, beginning of day (gathering or welcome song), end of day (closing song with review of day's highlights sung to a familiar tune). Music listening time can also be used as a reward for meeting certain classroom objectives.

Guidelines for Musical Experiences for Students with Cognitive Disorders

- **Vocal range:** Limited, usually within an octave and lower range. Build confidence in the lower range; then develop the upper range. Use simple syllable patterns, such as:
- **Melody:** Choose songs with small intervals and avoid large skips. Melodies with repeated patterns are often the most successful.

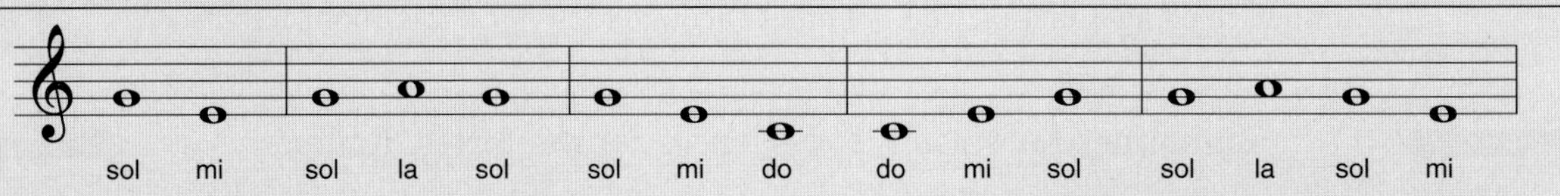

- **Rhythm**
  - Provide opportunities for experiences with rhythms on a variety of complexity levels. Allow extra time for the student to play an instrument. Example: While the rest of the class plays on beats 1, 2, 3, and 4, have the mentally challenged child play only on beat 1 or at the beginning of a line or phrase.
  - Allow the student to set the tempo of the rhythm and then follow the student. Example: Strum chords on the keyboard, Q-Chord, or guitar as the student plays a drum.
  - Allow two students, facing each other, to play a two-beat pattern on a drum. This focuses attention on one stimulus, even with the rest of the class participating (i.e., clapping), which may avoid confusion in attending to the task. You may also use the "peer model," with one of the drummers encouraging imitative response—this may also enhance the accuracy of the response.
  - Encourage students to create patterns for others to follow. The patterns can be based on classroom concepts or facts that are familiar—beat "Pres-i-dents of the U.S.A." using eighth, eighth, quarter, quarter, quarter, quarter, quarter, quarter. Also use familiar songs, students' names, days of the week, and activities of the days, for example.
- **Harmony:** Use limited chords on the keyboard, Q-Chord, or guitar. Identify chords with colors or use tactile materials (e.g., C chord = burlap, F chord = silk, G chord = velvet). Place chord names or symbols on charts and hang them around students' necks.
- **Word meanings:** Give special attention to word meanings and pronunciation. Choose songs

that are suitable for the *intellectual* age rather than the *chronological* age of the student. This is a challenge as students get older and their awareness of peer group music preferences becomes more astute. The teacher may need to seek out appropriate "pop" songs to listen to, play, and discuss as a means to guiding good music choices for these students.

- **Movement:** Proceed from large to small motor movements. Design movement activities with an emphasis on much repetition. Allow more time for the movement to occur (tempos may be somewhat slower).
- Assign or ask for willing and musically confident volunteers to help mentally challenged students who may be mainstreamed. With an able "peer model," many of these special learners may be able to function effectively in a "typical" music class; in some cases, outside/out-of-class tutoring may help to prepare the special needs student to feel confident and comfortable with the material (i.e., teaching the student music that the choir is singing so that the special needs student can participate in the school choir). Be sure to change helpers often and have a student assistant assigned to one particular activity.
- Do not talk down to students or use "baby" or "special" music; a Sousa march can draw the same strong rhythmic response from these students as from any others. However, teachers may need to modify their expectations regarding a coordinated physical response to the beat.

Students with Autism Spectrum Disorders (ASD)[3]

- Stability and predictability in activity sequence and physical environment are very important to this student.
- Attention span may be very short and may be intermittent even through the duration of a song or activity.
- Seating position may be vital to success. Placing either familiar people or no one in this student's "space" may prove to be most effective for facilitating the student's comfort and appropriate social behavior.
- These students often exhibit sensory stimulation behaviors that may distract other students—teacher may model appropriate responses for other students. These behaviors may increase when the student feels stressed or frustrated.
- Peer models are sometimes effective for helping the student begin social-skill development, keeping the student on task, and providing imitative models of the skills being used.
- Speech development is often delayed and students display echolalic responses, pronoun reversal (*you* instead of *I*), lack of verbs in sentences, and lack of reciprocal responses (saying "hello" to someone who says "hello").
- Students display sensory sensitivity, including aural (loud sounds), tactile (personal touch, even when it is unintentional), and visual (covering eyes) sensitivity.

[3] The term *autism spectrum disorders (ASD)* covers a number of different types of autism. Specifically, it describes a range of the characteristics displayed by children who have been diagnosed with autism, and the specific degree levels for each type of disorder. Classroom teachers can find additional information on the Autism Society of America's website (www.autism-society.org), which provides more specific diagnostic and current-treatment and behavioral strategies for working with this very diverse population and for planning adaptations for the classroom. Teachers are encouraged to check research cited and websites for specific information.

Guidelines for Musical Experiences for Students with ASD

- Students with ASD respond positively in music environments and often perform above their other established classroom levels when demonstrating musical skills.
- Music stimuli as a form of auditory stimulation and communication provide a more acceptable and comfortable form of expression for students with ASD. Question/answer songs and alternating lines of song lyrics are methods for helping students with ASD to develop reciprocal interactive communication skills.
- **Melody:** Many children with ASD have good to excellent pitch-matching ability and can recall melodies easily.
- **Rhythm:** Consistency in presentation, whether focusing on "beat" or "rhythm," will enhance the student's attention and performance while avoiding stress/self-stimulation behaviors. You may want to begin by imitating the student's spontaneous beat or rhythm patterns—modeling an "echo" response that can be shaped into a sharing of the "leading" role as the child is able to recognize this expectation.
- **Harmony:** Because of the unique perceptual processing of the student with ASD, the teacher should observe reactions/responses to certain harmonies that may trigger a negative response. Strong harmonic backgrounds or minor keys, for example, may cause the student to turn away or put hands over ears, or may trigger enhanced attention, curiosity, and exploratory behaviors.
- **Word meanings:** Sign language has been used to enhance communication and stimulate reciprocal communication for students with ASD. Signs can be paired with lyrics and can be performed by all students to provide a common-skill group experience.
- **Movement:** Caution should be used in this area until the student is very comfortable in the music environment and then should be carefully monitored so as not to overstimulate or overly stress the child. Structured movement may be introduced first (may be an extension of "sign language"); creative movement/improvisation may be enhanced by using a prop (ribbon dancer/stick, rhythm instrument, scarf).

Classroom teachers must assess each student's special needs and then devise ways to bring that student into the mainstream of activity. Musical experiences must involve all students, and the personal satisfaction is great for the teacher who sincerely tries to help a student overcome a challenge so that he or she can have success and pleasure with musical experiences.

Classroom teachers may wish to refer to the following publications, organizations, and websites for further information and current diagnosis-specific resources:

Publications

M. Ademek and A. Darrow, *Music in Special Education* (Silver Spring, MD: American Music Theory Association [AMTA], 2005)

Alice M. Hammel and Ryan M. Hourigan, *Teaching Music to Students with Special Needs: A Label-Free Approach* (New York: Oxford University Press, 2011)

Gail Schaberg (compiler), *Tips: Teaching Music to Special Learners* (Reston, VA: MENC: The National Association for Music Education, 1988)

Elise Sobol, *An Attitude and Approach for Teaching Music to Special Learners* (Raleigh, NC: Pentland Press, 2001)

Spotlight on Making Music with Special Learners (Reston, VA: MENC: The National Association for Music Education, 2004) (available from www.amazon.com)

Websites and Organizations

www.hammel.us
Dr. Alice M. Hammel

Click on "special learners" for a wealth of information based on the experience of Dr. Alice Hammel, a special needs music educator from Richmond, Virginia. This website includes tips on inclusion, adaptations for music activities, classroom management, and resources.

American Music Therapy Association (AMTA)
8455 Colesville Road, Suite 1000
Silver Spring, MD 20910
800-765-2268
www.musictherapy.org

This website offers several FAQ sheets and evidence-based statements supporting the use of music with special learners. You may also locate a music therapist in a specific area of the country through this website.

Council for Exceptional Children (CEC)
1110 North Gleve Road, Suite 300
Arlington, VA 22201
888-232-7733
www.cec.sped.org

This website is the official site for the Council for Exceptional Children. It offers some of the most up-to-date information on the terminology, legislation, and research affecting the education of children with special needs.

The Role of National and State Standards in Enhancing Musical Learning

One of the most important contemporary trends in music education has been the establishment of national and state standards for school music programs. The national standards, which have been used as a basis for establishing state standards, are designed to provide a foundation for building a balanced, comprehensive, and sequential curriculum in music. Nine basic national voluntary content standards have been set forth for school music programs:

1. Singing, alone and with others, a varied repertoire of music
2. Performing on instruments, alone and with others, a varied repertoire of music
3. Improvising melodies, variations, and accompaniments
4. Composing and arranging music within specified guidelines
5. Reading and notating music
6. Listening to, analyzing, and describing music
7. Evaluating music and musical performances
8. Understanding relationships between music, the other arts, and disciplines outside the arts
9. Understanding music in relation to history and culture

In addition to these national standards, teachers can acquire state music standards from their respective state departments of education, where they are available on-line. National and state standards serve as a guide for developing lessons for different grade levels. See *The School Music*

Program: A New Vision for more information on the national music standards for the various grade levels.[4]

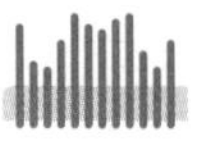

THE PLACE OF INSTRUCTIONAL TECHNOLOGY IN SUPPORTING MUSICAL LEARNING

Many types of instructional technology and student-owned devices found in schools today can increase the effectiveness of music instruction in the classroom. These are computers, including "tablet" computers, computer applications and software, on-line "cloud"-based resources and tools, iPods, smartphones, CD players, DVD players, MIDI pianos, video projectors, and Smart Boards.

Computers provide one of the most far-reaching instructional technology tools for the classroom. Innovative teachers are using computer-related technologies that include electronic musical instruments, sequencers, music notation software, computer-assisted instructional software (CAI), multimedia, digital audio workstations (DAWs), and the Internet to facilitate the process of music teaching and learning. These instructional technologies are helping students understand, perform, create, and respond to music. In addition, many technology-based resources offer opportunities for the interdisciplinary integration of music with other subject areas.

Tablet computers, such as the iPad, have revolutionized the consumer computer market. The intuitive touch-based interface of these devices makes them ideal for younger students and students with disabilities. Additionally, the wide variety of applications for these devices makes them incredibly

Suggested Software, Applications, and Web-based Resources

Music Recording and Podcasting

- "GarageBand": Software that is available for Apple computers, iPad, iPod, and iPhone
- "Mixcraft": PC equivalent to "GarageBand"
- "Audacity": Free recording software

Music Theory

- MusicTheory.net
- Music Ace

versatile in the classroom. Music applications such as "GarageBand" are reasonably priced to allow you and your students access to software that enables students to create and compose music in traditional and non-traditional notation.

Digital music players (DMPs) have all but replaced portable listening devices. DMPs, such as Apple's iPod, are small, portable devices that can store digital music, video, pictures; access the Internet; and run applications. The advantages of these devices are (1) the convenience of having all music needed for all classes in one small portable device; (2) the ease of procuring the music; (3) the ease of arranging music into lessons (playlists); (4) the high quality of the music; (5) the ability to have a backup of all the music on a computer/cloud; (6) the ability to capture pictures, audio, and video; and (7) the ability to download music applications for music creation and theory training;

[4] Consortium of National Arts Education Associations, *National Standards for Arts Education* (Lanham, MD: Rowman & Littlefield Education, 1984); and MENC: The National Association for Music Education, *The School Music Program: A New Vision* (Lanham, MD: Rowman & Littlefield Education, 1994). See website for the National Association for Music Education, www.nafme.org.

Smartphones are cell phones, such as the iPhone or Android phone, that can run applications, access the Internet, take photos and video, access documents, and manage your digital music.

Cloud-based resources and Web 2.0 tools, such as Google Docs and Google Music, allow users to access files and information from any device, anywhere, any time. Cloud-based file management has many instructional advantages for teachers in that it facilitates collaborative projects.

Digital video discs (DVDs) are found in homes and schools and allow for the presentation of extremely high-quality pictures and sound via discs the size of audio CDs. An increasingly large number of DVDs are available in music, including those demonstrating band and orchestra instruments, ballet and opera performances, and music of other cultures. These are especially effective because students can *see as well as hear* the musical presentation.

MIDI (musical instrument digital interface) is a technological term that identifies hardware and software capable of understanding music information from each other. An electronic musical instrument that is MIDI-compatible will be able to share information with a computer and any other MIDI device. Inexpensive MIDI synthesizers with built-in speakers make an excellent classroom accompanying instrument and allow students to respond to music instructional software by playing on the keyboard.

Television continues to play a role in school educational programs. Television programs of orchestras, operas, jazz, rock, and other popular styles of music occur frequently and can be used to effectively supplement lessons in the classroom.

Overhead and slide projectors have been available in schools for many years and are still an effective means of enhancing instruction by providing visuals for particular music lessons.

Presentation software, such as Microsoft's PowerPoint or Google Presentation, provides an easier means of preparation and professional presentation of teacher-created visual materials. Presentation software makes it possible to easily update materials, which is more difficult to do for lessons that have been prepared for overhead or slide presentation.

Interactive white boards, such as Smart Boards, are large interactive displays that connect to a computer and projector. A projector projects the computer's desktop onto the board's surface where users control the computer using a pen, finger, stylus, or other device. The board is typically mounted to a wall or floor stand. Using a Smart Board is similar to using a giant 5-by-4-foot iPad. This is great tool for elementary students and for special needs students in that it allows students to physically interact with computer programs.

Social media such as Facebook, Twitter, and YouTube continue to grow. Though perhaps not an effective instructional tool for elementary students, these social media sites can be an effective communication tool with parents and community members. Consider creating a "page" in Facebook for your class and invite your students' parents to "like" it. You can post their classroom projects and compositions directly to the page. You can also post links to handouts and other instructional tools.

Learning with a Single Computer in the Classroom

A single computer can be used to present material to a class. This is not unlike using videos or DVDs, except the computer presentation can be more interactive. When presenting with a computer, a large monitor or a video projector is needed so that all students can see. For accurate representation of musical sounds, high-quality speakers are also recommended.

Another way to utilize a single computer is through interactive group strategies. For example, individual students can take turns using the computer while the remainder of the class watches and verbally assists as needed in helping accomplish the task at hand. Another strategy that can be used with music software is to set up a game format involving teams of students who take turns answering questions, with points awarded for each correct answer. This can be a motivational way to engage students in a lesson.

A single computer in the classroom can also be set up as a learning station. This can be especially beneficial for student remediation or enhancement activities. If only a single student is using the computer at a time, use high-quality headphones so that the music from the computer does not disturb students working on other projects.

Learning in the Computer Laboratory

The school computer lab provides a means for all students in a class to work simultaneously in a hands-on situation with computer technology. Although most school computer labs do not have MIDI keyboards as part of their workstations, many instructional software packages and websites do not require MIDI keyboards; all that is necessary for many of these applications and sites to function as intended is a computer with a sound card. If software programs are used in a computer lab, enough copies for the entire class will be needed. Alternatively, a site license may be purchased and the software installed on the school's network server. Headphones for each student (or possibly for pairs of students at each computer) will be necessary for sound containment.

Learning Using Tablet Computers and Other Handheld Electronics

The creation of the iPod in 2001 and the more recent creation of the iPad and similar products have completely changed people's day-to-day use of electronic devices. The Apple App store and Android Market offer a myriad of helpful and instructive applications (or "apps") that may be downloaded and used to improve instruction. Types of apps range from playable instrument apps such as "PocketGuitar," theory apps such as "Nota," and recording and composition apps such as "GarageBand."

Computer-Based Assignments Extend the Learning Environment

Computer-based assignments, to be completed outside of class time, extend the learning environment to the home and community. Students will need access to the necessary computers and software through the school's media center or the local public library. Out-of-class assignments might work best as extra-credit or enrichment activities.

The Internet as a Learning Tool

The Internet is the single most important resource in education today. Materials are readily available to assist the classroom teacher in presenting lessons that include a wide variety of music and information about music, and that integrate and correlate music with other subjects. Most importantly, high-quality musical examples are readily available to support the teaching and learning of music.

Downloading Quality Musical Examples for Learning

Throughout the text the authors have referenced several performance pieces and suggested avenues by which they can be streamed or downloaded. The benefits of downloading or streaming musical examples include the ease of obtaining high-quality performances, the ability to collect all examples in one easy-to-find location, the advantage of being able to use the examples year after year, and portability.

Integrating Technology

The Music Education Premium Site contains chapter quizzing, Spotify playlists and downloads of free MP3s of noted songs. Visit CengageBrain.com to purchase an access code or enter the code provided with your text materials.

Web Resources

- Links to websites expand on the topics discussed within the chapter and offer additional teaching resources.

Videos

- Watch classroom videos that apply to the chapter content and access the YouTube playlist for videos referenced within the chapter.

Audio

- iTunes provides an easy way to download the music discussed within each chapter.
- Spotify playlists allow students to stream music referenced within each chapter.
- Music selections prepare you to hear and learn many of the songs in the text as children would sing them. These songs, which were previously supplied on CD, are now available as audio MP3s. Additional selections have been added, providing more than fifty songs in total. Songs within the chapter that are designated with an icon are available for downloading at no extra cost.

CENGAGE**brain**.com

Questions for Discussion

1. Give a musical example of psychomotor learning.
2. Give a musical example of cognitive learning.
3. Give a musical example of affective learning.
4. Discuss the differences between active and passive learning.
5. How do teacher-centered and student-centered learning differ?
6. Discuss each of the following and give a musical example:
   - Making what you teach meaningful
   - Organizing your material so that it is sequential
   - Experiencing something before placing a label on it
   - Developing conceptual learning
   - Cultivating a multisensory approach to learning
   - Developing a multicultural approach to learning
   - Stressing the importance of reinforcement in learning
   - Focusing on transfer of learning
7. What does the term *challenged* mean and how is it applied to students in the classroom?
8. How might a gifted student in music (or in mathematics, reading, science, or any other subject) be kept interested when she or he already knows what you have to offer?
9. Discuss ways that you might adapt a music lesson for a student who is physically, visually, aurally, or mentally challenged.
10. Discuss why guidelines are important for the teacher to know when dealing with students who have special needs.
11. Why are national and state standards important for music learning in elementary schools? Briefly discuss the national music standards and your own state's music standards.
12. What role can instructional technology play in improving musical learning? Give some specific examples.

CHAPTER 2

Guidelines for Teaching Music

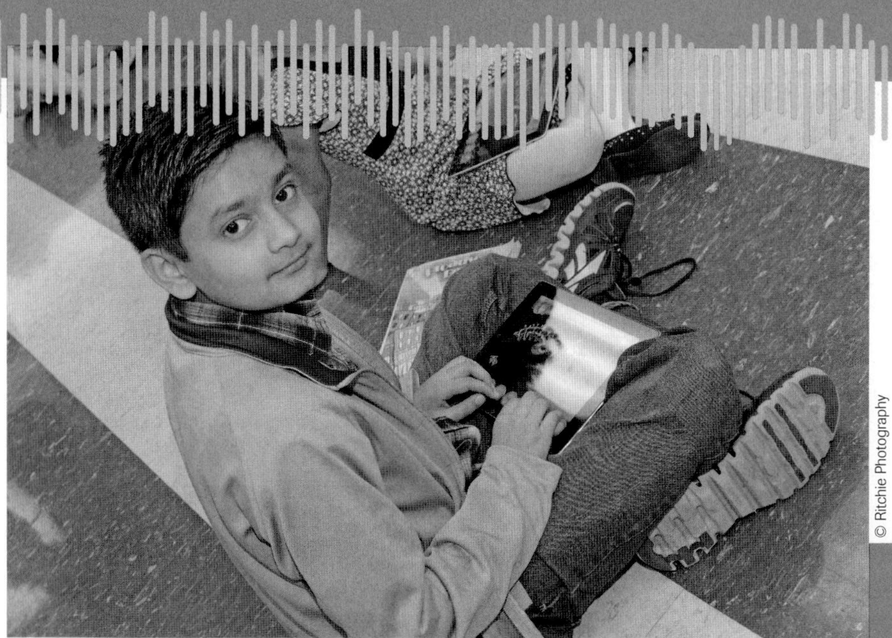

Objectives

Students will be introduced to guidelines for teaching music:

- Key elements in designing integrated learning experiences with music
  - Identifying long- and short-term goals
  - Deciding on musical concepts
  - Developing objectives
  - Choosing appropriate musical materials and activities
  - Teaching and learning in a logical sequence
  - Deciding on length and frequency of lessons
  - Relating music to student's personal lives
  - Developing multisensory experiences
  - Including multicultural experiences
  - Using instructional technology
  - Bringing closure to the learning experience
  - Assessing learning
- Writing lesson plans
- Reminders for planning and teaching lessons
- Making good teaching great teaching

National and State Music Standards

This chapter focuses on the following national music standards and related state music standards:

- Singing, alone and with others, a varied repertoire of music
- Performing on instruments, alone and with others, a varied repertoire of music
- Listening to, analyzing, and describing music

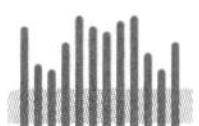

DESIGNING INTEGRATED LEARNING EXPERIENCES WITH MUSIC

As you begin to think about teaching music in an elementary school classroom, you need to consider the following key elements:

- Identifying long- and short-term goals
- Deciding on musical concepts
- Developing specific objectives related to the learning abilities of various age levels
- Choosing interesting and appropriate musical materials and activities that can be integrated with other classroom experiences
- Involving students in logical and sequential activities that will enable them to learn easily and effectively
- Deciding on length and frequency of lessons that focus on musical ideas or concepts
- Relating music and activities to the lives of the students
- Involving students in multisensory activities that focus on seeing (visual), hearing (auditory), and moving (psychomotor)
- Including multicultural experiences for students
- Using instructional technology to enhance the lesson
- Bringing review and closure to the learning experience
- Assessing to ascertain if objectives have been met

Identifying Long- and Short-Term Goals

The first task in teaching a music lesson is to formulate long- and short-term goals. Goals are generally concerned with what is desired in terms of musical interest and behavior over a period of time.

Long-Term Goals

As implied in the name, long-term goals are designed to assist the teacher in clearly specifying what is ultimately to be achieved in a learning environment. For example, "students will develop an appreciation of jazz" might be a long-term goal. Other long-term goals might be "to foster perceptive listening so that students will interact with the art of music with ever-increasing satisfaction and meaning," "to develop musical skills and understanding," and "to appreciate music of different styles and cultures." Long-term goals use statements with verbs such as *develop, foster, appreciate, understand,* and *enjoy.* These statements represent the philosophy of the educator and the school system, and it is from these long-term goals that short-term goals and more specific objectives are derived.

Short-Term Goals

Short-term goals are related to long-term goals but are generally attained within a specified time frame. Short-term goals often indicate what needs to be accomplished in a particular week or lesson. Examples of short-term goals might be "using classroom instruments, students will create and perform a sound piece" or "using the solfège system of music reading, students will successfully sing songs appropriate to their age."

Teachers who take time to formulate long- and short-term goals tend to have a clearer sense of direction about what students are to learn. Without goals it is easy for both teachers and students to wander aimlessly and haphazardly through a series of musical activities without much learning taking place.

Deciding on Musical Concepts

A concept is "a collection of experiences or ideas that are grouped together based on some common properties."[1] One of the first decisions a teacher makes about a music lesson is what concept or concepts to cover. Principal musical concepts include rhythm, melody, dynamics, tone color or timbre, texture, and form. (See Chapter 3.)

Developing Objectives

In developing lessons for the classroom, state what children are to learn in terms of specific objectives to be accomplished. Objectives should be stated in terms of observable behavior so that the teacher can actually observe what students are doing to demonstrate what they have learned. For example, an objective might read: "Students will demonstrate an understanding of AB form by using sheets of colored paper to outline the formal design in the song 'Home on the Range' (p. 51)." Other examples of objectives might be "Students will use alphabet cards to identify the ABACA sections of Mozart's *Horn Concerto no. 3 in E-flat Major* (third movement, Rondo; [iTunes/Spotify])" or "Students will demonstrate their understanding of rests by clapping their hands on the appropriate rests in the song 'If You're Happy' (p. 374)." In each case, the teacher can clearly observe what the students are doing to indicate that learning has taken place.

Choosing Appropriate Musical Materials and Activities

As you prepare lessons to teach to children, it is important to choose musical materials and design activities that (1) are within the capabilities of a particular class, (2) are interesting and fun, (3) can be integrated with other classroom subjects and experiences, and (4) emphasize active involvement in musical experiences such as singing, playing instruments, and moving to music. An important consideration must be recognizing the difference between "presenting" and "teaching." *Presenting* is generally teacher-centered, whereas *teaching* focuses on the child. This book focuses on the latter, with many suggestions for ways to involve children in successful musical experiences.

Teaching and Learning in a Logical Sequence

Children learn best when ideas progress logically from simple to complex. As you plan lessons, consider what should come first, second, third, and so on. For example, you can introduce a song by performing it (or playing a recording of it) and then teach students the melody, words, and rhythms by using the rote, rote-note, or note approach.

In developing the sequence within lessons, you will need to consider presenting the same idea in many different ways. For example, to teach students the rhythm of a specific song (such as one in 2/4 meter):

- Ask students to play the beat on the drums.
- Have students experience the strong and weak beats by tapping thighs and clapping hands.
- Have one student play the strong beat on a tambourine and another play the weak beat on the claves.
- Ask students to speak the words in the rhythm of the song, accenting the first beat of each measure.
- Use a rhythm chart with notes or some type of graphic to help students see the beat.

[1]Anita Woolfolk and Lorraine Nicolich, *Educational Psychology for Teachers* (Englewood Cliffs, NJ: Prentice Hall, 1980), p. 596.

Some Long-Term Goals for Various Grade Levels

Following are some long-term goals that reflect expectations for various grade levels. You will need to develop short-term goals and specific objectives for individual classes.

Preschool/Kindergarten
Students will:

1. Sing short songs in tune, with good breathing habits and tone quality.
2. Perform rhythms with a steady beat.
3. Perform music expressively.
   a. Loud–soft
   b. Fast–slow
   c. Legato–staccato
4. Respond to expressive qualities of music through movement.
   a. Duple meter and triple meter
   b. Strong accents and changing accents
   c. Steady beat
   d. Changing dynamics
5. Play simple rhythmic-melodic patterns on classroom instruments.
6. Sing, play, move, and create music expressive of individual imaginations.

Grades 1 and 2
Students will:

1. Sing short songs in tune, with good breathing habits and tone quality.
2. Distinguish between high and low, fast and slow, and instrumental tone colors.
3. Identify expressive use of repetition and contrast in simple songs and short listening examples.
4. Express through creative movement musical concepts such as:
   a. Steady beat
   b. Accent
   c. Crescendo or decrescendo
   d. Staccato
   e. Legato
5. Engage in singing games.
6. Play simple rhythmic-melodic patterns on classroom instruments.
7. Read and create simple music notation.

Grades 3 and 4
Students will:

1. Sing short songs in tune, with good breathing habits and tone quality.
2. Sing simple rounds and descants in tune.
3. Sing songs expressive of text.
   a. Legato and staccato
   b. Dynamics
   c. Phrasing
4. Analyze music in terms of elements.
   a. Melodic phrases
   b. Tone colors
   c. Formal structure
5. Read or create simple music notation.
6. Engage in singing games and dances.
7. Play simple melodies and rhythmic accompaniments on classroom instruments.

Grades 5 and 6
Students will:

1. Sing songs in tune, with good breathing habits and tone quality.
2. Sing songs in two and three parts.
3. Demonstrate rhythmic sense by:
   a. Identifying simple-to-complex rhythms (both verbally and aurally)
   b. Playing rhythms in 2/4, 3/4, 6/8, and mixed meter
4. Play simple harmonic accompaniments on guitar, keyboard, or Q-chord.
5. Play simple melodies and descants on melody bells or recorder.
6. Identify music from other parts of the world according to their use of rhythm, melody, dynamics, tone color, texture, and formal structure.
7. Develop musical leadership by taking part in musical plays.
8. Read and write music notation.

Any or all of these ideas can be used in a logical sequence of events that proceeds from the introduction of a song or larger composition to a deeper understanding of the piece.

Deciding on Length and Frequency of Lessons

The length of lessons will depend on the age and grade level of the students. In general, younger children will need to have shorter lessons than older students, who have longer attention spans.

For kindergarten through third grade, a lesson length of 20 to 25 minutes is recommended. Lessons for students in grades 4 through 6 may be 30 to 40 minutes. The decision about lesson length, however, needs to be carefully tailored to each particular class of students.

When planning, determine the approximate number of minutes needed for each segment of the lesson—for example, 5 minutes for introductory discussion and 10 minutes for singing a song and adding accompaniment. Such guides ensure that the various segments of the plan receive their fair share of time. Further, both teachers and students will be kept on track and will not wander significantly from the major points of the lesson.

Frequency of lessons is another important consideration in organizing music instruction. In general, students need to have lessons scheduled close enough for continuity of learning to be maintained. Further, it is generally better to have frequent short lessons than long lessons with considerable time gaps in between. The frequency of lessons is also related to the age and grade level of the students. Younger students need to have instruction more frequently than do older students. All students seem to do best with some music instruction as part of each school day.

Relating Music to Students' Personal Lives

Relating music to the personal lives of students often occurs in preliminary activities as well as in the lesson itself. Many times, preliminary activities will lead students to an understanding of the concept being taught. Preliminary activities normally call for teachers to present something familiar to students, with the idea of letting that experience act as a bridge to the principal part of the lesson. For example, if you are going to talk about contrast in music, the lesson might have preliminary activities that involve students in looking for contrast in the classroom—in clothing, in a poem, in a visual artwork, or in movement. When the concept is clear in the minds of students, you can then involve them in appropriate experiences with musical sounds.

Developing Multisensory Experiences

Children often learn more effectively if several of their senses are involved, rather than just one. For example, in an age in which television often dominates the lives of children, developing and using the visual sense becomes an important teaching method. A visual cue is often helpful because it does not go away; it remains where you put it, and the student can leave the room either mentally or physically and return to find the visual cue in the same place. On the other hand, music involves sound; it passes through time and is gone. Thus, using the visual sense as well as the aural offers children increased opportunities for understanding and success. The tactile sense is of particular interest to students who have some form of visual challenge and provides opportunities to relate sounds to touch. You can compare smooth sounds to silk, or jagged or rough sounds to burlap or hickory bark.

Including Multicultural Experiences

Through television, the Internet, and a variety of printed material, we are becoming increasingly aware of the proximity of other peoples of the world. Many of the world's cultures are present in the United States, where hundreds of different ethnic groups make up the American cultural mosaic. Studying the multicultural musical environment both of the world and of our own country is a wonderful way for students to learn a variety of new kinds of music. It also provides a distinctive opportunity for students to broaden their understanding of other cultures and to develop sensitivity and tolerance toward one another.

Using Instructional Technology

Integrating technology into a lesson is an effective means of engaging today's digital generation as well as a useful way of improving teaching. Traditional digital media, such as CDs and DVDs, can greatly enhance instruction in the classroom. And, with increasingly available music content online, teachers can access videos from a number of websites, including TeacherTube and YouTube. Software programs and websites can provide drill and practice on previously learned information and also serve as a tutorial for new concepts and skills. Further, these tools are highly effective at providing differentiated instruction (i.e., individualized instruction) and the teaching of sequential material that moves from low- to higher-level knowledge and skills. In addition to teacher use of technology to improve engagement and overall instruction, a particularly rewarding classroom experience is for students to actually interact with the technology itself. Interactive use of technology can be explored through various websites (e.g., www.dsokids.com/), where students learn about instruments and composers), interactive whiteboards, electronic instruments, digital recorders, and CD and MP3 players. Explore what your school has in terms of technology, see how you can use these resources for music instruction, and carefully write instructional technology applications into your lesson plans.

Bringing Closure to the Learning Experience

Near the end of a lesson, schedule a summary or closing activity in which to pull together the separate parts of the lesson and give students a feeling of finality. Quite often such closure is accomplished by students performing a piece in its entirety after having worked on separate segments during the lesson.

Assessing Learning

Assessing learning in music is based on how well students meet national and state music standards (as outlined in Chapter 1). Thus, music standards are given for each of the sample lessons in this book. Assessment tells you if the goals you identified for a lesson have been achieved, and ultimately it tells you how effective you have been in your teaching. Often you will discover that you have been successful with some aspects of a presentation and not as effective with others. By systematically assessing students, you learn what changes need to be made in materials and teaching strategies to ensure that students make satisfactory progress in all areas of study.

For students, periodic assessment is crucial for letting them know how well they are progressing in their musical study. Children need a sense of accomplishment, and a regular program of assessment gives them needed feedback. One of the most helpful aspects of assessment for students is that they become aware of strengths and weaknesses—in effect, discovering areas in which they excel and areas to which they need to give more attention.

You will want to assess students with respect to the following:

- Musical performance skills
- Perception and understanding of musical concepts
- Acquisition and retention of information about music

In performance, assessment focuses on progress made in singing and playing instruments. For example, is there steady improvement in students' ability to sing on pitch and with good tone quality? Can students physically execute duple and triple meter? Are students able to satisfactorily accompany pieces using classroom instruments?

Perception and understanding of musical concepts can be assessed through such techniques as a listening chart (see Chapter 6), in which students are asked to discriminate between contrasting phenomena (loud and soft, duple and triple, violin and trumpet) as they listen to a piece of music. Understanding is often demonstrated by students actually *doing* something, such as creating a "sound composition" illustrating rondo form. Still another way of demonstrating perception and understanding is to ask students to identify a similar concept (such as unity through repetition) in art forms such as music, painting, and poetry.

You can give periodic quizzes to determine how well students have assimilated and retained information about music presented in class. In general, it is better to give short quizzes at frequent intervals than to wait for long periods of time and give lengthy tests.

WRITING LESSON PLANS

As you begin to write a lesson plan to teach music, you need to ask yourself the following questions:

1. What is the activity? (e.g., singing a song)
2. Who will receive the lesson? (grade level)
3. What concepts do you want to teach?
4. What materials do you need? (to be completed last)
5. What do you want to do? (objectives)
6. How are you going to do it? (procedures)
   a. Preliminary
   b. Main content
7. How will you tie everything together? (closure)
8. Did you teach what you thought you were going to? (assessing both yourself and your students)

As in all lesson plans, detail is critical, especially at the beginning, so don't leave anything to chance. Following are some sample lesson plans to help you see how a typical lesson might be set up.

Lesson Planning Tips

- Use a computer to write lesson plans. Make a "template" that contains all of the repetitive parts of a lesson plan. Computers provide the flexibility to review plans after they have been taught and to adjust them so that the next time they are used they will be improved.
- Keep a bank of instructional goals and objectives in a separate file. The twofold purpose of this is to serve as a reminder of long-term instructional goals and to make it easy to copy and paste the goals and/or objectives into the current lesson plan.
- Use a database to organize and find teaching materials.
- Use a spreadsheet to create schedules.
- Use a music notation program to construct professional-looking musical examples.
- Use the Internet to acquire music and pictures of other cultures.

LESSON PLAN
Performing a Song

Activity: Performing a song
Grade: 2
Concepts: Ascending and descending patterns

Key: F
Starting pitch: C
Meter: 4/4, begin on 1

"Five Little Pumpkins"

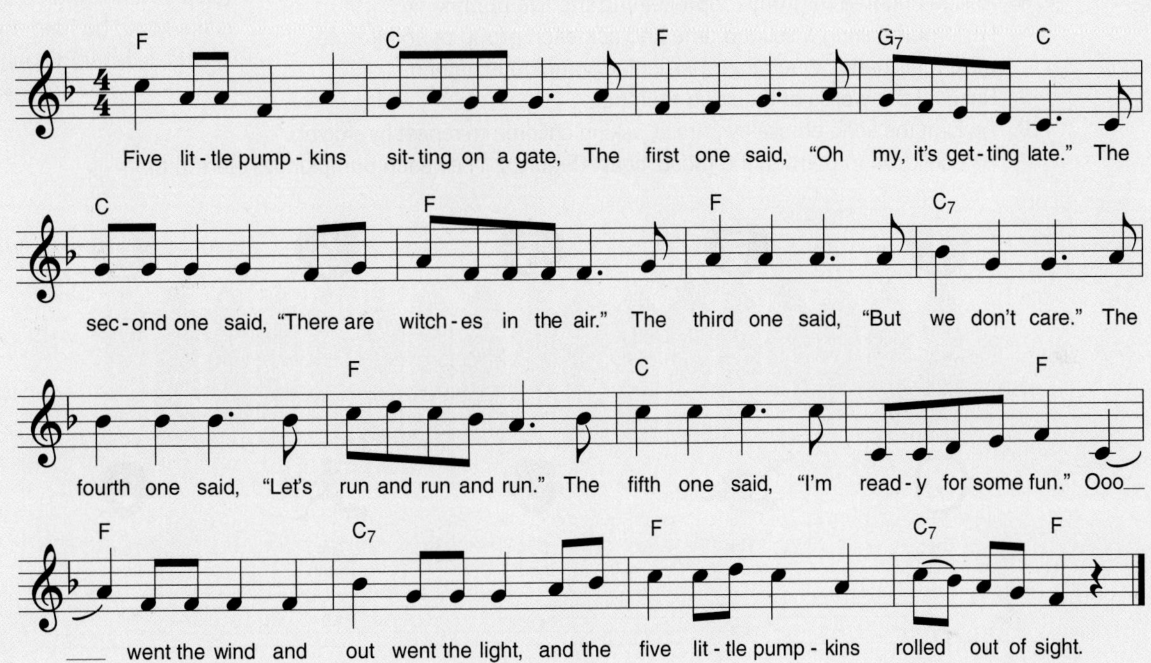

NATIONAL AND STATE STANDARDS

1. Singing, alone and with others, a varied repertoire of music
2. Performing on instruments, alone and with others, a varied repertoire of music

OBJECTIVES

Students will:

1. Identify the upward motion of the beginning pitches of musical phrases from *one* to *five* little pumpkins.
2. Play the pitches F G A C on the xylophone as each occurs.
3. Create appropriate motions to the song using pumpkins as a guide.
4. Sing with good tone quality.

MATERIALS

- Pictures of pumpkins or real pumpkins
- Pumpkin note heads with numbers
- Xylophone
- Fence or gate

PROCEDURES

Preliminary Activities

1. Ask children to sit on the floor around you.
2. Show pictures of pumpkins or show several real pumpkins that are similar in size.
3. Announce "Today we are going to learn a song about pumpkins."

Main Content

Special Learner Note

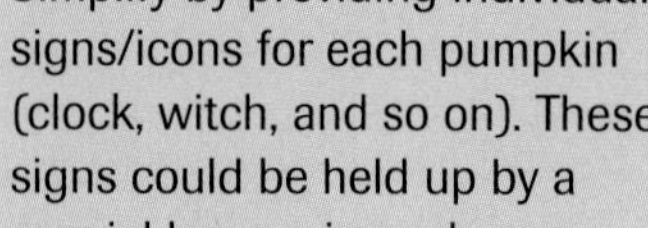

Simplify by providing individual signs/icons for each pumpkin (clock, witch, and so on). These signs could be held up by a special learner in each group.

1. Sing the song "Five Little Pumpkins." Indicate pitches with hands.
2. Discuss the five pumpkin faces identified in the song.
3. Assign children to groups representing the five pumpkins.
4. Perform the song a second time and ask each group of children to raise their hands when their particular pumpkin is named.
5. Read all the words of the song together.
6. Perform the song phrase by phrase, asking children to repeat by singing.
7. Ask children to point to the music chart (Figure 2.1) as each pumpkin is referred to.

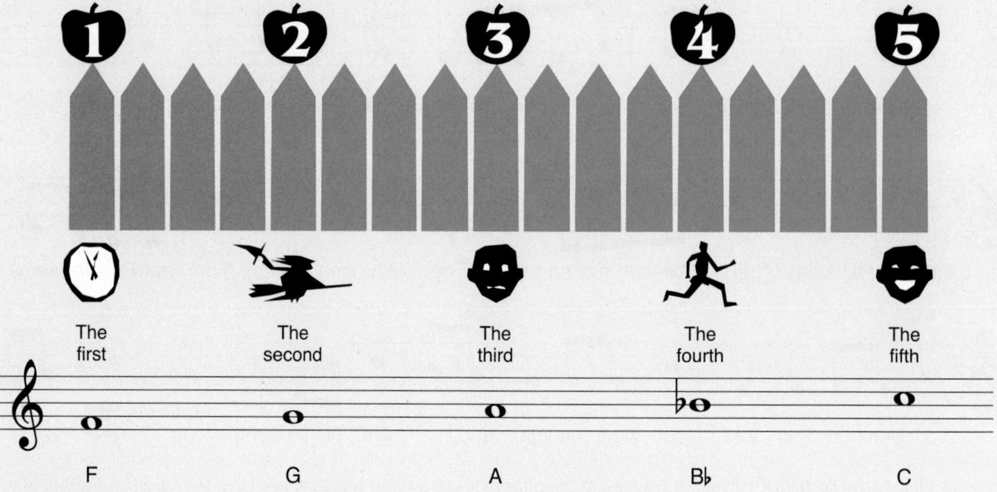

Figure 2-1

8. Have the class perform the song as a child plays the xylophone notes F G A C at appropriate times, noting that pitches are ascending.
9. Have the class perform the song as a child points to the appropriate pumpkin face.
10. Ask children to sing the words and music to "Ooo went the wind and out went the light, and the five little pumpkins rolled out of sight." Discuss which way "rolled out of sight" occurs (ascending or descending):

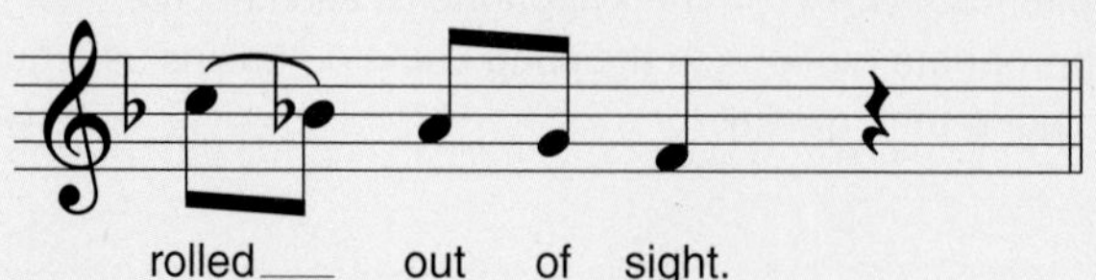

11. Ask children to create a motion for "rolled out of sight."
12. Ask children to create motions for each musical phrase. For example, "five little pumpkins" could be five fingers: one finger = watch; two fingers = witch; three fingers = child doesn't care; four fingers = run; five fingers = ready for fun. The ending could be a swish with hands to snuff out the candle, then five fingers, hand over hand.
13. Closure: Have the class perform the entire song with motions.

ASSESSMENT

1. Do the beginning pitches of each phrase go up or down?
2. What are the names of these pitches?
3. Do the last five pitches go up or down?
4. Does the class perform the song with the correct pitches and rhythms?
5. Does the class perform the song with good tone quality?

ADDITIONAL INTEGRATIVE AREAS

Reading, visual art, Halloween, mathematics, farming

Special Learner Notes

Match xylophone bars with pictures on a chart (put picture on bar); assign an individual student to each bar.

Use Boomwhackers® (see page 131) instead of the xylophone for more individualized participation (color/visual) and for ease of playing. (Holding a Boomwhacker can be easier for students who have difficulties with fine motor skills.)

LESSON PLAN
LISTENING TO FAST AND SLOW MUSIC

Activity: Listening to music
Grades: 1–2
Concepts: Fast/slow

NATIONAL AND STATE MUSIC STANDARD

1. Listening to, analyzing, and describing music

OBJECTIVES

Students will:

1. Visually identify objects that move fast and slow.
2. Demonstrate through body movements fast and slow, getting faster, and getting slower.
3. Verbally identify sounds that are fast and slow and sounds that move gradually faster and gradually slower.
4. Identify expressive uses of fast and slow, getting faster, and getting slower in the recorded music used.

MATERIALS

- Recordings [iTunes/Spotify]
  - Saint-Saëns, "The Swan" from *Carnival of the Animals* (slow)
  - Rimsky-Korsakov, "Flight of the Bumblebee" (London Philharmonic) (fast)
  - Honegger, "Pacific 231" (fast/slow)
- Computer, iPad, iPod
- Pictures that suggest fast (auto racing, jogging, airplane taking off) and slow (turtle, person walking, leaf floating to the ground)
- Word cards (*fast, slow, getting faster, getting slower*)

PROCEDURES

Preliminary Activities

1. Show pictures that suggest fast and slow.
2. Ask students to move their arms slowly, then quickly; have them run and then slow down to a walk.

3. Ask students to dramatize a rosebud gradually opening or a candle melting down, a racehorse bursting through the starting gate or a football player running for a touchdown.

Main Content

1. Ask students to create slow sounds and then fast sounds. Experiment with sounds that start slowly and gradually get faster and with fast sounds that gradually slow down.
2. Space students around the room. Ask them to move creatively as you play a fast or slow pattern on a drum. Invite individual students to take turns playing creative drum rhythms (fast–slow, getting faster–getting slower).
3. Download and play Saint-Saëns's "The Swan." Discuss the composer's choice of a slow tempo to represent a swan swimming on a pond.
4. Download and play Rimsky-Korsakov's "Flight of the Bumblebee." Discuss the composer's choice of a fast tempo to represent a bumblebee flying past you.
5. Download and play Honegger's "Pacific 231." Ask students to place appropriate words on the writing board (fast, slow, getting faster, getting slower) as they listen to the music. After they have listened, discuss the composer's use of fast and slow to represent a train starting, traveling down the track, and then slowing down.

Technology Enhancement

Prior to the students arriving to class, do an Internet search for the word "speed." Choose four or five random images related to speed, such as a car, motorcycle, or cheetah. Download the images and have them displayed on a video projector. When students arrive, ask them to identify similarities between the different images, guiding them toward the idea of "speed."

CLOSURE AND ASSESSMENT

Play excerpts from "The Swan," "Flight of the Bumblebee," and "Pacific 231." Choose appropriate cards (with captions *fast, slow, getting faster,* and *getting slower*) and ask students to place them on the chalkboard as you play the selections. (Record the selections so that they occur one after the other.)

Special Learner Note

Observe students' attention spans during recording/listening; you may want to shorten the actual listening time and repeat the listening experience in between other activities or classroom tasks.

ADDITIONAL INTEGRATIVE AREAS

Visual art, transportation

Reminders for Planning and Teaching Lessons

- Visuals must be large enough to be seen from the back of the room. Do not use yellow or orange as a color for printed text; they cannot be seen on white paper. The same is true of black on blue or purple paper.
- Be sure that the lesson is appropriate in content and musical concepts for the maturity level of the students. A song with a very wide range, such as "The Star-Spangled Banner," is not suitable musically for young children. Many can't sing that high or that low.
- Remember that kindergarten, first-grade, and even second-grade students in general do not read well and need help in following a chart.
- You are a *leader* in teaching. Be involved in the lesson. Get the children involved in doing something, responding in some way.
- Be involved in the listening; don't just stand and gaze at the floor or look out the window.
- *Always use a mechanical source for the pitch of a song.* Otherwise, most of the time you will pitch the song too low because adult voices are generally lower than children's voices.
- Be sure that you start the song on the pitch given. If the recorder is difficult for you, use a guitar, keyboard, or pitch pipe for the starting pitch.

- Avoid overusing colloquialisms, such as "okay" and "you guys."
- Be accurate in teaching rhythm and melody.
- If you use a recording of a song, be sure to give the pitch and either mouth or sing the song along with the recording.
- Be sure that the lesson has sequence; don't leapfrog from one thing to another.
- Every lesson should have closure; avoid just stopping. Review to determine whether you have achieved your objectives.
- Use terms accurately. For example, a *song* must have, or originally have had, words (if it is imbedded in a large piece). Everything else is a *composition* or a *piece*. In other words, Beethoven's Symphony no. 5 is not a song but a piece.
- Understand your audio/video equipment and practice using it.
- Visit websites before using them and chart the path(s) to be used through a site.
- Always preview videos/DVDs before using them in instruction.
- Recognize the cultural diversity that may be in your classroom and include music relevant to Native American, African American, Hispanic, Asian, or other students.

Some Options to Use When Teaching Music

If you do not play an instrument:

- Sing the song yourself.
- Play a recording.
- Ask a child to play the song on the piano or other keyboard instrument. (Many children take piano lessons and are delighted to have a reason to practice.)
- Ask a friend to record the song (melody, accompaniment, or both).

If you can't sing in a high register:

- Use a recorder or melody bells.
- Play a recording.
- Use a child to help you start the song.
- Indicate with your hand when the pitch should be high.
- Guide children to sing an octave higher than you sing (if you are a man).

If you have a poor sense of rhythm:

- Use a child to help you keep a steady beat.
- Use a metronome to help you practice the rhythmic and melodic patterns.
- Use a metronome in class to help keep the class together.

If you can't read music quickly or accurately:

- Teach songs that you have learned accurately by ear. (Save your music-reading practice for when you are alone.)
- Use recordings.
- Try to feel the contour of the melody with your hands; don't depend on the music notation.

If you have difficulty singing a song in tune:

- Use a recording.
- Play the song on melody bells or a recorder.
- Use small groups of children as your leaders.

If you feel insecure in finding the starting pitch and getting the children to sing together:

- Practice using melody bells or a recorder.
- Play the key note of the song (D for key of D major, F for key of F major, and so on).
- Play notes 1, 3, and 5 of the scale (e.g., C, E, and G in the key of C major). You may wish to sing the syllables *do, mi, sol* (1, 3, 5) to establish the tonality.
- Play the first two notes of the song.
- Sing the first two notes of the song.
- Establish the tempo and say, "Ready, sing."

If you don't know what to do when children won't sing:

- Be enthusiastic.
- Give clear directions.
- Select songs that need a lot of energy and are fairly fast.
- Select songs that are fun to sing.
- Select songs that have meaning to them and aren't just silly.
- Set an example by singing or playing the song.
- Add instruments as accompaniment (both harmonic—keyboard, Q-chord, or guitar—and percussion).
- Be sure the songs are within the children's vocal range.

Making Good Teaching Great Teaching

- Know what you can expect from children at each grade level. Know each child in your classroom. Care about them.
- Be an example. Students look up to you and seem to have a way of knowing whether you measure up to what they expect of you.
- Be energetic and industrious. Stay fresh and inspired. Never stop reading and learning. Burnout is a product of an uninspired person. Read! Attend conferences! Give above and beyond yourself. Remember: *The only things we really have are those we give away.*
- Learn to motivate both your students and the people with whom you work.
- Be a dedicated teacher. Never count your time, and remember that the student is the most important person in the classroom.
- Give freely of your love and your time.
- Be the best musician you can be. Learn about music by performing it and attending concerts. There is no substitute for knowing what you are teaching.
- Be active in teaching organizations. Learn all you can from others.
- Use activity teaching. Students learn by doing.
- Use top-quality music in your classroom. High-quality music and materials are the foundation of good teaching.
- Use first-rate supplementary materials. Develop a library of visuals that will enhance your teaching.
- Use a variety of musical styles: jazz, folk, electronic, blues, and so on.
- Build your classroom teaching skills and a program that is educationally sound.
- Be a firm, fair, and kind disciplinarian. Remember that you are the leader and that you determine what happens in your classroom. Everything begins at the top—and that means you.
- Reward all good work. Don't make your awards necessarily competitive. Keep it simple—maybe a smile from the teacher or a star on a good paper. Remember that praise is the very best reward.
- Show that you care about each student (even those who try your patience). Be sincere and interested in each life.
- Believe in the value of what you are doing. It is an anchor when the going gets rough.

Integrating Technology

The Music Education Premium Site contains chapter quizzing, Spotify playlists, and downloads of free MP3s of noted songs. Visit CengageBrain .com to purchase an access code or enter the code provided with your text materials.

Web Resources

- Search the Web for information on music instruction. See classroom videos that apply to the chapter content.

Videos

- Watch classroom videos that apply to chapter content.

Audio

- Download music discussed in this chapter from the iTunes Store.
- Spotify playlists allow students to stream music referenced within each chapter.

CENGAGE**brain**.com

Questions for Discussion

1. Discuss the meaning of such terms as long-term goals, short-term goals, musical concepts, objectives of a music lesson, preliminary experiences, closure, and assessment.
2. Why are visuals helpful for enabling a child to understand music?
3. If you are assigned to a class of kindergarten children, what kinds of musical expectations would you have? How are various classes different and still the same? What kinds of expectations would you have for grades 1 and 2, 3 and 4, and 5 and 6?
4. Discuss how you would decide on the length and frequency of music lessons.
5. Discuss how you might use multisensory and multicultural experiences and materials in your class.
6. Discuss how you might use instructional technology to enhance teaching music.
7. Discuss key points to remember in the writing of lesson plans.

Assessment

Review ways the music standards listed at the beginning of this chapter have been met.

CHAPTER 3

Fundamentals of Music

Understanding How Sounds Are Organized in a Musical Composition

© Ritchie Photography

Objectives

Students will learn the basic elements of music through experiences with rhythm, melody, dynamics, tone color, texture, and form:

- Experiences with rhythm
  - Beat
  - Tempo
  - Meter
  - Reading rhythms
  - Syncopation
- Experiences with melody
  - A melody moves by steps or skips
  - A melody has shape
  - A melody has range
  - A melody is made up of phrases
  - A melody is based on a scale
- Experiences with dynamics
- Experiences with tone color
  - Tone color varies with the type and size of material producing the sound
  - Tone color varies with different types of instruments
  - Tone color varies with different types of voices
  - Exploring tone colors
- Experiences with texture
  - Monophonic
  - Homophonic
  - Polyphonic
- Experiences with musical forms
  - Binary form
  - Ternary form
  - Rondo form
  - Fugue form
  - Theme-and-variation form

National and State Music Standards

This chapter provides experiences with the following national music standards and related state music standards:

- Singing, alone and with others, a varied repertoire of music
- Performing on instruments, alone and with others, a varied repertoire of music
- Composing and arranging music within specified guidelines
- Reading and notating music
- Listening to, analyzing, and describing music

Music is an aural art form consisting of the organization of sounds in time. An understanding of music begins with the perception of its basic elements, which include rhythm, melody, dynamics, tone color, texture, and form. This chapter explains some of the basic characteristics of these elements and provides musical examples. You are encouraged to *experience* the characteristics of the elements through actual performance. When you finish this chapter, you should be able to perform or listen to short musical compositions and describe them in terms of their basic elements.

Technology Enhancement

A great website covering basic elements of classical music (notation, instrumentation, harmony, tonality, rhythm, meter, melody, and texture): http://www.bbc.co.uk/schools/gcsebitesize/music/elements_of_music.

Additionally, http://www.teoria.com/ is a website devoted to music theory tutorials and exercises as used in classical music, though it may be more beneficial for teacher preparation than student use.

EXPERIENCES WITH RHYTHM

Rhythm refers to the organization of musical sounds in time. It is composed of a number of subareas including *beat, tempo,* and *meter,* along with distinctive features such as syncopation.

Beat

The ongoing pulse in music is called the *beat*. Sometimes teachers refer to the beat as the "steady beat" to help students realize that the feeling of the beat is even.

ACTIVITIES

1. Download or stream [iTunes/Spotify] and play a recording of "Stars and Stripes Forever" by John Philip Sousa. Call attention to the strongly felt beat in the music. Ask students to march to the music.
2. Sing or play Brahms's "Lullaby" and ask students to sway gently from side to side as if they were attempting to put a baby to sleep. Call attention to the weakly felt beat in the music.
3. Model nonlocomotor beat movements to recorded music for students to copy. These beat movements can be patting, clapping, tapping the head, moving arms up and down, rubbing hands together, opening and shutting the hands, and any other nonlocomotor beat movements students can mimic. (See page 17–19, 24–27 for the "four-step language process" of teaching nonlocomotor movements developed by Phyllis S. Weikart.) Choose recorded music that has a fairly brisk tempo (around 130 beats per minute) for beginning activities. As students become more proficient at keeping the beat, the speed of the recordings can be varied. (Suggested downloads from [iTunes/Spotify]: Bach's "Badinerie" and Kodály's "Viennese Clock".)
4. Invite children to lead nonlocomotor beat movements to recorded music for the class to follow. Play a game where one child hides his or her eyes as the teacher chooses another child to lead the beat movements for the class to follow. When the hiding child returns, he or she must then determine who the leader is.
5. Keep the beat to known songs and chants by using nonlocomotor (e.g., patting and clapping) and locomotor (e.g., walking and marching) beat movements. (Suggested songs: "Camptown Races" [p. 218], "Erie Canal" [p. 430], "Galway Piper" [p. 319], "Pop Goes the Weasel" [p. 249], "Yankee Doodle" [p. 368], and "Hickory Dickory Dock" [p. 46].)
6. Play the beat to known songs and chants and to recorded music on various small percussion instruments, including drums, maracas, woodblock, guiro, and sand blocks. (See steps 3 and 5 for a suggested repertoire.)

7. Provide visual icons that represent the beat. Invite students to point to the icons for the beat of recorded music, songs, and chants.

8. Read books that have a feeling of beat. (Examples: *Hand, Hand, Fingers, Thumb* by Al Perkins and Eric Gurney [New York: Random House for Young Readers, 1969] and *Chicka Chicka Boom Boom* by Gill Martin et al. [New York : Beach Lane Books, 2009]).
9. Use a "counting out" chant to choose who goes first in line.
   Example:
   Bee bee bumble bee,
   Stung a man upon his knee,
   Stung a pig upon his snout,
   I declare that you are OUT!
   Point to one child on each beat of the chant. The child who gets the beat "out"—is out. Repeat the process until there is only one child left. That child will then be the line leader.
10. Compare music that has a strong feeling of beat with music that does not have a feeling of beat. (Suggested recording downloads [iTunes/Spotify]: Greig's "In the Hall of the Mountain King" and Debussy's *La Mer.*
11. More beat activities can be found on page 35.

Special Learner Note

Model clapping to the beat in an exaggerated manner; vary the presentation to reinforce kinesthetic experience by tapping hands on knees, marching or lifting knees while seated, or tapping hands on desktop or wheelchair tray.

Use scarves or streamers to enhance the visual cue for movement.

Specific motions to express strong and weak beats could include leaning forward and back, putting arms in front, down, up, in lap, and so on.

Tap the beat on the student's shoulders; put your hands over the student's hands and clap the beat; use Velcro to attach an instrument (e.g., rattle) to the student's hands—have him or her follow the beat with the instrument.

Tempo

The speed with which the beat recurs in music is called *tempo*.

ACTIVITIES

1. Follow the moderately fast tempo in "Stars and Stripes Forever" and compare it with the much slower tempo of Brahms's "Lullaby."

America the Beautiful

Words by Katharine Lee Bates
Music by Samuel A. Ward

Key: C
Starting pitch: G
Meter: 4/4, begins on 4

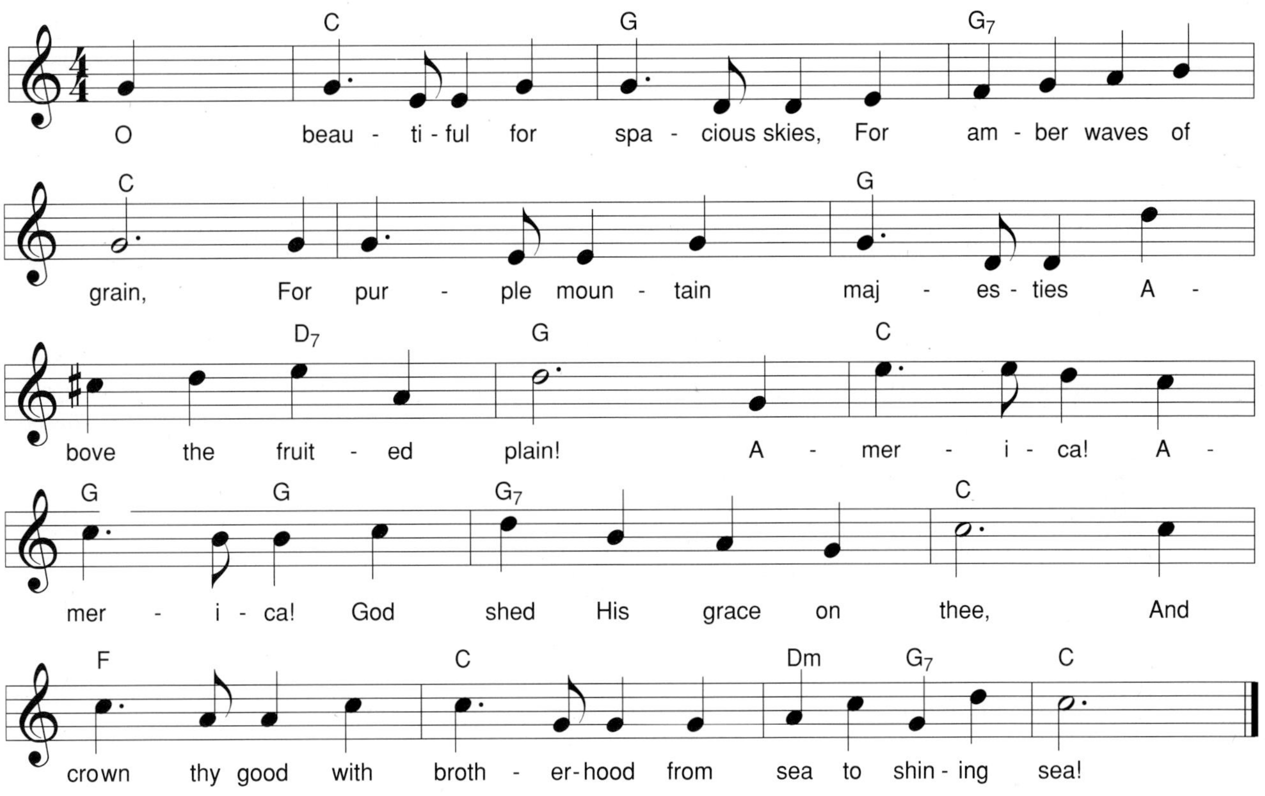

2. Sing or play a familiar song, such as "America the Beautiful," and experiment with musical effects created by performing it at different tempos (slow, medium, and fast).
3. Listen and compare the tempos of "The Swan" and "Fossils" in Saint-Saëns's *Carnival of the Animals* [iTunes/Spotify].
4. Sometimes the tempo gradually gets faster or slower. Listen to Honegger's "Pacific 231," a musical composition about a train [iTunes/Spotify]. Notice the gradual increase in tempo at the beginning of the composition as the train starts up and the gradual decrease in tempo near the end of the piece as the train slows down.

Special Learner Note

Use pictures of animals and/or videos of animals moving to illustrate different types of motion.

A "moving train" video (see www.youtube.com) may enhance students' understanding before listening to "Pacific 231." Also, demonstrating physical movements as a way to model changes in tempo will reinforce understanding and may encourage more effective listening.

Meter

As the beat recurs in most music, certain pulses are emphasized or accented. The accenting of specific pulses establishes a pattern of strong and weak beats. This recurring pattern of accented and unaccented beats in music is called *meter*.

Two common types of meter are *duple meter,* in which the pattern of strong and weak beats is grouped into twos; and *triple meter,* in which the pattern of strong and weak beats is grouped into threes. *Bar lines* are used to divide the pattern of beats into measures.

A *meter signature* is placed on the musical staff. The top number indicates the number of beats in a measure, and the bottom number indicates the type of note receiving a single beat. For example, in

"Hot Cross Buns," the meter signature of 2/4 indicates that there are two beats in a measure and that the quarter note receives one beat, whereas in "America," the meter signature of 3/4 means that there are three beats in each measure with the quarter note receiving one beat.

Hot Cross Buns

England

Key: G
Starting pitch: B
Meter: 2/4, begins on 1

G D7 G G D7 G D7 G D7 G
Hot cross buns, hot cross buns, One a pen - ny, two a pen - ny, hot cross buns.
England 1798

America

Arranged by Henry Carey
England c. 1690–1743

Key: G
Starting pitch: G
Meter: 3/4, begins on 1

G D7 G D7 G

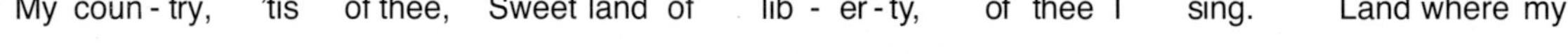
My coun - try, 'tis of thee, Sweet land of lib - er - ty, of thee I sing. Land where my

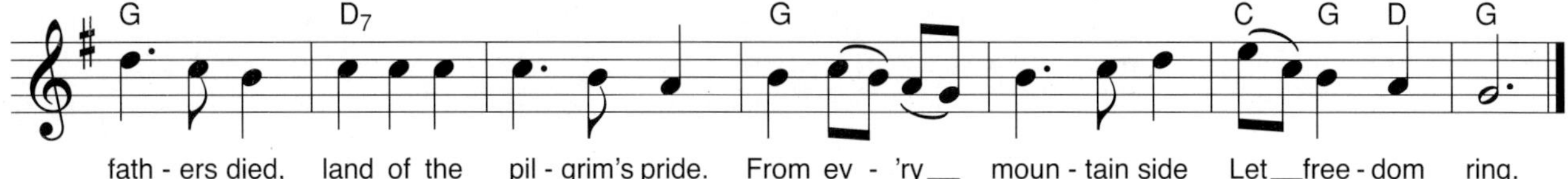
G D7 G C G D G
fath - ers died, land of the pil - grim's pride. From ev - 'ry moun - tain side Let free - dom ring.

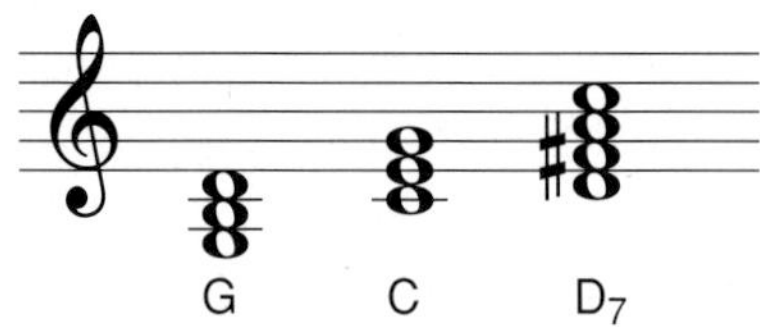
G C D7

ACTIVITIES

1. Ask students to stand in a circle.
   - Invite students to jump whenever the teacher plays a loud drum beat. The teacher then plays many soft beats and random loud beats. The teacher purposely lifts the mallet high before playing each loud beat. Students notice that it is easy to tell when the loud beats are coming because of the way the teacher lifts the mallet before playing the loud sound.
   - The teacher asks students to repeat the activity, but now with eyes closed. The students find it more difficult to jump with the loud beats.
   - Then, the teacher plays *patterns* of loud beats starting with *loud, soft, soft.* The students identify that the beats are grouped in threes. The activity is then repeated for patterns of two beats (loud, soft). Students find it easy to jump on the loud beats because they can hear the patterns of three and two beats defined by the loud and soft sounds played on the drum.
   - Students conclude that some beats have a stronger feel than others and can make patterns of three and two beats.
2. Ask students to sit in a circle all facing counterclockwise.
   - Students then take off their shoe from the foot that is on the inside of the circle.

- In order to get the feeling of strong and weak beats, students march in the circle, step to the beat, and say the following chant:

  Deedle deedle dumpling, my son John,
  Went to bed with his stockings on,
  One shoe off and one shoe on,
  Deedle deedle dumpling, my son John.

- Students describe how the beats felt when they were walking with one shoe on and one shoe off. Did one foot feel heavier than the other? The answer will be *yes*. Students may disagree about which foot felt heavier, but they will all agree that the activity helped them feel heavier and lighter beats.
- Repeat the activity, asking students to start stepping with the foot that felt heavier. This will allow them to get a heavy-light feeling to go with the chant.
- Students conclude that the beats for "Deedle Deedle Dumpling" are grouped in a pattern of two.

3. Ask students to find ways to use body percussion (pats, claps, and snaps) to show beats grouped in twos and threes. Require students to use the "pat" for the first beat of each group. (Examples: pat-clap or pat-snap for groups of two beats; pat-clap-clap, pat-snap-snap, or pat-clap-snap for groups of three beats.)
4. Have students chant the following in duple meter:

   Arthur, Arthur has a quarter. Jenny, Jenny has a penny.

Ar - thur, Ar - thur has a quar - ter. Jen - ny, Jen - ny has a pen - ny.

   - Have them chant the preceding line and play a drum or pat their thighs on the strong beats.
   - Have them pat their thighs on beat 1 and clap or snap on beat 2.

5. Sing "Hot Cross Buns." Have the students sit in a circle, each with a rhythm stick (or stone) placed at the right knee. As they sing the song, have them pick up the stick or stone on beat 2 (beginning with "Hot -Cross") and put it, on beat 1, in front of the left knee of the person sitting to their right ("buns"). Continue to pass the stick or stone around the circle as the song is sung over and over. Call attention to the fact that the beats are grouped into "twos" (duple meter).
6. Have students chant the following in triple meter:

   David and Jonathan like to play golf again.
   Leroy and Christopher play on the hockey team.

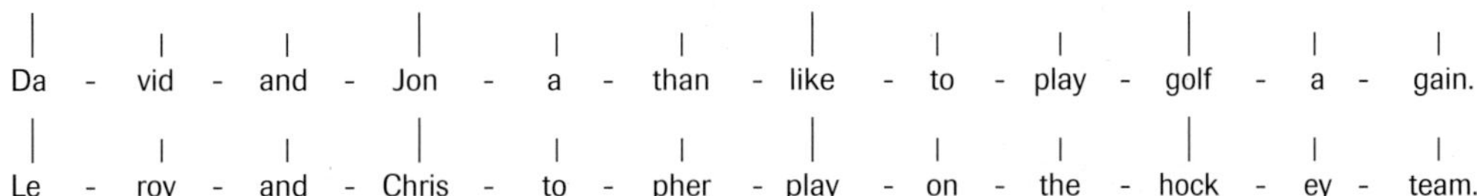
Da - vid - and - Jon - a - than - like - to - play - golf - a - gain.
Le - roy - and - Chris - to - pher - play - on - the - hock - ey - team.

   - Have them chant the above and play the drum or pat their thighs on the strong beats.
   - Have them pat their thighs on beat 1 and clap or snap on beats 2 and 3.

7. Ask students to sing "Hot Cross Buns" and then "America" employing body percussion in duple and triple meter, respectively.
8. Place the following terms on the chalkboard:

   Duple meter = 2 beats in a group, with the first beat being the stronger beat.
   Triple meter = 3 beats in a group, with the first beat being the strongest beat.
   More activities for meter can be found on page 38.

Reading Rhythms

Music notation was created (and has evolved over the centuries) to show both the pitch of the sound (whether it is high or low) and how long it is supposed to continue (duration). Musicians have created a series of symbols to represent how long a sound is to last. Figure 3.1 illustrates this system. Each of these notes has a name based on the idea of a "whole."

In Figure 3.1 each symbol represents half the value of the previous symbol; thus, two half notes equal one whole note (𝅗𝅥 + 𝅗𝅥 = 𝅝); two quarter notes equal one half note (♩ + ♩ = 𝅗𝅥); two eighth notes equal one quarter note (♪ + ♪ = ♩); and two sixteenth notes equal one eighth note (𝅘𝅥𝅯 + 𝅘𝅥𝅯 = ♪).

A dot (.) after a note is a symbol that lengthens that note by half its value. Thus, if a half note is to receive a duration of two counts, a dot placed next to it indicates that it will now receive three counts.

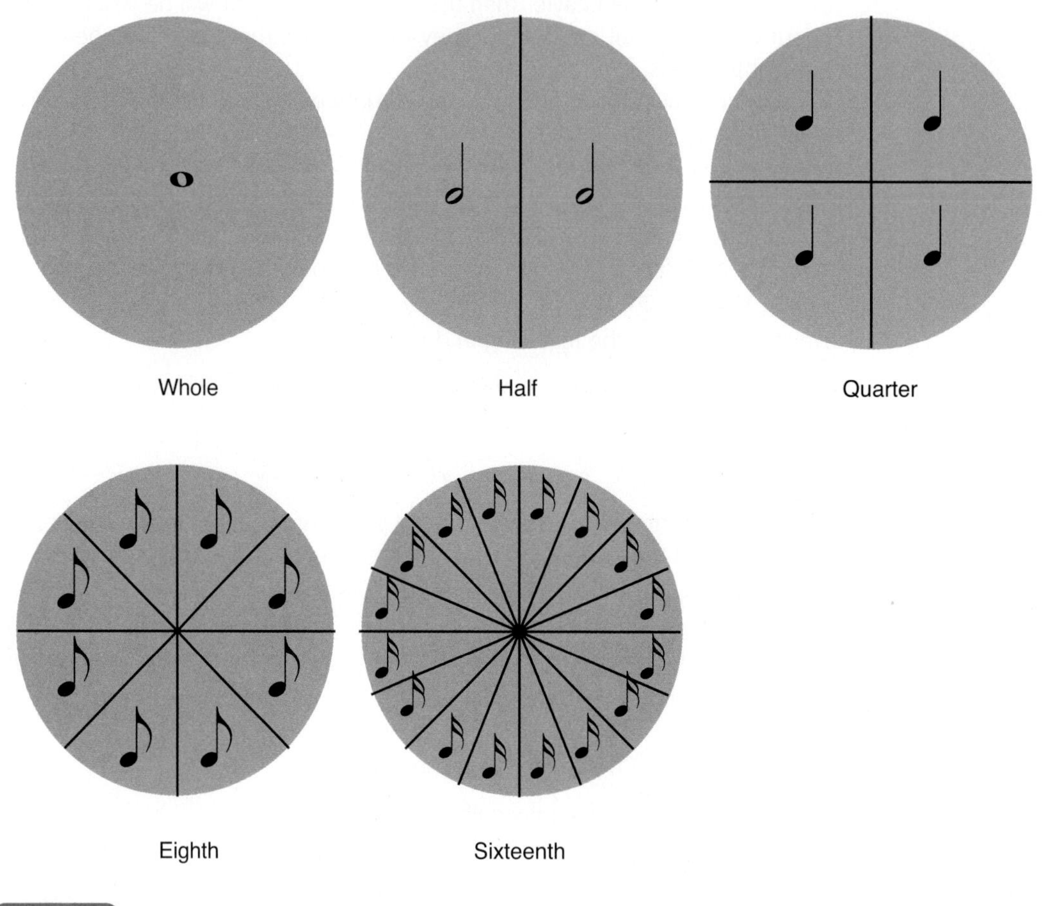

Figure 3-1 Symbols of duration: music notation

ACTIVITIES

1. Echo clap four-beat rhythm patterns, using patterns you want to teach. When echo clapping, the teacher claps a four-beat pattern, and then the students clap the same pattern. For a more advanced activity, echo clap patterns in canon. When echo clapping in canon, the teacher never stops clapping patterns and the students echo without stopping.
2. Clap the rhythm of a song for students to identify. For example, the teacher claps the rhythm for "Yankee Doodle" (p. 135). Students listen and determine the name of the song. (Earlier in the lesson, sing the song you plan to clap as preparation for the activity.)
3. Create a rhythmic "machine." One student starts the "machine" by creating a four-beat rhythm pattern and a movement for the pattern. A second student then joins with a different pattern and movement, but something that fits with the first pattern. Continue to add students, rhythm patterns, and movements until the whole class has joined. The teacher can help by tapping a steady beat on a drum.
4. The teacher taps either a steady beat or a rhythm on a drum for students to identify as either "steady beat" or "rhythm." Invite students to take over the role of the teacher and tap either a beat or a rhythm on the drum for the class to identify.

5. Here are some examples for you to try. Remember that 4/4 meter indicates that there are four beats to a measure and that the quarter note receives one beat.

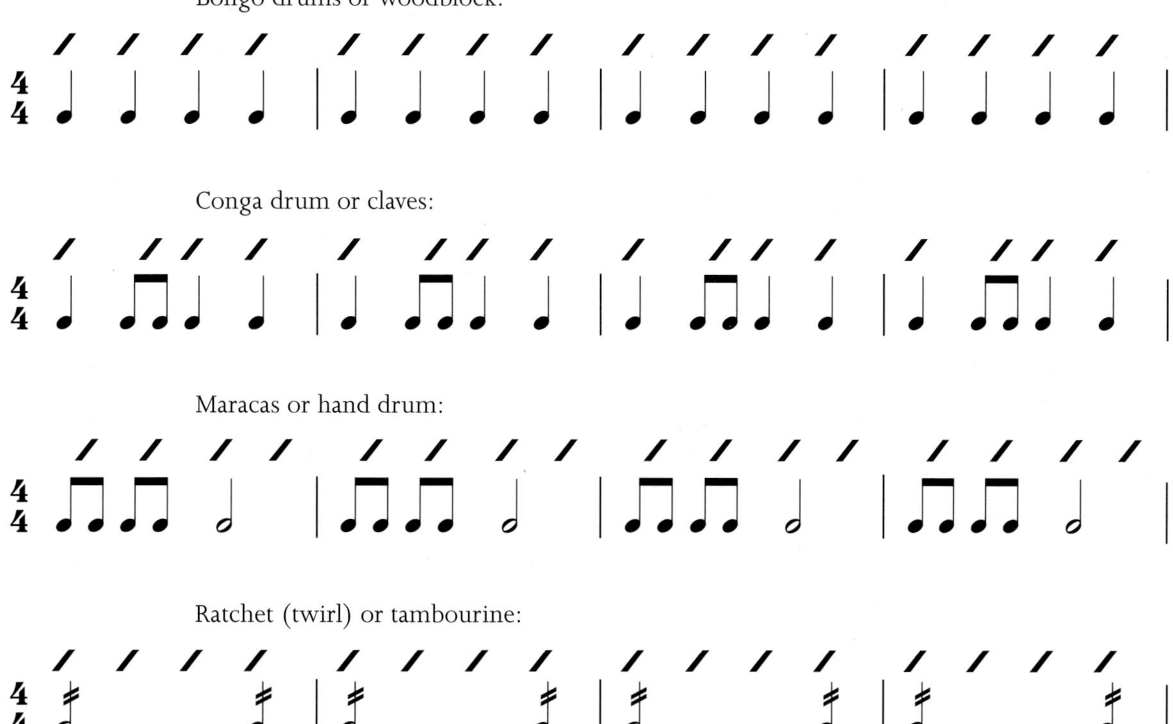

Music would be very dull if we heard only sound and no moments of silence. Silences in music are called *rests,* and there is a rest equal to every note. Examine the following table and notice the shapes of the various rests.

DURATION OF NOTES	AND RESTS
Whole note	Whole rest
Half note	Half rest
Quarter note	Quarter rest
Eighth note	Eighth rest
Sixteenth note	Sixteenth rest

ACTIVITIES

1. Invite students to do a work movement such as hammering, sawing, or turning a screwdriver to the steady beat provided by the teacher. (The teacher may play the steady beat on a drum or other small percussion instrument.) When the teacher calls out a number, the "workers" must stop for that number of beats. Repeat the activity, but this time the students also make a sound to accompany their movement. Finally, do the activity without the support of the teacher's beat; students must internalize the beat. As before, when the teacher calls out a number, the "workers" stop for that number of beats. Listen to the silence!
2. Teach the students a chant that has a quarter rest in it, for example, "Pease Porridge Hot." Draw beat slashes over the beats for the chant.

   / / / /
   Pease porridge hot. 𝄽

   / / / /
   Pease porridge cold. 𝄽

   / / / /
   Pease porridge in the pot.

   / / / /
   Nine days old. 𝄽

   Students say the chant and pat the beat. Students blink on the beats where there are no words. Students discover that some beats have no sound.
3. Here are some notated rhythmic examples to try (use the instruments listed or choose your own):

   You may also create your own rhythms.
4. More activities for rhythm can be found on pages 277–278, 278–279, and 280–281.

Technology Enhancement

Use available composition software, such as "GarageBand," or websites, such as Aviary.com, to have students create simple compositions that demonstrate various elements of rhythm that they have learned. For example, ask students to create an eight-measure drum beat in a fast tempo. Have them change the tempo of their composition and reflect on how the tempo changes the music. Also have students create drum beats in various meters (e.g., 2/4, 3/4), noticing how different rhythmic groupings affect the way music sounds.

Syncopation

Accenting beats or portions of beats that would normally be unaccented produces *syncopation.*

Five Green and Speckled Frogs

Words by Louise Binder Scott
Music by Virginia Pavelko

Key: C
Starting pitch: G
Meter: 4/4, begins on 1

C F

1. Five green and speck - led frogs
2. Four green and speck - led frogs
3. Three green and speck - led frogs
4. Two green and speck - led frogs
5. One green and speck - led frog

Sat on a speck - led log

C G_7 C

Eat - ing some most de - li - cious bugs. (Yum, yum!) 1.–4. One jumped in - to the pool,
5. He jumped in - to the pool,

F C G_7 C

Where it was nice and cool.

1. Then there were four green speck - led frogs.
2. Then there were three green speck - led frogs.
3. Then there were two green speck - led frogs.
4. Then there was one green speck - led frog.
5. Then there were no green speck - led frogs.

(Glub, glub!)

ACTIVITIES

1. Ask students to keep the basic pulse (1, 2, 1, 2, etc.) with their feet, while clapping and counting the following pattern. Emphasize the strong portion of the beat indicated by the accent (>).

2. Ask students to keep the basic pulse (1, 2, 1, 2, etc.) with their feet, while clapping and counting the following pattern. Emphasize the weak portion of the beat indicated by the accent (>).

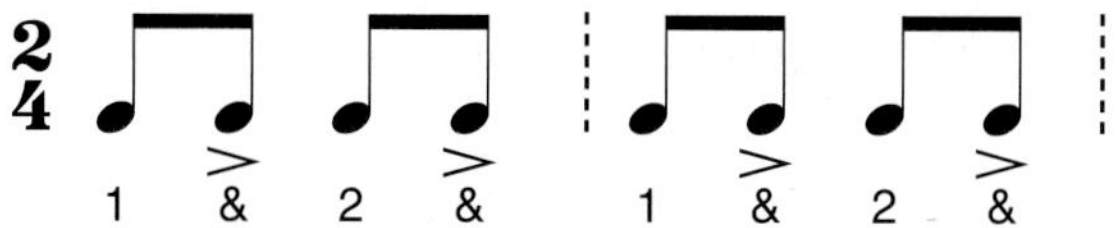

3. Repeat step 2, tying together the second and third eighth notes in each measure:

4. Ask students to clap and count the above rhythm with the tied eighth notes now written as quarter notes. Have them recite
"syn-co-pah" as they clap.

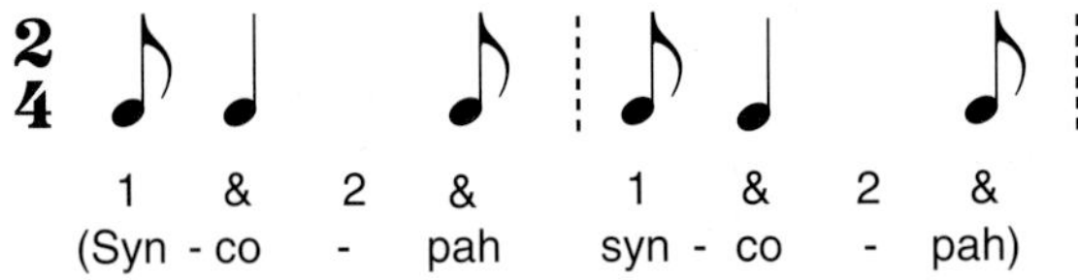

5. Sing "Five Green and Speckled Frogs." When the song is known, sing the song and clap the rhythm.
6. Provide opportunities for students to experience the syncopated rhythm aurally, visually, and kinesthetically.
   - Help students aurally identify the uneven pattern of "Five green and" in the first line by clapping the pattern and feeling the *short-long-short* pattern. Determine that the *short-long-short* pattern has three parts or sounds.
   - Identify the song visually by using rhythm icons:

   - Sing the song on "short" and "long." For example, the first line would be: *short-long-short short-short long*. Point to the icons as the children sing.
   - Write traditional notation above the icons. Sing the song again replacing all of the "*short-long-short*" patterns with "syncopah."
   - Find the "syncopah" rhythm in other songs, for example, "Kye, Kye Kule" (p. 293).

Special Learner Note

Play recorded examples of syncopation from current pop/country/folk music and encourage movement, playing along, and singing along with the recordings. Once accuracy of rhythm is coordinated with the recording, notation of the rhythm being sung/played may be introduced and pointed out as it occurs in the recording. (Example: Use the opening introduction to "My Girl" [iTunes/Spotify], which can be continued as a pattern under the melody/singer once the song begins.)

EXPERIENCES WITH MELODY

A *melody* is a succession of musical sounds that are perceived as belonging together. Melodies are familiar to all of us. We sing, whistle, and play melodies from the time we are little children. Whereas the rhythm or beat of a piece of music may dominate our physical response to it (toe-tapping, nodding), we generally recognize a composition by its melody. As you pay close attention to the features of the melodies discussed here, you will increase your understanding and experience greater pleasure in performing and listening to music.

A Melody Moves by Steps or Skips

Fundamentally, melodies in musical compositions move either by step or skip from one note to another.

ACTIVITIES

1. Sing the song "Hot Cross Buns" (p. 38) and the segments of "Row, Row, Row Your Boat" and "Joy to the World" below noticing how these melodies move basically by steps.
2. Then sing the song "Reveille," noticing how the melody moves basically by skips.

Reveille

U.S. Army Bugle Call

Key: G
Starting pitch: D
Meter: 2/4, begins on "and" of 2

A Melody Has Shape

ACTIVITIES

Melodies may move up or down.

1. Sing the first section of "Row, Row, Row Your Boat" and listen to the melody going up.
2. Sing the first section of "Joy to the World" and listen to the melody going down.
3. Sometimes melodies move like a pendulum, up and down around a particular note. Sing the first line of "Hickory Dickory Dock." Listen to the pendulum-like movement of the melody. "Map" the melody with your hand in the air.

Special Learner Note

Use body motions (i.e., bending knees, up on toes) to enhance rhythm and direction of the melody. Keep the tempo slow and gradually increase as group is able to keep up.

Row, Row, Row Your Boat

English, c. 1852

Key: C
Starting pitch: C
Meter: 6/8, begins on 1

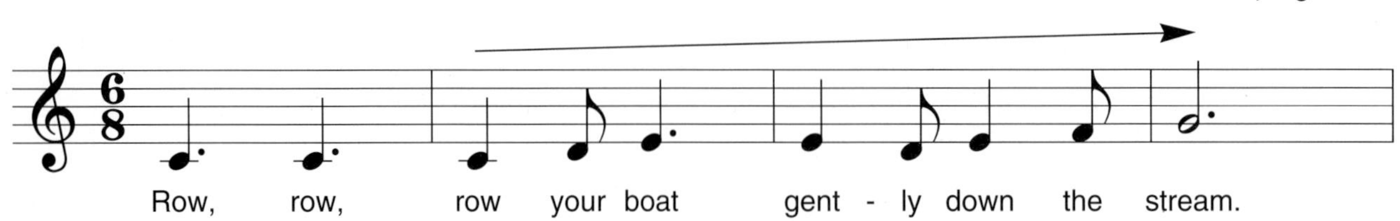
Row, row, row your boat gent - ly down the stream.

Joy to the World

English, c. 1839

Key: C
Starting pitch: C
Meter: 2/4, begins on 1

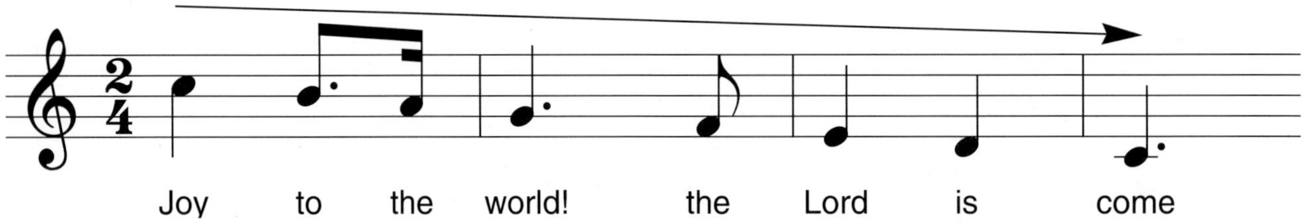
Joy to the world! the Lord is come

Hickory Dickory Dock

J. W. Elliott
English nursery rhyme, c. 1744

Key: F
Starting pitch: A
Meter: 6/8, begins on 1

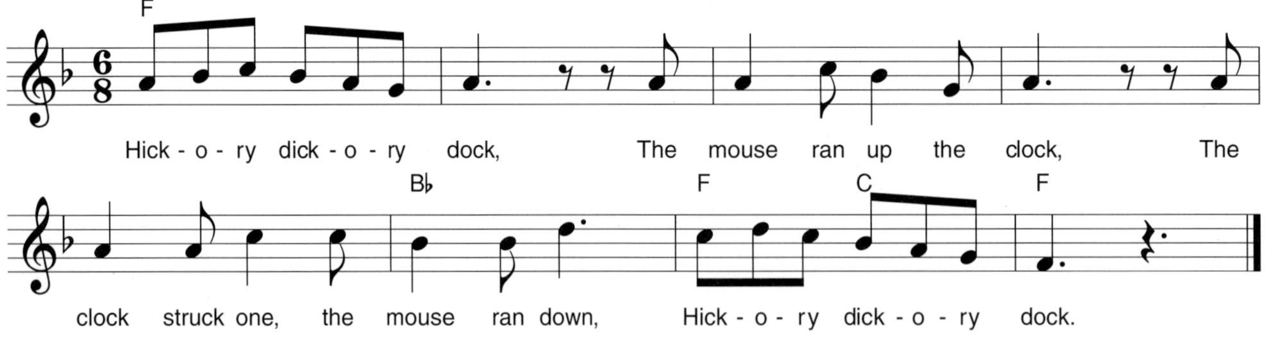
F
Hick - o - ry dick - o - ry dock, The mouse ran up the clock, The
B♭
F
C
F
clock struck one, the mouse ran down, Hick - o - ry dick - o - ry dock.

A Melody Has Range

As you trace the shapes of melodies, you will discover that the distance from the lowest to the highest note is sometimes large and other times small. The term *range* is used to describe these distances. Some melodies have a small range, whereas other melodies have a large range.

ACTIVITIES

1. Sing "The Star-Spangled Banner," noticing the large range of the melody (low to high).

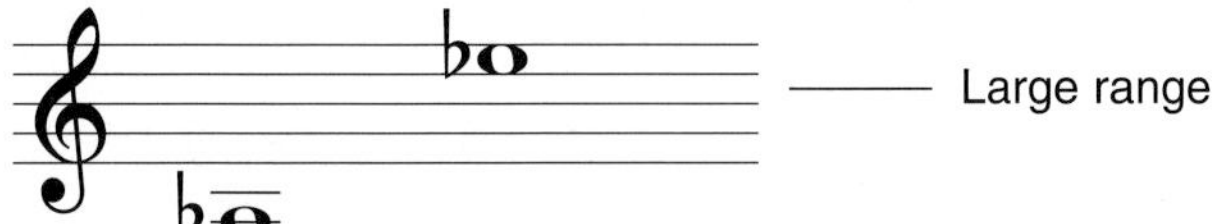

Play the lowest and highest notes on a melody instrument.

2. Sing the song "Old MacDonald Had a Farm," noticing the relatively small range of the melody (D to B).

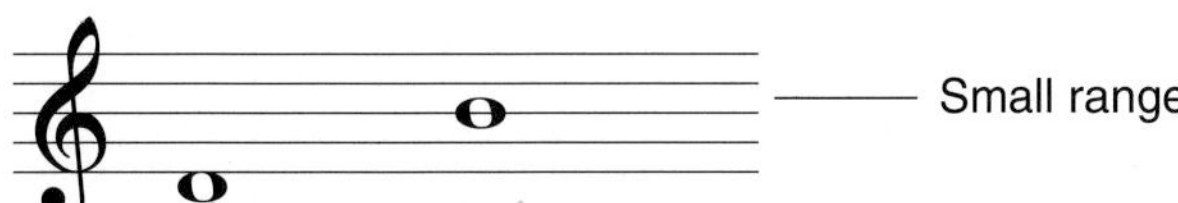

Again, play the lowest and highest notes on a melody instrument.

The Star-Spangled Banner

Music by John Stafford Smith
Text by Francis Scott Key

Key: Ab
Starting pitch: Eb
Meter: 3/4, begins on 3

Fm Bb7 Eb Eb7 Ab Db F7 Bbm Bb7
flag was still there. Oh, say, does that __ Star - Spang - led Ban - ner __ yet __
Ab Eb Eb7 Ab Fm Bb7 Ab Eb7 Ab
wave __ O'er the land __ of the free and the home of the brave?

Old MacDonald Had a Farm

United States

Key: G (Pentatonic)
Starting pitch: G
Meter: 4/4, begins on 1

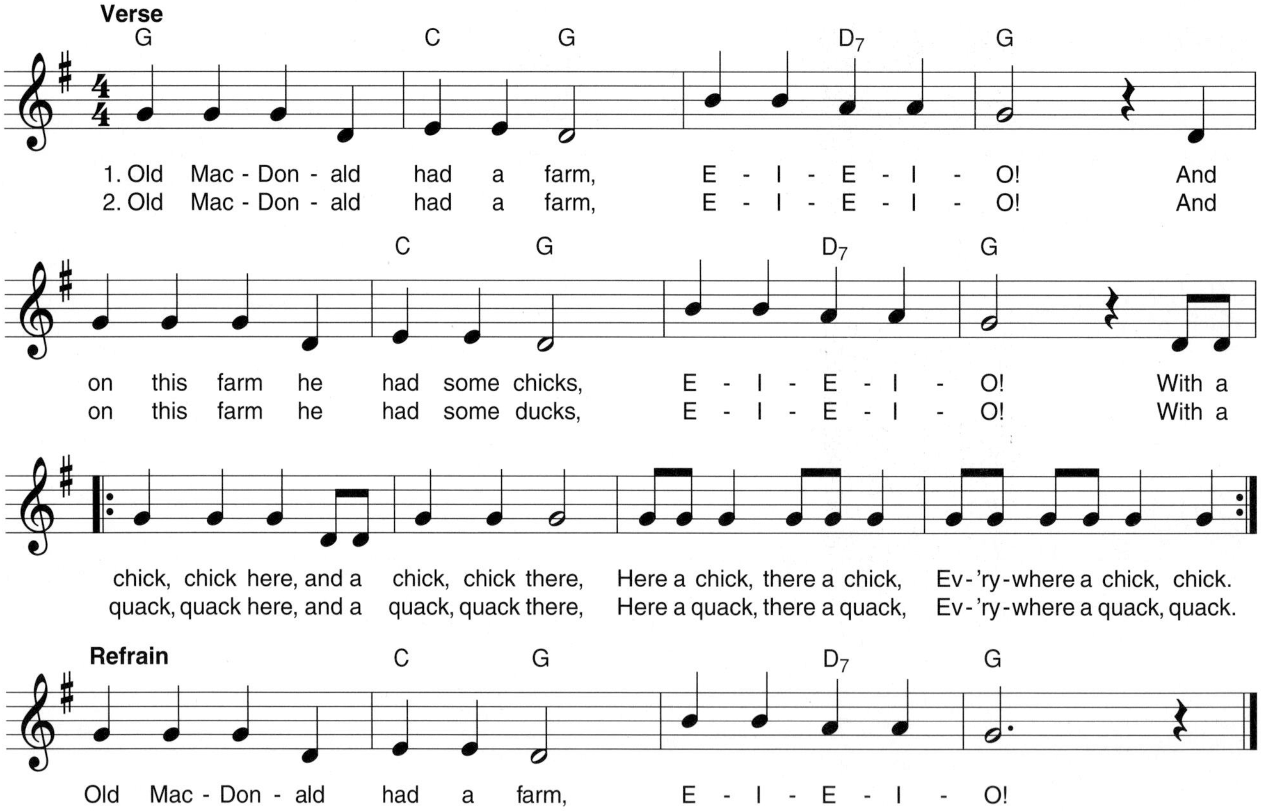

Verse

G C G D7 G

1. Old Mac - Don - ald had a farm, E - I - E - I - O! And
2. Old Mac - Don - ald had a farm, E - I - E - I - O! And

C G D7 G

on this farm he had some chicks, E - I - E - I - O! With a
on this farm he had some ducks, E - I - E - I - O! With a

chick, chick here, and a chick, chick there, Here a chick, there a chick, Ev-'ry-where a chick, chick.
quack, quack here, and a quack, quack there, Here a quack, there a quack, Ev-'ry-where a quack, quack.

Refrain

C G D7 G

Old Mac - Don - ald had a farm, E - I - E - I - O!

Special Learner Note

Begin by teaching the "E-I-E-I-O" part first, using a visual cue to help students sing it. Add "Old Mac" phrases next. The "with a . . . here and a . . . there" may be too fast for some students; simplify by "stretching" the lyric and eliminating "here a . . . there a . . . ." Example:

"With a chick here . . . (time for response instead of "chick there"). There a chick, everywhere a chick."

A Melody Is Made Up of Phrases

Melodies often have several sections, set off from one another by a slight pause or point of rest. These subsections, called *phrases,* function in a similar fashion to the phrases in a sentence.

ACTIVITIES

Sing "O Susanna," particularly noticing the four phrases. Outline the phrases by moving your hand from left to right in the air as you perform the piece. Using a flannel board, select different-colored objects, and as each phrase occurs, place one object on the board. Point out that each object (color) represents a phrase in the melody.

O Susanna

Stephen C. Foster

Key: F
Starting pitch: F
Meter: 2/4, begins on "and" of 2

A Melody Is Based on a Scale

Melodies are based on scales, which are arrangements of pitches in an order from low to high. The two most common scales in Western music are *major scales* and *minor scales.*

Major Scale

ACTIVITIES

1. Place the pitches of the following major scales on a chalkboard. Write the note names beneath each note. Have students sing the scales with a neutral syllable, such as "Loo," and then with note names. Ask students to take turns playing the scales on melody bells.

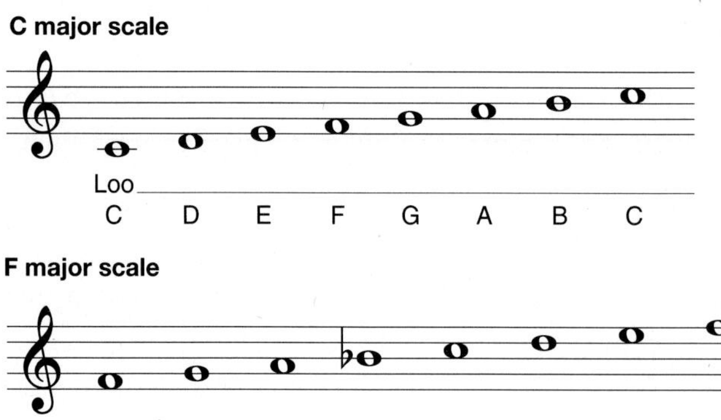

Loo
F G A B♭ C D E F

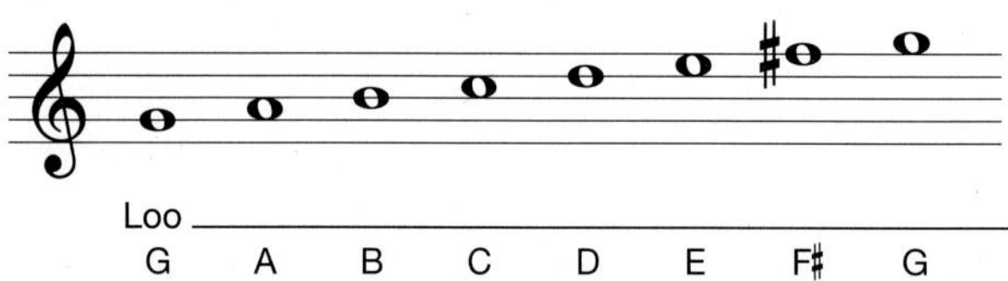

Loo
G A B C D E F♯ G

2. Point out that the distinctive quality of the *major scale* is due to its particular pattern of whole and half steps. Place a diagram of a keyboard on the writing board. Point out that the keyboard has twelve tones consisting of seven white keys (without any duplication of pitches) and five black keys. Between some notes, such as C and D, is an intervening black key; between others, such as E and F, there is none. If a black key intervenes between two consecutive white keys, the interval is described as a *whole step.* If no key occurs between two consecutive pitches, such as E to F (or C to C#), the interval is described as a *half step.* The scale shown below has the following whole- and half-step pattern: W-W-H-W-W-W-H. It is described as a *major scale.* All major scales, regardless of the pitch on which they start, have the same pattern of whole and half steps.

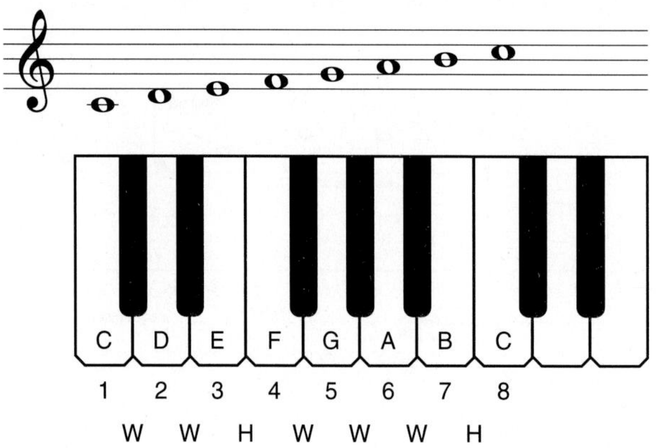

3. Have students sing songs based on major scales, such as "Sweet Betsy from Pike," "Home on the Range," and "Old MacDonald Had a Farm" (p. 48).

American

Sweet Betsy from Pike

Key: C major
Starting pitch: C
Meter: 3/4, begins on 3

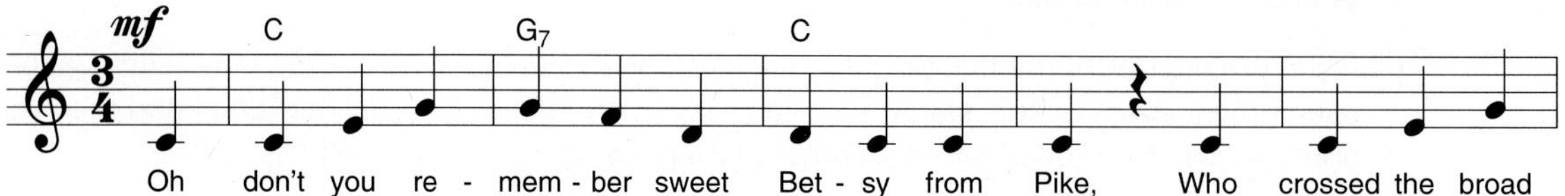

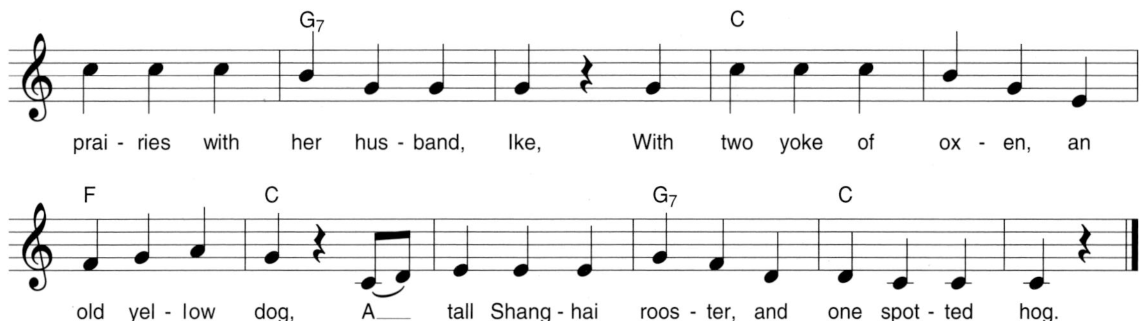

prai - ries with her hus - band, Ike, With two yoke of ox - en, an

old yel - low dog, A tall Shang - hai roos - ter, and one spot - ted hog.

Home on the Range

Traditional

Key: F major
Starting pitch: C
Meter: 6/8, begins on 6

A
F
B♭
F
G7
C7
1. Oh, give me a home where the buf - fa - lo roam, Where the deer and the an - te - lope play; Where
sel - dom is heard a dis - cour - ag - ing word, And the skies are not cloud - y all day.
B Chorus
Home, home on the range, Where the deer and the an - te - lope play; Where
sel - dom is heard a dis - cour - ag - ing word, and the skies are not cloud - y all day.

1. How often at night, when the heavens are bright
From the light of the glittering stars,
Have I stood there, amazed, and asked as I gazed
If their glory exceeds that of ours.

2. Where the air is so pure and the zephyrs so free
And the breezes so balmy and light;
Oh, I would not exchange my home on the range
For the glittering cities so bright.

3. Oh, give me a land where the bright diamond sand
Flows leisurely down with the stream;
Where the graceful white swan glides slowly along,
Like a maid in a heavenly dream.

Minor Scale

In addition to the major scale, the other most common scale in Western music is the *minor scale*. The minor scale differs from the major scale in the pattern of whole and half steps. In the following D minor scale, for example, the pattern of whole and half steps is W-H-W-W-H-W-W.

D minor scale

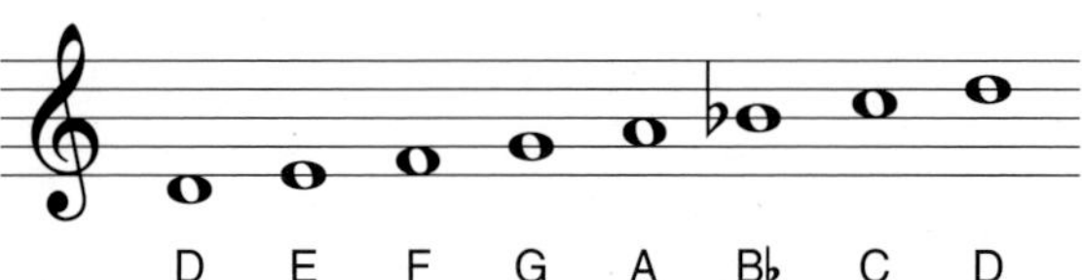

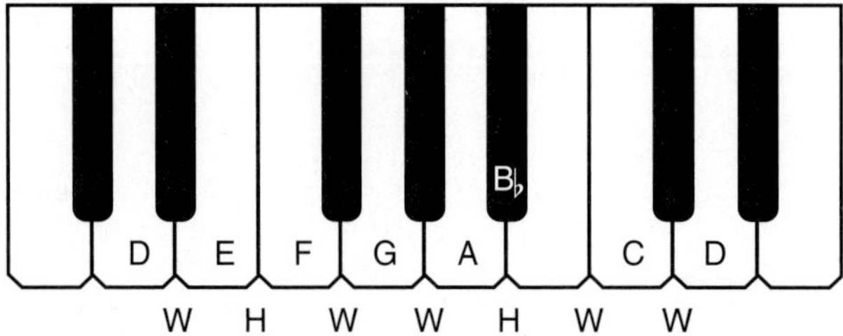

In many songs written in a minor key, the seventh degree of the scale will be raised (sharped) a half step. In the scales below, notice that G, the seventh degree, is raised (sharped); when a minor scale has the seventh raised, it is known as a *harmonic minor scale*.

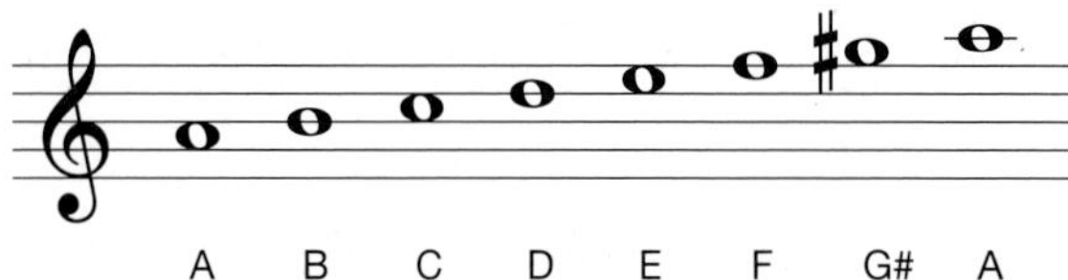

ACTIVITIES

1. Place the pitches of the D minor and A minor scales on the chalkboard. Write note names beneath each note. Have students sing the scales with a neutral syllable and then with note names. Ask students to take turns playing the scales on melody bells.
2. Perform the following songs based on minor scales: "Go Down Moses," A minor (p. 53); and "The Peddler" (Korobushka), D minor (p. 141).

A melody is also identified as being in a particular key, a term that refers to the scale on which it is based.

ACTIVITIES

1. Sing the song "Sweet Betsy from Pike" (p. 50), noticing that the piece is based on a major scale with "C" as the home tone. This composition is said to be in the key of C major. .
2. Sing the song "Go Down, Moses" (p. 53), noticing that it is based on a minor scale with "A" as the home tone. This composition is said to be in the key of A minor.

Notice that the *key* is indicated in the upper right corner of each song in this book.

Spiritual

Go Down, Moses

Key: A minor
Starting pitch: E
Meter: 4/4, begins on 4

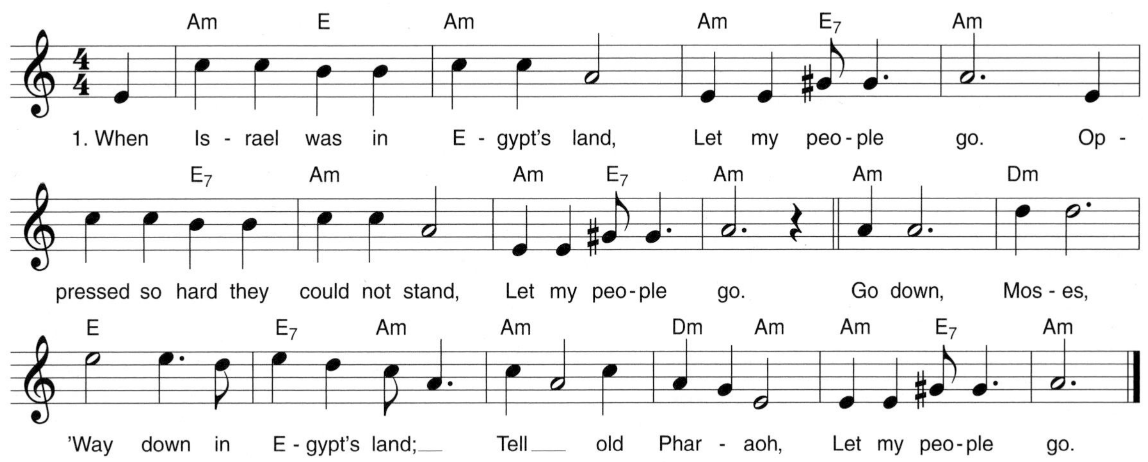
Am E Am Am E7 Am
1. When Is - rael was in E - gypt's land, Let my peo - ple go. Op -
E7 Am Am E7 Am Am Dm
pressed so hard they could not stand, Let my peo - ple go. Go down, Mos - es,
E E7 Am Am Dm Am Am E7 Am
'Way down in E - gypt's land; Tell old Phar - aoh, Let my peo - ple go.

Pentatonic Scale

In addition to the seven-tone major and minor scales, melodies sometimes have other types of scales, such as the five-tone, or *pentatonic,* scale, which is extremely common in the music of China and Japan as well as in American folk music.

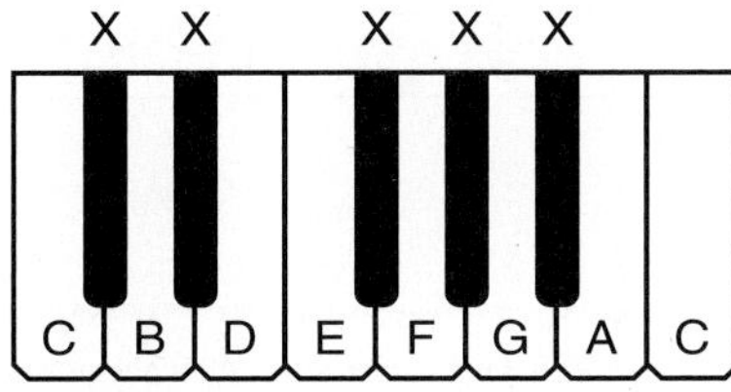
X X X X X
C B D E F G A C

Pentatonic scale

ACTIVITIES

1. Play the five black keys on the piano keyboard and listen to the distinctive quality of the pentatonic scale.
2. Play a pentatonic scale on the white keys of the piano, the pitches C D F G A.
3. Create a melody on a xylophone using only the pitches C D F G A. You may wish to play some pitches more than once, or you can extend the melody higher or lower by using the same pitches. The melody will sound more interesting if you place it in a meter.

Special Learner Note

In addition to having individuals creating melodies, you may want to pair students with peer models to create melodies. You can also use the entire group (self-contained special learner class) and assign each student a note with a color coding. Using the color coding, the group "song" could be transferred to Boomwhackers (see p. 131) or other similarly color-coded instruments for additional repetition of material.

Technology Enhancement

Using available music software, such as "GarageBand," or websites, such as Aviary.com, have students create pentatonic melodies using only the "black keys" of a MIDI piano.

4. Sing the well-known Korean song "Ahrirang," which has the following pentatonic scale:

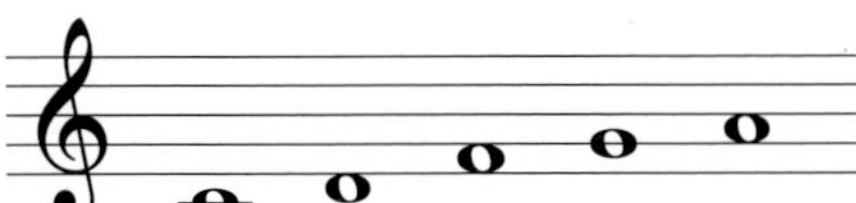

Ahrirang
Folk Song from Korea
English Words by Alice Firgau
Key: Pentatonic (C D F G A)
Starting pitch: C
Meter: 3/4, begins on 1
3
Ah - ri - rang, ah - ri - rang, ah - ra - ri - yo.
O - ver the hills of Ah - ri - rang.
Voic - es call me from far a - way.
I must fol - low I can - not stay.

EXPERIENCES WITH DYNAMICS

The term *dynamics* describes the degree of softness or loudness in music. Composers use different dynamic levels to express various moods in music and provide variety or contrast in musical works.

ACTIVITIES

1. Sing the American spiritual "Steal Away" (next page), exploring soft and loud dynamic levels. Note that this song was sung by slaves on plantations and that it focuses on an afterlife with the words "I don't have long to stay here." Notice how the mood of the piece changes with different dynamic levels for various sections of the lyric. For example, sing softly the words "I don't have long to stay here" and loudly the words "He calls me by the thunder; The trumpet sounds within-a my soul."

2. Use a megaphone (or make one out of cardboard). Talk into the small end for the sound to be louder, or talk into the large end for the sound to be softer.
3. Explain that a composer indicates "to get louder"—a *crescendo*—or "to get softer"—a *decrescendo*—with similar symbolic shapes:

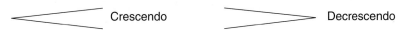

Draw the shapes on the board.
4. Sing "Steal Away" again, this time adding the suggested crescendos and decrescendos.
5. Create a short piece of music with classroom instruments, using different dynamic levels to provide variation or contrast.

Steal a - way, steal a - way, steal a - way to Je - sus.

EXPERIENCES WITH TONE COLOR

Musical tones are distinguished from each other by the quality of their sounds. In music, this is called *tone color,* or *timbre* (pronounced "tam-ber").

Tone Color Varies with the Type and Size of Material Producing the Sound

ACTIVITIES

1. Explore ways to produce different sounds; for example, strike two sticks together, shake pebbles in various-sized cans, blow air across different sizes of pop bottles.
2. Listen to each sound and describe it with words.
3. Make a list on the writing board of all the different qualities of the sounds you make. Notice that the tone color varies with the type and size of the material producing the sound.

Special Learner Note

Students with visual impairments will gain more from this experience if they are allowed to touch and play the instrument.

Students with hearing impairments will gain more from this experience if they are allowed to play the instrument to feel the vibrational quality of the sound.

Overall, students will benefit more from this activity if allowed to see, touch, feel, and create the sounds with the instruments. Once an interest in a certain instrument or sound is observed by the teacher, that student may be able to "earn" playing time on that instrument for other appropriate classroom effort or behavior. Use this "preferred activity" to reinforce the student's appropriate behavior in a less preferred activity.

Tone Color Varies with Different Types of Instruments

Musical instruments can be classified on the basis of the *quality* of their sounds. For example, on *stringed instruments,* the distinctive sound is produced by vibrating strings, which are set in motion by being either bowed or plucked. *Wind instruments* produce their distinctive sounds with a vibrating air column, which is set in motion by vibrating a reed, "buzzing the lips," or simply blowing across a notch or other opening. On *percussion instruments,* the sounds are produced by striking the instruments with either the hand or a mallet or by striking several objects together.

ACTIVITIES

1. Find instruments at home or at school, or make your own instruments for the class to listen to and classify.[1]
2. Listen to some examples of musical instruments from around the world and describe their distinctive tone colors. Include some electronic instruments such as those found in current popular music.

Tone Color Varies with Different Types of Voices

Singers can also be classified according to the tone color or quality of the musical sounds they produce.

ACTIVITIES

1. Listen to different vocal tone colors produced by individuals in your class, taking turns singing a familiar song.
2. Listen to recordings of women and men singing. Think of some words to describe the different tone colors of women's and men's voices. (Women's voices are generally lighter and thinner than the heavier, fuller sounds of men.)
3. Play recordings of singers from different areas of the world (such as Africa, China, and India) and discuss differences in tone color.

Exploring Tone Colors

ACTIVITIES

1. Sing the song "The More We Get Together."

[1] Bart Hopkins, *Making Musical Instruments with Kids: 67 Easy Projects for Adults Working with Children.* Tucson, AZ: See Sharp Press, 2009.

2. Create an accompaniment, first with tone colors created by mouth—for example:
   a. Oom-pah-pah.
   b. Oom-ss-ss.
   c. Oom-deedle-eet.
3. Perform as an accumulative song—for example:
   a. Begin with Oom-pah-pah.
   b. Add Oom-ss-ss.
   c. Add Oom-deedle-eet.
   d. Add the melody of "The More We Get Together."
4. Create an accompaniment with the different tone colors of classroom percussion instruments—for example:
   a. Use bongo drums with Oom-pah-pah.
   b. Use sand blocks with Oom-ss-ss.
   c. Use a tambourine with Oom-deedle-eet.
5. Perform as an accumulative song as in step 3.

Technology Enhancement

Using available music software, such as "GarageBand," or websites, such as Aviary .com, have students use various instrument loops to create a short composition. Have students describe the differences in timbre among their various instrument parts.

Germany

The More We Get Together

Key: D major
Starting pitch: D
Meter: 3/4, starts on 3

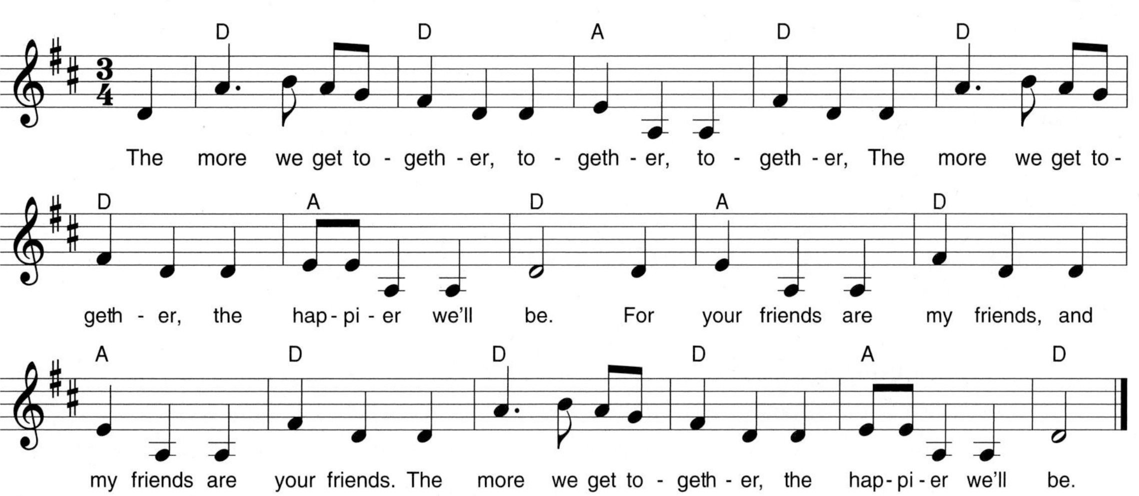
D D A D D
The more we get to - geth - er, to - geth - er, to - geth - er, The more we get to -
D A D A D
geth - er, the hap - pi - er we'll be. For your friends are my friends, and
A D D D A D
my friends are your friends. The more we get to - geth - er, the hap - pi - er we'll be.

Oom - pah - pah
Oom dee - dle - eet

EXPERIENCES WITH TEXTURE

Texture is a musical term used to describe the relationships among various musical lines.

Monophonic

The simplest type of texture is known as *monophonic* (*mono* = one; *phonic* = sound). In monophonic texture there is just one musical line.

For example, sing "America" (p. 38) together in unison without accompaniment, and notice the distinctive quality of monophonic texture.

Homophonic

Much of the music that we perform and listen to, however, has multiple lines of music. Most often there is a melody accompanied by chords, and this type of texture is called *homophonic texture.*

Chords most often consist of three pitches, each a third apart above any pitch. For example, a chord can be constructed on the note C by adding at the same time the notes E and G:

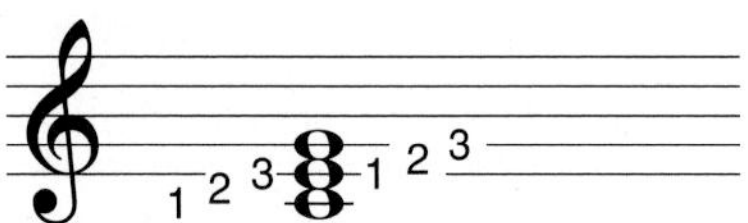

Chords are identified by their lowest note. Thus, the chord above is called a *C chord.* Construct and play chords by using melody bells.

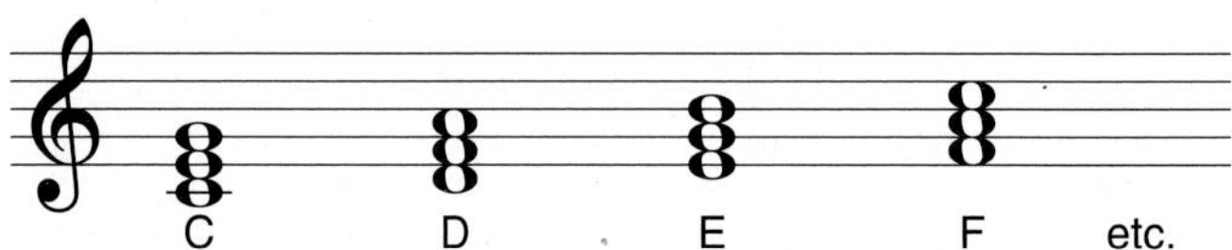

In accompanying songs, chords sometimes have four pitches. Such chords are called *seventh chords* because the distance between the lowest and highest pitches is seven notes.

Construct a seventh chord on the note G. Play it using melody bells and notice the distinctive quality. This chord is identified as a G_7.

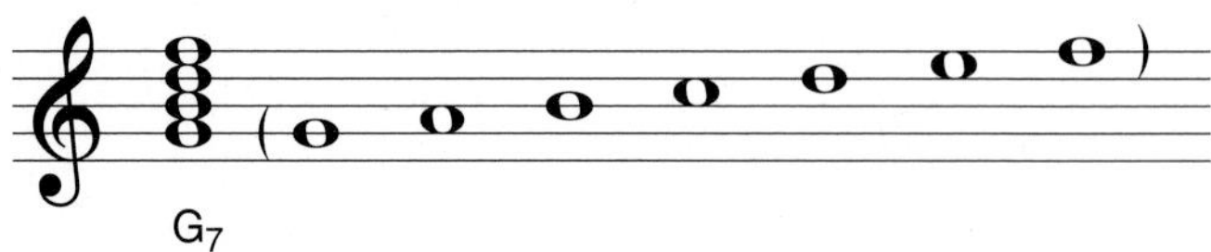

Technology Enhancement

1. Visit the New York Philharmonic's Kids Zone's "Instrument Storage Room" Web page at http://www.nyphilkids.org/lockerroom or Dallas Symphony Orchestra for Kids website and go to the Listen by Instrument page: http://www.dsokids.com/listen/instrumentlist.aspx.
2. Have students do an exploratory project in which they listen to the different instruments and identify similarities and differences between like instruments such as violin and cello. Have them explore and then explain why they believe these instruments sound alike or different based upon their observations, listening, and research.

ACTIVITIES

The songs in this book have chords indicated above the melody.

1. Accompany "Merrily We Roll Along" by playing the C and G7 chords on the resonator bells, keyboard, or Q-chord.

Traditional

Merrily We Roll Along

Key: C major
Starting pitch: E
Meter: 4/4, starts on 1

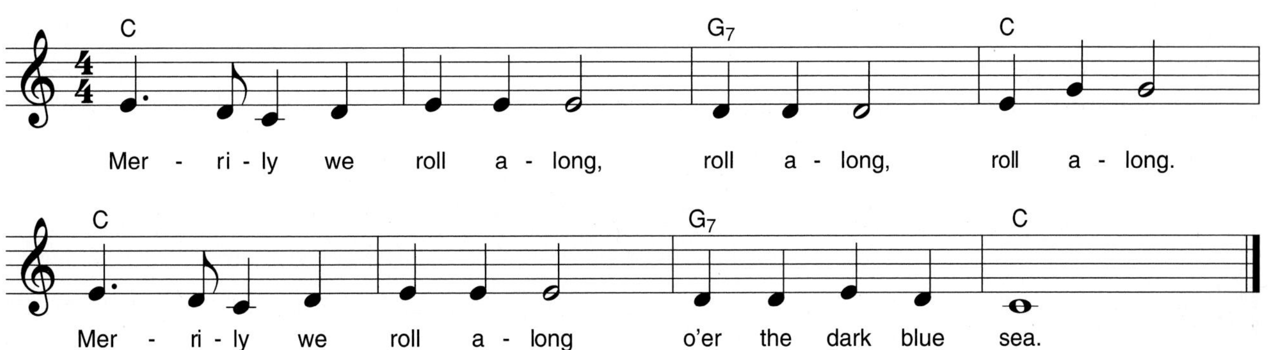

C
G7
C
Mer - ri - ly we roll a - long, roll a - long, roll a - long.
C
G7
C
Mer - ri - ly we roll a - long o'er the dark blue sea.

2. Play the chords C (C E G) and G7 (G B D F) to accompany "My Hat."

Germany

My Hat

Key: C major
Starting pitch: G
Meter: 3/4, begins on 3

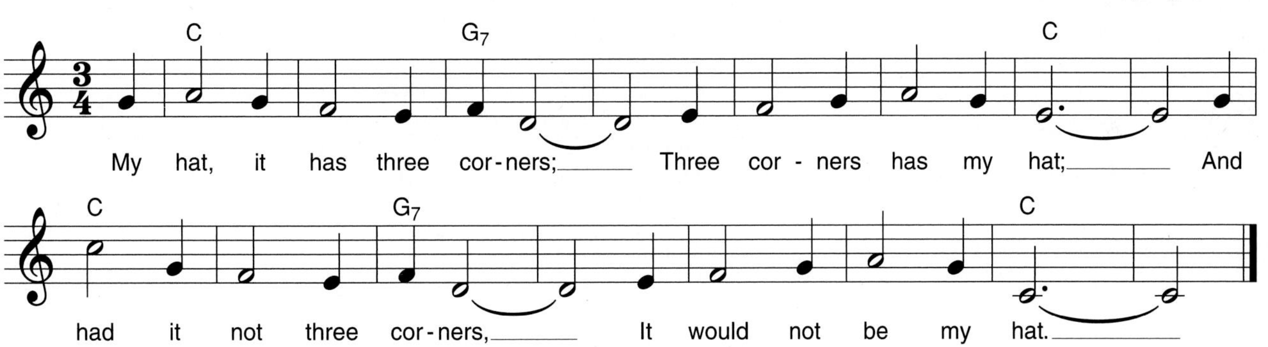

My hat, it has three cor-ners; Three cor - ners has my hat; And

had it not three cor-ners, It would not be my hat.

3. Play the chords G (G B D), C (C E G), and D7 (D F# A C) to accompany "Yankee Doodle" (p. 368).

Polyphonic

Sometimes musical compositions have several melodic lines, each with a distinctive rhythm, sounding at the same time. Such texture is called *polyphonic* (*poly* = many; *phonic* = sounds).

ACTIVITIES

1. Sing "Row, Row, Row Your Boat" as a three-part round. (The class is divided into three sections.) Notice that when everyone is singing there are three different lines of music.
2. Listen to Bach's "Little" Fugue in G Minor (p. 64), particularly noticing the distinctive quality of the many melodies sounding at the same time, each with a distinctive rhythm.

Row, Row, Row Your Boat

Traditional

Key: C
Starting pitch: C
Meter: 6/8, begins on 1

Row, row, row your boat gent- ly down the stream Mer- ri - ly, mer- ri - ly, mer- ri - ly, mer- ri - ly,
Row, row, row your boat gent - ly down the stream
Row, row, row your boat
Life is but a dream.
Mer- ri - ly, mer- ri - ly, mer- ri - ly, mer- ri - ly, Life is but a dream.
gent - ly down the stream Mer- ri - ly, mer- ri - ly, mer- ri - ly, mer- ri - ly, Life is but a dream.

EXPERIENCES WITH MUSICAL FORMS

The term *form* refers to how a composition is put together. Most forms are based on repetition and contrast. Repeated musical ideas unify compositions, and contrasting ideas provide variety.

Some of the most common musical forms are binary, ternary, rondo, fugue, and theme-and-variation.

Binary Form

As the name implies, musical compositions in *binary form* have two principal sections: The first is often labeled A, and the second, B.

ACTIVITIES

1. Sing "Home on the Range" (p. 51) and listen and look for the two contrasting sections, A and B.
2. Diagram the form by having students place sheets of red (A) and blue (B) paper on the board.

A
B

Ternary Form

In many musical compositions, an A section of music is followed by a B section, and then there is a return to the A section. In effect, such compositions consist of three sections, and the form is described as *ternary*.

ACTIVITIES

1. Sing "We Wish You a Merry Christmas" (below).
2. Diagram the form with colored paper.
3. Explain that repeating the A section helps tie together or unify the piece. The B section is designed to provide contrast or variety.

A
B
A

Technology Enhancement

When using listening examples such as Mozart's Horn Concert no. 3, try finding a video of a performance on YouTube or another site. If you are unable to access YouTube while at school, try downloading the YouTube video at home and bringing it to school on a flash-drive. A great downloading tool for YouTube videos is FastestTube (http://kwizzu.com/). It is a free browser extension that adds a "download button" below YouTube videos.

English

We Wish You a Merry Christmas

Key: A
Starting pitch: E
Meter: 3/4, begins on 3

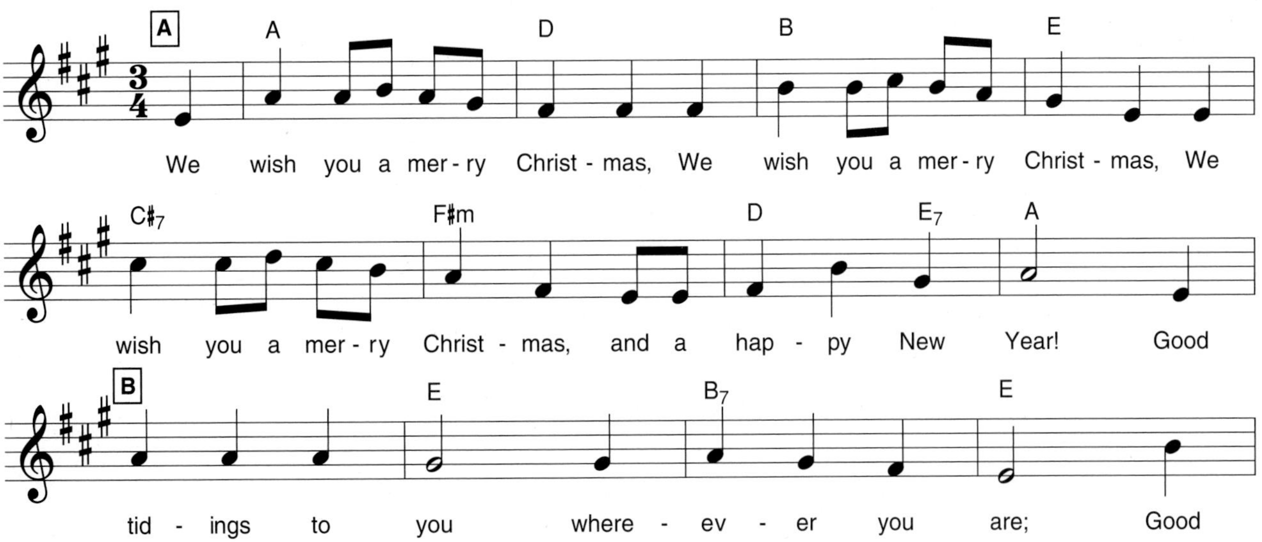
A
A
D
B
E
We wish you a mer - ry Christ - mas, We wish you a mer - ry Christ - mas, We
C♯7
F♯m
D
E7
A
wish you a mer - ry Christ - mas, and a hap - py New Year! Good
B
E
B7
E
tid - ings to you where - ev - er you are; Good

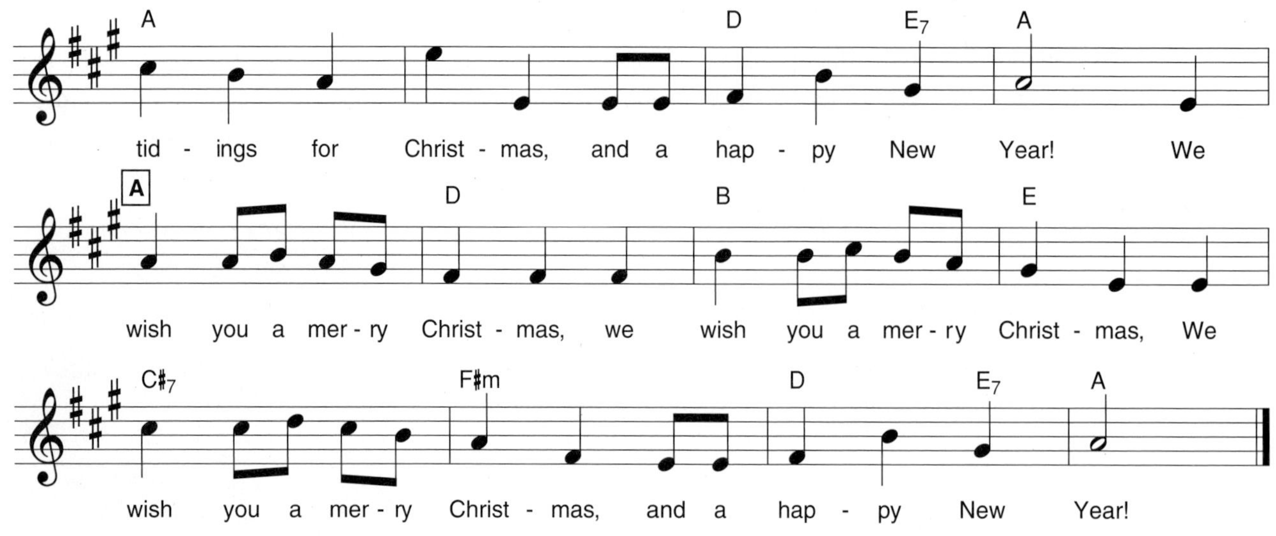
A
D
E7
A
tid - ings for Christ - mas, and a hap - py New Year! We
A
D
B
E
wish you a mer - ry Christ - mas, we wish you a mer - ry Christ - mas, We
C♯7
F♯m
D
E7
A
wish you a mer - ry Christ - mas, and a hap - py New Year!

Rondo Form

A *rondo* is a musical form in which there is an A section, followed by a contrasting B section, a return to the A section, followed by another contrasting C section, and then a return to the A section again. The recurring A section helps to "tie" the music together and provide a sense of unity, while the contrasting B and C sections provide variety in the musical composition.

Listening Guide: Mozart's Horn Concerto no. 3 (third movement)

Paper	Letters	Musical Idea
Red	A	Horn with orchestral accompaniment playing pulsating, driving theme
Blue	B	Contrast provided by smooth, lyrical theme played by horn with orchestral accompaniment
Red	A	Return to pulsating A theme
Green	C	Lyrical, contrasting section
Red	A	Pulsating theme from beginning

THEME	CONTRASTING IDEA	THEME	SECOND CONTRASTING IDEA	THEME
A	B	A	C	A

ACTIVITIES

1. Using a drum to keep the beat, ask students to walk around the room. On a signal, they should change the way they walk (backward, sideways, on tiptoe, on their heels, and so on). On a second signal, they should return to the way they walked at the beginning. On a third signal, they should walk a different way.
2. Repeat, having one student hold colored cards marked A B A C A. As each card is held up, students walk in the appropriate fashion.
3. Listen to the third movement of Mozart's Horn Concerto no. 3 in E-flat Major [iTunes/Spotify], having the students make up movements to follow the form. Diagram the form on the board with sections of colored paper and letters, or place on a transparency or PowerPoint slide.

Special Learner Note

Students who are unable to walk may be the card holders or drummers who control the walking of the ambulatory students.

ACTIVITIES

1. Have the students listen to a song that is popular on the radio (you can ask them the day before what songs are their favorites and then preview and download or stream them from iTunes, Spotify, or YouTube).
2. Diagram the form by having students place sheets of red (A), blue (B), and yellow (C) on the board.

Fugue Form

The *fugue* is another musical form based on repetition and contrast. The first section of the fugue is known as the *exposition*. In the exposition the *subject* (musical idea) is stated in one musical line and then imitated in other musical lines. For example, in Bach's "Little" Fugue in G Minor, the melody begins in the soprano line and then imitatively repeats in the alto, tenor, and bass lines.

Following the exposition, segments of contrasting musical ideas known as *episodes* alternate with periodic returns of the subject. The episodes are particularly important for providing variety in the musical work. The repetition of the subject from time to time helps tie the musical composition together and provides a sense of unity.

Technology Enhancement

Watch and listen to Bach's "Little" Fugue in G Minor" on YouTube at http://www.youtube.com/watch?v=pVadl4ocX0M

This video shows a visual representation of the notes as rectangles (MIDI notes), helping students to see the layering of the melody.

ACTIVITY

Play a recording of Bach's "Little" Fugue in G Minor [iTunes/Spotify]. Follow the diagram of events in the composition. (See the Listening Guide on next page.) If you wish, have students provide a visual response to their listening experience by asking half the class to raise their hands whenever they hear the subject, and the other half to raise their hands whenever they hear the episodes.

Listening Guide: Bach's "Little" Fugue in G Minor

Place on the board, or on a transparency or PowerPoint slide.

Call Number	Events
1	Exposition, main melody (subject) stated four times (in soprano, alto, tenor, and bass lines)
2	Episode: section designed to offer variety, contrast (main melody not heard)
3	Subject with accompanying melodies
4	Episode
5	Subject with accompanying melodies
6	Episode
7	Subject with accompanying melodies
8	Episode
9	Subject with accompanying melodies
10	Episode
11	Subject with accompanying melodies

Theme-and-Variation Form

In *theme-and-variation form,* the theme is generally stated at the beginning of the piece, and thereafter repeated over and over, but with changes each time to provide contrast.

ACTIVITIES

1. Explore the theme-and-variation form through the following:
   - **a.** Have students draw circles on the chalkboard or on paper and then create many different ways (variations) of changing the circle.
   - **b.** Have students print their names in at least eight different ways (using a different color, a different shape, a different-sized script, curved lines, straight lines, and so on).

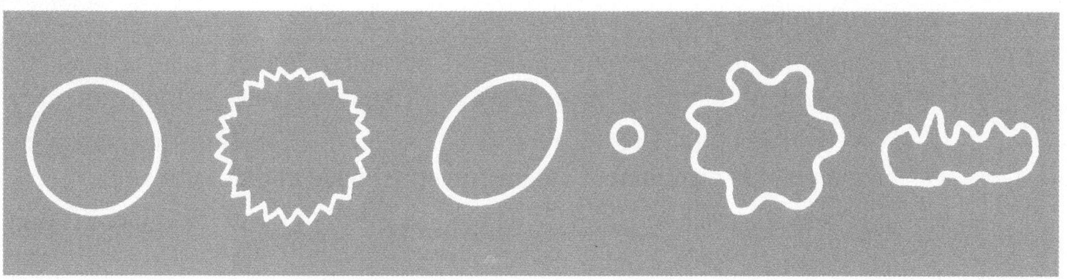

2. Sing the song "Simple Gifts." Explore ways of creating variety in the song by singing it faster or slower, louder or softer.

Shaker Melody

Simple Gifts

Key: F
Starting pitch: C
Meter: 2/4, begins on 2

F C7
'Tis the gift to be sim-ple, 'tis the gift to be free, 'Tis the gift to come down where you want to
F C7
be, And when we find our - selves in the place just right, 'Twill be in the val - ley of love and de-

F F C7
light. When true sim - pli - ci - ty is gained, To bow and to bend we shan't be a -

F C7 B♭ F
shamed, To turn, turn will be our de - light, Till by turn - ing, turn - ing we come 'round right.

3. Listen to variations on "Simple Gifts" Aaron Copland's ballet *Appalachian* [iTunes/Spotify]. This orchestral selection, which is based on the "Simple Gifts" melody, is cast theme-and-variation form. Listen carefully to see can identify ways in which the composer changes appearance of the tune.

   a. Place pictures of the following instruments on bulletin board:
      Clarinet
      Oboe
      Bassoon
      Strings (violin, viola, cello, bass)
      Trumpet
      Full orchestra

   b. Ask students to pretend that they are playing a clarinet, violin, or trumpet. Have them hum the tune of "Simple Gifts" as they "play" their imaginary instruments.

   c. As students listen to Copland's Variations on "Simple Gifts," have them circle each variation and point to picture(s) of the instrument(s) used in that variation.

Special Learner Note

Each student has a card with an instrument pictured on it. As an instrument is heard, a student who has a picture of that instrument holds up the card. This activity may require some cueing at first—or pairing with a peer model.

Listening Guide: Copland's *Appalachian Spring*, Variations on "Simple Gifts"

Place on the board, or on a transparency or PowerPoint slide.

Theme	**"Simple Gifts" Played on the Clarinet**
Variation 1	Variation (contrast) in tone color with "Simple Gifts" in oboe and bassoon
Variation 2	Variation (contrast) in tone color with "Simple Gifts" in stringed instruments; theme augmented
Variation 3	Variation (contrast) in tone color with "Simple Gifts" in trumpet
Variation 4	Variation (contrast) in tone color with "Simple Gifts" in clarinet and bassoon
Variation 5	Variation (contrast) in tone color and texture with "Simple Gifts" in the full orchestra

Integrating Technology

The Music Education Premium Site contains chapter quizzing, Spotify playlists, and downloads of free MP3s of noted songs. Visit CengageBrain.com to purchase an access code or enter the code provided with your text materials.

Web Resources

- Search the Web (www.google.com) for information on musical elements.

Videos

- Watch classroom videos that apply to the chapter content and access the YouTube playlist for videos referenced within the chapter.

Audio

- Download music discussed in this chapter from the iTunes store.
- Spotify playlists allow students to stream music referenced within each chapter.
- Download free audio MP3s for the songs noted in the chapter.

CENGAGE**brain**.com

Questions for Discussion

1. Briefly define the following musical concepts:
   - Rhythm
   - Melody
   - Dynamics
   - Timbre (tone color)
   - Texture
   - Form
2. Discuss experiences with *rhythm* that you could present in the classroom.
3. Discuss experiences with *melody* that you could present in the classroom.
4. Discuss experiences with musical *dynamics* that you could present in the classroom.
5. Discuss experiences with *musical timbre (tone color)* that you could present in the classroom.
6. Discuss experiences with musical *texture* that you could present in the classroom.
7. Discuss experiences with musical *form* that you could present in the classroom.

Assessment

Review ways the music standards listed at the beginning of this chapter have been met.

CHAPTER 4

Teaching Music through Singing

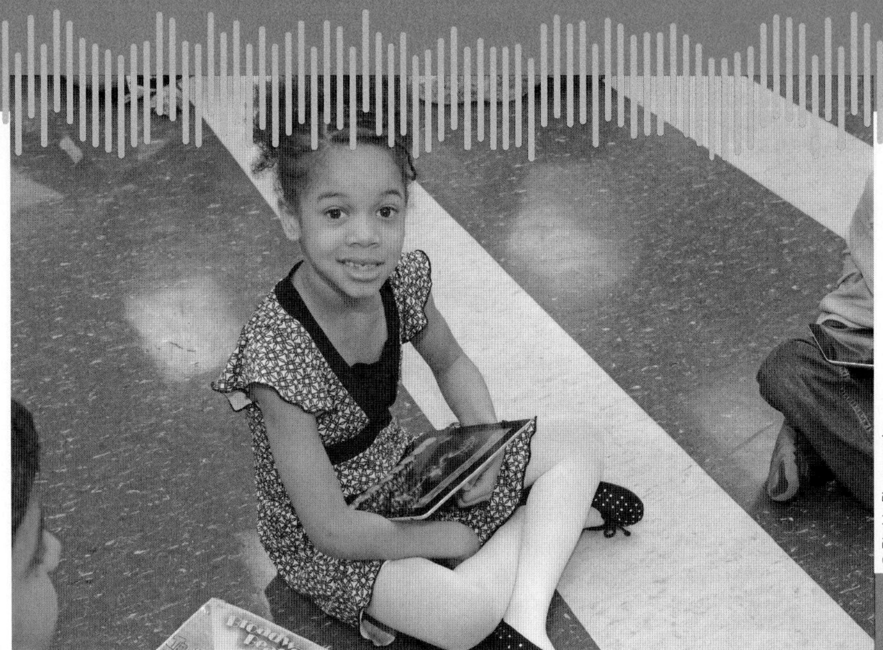

© Ritchie Photography

Objectives

Students will explore ideas for developing lessons based on:

- Characteristics of the child voice and children's song interests
  - Preschool and kindergarten (ages 4 and 5)
  - Early primary: first and second grades (ages 6 and 7)
  - Intermediate: third and fourth grades (ages 8 and 9)
  - Upper elementary: fifth and sixth grades (ages 10 and 11)
- Techniques for teaching children to sing
  - Creating an environment for singing experiences
  - Improving posture
  - Teaching good breathing habits to support the tone
  - Finding the head voice
  - Developing the ability to match tones
  - Developing the concepts of high and low
  - Discovering patterns
- Preparing to teach a song
- Leading a song
- Teaching songs to children
  - Teaching a song by rote
  - Teaching a song by rote-note
  - Teaching a song by note: the Kodály approach
  - Singing additive songs
- Teaching part singing
  - Lining out a song
  - Singing canons
  - Singing dialogue songs or echo songs
  - Singing call-and-response songs
  - Adding descants/countermelodies
  - Singing ostinato chants
  - Singing rounds
  - Singing partner songs

National and State Music Standards

This chapter provides experiences with the following national music standards and related state music standards:

- Singing, alone and with others, a varied repertoire of music
- Performing on instruments, alone and with others, a varied repertoire of music

From a very young age, children express their feelings through play chants and sound patterns that they experience alone or share with other children. Because singing is an intimate, highly expressive experience, it is an important way for a child to convey happiness, love, dreams, joy, and sadness.

Songs provide a rich storehouse of musical and literary treasures. Folk songs tell us of the ways peoples from other cultures, times, and places have lived and worked, whereas art songs may describe such things as a waterfall or a butterfly. Hymns, chorales, and spirituals provide opportunities to express feelings of awe, inspiration, praise, and thanksgiving.

Children should sing for sheer fun and pleasure in a variety of recreational activities, such as games, folk songs and dances, and musical plays. They should also learn musical concepts such as melody, rhythm, and form through the pieces that they perform.

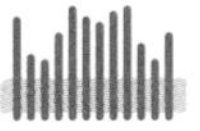

CHARACTERISTICS OF THE CHILD VOICE AND CHILDREN'S SONG INTERESTS

Teachers need to understand children's vocal characteristics and song interests to set realistic musical expectations and develop appropriate teaching strategies.

The singing voice of a young child (boy or girl) is relatively high, light in both quality and volume, and often limited to an octave or less in *range* (lowest note to highest note). A clear, flute-like quality is desirable and should be promoted. Many children in today's television- and movie-oriented society have been greatly influenced by pop singers, and some will try to imitate their sounds. The teacher should encourage and nurture the beauty of the child voice, however, and not an imitation of the adult voice.

Major differences develop between a girl's voice and a boy's voice as they mature through childhood. Initially, the girl's voice is light and thin and has a slightly translucent quality. As she matures, she is capable of creating a bigger sound but retains the same light quality. When a girl enters adolescence, her voice becomes breathy, and she often temporarily loses the ability to sing high notes. By the age of fifteen, she begins to develop the mature voice of a woman, and at this time the true soprano and alto qualities start to emerge.

A boy's voice is similar to a girl's until the age of nine, when it begins to develop the fullness and power we associate with musical groups such as the Vienna Boys' Choir. A boy's voice reaches its peak of clarity and brilliance *just before it begins to change*. American boys tend to want to sing lower than their European counterparts, and it is not unusual for a young boy, speaking in a high unchanged voice, to announce that he would like to sing bass. Allowing a boy to sing low before he is vocally ready is not advised. We need to acknowledge his wish to be grown-up yet suggest that he sing the "lower" part of the song, as opposed to the "lowest."

It is generally agreed that, if they are to be confident singers as adults, children must learn to match pitches and sing short musical phrases before the age of nine. By the age of nine, a child is becoming much more sensitive and self-conscious about singing alone. The ability to sing in tune and to sing increasingly complex melodies depends on carefully constructed singing experiences that follow the basic physical development of the child.

A child's vocal range varies a great deal. Contributing factors include natural talent, maturity, and musical experience.

The appropriateness and interest of songs also varies with the talent and interests of students. Most of the songs in the basal series books have been found to work well throughout the United States in a variety of teaching situations. A teacher should also consider whether a particular song can enhance lessons in other areas, such as social studies, language arts, or science.

Children singing.

As you gain experience in analyzing and teaching songs to children of different ages, you will want to refer frequently to the following outline of musical expectations.

Preschool and Kindergarten (Ages Four and Five)

Vocal Characteristics and Abilities

- Voices are small and light.
- Children are generally unable to sing in tune.
- Singing range is D–A for most; D–D for some.

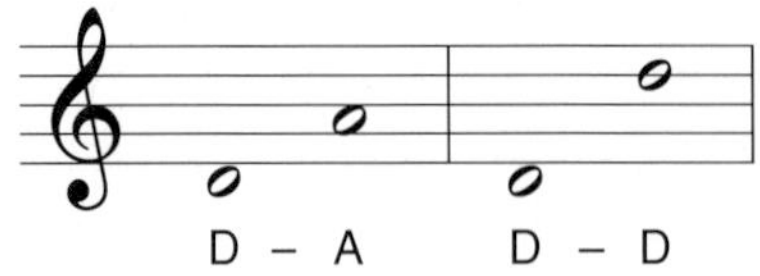

- Children can sing play chants and easy tonal patterns.

Special Learner Note

Microphones (real or toy-like) may be used to encourage singing. Students with hearing impairments may be helped by feeling the throat of a peer or the teacher to understand the way they are supposed to feel as they make the sounds. Many students with hearing impairments or mental retardation may begin vocalizing with a monotone sound and will need vocal "games" with exaggerated high and low pitches to feel/hear the differences in pitch that they are capable of producing.

- Children can sing short melodies in major, minor, or pentatonic scales.
- Children can sing melodies with one note to a syllable.
- Children can sing with an awareness of a steady beat.
- Children can sing repeated rhythmic patterns accurately.
- Children can sing softly and loudly.
- Children can sing melodies with or without a simple accompaniment.

Song Interests: Opportunities for Classroom Integration

Preschool children like songs that tell a story. Consider how many nursery rhymes are little dramas: "Jack and Jill," "Little Jack Horner," and "Polly, Put the Kettle On." Little children enjoy songs that give them an opportunity for natural expression. When they act out "Three Little Kittens Who Lost Their Mittens," they really become the little kittens. They are very much at home in the land of make-believe. Children also like songs that deal with familiar experiences: bedtime and wake-up songs; helping songs; and songs about friends, family, animals, the seasons, and special occasions.

Early Primary: First and Second Grades (Ages Six and Seven)

Vocal Characteristics and Abilities

- Most voices are light and high; a few may be low.
- Many children are still unable to sing in tune at age six.
- By age seven most children will be able to sing at least short phrases in tune and will begin to sing alone.
- Children can understand high and low pitches.
- Children can sustain a single pitch.
- Range expands from five to six consecutive pitches (D–B) to a full octave (D–D).

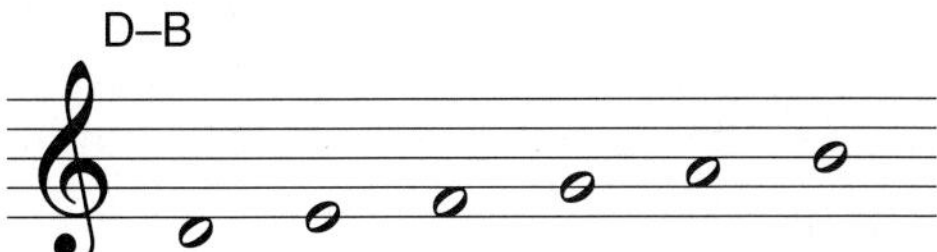

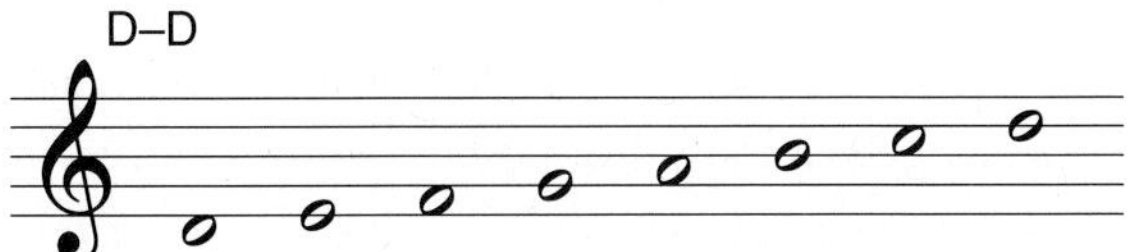

- Children understand the difference between a playground-shouting voice and a singing voice.
- Children begin to understand the importance of breath in singing.
- Children can sing melodies in major, minor, and pentatonic scales.
- Children can sing call-and-response songs, as well as songs in two- or three-part form.
- Children sing with attention to dynamics and changes in tempo.
- Children can sing rhythmically, accenting strong beats and performing simple syncopation.
- Children can sing from simple music notation.
- Children can sing melodies with simple harmonic or rhythmic accompaniment.

Song Interests: Opportunities for Classroom Integration

At six and seven, children enjoy songs about animals, community, friends, action (with movement or creative motions), pretending, folk games from around the world, and special occasions.

Intermediate: Third and Fourth Grades (Ages Eight and Nine)

Vocal Characteristics and Abilities

- Most children can sing a song in tune.
- Girls' voices continue to be very light and thin.
- Boys' voices begin to develop the rich resonance of the mature boy soprano-alto voice.
- Some children can sing rounds, partner songs, canons, and descants. There is little use of alto or lower parts.
- Some children have much more control over expressive qualities of singing, for example, legato, dynamics, and sustained phrases.
- Some children are capable of singing melodies or parts from music notation.
- Some children can harmonize parts or chords by ear, such as thirds and sixths.
- Some children can sing songs with more complex rhythms.

Song Interests: Opportunities for Classroom Integration

At eight and nine, children enjoy songs about early America (Native Americans, Pilgrims), transportation, geography (New England, the West, the South), the circus, planets, and people and songs that express emotions. Songs from other lands (such as Mexico, Africa, China, and Japan) are appealing because of their contrasting styles.

Upper Elementary: Fifth and Sixth Grades (Ages Ten and Eleven)

Vocal Characteristics and Abilities

- Unchanged voices remain clear and light; boys' voices become more resonant.
- Some children show greater ability to sing in two and three parts.
- Some children have a heightened rhythmic sense and respond to music with strong rhythms.
- Many children tend to imitate the quality and style of pop singers.
- Some voices begin to change—that is, boys' voices become lower, and girls' voices become very breathy.
- Some children can read simple music notation.

Song Interests: Opportunities for Classroom Integration

Children enjoy songs related to adventure, work, transportation, history, and feelings such as happiness, sadness, and love, as well as songs from other cultures and countries. Children also enjoy folk songs from America, songs about places or events, and contemporary popular songs. They like to harmonize and accompany songs with classroom instruments, especially guitar, keyboard, Q-chord, and recorder. They are enthusiastic about dramatics and producing musical plays.

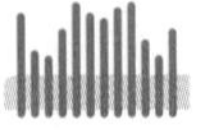

TECHNIQUES FOR TEACHING CHILDREN TO SING

Although many children can sing naturally, others require guidance and help in learning to use the head voice, singing in tune, and developing good tone quality.

Creating an Environment for Singing Experiences

There are many ways to help children achieve readiness for singing. Songs sung to them by a parent, teacher, or friend provide an effective model for them to follow. Recordings of children's voices found in the many music series books, as well as recordings of children's choirs, should be used during the day, both before and during class periods. Children learn to reproduce tonal sounds by imitation. Hearing songs repeatedly will help them relate to pitch, melody, and rhythm. In other words, children should be surrounded with interesting songs and many models of good singing.

Technology Enhancement

With the popularity of shows like "Glee" and "American Idol", as well as musical video games such as "Sing Star" or "Rock Band," more students than ever enjoy listening to and singing songs of all types. Choosing a song recently heard or seen on "Glee" can be a great way to encourage reluctant singers or reward students for their efforts. Using "Sing Star" or "Rock Band" as a classroom reward can also be a highly effective way to reward and encourage your students.

Musical Video Games:

"Sing Star"

"Rock Band"

"Guitar Hero"

Apps for Singing:

"Glee Karaoke"

"Disney Spotlight Karaoke"

"Soulo Karaoke"

Improving Posture

Because the body is the "instrument" for singing, it must be held upright; that is, a child must sit or stand with shoulders erect, head up, and spine straight. Create games and draw analogies to improve posture. For example:

1. Ask children to reach for an imaginary bar above their heads and to pull their bodies upward toward it. They should then relax and put their arms down to their sides.
2. Have children pretend they are puppets that have collapsed on the floor. Then have them pretend that they are being pulled up with a string attached to the backs of their necks. (Children can take turns being puppets and puppeteers.)
3. Have them pretend that they are inflated balloons just ready to leave the ground.

Teaching Good Breathing Habits to Support the Tone

Most children who cannot sing in tune, or in their head voice, have not developed the ability to support a tone with their breath. As they learn to "feel" the pitches, they will be better able to "match" the pitches. Have students imitate you in the following exercises:

1. Sip air as if through a soda straw and release it with a hissing sound. Be sure to keep the sound steady and not like a radiator that has sprung a leak.
2. Sip air as if through a soda straw and let the air out on a high "Ooo" sound, descending to a low sound. Use this same technique to imitate sirens.
3. Pretend that your finger is a lighted candle. Fill your lungs with air and blow gently on the "candle" so that the "flame" flickers but does not go out.
4. Inhale quickly, as if you see a fumble made on the one-yard line by your favorite football team.
5. Lean over from the waist, letting your arms dangle. Breathe deeply, expanding the ribs. Straighten up and exhale slowly and steadily.

Finding the Head Voice

Children who cannot sing in tune share a common problem: They are unable to manipulate their voices so that they can match the musical sounds they hear. Before a child can sing comfortably, he or she must learn how it feels and sounds to use the *head voice.*

One way of helping children find their head voice is to strengthen the concept of different "voices." Try the following games:

Teacher:	*Let's see if you can use your different voices. First, listen to me . . . .*
	This is my whispering voice.
Child (in a whisper):	*This is my whispering voice.*
Teacher:	*This is my talking-low voice.*
Child:	*This is my talking-low voice.*
Teacher:	*This is my talking-high voice.*
Child:	*This is my talking-high voice.*
Teacher:	*This is my yelling voice.*
Child:	*This is my yelling voice.*
Teacher (on a single pitch):	*This is my singing voice.*
Child (same pitch):	*This is my singing voice.*

Different "voices" can also be used when saying selected chants. For example, the chant "1, 2, 3, 4, 5" can be spoken this way:

Regular voice:	*1, 2, 3, 4, 5, once I caught a fish alive. 6, 7, 8, 9, 10, then I let it go again.*
Low voice:	*Why did you let it go?*
High voice:	*Because it bit my finger so.*
Low voice:	*Which finger did it bite?*
High voice:	*The little finger on the right.*

A second approach is to help children discover speech inflection. Start with speaking small phrases, such as Good ↗ morn ↘ ing. How are ↗ you? Gradually develop these phrases into tonal intervals, such as the following (either sing or play the pattern on melody bells):

Good Morn - ing. How are you?

A third approach involves imitating familiar sounds, such as the swooping up and down of a siren or the calls of the bobwhite, cuckoo, and cardinal.[1]

A fourth approach includes using children's literature to help children explore their voices. Use a variety of voices for the animal and environment sounds in the following books:

- Create different sounds for the mooing of cows in Dr. Seuss's *Mr. Brown Can Moo! Can You?* (New York: Random House, 1970).
- Create ten different doggie sounds from Sandra Boynton's *Doggies* (New York: Little Simon, Board edition, 1984).
- Inflect the voice up on the question words in Chris Raschka's *Yo! Yes*? (New York: Orchard Books, 1993).

[1] Additional songs and ideas can be found in *One, Two, Three . . . Echo Me*! by Loretta Mitchell (West Nyack, NY: Parker Publishing, 1991), pp. 1–28. Especially useful are the ideas for using puppets to teach the differences between singing and speaking.

Developing the Ability to Match Tones

The ability to match tones is directly related to breathing techniques, ear training, a relaxed jaw, and singing with energy. Most children have sung childhood chants, such as:

You can use similar chants to help children learn to match tones.

ACTIVITIES

1. Using a few pitches (such as G E A, in the chant illustrated above), create question-and-answer games. Because most adults sing too low for children, it is wise to use a pitch pipe, recorder, or melody bells to give the starting pitch or the beginning melodic phrase. If possible, avoid using the piano; the tone is too heavy for young voices and they have trouble matching it. If a child cannot sing the response in the key in which you play or sing it, try to match his or her range and work from there.

Where is Jim - my? I'm here.

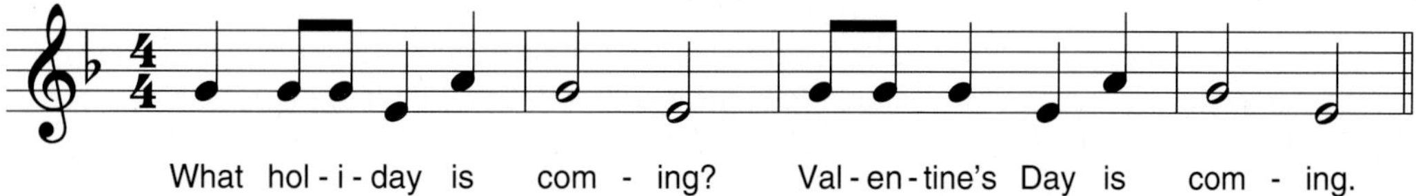

What hol - i - day is com - ing? Val - en - tine's Day is com - ing.

2. Using two toy telephones, create a telephone game. Play or sing a chant, such as "Hello, how are you?" Have the child answer, "Hello. I'm fine," for example.
3. In the song "Listen to the Wind," invite children (grades K–1) to match tones on the pitches C and A on the word *Whoo-ee:*

Note that *who* is the easiest sound for children to sing and is the most effective for developing the head voice. Playing these two pitches on resonator bells, melody bells, or recorder enables the child to hear the pitch he or she is trying to match. (See Chapter 5, "Teaching Music through Playing Classroom Instruments," for a detailed discussion and suggested activities.) Many times even a young child can play these two pitches on the bells. You may need to mark the proper pitches with colors to aid in identification.

German Folk Tune: Cuckoo
Words by Joy E. Lawrence

Listen to the Wind

Key: F (Pentatonic)
Starting pitch: C
Meter: 3/4, begins on 1

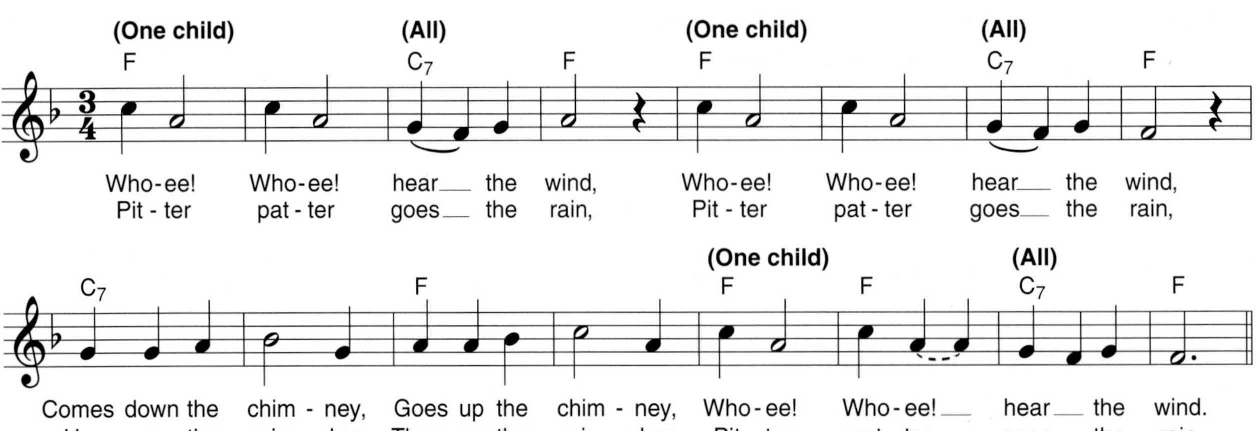

Who-ee! Who-ee! hear the wind,
Pit - ter pat - ter goes the rain,
Comes down the chim - ney, Goes up the chim - ney, Who-ee! Who-ee! hear the wind.
Here on the win - dow, There on the win - dow, Pit - ter pat - ter goes the rain.

You may wish to add the following percussion accompaniment to the song:

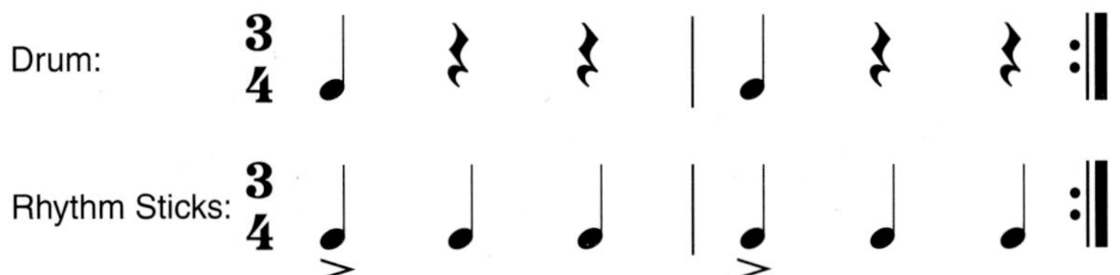

4. "Hello, There!" is an easy tone-matching song that is especially appropriate for kindergarten children, many of whom have played "echo" in the woods or in a cavern of some kind. Here the teacher sings, and the children "echo" to help with the tone-matching process. Have children sit in a circle as you sing the song. (You may want to place tape on the floor to aid the children in forming a circle.) Choose one child to cover his or her eyes and sit in the center and another child to be the echo. The child who is "it" tries to identify the child who sings the echo after the teacher. Continue the game by taking turns with a new child being "it" and a second child singing the echo.

Traditional

Hello, There!

Key: C
Starting pitch: G
Meter: 2/4, begins on "and" of 2

C
G7
Hel - lo, there! (Hel - lo, there!) How are you? (How are you?) It's so good (It's
so good) To see you (To see you) We'll sing and (We'll sing and) be
hap - py (be hap - py) That we're all here to - geth - er a - gain.

5. A simple echo song that can be used with younger children is "Charlie Over the Ocean."[2] This is a chase-game song. When the children know the song, play the game.
   - One child sings the call and walks around the outside of a circle carrying a handkerchief.
   - The rest of the children are seated on the floor. They sing the echo.
   - On "Can't catch me," the child drops the handkerchief behind a seated child.
   - The seated child picks up the handkerchief and chases the first child around the outside of the circle.
   - The first child then sits in the spot vacated by the child he/she chose.
   - That child then sings the calls with the class echoing and the game repeats.

From Lois Choksy and David Brummitt, 120 Singing Games and Dances for Elementary Schools (Englewood Cliffs, N.J.: Prentice-Hall, Inc., 1987), p. 60

6. Call-and-response songs are also useful when teaching matching tones. These songs provide short patterns for children to sing individually. A well-known example is "Michael, Row the Boat Ashore" (see p. 126), where the words "Michael, row the boat ashore" are the "call" and the "Alleluia" is the "response."[3]

---

[2] See John M. Feierabend and Tim Caton, *The Book of Echo Songs* (Chicago: GIA Publications, 2003).
[3] For more call-and-response songs, see John M. Feierabend and Tim Caton, *The Book of Call and Response* (Chicago: GIA Publications, 2003).

Developing the Concepts of High and Low

A basic skill in tone matching is to develop the concepts of high and low.

ACTIVITIES

1. Show pictures that illustrate the concepts of high and low, such as a plane and a car, a child stretching upward and one kneeling down, or a bird in a tree and a dog lying on the ground.

2. Create a variety of movements indicating low to high and high to low. For example, children could stand and stretch arms high, then stoop low to feel the ground:

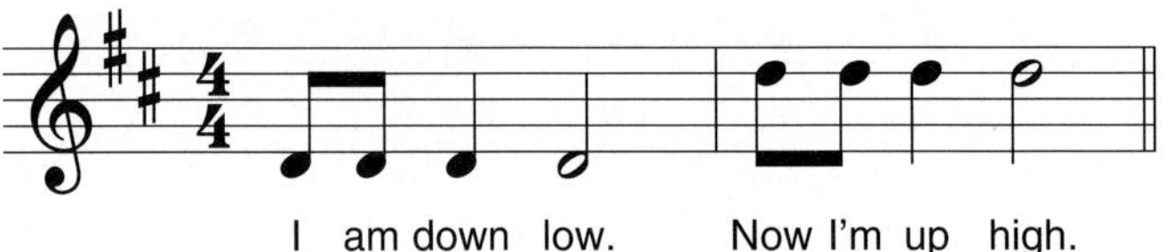
I am down low. Now I'm up high.

3. Ask children to be puppets on a string and pretend that their voices are being lifted up. Use a marionette to illustrate. Have different children "work" the voices of each other.
4. Have children sing "Ooo" as they pretend that they are watching their favorite baseball player hit a home run. Voices should rise as the ball goes into the upper stands.
5. For those who have difficulty hearing their own voice, give the following direction: Cup one hand behind your ear and place the other hand in front of your mouth. (This makes an echo chamber.) Sing "Ooo" into your hand so that it sounds high and then low.
6. Repeat the following simple chant several times:

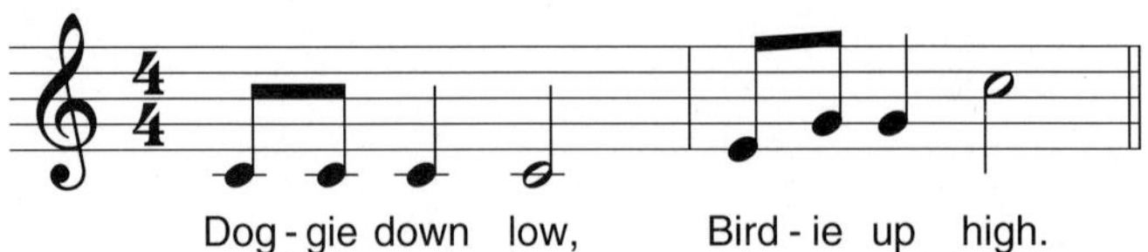
Dog - gie down low, Bird - ie up high.

Change keys each time, gradually getting higher.

7. Turn a xylophone so that the lowest pitches are to the left and the highest pitches are to the right. Play low C followed by high C. Play the full scale from bottom to top (C D E F G A B C) and then top to bottom (C B A G F E D C). Ask children to sing the ascending scale with syllables (*do re mi fa sol la ti do*). Ask the class if they sang high or low when they began. Compare singing the scale with a plant growing up tall. On a chalkboard or chart, place eight pictures of a plant or tree developing from seed to full maturity. Point to pictures as the children sing the scale.

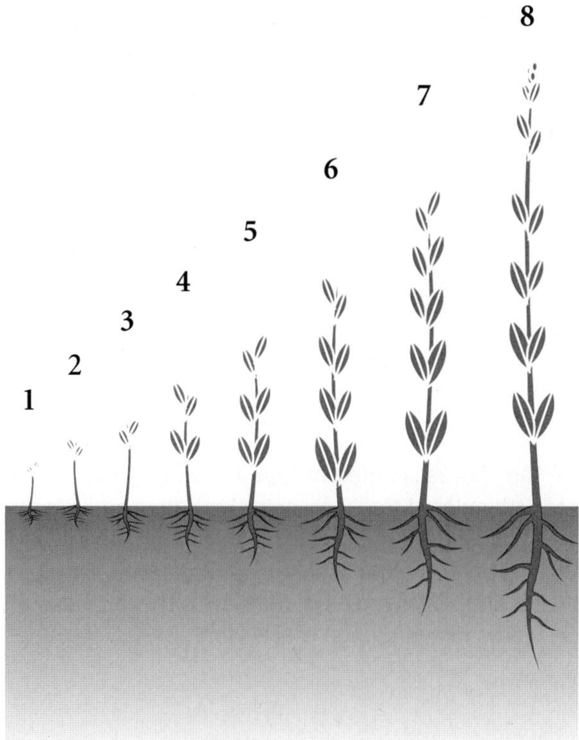

Discovering Patterns

All pieces of music have patterns that repeat. These patterns may be melodic, rhythmic, or harmonic. Teaching children to identify these patterns and then perform them shortens the time required for them to learn to sing songs or to listen perceptively to a larger musical composition.

ACTIVITIES

1. Examine repeated patterns on fabric or wrapping paper.
2. Show pictures with patterns that occur more than once.
3. Sing the well-known English song "Looby Loo." Point out the two rhythm patterns that are repeated. Have one child play the first rhythm pattern on a classroom percussion instrument such as rhythm sticks:

Pattern 1

Have another child play the second pattern on another instrument such as a triangle. Be sure to choose instruments with different tone colors.

Pattern 2

Ask children to count how many times each pattern is played. (Pattern 1 is performed six times, including the D.C. repeat, whereas pattern 2 is performed four times. Notice that exact repetition occurs twice, with the third and fourth times slightly altered.)

Put the following scale pattern on the chalkboard or a chart and point to the notes as the class sings the verse, to show how the song moves upward. These syllables correspond to the notes on the staff of F G A Bb C. (Showing a scale pattern helps children know which way to make their voices go—up or down.)

In "Looby Loo" the chorus is different from the verse both in melody and in rhythm. Give students flashlights with colored transparencies in them, and have children with one color "dance" their flashlights on the ceiling for the rhythm of the chorus and children with another color "dance" their flashlights for the verse. Of course, most kindergarten children will want to act out the words of the song and create additional verses of their own. This provides an easy link to rhyming and teaching the use of words in a language arts lesson.

English Singing Game

Looby Loo

Key: F
Starting pitch: F
Meter: 6/8, begins on 1

F C7 F

Here we go loo - by loo, Here we go loo - by light. Here we go loo - by loo

F C7 F *fine* F

All on a Sat - ur - day night.____ 1. I put my right hand in,____ I take my right hand
2. I put my left hand in,____ I take my left hand
3. I put my right leg in,____ I take my right leg
4. I put my left leg in,____ I take my left leg

F C7 F ***D.C. al fine***

out –____ I give my hand a shake, shake, shake, And turn my - self a - bout. Oh,
out –____ I give my hand a shake, shake, shake, And turn my - self a - bout. Oh,
out –____ I give my leg a shake, shake, shake, And turn my - self a - bout. Oh,
out –____ I give my leg a shake, shake, shake, And turn my - self a - bout. Oh,

4. Play or sing other songs with repeated rhythm patterns and have children clap the pattern or play it on percussion instruments. The repeated pattern in the song "Jack-o'-Lantern," for example, is:

This pattern occurs six times. Clap the pattern or play it on classroom percussion instruments as an ostinato. Use a drum to keep the steady beat:

Teach the words and melody of the song by imitation.

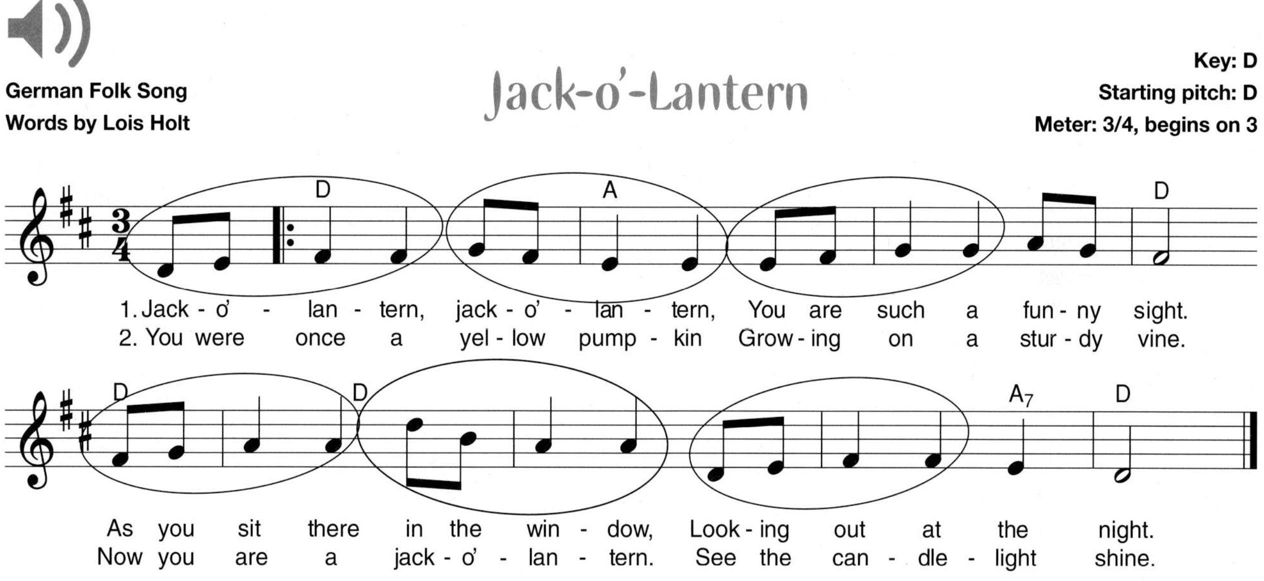
German Folk Song
Words by Lois Holt
Jack-o'-Lantern
Key: D
Starting pitch: D
Meter: 3/4, begins on 3
D A D
1. Jack - o' - lan - tern, jack - o' - lan - tern, You are such a fun - ny sight.
2. You were once a yel - low pump - kin Grow - ing on a stur - dy vine.
D D A7 D
As you sit there in the win - dow, Look - ing out at the night.
Now you are a jack - o' - lan - tern. See the can - dle - light shine.

PREPARING TO TEACH A SONG

Follow these steps when preparing to teach a song:

1. Choose an appropriate song for a specific class or grade level. (Refer to pp. 70–72 for musical expectations and song interests of various maturation levels.)
   a. Choose a song within a child's vocal capability (range and rhythm).
   b. Choose a song with an interesting and appropriate text.
   c. Choose a song that may increase the child's perception and understanding of music as an expressive art form.
   d. Choose a song that can be integrated with other activities (when possible).
2. Analyze the musical materials of the song—that is, range of melody, rhythmic patterns, formal structure, harmony, and expressiveness of text (see the sample analysis that follows).
3. Decide what musical concepts to emphasize, such as skips, rhythmic/tonal patterns, or repetition.

4. Decide what vocal techniques the class needs to work on, such as good breathing, using the head voice, tone matching, or posture.
5. Determine the approach you will use to teach the song (rote, rote-note, note). In the sample analysis that follows, "Tinga Layo" will be taught using the rote-note approach for grades 3–4.
6. Determine how you might integrate the song into other classroom activities, such as movement and social studies.
7. Prepare a lesson plan.

Sample Analysis: "Tinga Layo"

Expressiveness of Text

The song should be sung moderately fast with lots of energy. It is important to *observe* both legato ("Tinga Layo") and *staccato* ("Come, little donkey, come!") as you sing.

Melody

- There are two phrases in the refrain:
  - Tinga Layo! Come, little donkey, come!
  - Tinga Layo! Come, little donkey, come!
- There are two short phrases and one long phrase in the verse:
  - My donkey yes
  - My donkey no
  - My donkey stop when I tell him to go!
- The range of the melody is from C to C.
- The melody basically moves stepwise, with larger skips occurring in the verse.
- The melody is in the key of C major.

Rhythm

- The meter is duple: 2/4.
- The tempo is moderately fast.
- The meter is the same throughout.
- Repeated rhythm pattern occurs in measures 3 and 7.

Formal Organization

The song is organized in an ABA pattern.

Texture (Harmony)

The song can be accompanied on the keyboard or Q-chord. Classroom percussion instruments can be used to create variety and interest.

Chords are C, F, G7; or transpose to key of D (D, G, A7).

LESSON PLAN

Teaching a Song

Activity: Teaching the song "Tinga Layo"

Grades: 3–4

Concepts: Expressiveness/energy in singing, rhythm in patterns

NATIONAL AND STATE MUSIC STANDARDS

1. Singing, alone and with others, a varied repertoire of music
2. Performing on instruments, alone and with others, a varied repertoire of music
3. Reading and notating music

OBJECTIVES

Students will:

1. Sing with good tone quality.
2. Sing with accurate pitches and rhythms.
3. Identify rhythm patterns by sound and notation.
4. Accompany song on keyboard, Q-chord, or guitar and classroom percussion instruments.

MATERIALS

- Song
- Keyboard, Q-chord, or guitar
- Classroom percussion instruments
- Rhythm chart
- Chord chart

PROCEDURES

1. Emphasize the need for energy in singing. Review several breathing exercises:
   a. Sip through a straw and vocalize "Ooh" downward.
   b. Breathe and blow out two candles, one close to you and one at a distance.
2. Play or sing "Tinga Layo" for the class.
3. Play or sing the song again and ask children to tap their thighs and clap on beats 1 and 2 (duple meter). Repeat, using a drum or tambourine for meter beats.
4. Sing or play the first two phrases of the song. Accompany yourself on a chording instrument. Ask students to clap the melodic rhythm (the words) and accent as you do. Sing the first two phrases again and have students sing. Emphasize the need for good breathing and energy in singing.
5. Sing or play the verse and have students repeat after you.
6. Demonstrate the following rhythm:

   Using a rhythm chart, ask students to clap the rhythm.
7. Repeat, using a drum or maracas to play the rhythm pattern.
8. Ask students to find how many times the "musical picture" occurs in the song (four times if you include the repeat).
9. Ask the class to read both the English and the Spanish lyrics. Read with expression—for example, legato for "Tinga Layo" and staccato on "Come, little donkey, come!"
10. Introduce the chords C, F, and G7 (on a keyboard or Q-chord) or D, G, and A7 (on a keyboard or guitar). Provide each student with a chord chart showing where the chords are located on a guitar (see Appendix B).

    Practice singing the song and pushing down an imaginary chord bar (any one will do for this exercise) and strumming at the beginning of each measure. When students can sing and strum at the same time, ask selected students to accompany the song, using only a single chord wherever it occurs. For example, one student might play C, a second, F, and a third, G7. As skill increases, each student will be able to play all three chords to accompany the song.
11. Closure:
    a. Sing "Tinga Layo" accompanied by a chording instrument (keyboard, Q-chord, or guitar) and rhythm instruments. Emphasize again the importance of posture, good breathing, energy, legato and staccato singing, and the crisp rhythm of:

    b. Extend use of the song into movement activities and listen to other examples of calypso music.

Technology Enhancement

Web Exploration

Take your students to a lab or use your teacher computer to search the Internet to discover different facts about calypso. To bring more structure to the exploration, create a list of facts, pictures, or videos that the students need to find. The students can then either write down their findings or create a presentation in GoogleDocs or PowerPoint with their findings.

ASSESSMENT

1. What are some reasons why you need energy to sing?
2. Can you demonstrate duple meter? Triple meter?
3. Can you identify some rhythmic patterns that occur in the song "Tinga Layo"?

LEADING A SONG

Before you develop techniques for teaching children to sing songs, you need to be able to *lead* a song. As with all musical skills, this requires practice. The more you do it, the more comfortable you will be standing before a class and leading them in a song. You first need to analyze the song to determine the following:

- Whether you sing or play the melody accurately or should use a recording
- The starting pitch and how to find it on an instrument or with your voice
- The meter of the song (duple or triple)
- On what beat the song begins and on what beat to say "sing"
- What the text of the song is about and how it can be performed expressively (e.g., smoothly, loudly, softly, with or without accents)
- How to end the song together

The following guidelines for leading a song will contribute to your success and will also improve your students' singing.

1. Check students' posture, and be sure that they are looking at you. Assume a posture that reflects the mood of the song.
2. Sing the song, perform it on an instrument, or use a recording to establish the key, tempo, dynamic level, and mood. Perform the entire song unless students already know it. Be sure that you reflect energy and pride in your performance, whether you are actually playing or singing the song or using a recording.
3. Return to the starting pitch or pitches and play or sing them for the class. Then say "1, 2, ready, sing," or "1, 2, sing," depending on the meter and whether the song begins on an upbeat. Be sure that the speed (tempo) of your "1, 2, . . . " is the same as the tempo of the song—not too fast and not too slow. It is important for students to begin with the first word rather than drift in along the way.
4. Lift your arm to indicate your breathing so that students will also breathe and sing together. Remember: Good breathing, a lot of energy, and the desire to produce a pleasing sound are major factors in achieving good singing. The act of singing is *physical*, not mystical.
5. Give students a signal with your hand when they are to sing. You are *leading* a song, not just singing along with them. If you use a recording, be sure that you know the introduction well and that you can count the beats accurately.
6. Use the conducting patterns in Figure 4.1 to keep the singing together. Be sure that the downbeat is always on 1.
7. You may also consider "mapping" the melody—that is, raising or lowering your hands with the melody. Be sure that the style of the gesture fits the mood of the song.
8. So that they end together, give a clear signal to stop students at the end of the song.
9. Look at the students and be supportive. Praise students if they did well, but don't say "good" when the singing was poor. Give them specific suggestions for improvement and then try the song again.

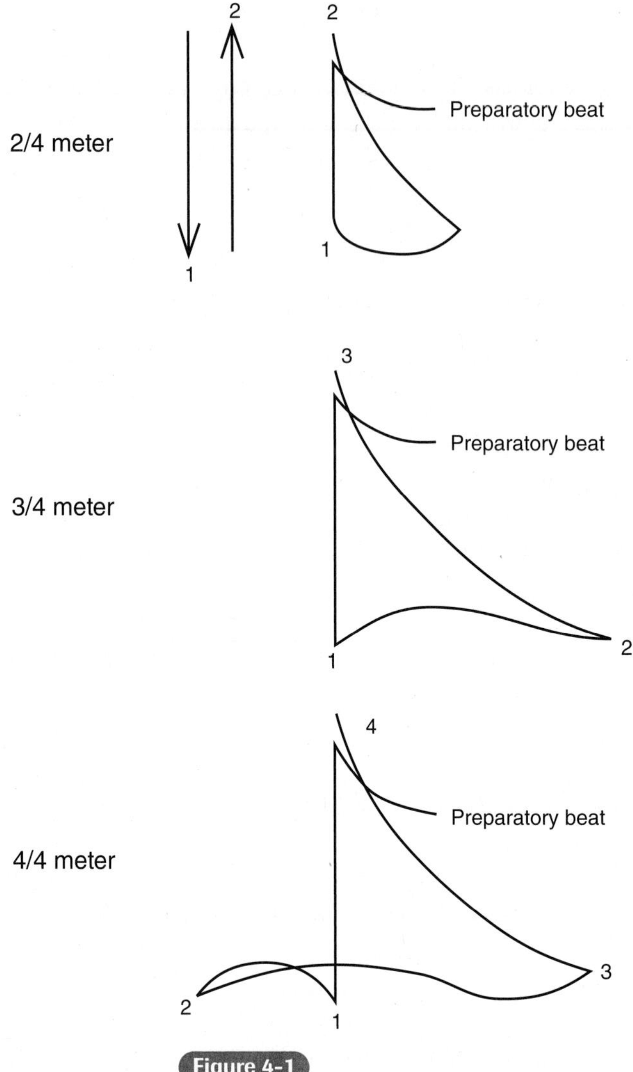

Figure 4-1

10. Use imagination when leading a song. If students miss the meaning of the song and just sing along, try different ways of singing so that students can express themselves with different moods.
11. Show pride in what you are doing. Become an actor or actress. Leave your troubles outside the classroom. Enjoy the music and make it fun. Both you and your students will enjoy it.
12. Practice leading the following song, "Jingle Bells," which is suitable for grades 3–5.

James Pierpont
Jingle Bells
Key: G
Starting pitch: D
Meter: 2/4, begins on 1
Introduction to Tempo: (2 measures) 1, 2, ready-sing
G C
Dash - ing through the snow in a one - horse o - pen sleigh, O'er the fields we
D7 G
go, Laugh - ing all the way. Bells on bob - tail ring mak - ing spi - rits
C D7 G
bright What fun it is to ride and sing a sleigh - ing song to - night.
G G C
Jin - gle bells, jin - gle bells, jin - gle all the way! Oh, what fun it
G A7 D7 G
is to ride in a one - horse o - pen sleigh! Jin - gle bells, jin - gle bells,
G C G D7 G
jin - gle all the way! Oh, what fun it is to ride in a one - horse o - pen sleigh!

TEACHING SONGS TO CHILDREN

There are many ways to teach songs. The three discussed here are rote, rote-note, and note approaches. You will find a number of ideas for teaching songs in the basal series textbooks. However, many of these approaches are not structured in perfect order for either you or your class, and you may find that adapting the activities will make them more suitable for your teaching skills and style. You may also wish to combine various methods with different songs. Remember that a multisensory approach, in which students hear, see, and physically respond, is one of the most effective.

Teaching students to read music is not very different from teaching them to read poems or stories. Teachers sometimes say, "But I don't read music," as if that were a permanent condition. You can learn to read music, and so can your students. The more songs you teach, the more confident and proficient you will become. Although the saying "Practice makes perfect" may not be totally true, it is a fact that practice can improve one's musical skill.

Teaching a Song by Rote

When you teach a song by *rote*, students learn through imitation. There are no materials in the students' hands; they learn the tune, rhythms, and words through aural memory. Short songs are usually taught in their entirety (whole-song approach); longer songs require teaching single sections or phrases, putting the sections together, and then singing the entire song. The following activities are intended simply to teach the song.

1. Play or sing the entire song.
2. Perform the song phrase by phrase and have children imitate each phrase in turn. Use your hands to "map" the melody, which gives children a visual reference that indicates whether their voices should be high or low and whether the duration is long or short.
3. Ask children to imitate the motions or actions you perform as you sing the song. Relate your actions to the words of the song so that they become cues to remembering the words. This method is appropriate for children in early childhood classes or primary grades.
4. As you perform the song several times, have children create movements or a game. Often students can perform the song quite soon, because they have heard it many times.
5. Perform the song and leave out a little motion, pattern, or word. Ask students to fill it in at the proper time.
6. As students listen to a performance of the song, ask them to arrange, in order, pictures or charts specified in the song.
7. Have students perform the entire song.

Guidelines for Teaching Songs to Children

As you teach songs to children, it is important to remember the following:

1. All children can experience some degree of success in singing activities.
2. If a child cannot match a pitch, it doesn't mean that the child cannot match any difference in pitch; it probably means that the child doesn't know what it feels like to match a pitch. Conduct tone-matching activities regularly and frequently.
3. Good singing, like good speech, requires controlled breath.
4. Good singing, like good speech, requires clear diction and articulation.
5. Choose songs with a limited range for young children and beginning singers.
6. Pitch songs for the children, not for the teacher. Generally, an adult voice is much lower than a child's voice. Use a mechanical source to find the pitch (a pitch pipe, recorder, keyboard, or Q-chord). Transpose melodies that are too high or too low. (See p. 152 for specific activities involving transposition.)
7. Choose a variety of songs representative of different moods, tempos, tonalities, forms, rhythms, and melodies.
8. Choose songs representative of different cultures—both Western and non-Western. Include folk, art, patriotic, fun, ethnic, popular, and children's songs.
9. Choose songs "for the moment" (popular) as well as songs of permanent value.
10. It will be helpful if you can answer the following questions when deciding to use a particular song:
    - **a.** Is it musically expressive? Does it have a sense of completeness and beauty?
    - **b.** Is the melody easily singable? Does it have a comfortable singing range? Are the intervals between notes easily singable?
    - **c.** Is the rhythm interesting?
    - **d.** Is there sufficient repetition and contrast to make the song interesting?
    - **e.** Are the text and length of the song appropriate for a child's maturity and musical abilities?
    - **f.** Do the words appropriately fit the melody and the rhythm?
    - **g.** Does the song fit the objectives for the lesson? For example, if your aim is to develop an awareness of ascending and descending melodies, the song must have these characteristics.

LESSON PLAN

Rote Learning

Activity: Singing the song "Michael Finnegan"

Grades: 2–4

Concepts: Rhythm: Duple meter
Harmony: Chords F, C
Melody: Repeated phrases

Michael Finnegan

Children's Game Song
Key: F
Starting pitch: C
Meter: 2/4, begin on upbeat

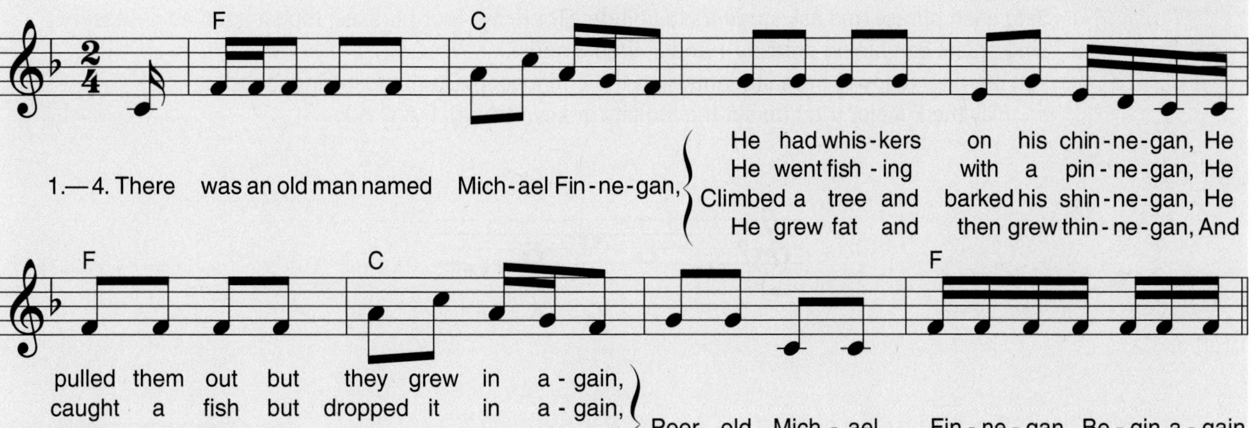
F
C
1.—4. There was an old man named Mich-ael Fin-ne-gan,
He had whis-kers on his chin-ne-gan, He
He went fish-ing with a pin-ne-gan, He
Climbed a tree and barked his shin-ne-gan, He
He grew fat and then grew thin-ne-gan, And
F
C
F
pulled them out but they grew in a-gain,
caught a fish but dropped it in a-gain,
lost a-bout a yard of skin-ne-gan,
then he died and that's the end-e-gan,
Poor old Mich-ael Fin-ne-gan. Be-gin a-gain.

NATIONAL AND STATE MUSIC STANDARDS

1. Singing, alone and with others, a varied repertoire of music
2. Performing on instruments, alone and with others, a varied repertoire of music

OBJECTIVES

Students will sing the song expressively with:

1. Good tone quality
2. Correct pitches
3. Correct rhythms
4. Correct words
5. Accompaniment provided by a chording instrument using F and C chords

MATERIALS

- Recorder or melody bells
- Keyboard, guitar, or Q-chord
- Classroom percussion instruments

PROCEDURES

1. Sing or play (recorder, melody bells, keyboard, Q-chord, or recording) the first verse.
2. Read the words to verse 1. Ask students to identify words that rhyme: *Finnegan, chinnegan, in again, begin again.*
3. Discover rhythm patterns that are repeated. Have students echo you as you chant/clap them.

Mich - ael Fin -ne -gan; on his chin -ne -gan; they grew in a -gain

4. Sing each phrase and ask students to imitate. (There are four phrases; repeat each as necessary.)
5. Sing again, combining phrases 1 and 2, then 3 and 4.
6. You are now ready to have students sing the entire song. Do the following in order:
   a. Play the F major triad (to set the tonality or key feeling): F A C A F.

F A C A F

   b. Play the first two notes of the song: C, F.
   c. Think about the tempo of the song (remember to keep the same tempo). Play four F major chords on the keyboard or Q-chord and at the same time say, "1, 2, 1, sing." (Note that the song begins on an upbeat.)
7. Sing or play the song again. This time ask children to clap the meter with you. It is in duple meter with two pulses per measure. Extension: Assign half the class to sing the song while the other half claps the duple meter, accenting the first beat. Switch assignments and sing through again. Add percussion instruments such as rhythm sticks or claves.
8. Accompany the song (F and C chords) on the keyboard, guitar, or Q-chord. Ask individual students to play these chords.
9. Follow the same procedure to teach each verse.
10. Closure: Sing the song and accompany on appropriate instruments.

Special Learner Note

On a chart with lyrics written in large letters, highlight the words or parts of words where the actual "beat" occurs (to cue the clapping or rhythm-stick playing). Example: There **was** an old **man** named **Michael Finnegan ....**

ASSESSMENT

1. Identify those melodic phrases that are the same.
2. Name the words that rhyme. Where do you find them?
3. What does 2/4 mean?
4. Create a pattern and clap it in duple meter. Create a second pattern and clap it in triple meter.
5. Play F and C chords on an instrument.

Teaching a Song by Rote-Note

Teaching a song by the *rote-note* method involves not only imitating what is heard but also recognizing short melodic or rhythm patterns. You can combine media such as flash cards or posters with the playing or singing of melodic and rhythmic patterns to introduce experiences with music notation.

LESSON PLAN

Rote-Note Learning

Activity: Singing the song "Michael Finnegan"

Grades: 2–4

Concepts: Melody: Repetition of phrases and pitches

NATIONAL AND STATE MUSIC STANDARDS

1. Singing, alone and with others, a varied repertoire of music
2. Performing on instruments, alone and with others, a varied repertoire of music
3. Reading and notating music

OBJECTIVES

Students will:

1. Recognize repeated phrases of the melody.
2. Recognize repeated pitches of the melody.

MATERIALS

- Accompanying instrument (keyboard, guitar, or Q-chord)
- Charts with repeated patterns
- Colored strips of paper
- Coloring materials
- Copies of song

PROCEDURES

1. Sing or play the song "Michael Finnegan."
2. Use colored strips of paper to represent each phrase—for example, use red for phrase 1, "There was an old man named Michael Finnegan"; yellow for phrase 2, "He had whiskers on his chinnegan"; red for phrase 3, "He pulled them out but they grew in again"; green for phrase 4, "Poor old Michael Finnegan. Begin again." Ask students which phrases are repeated (1 and 4).
3. Use copies of the song so that students can mark the music with colors. Ask them to mark the music with colors that correspond to the strips of paper.
4. Compare the notation of the contrasting phrases. What is different? What is similar? What is the same?
5. Play the five repeated pitches in the first measure of the song (F F F F F). Call attention to their being the same. Play the four repeated pitches in the second phrase (G G G G). Repeat the procedure for the third (F F F F) and the fourth (F F F F F F F) phrases.
6. Sing or play the song again. Give the starting two pitches (C and F) and ask students to sing the song, tracing in the air the outline of the melody as they sing.
7. Closure: Play or sing "Michael Finnegan" again.

ASSESSMENT

1. Invite students to raise their hands as they sing—when they hear four or more pitches that are the same.
2. Ask them to locate these repeated pitches on their copies of the song.
3. Have students locate phrases of the song where the pitches are not the same.

Teaching a Song by Note: The Kodály Approach

Teaching a song by *note* means to teach students to read the music notation. This requires preparation in understanding and conceptualizing the abstract symbols that represent the various elements in music, such as rhythm, melody, and harmony. In teaching most songs to elementary-age children, you will rely heavily on the rote or rote-note approach, but you should introduce the reading of music notation through icons prior to the first grade and formal notation starting in the first grade.

It is important that a child's experience with the sounds of music precede contact with visual symbols. Symbols of music notation take on meaning only when they can be connected to a tonal or rhythmic grouping that has been sung or played. The approach to music reading in this book is based on the Kodály system of tonal and rhythm syllables as practiced in American schools. It is an adaptation of a method of music education developed by the Hungarian composer/educator Zoltán Kodály (1882–1967), who created a method based on the Hungarian language and folk music. The method stresses good singing and music literacy—the ability to read music. And though rhymes and children's game songs are important, body movement is also an effective means of learning.

The Kodály approach focuses on a balance of singing, listening, playing, moving, thinking, and creating. In the Kodály method, steady beat and rhythmic echo clapping are taught first as preparation for rhythm reading, along with pitch discrimination and the concepts of high and low as preparation for melodic reading. Rhythmic duration syllables and hand signs (adapted from the Glover/Curwen approach) contribute to learning through a combination of eye (seeing), ear (hearing), and body (moving). The philosophy of the Kodály approach is as follows:

- All people capable of lingual literacy are also capable of musical literacy. Learning to read music, like learning to read words, is a taught skill. Knowing how to read this language increases the quality of life itself.
- Singing is the best foundation for musicianship. Singing is as natural an activity as speaking. It is through singing that musical knowledge can be internalized.
- To be most effective, music education must begin with the very young child. It is in his or her early years that a child acquires discrimination in pitch as well as language.
- The folk songs of a child's own linguistic heritage constitute a musical "mother tongue" and therefore should be the vehicle for all early instruction. The natural patterns of rhythm and melody are found in folk music of all cultures. Through folk music, children can gain a sense of identity with the present and continuity with the past.
- Only music of the highest artistic value, both folk and composed, should be used in teaching. All music used with children should have intrinsic value, for it is from this heritage that the child will learn to value good music.

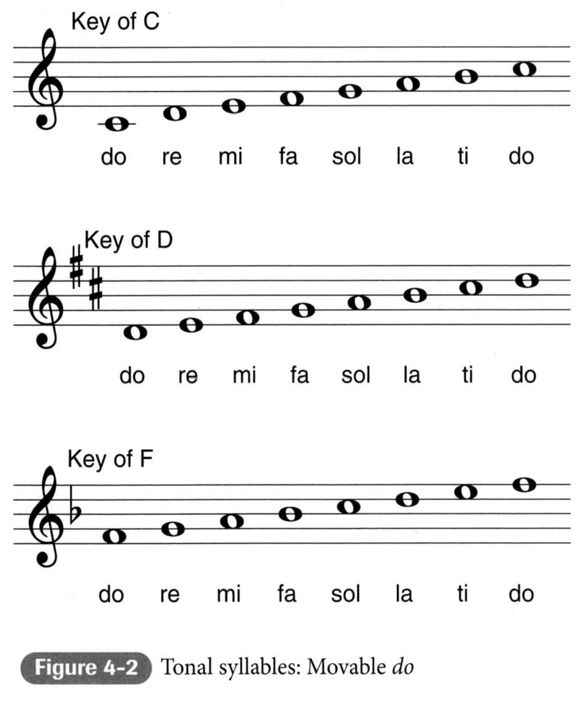

Figure 4-2 Tonal syllables: Movable *do*

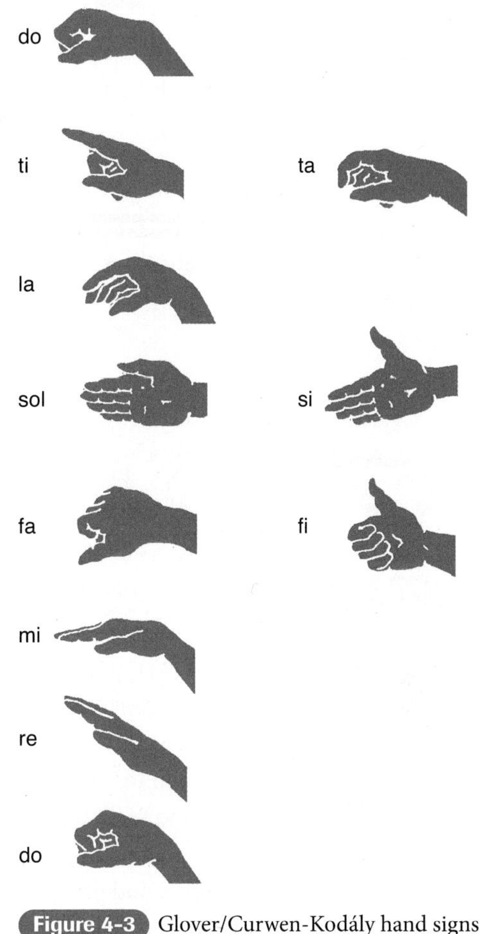

Figure 4-3 Glover/Curwen-Kodály hand signs

- Music should be at the heart of the curriculum—a core subject used as a basis for education. Music contributes to all phases of a child's development: emotional, intellectual, physical, and aesthetic.

The tools of the Kodály method are (1) the tonal syllables *do, re, mi, fa, sol, la, ti, do*; (2) hand signs; and (3) rhythm duration syllables.

The first tool, *tonal syllables*, is based on *tonality*. One purpose of this approach is to develop the ear to hear and perform tonal patterns (see Figure 4.2).[4]

The second tool of the Kodály approach is the use of *hand signs*. Originally developed by Sarah Glover and John Curwen in England, and somewhat modified for use in Hungarian schools, these hand signs have become an invaluable teaching aid (see Figure 4.3).

The third tool of the Kodály method is *rhythm duration syllables*. Rhythm is taught by patterns and by relative durations over the beat. The rhythm syllables (see Figure 4.4) are widely used in North America.[5]

[4] Lawrence Wheeler and Lois Raebeck, *Orff and Kodály Adapted for the Elementary School*, 3rd ed. (Dubuque, IA: Wm. C. Brown, 1985).

[5] For a detailed discussion of Kodály methodology, see Robert E. Nye and Vernice T. Nye, *Music in the Elementary School*, 6th ed. (Englewood Cliffs, NJ: Prentice Hall, 1992); and Lois Choksy et al., *Teaching Music in the Twenty-First Century* (Upper Saddle River, NJ: Prentice Hall, 2000).

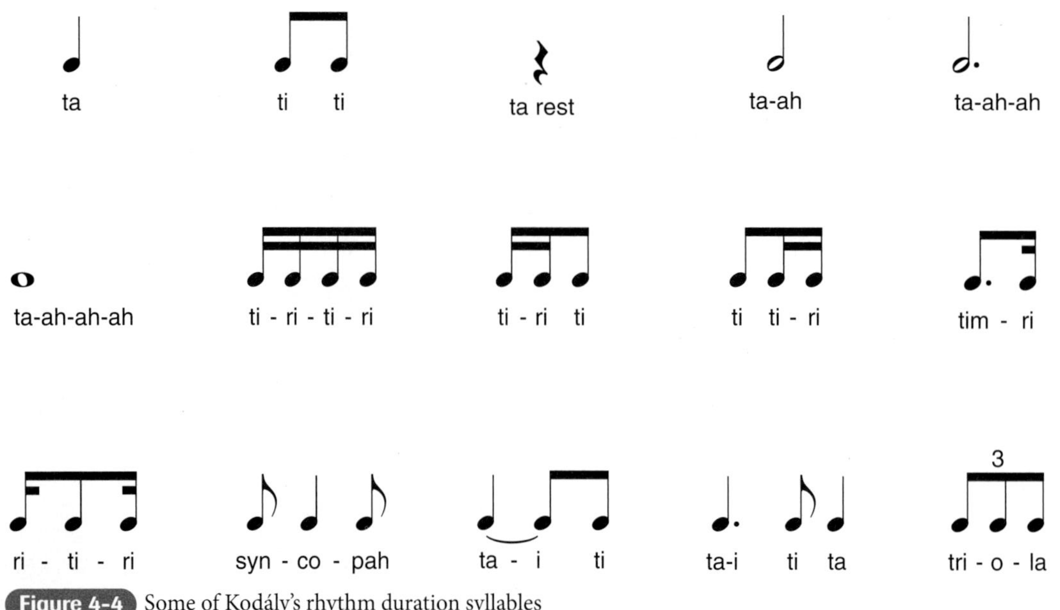

Figure 4-4 Some of Kodály's rhythm duration syllables

Kodály pedagogy emphasizes teaching rhythmic and melodic elements in a logical sequence on the basis of the folk repertoire of the mother-tongue culture of the students. Rhythm and melody are then taught using a *prepare, label*, and *practice* teaching sequence. Repertoire and prerequisite concepts are taught in the *preparation phase;* rhythm and tonal syllables as well as notation are taught in the *label phase*; and reading, writing, composition, and improvisation are explored in the *practice phase*. (The lesson plan ideas for "Bee, Bee, Bumble Bee," on the next page, provide examples of preparation, labeling, and practice activities, whereas the lesson plan ideas for "Michael Finnegan" are practice activities.)[6]

The following is a series of activities using the chant "Bee, Bee, Bumble Bee" that is based on Kodály pedagogy. These activities could become small parts of many lessons.

In order for you as the teacher to understand this teaching sequence, you need to know that *ta* (|) is one sound on a beat and *ti-ti* (⊓) is two sounds on a beat. You also need to be able to clap and read four-beat rhythm patterns that use *ta* and *ti-ti*, preferably patterns that are found in American songs and chants. These patterns include:

ta ta ti-ti ta	|	|	⊓	|
ti-ti ti-ti ti-ti ta	⊓	⊓	⊓	|
ta ta ta ta	|	|	|	|
ti-ti ti-ti ti-ti ti-ti	⊓	⊓	⊓	⊓
ta ti-ti ta ta	|	⊓	|	|
ti-ti ta ti-ti ta	⊓	|	⊓	|

[6] For an in-depth understanding of Kodály pedagogy, teachers are encouraged to take a series of courses that are offered in the summer throughout the United States. Go to the Organization of American Kodály Educators (OAKE) website at www.oake.org for more information about workshops, philosophy, and pedagogy. The book *An American Methodology: An Inclusive* Approach to Musical Literacy by Ann Eisen and Lamar Robertson (Lake Charles, LA: Sneaky Snake Publications, 1996) is a resource that outlines the Kodály approach, but is only a tool and cannot take the place of the summer workshop experience.

LESSON PLAN

Reading Rhythm Notation

Activity: Working with the rhythm of "Bee, Bee, Bumble Bee"

Grade: 1

Concepts: Rhythms have long and short sounds.

Rhythms have one and two sounds on a beat.

One sound on a beat is called *ta* (|) and two sounds on a beat are called *ti-ti* (⊓).

Prior Rhythm Knowledge: Steady beat, fast and slow

NATIONAL AND STATE MUSIC STANDARDS

1. Reading and notating music
2. Performing on instruments, alone and with others, a varied repertoire of music

OBJECTIVES

Students will:

1. Practice keeping the steady beat.
2. Read and perform rhythms with | (*ta*) and ⊓ (*ti-ti*).

MATERIALS

- "Bee, Bee, Bumble Bee" rhythm and beat icon charts prepared so that they can be used together or separately (overheads layered on top of each other are ideal)
- *Ta, ti-ti* rhythm flash cards (four beats each)
- Small, colored popsicle sticks (at least twenty-four per child)
- Grid for the popsicle sticks (one for each child):

PROCEDURES

Preparation-Phase Activities (Many Lessons)

1. Echo clap four-beat rhythm patterns with | (ta) and ⊓ (*ti-ti*), including | | ⊓ | (*ta ta ti-ti ta*) and ⊓ ⊓ ⊓ | (*ti-ti ti-ti ti-ti ta*) .
2. Say the chant "Bee, Bee, Bumble Bee" and play the game. (Point to one standing child for each beat. On the word "out," that child sits down. Continue until all children are sitting.)
3. Invite students to say the chant and pat the beat.
4. Invite students to say the chant and clap the words.
5. Invite one student to play the beat on a drum and a second student to tap the rhythm of the words on rhythm sticks.
6. Play a game: the teacher either pats the beat or claps the words—and the students identify "words" or "steady beat." (Note that the teacher and students consistently pat the beat and clap the words.)
7. Extend the game: the teacher plays the beat or the words on a drum—and the students identify "words" or "steady beat."

8. By listening to the rhythm and looking at the icon chart, students discover that some of the sounds for the words are long and some are short.
9. The students "read the chant" from an icon chart that shows the rhythm in bees, first on words, then on "long" and "short-short." The "long" is one sound on a beat and the "short-short" is two sounds on a beat. (For example, the first line would be "long, long, short-short, long.")

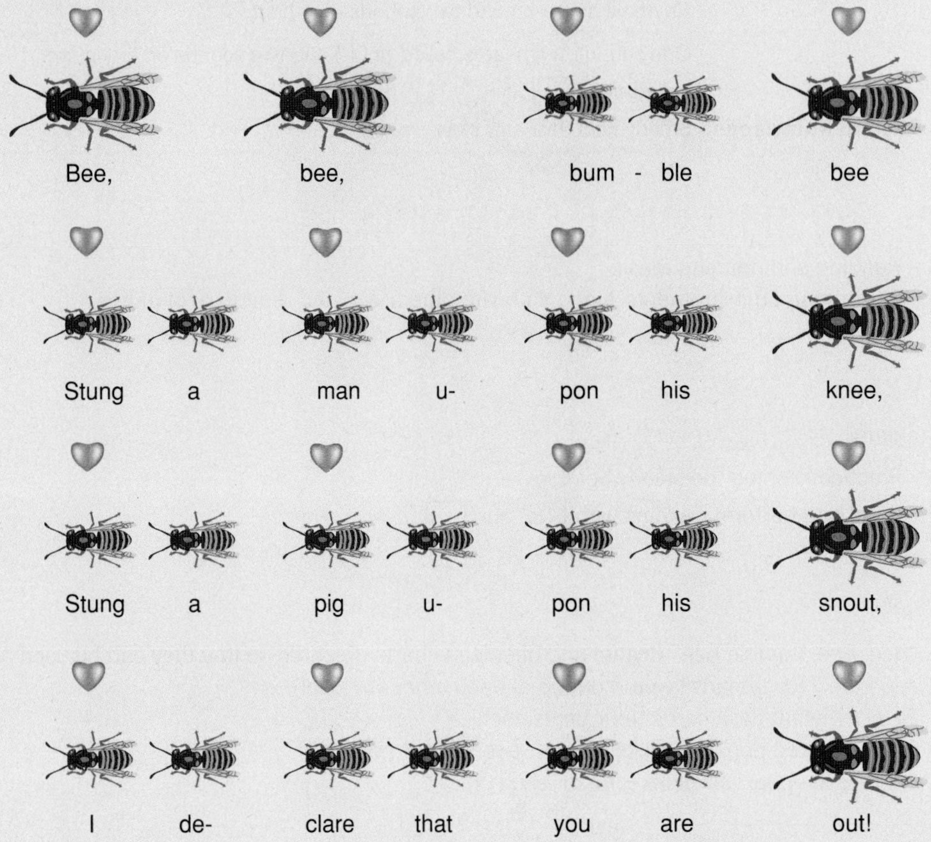

10. Students pat the beat as the teacher taps the rhythm on the rhythm icons. Repeat with the students clapping the rhythm and the teacher tapping the beat icons. (Students can also take the teacher's role and tap the beat or rhythm icons.)
11. Students discover that sometimes there is one sound on a beat and sometimes there are two sounds on a beat—by aurally hearing the one and two sounds on the beat as the teacher taps the beat icons, and by visually seeing the rhythm icons.

Labeling-Phase Activities (One Part of One Lesson)

1. The teacher has the beat icons and the rhythm icons prepared so that the rhythm icons can easily be taken away. If the teacher is using overheads (transparencies), then two overheads can be layered on top of each other. If the teacher is using PowerPoint, the rhythm icons can be animated to appear and disappear when needed.
2. Looking at the icon chart, students say, "Bee, Bee, Bumble Bee" and pat the beat as the teacher taps the rhythm icons. Repeat, with the students clapping the rhythm as the teacher taps the beat icons. Students rediscover that sometimes there is one sound on a beat and sometimes there are two sounds on a beat. (Students can also do the tapping.)

3. The teacher takes away the rhythm icons.
4. The teacher asks the students to say the chant again, clapping the rhythm, so he/she can draw lines to represent the rhythm.

5. The teacher says, "Musicians, call one sound on a beat *ta*" (as he/she points to the lines drawn for one sound on a beat), "and two sounds on a beat *ti-ti*" (as he/she points to the two lines drawn for the *ti-ti's*). "*Ti-ti's* are good friends, so they are connected with a line," the teacher says as he/she draws a horizontal line between the vertical *ti-ti* lines to create the rhythm symbol. The first introduction of *ta* and *ti-ti* are in stick notation as shown below.

6. The teacher demonstrates reading and clapping the patterns, pointing to the notation and saying the *ta's* and *ti-ti's*.
7. The students read and clap the rhythms using *ta* and *ti-ti*.
8. The students end the lesson by saying the chant, "Bee, Bee, Bumble Bee" with words.

Practice- and Assessment-Phase Activities (Many Lessons)

1. Read the rhythm of other known and new songs and chants that use only (*ta*) and (*ti-ti*) to practice and learn new four-beat *ta ti-ti* patterns. Examples: "Rain, Rain, Go Away" and "Starlight, Starbright" on p. 139, and the first line of "Lightly Row" on p. 126.
2. Analyze the form of "Bee, Bee, Bumble Bee" as A B B B or use other symbols such as cherry, banana, banana, banana.
3. Memorize the rhythm of "Bee, Bee, Bumble Bee" by reading the whole rhythm, and then erasing one line at a time.
4. Read four-beat rhythm flash cards with *ta* and *ti-ti* in stick notation.
5. Create an ostinato pattern that goes with "Bee, Bee, Bumble Bee." Example: "Bumble bee, bumble bee." Have the class say the ostinato pattern as you, the teacher, say the chant. Reverse roles.
6. Write | | ⊓ | (*ta ta ti-ti ta*) and ⊓ ⊓ ⊓ | (*ti-ti ti-ti ti-ti ta*) using small, colored popsicle sticks on a grid representing four beats:

7. Improvise and compose four-beat patterns using *ta* and *ti-ti*.

LESSON PLAN

Reading Music Notation

Activity: Working with the rhythm of "Tideo"

Grades: 2–3

Concepts: Rhythms have long and short sounds.

Rhythms have one, two, and four sounds on a beat.

One sound on a beat is *ta*, two sounds on a beat are *ti-ti*, and four sounds on a beat are *ti-ri-ti-ri*.

Stick and standard notation are used for quarter, two-eighths, and four-sixteenths notes.

Prior Rhythm Knowledge: Steady beat, fast and slow; *ta* has one sound on a beat, *ti-ti* has two sounds on a beat, *ta-rest* is one beat of silence

Key: D
Starting pitch: F#
Meter: 2/4, begins on 1

Ti-de-o

Chosky, L; Brummitt, D., *120 Singing Games & Dances for Elementary Schools,* 1st Edition, (c) 1987, p. 68. Reprinted by permission of Pearson Education, Inc., Upper Saddle River, NJ.

NATIONAL AND STATE MUSIC STANDARDS

1. Singing, alone and with others, a varied repertoire of music
2. Reading and notating music

OBJECTIVES

Students will:

1. Sing the song by reading the correct rhythms using rhythm syllables.
2. Sing the song with energy and enthusiasm.

MATERIALS

- A chart with the rhythm of the song "Tideo" displayed in icons
- A chart with the rhythm of the song "Tideo" displayed in stick notation, with a question mark used for the *ti-ri-ti-ri*

PROCEDURES

1. Sing "Tideo" and do the following movement activity:
   - Students stand in a double circle, facing a partner.
   - On the word "pass," students take one step to their right so that the outer circle moves counterclockwise and the inner circle moves clockwise.
   - Students stop and pat "Jingle at the," clap "window," and pat their partner for "Tideo."
   - On "Tideo, Tideo" students trade places, and then repeat the patting-clapping pattern for "Jingle at the window, Tideo."
   - On the second "Tideo, Tideo," students return to their original spot in the circle.
2. Invite students to clap the rhythm of the song "Tideo" to find the really fast notes. Students notice that the fast notes are at the beginning of "Jingle at the window, Tideo."
3. Students clap the rhythm of "Tideo" as the teacher points to icons representing the rhythm.

4. Students clap the rhythm of "Tideo," speaking the rhythm syllables they know and saying the words "Jingle at the"* for the new rhythm.

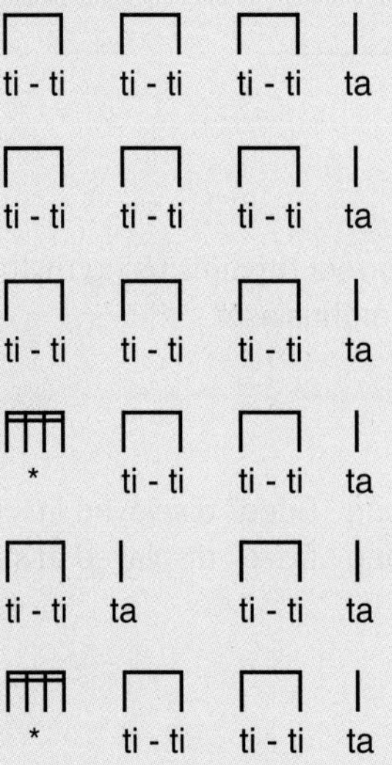

(* = "Jingle at the" or ti-ri-ti-ri)

5. Students determine that the new rhythm has four sounds on the beat.
6. The teacher writes the new rhythm in standard notation, showing students that two bars are drawn across the top and tells them the new pattern is called *ti-ri-ti-ri*.

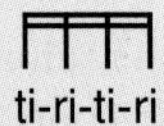

7. Students read the rhythm of the last line of the song on rhythm syllables using *ti-ri-ti-ri*.
8. Students read the rhythm of the whole song.
9. To end the lesson, students sing the song with words.

ASSESSMENT

1. How many sounds are on the beat for *ti-ti* and *ta*?
2. How many sounds are on the beat for *ti-ri-ti-ri*?
3. Write a four-beat rhythm pattern that uses *ti-ri-ti-ri*.
4. Read the rhythm of other songs that use *ti-ri-ti-ri*, for example, "Salamanca Market" on p. 106.

LESSON PLAN
Reading Music Notation

Activity: Working with melody and rhythm in the song "Michael Finnegan" (p. 89)

Grades: 3–5

Concepts: Tonal syllables (*do, re, mi, fa, sol, la, ti, do*)

Rhythm syllables:

NATIONAL AND STATE MUSIC STANDARDS

1. Singing, alone and with others, a varied repertoire of music
2. Performing on instruments, alone and with others, a varied repertoire of music
3. Reading and notating music

OBJECTIVES

Students will:

1. Sing the song by reading the correct pitches using tonal syllables.
2. Sing the song by reading the correct rhythms using rhythm syllables.
3. Sing the song with energy and enthusiasm.

MATERIALS

- Charts with tonal syllable patterns such as *do mi sol, mi re do, sol do, re sol do,* and *ti la sol*
- Chart with tonal scale
- Chart with rhythm syllables
- Keyboard, guitar, or Q-chord
- Resonator bells

PROCEDURES

1. Discuss the value of reading music and compare it to reading words. For example, reading music saves time and allows the student to learn many more songs. Reading music also provides the student with a skill that can enhance all musical experiences and activities.
2. Play or sing the song and have students pat-clap the meter beats (1 2 1 2).
3. Review the meter signature (2/4).
4. Echo sing patterns from the song in F.
5. Read patterns on the staff in F and establish F as *do*. Patterns can be placed onto large flash cards to facilitate presentation.
6. Appoint a student as leader to sing some of the song patterns and have the rest of the class echo.
7. Introduce rhythm patterns by playing or singing the following for students to imitate:

8. Introduce unusual rhythm syllables used in the song:

= ti

= ti-ri

9. Place the following patterns on flash cards and ask students to read them using rhythm syllables:

10. Place a copy of the song on a transparency and ask students to read the rhythm using syllables.
11. Using a chart with solfa syllables, sing *do, re, me, fa, sol* going up from *do*, and *do, ti, la, sol* going down from *do*.
12. Practice singing tonal syllables from the chart. Locate similar patterns in the song.
13. Sing the song using tonal syllables.

14. Speak the words of the song in rhythm.
15. Sing the entire song from notation.
16. Emphasize the need for singing with good tone color, enthusiasm, and energy.
17. Closure: Sing the song using tonal syllables and then sing it using rhythm syllables. Finally, sing the song using words.

ASSESSMENT

1. In the song "Michael Finnegan," where is *do*? Where are *re, mi, fa*, and *sol*?
2. In the song "Michael Finnegan," what are the rhythm syllables for eighth notes? For sixteenth notes?
3. What advantage do you have when you know tonal syllables? Rhythm syllables? How do they help you learn a song?
4. In the song "Michael Finnegan," what tonal syllables are used?
5. Finally, apply what you have learned to the song "Do-Re-Mi" (which is in the key of C).

Singing Additive Songs

An *additive song* is one that has several verses, each of which piggybacks on the previous verse—for example, "The Twelve Days of Christmas."

English Carol

The Twelve Days of Christmas

Key: F
Starting pitch: C
Meter: 4/4, (duple), begins on 4

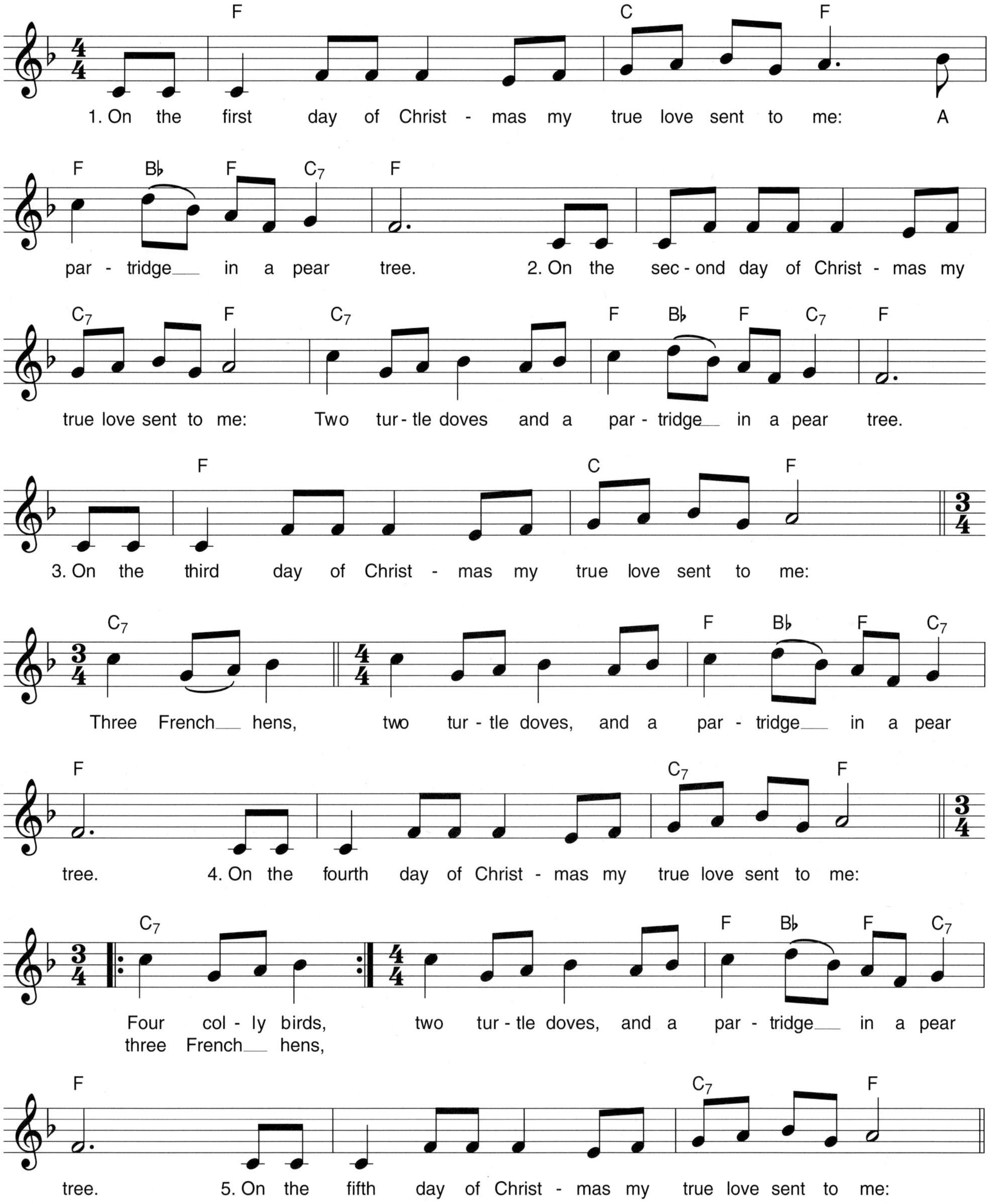

1. On the first day of Christ - mas my true love sent to me: A
par - tridge___ in a pear tree. 2. On the sec - ond day of Christ - mas my
true love sent to me: Two tur - tle doves and a par - tridge___ in a pear tree.
3. On the third day of Christ - mas my true love sent to me:
Three French___ hens, two tur - tle doves, and a par - tridge___ in a pear
tree. 4. On the fourth day of Christ - mas my true love sent to me:
Four col - ly birds, two tur - tle doves, and a par - tridge___ in a pear
three French___ hens,
tree. 5. On the fifth day of Christ - mas my true love sent to me:

F G7 C7 F B♭
Five gold - en rings, four col - ly birds, three French hens,

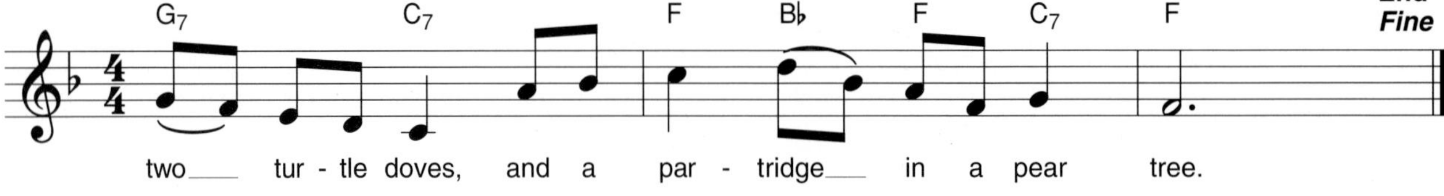
G7 C7 F B♭ F C7 F
End
Fine
two tur - tle doves, and a par - tridge in a pear tree.

Go back to the sign and sing to the end
D.C. al fine
F C7 F C7
6.–12. On the sixth day of Christ - mas my true love sent to me: 6. Six geese a - lay - ing,
(seventh, etc.)

7. Seven swans a-swimming,
8. Eight maids a-milking,
9. Nine drummers drumming,
10. Ten pipers piping,
11. Eleven ladies dancing,
12. Twelve lords a-leaping.

Extension Activity

Once students have mastered singing the melody of "The Twelve Days of Christmas" have them create new words to the melody. Work as a class or in groups to create "The Twelve Days of Middle School":

Example: "On the first day of middle school my teacher gave to me . . . "

The final song could be performed at a holiday concert or recorded and sent home with the students as a present to their parents.

TEACHING PART SINGING

Singing in parts adds an exciting dimension to musical experiences. It is important, however, that a child be able to sing a simple song in tune before trying to sing harmony; thus, part singing is seldom attempted before third grade. Each of the following approaches or songs can be used singly or in combination with a variety of age levels to teach this important skill.

Lining Out a Song

Lining out is a technique for learning a song in which each line is presented by a leader and then repeated by a group. If the note at the end of each phrase is sustained (with the voice or an instrument), lining out is a good first step in developing part singing. This is appropriate for grades 3–6.

1. Sing the song phrase by phrase, each time sustaining the pitch of the last note. Ask students to imitate each phrase after you sing it.
2. Divide the class in half and ask one half to begin the song and the other half to answer.

2. They've plowed and fenced
   My cattle range,
   And the people there
   Are all so strange

3. I'll take my horse, and I'll take my rope,
   I'll hit the trail upon a lope,
   Say "adios" to the Alamo,
   And turn my face toward Mexico.

Singing Canons

A *canon* is a contrapuntal (imitative) musical composition sung by two or more groups in which the melody is imitated exactly and completely by the successive voices, though not always at the same pitch. The song "Salamanca Market"[7] (which is based on the pentatonic scale: *do, re, mi, sol, la*) is a "canon" song.

[7] The Salamanca Market is in the city of Hobart, Tasmania, an island off the coast of Australia. The market was named after the British general Arthur Wellesley Wellington's victory over France at Salamanca, Spain, in 1812.

Singing Dialogue Songs or Echo Songs

Another way of teaching part singing to children is through dialogue or echo songs. As the name implies, in these songs a melody in one line of the music is mimicked in another line of music, thus creating several lines of music at the same time. Sing the song "Go, Tell It on the Mountain," noticing in particular the part singing in the refrain (section B) where the phrase "Go, Tell It on the Mountain" is first sung in the top part and then repeated in the lower line of music. Also sing "The Keeper," another dialogue song.

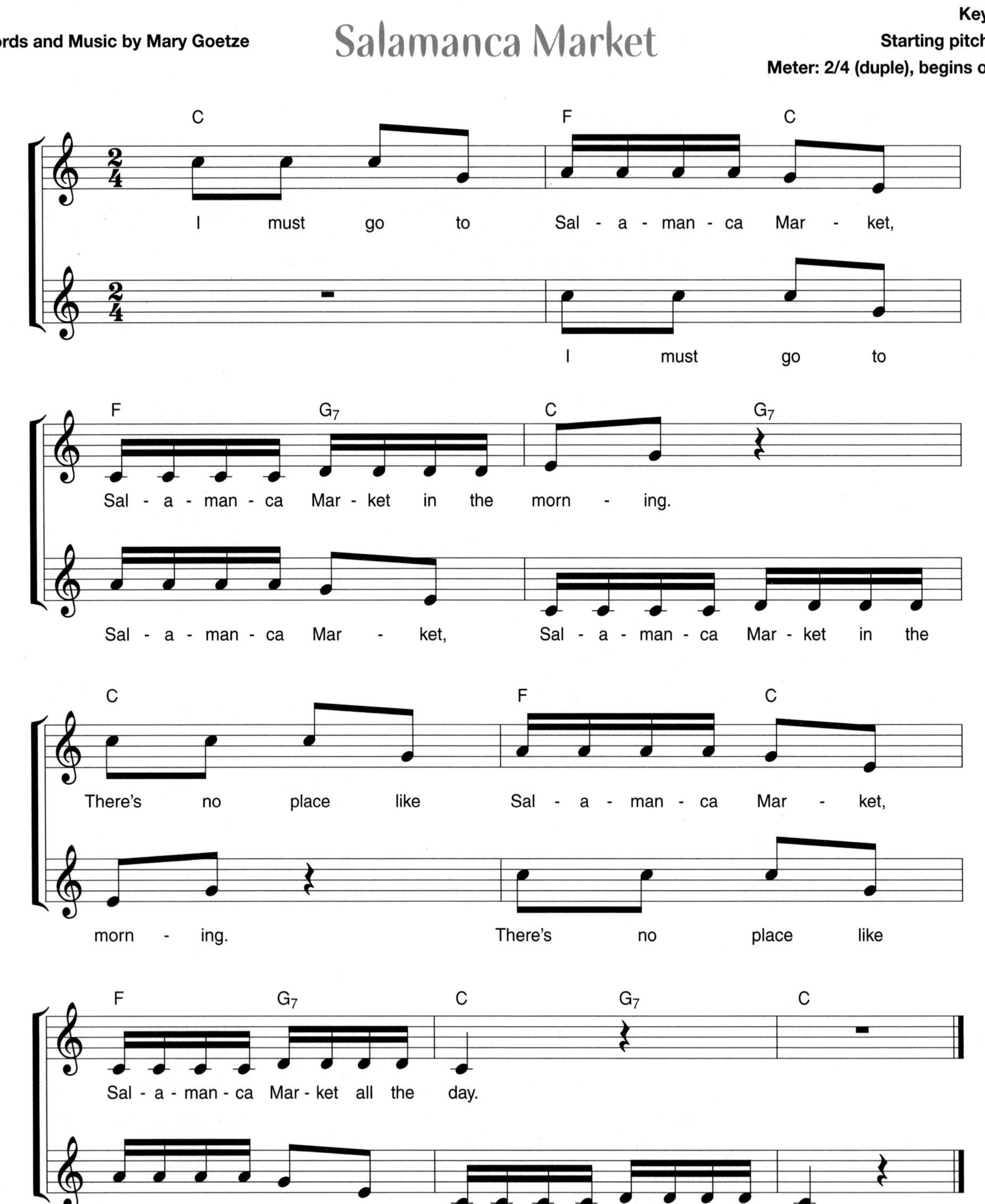

Spiritual

Go, Tell It on the Mountain

Key: F
Starting pitch: A
Meter: 4/4, begins on 1

(A)

Verse *(freely)*

F — C7 — F

1. When I was a seek - er, I sought both night and day. I
2. He made me a watch - man Up - on the cit - y wall. And

F — B♭ — C7

asked the Lord to help me, And He showed me the way.
if I serve Him tru - ly, I am the least of all.

(B)

Refrain *(in rhythm)*

F — C7 — F

Go tell it on the moun - tain, O - ver the hills and ev - 'ry - where.

Countermelody

Go, tell it on the moun - tain,

F — C7 — F

Go, tell it on the moun - tain, Our Lord in heav - en is born.

Go, tell it on the moun - tain, our Lord is born.

(A)

Drum

(B)

Tambourine

English Folk Song

The Keeper

Key: D
Starting pitch: A
Meter: 4/4, begins on 4

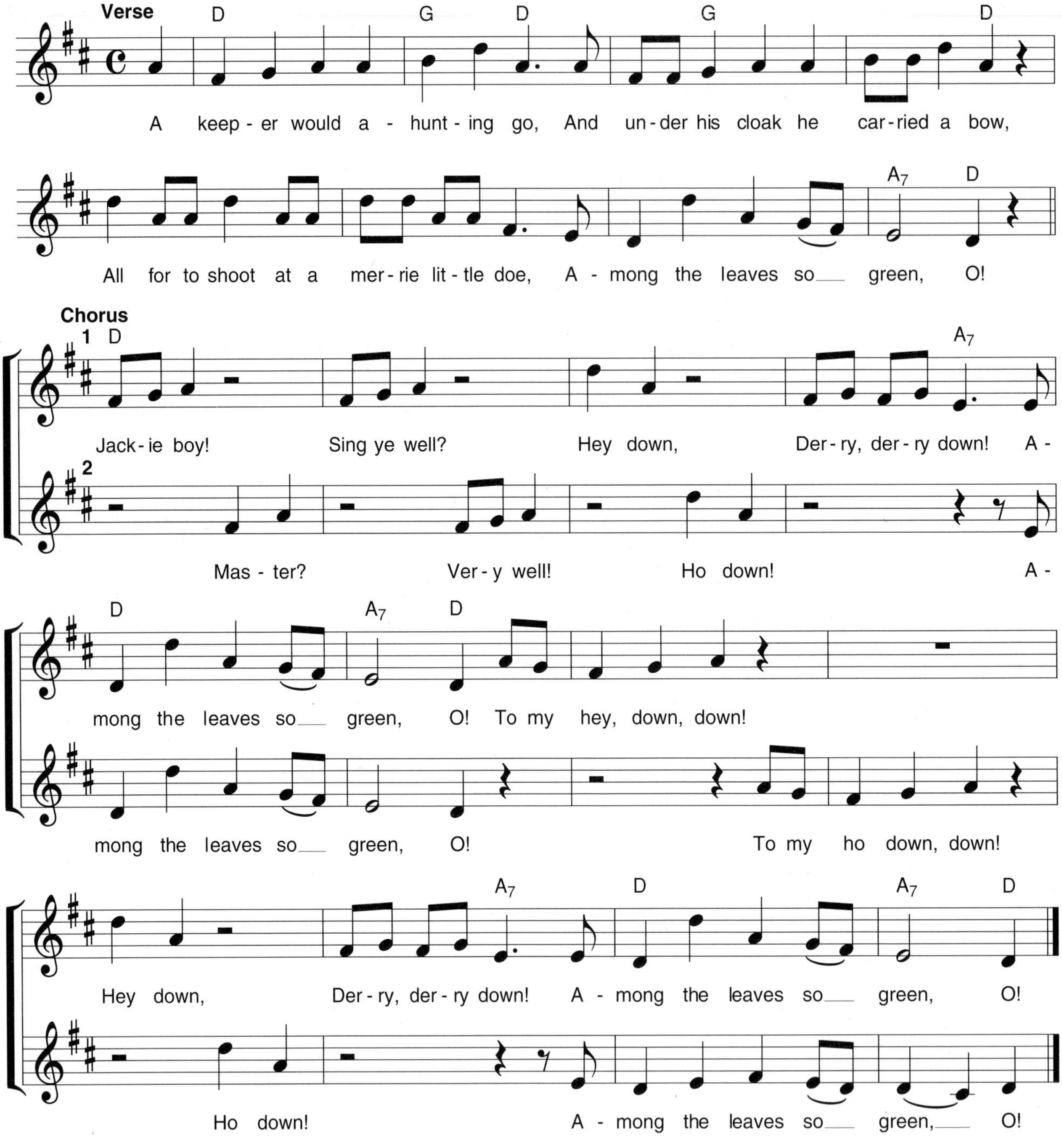

Verse

D G D G D

A keep - er would a - hunt - ing go, And un - der his cloak he car - ried a bow,

A7 D

All for to shoot at a mer - rie lit - tle doe, A - mong the leaves so___ green, O!

Chorus

1 D A7

Jack - ie boy! Sing ye well? Hey down, Der - ry, der - ry down! A -

2

Mas - ter? Ver - y well! Ho down! A -

D A7 D

mong the leaves so___ green, O! To my hey, down, down!

mong the leaves so___ green, O! To my ho down, down!

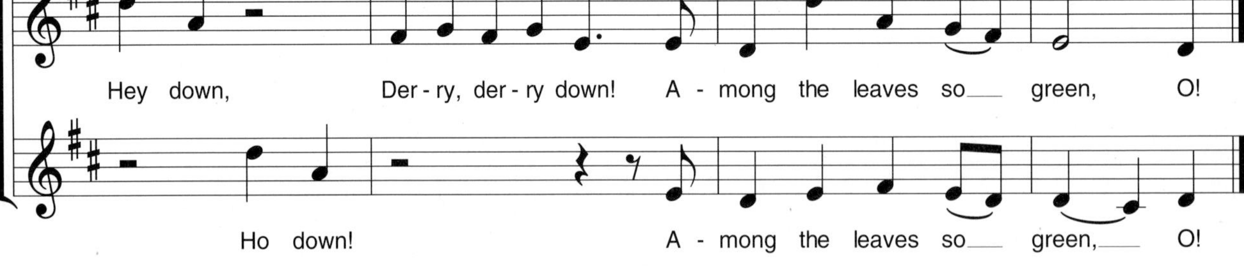

Add the following rhythmic accompaniment beginning at the "Chorus."

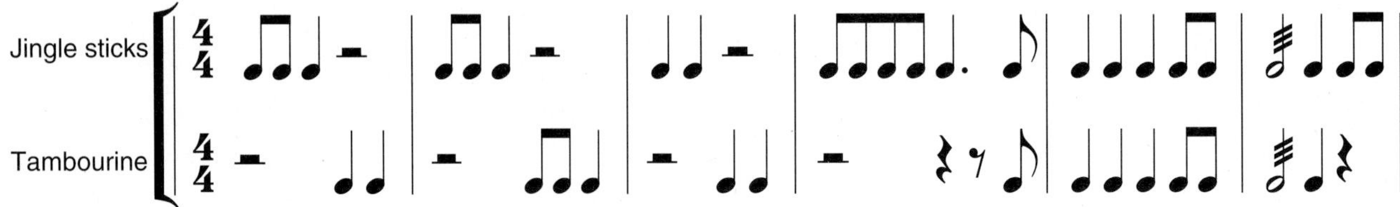

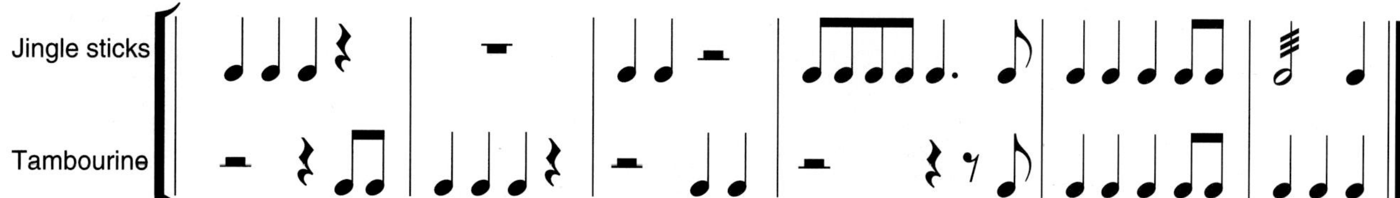

Singing Call-and-Response Songs

A *call-and-response* song is one in which a musical phrase is sung by a leader answered by a group, as, for example in "Kye, Kye Kule," (see p. 289) an African dance/game song.

Adding Descants/Countermelodies

A *descant* or *countermelody* is a melody that is sung or played above or below the primary melody. A simple descant can be created by using the individual notes of the song's chords with an occasional "passing" tone. In the following song, "Did You Ever See a Lassie?" a basic descant has been created from the fifth (C) and third (A) of the F chord, and the fifth (G) of the C7 chord. And, in the song "He's Got the Whole World in His Hands," the descant is created from just the chord roots.

German Folk Song
Arranged by Joy E. Lawrence

Did You Ever See a Lassie?

Key: F
Starting pitch: F
Meter: 3/4, begins on 3

Descant

F F C7 F F

Doo Doo Doo Doo Doo

Melody

Did you ev - er see a las - sie / lad - die a las - sie, a las - sie, Did you ev - er see a

F C7 F C7 F

Doo Doo Doo Doo Doo Doo Doo Doo Doo

las - sie do this way and that? Do this way and that way, do

C7 F F F C7 F

Doo Doo Doo Doo Doo Doo Doo Doo Doo Doo

this way and that way, Did you ev - er see a las - sie do this way and that?

The descant in "Did You Ever See a Lassie?" has been created from the following chords. The bottom pitch is the root. (See Chapter 5 for a more detailed discussion and suggestions for instruments.)

Spiritual

He's Got the Whole World in His Hands

Key: D
(Pentatonic)
Starting pitch: A
Meter: 4/4, begins on "and" of 3

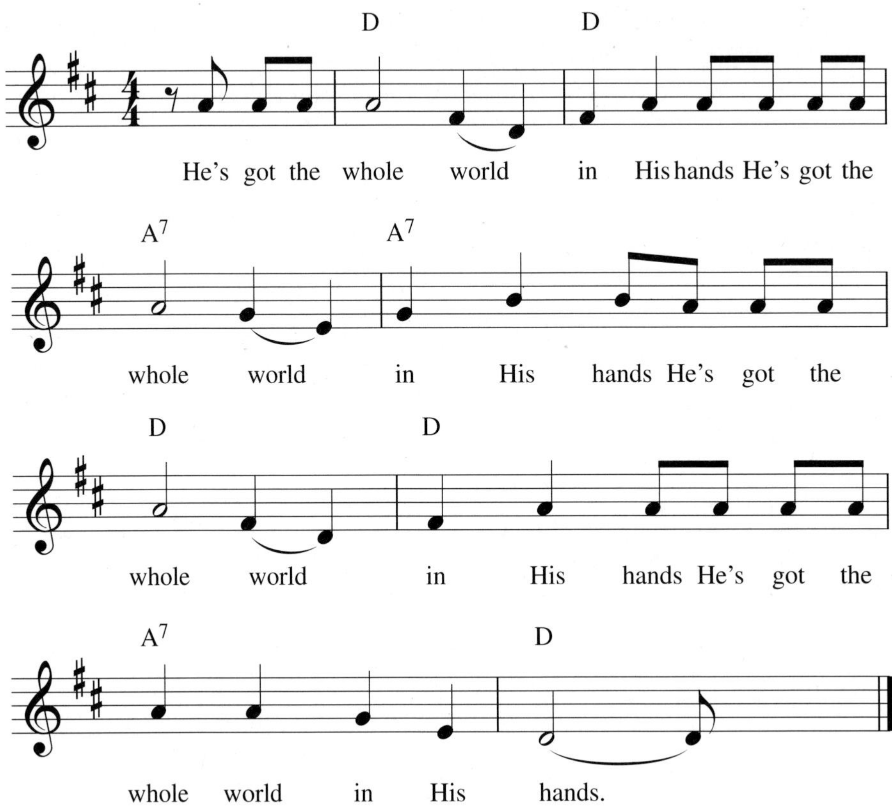

2. He's got the winds and rain in his hands. (3 times)
   He's got the whole world in his hands.

3. He's got you and me brother in his hands. (3 times)
   He's got the whole world in his hands.

4. He's got everybody in his hands. (3 times)
   He's got the whole world in his hands.

Boatner, Edward. Spirituals Triumphant, Old and New. Nashville: Sunday School Publishing Board, National Baptist Convention U.S.A., 1927.

Descant (created from chord roots)

D D C♯ C♯ D D C♯ D

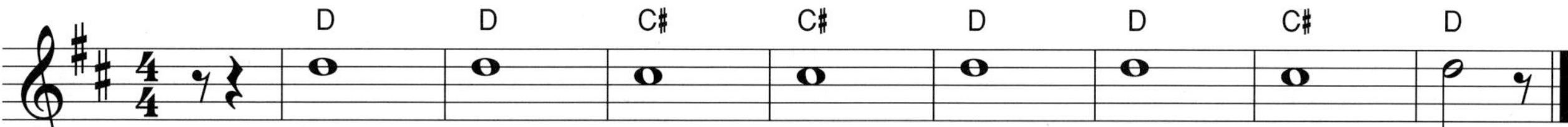

Descants may be complete melodies composed and performed along with the main melody. Sing "Did You Ever See a Lassie" again (p. 109), adding the descant played on the recorder (p. 137). Also, sing "America" (p. 142) and add the descant melody found on page 137.

Singing Ostinato Chants

Still another way of teaching part singing to children is through the use of an *ostinato*, a repeated melodic/rhythmic line that is sung against the main melody of a song. For example, sing the song "The Cuckoo" and add an ostinato part at the refrain. Then perform the song "Zum Gali Gali" with its ostinato pattern.

The Cuckoo

Austrian Folk Song
Ostinato by Joy E. Lawrence

Key: G
Starting pitch: B
Meter: 3/4, begins on 3

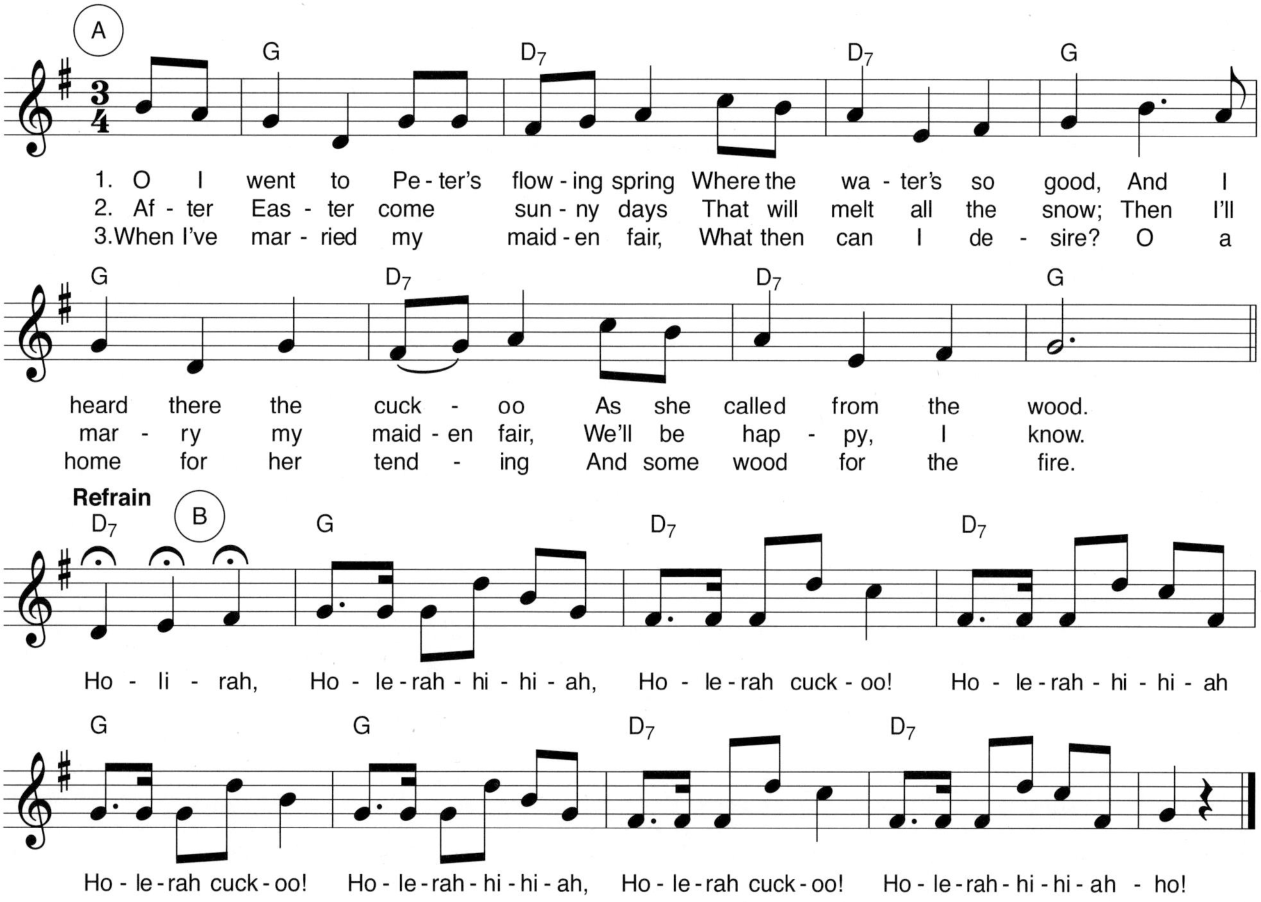

A
G D7 D7 G
1. O I went to Pe-ter's flow-ing spring Where the wa-ter's so good, And I
2. Af-ter Eas-ter come sun-ny days That will melt all the snow; Then I'll
3. When I've mar-ried my maid-en fair, What then can I de-sire? O a
G D7 D7 G
heard there the cuck-oo As she called from the wood.
mar-ry my maid-en fair, We'll be hap-py, I know.
home for her tend-ing And some wood for the fire.
Refrain
B
D7 G D7 D7
Ho-li-rah, Ho-le-rah-hi-hi-ah, Ho-le-rah cuck-oo! Ho-le-rah-hi-hi-ah
G G D7 D7
Ho-le-rah cuck-oo! Ho-le-rah-hi-hi-ah, Ho-le-rah cuck-oo! Ho-le-rah-hi-hi-ah-ho!

1. Have the class sing the song.
2. Accompany on keyboard, guitar, or Q-chord while the class sings the song.
3. Chant the word rhythms of the ostinato. Ask the class to imitate.
4. Sing the ostinato on pitches. Ask the class to sing the ostinato.
5. Have half the class sing or play the ostinato while the other half sings the refrain.

Rhythm Ostinato

Keyboard, guitar, or Q-chord

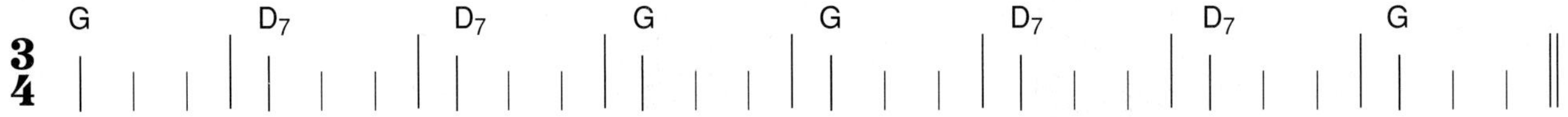

G D7 D7 G G D7 D7 G

3/4

Claves

3/4

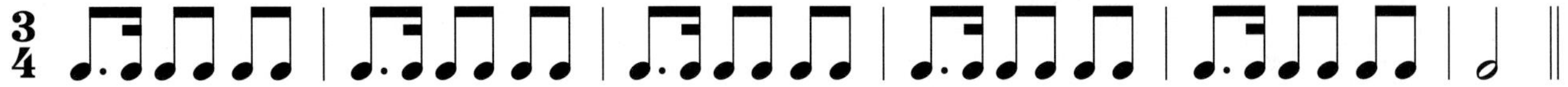

Melodic/Rhythmic Ostinato

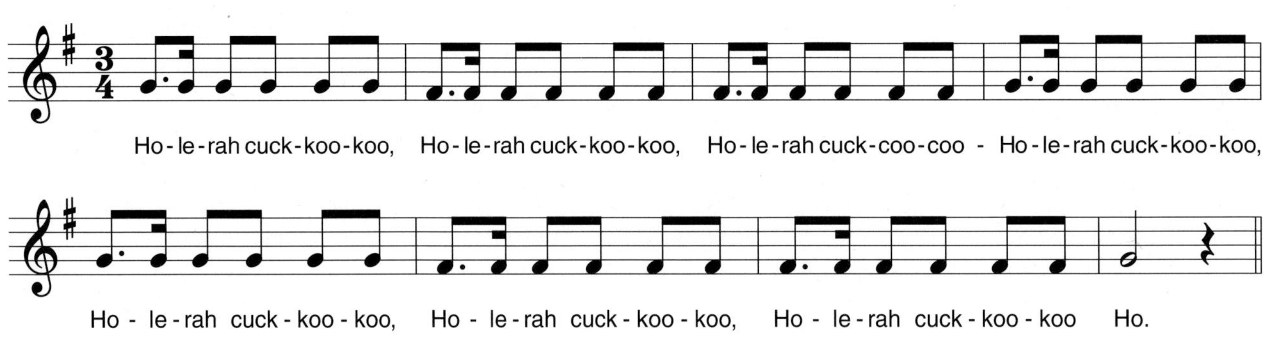

3/4

Ho-le-rah cuck-koo-koo, Ho-le-rah cuck-koo-koo, Ho-le-rah cuck-coo-coo - Ho-le-rah cuck-koo-koo,

Ho - le-rah cuck-koo-koo, Ho - le-rah cuck-koo-koo, Ho - le-rah cuck-koo-koo Ho.

Israeli Folk Song

Zum Cali Cali

Key: E minor (Pentatonic)
Starting pitch: E
Meter: 2/4, begins on 1

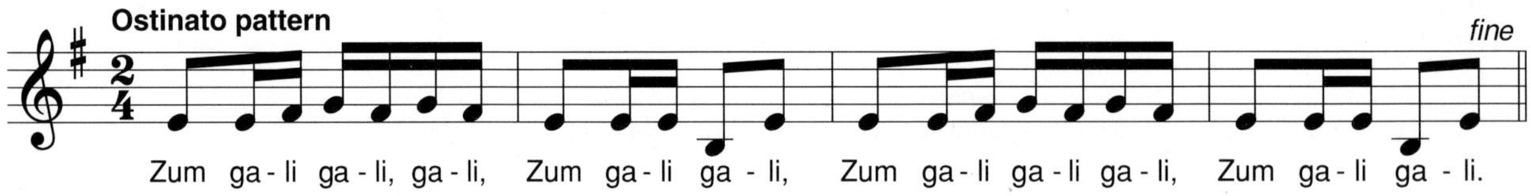

Ostinato pattern

2/4 *fine*

Zum ga-li ga-li, ga-li, Zum ga-li ga-li, Zum ga-li ga-li ga-li, Zum ga-li ga-li.

Melody
D.C. al fine
1. Pi - o-neers work hard on the land, Men and wom - en work hand in hand.
2. As they la - bor all day long, They lift their voice in song.
Ostinato
Zum ga - li ga-li, ga-li, Zum ga - li ga - li, Zum ga - li ga-li, ga-li, Zum ga - li ga - li.

1. Sing or play the ostinato used in "Zum Gali Gali."
2. Play the E minor chord on an accompanying instrument (e.g., keyboard) while the class sings the ostinato.
3. Perform the song with accompaniment. Have part of the class sing the ostinato while the rest sing the melody.
4. Add the following rhythms on drum, claves, and tambourine:

Singing Rounds

A *round* consists of exact imitation of a given melody sung one or two measures later. Singing rounds can help a child begin to comprehend the concept of harmony. There are several steps to follow for such singing to be successful:

1. The melody must be learned very well.
2. As children sing the song, play the melody as a round (that is, beginning a measure or two later). Use melody bells or a recorder, which will enable the children to hear the melody as a second part while singing.
3. Choose the best singers to sing the second part of the round. Encourage them to be on their own.
4. Do not try a three- or four-part round until children are secure with two parts.

Sing the following round. Begin with two parts, gradually adding a third or fourth part.

Round

Frère Jacques

Key: F major
Starting pitch: F
Meter: 4/4, begins on 1

Singing Partner Songs

Still another way to teach part singing to children is through *partner songs*. As implied in the name, in this type of part singing two songs are combined.

The creation of a partner song involves the following considerations:

1. The two songs must be the same length.
2. The two songs must be in the same key.
3. The meter must be the same; that is, both songs need to be in duple or triple meter.
4. The words may or may not be similar, but partner songs work best together when the text of one complements that of the other.
5. The harmonic structure (chords) given must match measure for measure.

Following are two partner songs, "Cielito Lindo" (which is partnered with the song "My Bonnie") and "All Night, All Day" (which is partnered with the song "Swing Low, Sweet Chariot" on pp. 264 and 328). With each partner song, have students learn to sing each individual song segment before combining them to produce part singing. Other partner song combinations that you may wish to explore include combining "Row, Row, Row Your Boat" (pp. 46 and 60) with "Three Blind Mice" and with "Farmer in the Dell" (p. 152).

Cielito Lindo

Mexican Folk Song

Partner: "My Bonnie"
Key: B♭
Starting pitch: F
Meter: 3/4, begins on 1

Combines an ostinato on the verse with the partner song on the chorus

B♭
F
B♭
F7
you will go down to Mex - i - co you will
Bring back my señ - or - i - ta.
B♭
F7
meet a gay señ - or - i - ta.
Bring back my señ - or - i - ta.
F7
In a while you will see her smile and her
Bring back my señ - or - i - ta.
B♭
name is Cie - li - to Lin - do.
Bring back, my señ - or - i - ta.
B♭
E♭
Ay, ay, ay, ay,
Bring back, bring back

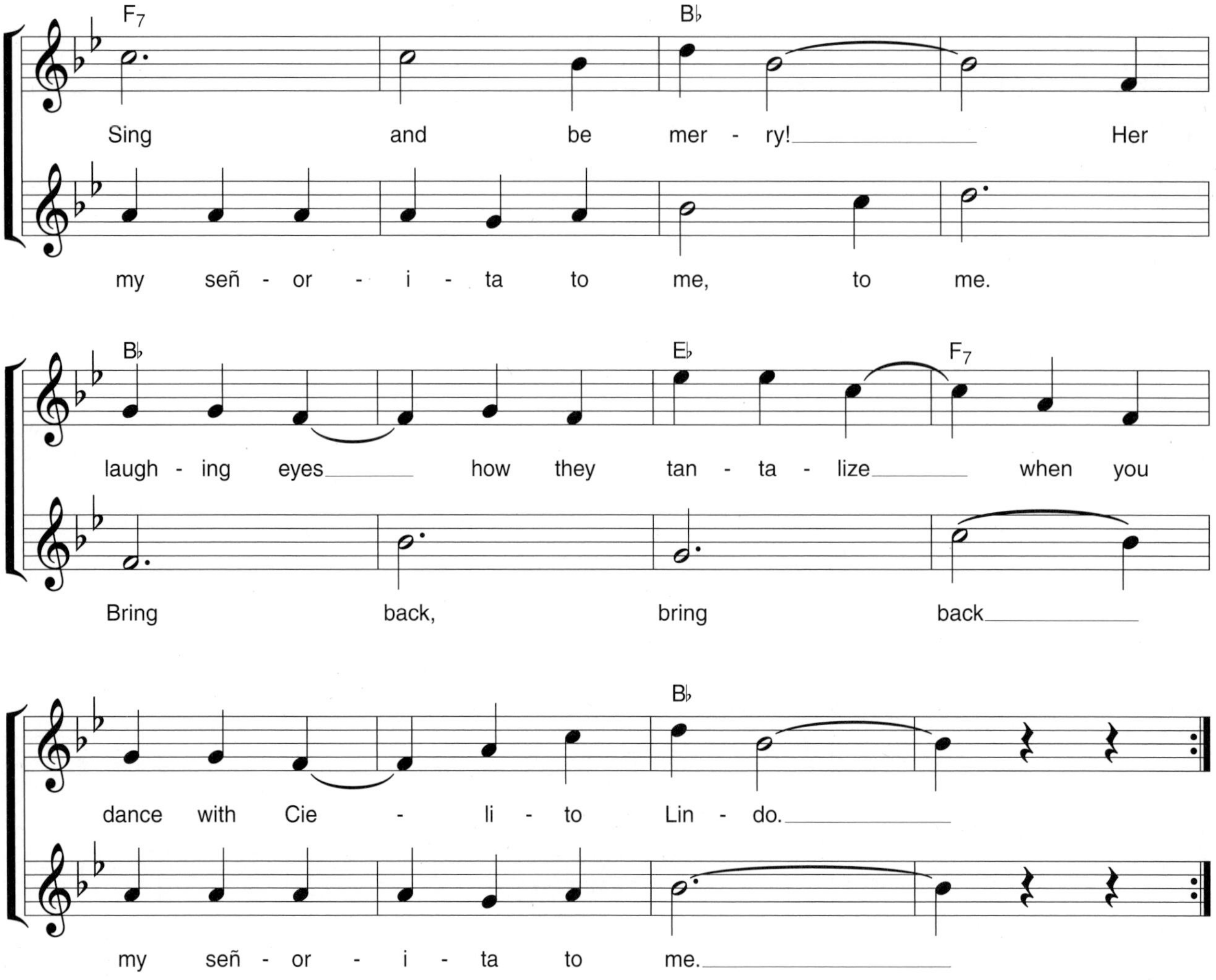

F7 B♭
Sing and be mer - ry! Her
my señ - or - i - ta to me, to me.
B♭ E♭ F7
laugh - ing eyes how they tan - ta - lize when you
Bring back, bring back
B♭
dance with Cie - li - to Lin - do.
my señ - or - i - ta to me.

Spiritual

All Night, All Day

Partner: "Swing Low, Sweet Chariot"
Key: F
Starting pitches: C, A
Meter: 4/4

F Dm B♭ F B♭
Al night, all day, An - gels watch - ing o - ver
Swing low, sweet char - i - ot, com - in' for to car - ry me

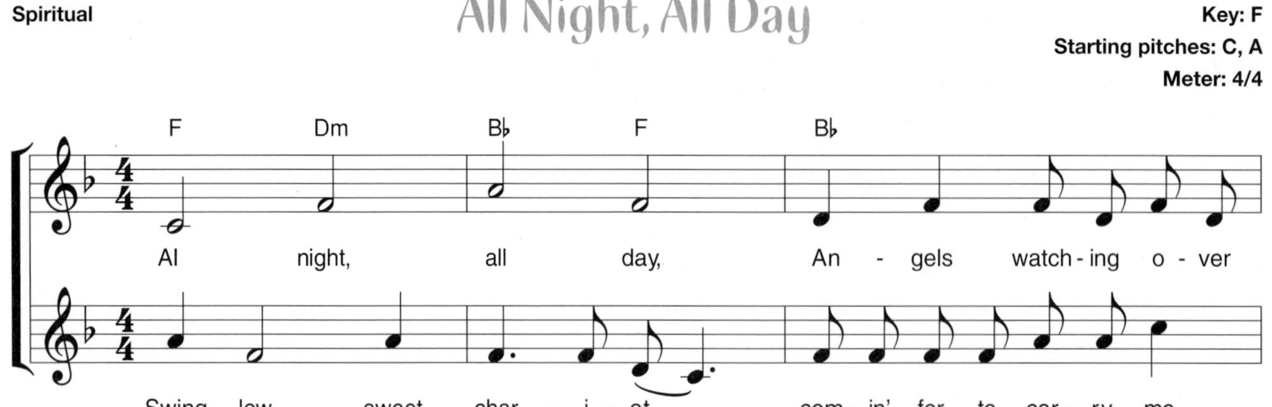

Gm C7 F Dm B♭ F
me, my Lord. All night, all day,
home! Swing low, sweet char - i - ot,
Am Dm B♭ C7 F B♭ F
Verse
F
An - gels watch - ing o - ver me.
1. Now I lay me
2. If I die be -
com - in' for to car - ry me home!
B♭ F B♭ Gm C7
down to sleep,
fore I wake,
An - gels watch - ing o - ver me, my Lord.
Com - in' for to car - ry me home.
F B♭ (G7) F Dm B♭ C7 F B♭ F
Pray the Lord my soul to keep,
Pray the Lord my soul to take,
An - gels watch-ing o - ver me.
pp
Com - in' for to car - ry me home.

F Dm B♭ F B♭
All night, all day, An - gels watch - ing o - ver
Swing low, sweet char - i - ot, com - in' for to car - ry me
Gm C7 F Dm B♭ F
me, my Lord. All night, all day,
home! Swing low, sweet char - i - ot,
Am Dm B♭ C7 F B♭ F
An - gels watch - ing o - ver me.
com - in' for to car - ry me home.

Integrating Technology

The Music Education Premium Site contains chapter quizzing, Spotify playlists, and downloads of free MP3s of noted songs. Visit CengageBrain.com to purchase an access code or enter the code provided with your text materials.

Web Resources

- Search the Web (www.google.com) for information on the Zoltán Kodály method of teaching music.

Videos

- Watch classroom videos that apply to chapter content.
- Try doing Internet searches to help you learn about the songs and to gather ideas on how to teach them.

Audio

- Download music in this chapter from the iTunes store.
- Spotify playlists allow students to stream music referenced within each chapter.
- Download free audio MP3s for the songs noted in the chapter.

CENGAGE**brain**.com

Questions for Discussion

1. Discuss the principal differences between a child's voice and an adult's voice.
2. What differences are there in the vocal abilities of children in grades 1, 3, and 6?
3. Discuss several ways for getting children to sing in tune.
4. Discuss ways that you could assist children in learning to sing harmony.
5. Why is "discovering patterns" a useful method for teaching a song? Discuss some examples of movement patterns, visual patterns, and patterns in literature that you could use to help teach patterns in music.
6. Briefly discuss some conceptual and nonconceptual ways of teaching a song.
7. If you wished to teach a song using a particular method (rote, rote-note, note), how would you go about it?.
8. Briefly outline some basic principles of the Kodály method for teaching music.

Assessment

Review ways the music standards listed at the beginning of this chapter have been met.

CHAPTER 5

Teaching Music through Playing Classroom Instruments

© Ritchie Photography

Objectives

Students will explore ideas for developing lessons that involve:

- Playing melodies
  - Piano and electronic keyboards
  - Melody bells
  - Step bells
  - Resonator bells
  - Xylophone
  - Glockenspiel
  - Metallophone
  - Handbells
  - Tone chimes
  - Recorder
- Using melody instruments in the classroom
  - Playing melodic ostinatos
  - Using melody instruments to play harmony
- Playing harmony instruments
  - Guitar
  - Q-Chord (Digital Song Card Guitar)
- Playing percussion instruments
  - Woods: rhythm sticks, claves, woodblock, maracas, sand blocks, guiro
  - Metals: cymbals, finger cymbals, triangle, tambourine, jingle bells, jingle sticks
  - Skins: hand drum, bongo drums, conga drum
- Playing rhythm accompaniments to songs
- Developing a rhythm ensemble (Grades K–3)
- Integrating instrumental experiences into the classroom
  - Language arts (Grades 4–6)
  - Science: Sound (Grades 4–6)
  - Social studies: American West (Grades 4–6)
- Sample lessons

National and State Music Standards

This chapter provides experiences with the following national music standards and related state music standards:

- Performing on instruments, alone and with others, a varied repertoire of music
- Singing, alone and with others, a varied repertoire of music
- Listening to, analyzing, and describing music

Students are usually enthusiastic about performing music on instruments, and you will generally find them highly motivated and very responsive. As with singing, playing instruments involves students directly in making music, spontaneously or from a musical score, alone or with a group. Experience is often the best teacher; students learn to listen attentively both to the music they are playing themselves and to the music performed by the total ensemble. Individual players come to rely on others and to respect their roles in the creative process of performing music together.

Development of motor coordination is essential for playing classroom instruments. Through such activities many students improve the effective use of their arms, hands, fingers, legs, and feet.

Classroom instruments function in a variety of ways. Some are used to play melodies (recorder, melody bells, xylophone, and glockenspiel), others to play harmony (guitar and Q-chord), and still others to play both melody and harmony (keyboard, handbells, tone chimes, and resonator bells). The many percussion instruments, such as drums, tambourines, claves, and triangles, are used to play rhythms.

As students learn to play instruments, they should develop the following skills.

- The ability to choose appropriate instruments for musical concepts such as:
  a. Steady beat
  b. Differences in dynamics
  c. Musical form
  d. Pitch and melody
- The ability to discriminate and select appropriate rhythm instruments for various types of music
- An awareness of the expressive potential of different instruments
- The ability to select and play instruments that can add to the expressiveness of music through accompaniment

Teachers need to learn the physical and musical characteristics of some of the most common classroom instruments and develop basic playing skills that will enable them to demonstrate these instruments and guide students in playing them.

The following guidelines will contribute to students' successful experiences with playing instruments:

1. Provide many aural experiences before using instruments.
2. Provide many opportunities for immediate success.
3. Reinforce each playing skill before going on to a new one.
4. Give *all* students an opportunity to play instruments.
5. Use instruments on a regular basis.
6. Encourage students to improvise.
7. Use instruments in musical ways.
8. Keep directions simple.
9. Avoid giving out all of the instruments at once.
10. Avoid asking students to "experiment" in creating sounds indiscriminately.
11. Avoid letting students mistreat instruments.
12. Avoid allowing students to "abuse" music by unmusical playing or behavior.
13. Ask students to "play" the instrument, not "hit" the instrument.

Careful attention to these guidelines will reward both you and your students with musically satisfying experiences.

This chapter focuses on general descriptions and functions of melody, harmony, and percussion instruments and techniques for teaching students to play them. It deals with selecting an appropriate instrument, playing rhythm accompaniments to songs, developing a rhythm ensemble, making your own instruments, and integrating instrumental experiences into the classroom. The chapter concludes with sample lessons.

Special Learner Note

Encourage students to articulate or sign the name of each instrument. A shortened version of the name may be used, but avoid calling all "shaken" instruments "shakers" or "rattles." Use the name—for example, *maraca*—and encourage at least an *m* sound or a signed *m* with a shaking motion.

PLAYING MELODIES

A number of different instruments can be used to play a melody, including piano and electronic keyboards, melody bells, step bells, resonator bells, xylophone, glockenspiel, metallophone, handbells, tone chimes, and recorder. In addition to playing a melody, these instruments can also be used to play melodic ostinato patterns, descants, and sometimes harmony parts.

Piano and Electronic Keyboards

The *piano* and *electronic keyboards* (such as those made by Casio, Yamaha, and Suzuki) are used primarily for playing melodies and simple accompaniments.

When you play the piano, depressing the keys causes hammers to strike strings. You can sustain the sound by depressing the right damper pedal, which raises the felt pads (called *dampers*) from the strings and allows them to continue to sound. When you release the pedal, the dampers return to the strings and stop the sound. When playing the following simple exercises and tunes, try to play a pitch on the piano and then press downward on the pedal. Remove your finger from the key and listen to it continue to sound. Then release the pedal with your foot and notice that the tone stops. Careful use of this pedal will allow you to play melodies smoothly. Too much pedal—that is, playing a melody with the pedal depressed throughout—will cause the tones to blur together. A little experimentation will make this principle clear to you.

Piano

Although an electronic keyboard is laid out in the same way as the piano keyboard, it offers a variety of tone colors to choose from. That is, the electronic keyboard can sound somewhat like a harpsichord, a piano, an organ, a violin, and so on. In this way electronic keyboards differ dramatically from the piano. Additionally, keyboard software applications are available on all mobile devices including smartphones, tablet computers (e.g., iPad), and MP3 players (e.g., iPod).

Keyboard

The Form of the Keyboard

Because the "form" of the keyboard (pattern of black and white notes) is also found on melody and resonator bells, you will want to become familiar with it. (See the keyboard template at the back of the book.)

Position yourself at the center of the keyboard. You will notice white keys and black keys grouped into twos and threes. This pattern is repeated throughout the keyboard:

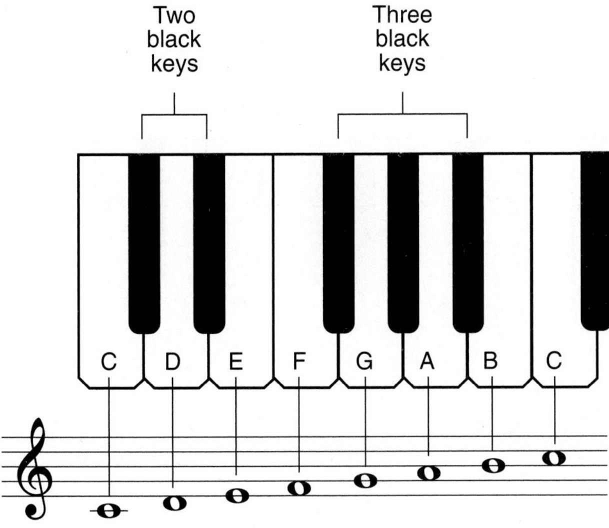

Special Learner Note

By adopting a standard color-coding system (use the same colors for notes as are used for Boomwhackers®, p. 131), you can easily adapt any melody instrument for students who are less able to read notation but very motivated to create melodies.

Each white key has a letter name that corresponds to a line or a space on the staff. Thus, the pitch name E represents the white key E on the keyboard. The piano keyboard is divided into a series of eight pitches to the octave, and there are eight octaves. The lowest pitch (to your left) is A. Play this note and then move up the keyboard, playing only the white notes. The pitches are A, B, C, D, E, F, and G; then you start over again.

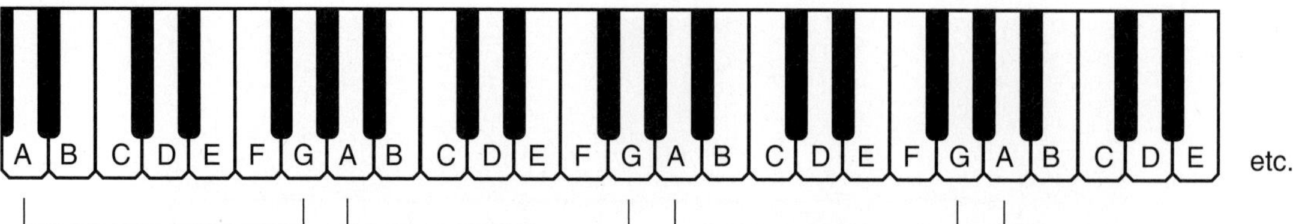

The octave A, B, C, D, E, F, G, A is divided into twelve semitones, or half steps. Raising a pitch a half step is called a sharp (#) (for example, F, F#), and lowering it a half step is called a flat (♭) (for example, G, G♭). Notice in the following example that a single black note may have two names (for example, F# and G♭).

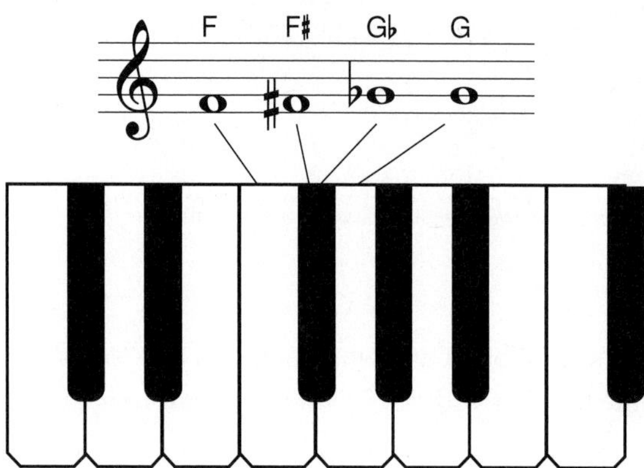

The pitch to the left of the two black keys in the center of the piano keyboard is called *middle C*. Place your right thumb on A (below middle C), followed by your middle finger on A#. Play the chromatic scale (half steps), alternating finger and thumb with each pitch. Next, play from A to B. Notice that this is a whole step (A# is in between). Play from C# to D#. Notice that this is a whole step with D in between. Locate and play other half and whole steps.

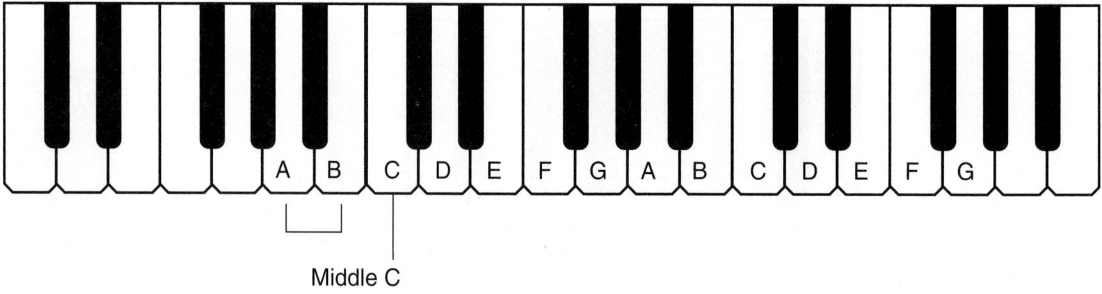

Fingering

To play a melody on a keyboard, you need to use the correct fingers. Follow these steps, and you will soon be able to play a melody:

1. Place your right hand on the keyboard with your thumb on middle C.
2. Curve your fingers above the keys, cupping your hand slightly as if over an orange, with the wrist flat.

3. Raise your thumb and "drop" it to the bottom of the key. Do not try to "push" the key down. The pitch should sound bright and clear.
4. Follow this same procedure with each of your five fingers playing successive pitches.
5. Now play the following exercise with your right hand, using the fingers indicated:

   thumb = 1
   index = 2
   middle = 3
   ring = 4
   little = 5

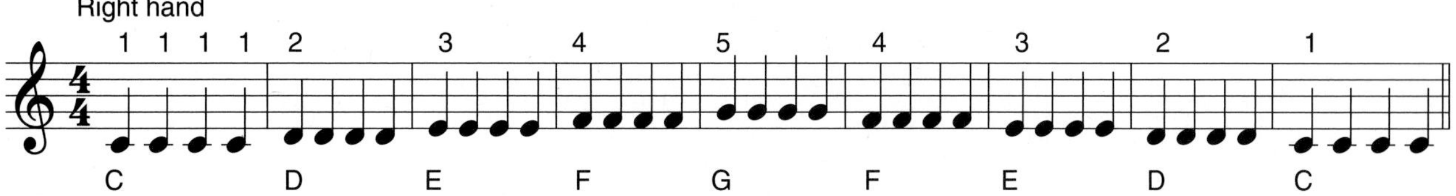

6. Now place your hand so that the thumb is on G and the little finger is on D. Repeat the above pattern with your hand in this position.

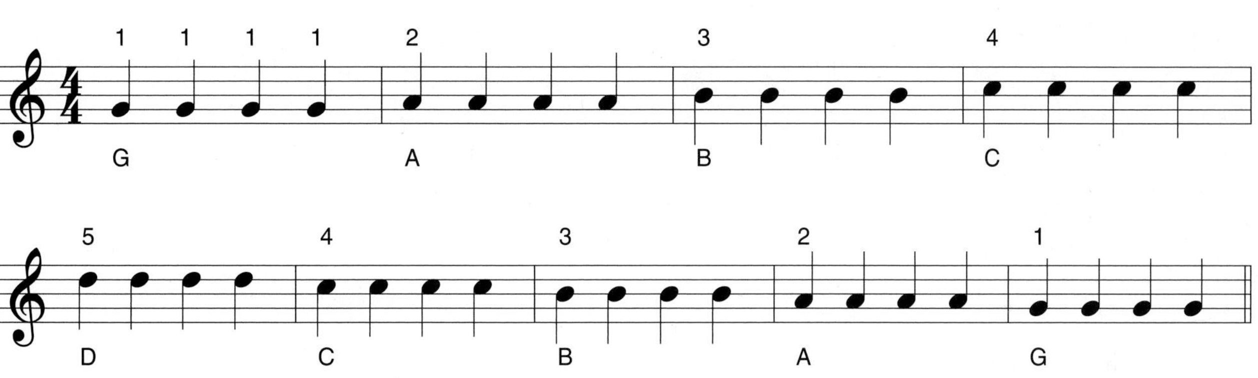

Now you are ready to play the following melodies. To ensure correct rhythm, be sure to count the beats out loud as you play.

Mary Had a Little Lamb

Sara J. Hale

Key: G
Starting pitch: B
Meter: 4/4, begins on 1

Key: G
Starting pitch: B
Meter: 4/4, begins on 2

Good News

Spiritual

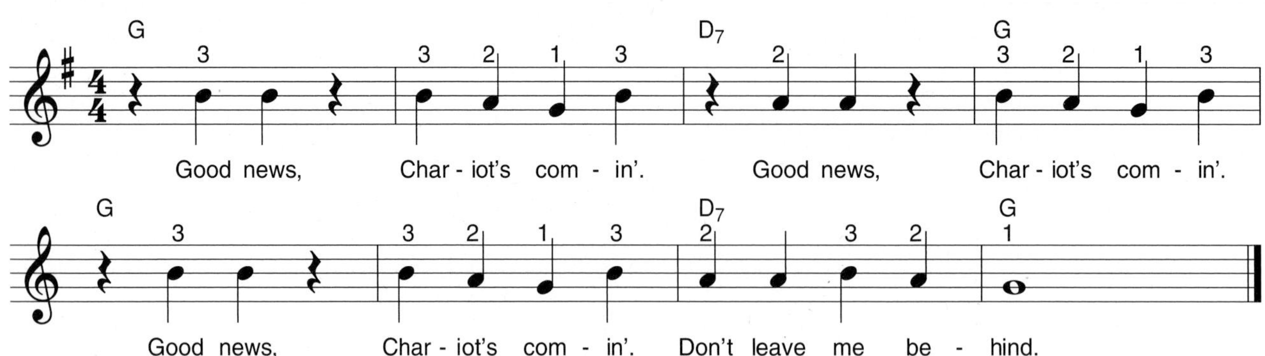
G D7 G
3 3 2 1 3 2 3 2 1 3
Good news, Char - iot's com - in'. Good news, Char - iot's com - in'.
G D7 G
3 3 2 1 3 2 3 2 1
Good news, Char - iot's com - in'. Don't leave me be - hind.

Key: G
Starting pitch: D
Meter: 2/4, begins on 1

Lightly Row

Germany

G D7 G D7
5 3 4 2 1 2 3 4 5
Light - ly row, Light - ly row, O'er the shin - ing waves we go.
G D7 G D7 G
5 3 4 2 1 3 5 1
Smooth - ly glide, smooth - ly glide on the si - lent tide.

Key: C
Starting pitch: C
Meter: 4/4, begins on 3

Michael, Row the Boat Ashore

Spiritual

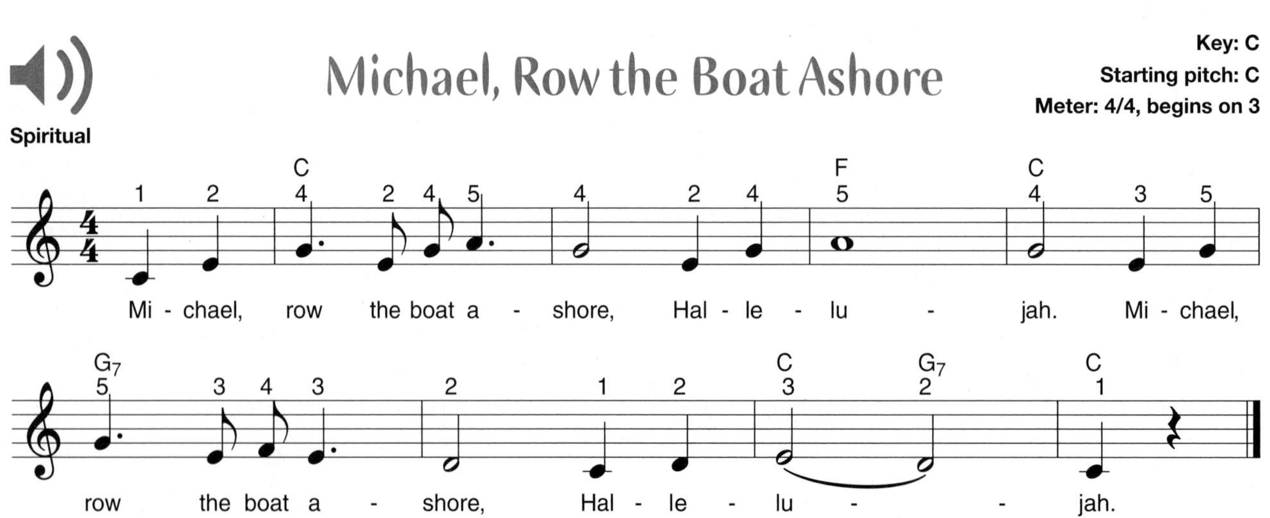
C F C
1 2 4 2 4 5 4 2 4 5 4 3 5
Mi - chael, row the boat a - shore, Hal - le - lu - jah. Mi - chael,
G7 C G7 C
5 3 4 3 2 1 2 3 2 1
row the boat a - shore, Hal - le - lu - - jah.

Melody Bells

A set of *melody bells* consists of a series of chromatically tuned metal bars mounted horizontally on a frame in the form of a keyboard. The smaller set contains pitches that range from C to G. Larger sets consist of two complete octaves. The lower pitches are to the left, and the higher pitches are to the right.

Twenty-five-note chromatic bells

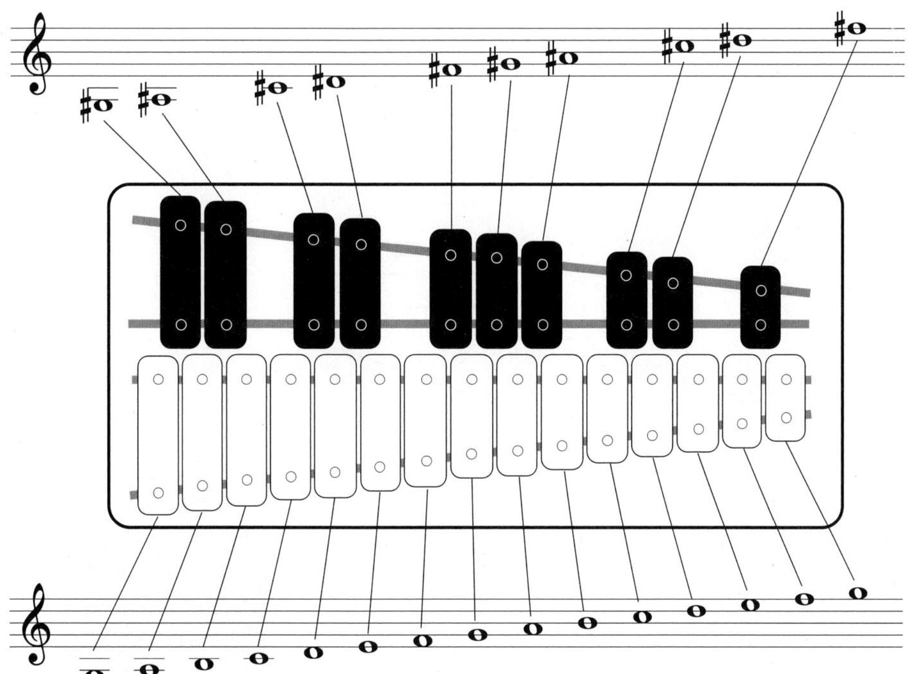

Melody bells

Step Bells

A smaller set of melody bells constructed vertically as "steps" encompasses only one octave (eight notes) without sharps or flats. The pitches go higher as the bells go "up the ladder." Many use a different color tone bar for each pitch.

Eight-note diatonic step bells

Step bells

Melody bells are played with a short stick with a mallet head made of wood, rubber, string, or yarn. The choice of mallet head determines the tone quality. A hard mallet will produce a bright, loud

Resonator bells

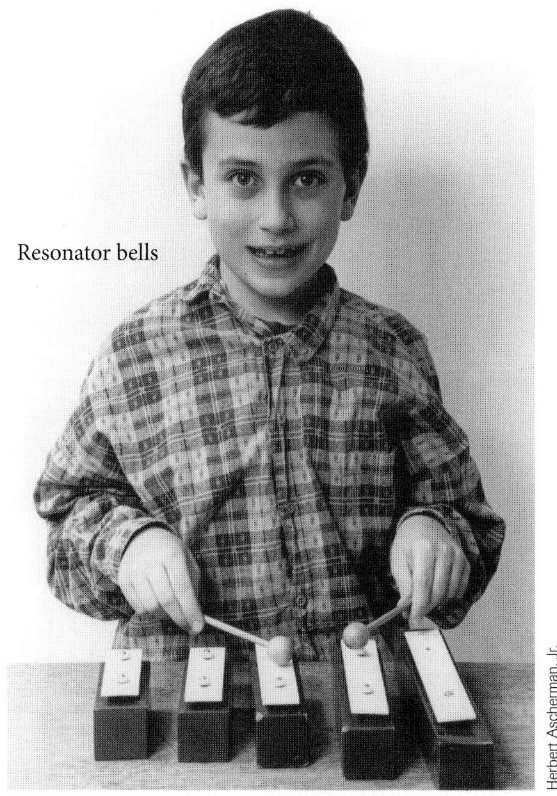

Herbert Ascherman, Jr.

Xylophone

Herbert Ascherman, Jr.

tone, whereas a soft mallet will produce a quiet, mellow tone.

To play melody bells, grasp the mallet with your thumb and one or two fingers. Keep your wrist flexible and strike the bell near the center, letting the mallet rebound instantly. If you hold the stick too tightly, the tone will lack resonance and brilliance. Have students practice striking the bells, holding the mallets in either hand until they can alternate L-R-L-R-L-R as they move up or down a melody pattern. It is important for students to develop the technique of playing with two mallets. A little practice will reward the student with a musically satisfying sound.

Resonator Bells

Resonator bells are tuned metal bars mounted individually on a block of wood or plastic that serves as its own resonator. When played as a melody instrument, resonator bells function in the same fashion as melody bells. Because they are not fastened to one another, however, individual bells can be removed and can also be used to play harmony as well as melodies.

Xylophone

The *xylophone* is a pitched instrument made from tuned wooden bars mounted individually on a frame. It does not have black bars (keys) like keyboards or melody bells but generally has the B-flat and F-sharp accidentals. You can purchase other accidentals to make it possible to play in several keys. Xylophones are especially useful for playing ostinato melodies, harmonic patterns, and descants. They are available as soprano, alto, and bass instruments.

You play a xylophone with the same technique as that used for melody bells, but with soft instead of hard mallets.

Glockenspiel

A *glockenspiel,* whose tones are clear and brilliant, is similar to melody bells in that it contains tuned metal bars mounted horizontally on a frame. Like xylophones, glockenspiels do not have sharps or flats; but the tone bars are removable, and you can purchase and add the B-flat and F-sharp accidentals. You can also add other accidentals to play

Glockenspiel

Herbert Ascherman, Jr.

Metallophone

Herbert Ascherman, Jr.

melodies in several keys. Glockenspiels are generally played with wooden or rubber mallets. There are both alto and soprano glockenspiels.

Metallophone

The *metallophone* is a large diatonic instrument that includes the chromatics B-flat and F-sharp. The tone bars are of aluminum and are tuned for perfect pitch and harmonics. They provide a full and resonant sound to the ensemble. The soprano and alto metallophones are smaller than the large metallophone, which has a deep bass sound.

Handbells

A set of *handbells* cast by Schulmerich, Malmark (American), Petit and Fritzen (Holland), or Whitechapel (England) is a fine addition to the classroom collection. They can have 25 chromatic bells (two octaves), 37 bells (three octaves), or 49 to 61 bells, which may be added one at a time.

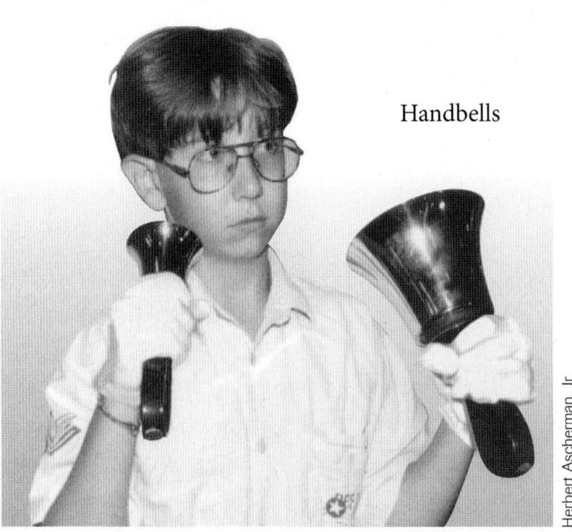
Handbells

Herbert Ascherman, Jr.

Boomwhackers

"Boomwhackers" is a registered trademark licensed to, and "Boomophone" is a trademark of Whacky Music, Inc. of Sedona, Arizona, the manufacturer of these musical instruments./Whacky Music, Inc.

Special Learner Note

Boomwhackers® are pitched, plastic tubes that have been gaining in popularity for groups of all ages. An individual can play one or two holding one in each hand. The tube is hit against a hard surface (floor, tray, table, desk) or body part (knee, leg, other hand) to produce the pitch indicated on the tube. The newer Boomophone Whack Pack (pictured) enables the tubes to be played like a xylophone. The color coding of the tubes makes integration with other instruments (melodic and harmonic) easier to manage. A music-notation software program is now available that uses the Boomwhacker® *color-notation system to notate music.*

Tone chimes

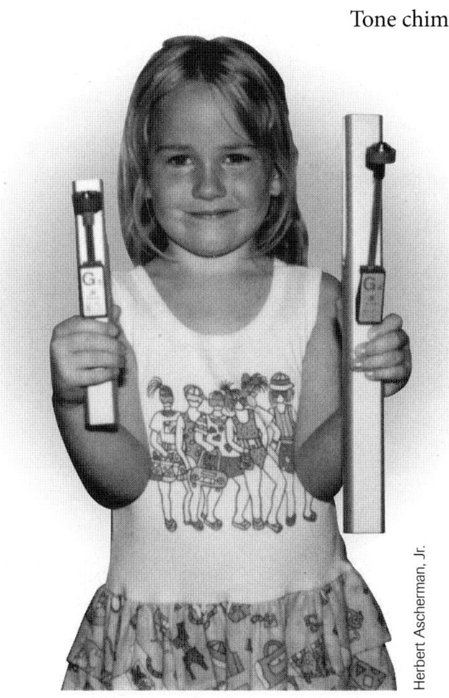

Herbert Ascherman, Jr.

Handbells can be used to play a single melody or for harmony, or to play a particular piece that involves melody and harmony.[1]

Handbells may be combined with other instruments, such as recorder, flute, Q-chord, or Orff instruments.

Tone Chimes

These have a variety of names, including choir chimes by Malmark and tone chimes by Suzuki. Like handbells, *tone chimes* are chromatic, but they are lightweight, durable, and have a clarity of sound. They come in chromatic sets of 25 (two octaves) or 37 (three octaves). Additional tone chimes may be purchased singly or as an octave set.

Recorder

The *recorder* has become increasingly popular as a melody instrument in elementary classes. It has a clear, pure tone that blends well with young voices. Any song is a potential recorder piece, and many music series books provide simple ostinato patterns and descants that can be played on either the soprano or the alto recorder.

The two kinds of recorders—Baroque and German—are identified by their fingering patterns. You can determine which kind of recorder you have by comparing the size of the fourth fingerhole with the fifth. If the fifth hole is larger than the fourth, it is a Baroque recorder, and you should use Baroque fingering (as in

[1] The reader is referred to the American Guild of English Handbell Ringers (AGEHR) for further information; see www.agehr.org.

Recorder

Technology Enhancement

Online Tutorials and Links

http://www.joytunes.com/ You can play online or download the JoyTunes Recorder Master app for the iPad.

http://www.monkeysee.com/play/10185-how-to-play-the-recorder

http://www.sandyn.com/play/play.htm

this book). If the fourth hole is larger than the fifth, it is a German recorder, and you must use German fingering. Recorder instruction texts generally provide both fingerings.

Children aged nine and older are most successful at playing recorders. Younger children typically do not yet possess the finger dexterity and coordination to play this instrument. The photo at top shows the correct way to place the instrument in the mouth.

Observe the following suggestions when playing the recorder:

1. Place the tip of the mouthpiece between your lips and in front of your teeth. Never place the mouthpiece between your teeth.
2. Blow gently.
3. Whisper the sound "too" or "doo" into the mouthpiece. Avoid a "whoo" sound. Use the tongue to stop or release the air.
4. Begin with a few pitches and gradually add notes. Avoid songs that contain middle C until students have perfected the technique of covering the holes tightly. (Middle C is a difficult pitch to play on the recorder.)

Fingering

The fingers of the left hand control the upper tone holes, while the fingers of the right hand cover the lower holes.

1. The thumb of the left hand has three positions:
   a. Covers the thumbhole
   b. Does not cover the thumbhole
   c. Covers only half of the thumbhole
2. The bottom two holes have double openings so that the player can play C-sharp and D-sharp.
3. You play pitches by covering the holes completely with your fingers. The slightest leak will create the wrong pitch or a high-pitched

Special Learner Note

Recorders may present a frustrating situation for many students. Introduction of kazoos as a pre-recorder experience may be appropriate; students may also use kazoos instead of recorders to integrate their sounds with the recorder ensemble. Kazoos are also very useful for students with respiratory disorders and some speech disorders; kazoos can encourage appropriate breathing and deeper breathing as well as early vocalization.

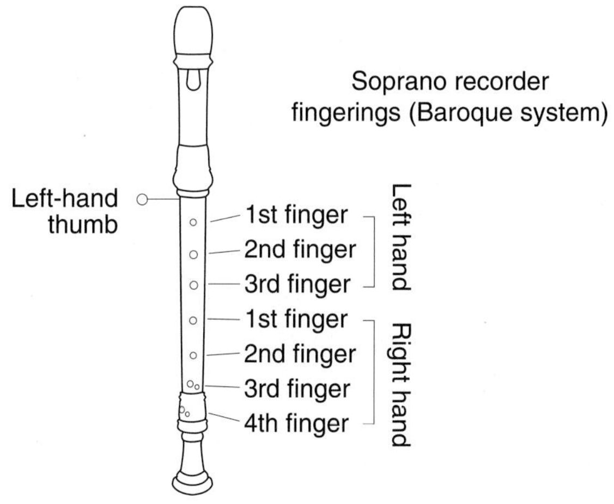

squeal. Minimize finger movements, because the higher you raise your fingers, the greater the possibility that a hole will become uncovered.

4. A simple thumb rest can be made by taping a piece of eraser to the back of the recorder. This provides for greater stability in holding the instrument.

Experiences

1. Introduce the recorder to students by having them play the following pitches:

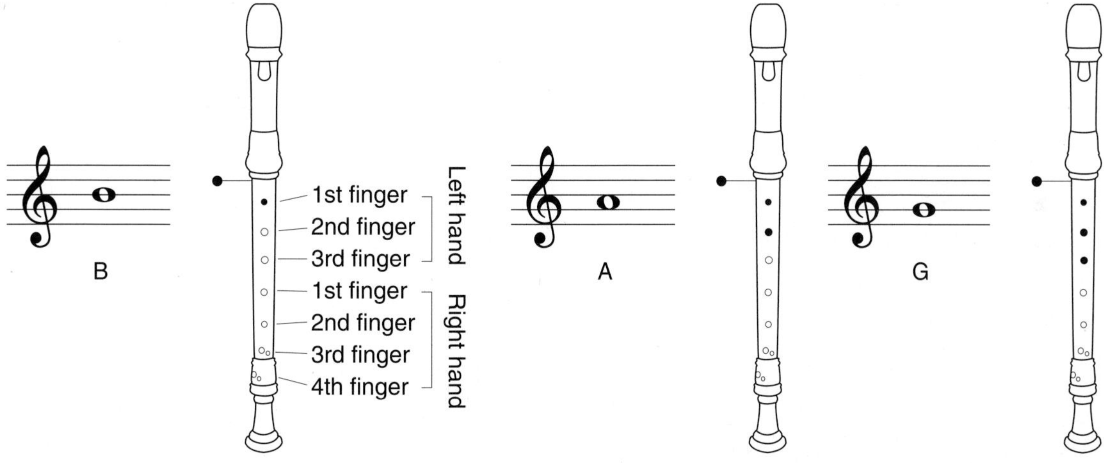

2. Sing "Hot Cross Buns" (p. 38), "Mary Had a Little Lamb" (p. 125), and "Good News" (p. 126); then play them by ear on the recorder.
3. Compose and perform additional tunes by using these three pitches. Use titles such as "BAG" or "GAB," which reflect the occurrence of these three pitches in the tune.

4. Gradually add the following pitches:

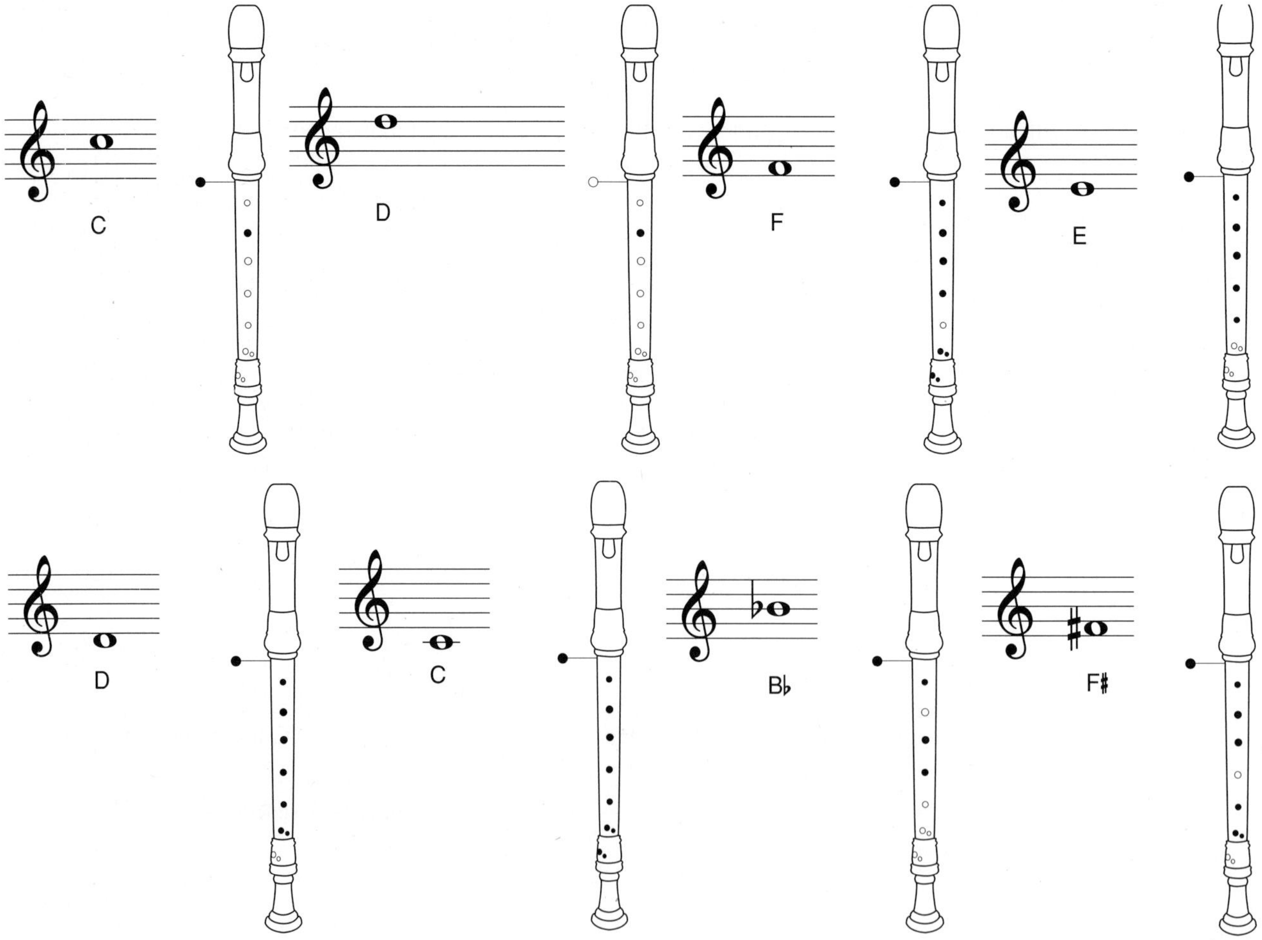

C D F E

D C B♭ F♯

5. Practice the following musical examples as you learn how to play new notes on the recorder.

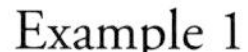

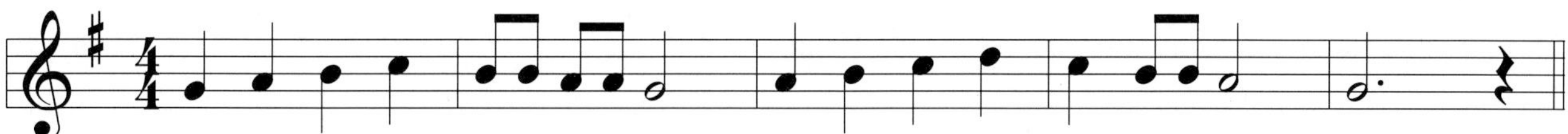

Example 2

Example 3

Example 4

6. Practice the following compositions on the recorder:

English nursery rhyme

Rain, Rain, Go Away

Skip to My Lou

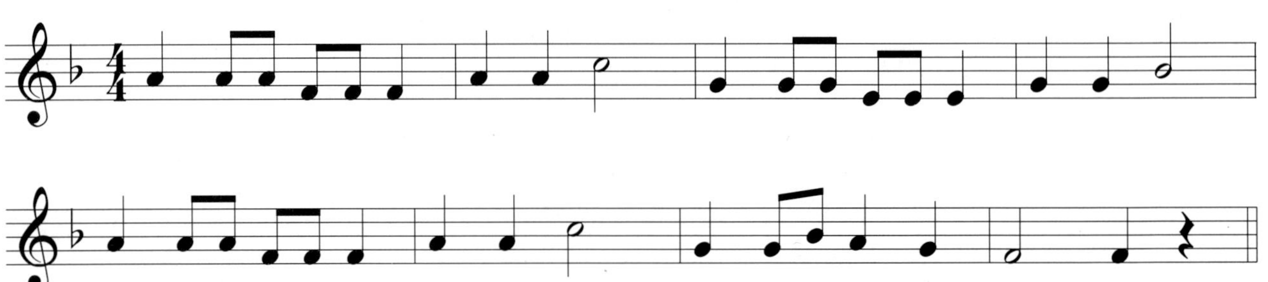

England, 1906

This Old Man

Jolly Old Saint Nicholas

Muffin Man

English

Ode to Joy (Ninth Symphony)

7. Play descants on the recorder to accompany songs:

   a. Descant for "Did You Ever See a Lassie?" (see p. 109)

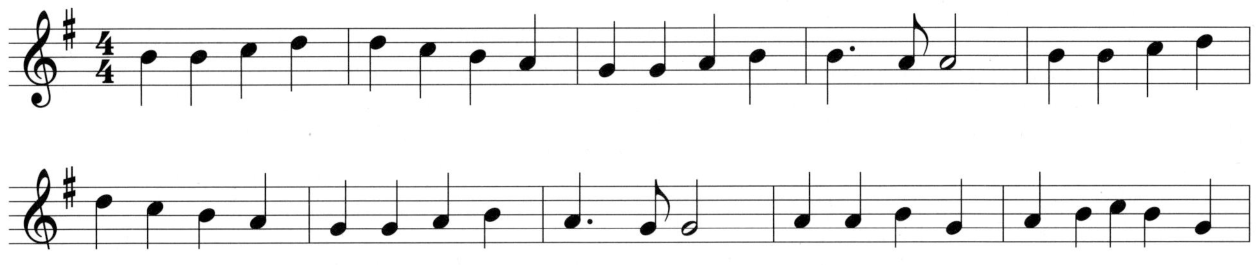

   b. Descant for "America" (see p. 142)

Additional Songs for the Recorder

3 Notes
"Rain, Rain, Go Away" (pitches E, G, A), p. 136, 138
"Starlight, Starbright" (pitches E, G, A), p. 139

5 Notes
"Did You Ever See a Lassie? (descant) (pitches F, G, A, B♭, c*), p. 109
"Eency, Weency Spider" (pitches D, G, A, B, d), p. 228
"The Farmer in the Dell" (pitches G, A, B, d, e), p. 152
"I Wish I Were a Windmill" (pitches C, F, G, A, c), p. 241
"Jolly Old Saint Nicholas" (pitches D, E, G, A, B), p. 136, 398
"Mister Turkey" (pitches G, A, B, c, d), p. 391
"Lightly Row" (pitches G, A, B, C, D), p. 126
"Hanukkah Is Here" (pitches D, E, F, G, A), p. 395
"Little Marionettes" (pitches D, G, A, C, d), p. 240
"Little Tommy Tinker" (pitches D, E, F♯, A, d), p. 228

6 Notes
"America" (pitches F♯, G, A, B, c, d), p. 142
"Five Fat Turkeys" (pitches D, G, A, B, C, d), p. 392
"Ode to Joy" (pitches D, G, A, B, c, d), p. 137
"The People on the Bus" (pitches D, E, G, A, B, d), p. 227
"The Peddler (Korobushka)" (pitches D, F, G, A, c, d), p. 141
"This Old Man" (pitches F, G, A, c, d), pp. 136, 142, 263

7 Notes
"Auld Lang Syne" (pitches C, D, F, G, A, c, d), p. 405
"Clementine" (pitches D, F♯, G, A, B, c, d), p. 150
"My Hat" (pitches C, D, E, F, G, A, c), p. 59
"Simple Gifts" (pitches C, E, F, G, A, B, c), p. 65

8 Notes
"Las Posadas Songs" (pitches C, D, E, F, G, A, B, c), p. 399
"O Come, All Ye Faithful" (pitches D, E, F♯, G, A, B, c, d), p. 401
"Sweet Betsy from Pike" (pitches C, D, E, F, G, A, B, c), p. 50, 140

9 Notes
"We Gather Together" (pitches C, D, E, F, G, A, B, c, d), p. 393

*Lowercase letters indicate a pitch in a higher octave.

8. Play the partner song, "All Night, All Day/Swing Low, Sweet Chariot" (see pp. 116, 265) on recorders.
9. For additional material on learning to play the recorder, see Bruce Pearson and Wendy Barden, *Recorder Excellence* (San Diego: Neil A. Kjos Music Company, 2006); www.kjos.com.

USING MELODY INSTRUMENTS IN THE CLASSROOM

Students should be encouraged to use classroom instruments to play familiar songs and simple melody patterns by ear. Short childhood chants are effective for developing the ear and for vocal tone matching. As children sing the chants, they should match them on melody bells, handbells, resonator bells, or tone chimes.

Rain, Rain, Go Away

English nursery rhyme

Rain, rain, go a - way, Come a - gain some oth - er day.

Starlight, Starbright

One of the advantages to using melody or resonator bells is that the letter names of the notes are stamped on each tone bar; thus, students can be guided to relate a letter name with each pitch. Because it is difficult to read music and play melody bells at the same time, however, teachers should encourage children to improvise melodies and play songs by ear. Descants and ostinatos can be taught from notation but are best performed from memory.

Playing Melodic Ostinatos

An ostinato is a repeated pattern that occurs throughout a composition. Select one of the following patterns to play on the xylophone or glockenspiel to accompany "Row, Row, Row Your Boat" (p. 46). The ostinato should be played initially by ear only, and later from music notation.

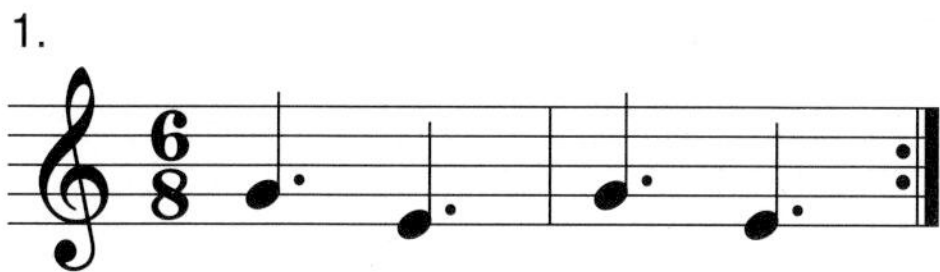

The song "Colorful Boats" (p. 301) is composed on the pentatonic (five-note) scale (shown below). Play the following melodic ostinato or have students create their own. Any combination of pitches may be used.

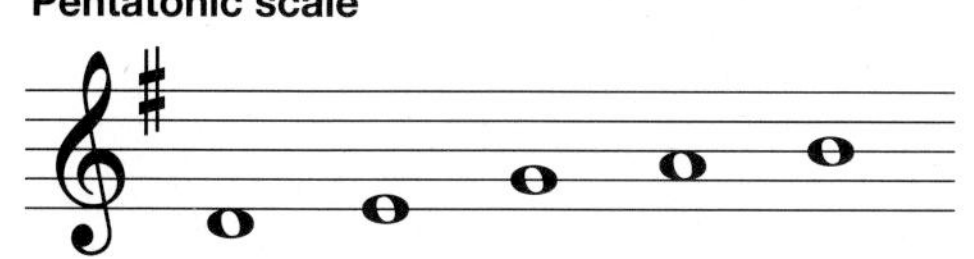

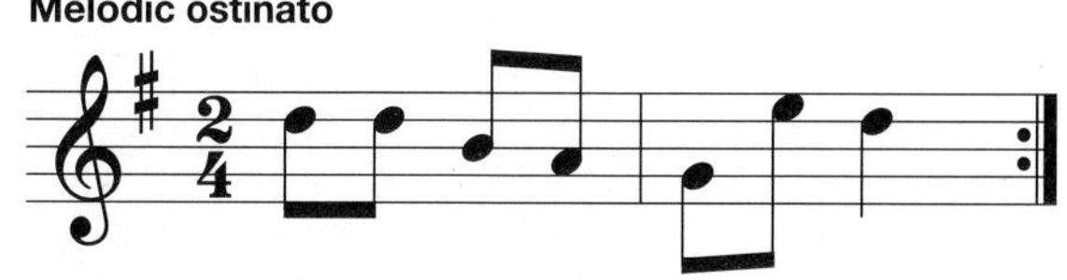

Play or sing "Good News" (p. 126), "Lightly Row" (p. 126), "Mary Had a Little Lamb" (p. 125), or "Sweet Betsy from Pike" (see below), adding the suggested accompaniments. You may wish to create your own rhythm pattern and choose different instruments.

Sweet Betsy from Pike
Key: C)
Starting pitch: C
Meter: 3/4, begins on 3
Traditional
C G7 C
Oh, don't you re - mem - ber sweet Bet - sy from Pike Who crossed the broad
G7 C
prai - ries with her hus - band, Ike, With two yoke of ox - en, an
F C G7 C
old yel - low dog, A tall Shang - hai roost - er and one spot - ted hog?

Descant: Glockenspiel

Bass xylophone/metallophone (Notice that these are written in the treble clef.)

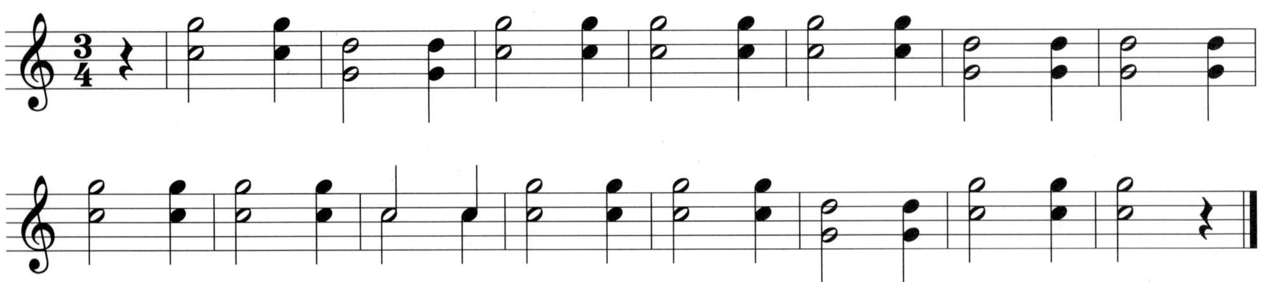

Using Melody Instruments to Play Harmony

Resonator bells can be used to play simple chords as harmonic accompaniments. Individual students can be assigned a single note of the chord, such as C, E, G, or G, B, D; thus, three students can play at the same time. Sing the following songs accompanied by chords played on the resonator bells, handbells, or tone chimes.

The Peddler (Korobushka)

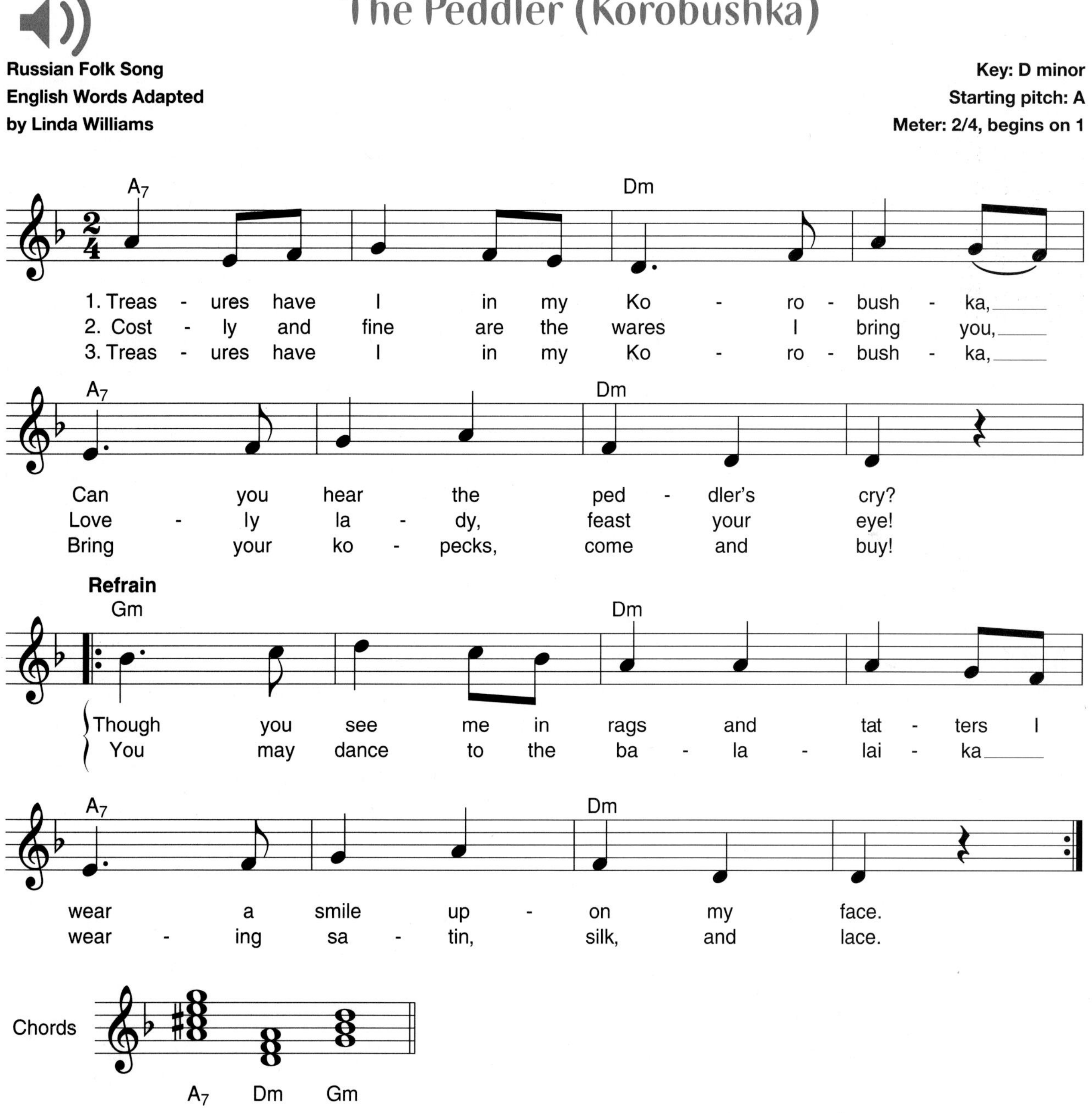

Russian Folk Song
English Words Adapted
by Linda Williams
Key: D minor
Starting pitch: A
Meter: 2/4, begins on 1
A7
Dm
1. Treas - ures have I in my Ko - ro - bush - ka,
2. Cost - ly and fine are the wares I bring you,
3. Treas - ures have I in my Ko - ro - bush - ka,
Can you hear the ped - dler's cry?
Love - ly la - dy, feast your eye!
Bring your ko - pecks, come and buy!
Refrain
Gm
Though you see me in rags and tat - ters I
You may dance to the ba - la - lai - ka
wear a smile up - on my face.
wear - ing sa - tin, silk, and lace.
Chords
A7 Dm Gm

America

Arranged by Henry Carey
England c. 1690–1743

Key: G
Starting pitch: G
Meter: 3/4, begins on 1

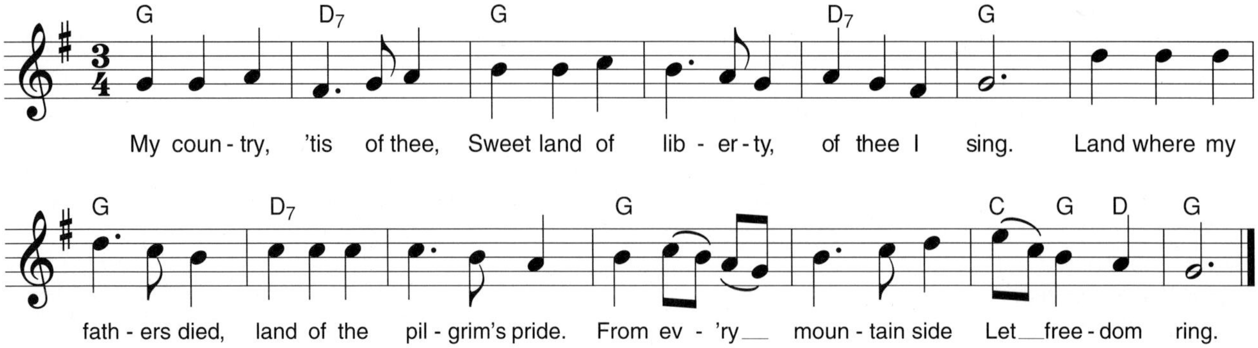

G D7 G D7 G

My coun - try, 'tis of thee, Sweet land of lib - er - ty, of thee I sing. Land where my

G D7 G C G D G

fath - ers died, land of the pil - grim's pride. From ev - 'ry moun - tain side Let free - dom ring.

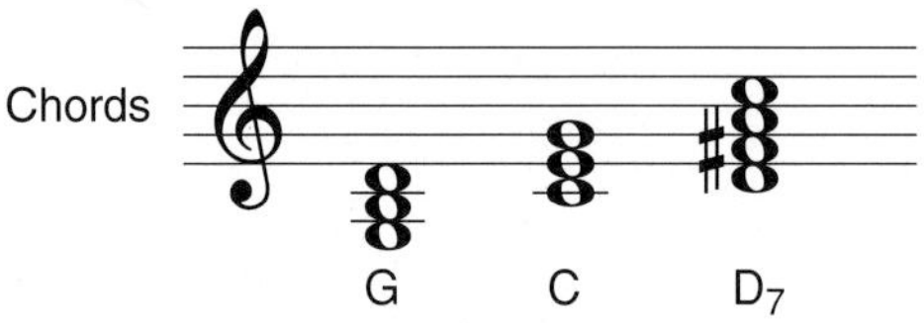

Chords
G C D7

This Old Man

Nursery Rhyme

Key: F
Starting pitch: C
Meter: 2/4, begins on 1

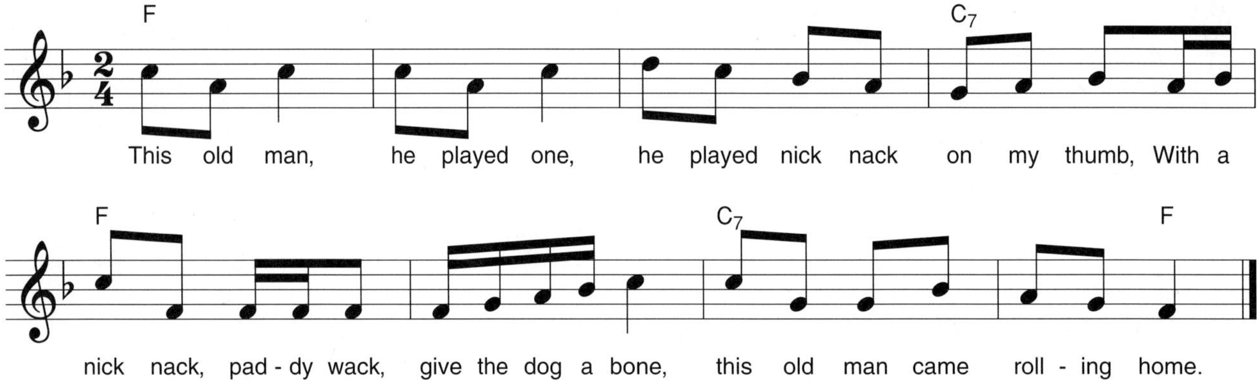

F C7

This old man, he played one, he played nick nack on my thumb, With a

F C7 F

nick nack, pad - dy wack, give the dog a bone, this old man came roll - ing home.

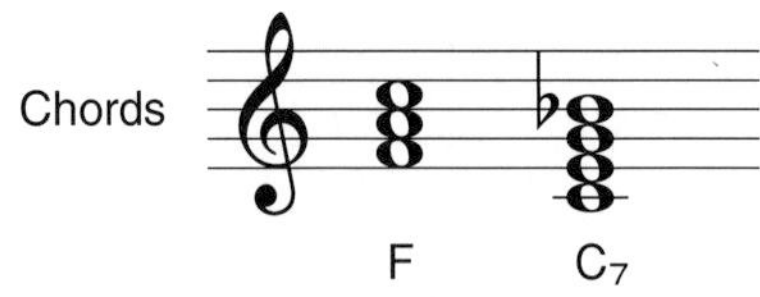

Other types of harmony that can be played on melody instruments include descants (a second contrasting melody), rounds, and simple alto or tenor harmony parts. After experimenting with different melody instruments, choose the one that is most satisfying to you and that produces the best musical result for each of the following:

- Descants
  "Did You Ever See a Lassie?" (p. 109)

- Rounds
  "Frère Jacques" (p. 113)
  "Row, Row, Row Your Boat" (pp. 46, 60)
- Simple harmony
  "Swing Low, Sweet Chariot" (pp. 265, 332)
  "Hahvah Nahgeelah" (p. 253)
  "I've Been Working on the Railroad" (p. 431)

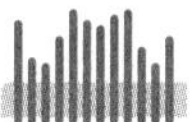

PLAYING HARMONY INSTRUMENTS

Instruments such as the guitar and Q-chord are referred to as *harmony* instruments because they can be used to play harmonic accompaniments to songs or to provide an introduction, an interlude, or a coda (ending) to a composition.

Guitar

The *guitar* is a popular instrument with children, and by third grade many have physically matured enough to hold it and begin to play simple chords.

There are many different types of guitars, including Hawaiian, twelve-string, folk, classical, steel-string, and electric. The two types of guitars most used in the classroom are the classical guitar with nylon or gut strings and the steel-string flattop guitar.

Contemporary rock groups use electric guitars. Both classical and steel-string guitars are *acoustic* (not amplified). The basic difference is in the tone quality—the classical nylon-string guitar having a more mellow quality and the steel-string flattop guitar having a bright and brassy sound. Because nylon strings are easier on the fingers, the classical guitar is usually recommended for beginners.

The basic function of the guitar in the classroom is to accompany songs. The guitar can provide an introduction, interlude, or ending to a song. The guitar's great advantages are that there are only six strings to tune and, because many students may own guitars, more instruments may be available for use in the classroom. A guitar player can move freely around the classroom.

This section provides an introduction to basic guitar skills that will enable you to accompany songs. Materials are limited to the use of eight chords (as used in the keys of D, G, E, and E minor). For detailed discussions and more advanced techniques, consult one of the many excellent publications that teach one how to play the guitar.

Additional Guitar Resources:

- http://www.guitaredunet.org/
- *Beginning Guitar for Adults* by Nick Vecchio
- *Teaching Classroom Guitar* by Steve Eckels
- http://www.guitaredunet.org/schmidarticle.html
- http://www.guitarmasterclass.net/Free online tutorials
- Do you have "GarageBand"? Try the using the Learn to Play lessons for guitar or piano.

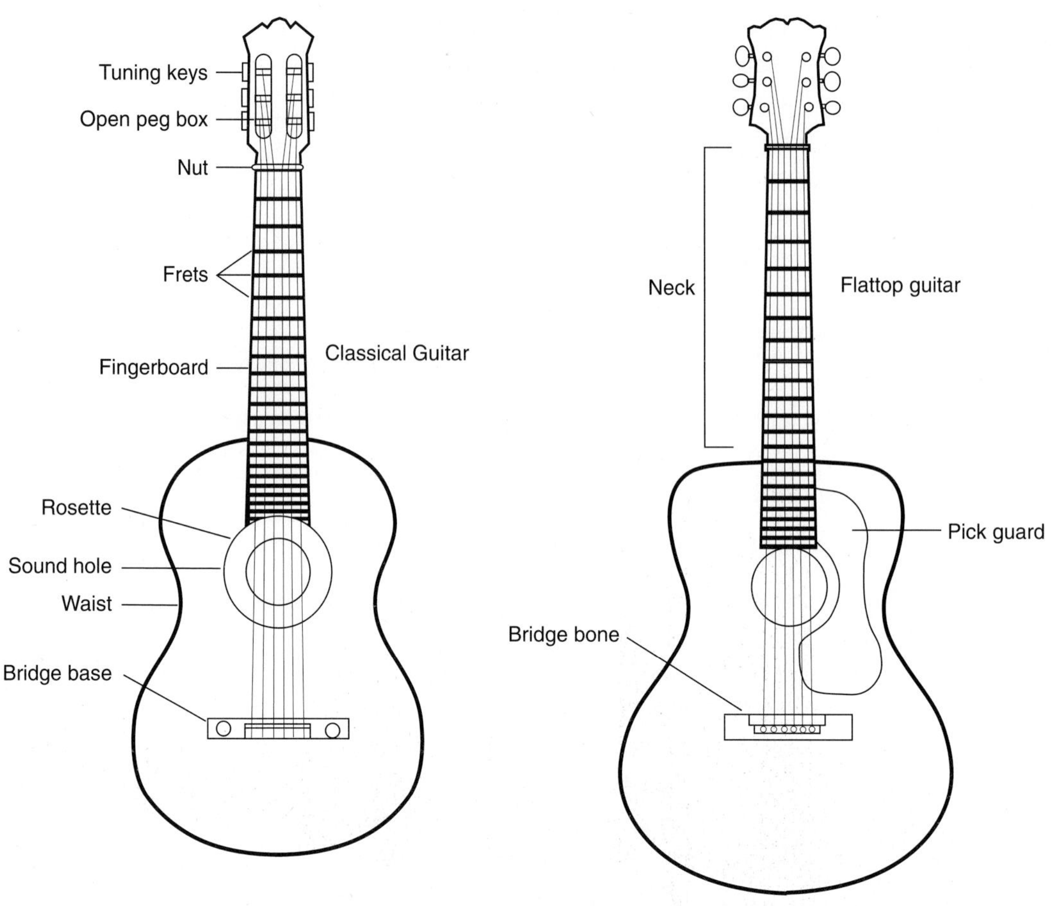

The six strings of the guitar are E A D G B E. The following diagram shows the matching pitches on the piano keyboard:

Tuning the Guitar

Tune the open strings to a piano that is in tune. If no piano is available, use a pitch pipe and tune the lowest string (E). Notice that the strings of the guitar are numbered from the highest pitch—1—to the lowest pitch—6. Guitar pitches are

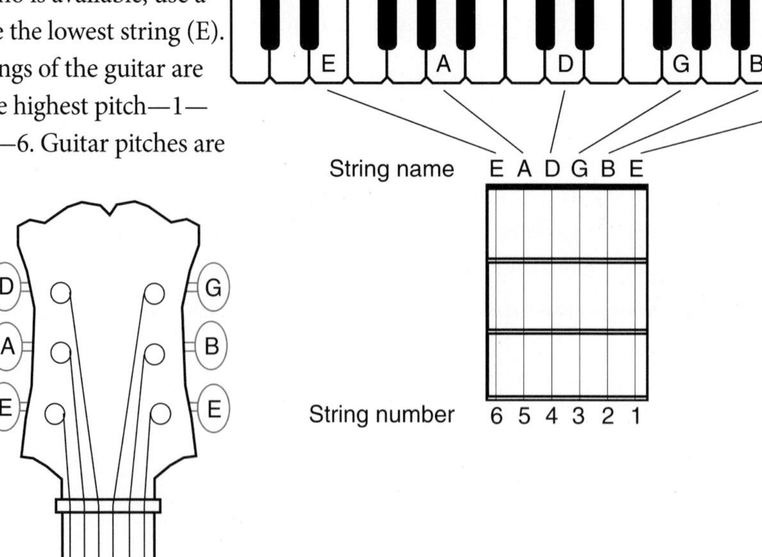

notated one octave higher than they actually sound. The pitch of each string is adjusted by turning the tuning peg. To lower the pitch, turn a peg toward you; to raise the pitch, turn it away from you.

The diagram at the bottom of the previous page shows which strings are controlled by each tuning peg.

By following the steps listed below, you will be able to tune a guitar accurately. The diagram below shows the finger positions you will use.

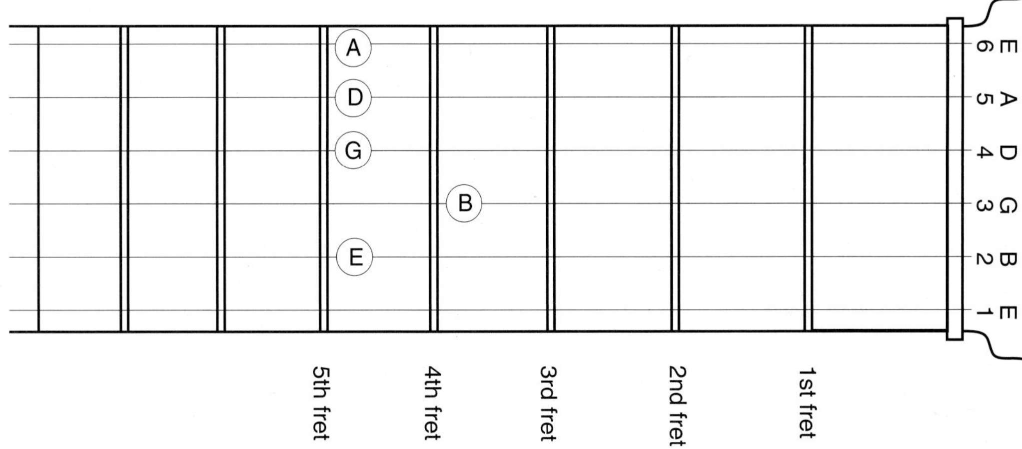

1. After you have tuned the bass E string, place your second finger (left hand) on that same string at the *fifth* fret. Match the next string (A) to that pitch. The open fifth string is now A.

2. Place your finger on the A string at the *fifth* fret. Match the next string (D) to that pitch.

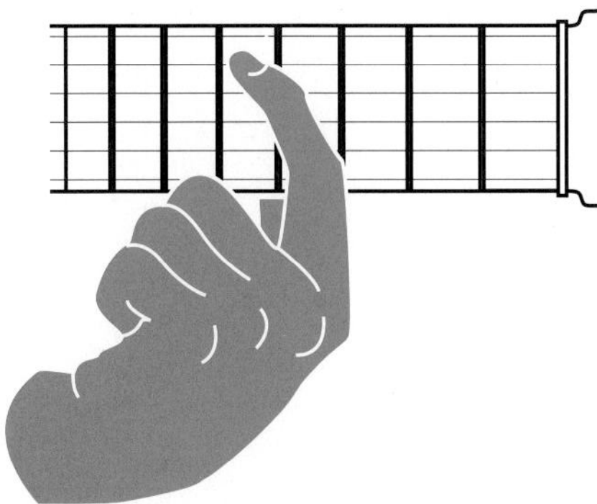

3. Place your finger on the D string at the *fifth* fret. Match the next string (G) to that pitch.

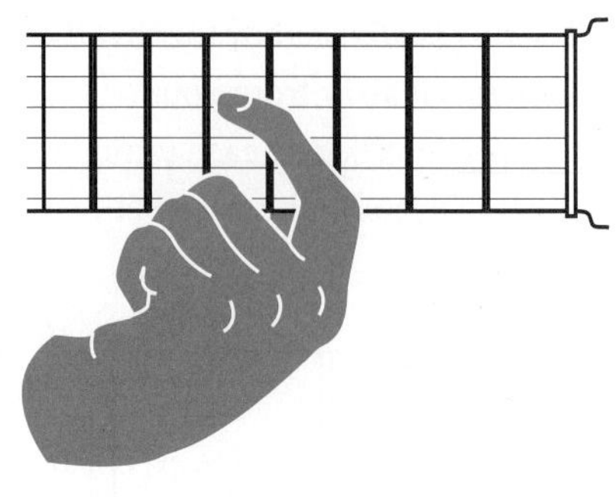

4. Place your finger on the G string at the *fourth* fret. Match the next string (B) to that pitch.

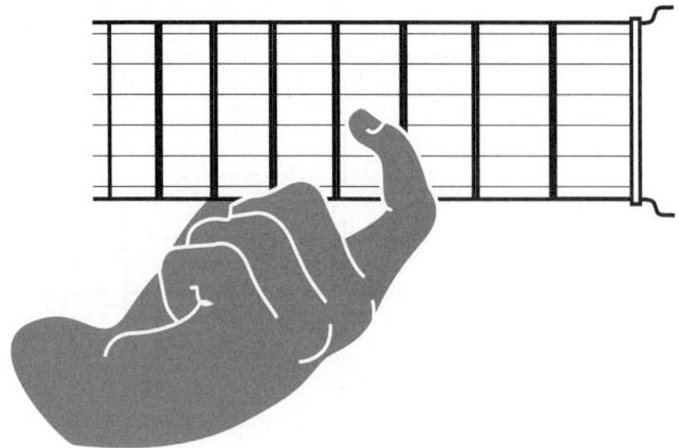

5. Place your finger on the B string at the *fifth* fret. Match the next string (E) to that pitch.

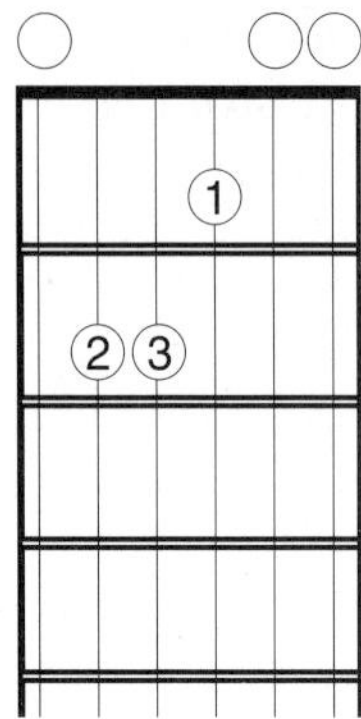

Now that you have tuned the guitar, you can try some simple chords. Chords are created by placing one or more fingers on designated frets. Place your index finger (1) on the third string, first fret; second finger on the fifth string, second fret; and third finger on the fourth string, second fret. Strings 1, 2, and 6 are open. Strum the E major chord.

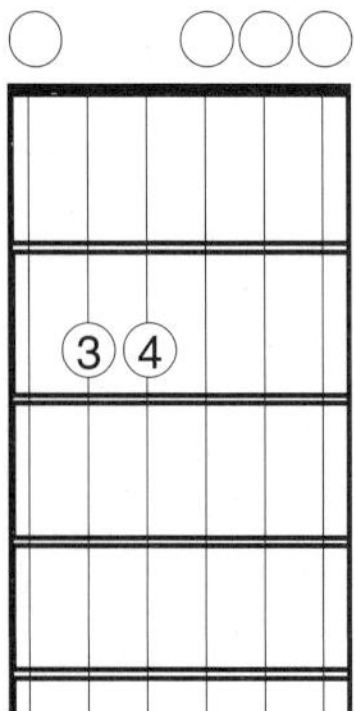

Place your second finger on the fifth string, second fret, and your third finger on the fourth string, second fret. Strings 1, 2, 3, and 6 are open. Strum the E minor chord.

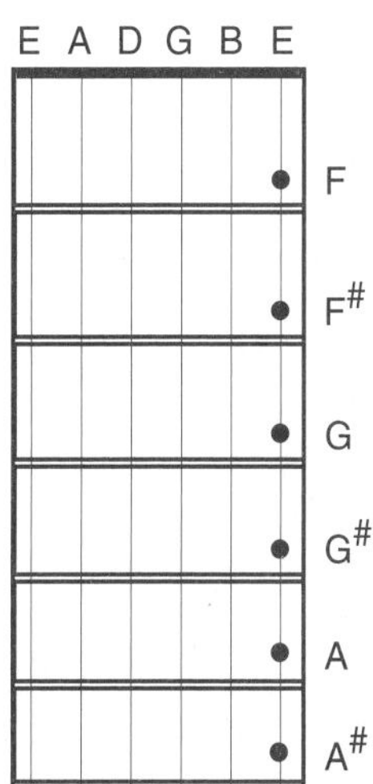

Each fret on the neck of the guitar represents a half step in the chromatic scale. Pluck the highest string (E). Now place your index finger on the string between the frets and pluck the string. You will now hear F. Move your finger up each fret and you will hear the pitch go up by half steps.

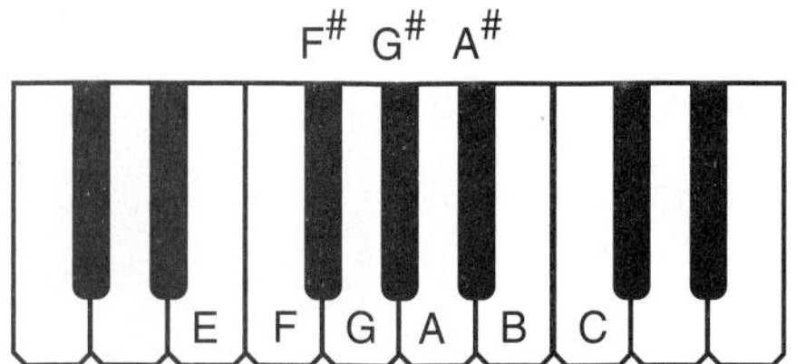

Follow the same procedure for each string and listen for the half steps.

Playing the Guitar

There are three basic positions for playing the guitar: (1) classical style, in which the player is seated and places a foot on a small stool or platform; (2) folk style, in which the player is seated and balances the guitar on a crossed leg; and (3) standing, where the player uses a neck strap. Regardless of the position you choose, the back of the guitar should remain flat against your body. Do not allow the neck of the guitar to drop below the horizontal position.

To play the guitar, you need to know how to strum with your right hand and form chords with your left hand. The notation, called *tablature,* indicates which strings are to remain open and which strings are to be fretted. An *X* indicates that the string is not sounded, whereas an *O* indicates that the string is open. The circle on the fretboard indicates where the fingers are to be placed. Left-hand fingers are identified as follows:

Folk-style position

Jonathan Poore

Classical-style position

Jonathan Poore

① = index finger
② = middle finger
③ = ring finger
④ = little finger

The thumb is not used in playing the guitar. You must use the tips of your fingers to press down the strings. They should be close above the frets that stop the string but should not touch the frets. Here are the diagrams for the other chords used in this book. (See Appendix B for a complete chord chart.)

Standing position

Jonathan Poore

G Major

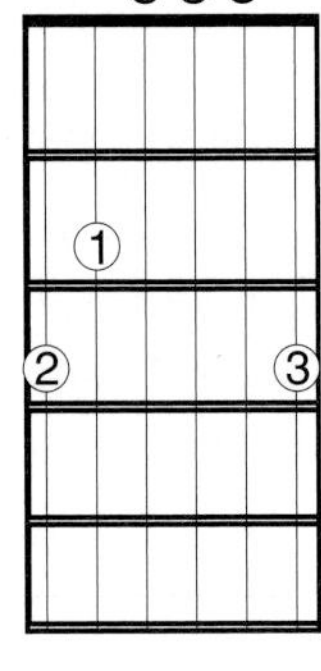
G

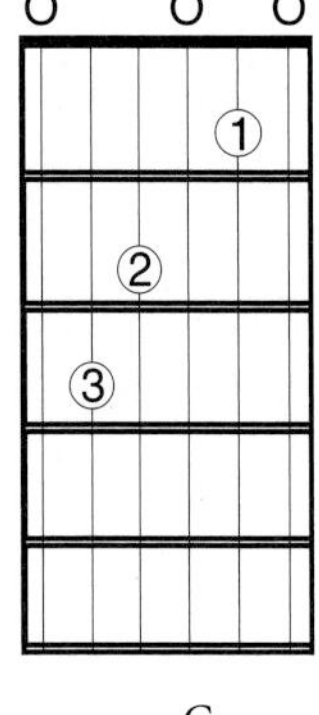
C

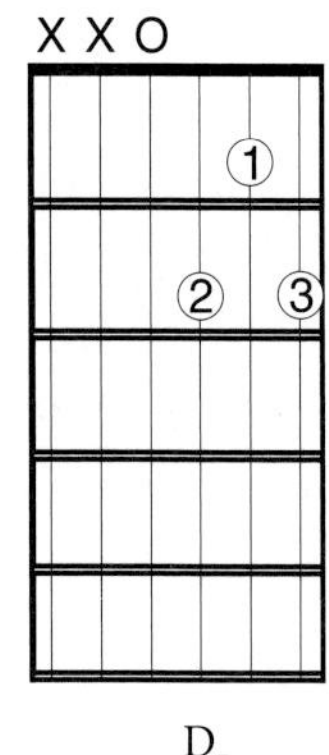
D_7

D Major

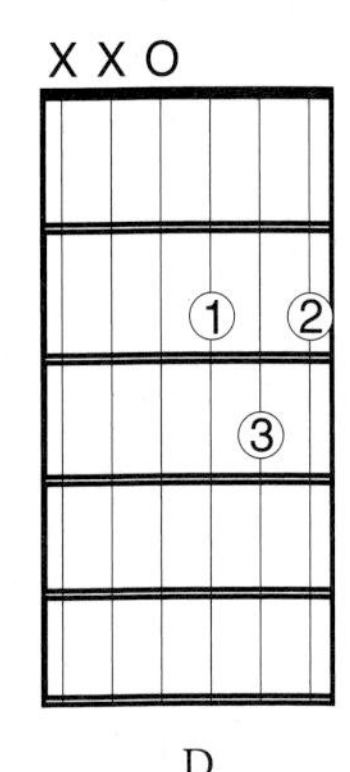
D

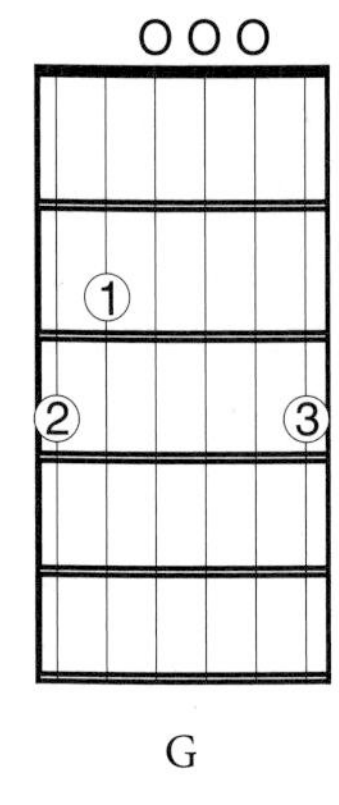
G

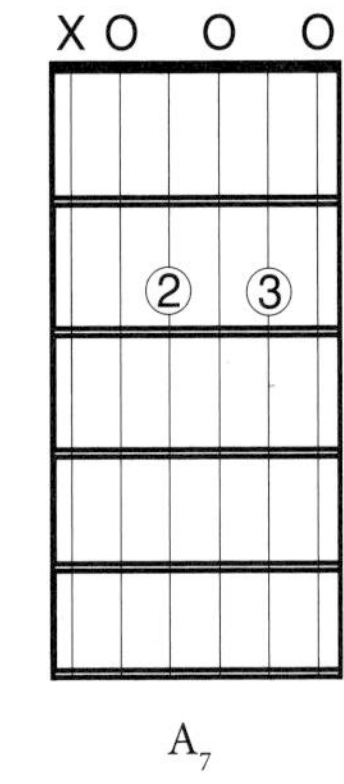
A_7

Strumming

The *sweep strum* is created by a downward motion of the thumb across all the strings. It can be used on accented beats as well as unaccented beats. The *brush strum* is created by using the backs of the fingernails across the strings. It is used on unaccented beats. A combination of sweep and brush strums can be used for duple meter (sweep-brush) and triple meter (sweep-brush-brush). The *pluck-sweep strum* involves plucking the root of the chord and strumming on the remaining chords. It is often done with a plastic pick.

Using a Capo

A *capo (capotasto)* is a device that clamps over the strings of a guitar and holds them down tightly at a new pitch level, instantly transposing a song into a higher key. When the capo is in place, chord fingerings are the same but the sounds are at a new pitch level. For example, if the capo is installed on the second fret (one whole step higher) and a D chord is played, it will sound like an E chord. If the capo is put on the third fret, chords will sound one and a half steps higher. Thus, if you know two chords in the key of D major, D and A_7, you could place the capo on the third fret and play in the key of F. The two chords would then sound as F and C_7 using the same fingering. Experiment with key changes by placing the capo on the appropriate fret to match the key in which you wish to play.

Guitar capo

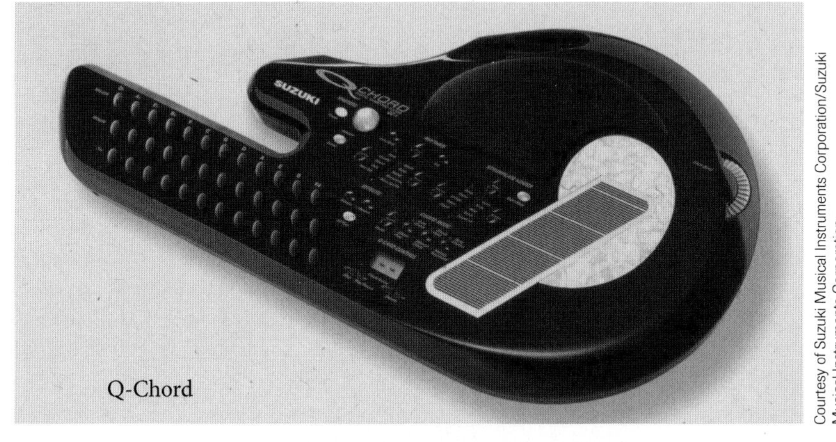
SUZUKI
Q CHORD
Q-Chord

Courtesy of Suzuki Musical Instruments Corporation/Suzuki Musical Instruments Corporation

Technology Enhancement

Q-Chord Links

http://www.qchord.net/

http://www.suzukimusic.com/education/qchord/

Q-Chord (Digital Song Card Guitar)

The *Q-chord* is characterized by marked chords that you can press down and play. It can play rhythms or can automatically execute chord combinations with a rhythm or walking bass line. You can play only chords on the Q-chord. The Q-chord is self-contained with a built-in amplifier and is completely portable.

There are many major, minor, and seventh chords on the Q-chord, as well as preset rhythm patterns such as waltz, march, and rock. Separate tempo and volume controls are provided for both chords and rhythms. The performer, however, must be careful to release each chord completely before moving to a different one or the chords will not change.

The electronic component enables you to select from the following tone colors: piano, guitar, banjo, organ, flute, chimes, brass, vibes, and synthesizer.

The Sonic Strings, a unique feature of the Q-chord, encompass four full octaves. These Sonic Strings play pitches of the chord selected. Thus, if the student plays a C major chord, the Sonic Strings can also be strummed to sound the pitches C, E, and G at more than one octave.

Playing Song Accompaniments

1. Play and sing "Shalom, Chaverim" accompanied by one chord (E minor). Another one-chord song you might play is "Zum Gali Gali" (p. 112).

Shalom, Chaverim
Israeli Folk Song
Key: E minor
Starting pitch: B
Meter: 4/4, begins on 4
Em
Sha - lom, cha - ve - rim! Sha - lom, cha - ve - rim, Sha - lom, Sha - lom! Le
hit ra ot, le hit ra ot, Sha - lom, sha - lom.

2. Practice changing back and forth from the G chord to the D chord (see previous page). Then try accompanying "Clementine," "La Raspa" (p. 330), or "Old Texas" (p. 105).

Clementine

United States

Key: G
Starting pitch: G
Meter: 3/4, begins on 3

G
D7
Oh, my dar - lin', oh, my dar - lin', Oh, my dar - lin' Clem - en - tine, You are
D7
G
D7
G
lost, and gone for - ev - er, Dread - ful sor - ry, Clem - en - tine.

3. Use the C and G chords to accompany "Mary Ann."

Mary Ann

Calypso

Key: C
Starting pitch: E
Meter: 4/4, begins on 1

C
G7
C
All day, all night Ma - ry Ann,
Down by the sea - shore sift - ing sand.
C
G7
C
Ev - en lit - tle chil - dren join in the band
Down by the sea - shore sift - ing sand.

4. Use the D and A_7 chords to accompany "Down in the Valley," "He's Got the Whole World in His Hands" (pp. 110, 151), and "Six Little Ducks" (p. 382). Now practice the following progression (D, A_7, D) using the pluck-sweep strum until it is smooth; then play "Down in the Valley" using this technique.

Down in the Valley

Traditional

Key: D
Starting pitch: A
Meter: 3/4, begins on 1

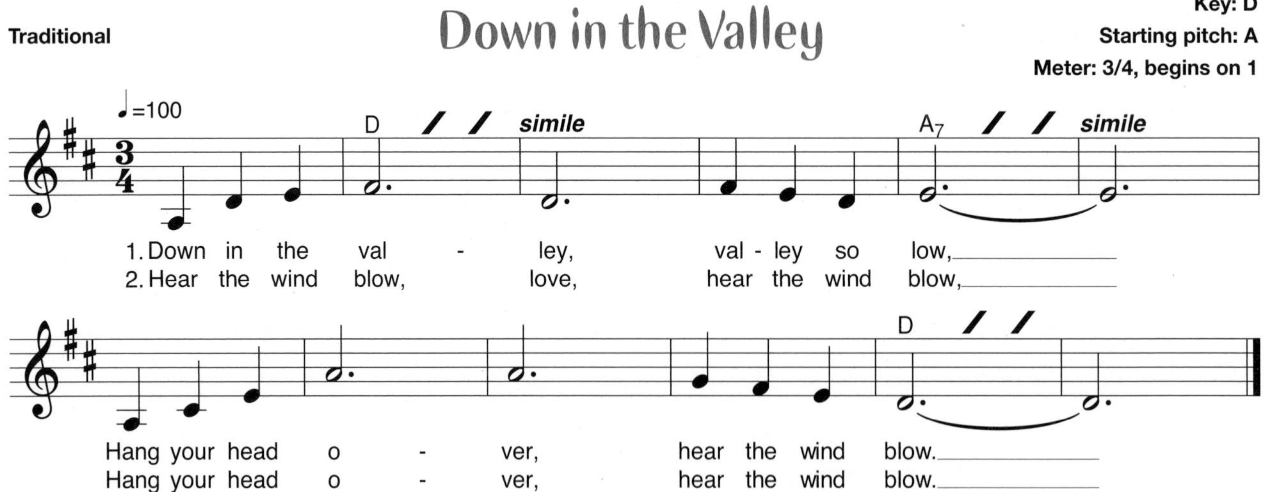
♩=100
D
simile
A7
simile
1. Down in the val - ley, val - ley so low,
2. Hear the wind blow, love, hear the wind blow,
D
Hang your head o - ver, hear the wind blow.
Hang your head o - ver, hear the wind blow.

Note: You can transpose this song into the key of G and use the chords G and D_7.

Spiritual

He's Got the Whole World in His Hands

Key: D (Pentatonic)
Starting pitch: A
Meter: 4/4, begins on "and" of 3

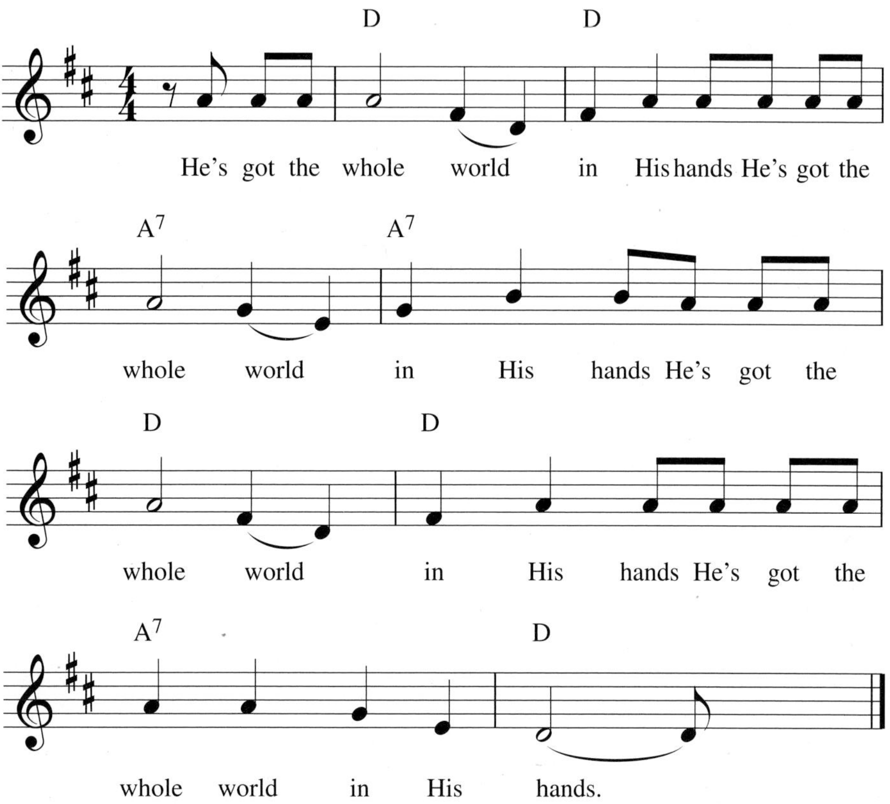
D D
He's got the whole world in His hands He's got the
A7 A7
whole world in His hands He's got the
D D
whole world in His hands He's got the
A7 D
whole world in His hands.

Boatner, Edward. *Spirituals Triumphant, Old and New.* Nashville: Sunday School Publishing Board, National Baptist Convention U.S.A., 1927.

2. He's got the winds and rain in his hands. (3 times)
   He's got the whole world in his hands.
3. He's got you and me brother in his hands. (3 times)
   He's got the whole world in his hands.
4. He's got everybody in his hands. (3 times)
   He's got the whole world in his hands.
5. Use the G, A_7, D, and D_7 chords to accompany "Muffin Man."

Muffin Man

England

Key: G
Starting pitch: D
Meter: 4/4, begins on 4

G A7 D
Oh, do you know the muf - fin man, the muf - fin man, the muf - fin man? Oh,
G A7 D7 G
do you know the muf - fin man that lives in Dru - ry Lane?

Transposition

Sometimes it is necessary to transpose a piece of music from one key to another. A common reason for transposition is to lower the pitch level of a song to make it easier to sing or to play.

The following song is shown first in the key of G major and then transposed down one whole step to the key of F major. Sing and accompany the song first in G major and then in F major.

The Farmer in the Dell
England
Key: G
G
The far - mer in the dell, The far - mer in the dell,
G D7 G
Hi! ho! the der - ry oh, The far - mer in the dell.
Key: F
F
The far - mer in the dell, The far - mer in the dell,
F C7 F
Hi! ho! the der - ry oh, The far - mer in the dell.

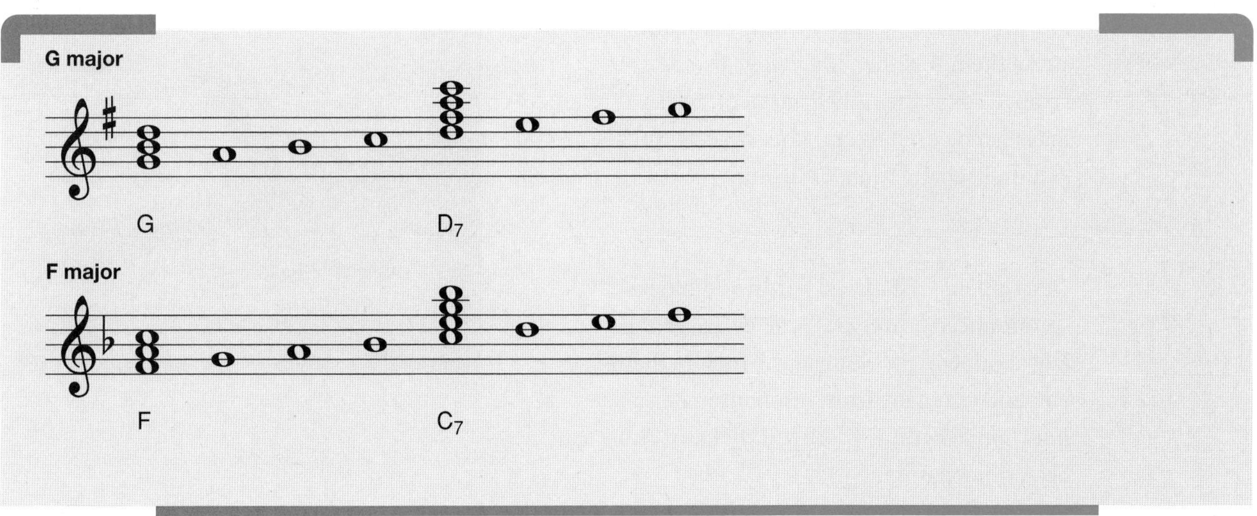

PLAYING PERCUSSION INSTRUMENTS

A third group of classroom instruments, *percussion* instruments, is used primarily to provide rhythmic accompaniments to songs. These instruments can also be used in ensembles and to play original musical compositions. They are divided into woods, metals, and skins.

Although most percussion instruments are commercially available, later in this chapter we include suggestions for the innovative teacher who wishes to make such instruments. Before using percussion instruments in the classroom, you should have a thorough knowledge of the types of musical effects that can be produced by each instrument. In the sections that follow, you will find brief descriptions of frequently used instruments, directions for playing them, and some functions they might serve.

Technology Enhancement

Helpful Links

http://www.vicfirth.com/education/ (Comprehensive website covering the playing and teaching of percussion instruments)

www.pas.org (Percussive Arts Society home page)

Rhythm sticks

Herbert Ascherman, Jr.

Woods

Wood percussion instruments include rhythm sticks, claves, woodblock, maracas, sand blocks, and the guiro.

Rhythm Sticks

Description: Sticks with both a smooth surface and a ribbed surface. They are usually 12 inches in length and are rounded.
Function: Beat, meter, special effects.

Playing: Hold one stick in each hand and strike them together. They may also be scraped (over the ribbed surface). Sticks may also be used to tap other objects, such as a desk, chair, book, or drum.

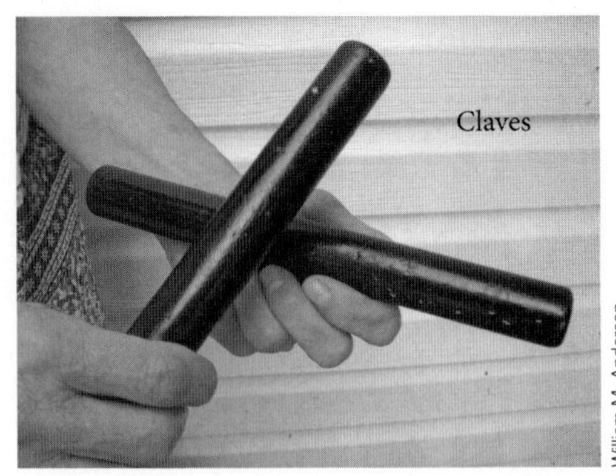
Claves

William M. Anderson

Claves

Description: Cylindrical hardwood blocks (pronounced "*clah*-vays"). They are generally about 6 inches long and 1 inch in diameter and are made from resonant material.
Function: Rhythms (particularly Latin American), beat, syncopation.
Playing: Hold one clave loosely on top of a partly closed hand and strike with the clave held in the other hand. Tap out the rhythm.

Woodblock

Description: Hollow block of wood that creates an interesting *clip-clop* sound.
Function: Beat, meter, syncopation, special effects.
Playing: Strike block with a hard mallet.

Woodblock

Herbert Ascherman, Jr.

Maracas

Description: Dried gourds with dried seeds inside, making a crisp, swishing sound.
Function: Rhythm patterns, Latin American music, syncopation.
Playing: Usually played in pairs by shaking.

Maracas

Herbert Ascherman, Jr.

Sand Blocks

Description: Small blocks of wood covered with varying grades of sandpaper. Handles for each are attached.
Function: Meter, beat, swishing effects.
Playing: Rub two blocks together.

Sand blocks
Herbert Ascherman, Jr.

Guiro

Description: An elongated wooden instrument with resonating holes and a serrated surface that is scraped with a stick to produce the sound (pronounced "gwee-ro").
Function: Used to accentuate rhythms in Latin American music.
Playing: Hold instrument in one hand while scraping the serrated surface with a stick held in the other hand.

Guiro
Herbert Ascherman, Jr.

Metals

Metal percussion instruments include cymbals, finger cymbals, triangle, tambourine, jingle bells, and jingle sticks.

Cymbals
Herbert Ascherman, Jr.

Cymbals

Description: Discs of brass with a depression in the center of each.
Function: Accents, crescendos, climax.
Playing: (1) Strike together by holding the left hand still and moving the right-hand cymbal in a slicing motion against the left-hand cymbal (reverse if left-handed); stop the sound by pulling the cymbals against the body. (2) Strike together and let sound continue on, as in a cymbal crash. (3) Hold onto cymbal and play with a soft mallet.

Finger Cymbals

Description: Tiny replicas of large cymbals.

Function: Special effects, soft accompaniment patterns.

Playing: Touch the rim of one with the rim of another, rather than trying to clap them together.

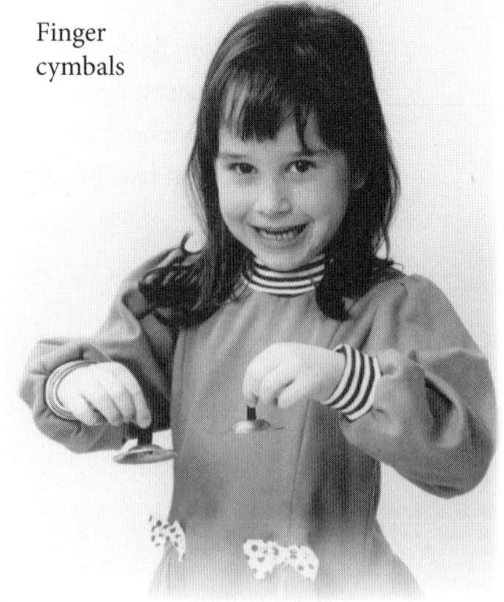
Finger cymbals

Herbert Ascherman, Jr.

Triangle

Description: A steel rod bent in the form of a triangle with one angle open. It is suspended on a string and played by striking it with a metal stick.

Function: Meter, accents, sustained sound, special effects.

Playing: Hold triangle by string and tap with metal striker. Be sure not to touch triangle with your hand, or the sound will be muted or stopped.

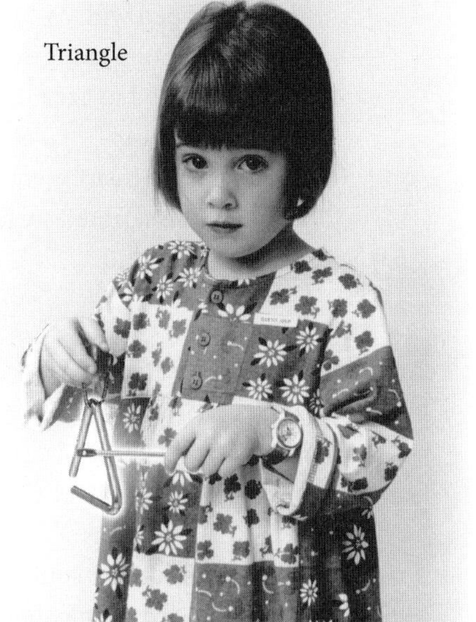
Triangle

Herbert Ascherman, Jr.

Tambourine

Description: A miniature drum with small metal discs attached to the wooden rim. The discs vibrate when the instrument is struck or shaken.

Function: Sustained sounds, accents, special effects, meter.

Playing: Shake, tap with a hand on the drum-head (if there is one), or tap the side of the rim with a hand.

Tambourine

Herbert Ascherman, Jr.

Jingle Bells

Description: Bells mounted on sticks, leather straps, or small frame.
Function: Rhythmic effects in Native American music; sleigh ride, beat, meter.
Playing: Shake or wear around wrists or ankles.

Jingle Bells

Herbert Ascherman, Jr.

Jingle Sticks

Description: Two metal discs attached to a stick.
Function: Meter, sustained sounds, beat, special effects.
Playing: Tap the wooden handle against the palm of the hand.

Jingle sticks

Herbert Ascherman, Jr.

Skins

The *skin* percussion instruments, called so because they are based primarily on striking stretched skins, include the hand drum, bongo drums, and the conga drum.

Hand Drum

Description: Metal or wooden cylinder covered with a head made of leather or plastic. The head is struck from one side only.
Function: Meter, beat, accents, tempo.
Playing: Strike with a hard or soft mallet, a stick, or the hands.

Hand drum

Herbert Ascherman, Jr.

Bongo Drums

Description: Two small drums of different pitches—one high, the other low. The head may be a membrane or plastic.

Function: Often used in Latin American music to play syncopated rhythms.

Playing: Place bongos between the legs of the seated player. Use fingertips and palms of hands to strike the heads. Striking the center of the drumhead and the rim produces different pitches and timbres.

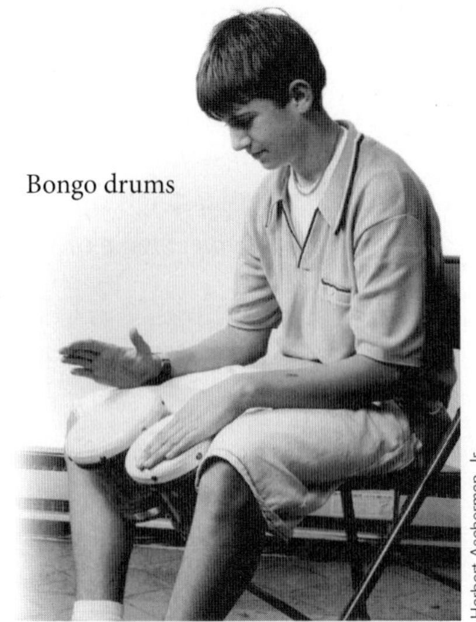
Bongo drums

Herbert Ascherman, Jr.

Conga Drum

Description: A tall, barrel-type drum with a membrane head. It has a deep, resonant tone quality. The drum may be placed directly on the floor, in a stand, or suspended from the shoulder by a strap.

Function: Used in both Latin American and African music for rhythm accompaniments.

Playing: Strike with fingertips, palms of hands, or even elbows. Striking the center of the drumhead, the rim, and the shell produces different pitches and timbres.

Conga drum

How to Select an Appropriate Instrument

The ability to play a musical instrument is directly related to a student's physical growth and coordination. Some questions to be considered in the choice of instruments include the following:

- What degree of eye-ear physical coordination is required? Playing melody bells from written notation requires a high degree of skill and coordination (ages ten to eleven), whereas playing a two- or three-note melodic pattern by ear or by letter or number is a task young children (ages five to nine) can handle.
- Is a large hand required? Many chords on the guitar require a large hand and the ability to stretch the fingers. A student must also be big enough to hold the instrument.
- What instruments use large muscle movements? Such instruments as drum, tambourine, cymbals, and rhythm sticks are appropriate for use by young students (ages five to seven).
- Can students move their fingers quickly from one chord bar to another while strumming chords on a Q-chord (ages nine to eleven)?
- Have students developed sufficient eye-finger dexterity and coordination to play the recorder? Their hands must also be large enough to cover all the fingerholes (ages nine to eleven).

Just as a composer must decide on the instruments to use in a composition, so teachers must guide students in the selection and playing of instruments appropriate to the expressiveness of the music. The following questions will serve as guidelines for determining this selection:

- Is there an ethnic (such as Latin American) influence in the music?
- What is the style of the music (march, waltz, calypso, rock)?
- Is the melody most expressive when played on a percussive instrument, such as melody bells or xylophone, or on a sustaining instrument, such as recorder or piano?
- Is a harmonic accompanying instrument (such as Q-chord, guitar, or keyboard) needed to maintain the tonality of the song?
- Can percussion instruments be used to create variety and interest through the playing of rhythm patterns or ostinatos?
- What is the nature of the text of the song? Does it portray, for example, activity, a quiet mood, or joyousness?
- What instruments can best be used to: (a) keep a steady beat; (b) express loud and soft; (c) show contrast in texture, mood, and tempos; or (d) illustrate musical form (such as AB, ABA, or rondo)?

Special Learner Note

When working with a "self-contained classroom" or a smaller group, introduce instruments one at a time—ideally with everyone in the group playing the *same* instrument at the same time. This will more easily reinforce the characteristic sound of each instrument, the appropriate method(s) for playing the instrument, and the name of each instrument while avoiding the confusion of too many different sounds, techniques, and names at one time.

Several music companies have developed a line of "adapted percussion instruments" that accommodate students with different physical disabilities. Check with a local music store/dealer to access a catalog—or check online for these companies.

Technology Enhancement

Using Software Instrument Applications

A fourth group of classroom instruments, *software instruments,* continues to gain ground in music education and in popular culture. Software instrument apps come in all types: Melody instruments, chordal accompaniments, and percussive. These software instruments are easily downloaded to handheld devices such as an iPod, iPad, tablet, or smartphone from either the Apple App store or Android Market.

Although many software instruments are paid-for apps, there are several great free applications that a teacher may employ. Before using electronic handheld instruments in the classroom, you should have a thorough knowledge of the specific apps you are going to use and how to manage the sound volume produced by the built-in speakers of the devices. For larger classroom demonstrations, the use of desktop speakers is encouraged. In the sections that follow, you will find brief descriptions of frequently used software instruments, directions for playing them, and some functions they might serve.

PIANO/KEYBOARD APPS:

MusicSparkles (Cost: Free)

- Xylophone with four octaves.
- Drum set.
- Vocal notes–play *Do* to *Do* with vocal notes and learn all about musical notes.
- Additional instruments available as in-app purchases.

Magic Piano (Cost: Free)

- From Bruno Mars to Mozart, you can play the various songs on this piano game.
- Get free songs every day and enjoy the largest catalog of songs.
- Turn on game mode to unlock achievements and free songs, or just relax and play your favorite tunes.
- Non-traditional notation.
- Great for Younger Students.

Dr. Seuss Band (Cost: Free)

- Two ways to play: Go for high scores in the Music Game or use Free Play to compose your own tunes.
- Ten original songs: Play along with the soundtrack from *The Cat in the Hat, Green Eggs and Ham, Dr. Seuss's ABCs, Hop on Pop* and more.
- Five unique horn Instruments: Play Seussian versions of the trumpet, french horn, clarinet, trombone and flute.
- Ten crazy horn effects: Customize the sound of your horn by adding fun effects like a fish bowl, train whistle, reverb and more.
- Mix and match horns: Swap parts of the horn while playing to create over 120 horn combinations.
- Three difficulty levels: Choose Easy for beginners, Medium for experienced players and Hard for experts.
- Twenty-six unlockables: Achieve high scores to unlock songs, horns and effects.

Virtuoso Piano Free 2 (Cost: Free)

- Six octaves of sampled concert grand piano.
- Robust bass, warm middles and crisp highs.
- Play along with your music library.
- Key labels (with colors).
- Play chords with up to five fingers.
- Slide your fingers to roll the keys.
- Free for unlimited period.

Piano (Cost: Free)

- Five octaves of sampled piano.
- Ten songs with animated music notation and background music (example songs includes "Mary Had a Little Lamb" and other simple songs.

Real Piano II (Cost: Free)

- Full 88 keys and amazing grand piano sound (best if using an external speaker).
- Multiple instruments including harp, marimba, guitar, bass, and music box.
- Smoothly move and zoom the keyboard by just sliding and pinching.
- Pedal and pedal lock.
- Expression support: volume-on-position and force/accelerometer.
- Three different keyboard layouts: Single, locked dual keyboard, and unlocked dual keyboard.
- Customizable key labels in different types and styles: C-D-E, c1-d1-e1, 1-2-3, or do-re-mi.
- Transpose to higher or lower key.

Drum Apps

Epic Drum Set (Cost: Free)

- Record your very own beats and play them back at any time.
- Save your recordings or choose any song in your [iTunes/Spotify] library and play along with it.
- For even more fun and creative options try creating your own beat, recording it and playing along with it.
- Choose from a range of four different drum sets (two free), standard, industrial, hard rock and junk! Each sound is professionally recorded and provides a realistic sound.

FingerDrums (Cost: Free)

- Choose from three amazing professionally recorded drum kits: rock, hip hop or dance.
- Play along with any songs on your music library.

DrumKit Lite (Cost: Free)

- Six-piece kit (snare, bass, hi-hat, crash, ride, splash).
- Visual feedback as you tap the drum head.
- Play multiple drums simultaneously.
- Add beats or fills as you play along with existing music.

Guitar

Epic Guitar (Cost: Free)

- Tap the buttons on the right to select the chord you want to play while you strum.

Smart Guitar (Cost: Free)

- Free acoustic guitar sound; available in-app purchase of other guitar styles.
- Choose to play chords with by playing using the chord button or form chords with ease letting Smart Guitar pinpoint the chords you mean to play.

Additional Resources:

http://www.ti-me.org/ (*TI:ME: Technology Integration Music Education website*)

Technology Integration in the Elementary Music Classroom by Amy Burns (*Book*)

http://musicroomburns.net/

Technology Guide for Music Educators by TI:ME (*Book*)

Technology Strategies for Music Education by Tom Rudolph, Floyd Richmond, David Mash, and David Williams. (*Book*)

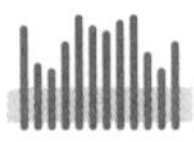

PLAYING RHYTHM ACCOMPANIMENTS TO SONGS

The following steps will contribute toward successful experiences in using percussion instruments to accompany songs.

1. Ask students to pat their thighs to keep the tempo beat (speed of song). Repeat using selected rhythm instruments such as rhythm sticks.
2. Ask students to pat their thighs and clap their hands in duple or triple meter. Add selected rhythm instruments and accent the first beat of each meter group.
3. Improvise patterns and ask students to imitate by clapping or playing instruments.
4. Ask students to improvise rhythm patterns on instruments within the meter beat pattern, such as triple meter:

> **Special Learner Note**
>
> **Technology and Special Learners**
>
> Technology advancements over the past several decades continue to lead to new accessibility for students of *all* abilities. With the proliferation of touch-based computer interfaces, technological devices have become intuitive and ideally suited for all students. Additionally, there are myriad of apps that cover a wide variety of curricula, assisting the teacher in providing individualized instruction for students.
>
> Additional information and resources about using technology with special needs students:
>
> http://www.apple.com/education/special-education/
>
> http://specialeducationtoday.com/category/ipad/

1. Decide on patterns to use for a selected song. Choose appropriate instruments. Apply these steps to "Rock-a My Soul" by using the instruments indicated.

Rock-a My Soul
Key: D
Starting pitch: F#
Meter: 4/4, begins on 1
Spiritual
♩ = 116
D
A7
etc.
Rock - a my soul in the bos - om of A - bra - ham, Rock - a my soul in the
bos - om of A - bra - ham, Rock - a my soul in the bos - om of A - bra - ham,
Fine
Oh, rock - a my soul. So high, can't get o - ver it, So low,
D.C. al fine
can't get un - der it, So wide, can't get a - round it, I must go in at the door.
Claves:
Hand drum:
Finger cymbals:

DEVELOPING A RHYTHM ENSEMBLE (GRADES K–3)

You can organize a classroom percussion ensemble to perform with recorded music. The choice of instruments will depend on musical characteristics such as high–low, strong beat–weak beat, dynamics, and accents. Expressiveness can be further enhanced by (1) alternating the total ensemble with a smaller group of instruments; (2) alternating the total ensemble or a smaller group of instruments with a solo instrument; and (3) contrasting different timbres (such as jingle sounds with wood sounds). Leadership skills can be developed by having individual students conduct the ensemble.

Students should listen to a selected composition many times. After each hearing, they should make decisions regarding their choice and use of instruments. The entire experience should be one of developing aural skill in hearing expressive changes in music. The following guidelines will assist you in this task:

Joy E. Lawrence

Rhythm ensemble

1. Select a musical composition that has a strong rhythm and a clear use of instruments.
2. Have students determine the meter (duple/triple).
3. Determine whether there are accents and if they are on the beat or off the beat (for example, syncopation).
4. Decide on instrumentation that is expressive of the composition.
5. Create a playing guide (as appropriate to grade level).

Musical compositions that are effective with a rhythm ensemble include the following (download or stream from [iTunes/Spotify]):

- Sousa marches
- Elgar, *Pomp and Circumstance*, "March #1"
- Mozart, Symphony no. 40 in G Minor (third movement, "Minuet")
- Bizet, "Farandole" from *L'Arlésienne Suite*
- Polkas: "Over the Waves," "Carnival of Venice," and "Varsoviana"
- Grieg, "In the Hall of the Mountain King" from *Peer Gynt Suite*
- Schubert, *Marche Militaire*
- Many popular pieces

In addition, consider organizing a "drum circle" for upper elementary school students using Will Schmid's *World Music Drumming* (available from www.amazon.com). This book contains a variety of songs from around the world complete with lesson plans, helpful teaching suggestions, and an instructional DVD on how to teach and use drums in the classroom.

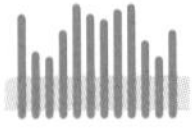

INTEGRATING INSTRUMENTAL EXPERIENCES INTO THE CLASSROOM

Playing instrumental accompaniments adds interest and variety to many songs and contributes toward perceptual and motor skills. The choice and use of appropriate instruments in musical experiences can enrich the study of history, geography, culture and people, poetry, feelings and moods, and holidays. Use the following suggestions as you plan your lessons.

Language Arts (Grades 4–6)

Use classroom instruments to express ideas and sounds in poems or stories, as in the following five examples:

1. Select classroom instruments to express appropriate sounds found in a Halloween story or poem, such as the following poem by Kay Maves. Encourage students to be creative in their choice of playing techniques.

   Gargoyles[2]
   Gargoyles perch by day on the rooftops,
   With frozen stone smiles, and long, lolling mouths ajar,
   No movements no sound 'til dark, and then GARGOYLE!
   Zipping, slipping through the night air!
   Laughing, leering tearing through the quiet air!
   Scaring cats, chasing bats 'til dawn
   When each one flits to his rooftop
   And stares with his cold stone eyes at the busy streets
   Through the only bright day,
   And knows that night will come when GARGOYLE!
   Laughing, leering tearing through the quiet air!
   Scaring cats, chasing bats,
   Reeling, spinning, shrieking, grinning GARGOYLE!

2. Dramatize "Five Little Pumpkins" (p. 27) and use music and text to determine rhythmic accompaniment and pitch relationships. Consider the following suggestions:

   a. Steady beat (rhythm sticks)
   b. Resonator bells (one for each pitch of the phrase):
      1 = F
      2 = G
      3 = A
      4 = B
      5 = C
   c. "Run and run and run" (play on melody bells):

   d. "Ooo went the wind" (glissando on xylophone)
   e. "*Out* went the light" (woodblock)
   f. "Rolled out of sight" (jingle sticks)

3. Read the story of *Peter and the Wolf*.[3] Select classroom instruments to represent each character. Decide on a rhythm, melody, or playing technique. Follow up by listening to Prokofiev's *Peter and the Wolf*. Discuss the composer's choice and use of instruments.

---

[2] Kay Maves, "Gargoyles," *New Dimensions in Music* (New York: American Book Co., 1970), pp. 107–108.
[3] Vladimir Vagin, *Peter and the Wolf* (New York: Scholastic Press, 2000).

4. Read the story *Little Toot* by Hardie Gramatky.[4] Select classroom instruments to represent the various boat sounds and types of boats. Use them to dramatize the story.
5. Read a children's story of your choice and select musical instruments to represent each character. Decide on a rhythm, melody, or playing technique for each.

Science: Sound (Grades 4–6)

Technology Enhancement

Video Resource
Bill Nye the Science Guy - Sound (Episode)
http://www.teachertube.com/viewVideo.php?title=Bill_Nye___Sound_Part_1_of_3&video_id=174563

1. Explore concepts of sound through the use of classroom instruments.
   a. Place the terms *sound, vibration, pitch,* and *frequency* on the chalkboard. Select a drum; as you strike the head, have students place their hands against the side of the instrument. They will feel and hear the *sound* produced by the *vibration* of the instrument. Explain that the vibration of the instrument produces the *pitch*—the highness or lowness of musical sounds. Select some instruments, such as the Q-chord, that produce both high and low sounds. Ask individual students to play them; then discuss why high or low sounds are produced (discovering that high sounds are produced by short strings or small instruments and low sounds by long strings or large instruments). Demonstrate how high-to-low pitches can be produced by lengthening an instrument. Have a student play a clarinet or flute first with just the mouthpiece and then add sections of the instrument, gradually lengthening the pipe and lowering the pitch. Pitch is directly related to the frequency of vibration. Sound vibrations move back and forth in a cycle; the number of cycles of vibration per second is known as the *frequency.* Some instruments produce sounds of low frequency, whereas other instruments produce sounds of high frequency.
   b. Explore various types of sounds by making your own musical instruments. Try for both high and low sounds. Also explore how sounds change depending on which material the musical instrument is made of. The box on the next page provides suggestions for making your own instruments.

[4] Hardie Gramatky, *Little Toot* (New York: G. P. Putnam's Sons, 2007).

How to Make Your Own Musical Instruments

Cymbals
Materials: Lids of pans
Directions: Make a hole in the lids with a nail and fasten a spool or piece of wood for the handle.

Triangle
Materials: Steel rod bent into a triangle blunt-end bolt
Directions: Strike bent rod with the blunt-end bolt.

Hand Drum
Materials: A quart or gallon can
Two pieces of canvas or leather 3 to 5 yards of heavy cord
Enamel or lacquer and brush
Leather punch
Directions: Remove the ends of the can and smooth the edges. Paint the can. Cut two pieces of canvas or leather about 4 inches larger in diameter than the can. Punch the same number of holes in each piece at least 1 inch from the edge. Place the two pieces of canvas or leather over the ends of the can and lace them together. Tie a cord securely around the ends of the drum and adjust the lacing until you get the desired sound.

Jingle Bells
Materials: 6-inch dowel
Three jingle bells
Two tacks
3-inch leather or plastic strap
Four pieces of thin wire
Directions: Punch holes in the strap and fasten the bells to the strap with the wire. Tack the strap to the dowel (use small tacks to avoid splitting the wood) or drill a hole through the wood and anchor the strap securely with the wire.

Claves
Materials: 1-inch dowels of hardwood, which give clear tone when tapped together: beech, mahogany, walnut, cherry, ash, or sycamore
Directions: Cut dowels into 6-inch lengths. Apply several coats of varnish or hard wax.

Rhythm Sticks
Materials: Hardwood dowels 3/8 inch to 5/8 inch in diameter
Directions: Cut dowels into 12-inch lengths. Carve ridges on one side and paint dowels in bright colors.

Woodblock
Materials: Small wooden box (such as a cigar box)
Directions: Fasten lid tightly onto hollow box. Strike box with stick or mallet.

Maracas
Materials: Ball of plasticine
Dowel
Tissue paper and newspaper
Paste or glue
Peas, buttons, rice, or pebbles
Directions: Shape the desired size of plasticine on a length of dowel. Apply small pieces of damp tissue paper and add small pieces of pasted newspaper. Build up layers of white or colored newspaper. When ball is dry, cut in half, and remove plasticine. Join the two halves together and glue. Drop a few hard objects into the shell and replace the dowel. Secure with strips of paper and paste. When dry, paint the maraca with bright colors.

Sand Blocks
Materials: 3-inch square blocks of wood, 3/4 inch to 1 inch thick
Sandpaper
Directions: Cover blocks of wood with various thicknesses of sandpaper (to get the desired effect). Add handles made from empty spools of thread or cabinet knobs.

African Rattle
Materials: Large gourd or papier-mâché shell mounted on a dowel
Buttons
Knotted string
Directions: Fasten buttons on knotted string and form into loose net. Mount on the outside of the gourd or shell.

Social Studies: American West (Grades 4–6)

1. Select songs that describe activities of the American cowboy, for example, roping, branding, herding cows, or eating around a campfire. The following are some song possibilities (download from www.musicnotes.com/sheet):
   "Home on the Range" (p. 51)
   "Red River Valley"
   "Get Along Little Dogies"
   "Old Paint"
2. Add Q-chord accompaniment to each.
3. Introduce the harmonica and have selected students accompany the singing by ear.

Technology Enhancement

Helpful Links

http://www.nyphilkids.org/lab

http://www.dsokids.com/athome/makeinstrument.aspx

http://www.atlantasymphony.org/aso/asoassets/downloadcenter/Symphony%20Street%20Activity%20Sheets.pdf

http://www.makingmusicmag.com/features/make-your-own-percussion.html

Search YouTube for "Build Your Own Instrument": http://www.youtube.com/watch?v=qf9WRGD8E-k

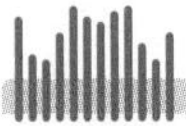

SAMPLE LESSONS

LESSON PLAN
Dynamics

Activity: Experiencing dynamics through the playing of instruments
Grades: 1–3
Concepts: Dynamics: Loud/soft

NATIONAL AND STATE MUSIC STANDARD

1. Performing on instruments, alone and with others, a varied repertoire of music

OBJECTIVES

Students will demonstrate an understanding of dynamics by their choice and expressive playing of classroom instruments.

MATERIALS

Prepare a chart with symbols:

- loud f
  soft p
  crescendo <
- decrescendo >
- accents 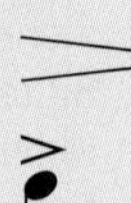

PROCEDURES

1. Engage students in an echo game:
   Teacher: Cup hands and call "Hello"
   Students: "Hello"
   Teacher: "Are you there?"
   Students: "Are you there? Are you there? Are you there?" (each time softer)

2. Echo clap the following rhythms:

3. Play or sing the echo song "Hello There!" (p. 75). Ask students to respond by:
   a. Singing an answer using tonal syllables
   b. Playing an answer on melody or resonator bells
4. Explore playing a single instrument loudly and softly.
5. Discover instruments that make loud sounds and those that make soft sounds.
6. Choose large cymbals and a pair of finger cymbals. Play an echo game: One child taps the large cymbal with a soft mallet; a second student answers by tapping the finger cymbals (on rim only). Apply to the words, such as the "Hello" in the song.
7. Invite children to choose instruments that could make a loud sound (drum, cymbals, woodblock) and those that could make a soft sound (sand blocks, jingle sticks). Divide class into two groups. Assign loud instruments to group 1 and soft instruments to group 2. Loud instruments will play on the first "Hello"; soft instruments will play on the second "Hello." Practice the rhythm:

Loud: ♪| ♫ 𝄽|

Soft: 𝄾 | 𝄽 𝄾 ♪| ♫

ASSESSMENT

Create a short piece of music with the students playing percussion instruments and using a variety of dynamic levels: loud, soft, crescendo, decrescendo.

LESSON PLAN
Repetition and Contrast

Activity: Playing instruments
Grades: 2–3
Concepts: Repetition and contrast

NATIONAL AND STATE MUSIC STANDARDS

1. Performing on instruments, alone and with others, a varied repertoire of music
2. Listening to, analyzing, and describing music
3. Singing, alone and with others, a varied repertoire of music

OBJECTIVES

Students will:

1. Identify contrasting melodies by playing selected instruments.
2. Demonstrate an understanding of form by creating a rhythm accompaniment involving contrasting timbres for each section.
3. Increase their ability to hear repetition and contrast of musical ideas in music.

MATERIALS

- Songs: "We Wish You a Merry Christmas" (p. 61)
- "Home on the Range" (p. 51)
- Recordings: Mozart, *Eine Kleine Nachtmusik*, "Rondo"; Herb Alpert, "Spanish Flea" (download or stream from [iTunes/Spotify])
- Geometric forms
- Classroom instruments:
  Group 1: Drum, tambourine, rhythm sticks
  Group 2: Triangles, jingle sticks, finger cymbals, jingle bells
- Bulletin board with pictures of the instruments

PROCEDURES

1. Provide a large table with two signs: *Heavy, Light.*
2. Explore the contrasting timbres of instruments. Each student plays and places an instrument in front of the appropriate sign. After all are in place, invite several students to play one instrument from each section. Ask the class to decide whether the instrument is in the right place or ought to be with the other group.
3. Play a game in which all of the instruments are placed at the rear of the classroom. Give each student an Instrument Sheet with pictures of the various instruments. (Pictures could also be placed on a chalkboard or bulletin board.) A selected student chooses an instrument and then plays it from the back of the room. Students circle the instrument on their worksheet or point to a picture on the board.
4. Select four students to play drum, tambourine, rhythm sticks, and cymbals in the following rhythm:

Special Learner Note

Signs/icons that represent the concepts of heavy (elephant) and light (bird) may help students understand these concepts.

5. Select four students to play the triangle, jingle sticks, finger cymbals, and jingle bells in the following rhythm:

6. Compare the sounds created by the two groups of instruments in steps 4 and 5.
7. Select instruments to play the contrasting sections of "We Wish You a Merry Christmas" (p. 61); one possibility would be jingle sticks (A), claves (B), jingle sticks (A).
8. Listen to Herb Alpert's "Spanish Flea." Play a steady beat on the hand drum for the main theme. Have students select categories of instruments to use for the contrasting theme (rhythm sticks, woodblock, claves; jingle bells, jingle sticks, tambourine, triangle; hand drum, conga drum, bongo drums, snare drum).
   a. Select a single instrument to play the main theme and other instruments to play the contrasting sections. Practice playing the following rhythm and changing on cue:

   b. Listen to "Spanish Flea" and accompany with the instruments. Alternate heavy and light instruments for the contrasting sections. Invite a student with a keen musical sense to direct the ensemble. Involve all students in playing the instruments. Provide the director with a conductor's baton.

ASSESSMENT

1. Create an ABA form by playing contrasting instruments.
2. Download and listen to Mozart's *Eine Kleine Nachtmusik*, "Rondo," and accompany the main melody and the contrasting melodies with heavy or light instruments. Involve all students in playing the instruments. Either the teacher or a student may conduct with a baton.

Integrating Technology

The Music Education Premium Site contains chapter quizzing, Spotify playlists, and downloads of free MP3s of noted songs. Visit CengageBrain.com to purchase an access code or enter the code provided with your text materials.

Web Resources

- Search the Web (www.google.com) for information and pictures of musical instruments.

Videos

- Watch classroom videos that apply to the chapter content and access the YouTube playlist for videos referenced within the chapter.

Audio

- Download music discussed in this chapter from the iTunes store.
- Spotify playlists allow students to stream music referenced within each chapter.
- Download free audio MP3s for the songs noted in the chapter.

CENGAGE**brain**.com

Questions for Discussion

1. What are some differences between melodic and harmonic instruments? Name two or three of each.
2. What are some guidelines for leading children in successful experiences with classroom percussion instruments?
3. Why is the guitar an excellent instrument to use for accompanying singing in the classroom?
4. When accompanying a song, why is it sometimes helpful to transpose the song to a higher or lower pitch?
5. What is the advantage of using a capo on the guitar?
6. What are the differences between melody bells, resonator bells, and step bells?
7. What is the difference between a xylophone and a metallophone?
8. Why is the recorder a good instrument for learning to play easy songs?
9. Play or write the guitar fingering for the following chords:
   - D
   - A_7
   - E minor
   - C
   - G
   - D_7
10. Name several two- and three-chord songs.
11. Summarize several ways in which you can use instruments to integrate music with other subjects.

Assessment

Review ways the music standards listed at the beginning of the chapter have been met.

CHAPTER 6

Teaching Music through Listening

© Ritchie Photography

Objectives

Students will explore ideas for developing listening lessons:

- The chain of events in musical expression
  - The composer
  - The performer
  - The composer/performer
  - The listener
- Sounds produced by voices
- Sounds produced by Western orchestral instruments
  - Stringed instruments
  - Wind instruments
  - Percussion instruments
  - Keyboard instruments
  - Electronic instruments
- Performing ensembles
  - Orchestra
  - Band
  - Chorus
- How to guide listening
  - The teacher's role
  - Guidelines for planning listening lessons
- Techniques for teaching students to listen to music
  - Visual representations
  - Written listening guides
  - The familiar song in a musical composition
  - Moving to music
  - Playing instruments
  - Sample lesson plans
- Integrating listening experiences into the classroom
  - Music and drama: opera
  - Music and drama: oratorio
  - Music and dance: ballet
  - Program music
  - Preparing students to attend a concert

National and State Music Standards

This chapter provides experiences with the following national music standards and related state music standards:

- Listening to, analyzing, and describing music
- Singing, alone and with others, a varied repertoire of music
- Performing on instruments, alone and with others, a varied repertoire of music
- Evaluating music and musical performances
- Understanding relationships among music, the other arts, and disciplines outside the arts
- Understanding music in relation to history and culture

In our society, radio and television, along with CD players, MP3 players, and tablet computers, surround us with music. Sometimes music serves as a background of sound while we wait in an office, ride in an elevator or car, or shop in a mall. At other times, such as when attending a concert, ballet, or opera, we must listen carefully to enjoy it fully. You might say that in the first instance we *hear* music, whereas in the second we *listen to* music.

Let us consider some differences between these two experiences. First, *hearing* is one of the five basic senses. Often we hear sounds without consciously identifying what they are: birds chirping, wind moving through trees, paper rustling, and so on. In a crowd we may hear a lot of talking without distinguishing any particular words or meanings. On the other hand, *listening* requires aural skills that include focusing attention on the sound source, remembering sounds, perceiving phenomena unique to sounds, and responding. A baby hears sound but must be taught to listen. Many a parent has said, "My child hears me when I speak, but doesn't want to listen." Listening to music requires focusing attention on its unique qualities. This takes energy and self-discipline; if our minds wander, we lose the meaning of what we are hearing.

A listening experience is very different from a visual experience. After viewing a picture, we can look out the window, leave the room, or think about something else, and when we return, the picture will be in the same place with the same colors, lines, and shapes. In music, however, unless we use a recording, no two performances are ever exactly the same. Music is also unique in that it passes through time and we hear it both in the present (as it is happening) and in our memory (as it has happened). Memory, then, is an important component of listening, for part of the pleasure derived from a musical experience is in recalling a musical theme, a harmony, or a distinctive tone color.

Children can be taught to listen to the expressive use of elements of music such as rhythm, melody, dynamics, tone color, texture, and formal structure. As they grow in their ability to perceive and understand musical phenomena, they have a greater potential for deeply satisfying aesthetic experiences.

A related outcome of a listening experience is learning how music expresses the time, place, and people who create it. For example, as children study and listen to "America," "Yankee Doodle," and "Chester," they can become more aware and sensitive to the events surrounding the American Revolution. Thus, for classroom teachers, music becomes a unique way of helping students understand important areas of the social studies curriculum.

Although there are many benefits to developing home listening libraries of music, nothing can really replace the thrill and excitement of attending a live performance. Throughout the United States, countless free concerts are given each year by colleges and universities, public and private schools, museums, churches, and others. Many symphony orchestras sponsor educational concerts for children at a nominal cost. It is important for the classroom teacher to seek out such opportunities so that children can attend live performances of music.

This chapter is designed to provide materials and techniques for preparing students to listen to music. It begins with a discussion of the chain of events in musical expression, followed by sections on sound sources for musical listening, ways to guide listening, and the integration of listening into the classroom.

Special Learner Note

Informally introduce music listening during other classroom activities to encourage familiarity with newer compositions. Background music can be intentionally selected to prepare students for a live music performance or concert attendance, or simply as a review of material from music class or other music experience.

THE CHAIN OF EVENTS IN MUSICAL EXPRESSION

Musical expression follows a chain of events that runs from composer to performer to listener.

The Composer

Music begins with an idea in the mind of a person called a *composer*. The idea may be a melody, a rhythmic motif, or a distinctive tone color. The composer must have the skill to organize these musical ideas in a logical and meaningful fashion that can be perceived and understood by the listener. All composers who have created lasting works of art have been able to achieve a high level of imagination and sensitivity in their works.

The Performer

Written music must be re-created from the musical score by the *performer*. The quality of the performance depends on (1) the performer's technical skill, (2) insights into the musical meanings that are expressed, and (3) understanding of the musical style of the composer. Although there is always somewhat of a personal stamp on any performance, the goal is to interpret the music as accurately and sensitively as possible according to the directions given by the composer.

The Composer/Performer

In many kinds of music, such as the oral traditions of Africa and India, as well as American jazz, the performer is often the composer. In such traditions, the musician creates or composes at the instant of performance. That is, the role of composer appears in the improvisations by the performer. These improvisations, while appearing to be spontaneous, are most often based on a catalog of musical ideas that have been stored in the musician's mind over a period of time. During performances the musician must organize both stored and newly created sound materials in logical and imaginative ways.

The Listener

The *listener* is one of the most important links in the chain of events of musical expression. The principal function of the listener is to receive, interpret, and respond to music. Learning to be an effective listener requires early and sustained training.

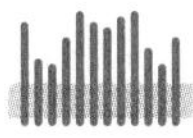

SOUNDS PRODUCED BY VOICES

People around the world produce a large number of different vocal sounds. Some are full and open, whereas others are pinched and nasal. In Western music women's voices are classified as *soprano* and *alto*, and male voices are divided into *tenor* and *bass*. Each of the following compositions can be used to illustrate various classical voice qualities [iTunes/Spotify]:

- Soprano: Giacomo Puccini, "Un Bel Di" (One Fine Day) from *Madame Butterfly*
- Alto: Felix Mendelssohn, "O Rest in the Lord" from *Elijah*
- Tenor: G. F. Handel, "Comfort Ye" from *Messiah*
- Bass: Jerome Kern, "Old Man River" from *Showboat*
- Bass, Tenor, Alto, and Soprano: "Tuba mirum" from Mozart's Requiem Mass in D minor, K. 626

Technology Enhancement

Often watching videos of singers and instrumentalists can be helpful for students in connecting "sounds" with how they are produced. Spending some time before your lesson searching for and previewing videos from YouTube, TeacherTube, or Vimeo can yield excellent examples of all types of music and musicians.

SOUNDS PRODUCED BY WESTERN ORCHESTRAL INSTRUMENTS

Sounds are produced by instruments in a variety of ways. In general, instruments are classified as stringed, wind, or percussion, depending on how their sounds are produced. In addition, some modern-day instruments produce their sounds electronically.

Stringed Instruments

Stringed instruments are usually played with a bow drawn across the strings. Placing the fingers of the left hand on the strings along the fingerboard changes the pitch. Each pitch is produced by a different finger position. Stringed instruments can also be plucked (called *pizzicato*). With pizzicato, the pitches are still created with fingers on the strings; however, the fingers of the right hand pluck the string instead of using a bow. This same technique of plucking is used when playing the Japanese *koto* or Indian *sitar*. Other instruments that can be plucked include the harp and the guitar.

Herbert Ascherman, Jr.

Violin

The *violin* is the soprano of the string family and is capable of a wide range of dynamics and expression. It has four strings, which are tuned by tightening or loosening pegs at the upper end of the instrument. *Musical example:* Mendelssohn, Violin Concerto in E Minor, Rondo (third movement) ([iTunes/Spotify], Academy of St. Martin in the Fields, Marriner/Bell).

Herbert Ascherman, Jr.

Viola

The *viola* is the alto of the string family. It is somewhat larger than the violin, and its strings are slightly thicker; therefore, its sound is lower and somewhat richer than the violin's. *Musical example:* Hindemith, *Der Schwanendreher* (The Swan Catcher) or Telemann, Viola Concerto in G (second movement) [iTunes/Spotify].

Herbert Ascherman, Jr.

Cello

The *violoncello* (usually called the *cello*) is the tenor member of the string family. Unlike the violin or the viola, which are supported by holding the instrument between the chin and the shoulder, the cello is placed upright with a peg at the base of the instrument resting on the floor. The cello's tone is warm and mellow. *Musical example:* Saint-Saëns, "The Swan" from *Carnival of the Animals* [iTunes/Spotify].

Herbert Ascherman, Jr.

String Bass

The *string bass* (double bass) is the lowest-sounding member of the string family of instruments. Although similar to the cello, the string bass is much larger, and players must either stand or sit on a high stool to play it. The sounds of the bass are among the lowest in the orchestra. *Musical example:* Saint-Saëns, "The Elephant," from *Carnival of the Animals* [iTunes/Spotify].

Rob Lewine/Corbis

Harp

The *harp* is a large instrument with forty-seven strings. These strings are tuned by pegs across the top of the instrument. A series of pedals on the bottom of the harp enable the player to change keys. *Musical example:* Tchaikovsky, *The Nutcracker,* "Waltz of the Flowers" [iTunes/Spotify].

Wind Instruments

The *wind* instruments are played by blowing into a tube whose length is controlled by the covering of fingerholes, the pressing down of valves, or, in the case of a trombone, the moving of a slide. They are divided into the woodwind family and the brass family.

Woodwinds

The *woodwinds* can be classified into three groups: those without reeds, those with single reeds, and those with double reeds.

The first group of woodwinds includes those without reeds. The *flute* is the soprano member of this group. Originally made of wood, it is now usually metal. Its tone in the lower register is warm and smooth, but as it proceeds up the scale the tone becomes brighter. *Musical examples:* Debussy, *Syrinx;* Prokofiev, *Peter and the Wolf,* "The Bird" [iTunes/Spotify].

The other member of the reedless group, the *piccolo,* looks like a small flute and sounds an octave higher. Composers use it for unusual effects because its sound can penetrate heavy masses of orchestral tone. *Musical example:* Sousa, "Stars and Stripes Forever," ending [iTunes/Spotify].

Herbert Ascherman, Jr.

© Ritchie Photography

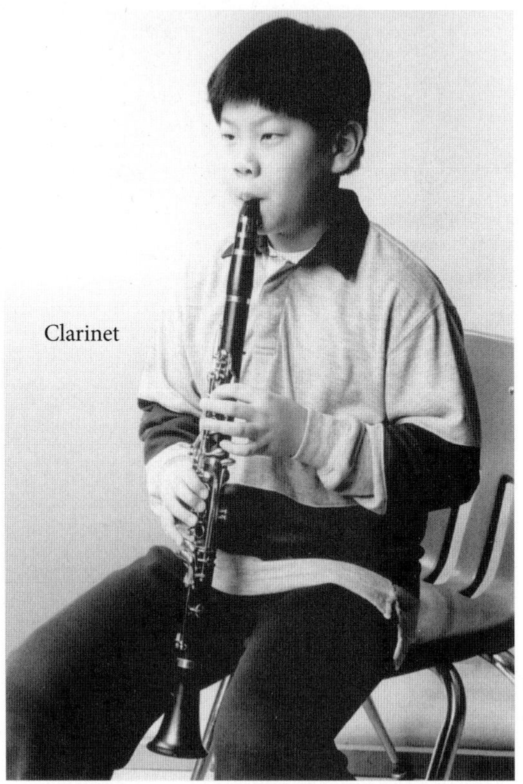

Herbert Ascherman, Jr.

Herbert Ascherman, Jr.

The second group of woodwinds includes those with a single reed. The *clarinet* is a single-reed instrument whose pitch and tone can vary from a low, dark, sonorous quality to brilliant high pitches. *Musical example:* Prokofiev, *Peter and the Wolf,* "The Cat" [iTunes/Spotify].

The *saxophone* is another single-reed instrument. It differs from the clarinet in that it is larger and is constructed from metal. Saxophones are found predominantly in bands but are occasionally played in orchestras. They come in several sizes, including alto, tenor, and baritone. *Musical example:* Mussorgsky, "The Old Castle" from *Pictures at an Exhibition* [iTunes/Spotify].

The third group of woodwinds includes those with a double reed. The *oboe* is a double-reed instrument with a bright tone color and a penetrating quality. *Musical example:* Pachebel, "Adagio" from Oboe Concerto in C Minor [iTunes/Spotify].

The *English horn* is larger than the oboe and therefore has a lower pitch and a darker tone color. *Musical example:* Dvořák, *New World Symphony,* second movement [iTunes/Spotify].

Herbert Ascherman, Jr.

English horn

David R. Frazier Photolibrary, Inc./Alamy

Herbert Ascherman, Jr.

Contrabassoon

Herbert Ascherman, Jr.

The *bassoon* is a still lower-pitched instrument; it is sometimes described as a tenor-sounding instrument. *Musical example:* Hindemith, Sonata for Bassoon and Piano [iTunes/Spotify].

The *contrabassoon* is the lowest-sounding member of the woodwind family. It is essentially the same as the bassoon, only larger, and it sounds an octave lower. Although it is 16 feet long, the instrument is constructed in coils so that it actually stands about 4 feet tall. *Musical example:* Ravel, *Mother Goose Suite,* "Beauty and the Beast" [iTunes/Spotify].

Brass

A second group of wind instruments are the *brass,* a name that refers to the material from which the instruments are made. There are four main brass instruments: trumpet, French horn, trombone, and tuba.

The *trumpet* is the soprano of the brass family and has a high, brilliant sound. *Musical example:* Purcell, *Trumpet Voluntary in D* [iTunes/Spotify].

Trumpet

Herbert Ascherman, Jr.

French horn

Herbert Ascherman, Jr.

The *French horn* is the alto member of the brass family. Its tone is lower and more mellow than that of the trumpet. *Musical example:* Mozart, Horn Concerto no. 3 in E-flat Major, K. 447 [iTunes/Spotify].

The *trombone* is the tenor member of the brass family. This instrument consists of a tube about 9 feet long, doubled on itself to about half that length. The performer uses a slide to alter the length of the tube and, therefore, the pitch. *Musical example:* "Bones Trombone," *Sounds of the Circus* [iTunes/Spotify].

The *tuba* is the bass member of the brass family and has a low and powerful tone. A special type of tuba, known as the *Sousaphone* (originally made from brass but today also from synthetic materials), is designed in circular fashion so that the instrument can be carried more easily in marching bands. *Musical example:* "Tuba Lullaby" by the Canadian Brass [iTunes/Spotify].

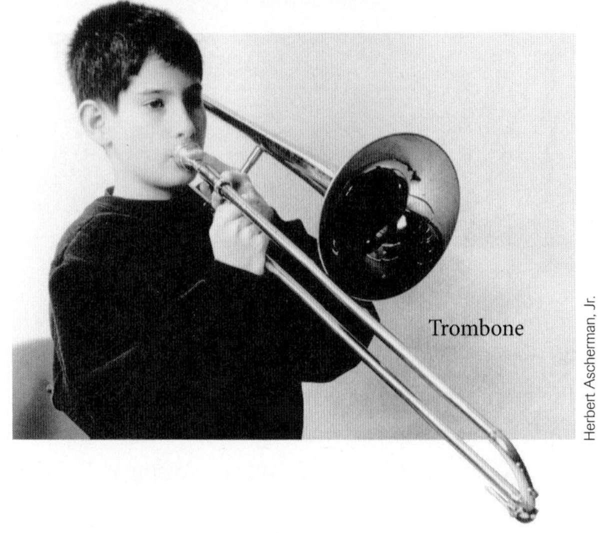

Trombone

Herbert Ascherman, Jr.

Tuba

Herbert Ascherman, Jr.

Sousaphone

Conn Sousaphone. Photo courtesy of United Musical Instruments, U.S.A., Inc.

Technology Enhancement

Additional Information and Examples of Orchestra Instruments

- *New York Philharmonic Kids Zone* – "Instrument Storage Room" section: http://www.nyphilkids.org/lockerroom
- *Arts Alive* – Instrument Lab section has pictures, audio, and videos about instruments and conductor. Also, under their "Activities and Games" section, there is a "Name the Instrument" game/quiz. http://www.artsalive.ca/en/mus/index.asp
- *Dallas Symphony Orchestra's* website for kids offers audio and pictures about orchestra instruments. http://www.dsokids.com/listen/instrumentlist.aspx
- *San Francisco Symphony's* website for kids offers pictures and audio about instruments of the orchestra as well as "Music Lab" sections that offer tutorials on musical topics including tempo, rhythm, pitch, harmony, and symbols. http://www.sfskids.org/
- "Sounds of the Orchestra" app for iPad/iPod/iPhone (cost: $1.99)
    - Tap on the colorful soundboard to learn the sounds of each instrument, or quiz yourself to train your ear to recognize them.
    - Explore the four sections of the orchestra, and learn about the individual instruments within each one while listening to some beautiful classical musical favorites.

Timpani

Herbert Ascherman, Jr.

Percussion Instruments

A fourth family of instruments, those that are struck or shaken, are known as *percussion*. Instruments that have a definite pitch are timpani, chimes, and xylophone. Instruments of indefinite pitch include the snare drum, bass drum, cymbals, triangle, gong, tambourine, and castanets.

Timpani

The *timpani* (kettledrums) are capable of definite and variable pitch. The player strikes the heads with different types of sticks that range in texture from hard to soft, according to the quality of tone required. The drums are tuned for the particular composition. *Musical example:* Prokofiev, *Peter and the Wolf,* "The Hunters Arrive" [iTunes/Spotify].

Chimes

Chimes consist of metal bars suspended on a frame and struck with a mallet. They are tuned to the chromatic scale, and the tone is very bright. *Musical example:* Tchaikovsky, *1812 Overture,* ending [iTunes/Spotify].

Chimes

Herbert Ascherman, Jr.

Xylophone

The *xylophone* consists of a graduated series of wooden bars suspended on a frame in two rows representing the white and black keys of the piano. It is played with hard mallets. *Musical example:* Saint-Saëns, *Carnival of the Animals*, "Fossils" [iTunes/Spotify].

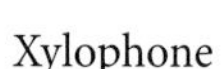

Xylophone

Herbert Ascherman, Jr.

Snare drum

Herbert Ascherman, Jr.

Snare Drum

The *snare drum* is a shallow cylinder of brass closed at either end by a membrane under tension. Metal strings (snares) are stretched across the lower head so that, when the drum is struck, they vibrate against the membrane, causing the familiar rattling effect. *Musical example:* Sousa, "Washington Post March" [iTunes/Spotify].

Bass Drum

The *bass drum* is made of wood or metal; its pitch is indefinite but very low. It is often used for special rhythmic emphasis. *Musical example:* Verdi, *Requiem,* "Dies Irae"[iTunes/Spotify] and "Bass Drum" (www.youtube.com).

Bass drum

Herbert Ascherman, Jr.

Cymbals

Cymbals are disks of brass with a depression in the center. They are used in pairs for rhythmic and tonal effects such as keeping the beat and dynamic contrasts. *Musical example:* Sousa, "Washington Post March" [iTunes/Spotify].

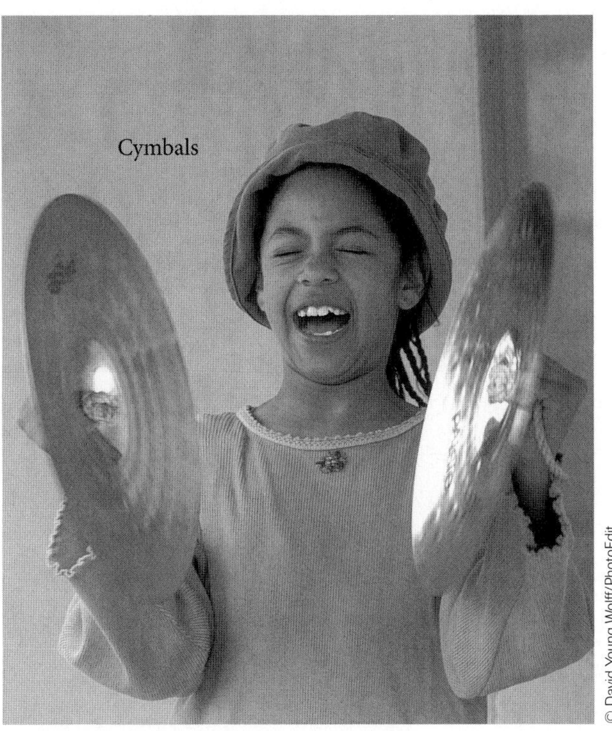
Cymbals

© David Young Wolff/PhotoEdit

Triangle

The *triangle* is a steel rod bent into a triangular shape with one angle open. It is suspended on a string and played by striking it with a metal stick. It has a brilliant, tinkling tone. *Musical example:* Verdi, *Il Trovatore,* "Anvil Chorus" [iTunes/Spotify] and "Triangle Musical Instrument" (www.youtube.com).

Triangle

Herbert Ascherman, Jr.

Gong

Herbert Ascherman, Jr.

Gong

The *gong* is a large, circular, metallic plate suspended by a cord and struck with a mallet. *Musical example:* Ravel, *Mother Goose Suite,* "Laideronette, Empress of the Pagoda" [iTunes/Spotify] or "Gong Musical Instrument" (www.youtube.com).

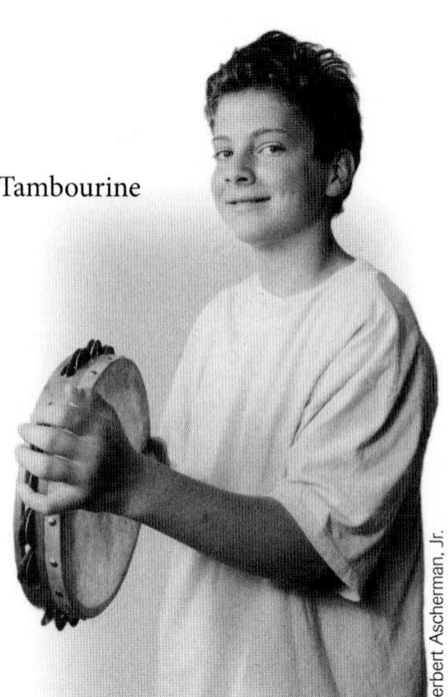
Tambourine

Herbert Ascherman, Jr.

Tambourine

The *tambourine* is a miniature drum with a single head. In the rim of wood are small metal discs that vibrate when the instrument is struck or shaken. *Musical example:* Verdi, *Il Trovatore,* "Anvil Chorus" [iTunes/Spotify] or tambourine (www.youtube.com).

Imagebroker/Alamy

Castanets

Castanets

Castanets are hollow shells that are always used in pairs. When clapped together rhythmically, they give a sharp, clacking sound. They are often used with dance music of Spain or Latin America. *Musical example:* "Flamenco Dance Song" [iTunes/Spotify].

Keyboard Instruments

Four keyboard instruments are the pipe organ, piano, harpsichord, and celesta.

Pipe Organ

The *pipe organ* consists of a set of pipes (one for each key) that produce different pitches. *Stops* activate the many pipes (flues, principals, reeds, and strings), and the player can use them to produce an enormous variety of tone colors. The player sits at a console, which may have several keyboards, including one called the *pedal* (played with the feet). Each one of these keyboards is connected to a division of pipes. These divisions are called *great, swell, positive, choir,* or *solo,* depending on the number of manuals (keyboards played by the hands). The organist manipulates stops and expression pedals (to get louder and softer) and selects tone colors from the various divisions to interpret the music. *Musical example:* Ives, *Variations on "America" for Organ* [iTunes/Spotify].

Steven A. Dieck/C.B. Fisk

Pipe organ

Piano

Image courtesy of Bosendorfer

Piano

The *piano* has eighty-eight notes and a single keyboard. Sounds are produced by hammers that strike strings stretched across the inner framework of the instrument. *Musical example:* Mozart, Variations on "Twinkle, Twinkle, Little Star" ("Ah! Vous dirai-je, Maman") [iTunes/Spotify].

Harpsichord

The *harpsichord* resembles a piano but is smaller and may have two keyboards. Instead of hammers striking strings, small plectrums, activated by the keyboard, pluck strings; thus the harpsichord has a much softer sound than the piano and a more limited dynamic range. *Musical example:* Couperin, "The Gnat" (from *Second Book of Harpsichord Pieces*) [iTunes/Spotify].

Harpsichord

Herbert Ascherman, Jr.

Celesta

Herbert Ascherman, Jr.

Celesta

The *celesta* looks like a small piano but has only a four-octave keyboard. When the keys are pressed, small hammers strike bell-metal bars. The sounds of this instrument are characterized by a light, bell-like quality. *Musical example:* Tchaikovsky, *The Nutcracker*, "Dance of the Sugar Plum Fairy" [iTunes/Spotify].

Electronic Instruments

Many acoustic instruments, such as the piano and the guitar, can be electrified. Much popular music today is performed on these electronic instruments.

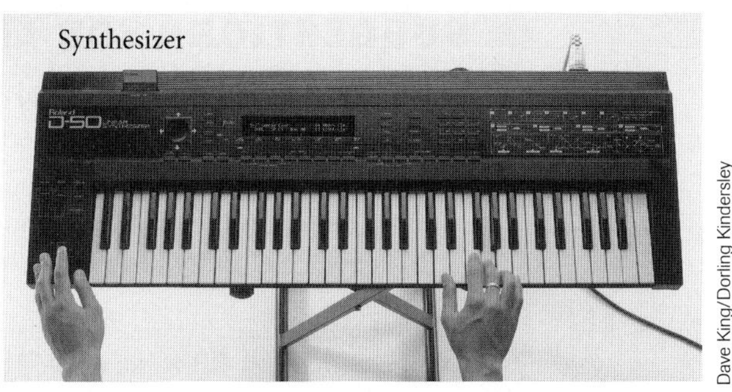

Synthesizer

Dave King/Dorling Kindersley

Another form of electronic instrument is the *synthesizer*. It can perform tasks beyond the capability of traditional instruments. For example, a composer can use a synthesizer to create melodies and rhythms extending beyond the pitch range of a traditional instrument—or faster than could be created by a human being. Synthesizers create new sounds and forms of music. *Musical example:* Kunzel, Cincinnati Pops Orchestra, "Synthesizer Effects" from the album *Chiller* ([iTunes/Spotify], Synthesizer Effects, Kunzel, Cincinnati Pops Orchestra).

Technology Enhancement

Showing students how instruments are made can help them connect how different materials are related to the sounds that are produced. The *How It's Made* TV series made several short videos about how various instruments are made. Search YouTube, TeacherTube, or Vimeo for "How it's made piano." Other instrument videos from *How It's Made* include: Alpine horn, accordion, acoustic guitar, banjo, clarinet, cymbals, drums, drum heads, drum sticks, electric guitar, electric violin, flute, French horn, guitar strings, harmonica, pipe organ, self-playing piano, steel drums, trombone, trumpet, tuba, and violin.

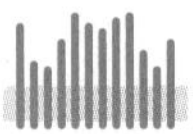

PERFORMING ENSEMBLES

Both instruments and voices are often grouped into large ensembles such as orchestras, bands, and choruses. Sometimes the ensembles are much smaller, such as duets (two performers), trios (three performers), and quartets (four performers).

Orchestra

The Western symphony orchestra is a large ensemble composed of stringed, brass, woodwind, and percussion instruments. Some principal stringed, brass, and woodwind instruments, arranged from "high sounding" to "low sounding," are given in the following table. Figure 6.1 shows a typical-seating arrangement.

Principal Orchestra Instruments

RANGE	STRINGS	BRASS	WOODWIND
Soprano	Violin	Trumpet	Flute
Alto	Viola	French horn	Clarinet/oboe
Tenor	Cello	Trombone	Bassoon
Bass	String bass (double bass)	Tuba	Contrabassoon

Instruments of the orchestra are often studied in terms of their general classification (strings, woodwinds, brasses) and their pitch ranges. Thus there are "soprano," "alto," "tenor," and "bass" instruments, as shown in the table.

In addition to the instruments listed in the table, orchestras have a variety of pitched and non-pitched percussion instruments with ranges from high to low. Often some keyboard instruments (such as celesta and piano) are also included in the orchestral ensemble.

SUGGESTIONS FOR LESSONS

1. Listen to and watch the DVD/video *The Orchestra* with Peter Ustinov.[1] Because the DVD/video has three parts, you may wish to teach the instruments over several days.

Part one includes (a) feelings about music and (b) the composer. Part two includes (a) the string family and (b) the woodwind family. Part three includes (a) the brass family, (b) special instruments, and (c) the conductor.

[1] The DVD/video *The Orchestra*, narrated by Peter Ustinov, is available from Friendship House, 29355 Ranney Pkwy., P.O. Box 450978, Cleveland, OH 44245; 1-800-791-9876; www.friendshiphouse.com.

Orchestra

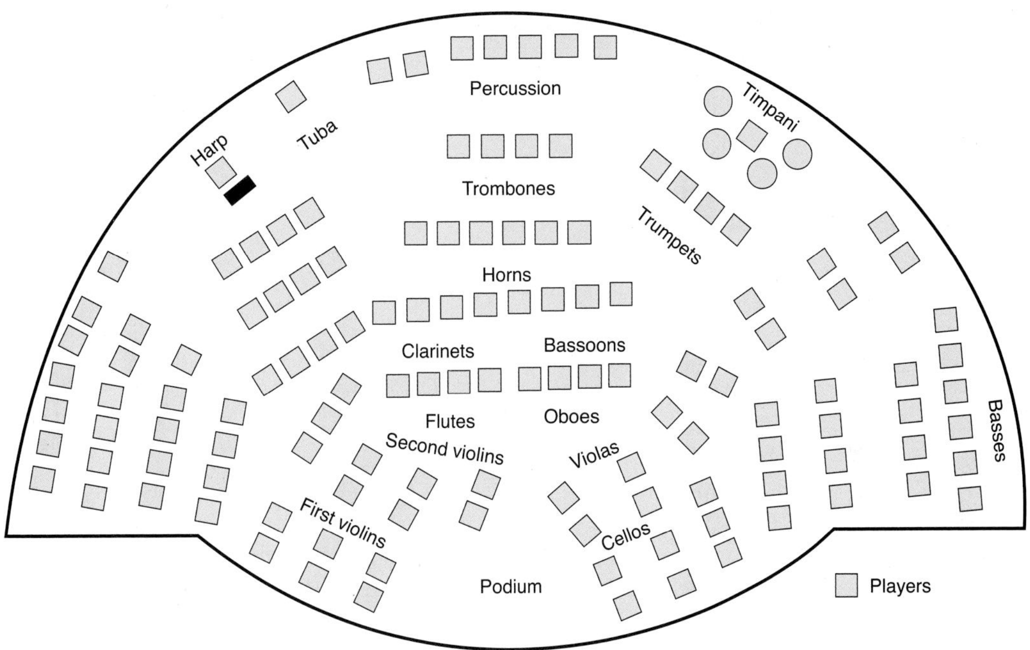

Figure 6-1 Typical Orchestra Arrangement.

2. Listen to Benjamin Britten's *The Young Person's Guide to the Orchestra,* subtitled *Variations and Fugue on a Theme of Purcell* (Purcell was an English composer, 1659–1695).[2] This composition features individual instruments and sections of the orchestra. Place the following diagram on a transparency or on the board and call out the number as each event occurs:

Technology Enhancement

The "Young Person's Guide to the Orchestra" interactive website is available through http://www.carnegiehall.org/ or directly at http://listeningadventures.carnegiehall.org/ypgto/index.aspx.

[2] Available from www.amazon.com.

Listening Guide: The Young Person's Guide to the Orchestra

1. Purcell theme played by the entire orchestra
2. Woodwinds play theme
3. Brasses play theme
4. Strings play theme
5. Percussion
6. Entire orchestra plays theme
7. Variations on the theme, each featuring a different instrument or instrument group as follows:

   a. **Woodwinds**
      Piccolo and flutes
      Oboes
      Clarinets
      Bassoons

   b. **Strings**
      Violins
      Violas
      Cellos
      Double basses
      Harp

   c. **Brasses**
      Horns
      Trumpets
      Trombones and tuba

   d. **Percussion**
      Kettledrums
      Bass drum and cymbals
      Tambourine and triangle
      Snare drum and Chinese block (brightly painted, wooden percussion instrument)
      Xylophone
      Castanets and gong
      Whip

   All percussion instruments together

8. A fugue, in which the theme is played by instruments entering one after the other, as follows:

   a. Piccolo
   b. Flute
   c. Oboe
   d. Clarinet
   e. Bassoons
   f. Violins
   g. Violas
   h. Cellos
   i. Double basses
   j. Harp
   k. Horns
   l. Trumpets
   m. Trombone and tuba

9. Brass instruments play the Purcell theme in a slow tempo, while remaining instruments continue with the fugal style

Band

In contrast to the large stringed instrument sections of the orchestra, a *band* has a large woodwind section consisting of clarinets, saxophones, flutes, piccolos, oboes, and bassoons. Brass instruments of the band include trumpets, French horns, trombones, and tubas. In addition, there are many different percussion instruments, particularly the bass drum and snare drums. Listen to the sound of a band in Sousa's "Stars and Stripes Forever" ([iTunes/Spotify].

© Ritchie Photography

Middle school band

Chorus

A *chorus* is an ensemble composed of many voices singing together. Large choruses, made up of soprano, alto, tenor, and bass voices, frequently perform works with an orchestra. Listen to the sound of a chorus in Handel's *Messiah,* "Hallelujah Chorus" [iTunes/Spotify].

Michael Newman/PhotoEdit

Elementary school chorus

Technology Enhancement

Selected Orchestra Websites

Explore the following orchestra websites for information on live performances for children, recordings, pictures, webcasts, YouTube segments, and other resources:

Atlanta Symphony, www.atlantasymphony.org

Baltimore Symphony Orchestra, www.bsomusic.org

Berlin Philharmonic, www.berliner-philharmoniker.de/en/

Boston Philharmonic, www.bostonphil.org

Chicago Symphony, www.cso.org

Chicago Symphony Explorers (for K–3), www.cso.org/orchestraexplorers

Cincinnati Symphony Orchestra, www.cincinnatisymphony.org

Cleveland Orchestra, www.clevelandorchestra.com

Dallas Symphony Orchestra, www.dallassymphony.com

Detroit Symphony Orchestra, www.dso.org

Florida Orchestra, www.floridaorchestra.org

London Philharmonic, www.lpo.co.uk

Los Angeles Philharmonic, www.laphil.org

Minnesota Orchestra, www.minnesotaorchestra.org

National Symphony, www.kennedy-center.org/nso

New York Philharmonic, www.nyphil.org

New York Philharmonic for Kids, www.nyphilkids.org

Orchestre Symphonique de Montréal, www.osm.ca

Philadelphia Orchestra, www.philorch.org

Saint Louis Symphony, www.stlsymphony.org

San Francisco Symphony, www.sfsymphony.org

Seattle Symphony, www.seattlesymphony.org

Vienna Philharmonic, www.wienerphilharmoniker.at

HOW TO GUIDE LISTENING

A teacher must have knowledge about the musical components of a piece of music. He or she needs to decide on the focus of the listening experience, choose materials appropriate to a given maturity level, and develop sequential and imaginative procedures. It is important for teachers to design listening lessons that are multisensory; that is, students need to do the following:

- Hear music
- See a visual that helps give meaning to the aural experience
- Be physically involved through movement
- Develop skill in verbally describing a musical experience

The Teacher's Role

When you teach a listening lesson, you are actually sharing a piece of music with students—in general, something that was unknown to them before. A piece of music may be familiar to some students. If so, the objective in the lesson could be to further their knowledge or understanding of the music. The same piece might be taught for different reasons at various grade levels. Each time students listen to a composition, they should grow in their understanding and interaction with the piece. Much, of course, depends on the music, for only music that bears repeating and is rich in musical information can be re-experienced with increasing satisfaction and enjoyment.

As you begin to organize and create listening lessons, it is important to keep in mind the following:

1. Have a cognitive understanding of the music. For example: Does the melody repeat exactly or repeat with variation? Are the rhythm patterns the same or different?
2. Understand how the music is expressive. Is the meaning found simply in the sound and construction of the melody, rhythm, and harmony, or is the composer trying to express an outside meaning as well? An example of the latter might be the way the composer Paul Dukas expresses, through musical sound, the story of *The Sorcerer's Apprentice* (see pp. 193–194).
3. Write clear objectives that enable students to focus on specific musical concepts or ideas.
4. Carefully and creatively plan steps that will contribute to learning.
5. Develop and implement evaluation tools that will determine whether the objectives have been met.

Guidelines for Planning Listening Lessons

The following suggestions reflect a basic philosophy: listening to music is *active* listening. The student must focus, concentrate, listen, and respond.

- Get students' attention. Intrigue them. Provide an exciting and stimulating beginning. Use pictures, charts, puppets, games, or creative experiences.
- Introduce the music. Remember, once you get students' attention, they want to hear this music that you are excited about. So don't talk forever. Part of teaching is pacing, knowing when to present an idea and when to hold back another idea.
- Listen to the music with students. Avoid looking out the window or deciding what you are going to do next. Your interest and enthusiasm will help keep them focused on the music.
- Get students involved physically and mentally. Ask them to respond in some way. They may clap the beat, trace the melody in the air, stand up or sit down on the verse or chorus, and so on. Repeat the music as necessary; one time is seldom enough.

- Keep the listening examples relatively short. Give specific directions about the kind of response you are seeking, such as "Place the arrows on the chalkboard to indicate the direction of the melody."
- Encourage spontaneous responses to music, such as swaying and finger tapping. Try to channel this behavior into desirable musical responses.
- Use only background information that contributes to musical understanding and is meaningful or important to the listener.
- Encourage students to listen to the music and not to you. Don't talk when you expect students to listen to music. Use the pause button if you must talk while playing a listening selection.
- Sensitivity develops gradually through repeated hearings; don't try to expose students to new music each week. You will probably be providing the first hearing of a piece for many students. You don't want it to be the last. Let them want to hear their "favorite pieces."
- Teachers need to plan ways to hear a piece of music (or parts of a piece) several times. For example, ask a question and then play 30–60 seconds of the music, focusing on that one thing (such as the instruments that are playing). Proceed with another task or problem to be solved (for example, listening to a distinctive melody or an aspect of the musical form), and play the music again. If there is a variety of student responses, play the music again to refine the answer/response.
- A class mirrors you. If you show interest and enthusiasm for the music, students are more likely to show interest. If you show insecurity, nervousness, and dislike of the music, they will often begin to talk, exhibit boredom, and perhaps become discipline problems.
- Fill the room with music. Be certain that students in all parts of the room are hearing a "near live" performance.
- When explaining a musical element such as form to students, compare it to familiar things. Metaphors such as blueprints, patterns in fabrics, and recipes can often help students understand musical form.
- Focus on building a repertoire of familiar music that the students want to return to often.

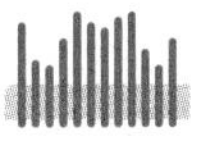

TECHNIQUES FOR TEACHING STUDENTS TO LISTEN TO MUSIC

There are many techniques for guiding perceptive listening. Some of these include (1) using visual representations, (2) using written listening guides, (3) learning a familiar song that is found in a composition, (4) moving to music, and (5) playing instruments.

Special Learner Note

Use pictures or icons to provide a visual tracking of the sections of the music. The teacher or a student (who may need some cueing) can point to these pictures as these sections of the music are heard. Students can then see the piece progressing as they move through the picture sequence, and may learn to anticipate certain parts, including recognizing when the end of the piece is near. (Figure 6.4 on p. 194 provides a very sophisticated example; it may be necessary to simplify pictures or icons for students to understand and visually process easily.)

Visual Representations

Visual representations are often highly effective in helping students follow events as they occur in music. For example:

1. *AB or ABA form:* Use familiar objects to diagram form.

2. *Duple meter* or triple meter: Create patterns of shapes or colors and place them on a chalkboard or bulletin board:

3. *Tone color:* Create cutouts of animals or instruments and mount them on tongue depressors (readily available from a drugstore or pharmacy). Use stick puppets to identify animals/instruments in selected compositions such as *Carnival of the Animals* and *Peter and the Wolf* [iTunes/Spotify].

Mapping Experiences

Mapping involves developing linear icons for events in a piece of music.

1. Figure 6.2 shows a "musical icon map" for the theme from Haydn's *Symphony no. 94* ("The Surprise"), second movement.
   a. Place the "map" onto a PowerPoint slide and project it onto a screen. Provide a link so that students can see it on their personal handheld device, such as smartphone or tablet.
   b. Download the music [iTunes/Spotify] and play with students "tapping" lightly on the "icons" as they follow the music.
   c. Have the students then look/listen for the similarities in the theme, identifying that "measures" 1–8 are essentially duplicated in 9–16, and that "measures" 17–24 are essentially duplicated in 25–32. Have the students diagram the melody on the board: A A B B.
2. Figure 6.3 shows a musical map for Mozart's *Eine Kleine Nachtmusik*, third movement. Place this map on a transparency. You may wish to use different colors to illustrate contrasting sections in the music [iTunes/Spotify].
   a. As you listen to the piece, ask students to move their right hands in the air as they follow the outline. You should guide the movement by using a pencil to follow the outline on the transparency.
   b. After students learn to follow the outline easily, call attention to the repetition, contrast, and then the larger ABA design by placing letters and geometric shapes on the board.

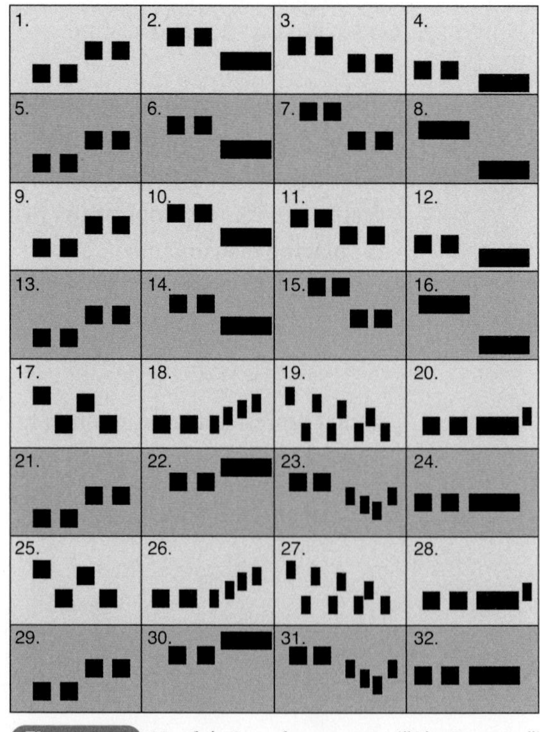

Figure 6-2 Haydn's *Symphony no. 94* ("The Surprise"), second movement.

Integrated Experiences

For an integrated experience, you could incorporate a variety of activities. For example:

1. Listen to Dukas's "The Sorcerer's Apprentice" [iTunes/Spotify].
2. Read the story of "The Sorcerer's Apprentice":

A sorcerer (magician) lives in a giant castle above the Rhine River. He spends most of his days preparing magic potions. His secrets are kept in a large book, which is placed in a locked box in his bookcase.

As the sorcerer's work increases, he decides that he needs an apprentice to help him. He hires a boy primarily to carry water from the river up to the castle. The boy has interest in becoming a magician himself but is somewhat lazy. He would rather sit along the river, play his flute, and stroke the sorcerer's cat.

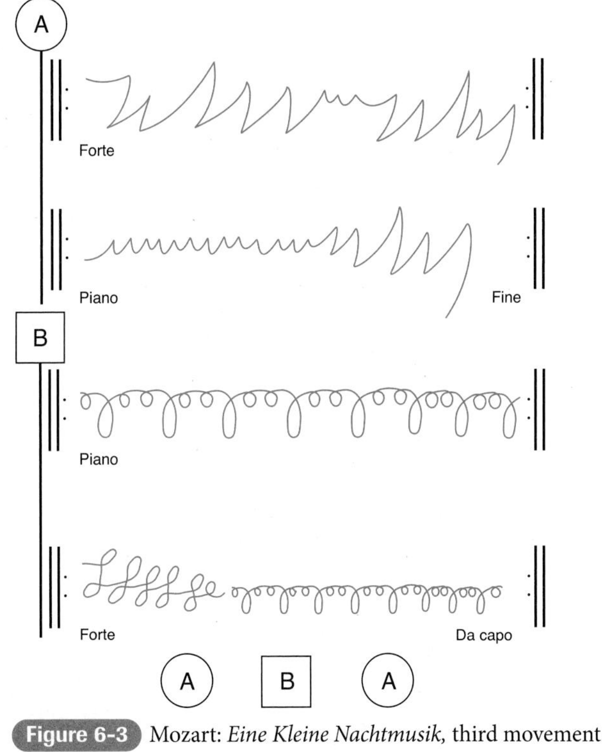

Figure 6-3 Mozart: *Eine Kleine Nachtmusik*, third movement.

One day the sorcerer has to be away from the castle on an important mission. He leaves his apprentice to look after things. When he is alone, the boy decides to investigate the magic book. He climbs up the ladder, opens the box, and removes the book. As he thumbs through the pages, he murmurs several of the magic words from the text, and suddenly there is a loud clap of sound that causes him to fall off the ladder. As he lies on the floor, the apprentice suddenly realizes that he has unleashed the magical powers of the book. He looks across the room and, as his eyes catch a glimpse of the broom, he has an idea. He quickly says the words "Abrah cadabrah," commanding the broom to pick up the pail and begin bringing water from the river up to the castle.

The broom obeys and begins to haul water. The apprentice is delighted and frolics around the castle while the broom continues to work. Everything is fine until suddenly the apprentice realizes that enough water has been brought to fill the huge tub, but the broom has not stopped its work. The boy repeats all the magic words but is unable to stop the rising water. He becomes frantic and grabs an axe, chopping the broom in half. To his enormous surprise, each of the resulting splinters of wood becomes a broom, picking up a pail and bringing more and more water.

The situation is now truly frantic, with everything in the castle afloat. All seems lost until the sorcerer suddenly reappears and, seeing the terrible mess, commands the water to recede. The castle is devastated, and the angry sorcerer gives his apprentice a sharp kick. The boy is sad but wiser, now realizing that his laziness and his opening of the magic book without the magician's approval led to his predicament.

3. Identify the main events in the story, and discuss how the composer might express these in music:
    a. Mysterious castle—soft strings and woodwinds
    b. Apprentice—loud, active melodies
    c. Brooms—melody played on bassoon, clarinet

1. Mysterious castle: Soft strings and woodwinds

2. Apprentice: Loud, active melodies

3. Broom: Melody played on bassoon

4. Water rises: Texture thickens

5. Water rises: Dynamics louder; texture thickens

6. Apprentice thinks, "How can I stop the broom?" Music continues in fast, agitated style.

7. Boy chops broom in half. Music stops.

8. Water continues to rise. Music becomes increasingly louder and higher.

9. Everything flooded. Music very loud and agitated.

10. Trumpets herald return of the Sorcerer.

11. Sorcerer's magic words: Softer, lower sounds

12. Water recedes; apprentice disciplined: Solo string; softer

13. Sorcerer kicks apprentice: Sudden loud chord

Figure 6-4 Images to accompany "The Sorcerer's Apprentice."

   d. Water rising—louder, higher
   e. Sorcerer—trumpets and horns, loud chorus
   f. Water receding—softer, lower, thinner
   g. "Kick in the pants"—sudden loud chord
4. Listen to "The Sorcerer's Apprentice" while following the pictures in Figure 6.4.
5. Show the DVD/video of "The Sorcerer's Apprentice" from Disney's *Fantasia* (www.amazon.com).

Written Listening Guides

Another effective way of helping students follow events in a musical composition is through a written listening guide. Here are some suggestions for creating a written guide for listening to theme-and-variation form in Franz Joseph Haydn's *Symphony no. 94* ("The Surprise"), second movement [iTunes/Spotify].

1. Listen several times to the second movement of *Haydn's Symphony no. 94* ("The Surprise"), each time focusing on particular musical elements.
   a. *Melody:* What are some characteristics of the melody (theme)? (Does it move by steps or skips? Is it major or minor?)
   b. *Rhythm:* What are characteristics of the rhythm (duple or triple meter, repeated patterns)?
   c. *Tone color (timbre):* What types of instrumental sounds are heard (strings, brass, woodwinds)?
   d. *Dynamics:* What types of dynamic changes occur?
   e. *Form:* How is the piece of music put together (e.g., theme with four variations)? How does the composer create each variation (add a second melody, change the tonality, add repeated notes, change the meter)?
2. From the analysis and discussion, list on the chalkboard the characteristics of each element as it applies to each variation.
3. Construct a listening guide such as the following:
4. Place the guide on a transparency or chart.

CALL NUMBER	MUSICAL EVENT
1. Theme	Main theme: mostly skips, repeated softly, played staccato
2. Variation 1	Countermelody in the high strings, stepwise melody, legato; contrasts with skips in the main theme
3. Variation 2	Melody changes from major key to minor key
4.	Countermelody added
5. Variation 3	Each melody note repeated as sixteenths; countermelody played by flute
6.	Returns to single-note melody
7. Variation 4	Full orchestra plays main melody; contrasts with ornamented melody (notes above and below the pitches of the main melody)
8. Ending (coda)	Sudden pause; return of main theme played by woodwinds

5. Select a student to point to the events that will be used to guide students' listening experience.
6. Listen to the piece and follow the guide.
7. Provide each student with an evaluation chart; ask them to circle the appropriate response as they listen to the piece again. Example:

THEME	MELODY MOVES MOSTLY BY STEPS	MELODY MOVES MOSTLY BY SKIPS
	Melody is played staccato	Melody is played legato
Variation 1	Countermelody Many skips	No countermelody Mostly stepwise
Variation 2	Major key	Minor key
Variation 3	Melody repeated with sixteenth notes	Melody as at the beginning
Variation 4	No ornamentation of melody	Much ornamentation of melody

The Familiar Song in a Musical Composition

One of the most effective ways to guide listening is to teach a song that is used by a composer in a musical composition (see pp. 200–201). As the student learns to sing the melody, it becomes easier to hear it in a larger context.

Technology Enhancement

Additional Techniques and Curriculum Materials for Guided Listening
http://www.carnegiehall.org/ORC/Games-and-Listening-Guides/

http://www.carnegiehall.org/ORC/Curriculum-Materials-List-View/

(additional curriculum materials)

Moving to Music

Although Chapter 8 is devoted to techniques for teaching music to students through movement, here are several suggestions for the teacher wishing to use movement as part of the listening experience. Young children in particular are in constant motion. They walk, run, jump, fidget, bounce, mimic, skip, and dance. Teachers can capitalize on this desire to move.

LESSON PLAN

Gould's "American Salute"

Activity: Listening to a piece of music as played by an orchestra; singing a song

Grades: 5–6

Concepts: Theme-and-variation
Familiar song in larger musical composition

When Johnny Comes Marching Home

Words and Music by Patrick S. Gilmore

Key: E minor
Starting pitch: E
Meter: 6/8, begins on 6

Gaily
mf
Em
Em
G
G
Em
When John - ny comes march - ing home a - gain, Hur - rah! Hur - rah! We'll give him a heart - y
Get read - y for the Ju - bi - lee, Hur - rah! Hur - rah! We'll give the he - ro

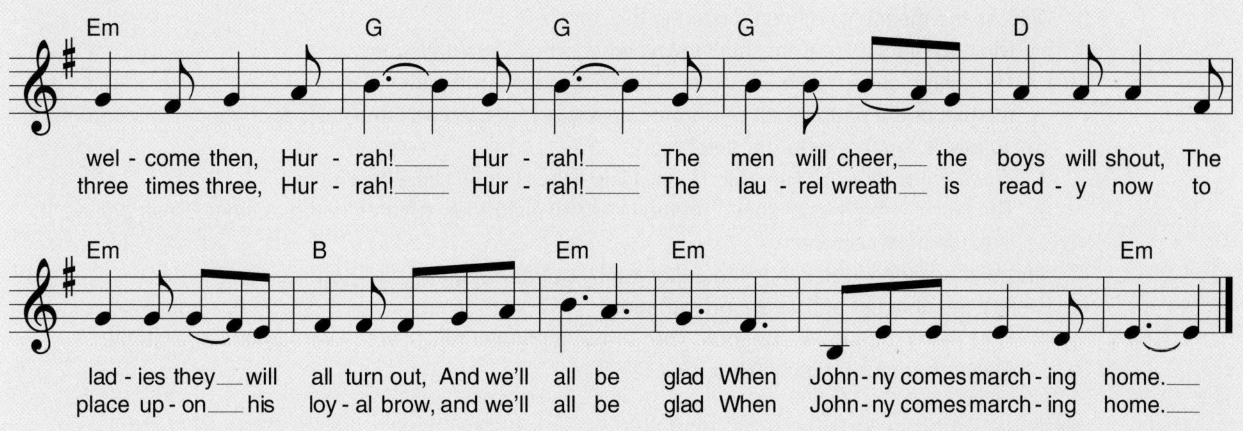

Em G G G D
wel - come then, Hur - rah! Hur - rah! The men will cheer, the boys will shout, The
three times three, Hur - rah! Hur - rah! The lau - rel wreath is read - y now to
Em B Em Em Em
lad - ies they will all turn out, And we'll all be glad When John - ny comes march - ing home.
place up - on his loy - al brow, and we'll all be glad When John - ny comes march - ing home.

NATIONAL AND STATE MUSIC STANDARDS

1. Singing, alone and with others, a varied repertoire of music
2. Performing on instruments, alone and with others, a varied repertoire of music
3. Listening to, analyzing, and describing music
4. Understanding music in relation to history and culture

OBJECTIVES

Students will:

1. Sing the song "When Johnny Comes Marching Home" with accurate pitches and rhythms.
2. Identify the song as popular during the Civil War.
3. Identify the song as a march.
4. Identify the meanings of jubilee, three times three, and laurel wreath.
5. Exhibit an understanding of form (theme-and-variation).

MATERIALS

- Musical score for "When Johnny Comes Marching Home"
- Pictures from the Civil War (download from www.images.google.com) and project
- Chart with words *march, jubilee, three times three,* and *laurel wreath*
- Keyboard, guitar, or Q-chord
- Blank 8½ × 11-inch white or colored paper
- Crayons or markers
- Writing board
- Examples of augmentation, diminution, fragmentation, accelerando, and syncopation on charts
- Recording of Morton Gould's *American Salute* [iTunes/Spotify]

PROCEDURES

1. Teach the song "When Johnny Comes Marching Home."
2. Show pictures from the Civil War and discuss the role (if any) of your state. Make students aware that the Civil War was between "brothers" in our country. "When Johnny Comes Marching Home" was one of the most popular songs to come out of the Civil War (along with "Dixie" and "Battle Hymn of the Republic"). The words were written by Patrick S. Gilmore, a bandmaster attached to General Benjamin Butler's command in New Orleans. It is a march with a strong beat.

3. Discuss the meanings of words used in the text.
   a. Most soldiers were from small towns where they were well known.
   b. The village church also served as a meeting house and place of assembly for the community, so the use of the church bell celebrated special events. We still ring bells for national celebrations.
   c. *Jubilee* is another word for celebration.
   d. *Three times three* = "Hip, Hip, Hurray! Hip, Hip, Hurray! Hip, Hip, Hurray!"
   e. The laurel wreath was placed on the heads of victorious athletes in the ancient Greek games. It is made of woven leaves.
4. Sing both verses of the song, accompanied by guitar, keyboard, or Q-chord.
5. Explore the concept of theme-and-variation:
   a. How many different ways could you "draw" the first letter of your last name? For example: Place examples on a chalkboard.

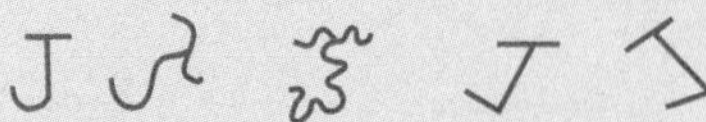

   b. How many ways could you draw a circle? For example:

   Place examples on a writing board.
   c. Using the "white sound" *chooo* held for 5 seconds, how many different ways could you alter it? For example:
   Staccato: *choo, choo, choo, choo,* etc.
   Scoop:

   d. How many different ways could you alter the melody of "When Johnny Comes Marching Home"? Examples: faster, slower, higher, lower, different voices, fragments. Experiment by playing the first phrase in different ways on the piano, melody bells, or recorder.
   e. Explain musical terms:
   Augmentation: Stretching out notes of the melody; for example, ♩♩♩ becomes 𝅗𝅥𝅗𝅥𝅗𝅥
   Diminution: Reducing the length of the notes of the melody; for example, 𝅗𝅥𝅗𝅥𝅗𝅥 becomes ♩♩♩
   Fragmentation: Breaking up the melody into small pieces
   Accelerando: Getting faster
   Syncopation: Emphasizing what is normally a weak beat
6. Download and listen to Morton Gould's *American Salute.* Follow the listening guide above. You can use individual guides, a transparency, or a large chart. Have a student identify each musical event by pointing to it as it occurs.

ASSESSMENT

1. Listen to *American Salute.* Ask students what *jubilee, three times three,* and *laurel wreath* mean.
2. Ask students how the composer creates each variation (fragments of the melody, faster, slower, changes in instruments, changes in meter, and so on).

Listening Guide: Morton Gould, *American Salute*, "When Johnny Comes Marching Home"

Call Number	Musical Event
1	Introduction is based on rhythmic fragments
2	Melody: Bassoon and bass clarinet
3	Bridge: Rhythmic fragments
4	Melody: English horn
5	Melody: Strings
6	Bridge: Brass and timpani play rhythmic fragments
7	Melody: High woodwinds (ornamentation)
8	Bridge: Woodwinds and strings play a crescendo
9	Melody: Use of rhythmic syncopation
10	Bridge: Meter changes from 3/4 to 4/4
11	Part one, melody: Trumpets and trombones (augmentation)
12	Repeats: Pianissimo
13	Part two, melody: Woodwinds (diminution)
14	Coda: Fragments of theme in imitation
15	Coda: Accelerando (gets faster)

Moving to Music

Although Chapter 8 is devoted to techniques for teaching music to students through movement, here are several suggestions for the teacher wishing to use movement as part of the listening experience. Young children in particular are in constant motion. They walk, run, jump, fidget, bounce, mimic, skip, and dance. Teachers can capitalize on this desire to move.

Songs Used in Larger Musical Compositions

Song	Composer	Composition[3]
"America" ("God Save the King")	Ludwig van Beethoven	*Wellington's Victory*
(American hymn)	Ludwig van Beethoven	Variations on "God Save the King"
	Claude Debussy	*Preludes*, Book II, no. 9, "Hommage"
	Charles Ives	Variations on "America"
	Max Reger	Variations on "God Save the King"
	Niccolò Paganini	Variations on "God Save the King"
Austrian Hymn	Franz Joseph Haydn	String Quartet, Opus 76, no. 3
(Austrian national anthem)	John Knowles Paine	Variations on "Austria"
"The Bear Went over the Mountain"	Ludwig van Beethoven	*Wellington's Victory*
("For He's a Jolly Good Fellow")	Virgil Thomson	*Symphony on a Hymn Tune*
	Virgil Thomson	Suite from *The River,* fourth movement
"The Birch Tree" (Russian folk song)	Peter Tchaikovsky	Symphony no. 4, fourth movement
"Camptown Races"	Aaron Copland	*A Lincoln Portrait*
(Civil War square dance)	Charles Ives	Symphony no. 2, third movement
"Chester" (American Revolution)	William Schuman	*New England Triptych*, third movement
"Columbia, the Gem of the Ocean"	Charles Ives	Symphony no. 2, third movement
(American Revolution)	Charles Ives	*The Fourth of July*
"Dixie" (Civil War/minstrel song)	Ernest Bloch	*America*
"The Farmer in the Dell"	Edwin Franko Goldman	*Children's March*
(play song)	Alec Templeton	Variations on "The Farmer in the Dell"
"Frère Jacques" ("Are You Sleeping?") (French round)	Gustav Mahler	Symphony no. 1, third movement
"Gaudeamus Igitur" (German student song)	Johannes Brahms	*Academic Festival Overture*
"Git Along Little Dogies" (American West)	Aaron Copland	*Billy the Kid*
"Goin' Home" (American folk song)	Antonín Dvořák	Symphony no. 9 (New World)
"Goodbye, Old Paint"	Aaron Copland	*Billy the Kid*
"Greensleeves" (English folk song)	Ralph Vaughan Williams	*Fantasia* on "Greensleeves"
	Buryl Red	*Greensleeves*
"Hail, Columbia"	Ernest Bloch	*America*
(American Revolution)	Charles Ives	"Putnam's Camp" from *Three Places in New England*
"Happy Birthday" (American)	Igor Stravinsky	*Greeting Prelude*
"Hatikvah" (Israeli national anthem)	Bedrich Smetana	*The Moldau*
"Irish Washerwoman" (Irish folk song)	LeRoy Anderson	*Irish Suite*, first movement
"Jesu, Joy of Man's Desiring" (German chorale)	J. S. Bach	Cantata no. 147
	Walter Carlos	*Switched-On Bach*
"Joy to the World" (English carol)	Charles Ives	Symphony no. 2, fifth movement
"Land of Hope and Glory" (English)	Edward Elgar	*Pomp and Circumstance*, no. 1
"London Bridge" (English)	Edwin Franko Goldman	*Children's March*
"Londonderry Air" (English)	Percy Grainger	*Irish Tune from County Derry*

[3] Most listening selections can be individually downloaded from Apple iTunes (www.apple.com/iTunes) or streamed from Spotify. Current recordings are also available in most record stores and public libraries, and on the Internet at www.amazon.com. Some musical selections also appear on YouTube (www.youtube.com).

"Mack, the Knife" (German opera)	Kurt Weill	*The Threepenny Opera*
	Andre Previn and J. J. Johnson	"Mack, the Knife"
	Louis Armstrong	"Mack, the Knife"
"March of the Three Kings" (French opera)	Georges Bizet	"Farandole" from *L'Arlésienne Suite*, no. 2
"The Marseillaise" (French national anthem)	Robert Schumann	*The Two Grenadiers*
	Peter Tchaikovsky	*1812 Overture*
	Hector Berlioz	*La Marseillaise*
"Mary Had a Little Lamb" (American)	Edwin Franko Goldman	*Children's March*
"The Metronome" (German)	Ludwig van Beethoven	Symphony no. 8, second movement
"A Mighty Fortress Is Our God" (German chorale)	J. S. Bach	Cantata no. 80
	Felix Mendelssohn	Symphony no. 5 *(Reformation)*
"Ode to Joy" ("Joyful, Joyful") (German)	Ludwig van Beethoven	Symphony no. 9, fourth movement
"Old Chisholm Trail" (American West)	Aaron Copland	*Billy the Kid*
"Old Hundredth" ("The Doxology")	J. S. Bach	*Cantata no. 130*
(fifteenth-century chorale)	Ernest Bloch	*America*
Henry Purcell-Clarke	Voluntary on	"Old Hundredth"
"On Springfield Mountain" (American folk song)	Aaron Copland	*A Lincoln Portrait*
"O, Susanna" (Civil War square dance)	Ferde Grofé	*Death Valley Suite*
"Pop, Goes the Weasel" (English)	Ernest Bloch	*America*
	Lucien Cailliet	Variations on "Pop, Goes the Weasel"
	Leo Sowerby	Variations on "Pop, Goes the Weasel"
"Sakura" ("Cherry Blossoms") (Japanese)	Eto	Variations on "Sakura"
"Simple Gifts" (Shaker hymn)	Aaron Copland	*Appalachian Spring*
"The Star-Spangled Banner" (U.S. national anthem)	Edwin Bagley	*National Emblem March*
	Charles Ives	"Putnam's Camp" from *Three Places in New England*
"Streets of Laredo" (American West)	Roy Harris	*Folksong Symphony*
	Virgil Thomson	*The Plow That Broke the Plains*, "Cattle" movement
"Toreador" (opera)	Georges Bizet	Overture to *Carmen*
"Twinkle, Twinkle, Little Star" (German-French)	Erno Dohnányi	Variations on a Nursery Song
	Wolfgang Mozart	Variations on "Ah! Vous dirai-je, Maman"
	Camille Saint-Saëns	*Carnival of the Animals*, "Fossils"
"When Johnny Comes Marching Home" (Civil War)	Morton Gould	*American Salute Overture*, "When Johnny Comes Marching Home"
"Yankee Doodle"	Ernest Bloch	*America*
(American Revolution)	James Hewitt	"Yankee Doodle" with Variations
	Charles Ives	*The Fourth of July*
	Charles Ives	"Putnam's Camp" from *Three Places in New England*
	Roger Sessions	Symphony no. 2, second movement

SUGGESTIONS FOR LESSONS

1. Listen to the Rondo from Mozart's *Horn Concerto no. 3 in E-flat Major* (third movement) [iTunes/Spotify]. Divide students into pairs and ask each pair to create a movement for A, B, or C. Be sure each pair keeps a steady beat. Practice the movement until students are comfortable with it; then have them perform with the recording. You may assist by pointing to shapes placed on the chalkboard.

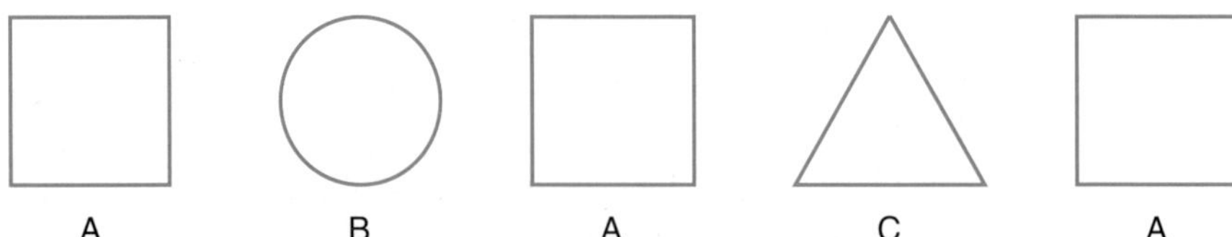

2. Invite children to respond physically to directions, such as, "Walk and change direction when you hear a new melody" (grades 4–6); "Pretend you are a rosebud opening as the music gets louder" (grades K–3); "Change partners when you hear a different meter or tonality" (grades 4–6).

Playing Instruments

Playing classroom instruments is a popular activity with children of all ages, and an important approach to listening to music.

SUGGESTION FOR LESSON: GRADES 1–3

Create an ensemble by combining several instruments. Orff instruments (designed by the German music educator Carl Orff) such as xylophones, drums, and glockenspiels can be used by either a few or many students to interpret larger musical compositions. For example, you may wish to use drums and triangles (or glockenspiels) to interpret the "Anvil Chorus" from the opera *Il Trovatore* by Giuseppe Verdi [iTunes/Spotify].

Drums

Triangles (or glockenspiels)

You may wish to alternate between the opening section, where all students can play, and the "anvil" section, where only a few students play selected instruments.

Sample Lesson Plans

The following sample lessons and teaching ideas are presented for use with lower elementary school students.

LESSON PLAN

Binary Form

Activity: Listening to binary form
Grades: K–2
Concepts: Binary form (AB)
Contrasting musical ideas

NATIONAL AND STATE MUSIC STANDARD

1. Listening to, analyzing, and describing music

OBJECTIVES

Students will:

1. Identify A and B sections of the music as being different from each other.
2. Identify like sounds and different sounds.
3. Identify melodies that are the same and melodies that are different.
4. Identify AB as the form of Berry's "Johnny B. Goode."

MATERIALS

- Pictures showing two contrasting ideas, such as winter/spring, boy/girl, red/green, or square/circle
- Cut-out letters *A* and *B* to mount on chalkboard
- Classroom instruments: wooden and jingling types
- Recording: "Johnny B. Goode" by Chuck Berry [iTunes/Spotify]

PROCEDURES

1. Show two contrasting pictures. Discuss how they are the same and yet different.
2. Show the letters *A* and *B*. Place them on the chalkboard.
3. Assign jingling instruments to five students and wooden instruments to a second group of five students. Ask one group to play (either by ear if in K–1, or from a chart if in grade 2) the following:

4. Select two children to be "machines" for A and two others to be "machines" for B. Children face each other and create a movement that will match the rhythm patterns.
5. Download and listen to the song "Johnny B. Goode" and follow the AB form. A and B sections repeat over and over: A = verse (music remains the same but words change with each repetition); B = chorus (music and words remain the same with each repetition).

ASSESSMENT

1. Ask what AB form means.
2. Ask students to name techniques used in class for identifying each of the A and B sections.

LESSON PLAN

Ternary Form

Activity: Listening to ternary form
Grade: 3
Concepts: Form: ternary (ABA)
Repetition and contrast

NATIONAL AND STATE MUSIC STANDARDS

1. Performing on instruments, alone and with others, a varied repertoire of music
2. Singing, alone and with others, a varied repertoire of music
3. Listening to, analyzing, and describing music

OBJECTIVES

Students will:

1. Identify the repetition of a musical idea.
2. Identify ABA (ternary) form.
3. Use classroom instruments to create a short piece in ABA form.
4. Identify ABA sections in Josquin's "El Grillo"; Chopin's op. 66, "Fantaisie-Impromptu"; and "We Wish You a Merry Christmas."

MATERIALS

- Recordings: Josquin Des Prez's "El Grillo" and Chopin's op. 66, "Fantaisie-Impromptu" [iTunes/Spotify]
- Score of "We Wish You a Merry Christmas" (p. 61)
- Rhythm instruments (jingle sticks, drums)
- Rhythm charts

- Colored and marked spoons (red = A, blue = B)

PROCEDURES

1. Clap the A rhythm and ask students to echo until they tire of it. Discuss why they got bored (same thing over and over).
2. Clap the B rhythm.
3. Perform three measures as ABA.

4. Choose rhythm instruments for each measure and play—for example, jingle sticks play A and drums play B.
5. Play "We Wish You a Merry Christmas." (Students without instruments should sing.) Discuss whether it is in AB form or ABA form. Does anything repeat?
6. Select two students to create a movement for A and another two students to create a movement for B. Match the movement to the rhythms. Perform together with instruments.
7. Closure:
   a. Listen to Josquin's "El Grillo" and Chopin's "Fantaisie-Impromptu." Raise red spoons for the A section and blue spoons for the contrasting B section.
   b. Ask students to diagram the ABA, or ternary, form as they listen.

ASSESSMENT

1. Discuss the meaning of ABA form. Ask selected students to create an example of ABA form using mouthed sounds or to rearrange materials in the room to reflect this concept.
2. Ask students the difference between AB and ABA form.
3. Ask students to identify a song in ABA form from the basal music series used in your school.

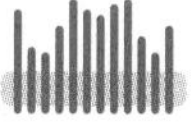

INTEGRATING LISTENING EXPERIENCES INTO THE CLASSROOM

Music and Drama: Opera

An *opera* is a story set to music. It incorporates staging, lighting, costumes, and scenery. In opera the dialogue between the characters is sung (in contrast to an *operetta,* wherein some of the dialogue is spoken). There are contrasts not only in the character roles but also in the types of music each sings. Some of the most significant musical sections are arias (or songs), which are accompanied by the orchestra. A favorite opera of children is Gian-Carlo Menotti's *Amahl and the Night Visitors,* which was written for television.

LESSON PLAN

Opera

Activity: Listening to an opera

Grades: 4–6 (This lesson should extend over two days.)

Concepts: Melody: direction, legato/staccato, range

Rhythm: tempo, meter, rubato

Tone color: female soprano (mother), boy soprano (Amahl), male trio (kings)

NATIONAL AND STATE MUSIC STANDARDS

1. Listening to, analyzing, and describing music
2. Understanding relationships between music, the other arts, and disciplines outside the arts

OBJECTIVES

Students will:

1. Exhibit an understanding of opera by dramatizing the story.
2. Identify techniques used by the composer to portray musical events:
   a. Descending musical line when Amahl goes to the door
   b. Slower tempo when mother goes to the door
   c. Use of trio when three kings sing
   d. Duple meter and brass instruments in "March"
   e. Contrast between legato and staccato, loud and soft, high and low

MATERIALS

- Recording: Menotti's *Amahl and the Night Visitors* ([iTunes/Spotify] and www.youtube.com)
- Chart with words *descending, ascending, staccato, legato, fast, slow*
- Stick or hand puppets: Amahl, mother, kings (Balthasar, Melchior, Kaspar), page, assistants

PROCEDURES

1. Tell the story of *Amahl and the Night Visitors:*

   Amahl, a poor shepherd boy who cannot walk without assistance, lives with his mother in a small, sparsely furnished house. He has a wonderful imagination and likes to tell wild make-believe stories. As the story opens, Amahl is seated outside the house, playing his flute and looking at the sky. After calling him several times, Amahl's mother becomes very angry and demands that he come into the house. Using his crutch, Amahl enters the house and, upon questioning by his mother, tells of seeing an enormous star. She doesn't believe him and tells him to go to bed. During the night Amahl hears singing and goes to the window. Looking out, he sees a procession in the distance. Soon there is a knock at his door. His mother tells him to go and see who it is. Amahl goes to the door, looks startled, and returns to tell his mother that there is a king outside. Again she doesn't believe him and sends him back. After two more trips to the door, he tells her there are three kings. When Amahl's mother looks for herself, she is greeted by the three kings and their page.

   She invites them into the house and soon leaves to find food and bring other shepherds to visit. Amahl asks questions of the kings–Balthasar, Melchior, and Kaspar. After the shepherds return with their gifts of food for the kings, two assistants entertain with a dance. Later, while the kings are asleep, the mother tries to steal gold from the kings for her child. A fight ensues between the mother and a page, who catches her in the act. The kings, however, tell her to keep the gold, for they are on their way to visit the Christ Child and He really won't need their gold. Amahl announces that he would like to go also, but that he has no other gift to give but his crutch. As he offers his crutch, Amahl is miraculously cured and runs and jumps in excitement. The opera closes as the mother waves to Amahl, who joins the kings on their journey.

Joy E. Lawrence/Kent State University

2. Use hand or stick puppets to dramatize this scene.
3. Download and play the opening section of the opera, through the part where the mother becomes impatient with Amahl and threatens to spank him.
4. Discuss what is different about this kind of conversation. (It is all sung.)
5. Point out that in an opera, the story is sung rather than spoken and that an orchestra provides the accompaniment.
6. Play the scene in which Amahl is going to the door to see the kings. Students should identify musical events:
    a. Descending melody to the door, ascending melody on return
    b. Staccato
    c. Repetition of "Mother, mother, mother come with me" text and melody
    d. Contrast of slower, legato, heavier sound when the mother goes to the door
    e. Smooth, legato singing in harmony by the three kings
7. Play the scene in which Amahl is asking the kings questions. Compare the musical answers of each king:
   Balthasar: Long melodic lines, smooth (bass)
   Melchior: Long, melodic lines, smooth (bass)
   Kaspar (who cannot hear): Fast, much repetition (tenor)
8. Create a procession of kings, page, and assistants carrying gifts. Play the "March" and identify the types of instruments used: trumpets, drums, woodwinds. Discuss the use of duple meter and staccato sounds.
9. The entire opera can be performed in 50 minutes. You will want to play a few scenes each day. Keep the students' interest with this continued story.
10. Closure: Play a recording of the opera and dramatize the events.

ASSESSMENT

1. Ask the meaning of the word *opera.*
2. Review the story of Amahl and ask students to point out the high voice of the boy soprano Amahl.
3. Ask students what musical techniques the composer used to tell the story (direction of melody, speed, legato, staccato, type of instruments used).

Music and Drama: Oratorio

An *oratorio* is also a large dramatic work, but it is performed in a concert hall without staging, costumes, or scenery. It is always based on a religious text and contains recitatives, arias, and choruses. One of the most famous oratorios is *Messiah* by George Frideric Handel.

LESSON PLAN

Oratorio

Activity: Listening to music
Grades: 5–6
Concepts: Recitative
Aria
Chorus
Text (word) painting
Homophonic and polyphonic texture
Jagged/smooth melody

NATIONAL AND STATE MUSIC STANDARDS

1. Listening to, analyzing, and describing music
2. Understanding relationships between music, the other arts, and disciplines outside the arts

OBJECTIVES

Students will:

1. Identify a recitative.
2. Exhibit an understanding of word painting in the aria "Every Valley Shall Be Exalted."
3. Distinguish between homophonic and polyphonic sections of the "Hallelujah Chorus."

MATERIALS

- Recording of Handel's *Messiah* ([iTunes/Spotify] and www.youtube.com)
- Chart with the words *aria, recitative, chorus,* and *word painting*
- Graphic listening guide

PROCEDURES

1. Explain to students that in an opera or oratorio most of the conversation or story is sung. In sections called *recitatives* the text is sung but with minimal accompaniment. The focus is on the expression of the text. Have the students experiment with composing a recitative.

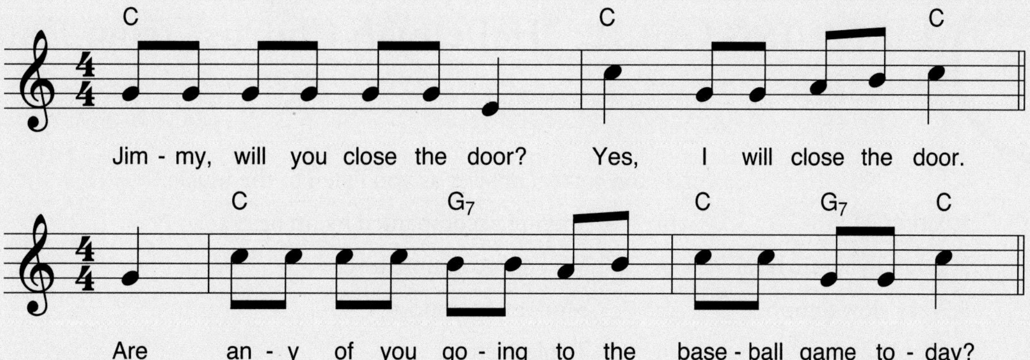

C
C
C
Jim - my, will you close the door? Yes, I will close the door.
C
G7
C
G7
C
Are an - y of you go - ing to the base - ball game to - day?

2. Download and listen to the recitative "Then Shall the Eyes of the Blind Be Opened" from the *Messiah*. Notice that it is relatively short and has little accompaniment.
3. In an oratorio, *arias* (an Italian word meaning "song") are interspersed with the recitatives. As implied in the name, in an aria the primary focus is on creating a beautiful piece of music with full accompaniment. Handel liked to use musical sounds to express the meaning of certain words. This is known as *text painting,* or *word painting*. Download and listen to "Every Valley Shall Be Exalted." Note that the word *crooked* is written with a jagged melody, the word *exalted* is conveyed in a long phrase with many repeated patterns, and the word *plain* is expressed with a sustained single-note melody.

   Write the words *crooked, exalted,* and *plain* on the chalkboard. Listen to the aria "Every Valley Shall Be Exalted" and have students follow the melody with their hands in the air, noticing how the music portrays the words.
4. A *chorus* is still another type of composition in an oratorio. It is sung by a large group of singers. Download and listen to the "Hallelujah Chorus" from Handel's *Messiah* using the following listening guide.

ASSESSMENT

1. Have the class briefly discuss what types of compositions are found in an oratorio (recitative, aria, and chorus).
2. Discuss what the term *text painting,* or *word painting,* means. On which words in "Every Valley Shall Be Exalted" would you use a "jagged" melody, and on which words would you use a "smooth" melody? Give a reason for your choice.

Listening Guide: "Hallelujah Chorus" from Handel's *Messiah*

Circle the correct answer as you listen to the music:

1. Singing Only	or	Singing accompanied by orchestra
2. Loud dynamic level	or	Very soft dynamic level
3. Very slow tempo	or	Moderate tempo
4. Duple meter	or	Triple meter
5. One line of music	or	Many lines of music

Music and Dance: Ballet

Music and dance are combined in the art form called *ballet*. Even though the music is written for a specific function, it is also exciting to listen to without the visual dimension. As with program music, knowledge of the story adds to the listener's enjoyment.

LESSON PLAN

Ballet

Activity: Listening to music and dancing a square dance
Grades: 4–6
Concepts: Syncopation
Rests
Contrasting tone colors
Different phrase lengths

BACKGROUND INFORMATION

Rodeo by the American composer Aaron Copland is a ballet whose story centers on a rodeo in the West. The dancers portray cowboys and cowgirls. In one scene a champion roper displays his roping talents. Another of the principal scenes is a Saturday-night dance that the cowboys and cowgirls attend in their finest attire.

NATIONAL AND STATE MUSIC STANDARDS

1. Listening to, analyzing, and describing music
2. Understanding relationships between music, the other arts, and disciplines outside the arts

OBJECTIVES

Students will:

1. Identify accents, syncopation, and use of pauses to express a square dance in "Hoedown."
2. Identify contrasting instruments such as trumpets, piano, and xylophone.
3. Identify repeated patterns that give the piece unity.
4. Identify different-length phrases used to create a "jerky" motion.

MATERIALS

- Pictures of rodeos
- Xylophone
- Recording of Copland, *Rodeo,* "Hoedown" ([iTunes/Spotify] and www.youtube.com)
- Cards with terms: *accent, syncopation, pause, repeated pattern, loud, fast, slow*

PROCEDURES

1. Show pictures of a rodeo. Discuss some of the activities, such as cattle roping, steer riding, and chuckwagon races. Use a xylophone to create patterns of sound expressive of these events (wide skips, fast tempo, pauses—rider falls off horse). Help students create some syncopated patterns.
2. Form eight selected students into pairs for a square dance. Have the rest of the class clap a steady beat as the dancers go through some simple motions.
   a. Head couple and foot couple: forward and bow; back to place
   b. Side couples: forward and bow
   c. Face partners, right-arm swing
   d. Face partners, left-arm swing
   e. Couples one and three exchange partners; couples two and four exchange partners
   f. Repeat dance
3. Point out that Copland wrote a piece of music, called *Rodeo,* for a ballet, in which men and women wear costumes and dance. One of the sections is called "Hoedown." Review examples of accents, syncopation, pauses, and repeated patterns. Download and play "Hoedown" and place these terms, along with others such as *loud, fast,* and *slow,* on cards.
4. Play "Hoedown" a second time. Have students select the terms and place them on a chart as they hear the piece. Any student may choose a card at any time, or you may wish to create a competitive game with two teams alternating.
5. Play "Hoedown" a third time and make any necessary changes in the cards.
6. Closure: Listen to "Hoedown" from *Rodeo* and choose cards from the chalkboard that are appropriate to the music as it is played (for example, syncopation, fast, slow, pauses, and so on).

ASSESSMENT

1. Ask what is meant by the following terms:
   a. Accent
   b. Syncopation
   c. Patterns
2. What are some contrasting instruments?
3. Can you identify any melodic or rhythmic patterns that repeat?
4. Are the phrases of the same length?

Technology Enhancement

Program Music Links

http://www.bbc.co.uk/schools/gcsebitesize/music/western_tradition/programme_music1.shtml

Search YouTube/Vimeo/TeacherTube for examples of program music.

Program Music

Program music refers to instrumental music that describes a theme or title depicting, for example, an event in nature (e.g., Grofé's "Cloudburst" from *Grand Canyon Suite*), an animal (e.g., "The Elephant" from Saint-Saëns's *Carnival of the Animals*), or a season of the year (e.g., "Spring" from Vivaldi's *The Four Seasons*). Students enjoy the challenge of discovering the unique ways a composer depicts a story or theme through music.

LESSON PLAN

Program Music 1

Activity: Listening to program music

Grades: 2–4

Concepts: Identification of low strings, high strings, woodwinds, and brass
Low, high; fast, slow
Wide skips, stepwise melody
Steady beat
Dynamics: loud, soft

NATIONAL AND STATE MUSIC STANDARD

1. Listening to, analyzing, and describing music

OBJECTIVES

Students will:

1. Identify the sounds of instruments with appropriate animals, such as elephant, birds, and swan.
2. Identify sounds that are low or high, fast or slow, loud or soft.
3. Identify wide skips, range of melody, steady beat, and dynamics and associate them with appropriate animals.
4. Integrate the study of *Carnival of the Animals* with language arts and visual art.

MATERIALS

- Recording: Saint-Saëns, *Carnival of the Animals* [iTunes/Spotify]
- Pictures or puppets of the animals described, such as elephant, birds, cuckoo, swan, and fish
- Pictures of the orchestral instruments used in the composition, such as piccolo, string bass, trumpet, oboe, xylophone, and violins
- Chalkboard or bulletin board
- Cards with words *low, high, fast, slow, thick, thin, strings,* and *brass*
- CD player, iPod, or iPad

PROCEDURES

1. Download and play the selection "The Elephant" from *Carnival of the Animals.* Show a picture of an elephant and discuss its characteristics (big, lumbering, thick skin, large trunk, and so on).
2. Use a puppet of an elephant to show children how to move as an elephant might (slowly, with big steps).
3. Show pictures of instruments: piccolo, string bass, trumpet, oboe. Play recordings illustrating each. Discuss which instrument the composer might use to portray an elephant (string bass). Place the following words on the chalkboard:

low	*high*
fast	*slow*
thick	*thin*
string	*brass*

Play the selection "The Elephant" again. Have children choose appropriate words and place them on a chart with a picture of an elephant at the top.

4. Integrate the lesson with language arts by having children write a poem or paragraph describing an elephant. Integrate it with visual art by having children draw pictures of elephants.
5. Follow this procedure for other animals represented in the work—for example:
   - "The Lion": Low, fast, rise and fall to the melody, punctuates the pacing (steady) beat of the lions' walk, low strings, piano
   - "Kangaroos": Wide range, staccato (jumpy), many skips, accents, crescendo and decrescendo, suddenly loud, suddenly soft
   - "Aquarium": Smooth, harp, glissando, celesta represents rippling water, mostly steps
6. Closure: Make a recording on which you feature five short "animal" pieces from the larger work. Place five pictures of animals in the front of the room. Divide the class into two teams. Affix all the words to the chalkboard. As each selection is played, have team members decide on the words that best describe the music. One team member places them under the proper pictures. The total number of points possible is determined by the number of musical events identified.

   Additional compositions about animals include the following [iTunes/Spotify]:
   - Copland, *The Cat and the Mouse*
   - Debussy, *The Children's Corner Suite,* "Jimbo's Lullaby"
   - Griffes, *The White Peacock*
   - Hovhaness, *And God Created Great Whales*
   - Messiaen, *Oiseaux Exotiques* (*Exotic Birds,* for piano and orchestra)
   - Moussorgsky, *The Flea*
   - Prokofiev, *Peter and the Wolf*
   - Rimsky-Korsakov, "Flight of the Bumblebee"

ASSESSMENT

1. Review the composer's use of instruments to represent animals. Discuss ways the composer uses these sounds to represent the animal.
2. Play at random three animal themes from *Carnival of the Animals.* Ask students to identify the instruments used, how they are used, and what animals the music represents.

LESSON PLAN
Program Music 2

Activity: Listening to program music
Grades: 4–6
Concepts: Melody: repeated patterns, narrow range
Rhythm: repeated patterns, steady beat, duple meter
Dynamics: loud and soft, echo effects
Tone color: strings
Form: concerto grosso (small group of solo instruments alternates with the orchestra)

NATIONAL AND STATE MUSIC STANDARDS

1. Listening to, analyzing, and describing music
2. Understanding relationships between music, the other arts, and disciplines outside the arts

OBJECTIVES

Students will:

1. Identify techniques the composer uses to express nature.
2. Identify the contrasting sections of the concerto grosso (small group of instruments and all instruments).
3. Identify different techniques used by string instruments.

MATERIALS

- Poems about spring: birds, flowers, the sun
- Paper and markers to draw pictures of budding flowers
- Charts: concerto grosso
- Listening guide
- Recording: Vivaldi's *The Four Seasons,* "Spring" [iTunes/Spotify]

PROCEDURES

1. Read poems about spring: birds, flowers, the sun. Discuss how nature, which has been dormant all winter, comes to life again.
2. Draw pictures showing the budding process in trees to full leaf.
3. Point out the delicate colors of spring (light green leaves, pink dogwood blossoms).
4. Download and listen to Vivaldi's "Spring" from *The Four Seasons* [iTunes/Spotify] following the listening guide on p. 350. Additional compositions about the seasons include the following [iTunes/Spotify]:
   - Haydn's *The Seasons,* "With Verdure Clad"
   - Vivaldi's *The Four Seasons,* "Summer," "Fall," and "Winter"[4]
5. Closure: Compare another season (summer, fall, winter) with "Spring." Discuss the different techniques that the composer might use. How does the music sound different?

ASSESSMENT

Create an evaluation chart from the listening guide. You may wish to include other musical information that you have learned.

[4] See "The Four Seasons: Teacher Resource Kit" at www.artsalive.ca/pdf/mus/tour2004/vivaldi2004_en.pdf

Listening Guide: Honegger's "Pacific 231"

1. Strings, woodwinds, brass; soft; train starting up
2. Woodwinds and strings joined by low brass; speed increases; becomes louder
3. Steady beat; staccato; imitation; becomes louder
4. Steady beat; staccato; clarinet, bassoon, horn, strings, trumpet, and full orchestra
5. Long theme: staccato, bassoon
6. Orchestra staccato; gradually gets louder
7. Staccato theme with imitation in orchestra
8. Contrasting melody played by clarinet, followed by strings
9. Brass instruments play staccato theme; gradually gets louder
10. Strings play sweeping, contrasting melody; clarinet plays soft running notes
11. Orchestra gradually gets louder; driving beat; imitation
12. Orchestra plays loudly; horns and trumpets play high theme above orchestra melody
13. Gradually slows down as train approaches stop

FURTHER SUGGESTIONS FOR LESSONS

Trains: ***Honegger's Pacific 231*** *(Grades 1–4)*

1. Show pictures of locomotives. Ask students whether they have ever ridden on a train or whether they have toy trains. Discuss the characteristics of a locomotive engine beginning to pull slowly with a *choo, choo* sound, and so on.
2. For young students, play a game with a leader as locomotive and other students as cars attached behind. They can move their arms as if they are the wheels. Ask one child to be the whistle. Consider how the train might move when going up a hill, down a hill, starting out from the station, and coming in to the station.
3. Select classroom percussion instruments and accompany the dramatization.
4. Read the story *The Little Engine That Could* by Watty Piper.[5] Discuss the way tempo is used in an expressive reading of the story.
5. For older students, listen to Honegger's "Pacific 231."[6] Use the listening guide.
6. Additional compositions about trains include the following [iTunes/Spotify]:
   - Brubeck, "Cable Car" from *Time Changes*
   - Rouse, "Orange Blossom Special"
   - Villa Lobos, "Little Train of the Caipira"

---

[5] Watty Piper, *The Little Engine That Could* (New York: Platt & Monk, 2003).

[6] Available from Apple iTunes (www.apple.com/iTunes), streaming from Spotify, or on Silver Burdett Ginn, *The Music Connection* 4 (2000), pp. 142–143 (CD 6–5).

Listening Guide: Grofé's "Cloudburst" from *Grand Canyon Suite*

1. Lyrical melody played softly by strings (canyons with huge rock formations bask in calmness of clear, sunny day)
2. Oboe and strings play lyrical melody with harp accompaniment; crescendo
3. Low strings play long lyrical melody
4. Woodwinds play ornamental melody
5. Full orchestra, strings play melody; crescendo
6. Strings decrescendo; cellos play slow, soft melody; repetition of short, melodic fragments
7. Loud splashes of orchestral sound; strings and piano go up and down; rumbling of timpani represents thunder reverberating through canyons, rain splashing against rocks, and lightning
8. Brass build in tempo and dynamic level as orchestra expresses fury of storm
9. Storm ends with decrease in dynamics and a slower tempo

Nature: Grofé's "Cloudburst" from the Grand Canyon Suite (Grades 5–6)

1. Download and show pictures of the Grand Canyon. Discuss where it is located and its type of climate. Ask students who have visited this "wonder of the world" to describe it to classmates.
2. Discuss what is meant by the word *cloudburst*. Consider ways that a composer might describe such an event through instruments (lightning—loud, crashing cymbals; thunder—roll of drums). Use classroom percussion instruments to create a musical composition that describes a cloudburst. Write an original poem about a cloudburst and draw pictures that express this phenomenon in nature.
3. Download or stream Grofé's "Cloudburst" from *Grand Canyon Suite* [iTunes/Spotify]. Use the subsequent listening guide.
4. Additional compositions about nature include the following [iTunes/Spotify]:
   - Beethoven, Symphony no. 6 (movement 4, "The Storm")
   - Debussy, *La Mer* (The Sea)
   - Smetana, *The Moldau* (a river in Czechoslovakia)

Listening Guide: Williams's *Star Wars*

1. Introduction: full orchestra
2. Main theme: high brass accompanied by strings, low brass, and percussion
3. Theme 2: strings, legato, followed by crescendo in brass
4. Main theme: low brass, joined by strings and high brass
5. Bridge: rhythmic and melodic fragments; ascending melody
6. Ritard (slow down): solo violin
7. Crescendo: repeated rhythmic fragments; brass and percussion; ritard
8. Faster: steady beat in percussion; block chords in high brass
9. Strings: short melodic patterns played fast
10. Main theme: low brass; block chords in high brass; main theme repeats
11. Theme 2: strings
12. Main theme: low brass, block chords in strings and high brass
13. Theme 3: low strings, legato, softer; high strings play countermelody
14. Accelerando to main theme: high brass, repeats
15. Theme 2: altered; strings play ascending melody
16. Block chords in high brass accompanied by strings, percussion; ascending melodies
17. Block chords repeated by violins; slower, softer
18. Full brass, percussion; crescendo; closing loud chords, ends with sustained low strings

Space: Williams' Star Wars (Grades 4–5)

1. Show the beginning of the motion picture *Star Wars.*
2. Discuss the music of the film and consider the demands made on the composer (e.g., music reflecting the characters and interplanetary travel).
3. Listen to a recording of the main title of composer John Williams's *Star Wars* [iTunes/Spotify]. Use the following listening guide.
4. Additional compositions about outer space include the following [iTunes/Spotify]:
   - Holst, *The Planets*
   - Perrey-Kingsley, *The In Sound Way Out,* "The Little Man from Mars," "Spooks in Space," "Visa to the Stars"
   - John Williams, *Return of the Jedi, E.T., Close Encounters of the Third Kind, The Empire Strikes Back, Star Trek*

Camptown Races

Stephen C. Foster

Key: Eb⁷
Starting pitch: B♭
Meter: 2/4, begins on "and" of 2

With humor

1. The Camp-town la-dies sing this song, doo-dah, doo-dah! The Camp-town race track five miles long, Oh, doo-dah-day. Oh, see those hors-es round the bend, doo-dah, doo-dah! Guess that race will nev-er end. Oh, doo-dah-day.

Chorus

Going to run all night, going to run all day, I'll bet my mon-ey on the bob-tail nag, Some-bod-y bet on the bay.

Lincoln's Era: Copland's A Lincoln Portrait (Grades 4–6)

1. Download and show pictures of the Lincoln Memorial in Washington, D.C.
2. Play performances of "Battle Hymn of the Republic." Have the class sing the song (p. 418) and discuss its use during the Civil War.
3. Teach the songs "On Springfield Mountain" (p. 418) and "Camptown Races."
4. Discuss the difference in text and style of music (e.g., quiet, lively).
5. Play Part 1 of Copland's *A Lincoln Portrait* [iTunes/Spotify]. Ask students to identify the musical means by which Copland expresses Lincoln's early life (soft dynamic level, open harmony, large skips in the melody, thin texture).
6. Review social activities that existed during the middle of the nineteenth century (square dances, Saturday-night "military post" parties).
7. Play Part 2 of *A Lincoln Portrait*. Ask students to raise their hands when they hear the fragments of "Camptown Races" in the music. Discuss other ways the composer portrays a Saturday-night dance (strong rhythmic beat, use of "fiddles," much syncopation).
8. Play Parts 1 and 2. Discuss in what ways they are the same and in what ways different.
9. Ask students to read the excerpts from Lincoln's speeches that are heard in the composition:

Listening Guide: Copland's *A Lincoln Portrait* (Part 1)

1. Introduction: Short melodic fragment (brass; woodwinds; strings)
2. Texture gets thicker and dynamics louder
3. Melody: "On Springfield Mountain" (clarinet)
4. Melody: "On Springfield Mountain" (oboe and strings)
   Melody: "On Springfield Mountain" (trumpet)
5. Fragments of "Camptown Races"; faster, lighter (clarinet and oboe alternate with melody)
6. Fragments of "Camptown Races" (trumpets)
7. Melody: "On Springfield Mountain" (fragment) (trumpets and other brass)
8. Melody: "On Springfield Mountain," in imitation between low brass and high brass; strings play a high descant above

This is what Lincoln said:

"Fellow citizens, we cannot escape history. We of this Congress and this administration will be remembered in spite of ourselves. No personal significance or insignificance can spare one or another of us. The fiery trials through which we pass will light us down in honor or dishonor to the latest generation.

"We even, we here, hold the power and bear the responsibility.

"The dogmas of the quiet past are inadequate to the stormy present. The occasion is piled high with difficulty, and we must rise with the occasion. As our case is new so we must think anew, and act anew. We must disenthrall ourselves, and then we shall save our country.

"It is the eternal struggle between two principles, right and wrong, throughout the world. It is the same spirit that says 'you toil and work and earn bread, and I'll eat it.' No matter in what shape it comes. Whether from the mouth of a king who seeks to bestride the people of his own nation and live by the fruit of their labor, or from one race of men as an apology for enslaving another race, it is the same tyrannical principle.

"As I would not be a slave, so I would not be a master. This expresses my idea of democracy. Whatever differs from this, to the extent of the difference is no democracy."

Abraham Lincoln, sixteenth president of these United States, is everlasting in the memory of his countrymen. For on the battleground at Gettysburg, this is what he said:

"That from these honored dead, we take increased devotion to that cause for which they gave the last full measure of devotion. That we here highly resolve that these dead shall not have died in vain. That this nation under God, shall have a new birth of freedom, and that government of the people, by the people, and for the people shall not perish from the earth."

Preparing Students to Attend a Concert

Many communities throughout the United States offer educational concerts for students in grades 4, 5, and 6. These concerts may be performed by professional orchestras such as the Cleveland Orchestra, the New York Philharmonic, or the Philadelphia Orchestra. In smaller communities, local orchestras and college or university ensembles fulfill this function. The cost is usually defrayed by funding from corporations, and sometimes students pay a token ticket charge. Some larger communities provide "docents"—volunteers who visit schools to prepare students for what they will hear; most schools, however, rely on the classroom teacher, who may or may not have received audiovisual materials from the orchestra's educational department.

It is not the purpose of these lessons to suggest proper behavior or attire, but to provide an introduction to what students might see and hear at a concert.

SAMPLE CONCERT	
Slavonic Dance no. 1 in C Major	Antonín Dvořák
Violin Concerto no. 3 in E Minor, op. 64	Felix Mendelssohn
"Trumpeter's Lullaby"	Leroy Anderson
"Syncopated Clock"	Leroy Anderson
"Triplets" (xylophone and three marimbas)	George Hamilton Green
"The Little White Donkey," Histoires for Piano	Jacques Ibert
"The Entertainer"	Scott Joplin
"Hoedown," *Rodeo*	Aaron Copland

LESSON PLAN
Orchestra Concert 1

Activity: Listening to music

Grades: 3–5

Concepts: Instruments of the orchestra: strings, brass, woodwinds, percussion, keyboards
Placement of the musicians
Role of the conductor
Role of the concertmaster

NATIONAL AND STATE MUSIC STANDARDS

1. Listening to, analyzing, and describing music
2. Singing, alone and with others, a varied repertoire of music

OBJECTIVES

Students will:

1. Identify, by sight and sound, instruments of the orchestra.
2. Define the role of the conductor.
3. Define the role of the concertmaster.

MATERIALS

- Basal music series instruments of orchestras (pictures and recordings)
- Recording: Anderson's "Trumpeter's Lullaby" [iTunes/Spotify]
- Small cards with words such as *soft, loud,* and *smooth*
- Large card with title "Trumpeter's Lullaby"

PROCEDURES

1. Discuss the characteristics of the four families of instruments (strings, brass, woodwinds, and percussion) in the orchestra. Use pictures from the basal music series books or large charts showing instrument families.
2. Download and play the composition "Trumpeter's Lullaby" by Leroy Anderson and ask students to choose the solo instrument from either the book or the chart.
3. Discuss possible reasons for naming the piece a *trumpeter's lullaby* (for example, soft, smooth, quiet). Write the descriptive terms on cards and place them on the board under the title of the composition.
4. Show a picture of a large symphony orchestra and ask students to identify the various "families" of instruments. Which sections have the most instruments? Which have the fewest?
5. Ask students to sing a familiar song, such as "Row, Row, Row Your Boat." Do not give any indication of pitch, tempo, or dynamics. Discuss some of the problems they encountered. (They didn't sing together, little or no dynamic change, couldn't decide how fast to sing, and so on.)
6. Perform the song again, but this time invite one student to conduct the performance. Point out that the role of a conductor is important because the conductor controls how the music is played.
7. Invite the students to sing, whistle, or speak "Row, Row, Row Your Boat" whenever they like. The result will be cacophony. Now appoint a student to be the "concertmaster" and give the starting pitch. Have everyone in the class tune to (or match) that pitch. After the leader is sure of the pitch, ask the conductor to lead the performance.
8. Dramatize the members of the orchestra and trumpeter playing "Trumpeter's Lullaby."
9. Closure: Play "Trumpeter's Lullaby" in its entirety.

ASSESSMENT

1. What is the role of the conductor?
2. What is the role of the concertmaster?
3. How many "families" are there in the Western orchestra? What are they?
4. Which "family" in the Western orchestra has more instruments than any other?
5. What is the name of this piece?
6. What instrument does it feature as a solo?

LESSON PLAN

Orchestra Concert 2

Grades: 3–5

Concepts: The orchestra concert
The string family

NATIONAL AND STATE MUSIC STANDARD

1. Listening to, analyzing, and describing music

OBJECTIVES

Students will:

1. Identify the violin as the solo instrument in Mendelssohn's *Violin Concerto in E Minor* (Rondo).
2. Identify characteristics of the violin: can play a wide range; can play very loud and very soft; can play staccato or legato; does not have any frets; has only four strings.

MATERIALS

- Recording: Itzhak Perlman playing Mendelssohn's *Violin Concerto in E Minor* (third movement, Rondo) [iTunes/Spotify]
- Pictures of violin, viola, cello, and bass (download from www.images.google.com)
- Basal music series instruments of orchestra
- DVD/video: *The Orchestra* (Peter Ustinov, narrator), strings only[7]

PROCEDURES

1. Show pictures of violin, viola, cello, and bass. Discuss their differences in appearance.
2. Play examples of each using the DVD, *The Orchestra,* strings only section.
3. Show and discuss pictures of a violin, including fingerboard, bow, mute, and lack of frets.
4. Indicate that in a concerto, the solo instrument plays both with the orchestra and alone.
5. Play a recording of Perlman playing Mendelssohn's *Violin Concerto in E Minor* (Rondo) [iTunes/Spotify]. Ask students to diagram the form on the board (A B A C, etc.).
6. Discuss the relationship of Perlman's talent to his physical challenges due to polio, a disease that affects the nervous system.
7. Closure: Play "Rondo" and ask students to raise their hands when they hear the main melody.

ASSESSMENT

1. What instrument is featured as a solo?
2. What are some parts of the violin? (fingerboard, bow)
3. What is the form of the rondo that you heard? (A B A C A)
4. What is a concerto?

Integrating Technology

The Music Education Premium Site contains chapter quizzing, Spotify playlists, and downloads of free MP3s of noted songs. Visit CengageBrain.com to purchase an access code or enter the code provided with your text materials.

Web Resources

- Search the Web (www.google.com) for information on listening to music including orchestras, bands, musicals, and opera.

Videos

- Access the YouTube playlist for videos referenced within the chapter.

Audio

- Download music discussed in this chapter from the Apple iTunes store.
- Spotify playlists allow students to stream music referenced within each chapter.
- Download free audio MP3s for the songs noted in the chapter.

CENGAGE**brain**.com

[7] The DVD/video, *The Orchestra,* narrated by Peter Ustinov, is available from Friendship House, 29355 Ranney Pkwy., P.O. Box 450978, Cleveland, OH 44245; 1-800-791-9876; www.friendshiphouse.com.Littlefield Education, 1984).

Questions for Discussion

1. Discuss some general characteristics of the four families of instruments found in the Western orchestra.
2. How is the conductor of a musical ensemble such as a band, orchestra, or chorus involved in creative music expression?
3. Discuss characteristics of several Western keyboard instruments that you might find in a school and the community.
4. Briefly discuss several electronic instruments that you could use in the classroom.
5. Discuss several possible "levels of listening" to music.
6. Discuss some guidelines to follow when planning and teaching listening lessons.
7. Discuss some teaching advantages of giving a listening lesson based on a familiar song being used in a composition. Cite several specific compositions and the songs used in them.
8. Discuss some ways of listening to music at various grade levels: 1–2, 3–4, 5–6. Cite specific musical compositions.

Assessment

Review ways the music standards listed at the beginning of this chapter have been met.

CHAPTER 7

Teaching Music through Movement

© Ritchie Photography

OBJECTIVES

Students will explore ideas for developing lessons based on:

- Developing body awareness in space
  - Movement as an expression of problem solving
  - Movement as an expression of imagery
  - Movement with no external beat
  - Movement to a beat with a sense of timing
- Expressing musical concepts through movement: The Dalcroze approach
  - Concept: beat/meter
  - Concept: fast, slow, getting faster, getting slower
  - Concept: accents
  - Concept: dynamics
  - Concept: rhythm patterns
  - Concept: melodic contour
- Interpreting musical ideas through movement
  - What inspires interpretative movement?
  - Abstract interpretative movement
  - Dramatic interpretative movement
- Playing singing games and dancing

National and State Music Standards

This chapter provides experiences with the following national music standards and related state music standards:

- Singing, alone and with others, a varied repertoire of music
- Performing on instruments, alone and with others, a varied repertoire of music
- Listening to, analyzing, and describing music
- Understanding relationships among music, the other arts, and disciplines outside the arts

Rhythm is one of the most basic elements of music. Nature has innumerable rhythmic patterns to which we respond (night and day, changing seasons, ebb and flow of tides); our physical system is subject to rhythm (heartbeat, respiration, digestive system, sleep patterns); and everyday activities require a sense of rhythm (walking, jogging, playing tennis, throwing or catching a ball). Thus rhythm seems to be a widespread phenomenon and an integral part of our human existence.

Children exhibit simple rhythmic movements from infancy. Newborn babies move within their own time and space as they stretch their arms and fingers and kick their legs. Later, as children learn to organize their movements, they walk, run, and jump. With maturation they develop more complex rhythmic movements for swimming, dancing, playing basketball, or performing on a musical instrument.

This chapter focuses on the use of movement to (1) develop body awareness in space, (2) express musical concepts, (3) interpret musical ideas, and (4) develop skill in folk dancing. It is based on the premise that a child's body, mind, and emotions are integrated into natural rhythmic expression and that through guided experiences involving movement children will learn to identify what they hear with what they do, thus stimulating their interest in and developing their skill with every facet of musical learning.

Teachers often ask, "How do I begin?" The following guidelines will help you generate ideas and techniques for musical learning experiences that occur through the use of rhythmic bodily response activities.

- Encourage the child's natural inclination to move.
- Encourage the natural use of speech, gesture, and body language to express thoughts and emotions.
- Encourage the use of various levels of energy (dynamics) and timing in movement, speech, and gesture (for example, hurried but forceful speech).
- Allow children to explore and find ways to "live" particular elements of the music (such as an ascending melody) in movement.
- Identify elements, concepts, or other aspects of music that children should experience (such as repetition or contrast in music).
- Pay attention to children's individual responses. Sometimes a child's response is so imaginative that it is worth having the whole class try it.
- Allow children freedom and opportunities to express music with their bodies in spontaneous ways.
- Encourage the completion of structured tasks that will, in turn, result in musical learning.
- Choose music for rhythmic activities that causes children to respond instinctively by, for example, tapping a foot (Sousa, "Stars and Stripes Forever") or bouncing and catching a ball ("This Old Man").
- Use a variety of music (jazz, popular, folk, classical, Hispanic, African American, Native American). Begin early to find music you like and make a list of possible ways to move to it.

Special Learner Note

Students who have some knowledge of or who are learning sign language may create movements/dances based on exaggerated forms of the signs of selected lyrics. Vocabulary may be increased, or at least reinforced, by using the signs in this context. Students who may be having difficulty demonstrating signs with fluid, confident motion may improve when they put the melody and rhythm "into" their signs.

DEVELOPING BODY AWARENESS IN SPACE[1]

Some basic tasks that involve children with music and movement include (1) developing body awareness, which will enable the child to move freely in space, and (2) developing the rhythmic ability to feel and move to a beat. When children can use their bodies expressively in space and can successfully feel and move to a beat, they are ready to experience movement in more complex musical settings.

When developing the body awareness that allows them to move freely in space, without inhibition, children should be involved in both locomotor and nonlocomotor activities. *Locomotor movement* means to move from one place to another, whereas *nonlocomotor movement* means to move within a stationary position. The four stages in developing body awareness are (1) movement as an expression of problem solving, (2) movement as an expression of imagery, (3) movement with no external beat, and (4) movement to a beat with a sense of timing.

Movement as an Expression of Problem Solving

Expressive movement may be used as a response to challenging statements, questions, or situations. These activities can also reinforce visual/aural awareness.

SUGGESTIONS FOR LESSONS

1. Ask students to respond to questions such as:
   - How can your hand move?
   - How can your foot move?
   - How can your whole body move?
2. Invite students to imitate a leader:
   - My hand can go up or down.
   - My hand can go over and under.
   - My hand can go fast and slow.
3. Draw expressive responses with statements such as:
   - Lift your arm slowly.
   - Lower your arm quickly.
   - Draw a square with one foot.
   - Make an S with your whole body.
4. Play the game "Simon Says." Create interesting and expressive movements.
5. Play music on a radio and turn the volume down to stop the music. Ask students to move creatively when they hear the music and to "freeze" when it stops.
6. Improvise sounds on the strings of the piano (tap, pluck, glissando). Ask students to respond by moving their hands, feet, bodies, and heads creatively.
7. Using only the black keys on the piano or other keyboard instrument, improvise in the low, middle, and high registers. Ask students to express the concepts of high and low by moving their bodies.

[1] This material is based on the work of Phyllis Weikart in developing rhythmic and spatial concepts for teaching rhythm. See Phyllis S. Weikart, *Teaching Movement and Dance* (Ypsilanti, MI: The High/Scope Press, 1982), pp. 31–42; also see the 4th edition of the same book (Ypsilanti, MI: The High/Scope Press, 1998).

Movement as an Expression of Imagery

In movement associated with imagery, the student's imagination is challenged by activities related to something previously experienced. Responses are limited only by the student's frame of reference; thus, "Show me how a snowman melts to the ground" assumes that the student has seen a snowman and has a mental picture of how slowly it melts away.

SUGGESTIONS FOR LESSONS

1. Ask students to express the following:
   - Show how a turtle moves.
   - How would you move if you had to carry a heavy pack on your back?
   - How would you move your hand if you (a) touched a warm stove, (b) touched a hot stove, (c) touched a sizzling-hot stove?
2. Using musical examples such as the following, ask students to move creatively (download or stream from [iTunes/Spotofy]):
   - **a.** Rimsky-Korsakov, "Flight of the Bumblebee" (fast)
     Ideas for movement: Move hands in circular motion; fingers "run" across tabletop.
   - **b.** Debussy, "Jimbo's Lullaby" from *The Children's Corner Suite*
     Ideas for movement: Stretch from one side to another, walk slowly with heavy steps, swing arms from side to side.
   - **c.** "Orange Blossom Special" (Charlie Daniels Band, Fire on the Mountain) (bluegrass)
     Ideas for movement: Rapid circular motion of arms (as for wheels of train), vertical raising of arms to "pull train whistle."
   - **d.** Copland, "Hoedown" from *Rodeo* (fast, slow, pause)
     Ideas for movement: Clap a fast beat, walk slowly, lift knees high, "freeze" on pause with both arms outstretched.
3. Sing "The People on the Bus" and have students create appropriate motions that express the words. Create your own verses and additional motions.

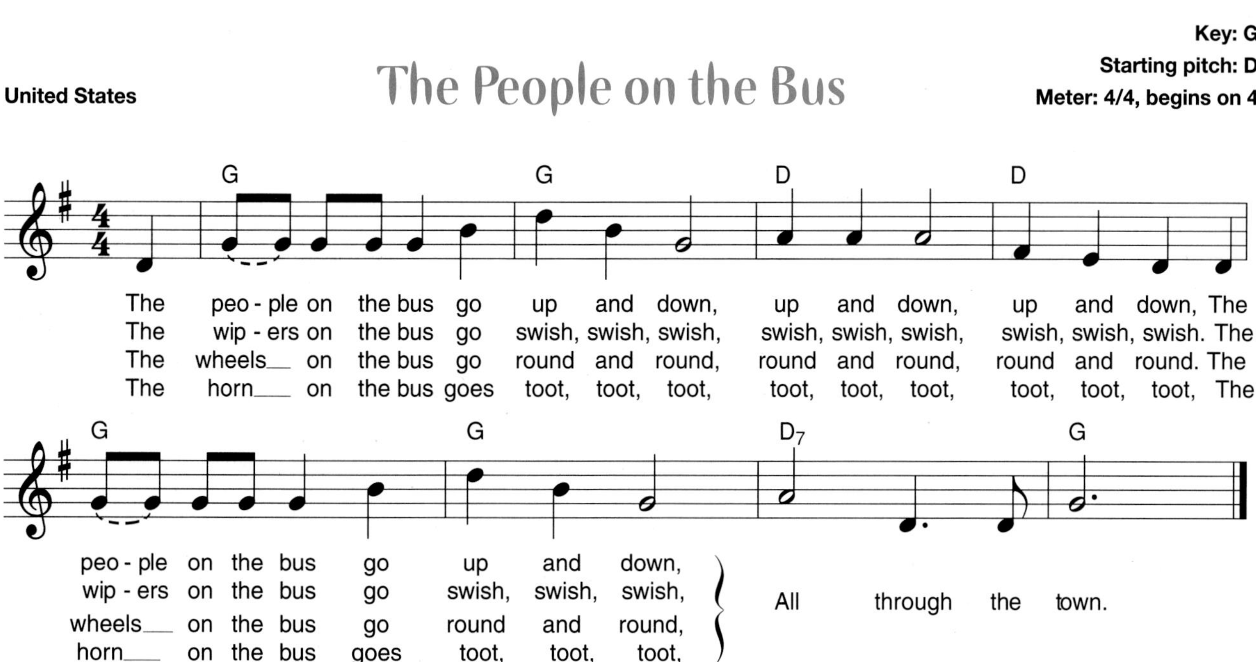
Key: G
Starting pitch: D
Meter: 4/4, begins on 4
United States
The People on the Bus
G G D D
The peo - ple on the bus go up and down, up and down, up and down, The
The wip - ers on the bus go swish, swish, swish, swish, swish, swish, swish, swish, swish. The
The wheels__ on the bus go round and round, round and round, round and round. The
The horn__ on the bus goes toot, toot, toot, toot, toot, toot, toot, toot, toot, The
G G D7 G
peo - ple on the bus go up and down,
wip - ers on the bus go swish, swish, swish,
wheels__ on the bus go round and round,
horn__ on the bus goes toot, toot, toot,
All through the town.

4. Sing "Little Tommy Tinker" and do the motions of raising hands high into the air on "Oh, Ma."
5. Sing "Eensy, Weensy Spider." The words of the song suggest movements that children might do. For example, the motion of the spider can be represented by touching the tip of the index finger on one hand to the tip of the thumb on the other, alternating hands as the "spider" goes up the water spout. Both hands, palms down, are lowered for "down came the rain." Have students create movements for the rest of the words.

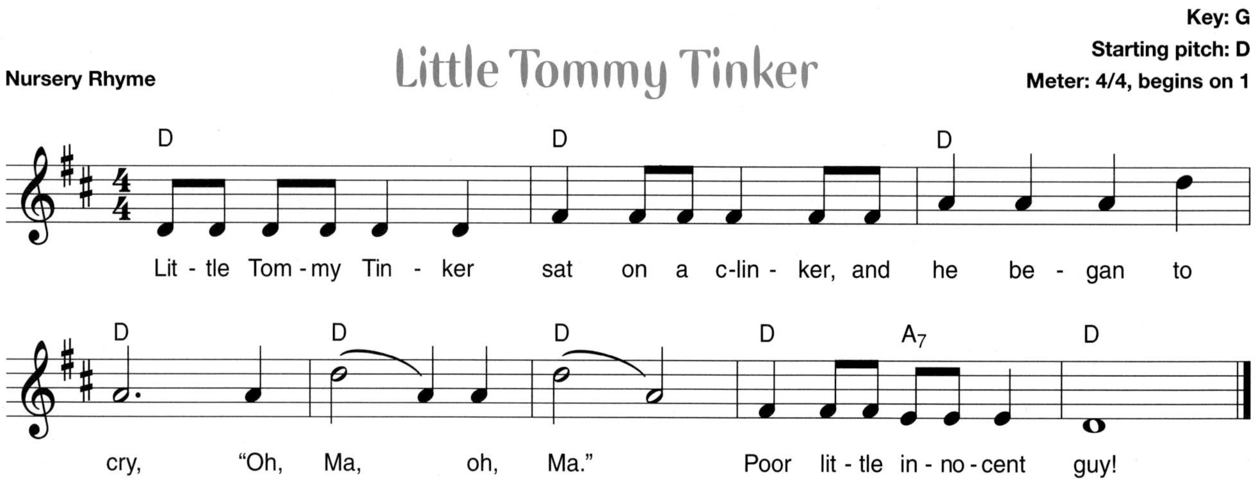

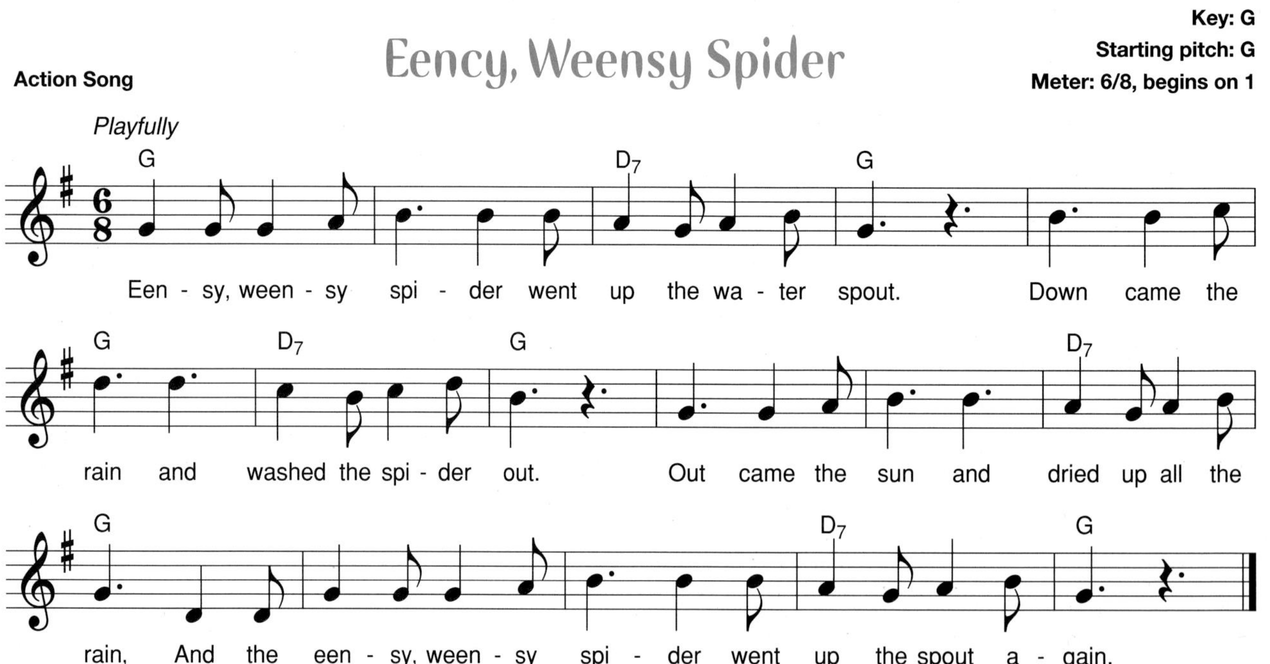

Movement with No External Beat

Another type of movement requires the students to move from one space to another freely and successfully according to their own beat or tempo.

SUGGESTIONS FOR LESSONS

1. Ask students to walk to the other side of the room as if walking a straight line. Play repeated chords on the keyboard or Q-chord.
2. Ask students to walk to the other side of the room as if walking a jagged line. Play black keys of the piano only—any series of skips.
3. Play or sing "We Wish You a Merry Christmas" (p. 61) and ask students to walk "happy." Sing "Lullaby" (p. 36) and ask students to sway slowly from side to side as if rocking a baby to sleep. Play or sing "I've Been Working on the Railroad (Dinah)" (p. 431); ask students to walk, letting their heads and arms be happy.

Movement to a Beat with a Sense of Timing[2]

In developing a sense of timing and the ability to move to a beat, it is first necessary to concentrate on the use of a single motion, such as patting the head. Use language as an organizer of movement and concentrate on bilateral motions (for example, "Both hands pat your head, both hands tap your shoulders"). Begin with body parts and create other activities. Sitting rather than standing contributes to a child's sense of security and confidence.

SUGGESTIONS FOR LESSONS

1. Perform the following simple movements and ask the children to echo them.

Teacher (says):	*"Head," points to head with both hands.*
Students (say):	*"Head," point to head with both hands.*
Teacher (says and does):	*"Pat, pat, pat head."*
Students (say and do):	*"Pat, pat, pat head."*
Teacher (whispers and does):	*"Pat, pat, pat head."*
Students (whisper and do):	*"Pat, pat, pat head."*
Teacher (silently):	*"Pat, pat, pat head."*
Students (silently):	*"Pat, pat, pat head."*

2. After many experiences with bilateral motions, add a drumbeat to a song or musical composition that has a strong and steady beat. Good examples include "Hahvah Nahgeelah" (p. 253) and *Grease* [iTunes/Spotify].
3. As perceptual-motor skills become more developed, create rhythmic sequences from the following more complex sequences of movement.

   Alternate motions: One hand or the other; one foot or the other

   Double alternate motions: Both hands alternate with both feet; two foot taps alternate with two shoulder taps

   Combined double alternate motions: Right hand to head/left hand to head; both hands to waist; left foot tap, right foot tap/both hands clap

4. Use such motions to express form, as in the following example. Phrases of eight or sixteen beats and clear repetition of sections help students discriminate among their movements.

   Musical example: Scott Joplin, "The Entertainer" [iTunes/Spotify] (4/4 meter, quasi-rondo: ABACA)

   Main theme, A: Pat head, tap shoulders

   Contrasting melody, B: Slap thighs, clap hands

   Contrasting melody, C: Tap chest, clap hands

---

[2] Based on the four-step language process developed by Phyllis S. Weikart, *Teaching Movement and Dance* (Ypsilanti, MI: The High/Scope Press, 1982), pp. 17–19, 24–27.

5. Sing "The Little Shoemaker." Ask half the class to tap a steady beat throughout. The other half of the class should tap the word rhythms.

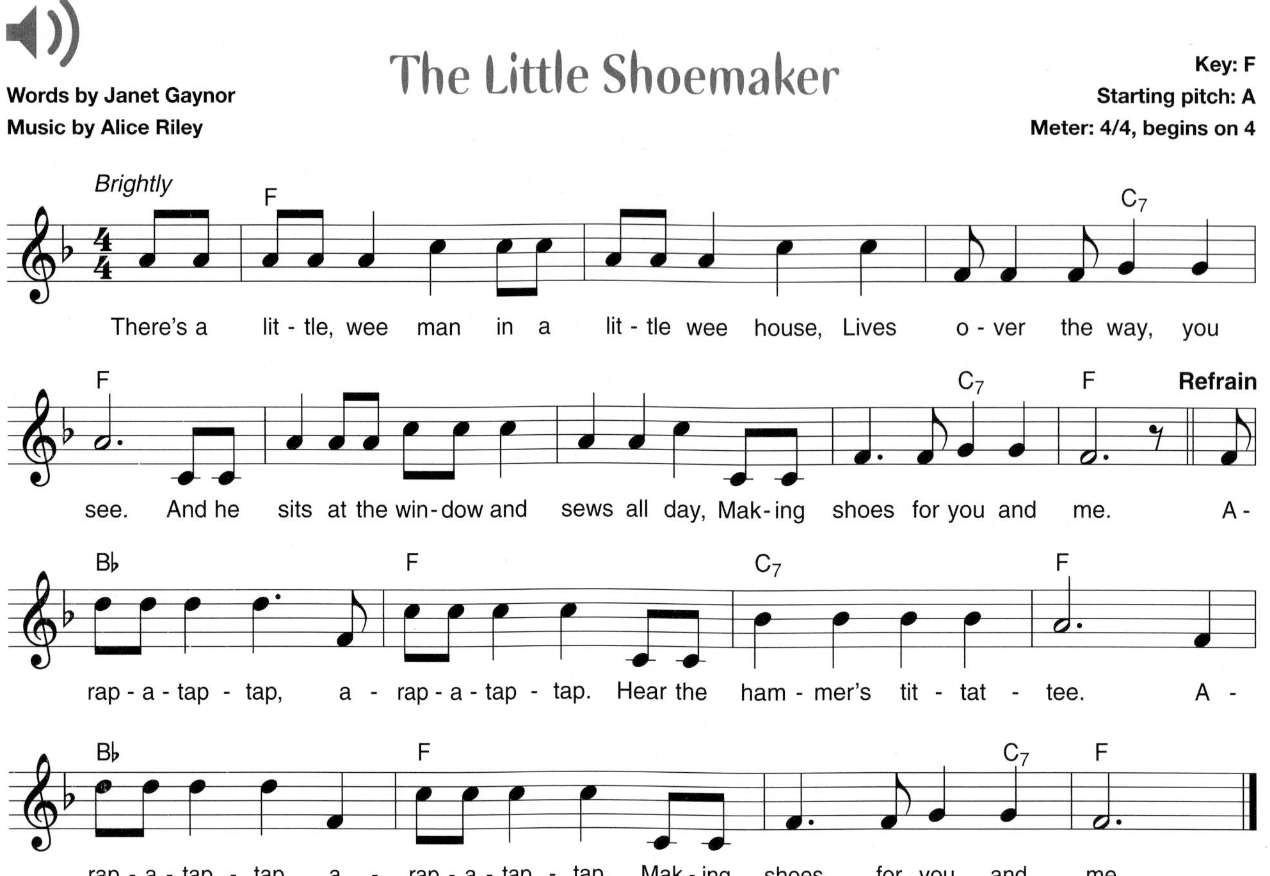

The Little Shoemaker
Words by Janet Gaynor
Music by Alice Riley
Key: F
Starting pitch: A
Meter: 4/4, begins on 4
Brightly
F
C7
There's a lit - tle, wee man in a lit - tle wee house, Lives o - ver the way, you
F
C7
F
Refrain
see. And he sits at the win - dow and sews all day, Mak - ing shoes for you and me. A -
B♭
F
C7
F
rap - a - tap - tap, a - rap - a - tap - tap. Hear the ham - mer's tit - tat - tee. A -
B♭
F
C7
F
rap - a - tap - tap, a - rap - a - tap - tap, Mak - ing shoes for you and me.

EXPRESSING MUSICAL CONCEPTS THROUGH MOVEMENT: THE DALCROZE APPROACH

Émile Jaques-Dalcroze (1865–1950) was a well-known Swiss educator and a pioneer in teaching music based on the premise that rhythm is the primary element.[3] His approach to teaching music consisted of three parts: eurhythmics (rhythmic movement), solfège (ear training), and improvisation. Through his teaching Dalcroze advocated developing the whole child, which he saw as involving physical and muscular control, mental awareness, social consciousness, and emotional health.

Technology Enhancement

"Dance Dance Revolution (DDR)" video game: Many school physical education teachers are already utilizing this video game to get students moving. Music educators can utilize the game to help re-enforce and motivate students to move in time with the beat of a song. This can also be a great "reward" activity at the end of a unit or after a major performance. In most major metropolitan areas, party rental businesses will rent out complete DDR systems for a minimal cost. If you do not have DDR rental in the budget, borrow one from a student or parent and simply place carpet squares or colored paper on the floor for students to practice on.

[3] See Virginia H. Mead, *Dalcroze Eurhythmics in Today's Music Classroom* (New York: Shott, 1994).

Creatas/PhotoLibrary

The system known as *eurhythmics* (meaning "good rhythm") focuses on developing the child's rhythmic potential through the use of his or her own body. Through experiences with natural movement, eurhythmics offers opportunities for developing keener hearing, concentration, mental alertness to musical elements, rhythmic control, coordination, flexibility, recognition and understanding of musical symbols, and appreciation of expressive qualities of music. Students are also asked to improvise rhythm patterns on a pitch or pitches and to improvise melodies, rondos, and moods by using percussion instruments. The study of eurhythmics is based on the following concepts:

1. The use of the whole body, involving the larger muscle groups, ensures a more vivid realization of rhythmic experience than does the more customary use of the extremities, such as the hands in clapping and the feet in tapping.
2. The physical coordination developed in the well-directed rhythm class gives the individual power to control his or her movements in related activities. This is especially true in regard to instrumental skills, where coordination is difficult and specialized.
3. Bodily movement acts as a reference for the interpretation of rhythm symbols, which become truly significant when learned as the result of a vital rhythmic experience.
4. Children develop habits of listening as they engage in the process of identifying what they *hear* with what they *do*.
5. Body, mind, and emotion are integrated in rhythmic expression.
6. The freedom of expression that is a cardinal principle in eurhythmics stimulates the creative impulse in every department of musical learning.[4]

The following section includes some basic concepts of rhythm, with specific suggestions for presentation to students according to Dalcroze's ideas. More information about Dalcroze and his philosophy, as well as workshops and training programs, can be found on the Dalcroze Society of America website at www.dalcrozeusa.org.

[4] Elsa Findlay, *Rhythm and Movement* (Easton, IL: Summy-Birchard, 1971), p. 2.

Concept: Beat/Meter

As students' perceptions of music are developed, their attention should be focused on the steady beat in music. A *beat* is a regularly recurring pulse in music, which may be strong, with heavy accents, or weak, with little or no accent. Grouping beats according to accents creates *meter,* which may be in groups of twos or threes or in combinations of four, five, six, seven, and so on.

SUGGESTIONS FOR LESSONS

1. Feeling the beat: Set a pendulum (or metronome) in motion. Have students say the word *swing* as they move to it. Vary the speed. Add something as simple as a finger cymbal or two pitches on a xylophone for each swing. Use familiar music with a strong beat, and encourage students to speak, chant, swing their arms, and move their whole body to the beat.
2. Feeling accents:
   - **a.** Sing, play, or listen to the songs "Yankee Doodle" (pp. 135, 368), "I'd Llike to Teach the World to Sing," and "Chim Chim Cher-ee (from *Mary Poppins*)" [iTunes/ Spotify]. Put a gentle push or weight on the first beat of every measure. Ask students to listen and respond by "lifting a low-hanging cloud back up into the sky" when they feel the music "lift."
   - **b.** Sing, play, or listen to "76 Trombones" (from *The Music Man* by Meredith Willson) or "Bicycle Built for Two" [iTunes/Spotify]. Give balloons to small groups of four or five children. Ask them to "lift" the balloons when the music seems to say "lift" (on the accent).
3. Feeling meter:
   - **a.** Use balls for developing coordination and discovering a feeling for beat. Individually or with partners, have students bounce a ball on the accent and then catch it. (You could play beats on drums or chords on a piano; caution students not to bounce the ball indiscriminately.) As the students say "One" on the accented beat, they will develop a feeling for groupings of twos and threes.

```
>       >
1   2   1   2
>           >
1   2   3   1   2   3
```

     After students can feel duple and triple meter, ask them to bounce the ball to changing meters. Have them say "Bounce, catch" (duple), or "Bounce, catch, hold" (triple).

```
>       >       >           >
1   2   1   2   1   2   3   1   2   3
```

   - **b.** Have students use their arms and upper bodies to find a swing in twos (two beats), then to find a swing in threes.
   - **c.** Have students find the accent and move their bodies or bounce balls to the following meters (music available from [iTunes/Spotify]).
     - *Duple meter:* Current rock or country-and-western, and songs such as "Consider Yourself" from *Oliver,* "It's a Small World," "This Land Is Your Land," "I'd Like to Teach the World to Sing," and "The Candy Man."
     - *Triple meter:* Songs such as "Edelweiss" from *The Sound of Music,* "Roll On, Columbia" (p. 388), and "Did You Ever See a Lassie?" (p. 109).

Concept: Fast, Slow, Getting Faster, Getting Slower

SUGGESTIONS FOR LESSONS: GRADES K–3

1. Download and play "The Little Shepherd" from *The Children's Corner Suite* by Debussy [iTunes/Spotify]. Ask students to respond with small and larger movements of hands, arms, and bodies as the music varies from slow to fast. Explore other types of physical expression, such as walking quickly and then slowly as the music changes. Use fingers to do the walking or running over the desktop.
2. Download and play "Little Train of the Caipira" by Villa Lobos, *Bachianas brasileiras no. 2, Toccata* [iTunes/Spotify]. Ask students to sit in a circle. Pass a large yarn ball to the right when the music gets faster and to the left when the music gets slower.
3. Try similar experiences with the following pieces [iTunes/Spotify].
   - Saint-Saëns, "Tortoises" from *Carnival of the Animals* (slow)
   - Rimsky-Korsakov, "Flight of the Bumblebee" (fast)
   - Grieg, "In the Hall of the Mountain King" from *Peer Gynt Suite,* op. 46, no. 1 (slow, becoming fast)

SUGGESTIONS FOR LESSONS: GRADES 4–6

(Download or stream from [iTunes/Spotify]):

1. Play sections of "Pacific 231" by Honegger. As the tempo changes from slow to fast to slow, ask students to respond by raising or lowering their arms. Point out the tension at both slow and fast tempos.
2. Dramatize the opening train scene from the musical *The Music Man.* Students should illustrate through their movements a train starting slowly, becoming fast, and then slowing down.
3. Many other musical compositions use tempo to express a mood, idea, or feeling. Encourage students to improvise free, creative movements as expressions of slow, fast, or slow-fast-slow, using the following pieces:
   - Chopin, "Fantaisie-Impromptu," op. 66 (fast-slow-fast)
   - Prokofiev, Sonata no. 7 (III) (fast)
   - Mozart, Clarinet Concerto in E-flat (II) (slow)
   - Tchaikovsky, "Arabian Dance" from *The Nutcracker* (slow)

Concept: Accents

Many musical compositions use *accents* as an expressive device. Encourage students to use free, creative movements to express accents as they occur in music.

SUGGESTIONS FOR LESSONS: GRADES K–3

1. Play the following rhythms on a drum. Ask students to sit in a circle and raise or lower yarn balls as accents are played.

2. Download or stream and play "Golliwog's Cakewalk" from *The Children's Corner Suite* by Debussy [iTunes/Spotify]. Ask students to make tight fists and then open their hands suddenly as they hear accents. Then have them stand and relax their bodies, with arms hanging loosely at the sides, and tighten their muscles for the accents.

SUGGESTIONS FOR LESSONS: GRADES 4–6

1. Invite students to create a designated movement on the accents in each of the following:

2. Apply movements denoting proper accents to any of the following pieces [iTunes/Spotify]:
   - Stravinsky, "Adoration of the Earth/Harbingers of Spring" from *Rite of Spring*
   - Bernstein, "America" from *West Side Story*
   - Bruch, Violin Concerto in G Minor, op. 26, no. 1 (III: Finale)

Concept: Dynamics

The body is an important means by which a child can be made aware of the role of *dynamics* in music. Movement experiences should include quiet, slow movements as well as sudden and gradual changes in energy levels.

SUGGESTIONS FOR LESSONS: GRADES K–3

1. Ask students to draw a big circle when the sound is loud and a small circle when the sound is soft. Play an echo game with movement as the response.
2. Download or stream and listen to the song "Frosty the Snowman" [iTunes/Spotify]. Discuss how the music gets softer when expressing the words "but he waved good-bye." Have students pretend to be snowmen and melt to the ground as the music gets softer.

SUGGESTIONS FOR LESSONS: GRADES 4–6

[iTunes/Spotify]

1. Download or stream and play portions of Beethoven's "The Storm" from Symphony no. 6 (*Pastorale*) or Grofé's "Cloudburst" from *Grand Canyon Suite*. Ask students to decide how to move in their own space in such a way that they show more energy as the storm intensifies and less energy as the storm recedes. Follow up this activity with a discussion about how students decided on the amount of energy to use, when to change it, and what in the music caused the change (dynamics: loud/soft/accents).

2. Download and listen to Debussy's "The Sunken Cathedral" from *Preludes* Book I. It begins softly as the mystical cathedral rises through the mist. The music gets louder as the cathedral comes into full view with its bells tolling, and then gradually gets softer as the cathedral vanishes from view. Ask students to interpret the dynamics of this piece with their bodies. You might begin by having them lie on the floor, curled up tightly to represent the soft dynamics of the beginning. As they stretch and expand their bodies with larger motions, they may express louder dynamics. Returning to the still, quiet position on the floor signifies the return of the cathedral to the hidden depths of the imagination and the soft dynamics of the ending.

Concept: Rhythm Patterns

When long and short sounds are put together and then repeated, a *rhythm pattern* results. If this pattern is placed in a melody, *melodic rhythm* is created. For example: ♫ ♩ is a melodic rhythm in the song "Jingle Bells" (p. 87).

SUGGESTIONS FOR LESSONS: GRADES K–3

1. To prepare students for stepping rhythmic patterns, have them walk, run, take giant steps, or "swim," skip, and gallop to improvised music played on the drum, piano, or other instrument. When improvising for basic rhythmic movement, the "walk" is a quarter note, the "running" is eighth notes, the "swims" are half notes, and the "skip" and "gallop" are dotted rhythms fitting within a quarter beat.
   a. Play stop-and-go games: The teacher plays for a movement and the students do the movement indicated by the teacher's improvisation, stopping and moving with the sound of the music. Students may move in a circle or randomly around the room.
   b. Students form short lines of four to six children. The teacher plays for basic rhythmic movement. The students move with the music and stop when the music stops. On the stop, the child who is the line leader continues to move and goes to the end of the line, thus designating a new leader.
   c. The teacher assigns rhythm values to the movements as follows:

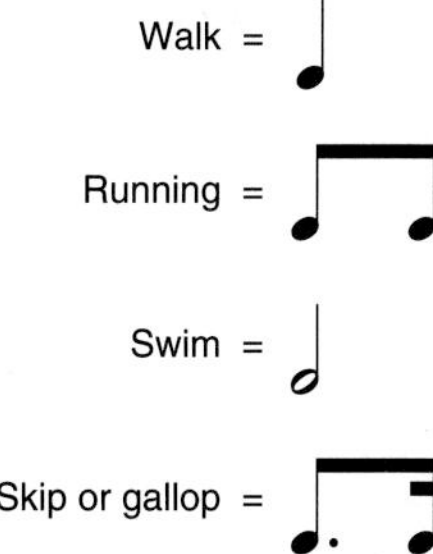

2. Have students step the rhythm for "Are You Sleeping?" and determine the movement words that are used. Translate the movement words into rhythmic notation as follows:

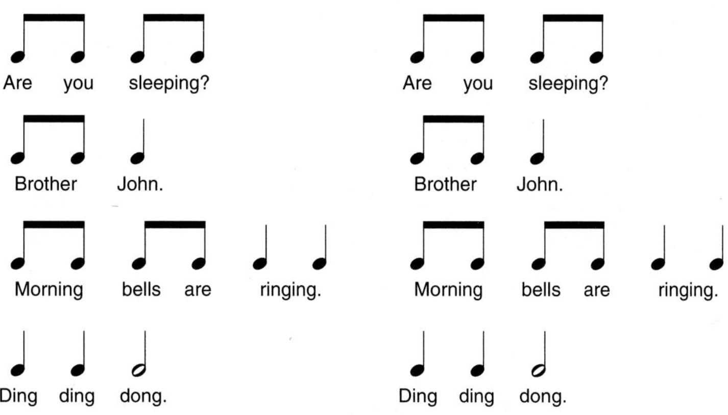

3. Use children's names or seasonal words to put note values together.

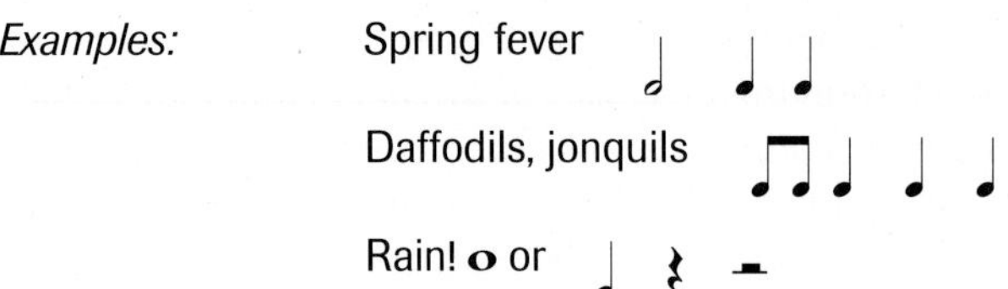

Let children respond aurally and physically before they are shown the patterns. Then put patterns together in various combinations.

4. Have students step characteristic rhythm patterns as they learn songs. The more precisely students can step a pattern fully with their bodies, the better they feel it in preparation for visual and intellectual understanding.

5. Make up word patterns. Practice stepping, clapping, and speaking the patterns, then remove the words and speak the patterns with rhythm syllables.

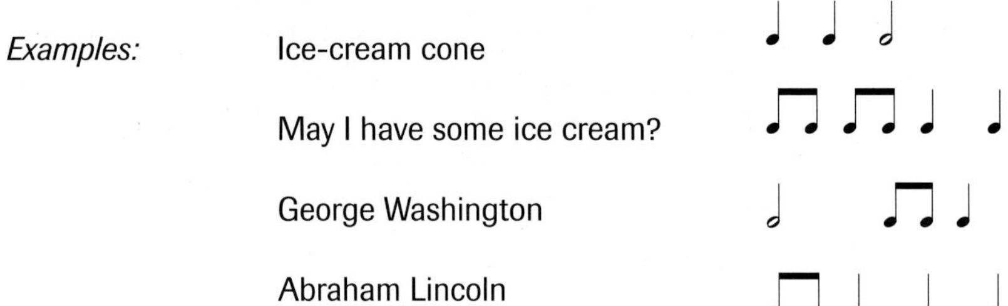

6. A 𝄽 is a *rest,* which is a silent pause in music. Help children feel the rest with their bodies but without a sound. An idea for small children is to "clap" and to touch temples gently on the rest. Then repeat the activity, walking and touching the temples.

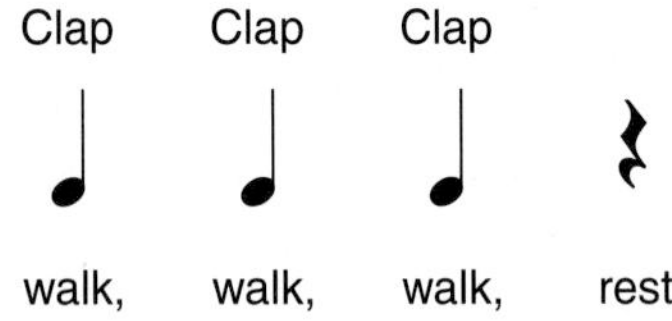

7. Start a beat ♩ ♩ ♩ ♩ and then add words to help you remember the following patterns. Locate the patterns in familiar songs.

SUGGESTIONS FOR LESSONS: GRADES 4–6

1. Sing "Erie Canal" (p. 430) and clap the rhythm. Aurally discover the syncopated patterns. Ask students to determine whether the syncopated pattern appears seldom or often in the song. Ask students to circle the following repeated pattern: ♪♩. Count the number of times this pattern ♪♩ occurs (nine). Perform part one of the song for students. Ask them to create a motion for the ♪♩ (syncopation).
2. Present part two of "Erie Canal" on a transparency. Ask students to circle the following repeated rhythmic pattern: ♪. ♬ Count the number of times it occurs (fifteen). Perform part two of the song for students. Ask them to create a different motion for the rhythmic pattern ♪. ♬ (The motion will need to be short.)
3. Divide the class in half. Perform the song again and ask half the class to do the motion for ♪♩ and the other half to do the second motion for ♪. ♬.
4. Perform the song with the class singing (without the motions); then perform the song with the motions.

Concept: Melodic Contour

Movement can be a major activity in learning the melody of a song. Moving their hands or "mapping the melody" helps students feel the *melodic contour,* which is when the melody moves up or down.

SUGGESTIONS FOR LESSONS: GRADES K–3

1. Ask students to apply movement to the phrase "Oh, Ma" in "Little Tommy Tinker" (p. 228).
2. Ask students to place their hands on feet, ankles, knees, waist, shoulders, jaw, eyes, and top of head as they sing/listen to the song "Do-Re-Mi" from *The Sound of Music* [iTunes/Spotify].

INTERPRETING MUSICAL IDEAS THROUGH MOVEMENT

Interpreting musical ideas through movement focuses on the simple expressiveness of musical elements, text, or programmatic ideas in music. The bodily movement may be free and creative or carefully planned and either abstract or dramatic. Essential to this type of expression is skill and comfort in using the body in a spatial environment. Many techniques for exploring the use of the body in space are discussed in "Developing Body Awareness in Space" earlier in this chapter. Children will find increased pleasure and satisfaction in musical experiences as they become comfortable with physical movement to music and are no longer self-conscious.

What Inspires Interpretative Movement?

Inspiration for creating movement patterns or expressiveness comes from the musical elements inherent in the piece of music. Questions to be asked by the teacher include:

1. What is the rhythm (beat, meter, syncopation)?
2. What is the tempo?
3. What kinds of rhythm patterns are used?
4. What is the text about? Are there programmatic ideas in the music?
5. What are the characteristics of the melody/melodies (steps, skips, up, down, legato, staccato, phrase length)?
6. What is the form (AB, ABA, rondo, theme-and-variation)?
7. How would you describe the dynamics (loud, soft, gradually getting louder, softer)?

As you study and analyze the qualities of a musical composition, you need to decide how you will use such basic rhythmic activities as walking, marching, clapping, slapping, snapping, stretching, bending, and swaying.

One type of interpretative movement is free and creative, a type in which students are encouraged to respond in an appropriate way to a given musical composition. Music may contain programmatic ideas to which children relate, or it may be abstract.

- *Music examples (programmatic):* Moussorgsky's "Ballet of the Chicks in Their Shells" from *Pictures at an Exhibition;* Sondheim's "Send in the Clowns" from *A Little Night Music;* Grofé's "Sunrise" from *Grand Canyon Suite* [iTunes/Spotify]
- *Music examples (abstract:* Chopin's "Fantaisie Impromptu," op. 66; Prokofiev's *Classical Symphony, Gavotte;* J. S. Bach's "Jesu, Joy of Man's Desiring" [iTunes/Spotify]

A second type of movement is structured, as determined by the students, the teacher, or both together. The movements are the same from performance to performance and are done together. Structured movement may be abstract or dramatic. In the former, basic rhythmic activities, such as snapping, clapping, and swaying, dominate the interpretation, whereas in the latter, movements are determined by a literal interpretation of the text or programmatic idea. Songs are popular sources for structured movement. The following general guidelines will help you use movement to involve students in experiencing music.

General Guidelines for Planning Movement Experiences

- Keep movement within the skills and capabilities of the student (for example, use bilateral motions for young children). These movements may range from the very simple to the highly complex.
- Choose musical compositions that lend themselves, through text or programmatic ideas, to interpretative movement. Be careful not to impose a story meaning on a simple melody.
- Plan movements so that they flow freely from one to another.
- Plan movements carefully. Sometimes children will improvise movement as a part of the learning process, whereas at other times you will want them to follow a planned pattern of movements.
- Ask children to help decide on appropriate interpretative movements and to chart them with stick figures and captions that give specific directions, along with the text of the song (if there is one).
- Make sure children learn each movement well; children must concentrate on the interpretation and not on "What do I do next?"
- Be sensitive to children's ages. Do not choose a movement that will be awkward or embarrassing to them.
- For performance experiences, you may wish to use simple costumes.
- Emphasize important words or syllables. You may choose to do the movement on a strong beat or on a particular word.
- Enhance the rhythm of the song with coordinated movement (that is, everyone doing the same thing at the same time).

Abstract Interpretative Movement

"Rock-a My Soul"

Activity: Slapping, clapping, and snapping fingers to music
Grades: 4–6
Concepts: Rhythm: beat, syncopation, melodic rhythm
Form: ABA

Special Learner Note

Props may help students "stay together" and may encourage "larger" motions by providing a visual representation of the movement as they perform it. Props may be streamers, scarves, hats, or cardboard or construction paper shapes.

SUGGESTIONS FOR LESSONS

1. Sing "Rock-a My Soul" (p. 163).
2. Say the text out loud to feel the beat and develop ideas for movement.
3. Determine the form (ABA) and create two sets of contrasting rhythmic motions as follows:

MEASURES	MOVEMENTS
A Section	
Measures 1–8	Slap thighs on beats 1 and 3; clap hands on beats 2 and 4
B Section	
Measures 9–10	Snap fingers on beats 2 and 4, arms in front
Measures 11–12	Snap fingers on beats 2 and 4, arms left
Measures 13–14	Snap fingers on beats 2 and 4, arms right
Measure 15	Arms at side
Measure 16	Clap hands on beats 2 and 3
A Section	
Measures 1–8	Repeat motions for measures 1–7; end with two claps on measure 8

"I'm Gonna Sing When the Spirit Says Sing"

Activity: Stretching, crossing arms, clapping
Grades: 4–6
Concepts: Rhythm: beat, accent, melodic rhythm

Spiritual

I'm Gonna Sing When the Spirit Says Sing

Key: G
Starting pitch: D
Meter: 4/4, begins on "and" of 3

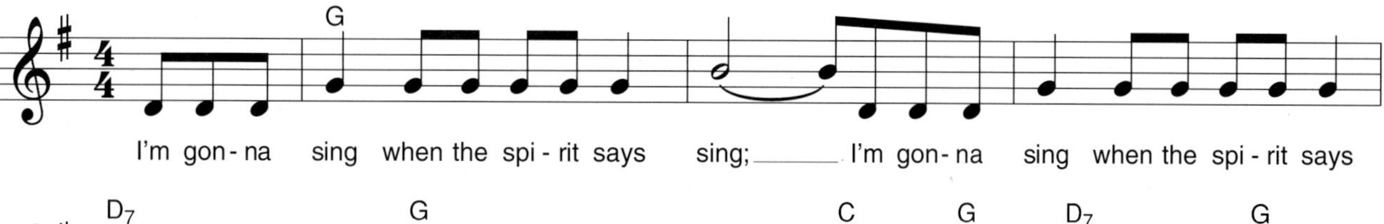
G
I'm gon-na sing when the spi-rit says sing; I'm gon-na sing when the spi-rit says

D7 G C G D7 G
sing; I'm gon-na sing when the spi-rit says sing, and o - bey the spi-rit of the Lord.

SUGGESTIONS FOR LESSONS

1. Sing the song.
2. Create movements that follow the text; for example:

   I'm gonna Hands and arms in ready position
   Sing Both hands and arms stretch out and up

Spirit	Both hands cross chest
o-bey	Clap
Lord	Both hands and arms outstretched in front, palms up

3. Chart the movements with stick figures to help students remember them.

Dramatic Interpretative Movement

Most children enjoy creative dramatics. They like to be something or someone else and experience great pleasure in acting out a song. Adding some visuals, costumes, and movement can generate a tremendous amount of excitement in the classroom, and because children have vivid imaginations, the teacher's role is minimized. Although dramatic movement can be added to any song, songs that lend themselves especially well to such treatment are those that (1) tell a story (ballad or multiple verses), (2) have contrasting phrases or sections, (3) feature a particular event or time in history, or (4) portray a strong human emotion or action.

In the following songs, ideas for dramatic interpretative movement can be found in the text or musical concepts.

"Little Marionettes"

Activity: Staccato finger movements, clapping, smooth hand motions
Grades: K–2
Concepts: Tempo: quick
Melody: staccato, short phrases, skips
Rhythm: steady beat, duple meter

Key: G
Starting pitch: G
Meter: 2/4, begins on 1

French Nursery Song

Little Marionettes

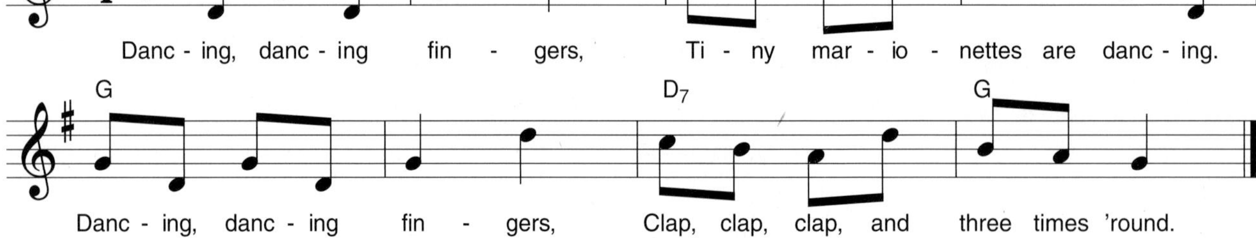
♩=84
G
D7
G
Danc - ing, danc - ing fin - gers, Ti - ny mar - io - nettes are danc - ing.
G
D7
G
Danc - ing, danc - ing fin - gers, Clap, clap, clap, and three times 'round.

SUGGESTIONS FOR LESSONS

1. Have students pretend that their fingers are marionettes on strings. Have students dance, stressing the first beat until the words "clap, clap, clap," when they should clap hands.

2. Have students circle one hand with the other at the words "three times 'round."

"I Wish I Were a Windmill"

Activity: Swaying, moving arms up and down

Grades: K–2

Concepts: Rhythm: steady beat, duple meter

Text: windmill, move my arms like this

Key: F
Starting pitch: C
Meter: 4/4, begins on 4

SUGGESTIONS FOR LESSONS

1. Have students choose partners and face each other.
2. Each should clasp the right and left hands of his or her partner and raise them overhead to form the "blades" of the windmill.
3. Have each pair move their arms up and down, swaying right and left with the beat.

"Aizu Lullaby"

Activity: Rocking, swaying

Grades: K–3

Concepts: Rhythm: steady beat, duple meter

Tempo: slow

Melody: legato

Text: rocks her/his sweet little baby

Japan

Aizu Lullaby (Aizu Komori Uta)

Key: D
Starting pitch: B
Meter: 4/4, begins on 1

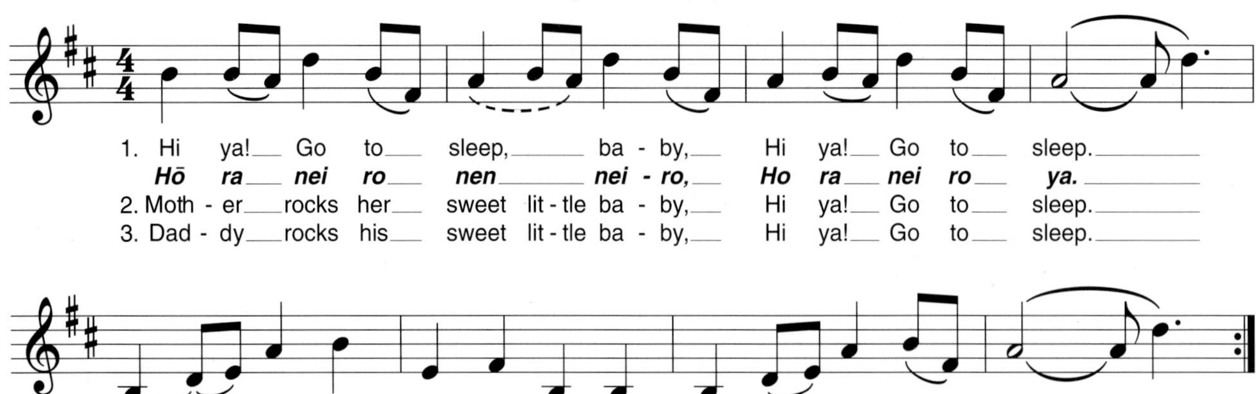
1. Hi ya! Go to sleep, ba - by, Hi ya! Go to sleep.
Hō ra nei ro nen nei - ro, Ho ra nei ro ya.
2. Moth - er rocks her sweet lit - tle ba - by, Hi ya! Go to sleep.
3. Dad - dy rocks his sweet lit - tle ba - by, Hi ya! Go to sleep.
Go to sleep my sweet ba - by, Hi ya! Go to sleep.
Nēn nei ro nen nei ro, Ho ra nei ro ya.

Betty Warner Dietz and Thomas Choonbai Park, *Folk Songs of China, Japan, and Korea.*

SUGGESTION FOR LESSON

1. Students take turns rocking a baby doll to sleep. Have them follow the quadruple meter and sway right and left on beats 1 and 3.

PLAYING SINGING GAMES AND DANCING

One of the most enjoyable ways of involving students in moving to music is through singing games and dances. Learning to coordinate body movements and music provides an excellent way for students to improve their listening skills.

Following are some popular singing games and folk dances for various grade levels. Although some are accompanied by recorded music, most have songs that are to be sung by the students as they participate in the movement. It is suggested that students learn the songs and are comfortable singing them before adding appropriate movements.

SUGGESTIONS FOR LESSONS: GRADES K–3

1. Sing "Did You Ever See a Lassie?" (p. 109).
2. Students form a circle, alternating boys and girls, with hands joined; one student is placed in the center.
3. As the students sing each phrase of the song, have them perform the corresponding action:

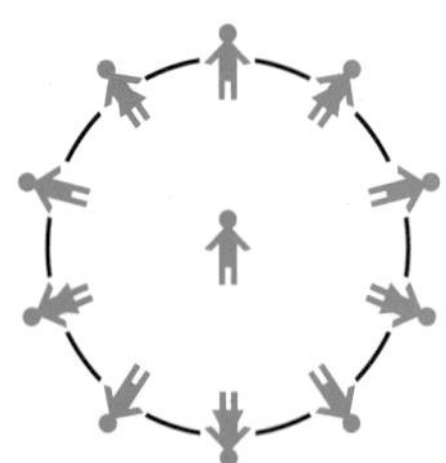

"Did you ever see a lassie, a lassie, a lassie,"	Students move to the left four steps in time to the music.
"Did you ever see a lassie do this way and that?"	Students move to the right four steps in time to the music.
"Do this way and that way, do this way and that way,"	Student in center makes some movements while those in the circle stand still.
"Did you ever see a lassie do this way and that?"	Students in circle imitate movements of student in the center.

While the students are performing the last phrase, the student in the center points to a student in the circle who will change places with him or her at the end of the phrase. Then the song and dance repeat.

SUGGESTIONS FOR LESSONS: GRADES K–2

1. Play a recording of the song "Wild Bird" (Silver Burdett Ginn, *World of Music*, CD 2-4).
2. Teach the song.
3. Experiment with listening to various voices to determine whom they belong to. (*Examples:* Jimmy has a low, throaty voice; Yolanda has a high, thin voice.)
4. Have students form a circle or "cage" for the bird. (Face inward, hands joined.) One child (the bird) sits in the center with eyes closed. As students in the circle move to the left, they stop when they sing "free." A single student who is directly behind the bird sings or says the rest of the song as a solo. The student who is sitting in the middle then tries to identify the singer (or speaker). If the student in the center is correct, they change places and play the game again. Otherwise, the student in the center remains the bird.

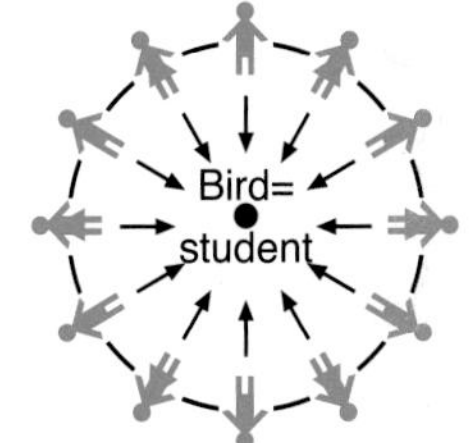
Bird=
student

5. Play the game and ask the children who are not the bird to sing.

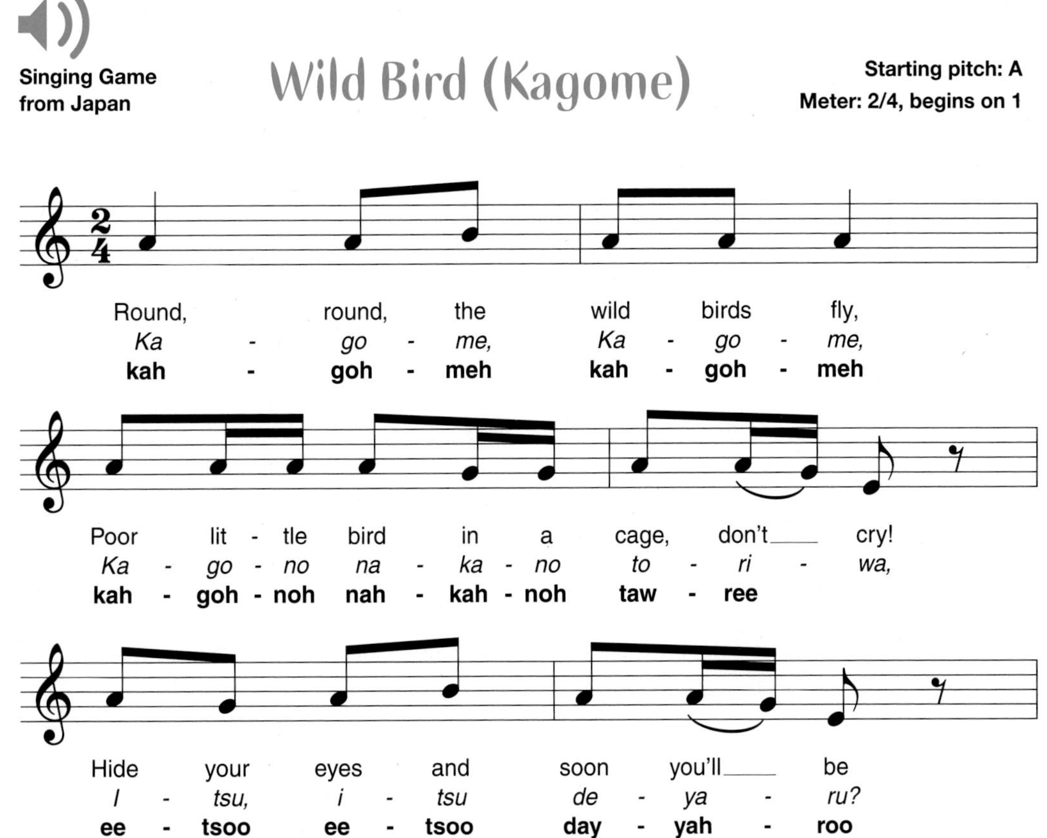
Singing Game
from Japan
Wild Bird (Kagome)
Starting pitch: A
Meter: 2/4, begins on 1
Round, round, the wild birds fly,
Ka - go - me, Ka - go - me,
kah - goh - meh kah - goh - meh
Poor lit - tle bird in a cage, don't cry!
Ka - go - no na - ka - no to - ri - wa,
kah - goh - noh nah - kah - noh taw - ree
Hide your eyes and soon you'll be
I - tsu, i - tsu de - ya - ru?
ee - tsoo ee - tsoo day - yah - roo

With the wild birds, fly - ing free.
Yo - a - ke - no ba - n - ni,
yoh - ah - kay - noh bah - nee
Solo
Who's stand - ing back of you, can you___ say?
Tsu - ru to ka - me to sub - be - ta.
tsoo - roo toh kah - meh toh soob - beh - tah
If you guess the name you can fly a - way!
U - shi - ro - no sho - men da - re?
oo - shee roh - noh shoh - mehn dah - reh

SUGGESTIONS FOR LESSONS: GRADES K–1

The Mulberry Bush

Key: G
Starting pitch: G
Meter: 6/8, begins on 1

England

G
D7
Here we go 'round the mul - ber - ry bush, the mul - ber - ry bush, the mul - ber - ry bush.
G
D7
G
Here we go 'round the mul - ber - ry bush, so ear - ly in___ the morn - ing.

1. Sing "The Mulberry Bush."
2. Have students form a circle, facing inward, with hands joined.
3. As students sing, have them perform the indicated actions or movements:

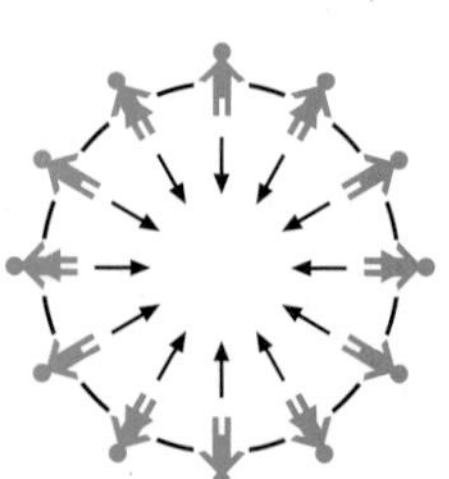

"Here we go 'round the mulberry bush, the mulberry bush, the mulberry bush. Here we go 'round the mulberry bush, so early in the morning."	Students move counterclockwise in time to the music.
"This is the way we wash our hands, wash our hands, wash our hands. This is the way we wash our hands, so early in the morning."	Students pantomime each verse of the song.
(Repeat first verse above.)	
"This is the way we brush our teeth, brush our teeth, brush our teeth. This is the way we brush our teeth, so early in the morning."	
(Repeat first verse.)	
"This is the way we comb our hair, comb our hair, comb our hair. This is the way we comb our hair, so early in the morning."	
(Repeat first verse.)	
"This is the way we sweep the floor, sweep the floor, sweep the floor. "This is the way we sweep the floor, so early in the morning."	
(Repeat first verse.)	

SUGGESTIONS FOR LESSONS: GRADES K–1

1. Sing "The Farmer in the Dell" (p.152).
2. Have students form a circle, facing inward. Boys alternate with girls and join hands. Select one student to be the farmer; he or she stands in the center of the circle.
3. As students sing, have them perform the indicated actions or movements:

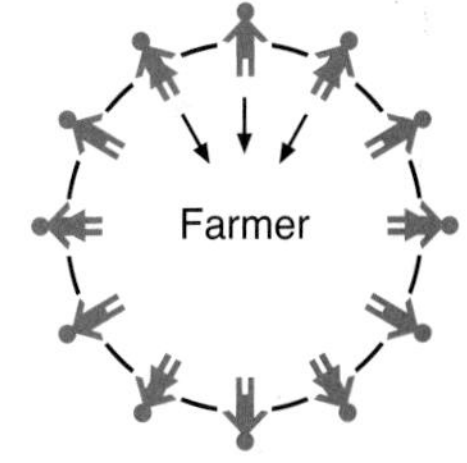

"The farmer in the dell, The farmer in the dell, Hi! ho! the derry oh, The farmer in the dell."	Students walk to right in time to music.
"The farmer takes a wife, The farmer takes a wife, Hi! ho! the derry oh, The farmer in the dell."	Students walk to right in time to music; "farmer" moves to the circle and takes a "wife"; farmer and wife return to center of circle.
"The wife takes the child, The wife takes the child, Hi! ho! the derry oh, The farmer in the dell."	Students walk to right in time to music; "wife" moves to the circle and takes a "child"; wife and child return to center of circle.

"The child takes the nurse, The child takes the nurse, Hi! ho! the derry oh, The farmer in the dell."	Students walk to right in time to music; "child" moves to the circle and takes a "nurse"; child and nurse return to center of circle.
"The nurse takes the dog, The nurse takes the dog, Hi! ho! the derry oh, The farmer in the dell."	Students walk to right in time to music; "nurse" moves to the circle and takes a "dog"; nurse and dog return to center of circle.
"The dog takes the cat, The dog takes the cat, Hi! ho! the derry oh, The farmer in the dell."	Students walk to right in time to music; "dog" moves to the circle and takes a "cat"; dog and cat return to center of circle.
"The cat takes the rat, The cat takes the rat, Hi! ho! the derry oh, The farmer in the dell."	Students walk to right in time to music; "cat" moves to the circle and takes a "rat"; cat and rat return to center of circle.
"The rat takes the cheese, The rat takes the cheese, Hi! ho! the derry oh, The farmer in the dell."	Students walk to right in time to music; "rat" moves to the circle and takes a "cheese"; rat and cheese return to center of circle.
"The cheese stands alone, The cheese stands alone, Hi! ho! the derry oh, The farmer in the dell."	Everyone returns to the circle except the "cheese"; all stand still facing the cheese.

4. The above steps can be repeated, with the "cheese" becoming the "farmer."

SUGGESTIONS FOR LESSONS: GRADES K–1

1. Sing "The Hokey Pokey" (p. 376).
2. Have students form a circle facing inward.
3. Have students sing along with a recording of the song "The Hokey Pokey," pantomiming the words for each verse and performing the refrain as follows:

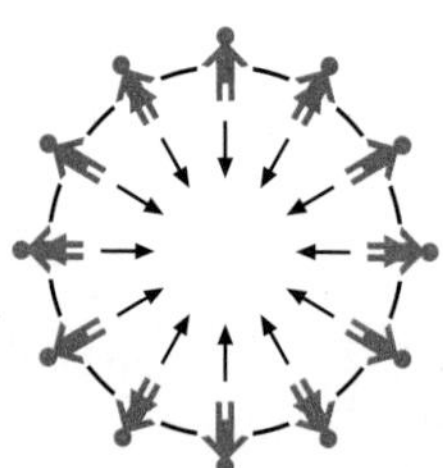

"And then you do the hokey pokey And you turn yourself about; And that's what it's all about.	Wave both hands over head. Keep both hands up and turn around.
Hey!"	Drop hands and return to circle.

SUGGESTIONS FOR LESSONS: GRADES K–2

Shoemaker's Dance

Danish Folk Song

Key: F
Starting pitch: C
Meter: 2/4, begins on 1

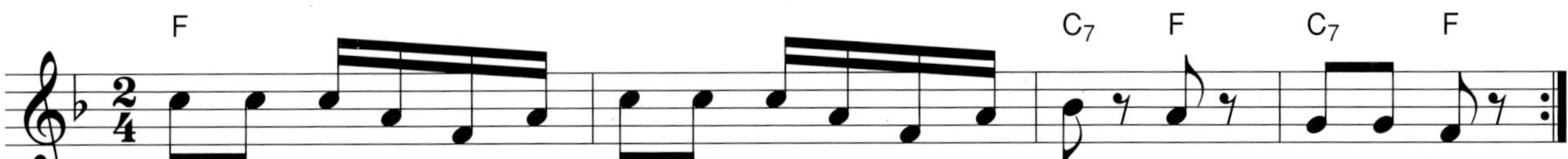

F
C7
F
C7
F
Wind and wind the thread and wind and wind the thread And pull, pull, tap, tap, tap.

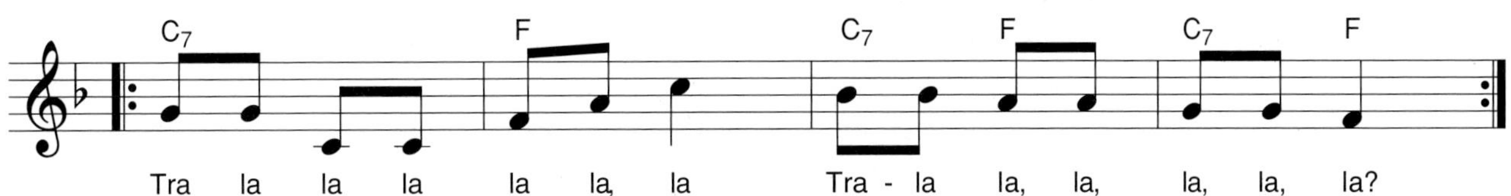

C7
F
C7
F
C7
F
Tra la la la la la, la Tra - la la, la, la, la, la?

1. Sing "Shoemaker's Dance."
2. Have students form two circles, with boys on the inside and girls on the outside; have partners face each other.
3. As students sing, have them perform the indicated actions or movements:

"Wind and wind the thread and"	Students pantomime by making fists, which they roll forward around each other four times.
"wind and wind the thread	Reverse fist movement, now backward four times.
And pull, pull,	Pull twice with both hands as if pulling up shoelaces.
tap, tap, tap."	Tap fists together three times.
(Repeat.)	
"Tra, la, la, la, la, la, la, Tra, la, la, la, la, la, la, la, Tra, la, la, la, la, la, la, la, Tra, la, la, la, la, la, la, la."	Boys' right hands join with girls' left hands; partners skip counterclockwise around the circle in time to the music.

SUGGESTIONS FOR LESSONS: GRADES 1–3

Round and Round the Village

United States

Key: F
Starting pitch: A
Meter: 2/2, begins on "and" of 2

F
C7
F
1. Go 'round and 'round the vil - lage, Go 'round and 'round the vil - lage, Go
2. Go in and out the win - dows, Go in and out the win - dows, Go
3. Now kneel and say "Good morn - ing," Now kneel and say "Good morn - ing," Now
4. Now fol - low me to Lon - don, Now fol - low me to Lon - don, Now
5. Shake hands be - fore you leave her, Shake hands be - fore you leave her, Shake

F
C7
F
'round and 'round the vil - lage,
in and out the win - dows,
kneel and say "Good morn - ing," As we have done be - fore.
fol - low me to Lon - don,
hands be - fore you leave her,

1. Sing "Round and Round the Village."
2. Divide the class into two groups. Half of the students form a circle; the other half stands in a line outside the circle.
3. As students sing, have them perform the indicated actions or movements:

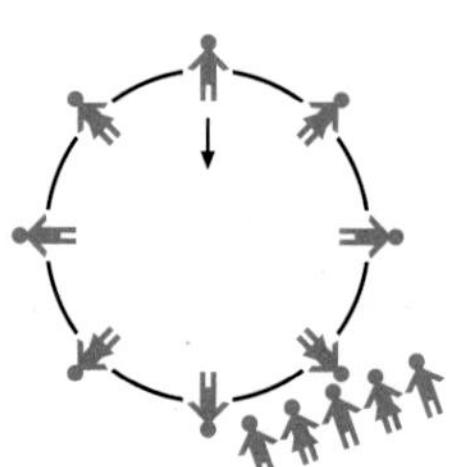

"Go 'round and 'round the village, Go 'round and 'round the village, Go 'round and 'round the village, As we have done before."	Outside group moves to the right (counterclockwise) around the circle as students in circle slap hands to beat.
"Go in and out the windows, Go in and out the windows, Go in and out the windows, As we have done before."	Students in circle join hands and raise arms to form "windows"; outside group goes *in* and *out* of the windows; at the end outside group should be *inside* the circle.
"Now kneel and say 'Good morning,' Now kneel and say 'Good morning,' Now kneel and say 'Good morning,' As we have done before."	The "new" inside group kneels, facing the outer circle (forming partners).
"Now follow me to London, Now follow me to London, Now follow me to London, As we have done before."	Students join right hands and skip together around in a circle.
"Shake hands before you leave her, Shake hands before you leave her, Shake hands before you leave her, As we have done before."	Each student in inside circle shakes hands with partner, then they change places with each other and the dance is repeated.

SUGGESTIONS FOR LESSONS: GRADES 1–3

England

Pop, Goes the Weasel

Key: C
Starting pitch: A
Meter: 6/8, begins on 1

C G7 C G7 C G7
1. All a-round the cob - bler's bench, the mon - key chased the wea - sel; mon - key thought 'twas

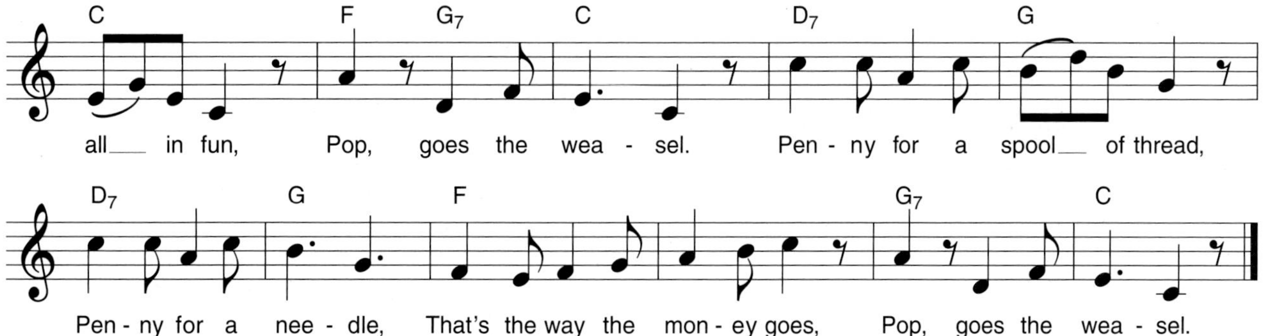
C
F
G7
C
D7
G
all___ in fun, Pop, goes the wea - sel. Pen - ny for a spool___ of thread,
D7
G
F
G7
C
Pen - ny for a nee - dle, That's the way the mon - ey goes, Pop, goes the wea - sel.

1. Sing "Pop, Goes the Weasel." Legend tells us that this song originally did not refer to an animal but to a tool used by London hatters and tailors called a "weasel," which they would pawn, or "pop," when they were short of funds and needed money to tide them over.
2. Have children form two lines facing each other.

Head couple
Peel left
Peel right

3. As students sing, have them perform the indicated actions or movements:

"All around the cobbler's bench,"	Head couple joins hands and slides to foot of row.
"the monkey chased the weasel; monkey thought 'twas all in fun,"	Return to original position;
	head couple slides down the row a second time.
"Pop, goes the weasel."	All clap hands on "Pop."
"Penny for a spool of thread," "Penny for a needle," "That's the way the money goes,"	From this position, head couple peels off to right and left; rest of students follow; head couple returns to head of line and continues down row, becoming new "foot couple."
"Pop, goes the weasel."	All clap hands on "Pop." Game begins again with a new head couple.

SUGGESTIONS FOR LESSONS

"Chiapanecas" (Mexican Hat Dance)

1. Listen to and then sing along with a recording of "Chiapanecas."[5]
2. Dance to "Chiapanecas." Have the students form a single circle, facing toward the center, around a large Mexican hat.

[5] Available for download from iTunes or streaming from Spotify, "Mexican Hat Dance," from the *100 Greatest Kidsongs Collection.*

3. For the first section of the song, students do the following:
    a. On the first phrase (four measures of three beats each), students sing "Oh Chiapanecas, Oh, Oh!" and then clap their hands two times.
    b. Students repeat the above three times.
4. For the second section of the song, students do the following:
    a. Turn to the right and step in a circle in time to the music (four measures of three beats each; repeated.) On the last beat students turn to face the center of the circle.
5. Repeat the entire sequence (first and second sections). In the first section, instead of claps, students stamp twice while putting their hands on their hips.

SUGGESTIONS FOR LESSONS: GRADES 3–6

O Susanna

Key: F
Starting pitch: F
Meter: 2/4, begins on "and" of 2

Stephen C. Foster

F, C7, F, C7, F

1. I___ came from Al - a - bam - a with my ban - jo on my knee, I'm___ going to Lou' - si - an - a my___ true love for to see.
2. It___ rained all night the day I left, the weath - er, it was dry; The ___ sun so hot I froze to death, Su - san - na don't you cry.

Chorus

B♭, F, C7, F, C7, F

O Su - san - na, O don't you cry for me, For I've come from Al - a - bam - a with my ban - jo on my knee.

1. Sing "O Susanna."
2. Have students form a circle, alternating boys and girls, facing inward.
3. As students sing, have them perform the indicated actions or movements:

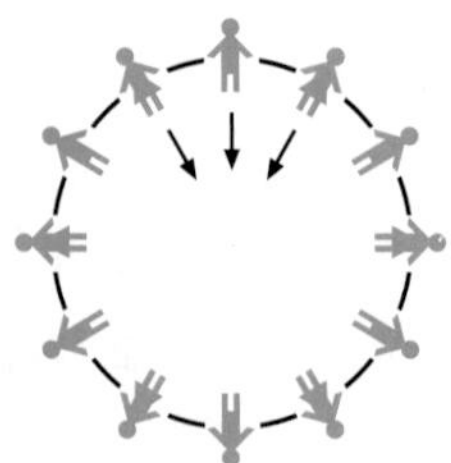

"I came from Alabama with my"	In time to the music, girls move four steps into the circle; boys clap beat.
"banjo on my knee,"	Girls move four steps back to their original place in the circle; boys clap beat.
"I'm going to Lou'siana my"	Boys move four steps into the circle; girls clap beat.
"true love for to see."	Boys move four steps back to their original place in the circle; girls clap beat.
"It rained all night the day I left, the weather, it was dry;"	Grand right and left: Boys face clockwise, girls face counterclockwise, join right hands and move around circle, alternating left and right hands; on "me," take new partners.
"The sun so hot I froze to death, Susanna don't you cry."	
"O Susanna, O don't you cry for me, For I've come from Alabama with my banjo on my knee."	New partners promenade eight walking steps counterclockwise; on the last beat, everyone faces inward ready to repeat the dance.

SUGGESTIONS FOR LESSONS: GRADES 4–6

La Cucaracha

Mexico

Key: G
Starting pitch: D
Meter: 3/4, begins on "and" of 2

Chorus

G
La cu - ca - ra - cha, la cu - ca - ra - cha. yo no quie - ro ca - mi -

D7 G *Fine*
nar, Por - que no tie - ne, por - que le fal - ta di - ne - ro pa - ra gas - tar.

Verse

G D7
U - na cu - ca - ra - cha pin - ta La di - jo a u - na co - lo - ra - da

G *D.C. al fine*
Va - ma - nos pa - ra mi tie - rra A pa - ser la tem - po - ra - da.

1. Sing "La Cucaracha."
2. Have students form two circles, boys on the inside and girls on the outside. Students face counterclockwise; boys put their hands on their hips, girls hold their skirts with left hand and castanets in right hand.
3. As students sing, have them perform the indicated actions or movements:

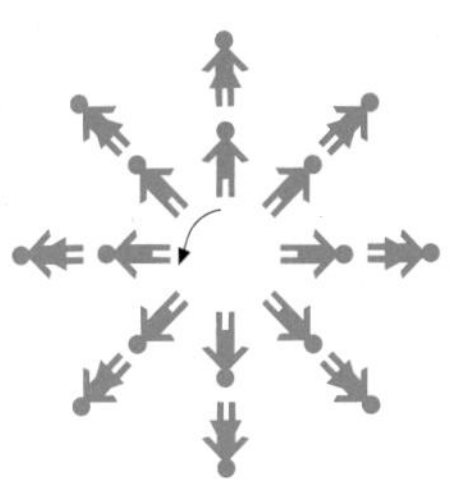

"La cucaracha, la cucaracha,"	Partners move sideways one step away from each other and back.
"Yo no quiero caminar,"	Partners take six running steps forward, and clap on rest.
"Porque no tiene, porque le falta"	Repeat side steps.
"dinero para gastar."	Repeat running steps and clap.
"Una cucaracha pinta La dijo a una colorada,"	Partners face each other, left hand behind back, right hand over head; boy circles left, girl stands still and clicks castanets for twelve counts.
"Vamanos para mi tierra A pasar la temporada."	Boy changes direction, circles right; girl clicks castanets for twelve counts.
(Repeat chorus.)	Repeat actions for chorus.

SUGGESTIONS FOR LESSONS: GRADES 5–6

Hahvah Nahgeelah

Jewish Folk Song

Key: G minor
Starting pitch: D
Meter: 4/4, begins on 1

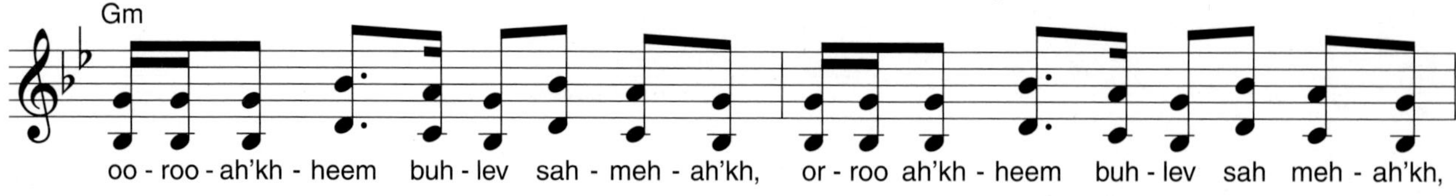

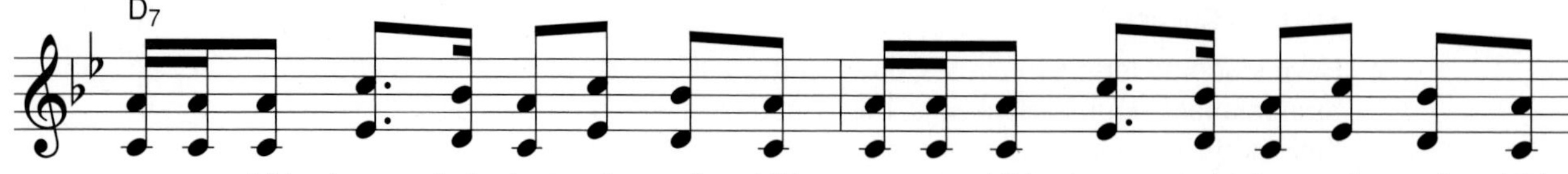

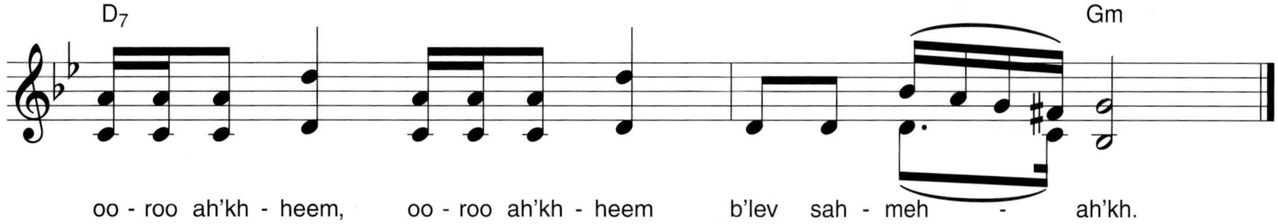
D7
Gm
oo - roo ah'kh - heem, oo - roo ah'kh - heem b'lev sah - meh - ah'kh.

1. Sing "Hahvah Nahgeelah."
2. Have students form a circle, alternating boys and girls, facing toward the center, hands joined.
3. Repeat the following movements throughout the song:
   a. Move left foot one step to the left; step on right foot crossing behind left foot.
   b. Move left foot one step to the left; hop on left foot while swinging the right foot across the front of the left foot.
   c. Move right foot one step to the right; hop on right foot while swinging the left foot across the front of the right foot.
   d. Repeat movements.

SUGGESTIONS FOR LESSONS: GRADES 5–6

1. Sing "Galway Piper" (p. 319).
2. Have students form two lines, boys in one and girls in the other, with partners facing each other and hands on hips.

3. As students sing, have them perform the indicated actions or movements:

"Every person in the nation, Of a great or humble station, Holds in highest estimation, Piping Tim of Galway."	Partners skip four steps forward toward each other then skip four steps backward from each other, returning to places in line (repeat).
"Loudly he can play or low."	Each student hops four times on left foot while at the same time tapping the right toe on the floor (forward, side, back, close).
"He can move you fast or slow,"	Repeat with the right foot while tapping the left toe on the floor (forward, side, back, close).
"Touch your hearts or stir your toe,"	Repeat four hops on left foot as above.
"Piping Tim of Galway."	Repeat four hops on right foot as above; add a clap on last beat.

SUGGESTIONS FOR LESSONS: GRADES 4–6

Cielito Lindo

Key: A
Starting pitch: A
Meter: 3/4, begins on 1

Mexican Folk Song

From Leon Dallin and Lynn Dallin, *Heritage Songster,* 2nd ed. (Dubuque, IA: Wm. C. Brown, Co., 1980).

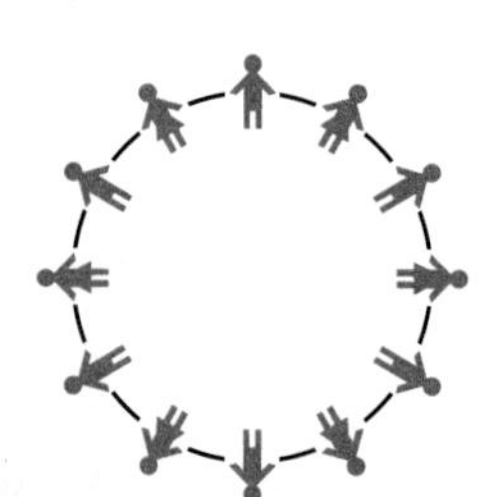

1. Sing "Cielito Lindo."
2. Have students form a circle and join hands.
3. As students sing, have them perform the indicated actions or movements:

"De la Sierra Morena, Cielito Lindo vienen bajando."	Join hands and walk counterclockwise seven steps; on step eight, change direction.
"Un par de ojitos negros Cielito Lindo, de contrabando."	Walk clockwise seven steps; stop on step eight and face center of circle.
"Ay, ay, ay, ay,"	Take four steps to center, raising arms high.
"Canta y no llores."	Take four steps backward, lowering arms.
"Porque cantando se alegran,"	Four students (two boys, two girls) join right hands and circle four steps to right.
"Cielito Lindo, los corazones."	Change hands (left hands); circle four steps to left.
	Repeat dance.

See Chapter 9, "Integrating Music with the Study of Peoples, Places, and Cultures," for additional singing games and dances:

- African game song "Tue, Tue" (p. 291)
- African game song "Kye, Kye Kule" (p. 293)
- Native American song "Mos', Mos'!" (p. 322)
- American square dance (p. 343)
- Greek dance (p. 331)
- Mexican dance to "La Raspa" (p. 330)

Technology Enhancement

Using Video Games to Teach Music through Movement

With the rapid advancement of video game systems such as PlayStation and the Wii, people are physically interacting with technology in a real way. One of the best video games for teaching music through movement is "Dance Dance Revolution (DDR)". Available on a wide variety of gaming systems, "DDR" has the players move their feet in time with music while standing on a dance platform that is connected to the game system. A wide variety of genres and ability levels can be used to re-enforce musical skills such as tempo, rhythm, syncopation, style, etc. DDR is already in wide use by school fitness education teachers and classes. With a little research, you may also find local party centers that rent out a complete DDR set-up (TV, game system, DDR, dance platforms).

Re-Enforcing Musical Concepts Through Line Dancing

Popular line dances are a great way to reach difficult students, re-enforce concepts, and prepare students for school dances! Here are some of the most popular line dances that could be used:

- *Achy Breaky Heart.*
- *At the Hop.*
- *Boot Scootin' Boogie.*
- *Cha Cha Slide.*
- *Cupid Shuffle.*
- *Electric Slide.*
- *La Bamba.*
- *Loco-Motion.*
- *Macarena.*
- *Mashed Potatot.*
- *Shou.*
- *YMCA.*

For Teaching Line Dancing:

http://dance.lovetoknow.com/Popular_Line_Dances

Integrating Technology

The Music Education Premium Site contains chapter quizzing, Spotify playlists, and downloads of free MP3s of noted songs. Visit CengageBrain.com to purchase an access code or enter the code provided with your text materials.

Web Resources

- Search the Web (www.google.com) for information on music and movement, including singing games.

Audio

- Download music discussed in this chapter from the Apple iTunes store.
- Spotify playlists allow students to stream music referenced within each chapter.
- Download free audio MP3s for the songs noted in the chapter.

Videos

- Watch classroom videos that apply to chapter content.

CENGAGE**brain**.com

Questions for Discussion

1. Discuss how movement is related to rhythm, one of the basic elements of music.
2. In what ways is movement natural for young children?
3. Discuss the meaning of the phrase "developing body awareness in space."
4. How can movement be used with young children to teach imagery? With older children (grades 5–6)?
5. Discuss ways that movement can be used to express rhythm, melody, texture, form, and tone color in grades 1–3 and 4–6.
6. Do children in grades 1–3 express musical ideas through movement in the same ways that children in grades 4–6 do?
7. Why do children sometimes have difficulty with the word "dancing" but not with the words "games" or "movement"?
8. What are some guidelines for generating ideas and techniques for moving to music?
9. Discuss why children have difficulty doing two things at the same time—for example, singing a song and simultaneously moving to the same song. How would you approach preparing a lesson that would have students both singing a song and doing movement to that same song?
10. Name some songs that could be accompanied by appropriate movements and that would be successful in both the early and later grades of elementary school.
11. Discuss some characteristics of the Dalcroze approach to teaching music.

ASSESSMENT

Review ways the music standards listed at the beginning of the chapter have been met.

CHAPTER 8

Creativity and Music

© Ritchie Photography

Objectives

Students will explore ideas for developing lessons based on:

- The Orff approach to musical learning
- Improvising and organizing sounds
  - Rhythm in speech
  - Rhythm speech canons
  - Improvising melodies
  - Ostinato patterns (rhythmic and melodic)
  - Improvising an accompaniment to a song
  - Improvising rhythms with classroom instruments
- Creative experiences with vocal sounds
- Creative experiences with instrumental sounds
- Creative experiences with environmental sounds
- Creative experiences with body sounds
  - Creating a musical video
  - Creating a percussion accompaniment to a song
  - Creating a percussion composition
- Creative experiences with writing melodies or songs
  - What makes an interesting melody?
  - Preparing students to write melodies or songs
  - Writing a melody using a pentatonic scale
  - Writing a melody using a seven-note scale (major/minor)
  - Writing an original poem

National and State Music Standards

This chapter provides experiences with the following national music standards and related state music standards:

- Singing, alone and with others, a varied repertoire of music
- Performing on instruments, alone and with others, a varied repertoire of music
- Composing and arranging music within specified guidelines
- Reading and notating music
- Listening to, analyzing, and describing music

Creating music can be an exciting and rewarding experience for students because it is a personal expression of their own feelings and ideas. Being involved in the creative process requires self-discipline, imagination, sensitivity, an understanding of the functions and possibilities of sounds, and the ability to organize materials into logical form. As students explore the realm of sound and focus their efforts on creating a musical work, they experience pleasure and satisfaction in having achieved a goal. Creating a musical composition requires that students use their current musical skills, and it may motivate them to learn new ones.

As in all creative effort, *a musical composition must begin with an idea.* This may be generated out of a student's interest in innovative ways of creating sounds, mixing instrumental or vocal sounds with environmental ones, writing a poem and setting it to music, creating a percussion accompaniment for a song, or expressing a dramatic idea or event. The teacher needs to encourage this type of creativity and at the same time set parameters for the musical effort being undertaken.

For instance, after being given an example of playing a drum by tapping the rim, students might be asked to explore three other ways of playing the drum (such as playing in the center of the drum with a drumstick, tapping the drum with fingers, or scratching the drumhead with fingernails). When students are given the opportunity to be creative, their activity has a focus. This is far more desirable than saying, "You have 5 minutes to play these instruments. Do anything you want to." With such a procedure, chaos is sure to result. Without some sort of direction, it is impossible, for instance, for students to be successful in writing a song. They simply do not know where to begin.

This chapter is directed toward developing skills for creative musical experiences. Students need to (1) have many opportunities to develop techniques for improvising and organizing sounds; (2) produce and use a rich variety of sounds—vocal, instrumental, environmental, body, and recorded; and (3) create songs, song accompaniments, and musical compositions that express feelings and ideas. The following materials and suggestions can be adapted to planning creative musical experiences for students in grades K–6.

THE ORFF APPROACH TO MUSICAL LEARNING[1]

Carl Orff (1895–1982) was a German composer/educator who believed that it is important from the very beginning that students *physically* experience beat, meter, and rhythmic patterns and that they express these by dancing and playing instruments. Orff agreed with Jaques-Dalcroze's belief that rhythm is a foundation of musical growth, and he developed an approach that begins with speech rhythms already known to the child, such as names and familiar words. These rhythms are used to create original pieces and accompaniment patterns. Orff believed that the study of traditional musical instruments should begin only when the learner can perform simple rhythms on percussion instruments or sing basic tonal patterns and intervals.

The pentatonic (five-note) scale was popular with Orff. In the Orff system, students are asked to create melodies or accompaniments in major or minor tonalities only after they have learned to create melodies and accompaniments within the pentatonic scale.

Orff advocated asking students to create introductions, codas, and accompaniments for folk songs within the student's ethnic tradition. He designed percussion instruments of high quality to form an ensemble. Some of these instruments are the glockenspiel (soprano and alto), xylophone (soprano, alto, bass), metallophone (soprano, alto, bass), and assorted drums, jingle bells, and jingle sticks.

[1] The material in this section is based on Lois Choksy et al., *Teaching Music in the Twenty-First Century* (Upper Saddle River, NJ: Prentice Hall, 2001). For more information, see the American Orff-Schulwerk Association website (www.aosa.org); Jane Frazee and Kent Kreuter, *Discovering Orff: A Curriculum for Music Teachers* (Mainz/London: Schott, 1987); and Arvida Steen et al., *Exploring Orff: A Teacher's Guide* (New York: Schott, 1992).

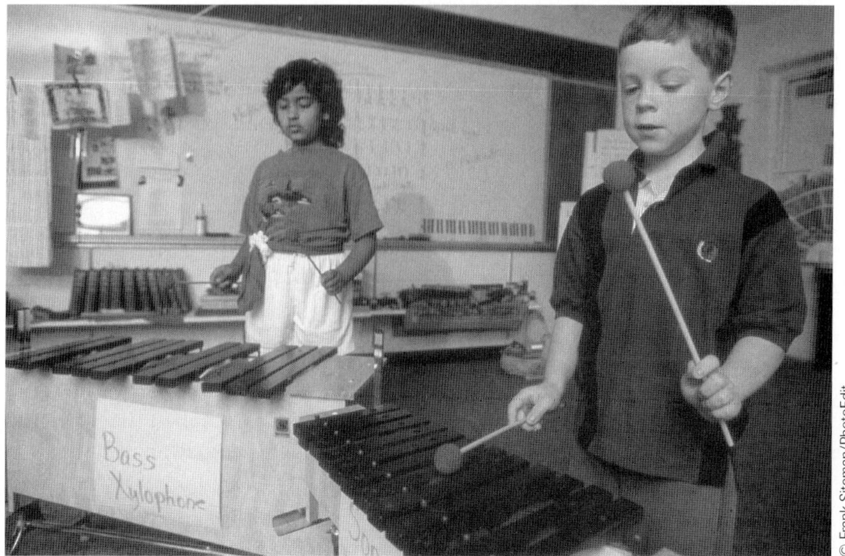

© Frank Siteman/PhotoEdit

The word *process* is paramount in Orff's system, and the keys to this process are *exploration* and *experience*. Students are encouraged to explore space, sound, form, and creativity. The most important instrument in the Orff approach is the body, followed by the voice. The Orff process at every maturity level includes movement, voice and instruments, and improvisation.

The extensive use of language that is found throughout the Orff process makes this system of teaching music especially accessible and useful for classroom teachers. Music and classroom teachers are trained to use the Orff process through Saturday and summer workshops. More information about Orff and workshops can be obtained by going to the American Orff-Schulwerk Association website at www.aosa.org.

IMPROVISING AND ORGANIZING SOUNDS

Improvising involves creating something spontaneously at a given moment. Experiences in improvising rhythms, melodies, and musical forms contribute to a student's confidence and skill in singing, playing instruments, and moving to music, as well as to greater perception and understanding of music created by others. It is essential that the teacher lead students carefully from simple to more complex experiences and provide them with many opportunities to explore sounds (e.g., high/low, fast/slow). Guidelines for improvisation activities include providing a framework for the activity (*examples*: given a steady beat, students will improvise rhythm patterns; using only the black keys of the piano, students will improvise a melody). As students gain confidence in improvising with their voices and classroom instruments, they will expand their understanding of music and find increased satisfaction and pleasure in the creative process. Following are some techniques for encouraging early experiences with improvisation.

1. Students echo clap four-beat rhythm patterns with the teacher. Next, the teacher invites students to be stubborn and refuse to clap the same patterns as the teacher—to clap something different. (This activity naturally encourages students to improvise patterns.) The teacher continues to clap four-beat rhythm patterns, but students answer by clapping improvised patterns.
2. Students keep a steady beat in duple meter (pat-clap) and say the following chant, leaving four beats of silence after each line:

1, 2, tie my shoe, XXXX
3, 4, shut the door, XXXX
5, 6, pick up sticks, XXXX
7, 8, lay them straight, XXXX
9, 10, a big, fat hen. XXXX

Repeat, but this time the teacher improvises four-beat patterns on the silence. Repeat again, but this time students improvise four-beat patterns on the silence.

Rhythm in Speech

An excellent way to introduce children to rhythm is through speech patterns.

SUGGESTIONS FOR LESSONS

1. Create word phrases and clap them in rhythm; then ask students to imitate. For example:

   | | | | | | |

   Teacher: I like pop - corn.

   Students imitate.

   Teacher: I like ap - ple pie.

   Students imitate.

   Invite students to create word phrases for the class to imitate.

2. Ask students to create other word phrases that fit a pattern. The pattern may be played by the teacher or a student. For example:

   Leader:

   Student word rhythms:

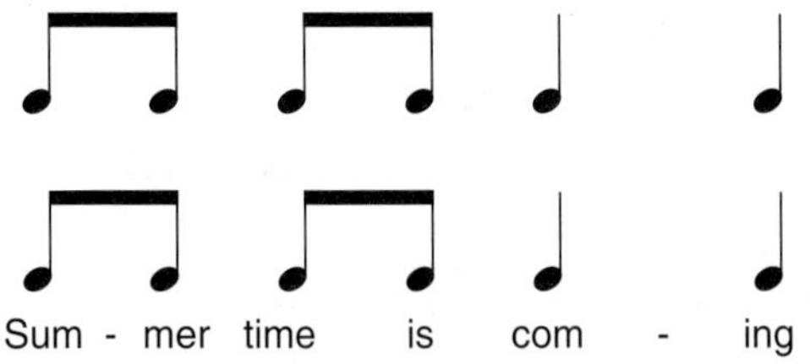

   Sum - mer time is com - ing

3. Ask students to create a short speech pattern and then a rhythm to go with it. For example:

4. Experiment with changing the number of beats in a measure according to a speech pattern:

I want to go swim - ming, swim - ming in the pool, in the pool.

5. Play a game in which one student says his or her name and a second student plays the rhythm on a percussion instrument. For example:

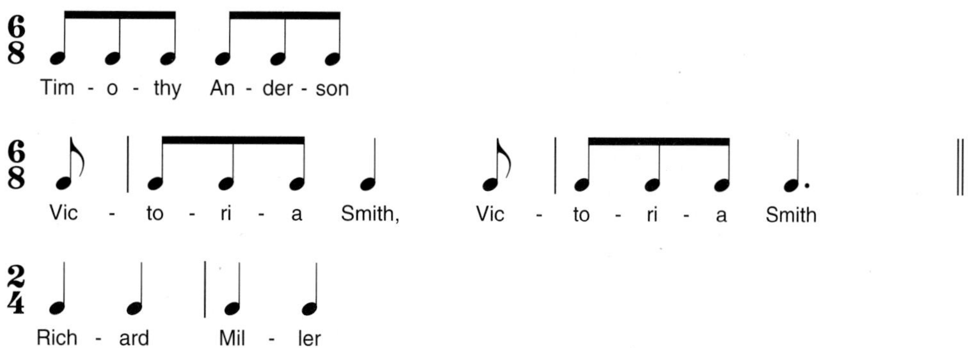

Tim - o - thy An - der - son
Vic - to - ri - a Smith, Vic - to - ri - a Smith
Rich - ard Mil - ler

6. Add a speech ostinato to a known chant. For example, start by inviting students to say the chant "Wee Willie Winkie."

Wee Willie Winkie
Runs through the town.
Upstairs, downstairs
In his nightgown.
Knocking at the windows
Peeping through the locks,
Are the children in their beds,
For it's 8 o'clock!

Then, invite students to say and clap, "8 o'clock, 8 o'clock" over and over as the teacher says the chant. Try other speech ostinatos, such as "Running through the town" or "Knocking at, peeping through."

Rhythm Speech Canons

A canon is a repeating form in which the same thing is sung or said at a precise interval of time.

SUGGESTIONS FOR LESSONS

1. In the following short "geographic" canon, have half the class begin and the second half enter one measure later. Speak the example as a rhythmic speech canon.

Geographic canon

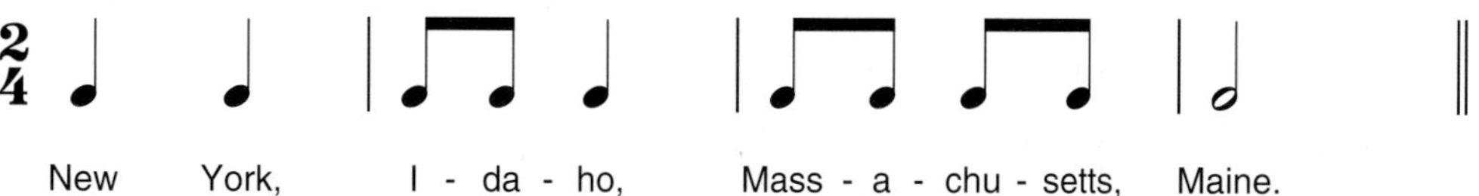

New York, I - da - ho, Mass - a - chu - setts, Maine.

2. Try other types of canons, such as the following winter and spring canons. You might wish to make up your own. Experiment with using instruments instead of your voice and try various types of movement for each measure.

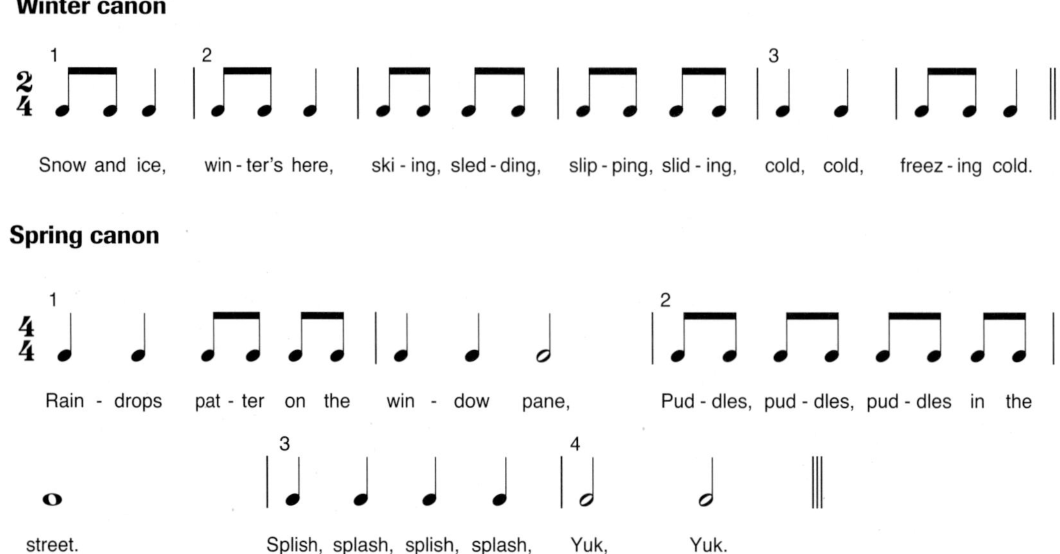

Winter canon
1 2 3
Snow and ice, win - ter's here, ski - ing, sled - ding, slip - ping, slid - ing, cold, cold, freez - ing cold.
Spring canon
1 2
Rain - drops pat - ter on the win - dow pane, Pud - dles, pud - dles, pud - dles in the
3 4
street. Splish, splash, splish, splash, Yuk, Yuk.

Improvising Melodies

To improvise a melody, begin improvising by using only two notes; for example, *sol-mi* or G-E (scale: C D E G A). Create a rap based on these two notes and a set rhythm; for example:

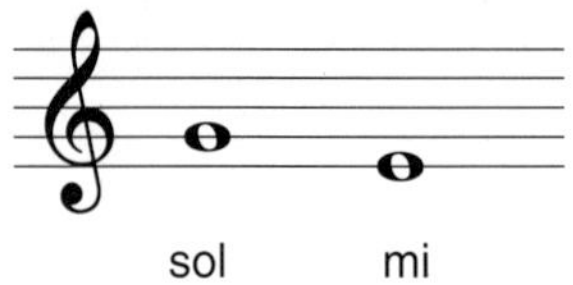

sol mi

Improvise on "We are going to school today" or another phrase of your choice. The music may be different each time. For example:

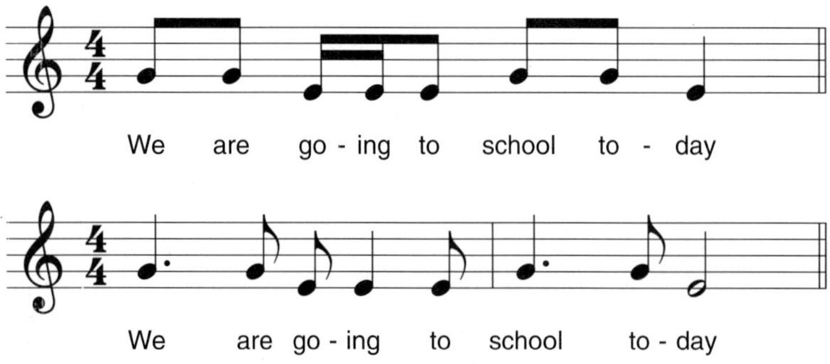

We are go - ing to school to - day
We are go - ing to school to - day

Try improvising on a three-note scale—*sol-mi-la* (G E A):

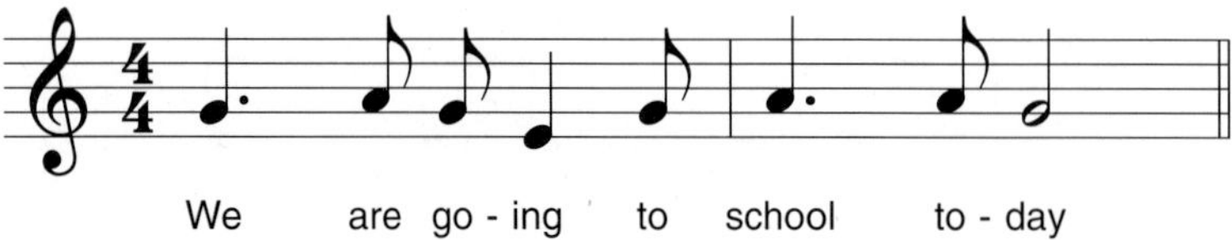

We are go - ing to school to - day

Next, using a five-note (pentatonic) scale, ask students to improvise a melody to a speech pattern or speech canon they have composed.

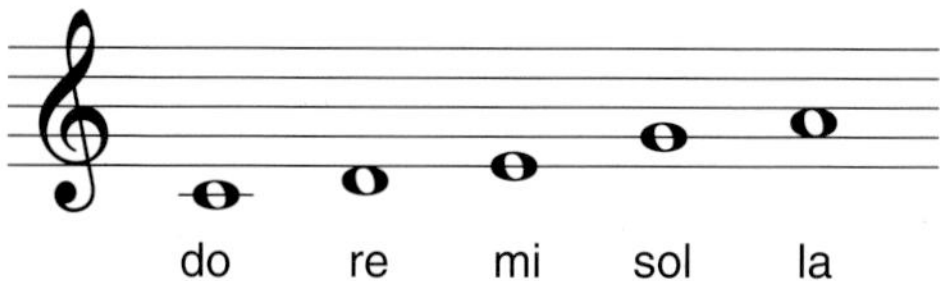

Play the song on any pitch, but perform to a prescribed rhythm. Any combination of pitches will sound pleasing. For older students, add a freely composed rhythmic accompaniment on classroom percussion instruments. Be sure to keep a steady beat on some instrument, preferably a drum.

Ostinato Patterns (Rhythmic and Melodic)

An *ostinato* is a melodic or rhythm pattern that is repeated throughout a song or larger musical composition.

SUGGESTIONS FOR LESSONS

1. Following are some examples of simple ostinato patterns to "This Old Man." Combine several and play them on classroom instruments, thus creating a small ensemble (appropriate for grades K–2).

Special Learner Note

Students may begin by using words they can easily articulate, nursery rhymes, or poems with which they are familiar to provide "rap" lyrics. Classroom themes and learning tasks can be reinforced by creating lyrics using the concepts/vocabulary being learned in the classroom. Teachers may also be able to assess learning by observing what material from the classroom the student is able and willing to integrate into his/her "song."

This Old Man

Key: F
Starting pitch: C
Meter: 2/4, begins on 1

2. Following are some ostinato accompaniments on a variety of instruments that can be used to accompany the song "Swing Low, Sweet Chariot." Try these accompaniments and then ask students to create their own ostinatos for familiar songs. (This material can be adapted for grades 3–6.)

Ostinato: xylophone

Ostinato: Glockenspiel

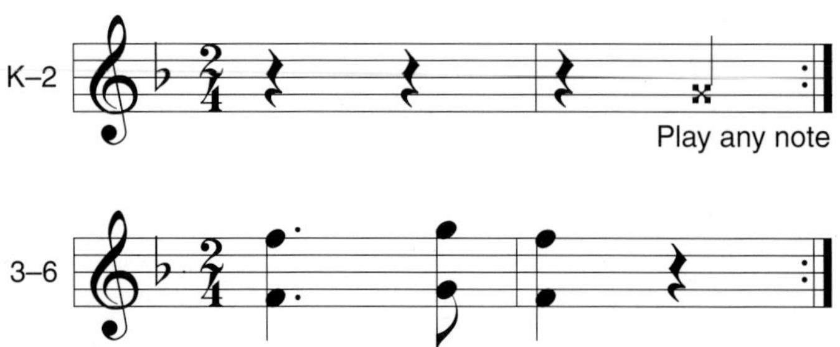

K–2
Play any note

3–6

Drum

ta ta ti - ti ta
("knick, knack on my thumb")

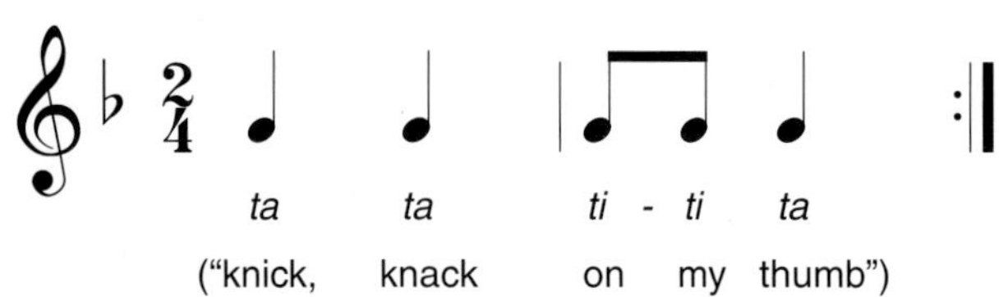

Spiritual

Swing Low, Sweet Chariot

Key: F
Starting pitch: A
Meter: 4/4, begins on 4

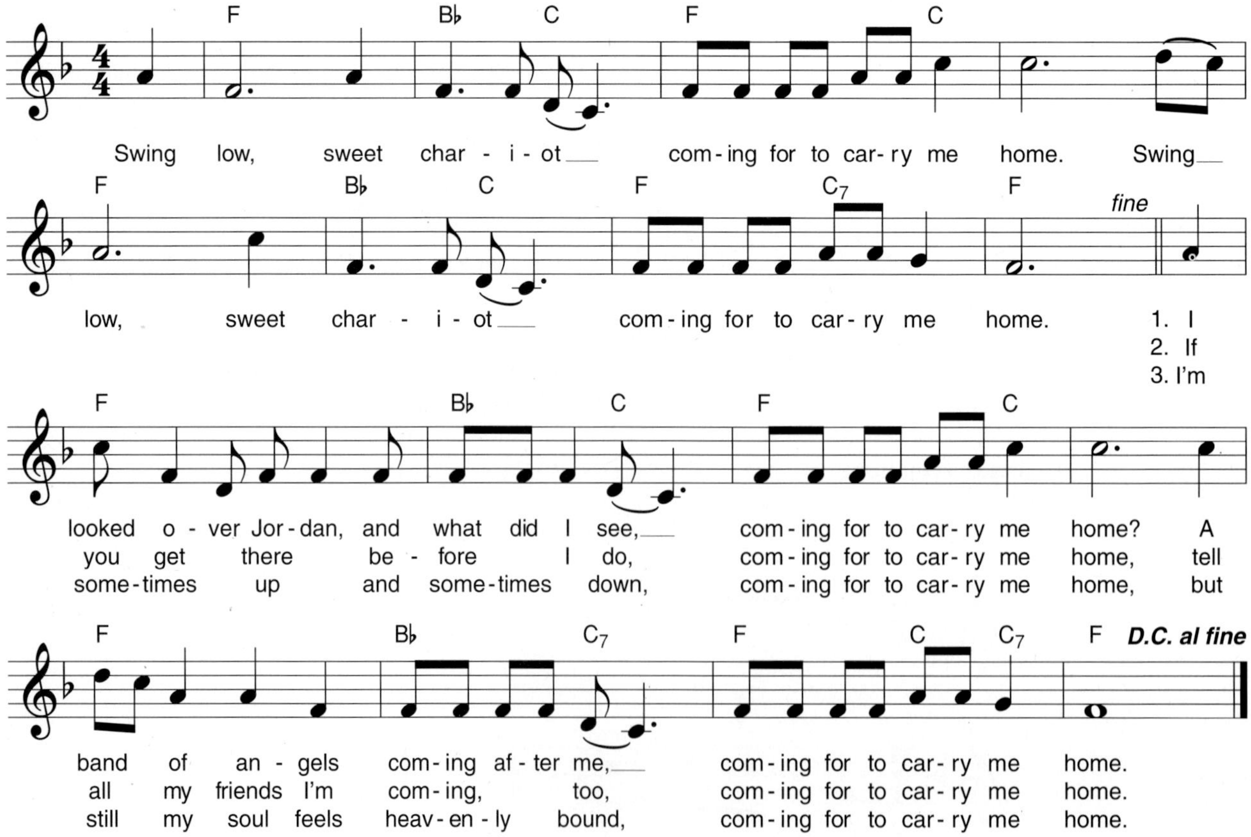

F Bb C F C
Swing low, sweet char - i - ot coming for to car- ry me home. Swing
F Bb C F C7 F fine
low, sweet char - i - ot com - ing for to car- ry me home.
1. I
2. If
3. I'm
F Bb C F C
looked o - ver Jor - dan, and what did I see, com - ing for to car - ry me home? A
you get there be - fore I do, com - ing for to car - ry me home, tell
some - times up and some - times down, com - ing for to car - ry me home, but
F Bb C7 F C C7 F D.C. al fine
band of an - gels com - ing af - ter me, com - ing for to car - ry me home.
all my friends I'm com - ing, too, com - ing for to car - ry me home.
still my soul feels heav - en - ly bound, com - ing for to car - ry me home.

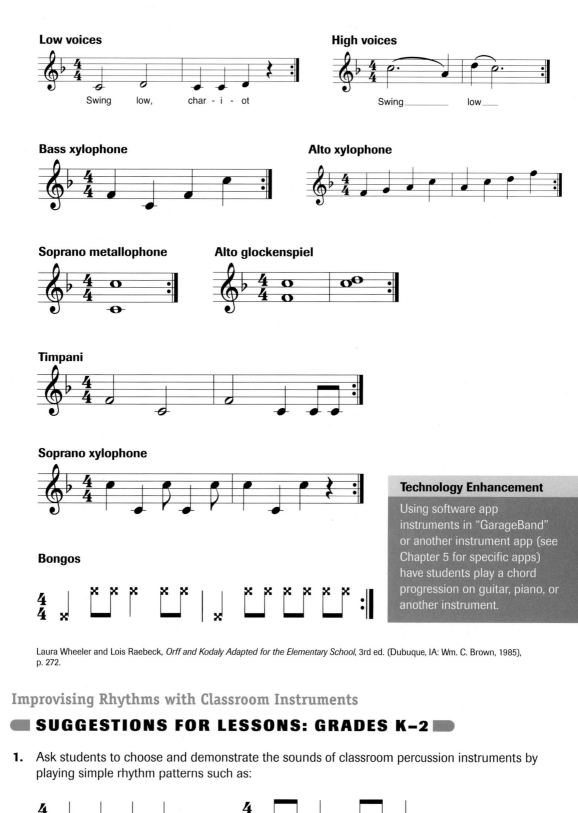

Low voices

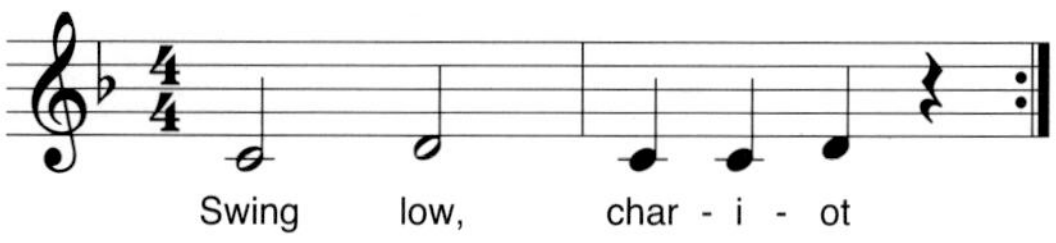

Swing low, char - i - ot

High voices

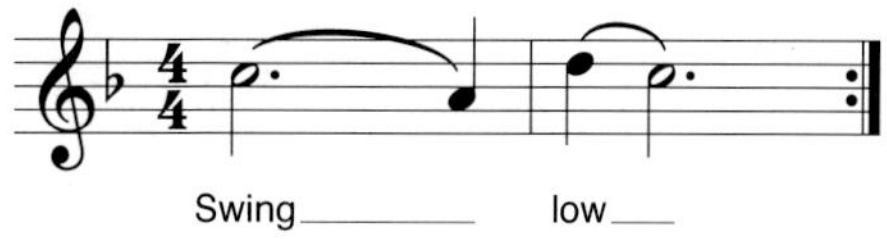

Swing______ low___

Bass xylophone

Alto xylophone

Soprano metallophone

Alto glockenspiel

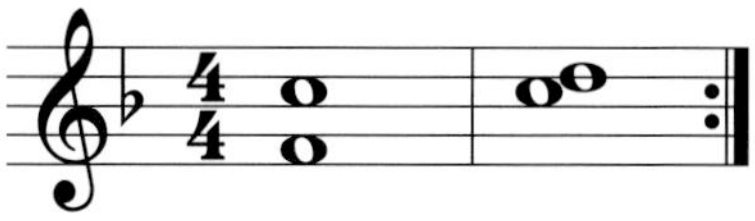

Timpani

Soprano xylophone

Bongos

> **Technology Enhancement**
>
> Using software app instruments in "GarageBand" or another instrument app (see Chapter 5 for specific apps) have students play a chord progression on guitar, piano, or another instrument.

Laura Wheeler and Lois Raebeck, *Orff and Kodaly Adapted for the Elementary School*, 3rd ed. (Dubuque, IA: Wm. C. Brown, 1985), p. 272.

Improvising Rhythms with Classroom Instruments

SUGGESTIONS FOR LESSONS: GRADES K–2

1. Ask students to choose and demonstrate the sounds of classroom percussion instruments by playing simple rhythm patterns such as:

2. Determine instruments that can sustain a sound (such as tambourine and triangle) and those that cannot (such as woodblock and rhythm sticks).
3. Divide the class into two groups. Assign group 1 nonsustaining instruments—woodblock, rhythm sticks; assign group 2 sustaining instruments—tambourine and triangle.
4. Ask individual students in group 1 to improvise a rhythm while keeping a steady beat. Give all students a chance to play. Repeat the procedure for group 2.

Technology Enhancement

Use software instrument apps such as "Music Sparkles: or "Epic Drum Set" as your instruments (see Chapter 5 for more instrument apps).

5. Create a duet by selecting students from each group to improvise a rhythm together. For example:

Tambourine: 4/4 (tr) ♩ ♫ (tr) ♩ (tr) ♩ (*tr* = shake)

Woodblock: 4/4 ♫ ♫ ♫ ♩

6. Experiment with rhythm in duple and triple meter. Have students who are not playing keep a steady beat. For example:
   Duple meter: Pat knees, clap
   Triple meter: Pat knees, clap, clap
7. As students sing familiar songs, take turns improvising rhythm patterns.

CREATIVE EXPERIENCES WITH VOCAL SOUNDS

Perhaps the most personal and individual sound is the human voice. We can make our voices sound high, low, nasal, or guttural. We can make our voice wail like a siren, bark like a dog, and sigh like the wind, and we can click, cluck, buzz, chirp, pop, and hiss. Almost unlimited vocal possibilities exist within our imaginations.

SUGGESTIONS FOR LESSONS: GRADES 4–6

1. Have students list the sounds that can be made by the human voice and perform them. Vary the pitch from high to low and the speed from fast to slow (tempo). Some suggestions:
   - Sighing
   - Whispering
   - Sneezing
   - Gurgling
   - Screaming
2. Have students use their voices to imitate or express an idea. For example:
   - We're going to the circus tomorrow, and I can hardly wait.
   - I'm a Martian from outer space.
   - Tonight's the night of Halloween. Boo!

3. Have students write a sentence and explore ways of saying it using different sounds. Possibilities for different sounds include the following:
   - Whisper
   - Shout
   - Shorten a word
   - Lengthen a word
   - Use a different pitch for each word
   - Accent selected words
   - Raise the pitch at the end of a sentence
   - Begin the sentence on a high pitch and end the sentence on a low pitch
4. Introduce a whoop sound, along with suggested notation, such as ↗↗. Ask students to create other ways of saying "whoop" and devise appropriate notation. Continue with other sounds, such as boom, tongue clicks, hiss, and whistle.
5. Use four contrasting sounds that can be performed in a variety of ways; for example, as a high-pitched sound on "whoop" (may be said/sung on a pitch with a swoop upward—siren effect); a low, heavy sound (*poom-poom* or *boom-boom*); tongue clicks with a variety of pitch levels; or hissing sounds (both short and long). Have students organize each set of sounds into a short pattern and perform it. Create symbols expressive of the sounds and use as notation. For example:

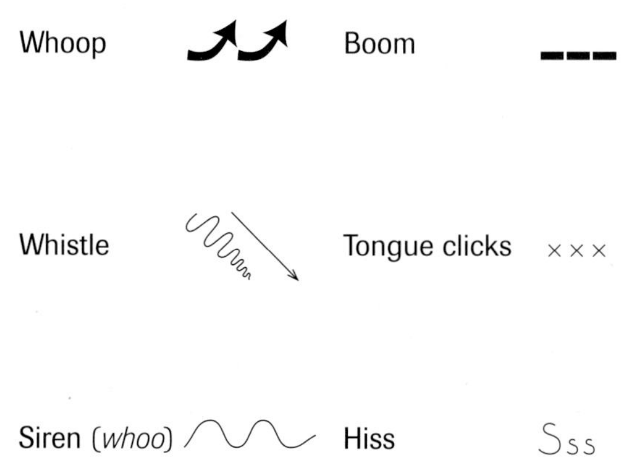

Technology Enhancement

Have students record their voices into "Myna," "GarageBand," or "Mixcraft." Have the students apply different effects to their voices such as echo, reverb, and pitch shift.

CREATIVE EXPERIENCES WITH INSTRUMENTAL SOUNDS

Exploring instrumental sounds involves not only traditional ways of creating sounds (such as playing the keys of a piano or blowing a horn) but also imaginative and nontraditional ways of making musical sounds. You may use not only traditional orchestral instruments, but also such instruments as the synthesizer, guitar, ukulele, banjo, and dulcimer. If available, explore the sounds of non-Western instruments (Japanese koto; African donno drum, agogo bells, or shekere rattle; Indian sitar and tabla). Encourage students to experiment with a variety of instrumental sounds and to create their own melodies, rhythms, tone colors, and dynamics.

Follow the Leader

Here are some icons that might be used with the voice to create a round.

There are four counts to a block, sixteen to a line. Divide the class into four groups. Group 1 begins on line 1. When group 1 begins line 2, group 2 starts line 1; when group 1 begins line 3 and group 2 line 2, group 3 begins line 1; and so on.

Line 1 (16 counts)	Whoop, whoop, whistle	Whoop, whoop, whistle	Siren	Whoop, whoop, whoop, pause
Line 2 (16 counts)	Boom Boom Boom Boom Boom Boom Boom Boom Boom Boom Boom Boom	BOOM BOOM BOOM BOOM	Boom Boom Boom Boom Boom Boom Boom Boom Boom Boom Boom Boom	BOOM BOOM BOOM BOOM
Line 3 (16 counts)	Tongue clicks (high/low at random)	Two high clicks, two low clicks	Tongue clicks	High clicks, low clicks
Line 4 (16 counts)	Sssss— Hiss...........	SsSsSs Hiss Hiss Hiss	Sssss— Hiss...........	SsSsSs Hiss Hiss Hiss

Group 1 performs lines 1–4 two times.
Group 2 performs lines 1–4, and then repeats 1–3.
Group 3 performs lines 1–4, and then repeats 1–2.
Group 4 performs lines 1–4 once only.

SUGGESTIONS FOR LESSONS: GRADES 3–6

1. Divide the class into small groups. Assign an instrument (such as Q-chord, drums, xylophone, and keyboard) to each group. Ask students to experiment with producing at least four different sounds on each instrument. Decide which sounds are similar among the instruments (if any) and which are the most contrasting. Organize the sounds into duple or triple rhythmic patterns and perform in a sequence, alternating tone color and meter.

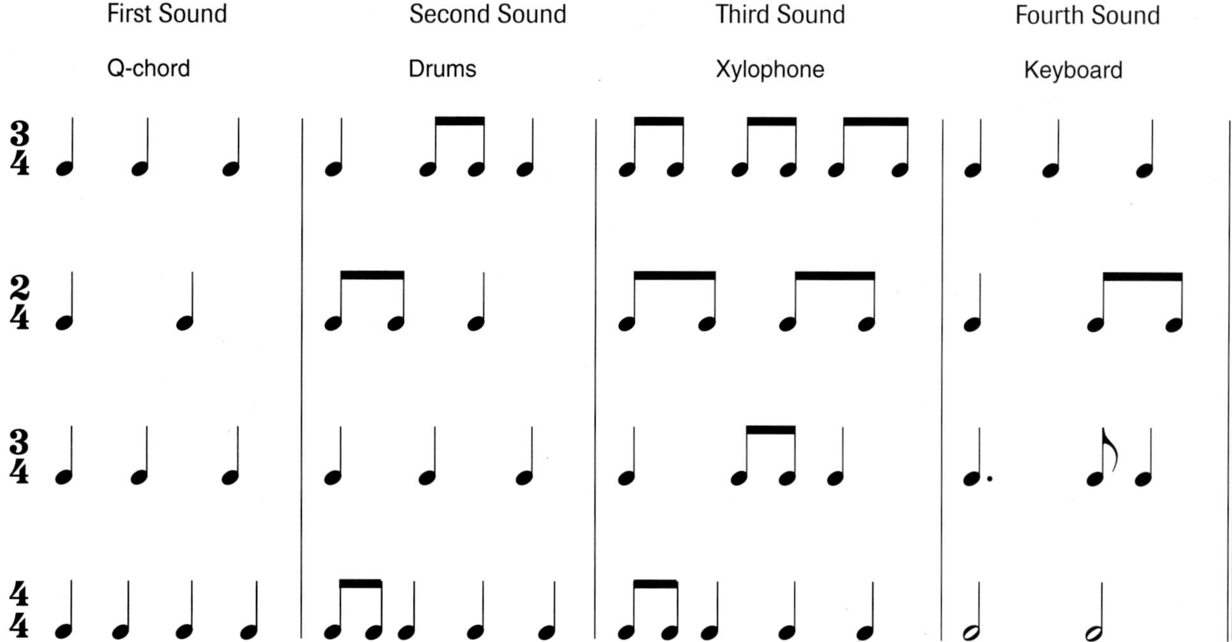

2. Divide students into small groups and assign to each a class of instruments (tambourines, jingle sticks; rhythm sticks, woodblocks; bongo drums, hand drums; maracas, castanets). Tell them to discover at least three ways of creating short sounds and three ways of creating long sounds. Ask each group to demonstrate for the class.
3. Have students create a musical composition in the form of a rondo: ABACA.

CREATIVE EXPERIENCES WITH ENVIRONMENTAL SOUNDS

The raw material of music is *sound*. Sounds in our environment often go unnoticed; yet if we pause to listen, there are many, each with a tone quality and rhythm all its own. Increasing perception of environmental sounds and how they can be used to create a musical composition can be a significant and enriching experience for students.

SUGGESTIONS FOR LESSONS: GRADES 4–6

1. Ask the class to be completely silent and listen to the sounds around them (clock ticking, a locker door slamming, bird chirping, jet airplane, car engine, coins dropping on the floor, animal sounds). Discuss which of these sounds are long, short, high, low, legato, staccato, loud, and soft.
2. Ask students to bring in a written description of the area they pass through on their way to school, along with sound-producing materials to express appropriate sounds—for example, in a factory district: whistle, machinery sounds (metal pipes), car horn. (See the example on the next page.) Discuss differences between sounds produced and heard in the morning and those produced and heard in the afternoon.
3. Decide on sounds and sound materials you wish to use in the musical composition. Create picture notation for each sound. Place all sounds into a time frame of four beats (see example).

Factory District in Sound

A few blocks from my house are a lot of big factories. They are in operation all day and all night. The early morning and late evening hours are quiet. There is always a light motor hum heard in the morning. After a while, the people begin to come to work. At first there are just a few, then more and more report for work. Occasionally, you hear a car horn blow in the parking lot, and the greetings of one worker to another. As the morning continues, the sounds from the factory become louder and more intense, spreading from section to section. In addition, there are sounds of people in the street. At the end of the day, there is a whistle signifying the end of one shift and the beginning of another. Then there is a gradual slowing down of machinery in the factory because not as many workers are employed on the evening shift. Gradually, the parking lot empties of cars, and the factory sounds return to the quiet hum of evening.

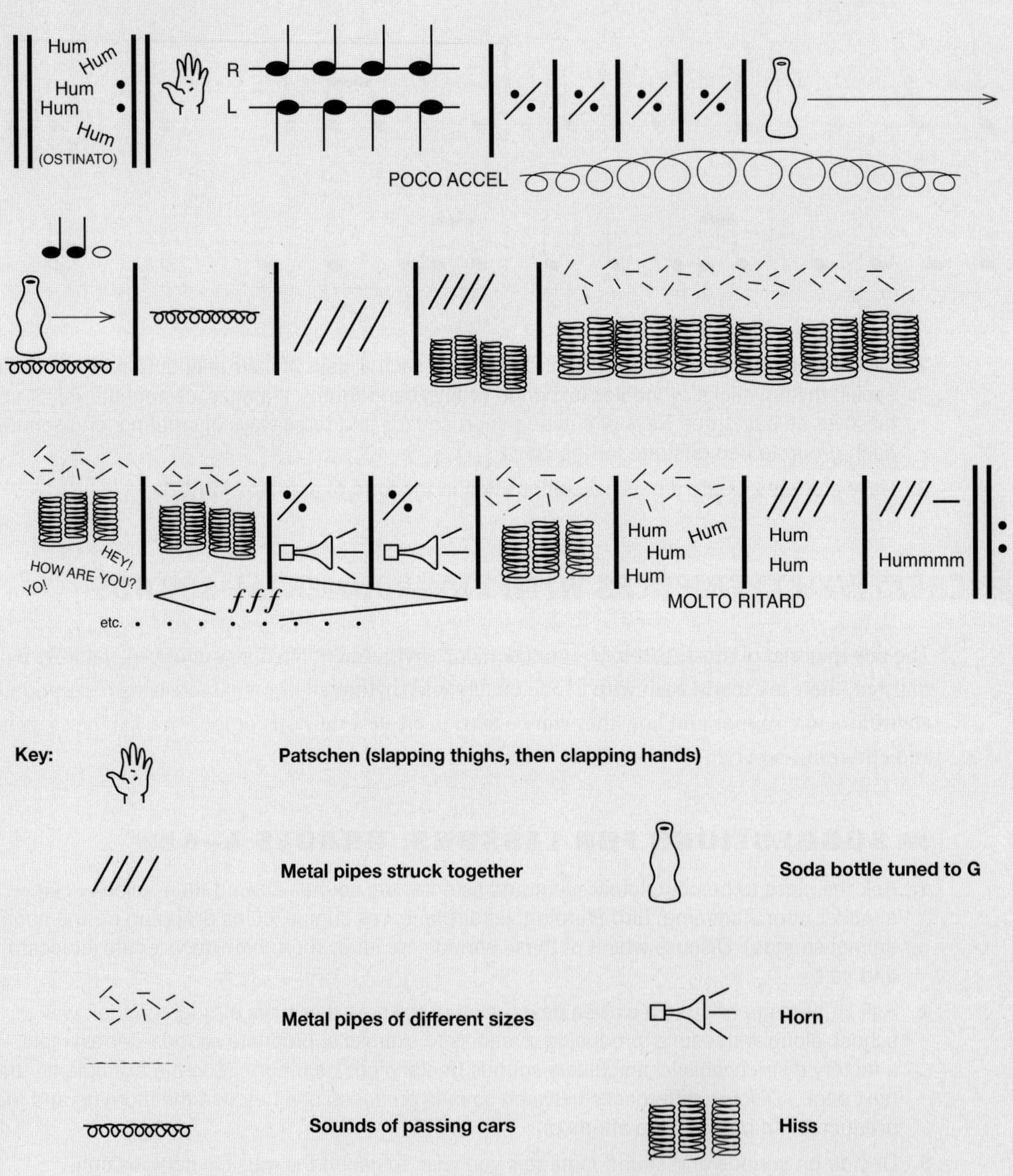

CREATIVE EXPERIENCES WITH BODY SOUNDS

Another category of sounds are those produced through body percussion. These include sounds such as clapping, tapping, patting, pounding, stamping, and snapping. Sometimes, when only the hands are used, body percussion is referred to as "hand jive." Many times body sounds are used in combination with vocal sounds or in combination with movement. Thus, students might walk in a circle and then stand still and clap a rhythm.

Creating a Musical Video

SUGGESTIONS FOR LESSONS: GRADES 3–6

1. Download or stream Pachelbel's *Canon in D Major* [iTunes/Spotify] and listen to the first four variations.
2. Decide how the composer created each variation—a high part (called a *descant*), broken chords in the bass, and so on.
3. Listen to the first four variations again and ask students which variation they would like to be.
4. Divide the class into four groups, each with a recording of their chosen variation on an MP3 player or tablet computer. As an ideal, there should be no more than five students in each group. If the class is large, you may want to have more groups and devices.
5. Assign an activity to each group (group 1, hands or fingers walking; group 2, using string; group 3, feet; group 4, sunflowers; and so on).
6. Ask each group to go into a separate corner of the room or into another space, such as the hall or a vacant room. Each group of five students should listen to its segment and then create a movement that matches the musical variation.
7. Each group should determine what props it needs and bring them the next day.
8. Each group practices the particular variation by using the props and activities it has decided on.
9. After each group practices the selected variation, bring students back together and make a video by using a Flip cam or built-in camera on an iPod/iPad/computer. Have the students review their videos and make changes to improve their dancing and video.
10. Make a final video and then splice together the different groups' videos and share with the class.
11. *Caution*: This project takes time and cannot be hurried. Often there is organized confusion. Allow at least two weeks (a half-hour per day) to make the musical video. Although this project is time-consuming, it is well worth the effort.

Creating a Percussion Accompaniment to a Song

It is essential in rhythmic experiences to establish the *tempo* (speed of the beat). Early on, students must feel and be able to clap (or move) to a steady beat. As students create rhythm patterns to accompany songs, they will need to develop techniques for playing and notating the rhythms.

SUGGESTIONS FOR LESSONS: GRADES 3–6

1. Teach the African folk song "Tue, Tue" (p. 287).
2. Have students tap their knees and clap the beats (duple meter: 1 2 1 2).

3. Decide on an instrument to play the beats, and notate. For example:

4. Explore rhythms that might fit the duple meter and play them on a variety of instruments. Make your choice and notate. For example:

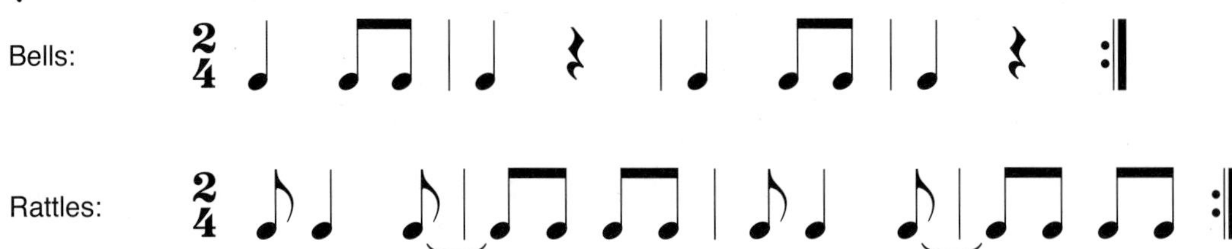

Write as a percussion score:

Conga drum: 2/4

Bells: 2/4

Rattles: 2/4

Creating a Percussion Composition

SUGGESTIONS FOR LESSONS: GRADES 4–6

1. Ask students to improvise a variety of rhythmic patterns in duple or triple meter.
2. Select four different patterns for use in the composition.
3. Discuss how you can extend a composition by repeating an idea or provide interest and variety by employing a contrasting idea. For example:

4. Have students practice clapping each pattern.
5. Decide on instruments to be used for each pattern. For example:

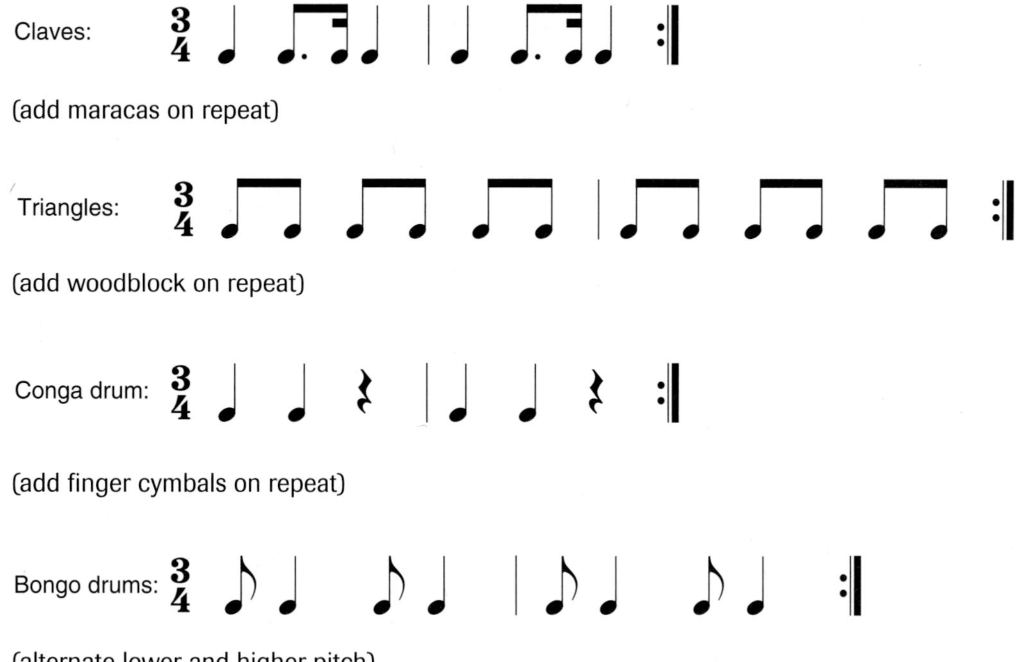

(alternate lower and higher pitch)

6. Begin with one instrument and add the rest one by one for a cumulative effect.
7. Discuss ways of creating a contrasting section, such as a slower meter or different instruments. For example:

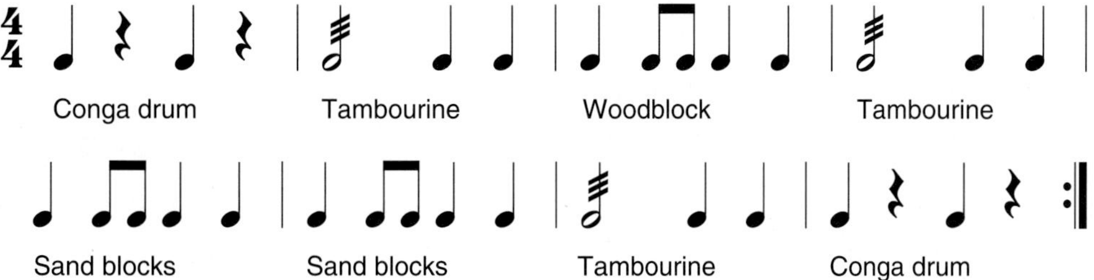

8. On the repeat of the contrasting section, ask one student to play a pattern in 3/4 meter, thus creating a polyrhythmic effect. Use a high-sounding instrument such as a high-pitched woodblock:

9. Add a closing section (coda) with elements of each section:

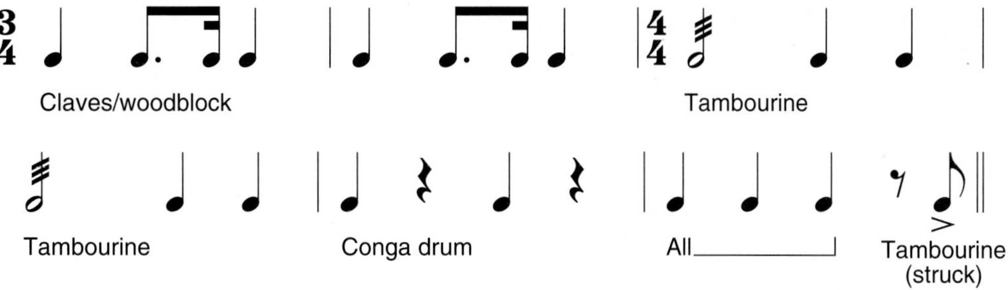

CREATIVE EXPERIENCES WITH WRITING MELODIES OR SONGS

Writing an original melody or song involves students in synthesizing their total response to music. It is a major means for developing concepts about melody, rhythm, harmony, and form, as well as for providing opportunities for creating expressive and formal relationships between words and music. All children create melodies. Just listen to them at play and you will hear them sing many chants and short melodic phrases.

As students create melodies or songs, they become involved as composers, performers, and listeners. Musical growth occurs as they become aware of possibilities for sound exploration and pattern development and use these in expressive ways. Although the process of composing is most important, the student should also be guided to achieve as expressive a product as possible.

Special Learner Note

Drum circles are an ever-growing music activity in many communities. People of all ages and abilities come together with drums (and occasionally other percussion instruments) of all sizes and shapes to create a one-time musical composition. All performers are encouraged to "create" their own part; solos are even part of some drum circles. Teachers are encouraged to look into drum circles for a quick and easy percussion composition experience.

What Makes an Interesting Melody?

Essentially, two elements contribute to a successful and interesting melody: repetition and contrast. A melody must also have a sense of coming to a rest or a close. This discussion focuses on writing a song melody, but the guiding principles may be used for writing instrumental melodies as well.

The use of repetition can extend the length of a melody, emphasize certain words, create rhythmic interest, and provide unity. Contrast can be achieved by techniques such as alternating melodic skips and steps, changing the direction of the melodic line, changing rhythms, and creating contrasting sections. If a melody is to be sung, one must also consider the range and its appropriateness for a given maturity level.

Preparing Students to Write Melodies or Songs

SUGGESTIONS FOR LESSONS: GRADES 3–6

1. Have students sing many songs and play classroom instruments to develop a feeling for tonality, rhythm patterns, tone color, and pitch.
2. Help students develop a sense of tonality and beat. Students in grades 4–6 should be encouraged to write out their responses in rhythm notation.
3. Sing or play a short phrase. Ask students to improvise a second phrase in the same meter, ending on the *tonic* (keynote of the scale). Explore in several keys, such as G, D, and F. For example:

4. Sing or play melody patterns and ask students to repeat exactly and then as a sequence (beginning on different pitches). For example:

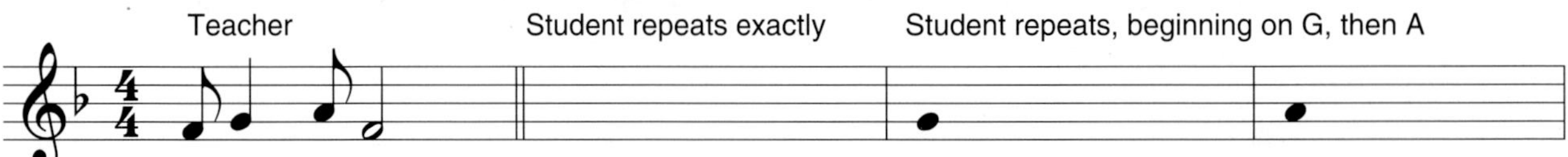

5. Sing or play rhythms and ask students to improvise a response. For example:

6. Sing or play a familiar melody and ask students to create ways of changing it—for example, by repeating a phrase, adding notes, or changing the rhythm:

Original melody (phrase):

Adding notes, changing rhythm:

Adding notes above and below:

Changing the meter from duple to triple:

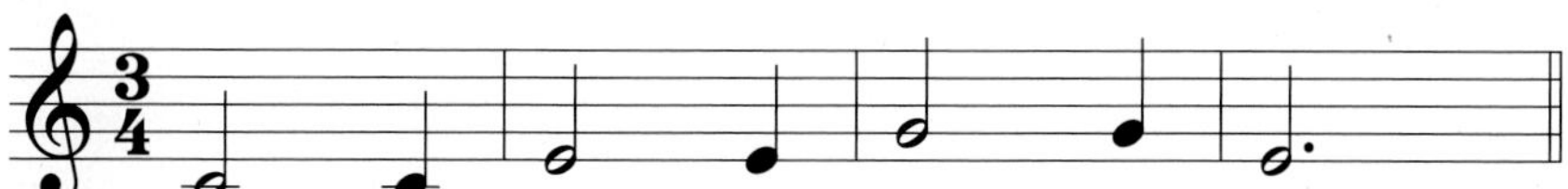

Changing the tonality from major to minor:

Writing a Melody by Using a Pentatonic Scale

It is easy to write a melody based on the pentatonic (five-note) scale because every combination will be satisfying to the ear. Some melodies, however, will be more interesting than others.

SUGGESTIONS FOR LESSONS: GRADES 4–6

1. Have students select a rhythm pattern and improvise a melody; then have them place the notation on a staff. It might look something like this (black keys only):

2. Help students explore the tonal possibilities of other pentatonic scales. For example:

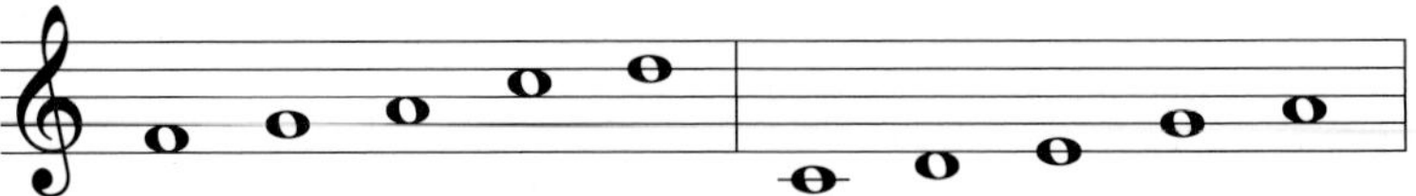

3. Add appropriate rhythms. For example:

Writing a Melody by Using a Seven-Note Scale (Major/Minor)

SUGGESTIONS FOR LESSONS

1. Prepare a handout with (1) a staff showing the C major scale and (2) a staff with a rhythm pattern above it.

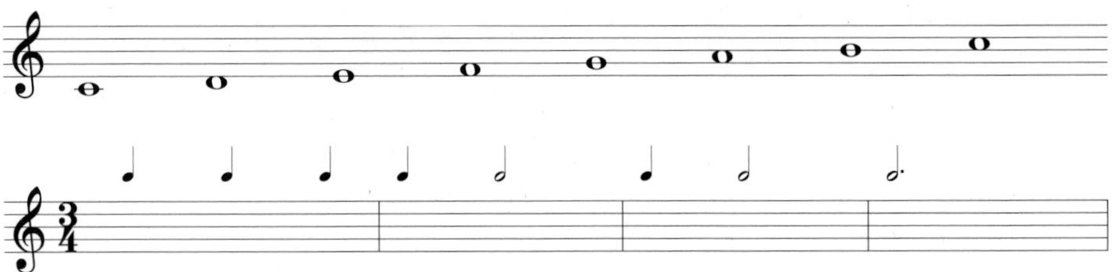

2. Tell students to begin on the first note of the C scale (C) and end on the last note (C). Use each pitch only once and place the pitches beneath the rhythm pattern. For example:

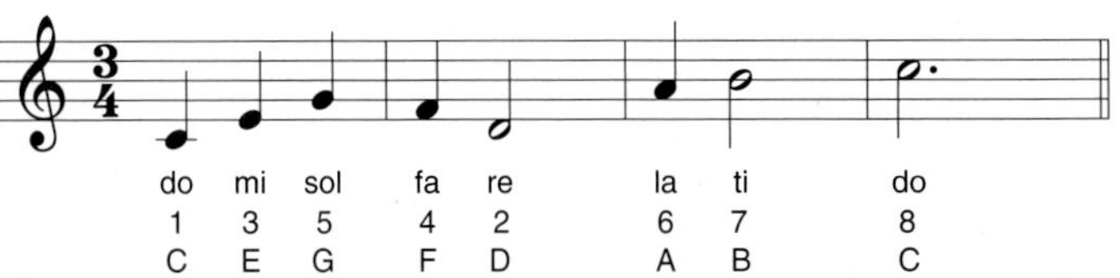

3. Choose a label (syllable, number, or letter) and name each note.
4. Play or sing the four-measure melodies of several students. Discuss the most interesting ones.
5. Experiment with a variety of rhythms for the melodies. Repeat a pitch when necessary to make the melody "fit" the rhythm.

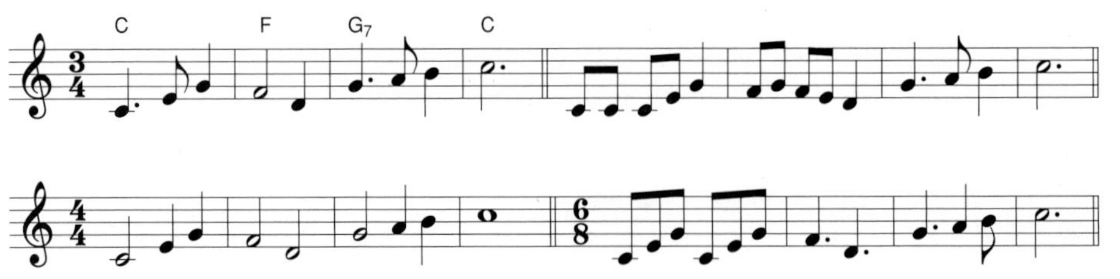

Special Learner Note

Use a standard color-coding system for all melody instruments (for example, Boomwhackers® color coding) for ease of transcription.

The group may create a melody by having each student pick a card with a color on it out of a "hat" and then pick from another "hat" a card with a type of note (whole, half, etc.) on it. The composition is created in the order that the notes are picked and then displayed on a board for all to see.

Create a chart by listing the notes of the scale across the top and the alphabet under the notes, as shown below. Each student is encouraged (or you may pair students with a peer model or aide) to create his/her own "name song" by matching the letters of the name with the appropriate notes on the chart.

A	B	C	D	E	F	G
A	B	C	D	E	F	G
H	I	J	K	L	M	N
O	P	Q	R	S	T	U
V	W	X	Y	Z		

6. Transpose the four-measure melody into different keys, both minor and major. For example:

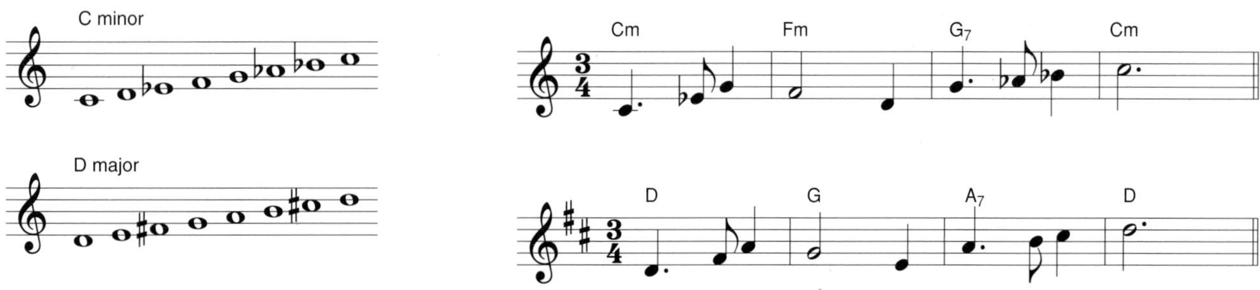

7. Review melodies previously learned (see the standard forms on next page) for ideas of what other composers have done.
8. Create a melody of eight measures. Measures 1–4 should end on the dominant (fifth tone of the scale), and measures 5–8 should end on the tonic (first tone of the scale). For example:

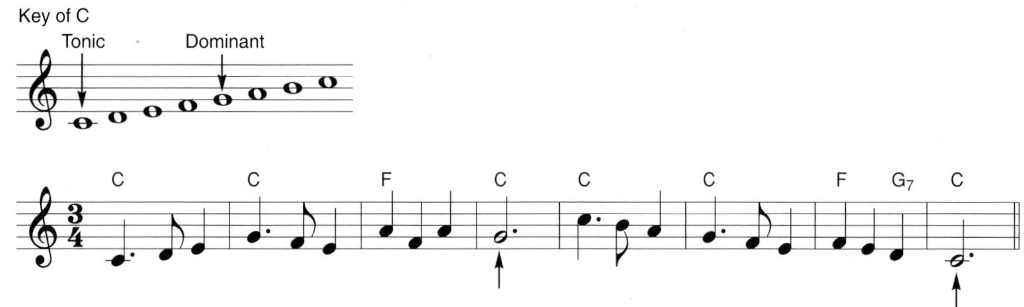

9. Add chords (C, F, G_7) and accompany on a keyboard instrument. Sing melody on "doo-be-doo" or play on recorders. Explore the possibilities of creating an AB or ABA form by adding a contrasting melody.

Writing an Original Poem and Setting It to Music

SUGGESTIONS FOR LESSONS: GRADES 4–6

1. Choose a subject for a poem; for example, nature, an event, an idea, or a person. Be sure that it has a strong rhythmic pulse. Following is an example of a poem (later set to music) by a fifth- and sixth-grade class:[2]

   We're America's children, and we're here to celebrate.
   Living, learning and growing in a land that's really great.
   Our land consists of different people, each unique in his own way,
   It matters not if you're short or tall, black or white, great or small—
   We're America's children, and we're here to celebrate.
   Living, learning and growing in a land that's really great.
   We all have a chance, you see, to be the best that we can be.
   Sing it loud, sing it proud, really great, celebrate.
   America, we love you.

2. After you have written a poem, mark the rhythmic pulses above the text. If necessary, adapt or change the text to fit this pulse:

[2] Written for the eightieth birthday celebration of the Cleveland Heights–University Heights School System, Ohio.

Standard Melody Forms

Arch form Haydn

Generally ascending Rodgers and Hammerstein

Generally descending "Joy to the World"

Undulating wave J. S. Bach

We're A-mer-i-ca's | chil-dren, and we're | here to cel-e- | brate. |
Liv-ing, learn-ing and | grow-ing in a | land that's real-ly | great. Our|
land con-sists of dif-f'rent | people, each u-|nique in his own | way, It |
mat-ters not if you're | short or tall, | black or white, | great or | small—- |
We're A-mer-i-ca's | chil-dren, and we're | here to cel-e-| brate. |
Liv-ing, learn-ing and | grow-ing in a | land that's real-ly | great. We|
all have a | chance, you see, to | be the best that | we can be.|
Sing it loud, | sing it proud, | real-ly great, | cel-e-brate.|
A-mer-i-ca, | we love | you. |

3. Before you begin composing the melody, note the repeated phrases (such as "We're America's children, and we're here to celebrate. Living, learning and growing in a land that's really great."). You will want to use the same melody for each.
4. Select a key (such as the key of C) and write the pitches on the chalkboard.
5. Experiment with different rhythm patterns within the two-pulse tempo beat and then notate your choice:

6. Using the pitches of your chosen scale, explore various tonal patterns and create a melody for each phrase. For example:

7. When you have completed the song, add accompaniment. Simple chords played on a keyboard instrument or guitar might be appropriate, or perhaps a music teacher could arrange a piano accompaniment.

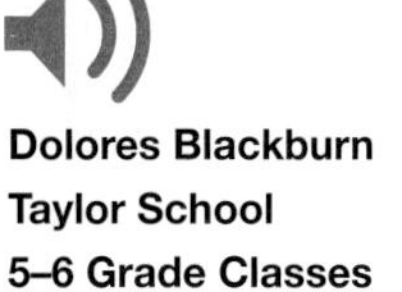

Dolores Blackburn
Taylor School
5–6 Grade Classes

We're America's Children

Key: C
Starting pitch: C
Meter: 4/4, begins on 1

F Am Am D D7 G G7
mat - ters not if you're short or tall black or white, great or small
C F G7
We're A - mer - i - ca's chil - dren and we're here to cel - e - brate.
C C F G7
Liv - ing, learn - ing and grow - ing in a land that's real - ly great. We
Am Dm G7
all have a chance, you see, to be the best that we can be.
C F G Am
Sing it loud, sing it proud, real - ly great, cel - e - brate. A -
C F G7 C C C
mer - i - ca, we love you.

Integrating Technology

The Music Education Premium Site contains chapter quizzing, Spotify playlists, and downloads of free MP3s of noted songs. Visit CengageBrain.com to purchase an access code or enter the code provided with your text materials.

Web Resources

- Search the Web (www.google.com) for information on the Orff approach to teaching music, and also the making of percussion instruments.

Audio

- Download music discussed in this chapter from the Apple iTunes store.
- Spotify playlists allow students to stream music referenced within each chapter.
- Download free audio MP3s for the songs noted in the chapter.

CENGAGE**brain**.com

Questions for Discussion

1. Discuss some ways in which you would approach music creativity in the lower elementary grades (K–3) and the upper elementary grades (4–6).
2. Choose a grade level and discuss how, for that grade, you might use some of Carl Orff's ideas about teaching music.
3. Discuss how you might teach improvisation of a melody to grades 2, 4, and 6 using such musical elements as tone color and rhythm.
4. Discuss why it might be better to begin improvising by using only two notes rather than seven. Discuss which two you might choose and outline how you might begin.
5. How do you think you might approach *assessment* for a musical lesson that is based on improvisation?

Assessment

Review ways the music standards listed at the beginning of this chapter have been met.

CHAPTER 9

Integrating Music with the Study of Peoples, Places, and Cultures

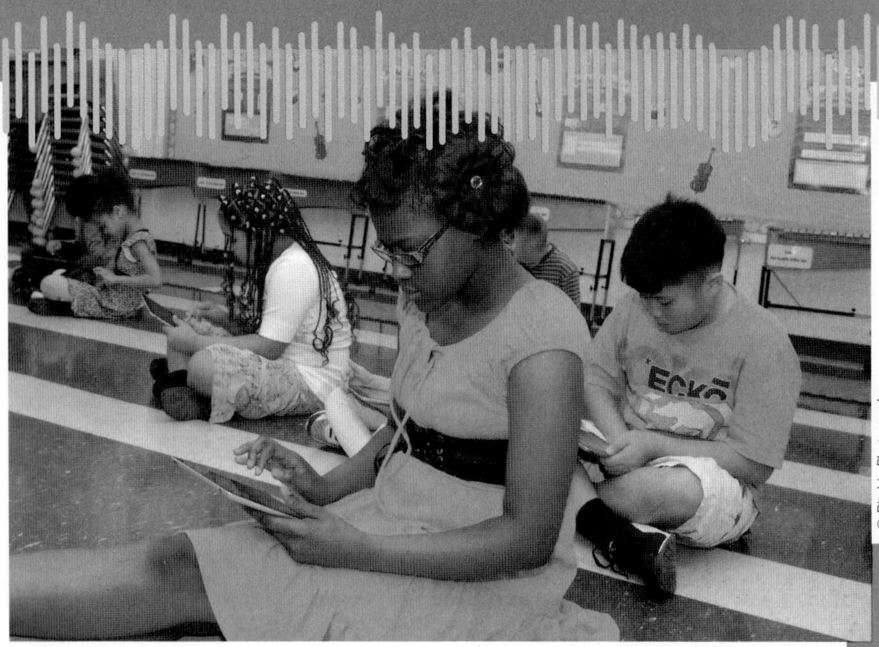

Objectives

Students will learn to develop lessons on music cultures from the following geographical areas:

- Africa
- Asia
- Europe
- America

National and State Music Standards

This chapter provides experiences with the following national music standards and related state music standards:

- Understanding music in relation to various cultures/geographical areas
- Singing a varied repertoire of music from different cultures/geographical areas
- Performing on instruments a varied repertoire of music from different cultures/geographical areas
- Listening to, analyzing, and describing music from different cultures/geographical areas

Students today are truly living in an international age. Almost every day, they encounter cultures from other areas of the world through television, radio, movies, books, magazines, and the Internet. Through new technology in communications satellites and the Internet, one part of our globe can be in instant contact with another. In many regions of our country, children are also coming to know large numbers of people from other places and cultures who now reside permanently in the United States. From its beginnings, this country has become home for immigrants from throughout the world, and demographic surveys today quickly reveal that while ours is indeed one nation, many cultures comprise it.

American schools traditionally have encouraged the study and appreciation of different cultural groups. Social studies, geography, and history curricula have directed attention to the contributions of many peoples of the world, and teachers at every grade level have sought to bring multicultural viewpoints to their classrooms. Reflecting this concern for keeping in touch with the international age in which we live, teachers have increasingly endeavored to present a greater variety of music representative of many different cultural groups. This trend has paralleled the work of music scholars, who have documented that music is a worldwide phenomenon occurring among all peoples

We now know that our planet contains a number of highly developed musical systems, of which the European-American classical tradition is just one. Such findings have clearly challenged many traditionally held views. It is evident that although music is an international phenomenon, it most certainly is not an international "language." Musical systems in other areas of the world are often constructed very differently from our own. If we wish to understand these different types of music, we must learn how they are constructed. Thus, one of the primary objectives in studying a variety of music is to help students understand that *there are many different but equally logical ways for organizing musical sounds.*

This chapter is devoted to providing musical experiences for the classroom from selected places or cultures of the world. We begin in Africa, move to Asia and Europe, and then to the Americas. For each of these geographic areas, musical examples and teaching strategies are provided. The experiences suggested may serve as a basis for musical study alone, although the intent is to help children perceive music as interrelated with other aspects of culture. Thus, as students study some examples of traditional Japanese music, they will also study other aspects of Japanese life and culture. Children enjoy learning about other peoples of the world, their customs and crafts, their architecture, dance, literature, painting, sculpture, and music. Through an integrated study of many aspects of a culture, children develop new and important understandings of other peoples. They begin to realize the integral place of the arts in other societies. Many teachers have also found that a combined study showing the interrelationships of culture and arts significantly enhances a child's interest in investigating and performing music.

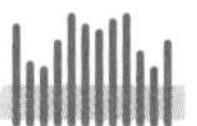

SOME SUGGESTED CLASSROOM EXPERIENCES

Along with studying the music of various ethnic groups, you may wish to introduce different cultural backgrounds through the following:

1. Prepare a bulletin board on each country studied. Place a map on the board and have students use pins to mark the major cities, mountains, rivers, deserts, and so on. Have students look for pictures of people, examples of the visual arts (architecture, sculpture, painting, dance, puppet theater), and photos of musicians. Arrange them in an attractive design on the board.

2. Have students search the Internet for information, pictures, and sounds of the music of various cultures.[1] Students can then create a PowerPoint, Google Presentations, or Prezi presentation using the information, pictures, videos, and music of these cultures.
3. Have students use Google Earth (www.google.com/earth) to locate specific continents, countries, and cities to orient themselves and relate new cultures to areas of the world they may know something about.
4. Invite guests from various countries and ethnic groups to speak to the class. Ask them to bring cultural items (especially musical instruments) to show to students.
5. Show DVDs/videos on different peoples and cultures. Search YouTube or TeacherTube for videos to use in your classroom.
6. Take a field trip or online "virtual tour" to a museum to see examples of the visual arts of various cultural groups.
7. Investigate the beliefs of various groups. For example, Buddhism is a major religion in China and Japan. Have the class explore the topic *What does it mean to be a Buddhist?*
8. Ask the physical education teacher to assist you in teaching dances from various cultures.
9. Have students look for stories from the various areas being studied. Read them in class and perhaps plan short dramatizations.
10. Plan imaginary trips to different countries. Make an itinerary of things you hope to see and do.
11. Have your school plan a multicultural or international festival. Include dress, dance, visual arts, food, and music.
12. Create a "World Music Drumming" ensemble. Visit www.worldmusicdrumming.com/.
13. Play geography games such as www.kidsgeo.com/geography-games/.

Technology Enhancement

Web Resources

Free lesson plans, PowerPoint presentations, and links to games about Africa: http://africa.mrdonn.org/lessonplans.html

Geography games for students: http://www.kidsgeo.com/geography-games/

Smithsonian National Museum of Natural History: African Voice Exhibit online. "African Voices is a permanent exhibition that examines the diversity, dynamism, and global influence of Africa's peoples and cultures over time in the realms of family, work, community, and the natural environment." The website contains an interactive historical timeline and cultural themes: http://www.mnh.si.edu/africanvoices/

MUSIC OF AFRICAN PEOPLES

Background Information for the Class

Africa is the second-largest continent in the world (see Figure 9.1), with a land mass stretching approximately 3,500 miles from north to south and almost 2,000 miles from east to west, an area approximately equal to Europe, China, and the United States combined.

The continent contains some of the most diverse land in the world. Its vast stretches of terrain contain the world's largest desert (the Sahara) and longest waterway (the Nile). Dense rain forests, receiving up to 8 feet of precipitation each year, result in vegetation so lush that the sun is almost totally obscured; whereas in bitterly cold regions, such as the mountain peaks of the Atlas and Ruwenzori ranges, snow falls for most of the year.

Africa is characterized by enormous ethnic diversity, which is clearly evident in the many countries and languages on the continent. Some ethnic groups, such as the Bantu, who reside in a number

[1] A good teacher resource for materials on various music cultures is World Music Press (www.worldmusicpress.com). Of particular interest at this website are "A Checklist for Evaluating Multicultural Materials" and links to a number of other companies that are publishing multicultural materials.

Figure 9-1 Africa

of countries south of the equator, primarily raise cattle and cultivate the land. Other groups, such as the Sudanese living between the equator and the Sahara, have built large metropolitan areas. One of the most powerful influences to affect the continent is the development of Islam and the migration of Arab peoples, especially along the northern and eastern areas of the continent.

Some General Characteristics of African Music

A great variety of music is found throughout the African continent. Music is a part of almost every aspect of life from birth to death. It is closely tied to festivals, work, politics, courtship, and recreation. Multi-art productions involving music, dance, and drama (with the latter two often involving brilliant visual effects in costuming and masks) occur frequently throughout the continent.

Because of the vast geographical and cultural differences on the continent, one can expect a considerable amount of diversity in music. The following general outline identifies some basic characteristics of much African music south of the Sahara and provides a resource for organizing a study of this music for the classroom.

- Much traditional African music is communal and functional; it is often associated with dance and games. Although there are some exceptions, the emphasis is on group rather than solo performance.
- Melodies are often short; longer melodies are often composed of short phrase units. A variety of scales is found: four-, five-, and seven-note scales occur, although pentatonic scales are

most common; intervals are predominantly seconds and thirds. Melodies tend to be syllabic (one syllable of text per note), and "resultant melodies" occur with pitches contributed by several individuals.

- There is a strong beat in much African music. Particularly in West Africa, there is often a driving, pulsating beat with a steady tempo throughout. Polyrhythms and syncopation are frequent. Repeated rhythmic patterns are common.
- Texture is monophonic (one musical line), heterophonic (simultaneous variations on a single musical line), and polyphonic (many musical lines). Harmony occurs in thirds, fourths, fifths, and sixths, although thirds are the most common. Both stratification of melodic and rhythmic lines and imitation are common.
- Form is often related to function (e.g., game songs, work songs); the call-and-response form is prevalent. The use of ostinato (repetition of melodies and rhythms) is common.
- Timbre is characterized by a wide variety of tone colors in the voice, but generally there is an open, relaxed quality in singing. Many percussion, stringed, and wind instruments are used; percussion instruments predominate. Music is often dominated by a percussive quality (e.g., individual tones are attacked strongly; many plucked stringed instruments are used). An important xylophone tradition is also present. A "buzzy" quality is created on some instruments (e.g., on xylophones through gourd resonators with spider-web membranes placed over holes, and button-like rattles added to the mbira).

Technology Enhancement

- BBC – GCSE Bitesize – Music of Africa: Website containing wonderful pictures, information, and audio examples of instruments and African musical concepts: http://www.bbc.co.uk/schools/gcsebitesize/music/world_music/music_africa1.shtml
- CIA's World Factbook: Information and maps about Ghana for teacher use: https://www.cia.gov/library/publications/the-world-factbook/geos/gh.html
- Lonely Planet: Interactive map, pictures, and information about Ghana and its people: http://www.lonelyplanet.com/maps/africa/ghana/

Teaching African Music: Sample Lessons

All of the sample lessons that follow are based on music from the West African country of Ghana. The overall goal, however, is to acquaint students with some of the many types of vocal and instrumental music present on the continent and to have them study these types in terms of the elements of music: rhythm, melody, timbre, texture, and form. Objectives are given for each of the sample lessons, along with performance and listening suggestions, some of which are coordinated with dance. In designing your own lessons for different school settings, you may wish to rearrange the order of presentation and adapt the teaching strategies suggested.

A number of songs are included in the lessons, and it is suggested that they be taught by rote. Teachers will need to practice the pronunciation of texts before presenting the pieces to the class.

African instruments, such as the mbira (kalimba), can be purchased in a number of music stores (also see www.amazon.com). Where authentic instruments are not available, suggestions for substitutes are given. Teachers and students may also wish to make some instruments, such as drums.

LESSON PLAN

African Music 1

Grade: 1–3

Tue, Tue
Key: F (Pentatonic)
Starting pitch: C
Meter: 4/4, begins on 1
Ghana
Tu - e Tu - e ba - ri - ma tu - e tu - e tu - e tu - e ba - ri - ma
(Too - ay Too - ay ba - ree - ma too - ay too - ay Too - ay too - ay ba - ri - ma)
tu - e tu - e A - bo - fra ba A - ma da - wa da - wa tu - e tu - e A - bo - fra
(too - ay too - ay A - boe - frah bah Ah - mah dah - wah dah - wah too - ay too - ay A - boe - frah)
ba A - ma da - wa da - wa tu - e tu - e Hai ba - ri - ma tu - e tu - e Hai ba - ri - ma
(bah Ah - mah dah - wah dah - wah too - ay too - ay Hey ba - ree - ma too - ay too - ay Hey ba - ree - ma)

NATIONAL AND STATE MUSIC STANDARDS

1. Singing, alone and with others, a varied repertoire of music
2. Performing on instruments, alone and with others, a varied repertoire of music

OBJECTIVES

Students will:

1. Learn some geographical characteristics of the continent of Africa and the country of Ghana.
   a. Sing the song "Tue, Tue."
   b. Add a rattle (shekere) accompaniment.
   c. Add body percussion.
2. Discuss the following musical characteristics found in much African music:
   - Strong beat
   - Pentatonic melody

MATERIALS

- Globe and map of Africa
- Rattle or shekere (see www.amazon.com)

William M. Anderson

Shekere

PROCEDURES

1. Using a globe or map, help students find the continent of Africa. Then have them locate the country of Ghana in western Africa. You may wish to place a map of Africa on the bulletin board and put a pin-flag on the country of Ghana. Assist students in looking for pictures and information about Ghana that can be added to a bulletin board.
2. Explain that in Ghana children learn many singing-game songs. The words of the song refer to the percussive clapping that accompanies the song.
3. Practice saying the words of the song:

Words:	Tu- e tu- e ba- ri- ma tu- e tu- e	(repeats)
Pronunciation:	Too-ay too-ay bah-ree-mah too-ay too-ay	
Words:	A- bo- fra ba A-ma da- wa tu- e tu- e	(repeats)
Pronunciation:	Ah-boe-frah-bah Ah-mah dah-wah too-ay too-ay	
Words:	Hei ba- ri- ma tu-e tu- e Hei ba- ri- ma	
Pronunciation:	Hey bah-ree-mah tu-ay tu-ay Hey bah-ree-mah	

4. Sing the song, particularly calling attention to the repetition of the musical phrases (measures 3 and 4 like measures 1 and 2; measure 7 like measure 5).
5. While singing, have the group keep the beat by clapping. Notice the strong feeling for the beat.
6. Accompany the song with a rattle sounding on each beat. Use an African shekere (pronounced "sha-kă-rāy") rattle or a substitute such as a maraca.

7. Add body percussion to the piece:
   a. Have the class divide into pairs.
   b. Place two student pairs together and have them clap in the following manner: Clap partner's hands on beats 1 and 2; hands against the thighs on beats 3 and 4.
   c. Repeat the pattern for measure 2.
   d. Change partners for measure 3 and, as before, clap hands on beats 1 and 2 and then against thighs on beats 3 and 4.
   e. In measure 4 repeat the pattern for measure 3.
   f. Change back to original partners in measure 5 and, as before, clap hands on beats 1 and 2 and then against thighs on beats 3 and 4.
   g. In measure 6 repeat the pattern for measure 5.
   h. In measure 7 change partners again and, as before, clap hands on beats 1 and 2 and then against thighs on beats 3 and 4.
   i. Repeat the clap pattern in the last two measures.
8. Draw attention to the fact that every syllable in the text of the song has one note. This gives a percussive effect to the music.
9. Have the students write out the pitches present in the song. Because there are five pitches, the scale is described as pentatonic. Have the students play the notes on a xylophone and sing along on the syllable "loo."

ASSESSMENT

1. Perform "Tue, Tue" with correct pitches and rhythms.
2. Discuss characteristics of African music in this piece (strong beat, pentatonic scale, shekere rattle accompaniment).

NATIONAL AND STATE MUSIC STANDARDS

1. Singing, alone and with others, a varied repertoire of music
2. Performing on instruments, alone and with others, a varied repertoire of music

OBJECTIVES

Students will:

1. Perform the song "Kye, Kye Kule" (from Ghana) and add dance movements.
2. Identify musical characteristics of "Kye, Kye Kule":
   - Short melodic phrases
   - Five-tone (pentatonic) scale

- Syncopation
- Call-and-response form

MATERIALS

- Shekere (www.amazon.com) or other rattle)

PROCEDURES

1. Explain to the students that music and dance are an important part of the lives of many people in Ghana. Children experience songs and rhythmic movement from the very earliest years.
2. Explain that "Kye, Kye Kule" is a dance/game song sung by children in Accra, the capital of Ghana. The words of the song refer to various areas of the body on which you place your hands.
3. Practice saying the words of the song:

Words:	Kye kye kule	"Hands on top of head"
Pronunciation:	Chay chay koo-lay	
Words:	Kye kye Ko-fi Nsa	"Hands on the shoulders"
Pronunciation:	Chay chay ko-fee nsah	
Words:	Ko-fi sa lan- ga	"Hands on the waist"
Pronunciation:	ko-fee sah lahn-gah	
Words:	Ke- te Kyi lan- ga	"Hands on the knees"
Pronunciation:	Kay-tay chee lahn gah	
Words:	Kum a- den-de	"Hands on the ankles"
Pronunciation:	koom ay-den-day	

4. Sing "Kye, Kye Kule" with the teacher leading in singing each musical phrase and students responding.
5. Accompany the singing with a shekere sounding on every other beat (beats 1 and 3).
6. "Kye, Kye, Kule" is accompanied by dance movements. Practice letting the body sway in time to the music with:
   - Hands placed on top of the head while singing "Kye, Kye, Kule"
   - Hands on top of the shoulders while singing "Kye, Kye Kofi Nsa"
   - Hands on the waist while singing "Kofi sa langa"
   - Hands on the knees while singing "Kete Kyi langa"
   - Hands on the ankles while singing "Kum adende"
7. Briefly discuss some of the characteristics of this African music:
   - Short melodic phrases
   - Call-and-response form: musical phrases given out by a leader and responses from the rest of the group
   - Syncopation: Sing and clap measure 3; place the notation on the board so the students can see syncopation

- Five-tone or pentatonic melody: Place the notes on the board; have students play the five tones on a melody instrument and then sing them on the syllable "loo"

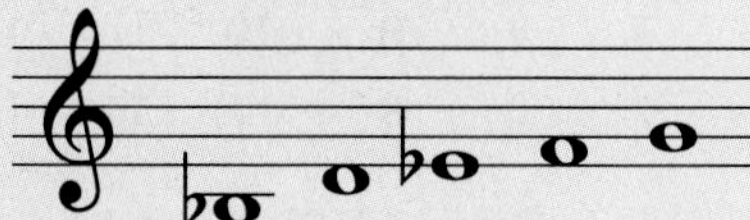

Technology Enhancement

Need help learning the melody or want to see students singing "Tue, Tue" or "Kye, Kye Kule"? Search YouTube and you will find several great videos of students performing both songs.

Learn to play "Tue. Tue" on the recorder.

http://www.monkeysee.com/play/19709-recorder-songs-learn-tue-tue

ASSESSMENT

1. Have the students perform the song with correct pitches and rhythms.
2. Have the students discuss some of the characteristics of African music that they have learned in this lesson.

LESSON PLAN
African Polyrhythm

Grades: 4–6

NATIONAL AND STATE MUSIC STANDARDS

1. Performing on instruments, alone and with others, a varied repertoire of music

OBJECTIVES

Students will:

1. Perform an example of African polyrhythm using agogo (bells), shekere (rattle), and several sizes of drums.
2. Listen to an example of polyrhythm and clap the rhythm played by the agogo (bells).

MATERIALS

- Instruments: agogo (also known as gankogui) (bells) in several sizes, shekere (rattle), and several sizes of drums[2]
- Recording of "Ewe Atsimivu" (download or stream [iTunes/Spotify])

PROCEDURES

1. Explain that the simultaneous sounding of highly contrasting rhythmic lines of music, known as polyrhythm ("many rhythms"), is common in African music.
2. Have students count each line of the following set of numbers, clapping on the boldface characters. Practice until the class can perform the entire example correctly, keeping a steady tempo throughout. Practice the example at several tempos: slow, medium, and fast.

[2] African instruments can be purchased from the House of Musical Traditions, 7010 Westmoreland Avenue, Takoma Park, MD 20912; (301) 270-9090; www.hmtrad.com. They are also are available from www.amazon.com.

1	2	**3**	4	**5**	**6**	7	**8**	9	**10**	11	**12**
1	**2**	3	**4**	**5**	6	**7**	8	**9**	10	**11**	12
1	2	**3**	**4**	**5**	**6**	**7**	**8**	**9**	**10**	**11**	**12**
1	2	**3**	**4**	5	**6**	**7**	8	**9**	**10**	11	**12**
1	2	**3**	4	**5**	6	**7**	8	**9**	10	**11**	12

3. Divide the class into five sections and have each section clap one line over and over in ostinato fashion. When all sections are combined, the class is performing polyrhythm.
4. Following is an example of the preceding rhythm in Western notation. Ask the class to clap the five lines one at a time; then divide the class into sections and have each section clap a line at the same time. The students can hear and see the polyrhythm.

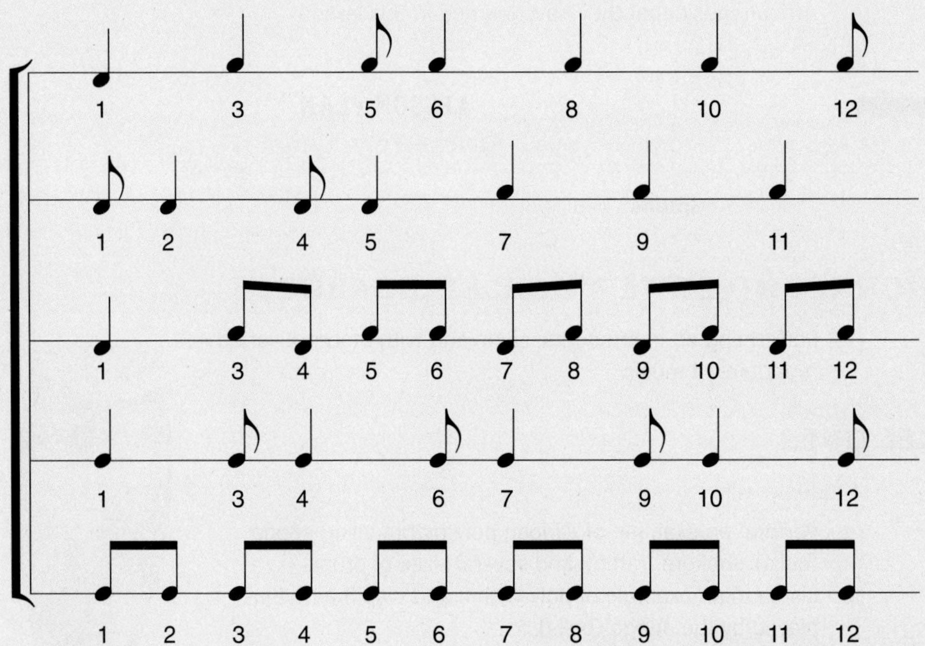

5. Play the following example with instruments.
   a. The first line is played on the metal percussion instrument known as an agogo ("ah-go-go"), or *gankogui* ("ghn-ko-gwee"). This instrument has two bell-shaped projections (one producing a lower pitch and the other a high pitch), which are struck with a stick to produce the sound.
   b. The second line of music is played on a larger and, therefore, lower-sounding agogo.
   c. The third line is played with a shekere. The agogo and shekere can be purchased in the United States, but teachers and students may wish to create their own instruments (see p. 162).
   d. Lines 4 and 5 are played with small and large drums, respectively.

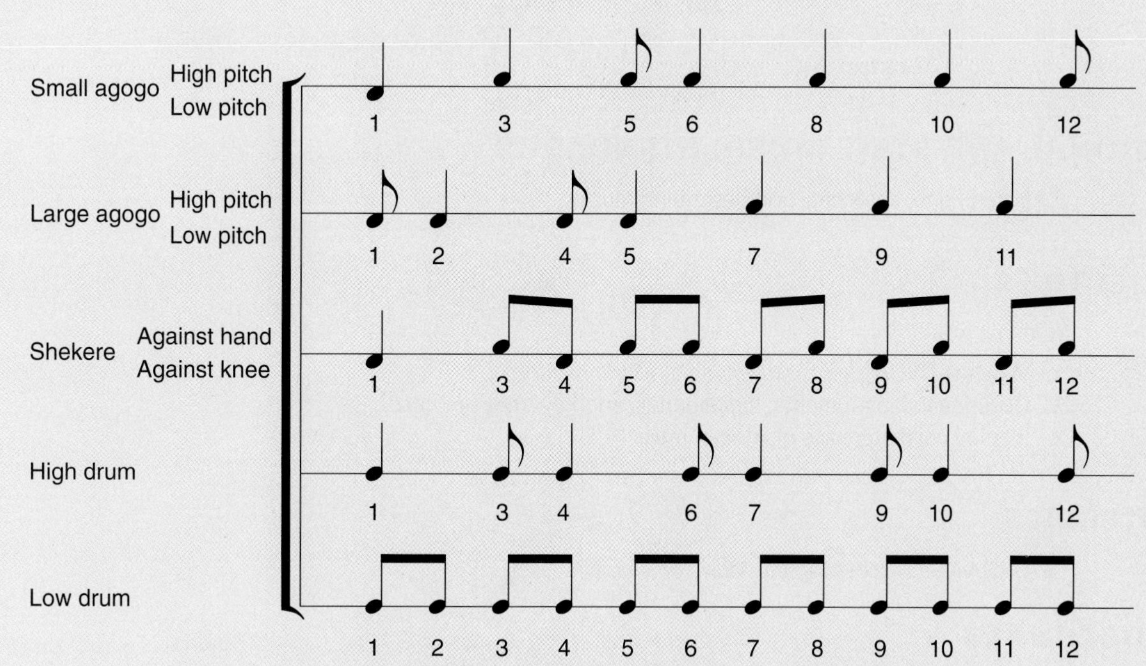

From Bruno Nettl, *Folk and Traditional Music of Western Continents*, 2nd ed. © 1973. Used by permission of Prentice Hall, Inc.

6. Perform the entire polyrhythm example several times, giving different students a chance to play the instruments. Other students in the class can clap along on a part while the instruments are being played. Perform the example at different tempos; each tempo must be maintained consistently throughout.
7. Download and listen to an example of polyrhythm in "Ewe Atsimivu," a musical selection from Ghana.
   a. This music accompanies the Agbeko ("Ahg-bek-o") dance of the Ewe ("a-wa-y") people of Ghana. You will hear a master drum, a supporting drum, and an agogo.
   b. As the students listen to the music, have them clap the rhythm played on the agogo:

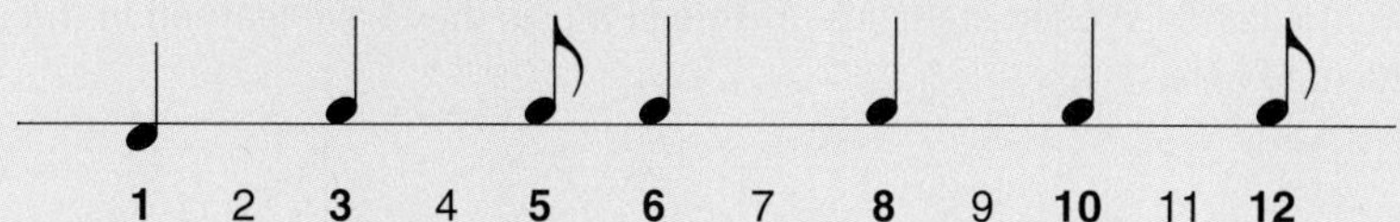

ASSESSMENT

1. Perform the polyrhythm example in this lesson with correct rhythms and with a steady tempo.

LESSON PLAN
The Music of Ghana

Grades: 5–6

NATIONAL AND STATE MUSIC STANDARDS

1. Listening to, analyzing, and describing music

OBJECTIVES

Students will:

1. View the DVD/video *Discovering the Music of Africa.*
2. Describe the instruments, their sounds, and how they are used.
3. Identify characteristics of African music.

MATERIALS

- DVD/video *Discovering the Music of Africa*[3]

PROCEDURES

1. This 22-minute DVD/video is about the music of Ghana. Have students find Ghana on a map of Africa.
2. Show the DVD/video, particularly noticing the drums, bells (agogo), and rattles (shekere) and the distinctive singing style and dance.
3. On the board place the following characteristics of African music as seen in the DVD/video:
   - Emphasis on percussion instruments and sounds
   - Call-and-response form
   - Open, relaxed quality of singing
   - Singing in harmony
   - Polyrhythm
   - Ostinato

ASSESSMENT

Have the class list characteristics of African music they have learned in the various lessons presented here.

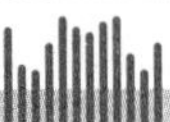

MUSIC OF ASIAN PEOPLES: CHINA AND JAPAN

Background Information for the Class

Among the largest and smallest countries of Asia are China and Japan, respectively (see Figure 9.2). China extends 2,700 miles from east to west and 2,600 miles from north to south, encompassing approximately the land mass of the United States and Mexico together. Within its borders live more than 1.3 billion people—more than in any other country in the world and four times the population of the United States. By contrast, the islands of Japan stretch 1,250 miles from north to south, but in total the land area encompasses only approximately that of Iowa and Minnesota. Within this relatively small land mass live more than 127 million people.

---

[3] *Discovering the Music of Africa* is available from http://store.discoveryeducation.com.

Figure 9-2 A portion of Asia

China and Japan have rich historical traditions, and over many centuries their peoples have made major contributions to the world. The Chinese invented paper and printing and have given the world silk, porcelain, and the compass. Both the Chinese and Japanese in recent times have made significant achievements in electronics, manufacturing, and other industries. Distinctive and highly prized artworks in painting, sculpture, theater, and music have been produced in both countries for several thousand years.

Many aspects of life in China and Japan have been subtly affected by the religions and philosophies of their peoples. Particularly evident in the arts have been (1) the Buddhist emphasis on simplicity of lifestyle, contemplation, peace, and tranquility; (2) the rules of order and personal conduct stemming from the philosopher Confucius; and (3) the religions of Taoism and Shintoism, which stress the importance of humans being in communion with nature. The tangible outcomes of these beliefs are present in several major thematic emphases in the arts.

One of the most persistent themes is *nature.* From the very earliest times, artists have sought to put themselves and their audiences in harmony with the "spiritual qualities" of the natural world. The theme of nature is evident in Asian architectural settings and building designs; in the visual arts of painting, sculpture, and flower arranging; in literature; and in music.

Another common tenet in both Chinese and Japanese arts is an emphasis on *understatement.* Artists seem to be directed toward simplicity, disciplined control, and attention to detail. In paintings bare outlines are often used to depict natural objects such as mountains and trees. Muted, pastel colors complement the delicacy and simplicity of the lines, and there are many blank, open spaces that viewers are left to imagine. It seems clear that many Chinese and Japanese artists wish to "suggest" through understatement with the hope of achieving maximum effect with minimal materials.

Some General Characteristics of Chinese and Japanese Music

Music has been an important part of Chinese and Japanese life from the beginnings of their recorded history. Several highly developed systems of traditional music are present today and are represented in a number of vocal and instrumental forms. Following are some general characteristics of traditional music.

- *Melody:* There is much use of five-tone (pentatonic) scales.
- *Rhythm:* Meter is most often duple.
- *Texture:* Texture is often monophonic (one-line) or heterophonic (simultaneous variations on a single line). Much emphasis is placed on distinct, delicate lines of music (unlike the thick, homogenous sounds of much Western orchestral music).
- *Dynamics:* Soft and loud dynamics are present. Soft dynamic levels reflect a general tendency toward understatement and delicate refinement in many types of traditional music. Very loud music can occur in some types of music, such as Beijing Opera.
- *Tone color:* A variety of instrumental and vocal tone colors are present. Stringed, percussion, and wind instruments are common, with stringed instruments most predominant. Tone color of singing is often somewhat pinched and nasal in quality.
- *Form:* Many compositions are programmatic (i.e., the music depicts a theme or title). Theme-and-variation and ABA form are also found.

Teaching Chinese and Japanese Music: Sample Lessons

The overall goal of the sample lessons that follow is to acquaint students with some of the many types of Chinese and Japanese traditional music. Students are encouraged to sing songs and listen to short selections of music, and to study them in terms of the basic elements of music: rhythm, melody, dynamics, tone color, texture, and form.

Several songs are included in the sample lessons, both in their native languages and in English. Although the songs are certainly to be enjoyed in both English and native languages, children should be encouraged to use the indigenous languages because doing so will enable them to identify more closely with the cultures and peoples that have produced the music. Although the songs are written out here, they are best learned through rote. Attention will initially need to be placed on correct pronunciation, which is provided through a phonetic spelling that appears below the native language.

For the listening selections, children should have a chance to see and discuss the instruments before listening to them. Pictures of the instruments are provided here and others can be found on the Web (www.images.google.com). These images can be downloaded to a computer and also projected onto a screen. Listening guides are given for each listening selection to help students focus on some principal musical events. Teachers may wish to duplicate a copy for each student or place a listening guide on a transparency or Microsoft PowerPoint slide so that it can be projected for the entire class to see.

In addition to the music selections given here, you may also wish to consult the current elementary music series for other examples from these cultures.

Technology Enhancement

Additional Web Resources about Chinese and Japanese Musical Instruments

PBS.org – Japan: Memoirs of a Secret Empire

www.pbs.org/empires/japan/instruments.html

Wikipedia – Traditional Japanese Musical Instruments

http://en.wikipedia.org/wiki/Traditional_Japanese_musical_instruments

Wikipedia – Koto (instrument)

http://en.wikipedia.org/wiki/Koto_(instrument)

Philmultic Management & Productions, Inc. – String Instruments from China

www.philmultic.com/home/instruments/

Wikipedia – List of Chinese Musical Instruments

http://en.wikipedia.org/wiki/List_of_Chinese_musical_instruments

LESSON PLAN
Chinese Music

Grades: 4–6

Colorful Boats

Melody Collected by William Anderson

Key: D (Pentatonic)
Starting pitch: A
Meter: 2/4, begin on 1

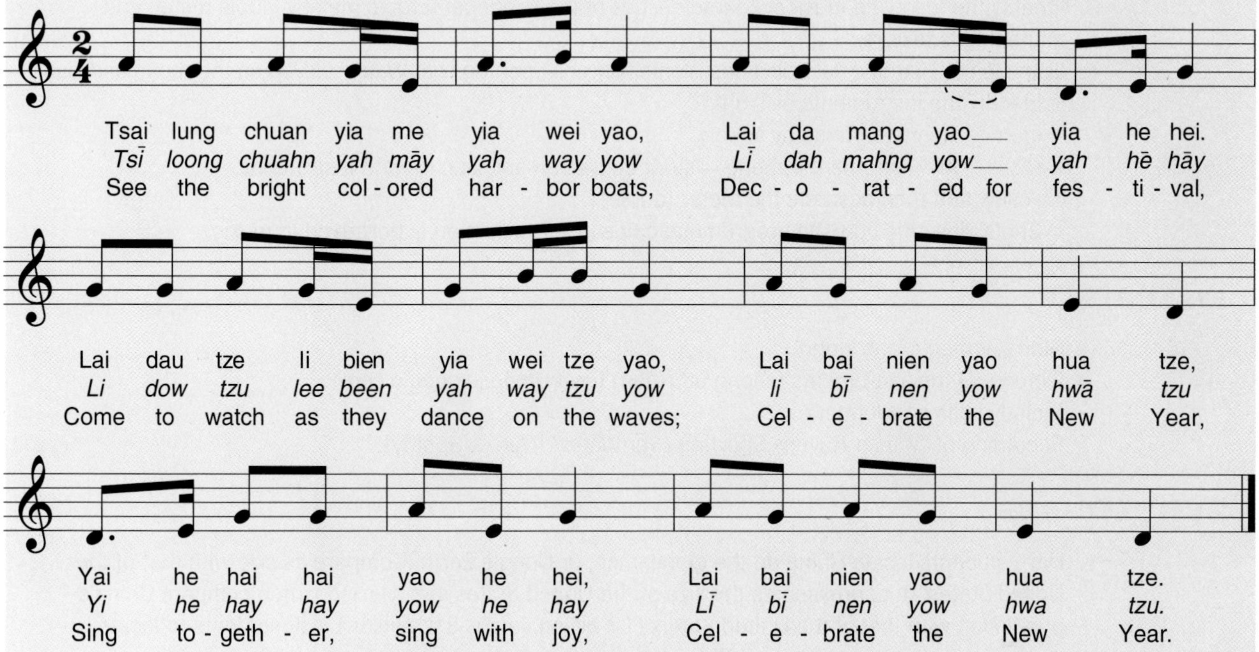

Tsai lung chuan yia me yia wei yao, Lai da mang yao___ yia he hei.
Tsī loong chuahn yah māy yah way yow Lī dah mahng yow___ yah hē hāy
See the bright col - ored har - bor boats, Dec - o - rat - ed for fes - ti - val,
Lai dau tze li bien yia wei tze yao, Lai bai nien yao hua tze,
Li dow tzu lee been yah way tzu yow li bī nen yow hwā tzu
Come to watch as they dance on the waves; Cel - e - brate the New Year,
Yai he hai hai yao he hei, Lai bai nien yao hua tze.
Yi he hay hay yow he hay Lī bī nen yow hwa tzu.
Sing to - geth - er, sing with joy, Cel - e - brate the New Year.

From *Silver Burdett Music Book 4.* © 1981. Reprinted by permission of William Anderson.

William M. Anderson

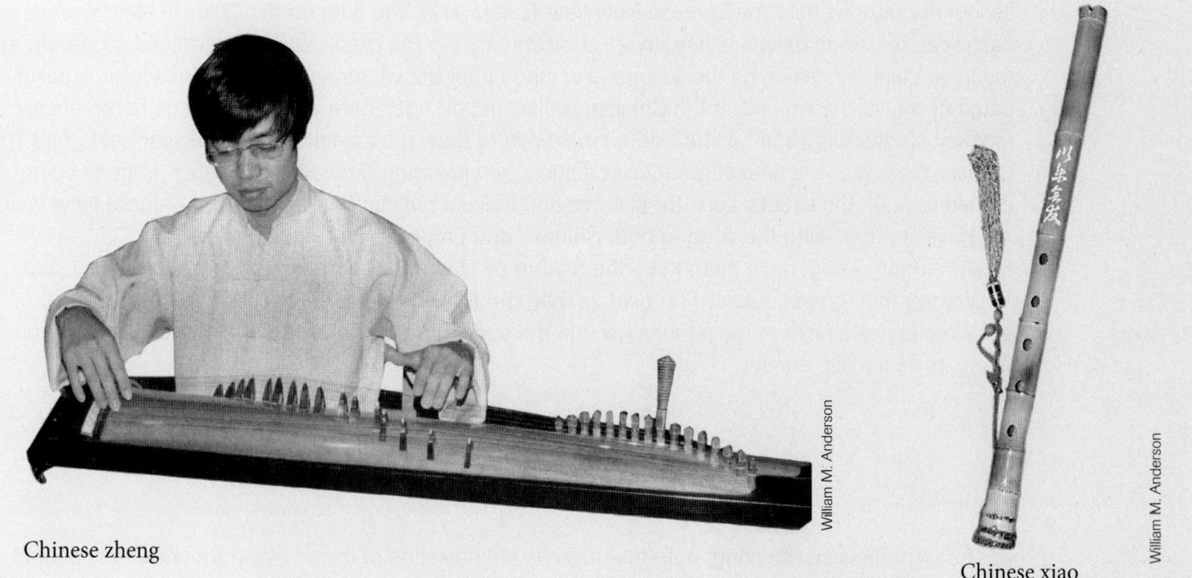

Chinese zheng

William M. Anderson

Chinese xiao

NATIONAL AND STATE MUSIC STANDARDS

1. Singing, alone and with others, a varied repertoire of music
2. Listening to, analyzing, and describing music

OBJECTIVES

Students will:

1. Be introduced to China, its geography, and culture.
2. Sing the song "Colorful Boats," using both English and Chinese languages.
3. Identify the following musical characteristics of the song: pentatonic melody, duple meter, and monophonic texture.
4. Listen to the instrumental selections "Winter Ravens Sporting over Water" played on the zheng and xiao.
   - Identify the instruments by sight.
   - Identify the instruments by sound.
   - Classify the instruments: zheng = stringed instrument, xiao = wind instrument.
   - Follow and then describe the meter (duple).
   - Briefly describe how the programmatic title of this selection is portrayed in music.

MATERIALS

- Globe or map of the world
- Pictures of the instruments (zheng and xiao) (www.images.google.com)
- Melody bells or xylophone
- Recording of "Winter Ravens Sporting over Water" [iTunes/Spotify]

PROCEDURES

1. Have students locate China on the globe, map, or Google Earth. Compare its size with that of the United States. (It approximates the size of the United States and Mexico.) Then compare China's population with that of the United States (1.3 billion versus 312 million). Ask students to locate some of the main cities (Beijing, Shanghai, and Guangzhou).
2. Make a "Characteristics of Chinese Music" chart on the writing board or bulletin board. As each piece of music is studied, list the important musical characteristics learned.
3. Sing the Chinese song "Colorful Boats," which is about boats decorated for a New Year's celebration. Lead a discussion about the Chinese New Year (see p. 412). The date for the Chinese New Year varies each year, occurring between January 21 and February 19. The exact date is determined according to the lunar calendar, falling on the second new moon after the winter solstice. Each new year is designated by one of the animals of the Chinese zodiac: rat, ox, tiger, hare, dragon, serpent, horse, sheep, monkey, rooster, dog, and boar. (Children may wish to draw the animal of the particular new year.) The Chinese New Year is a time of great celebration, often involving fireworks and paper dragons being carried through the streets. Look for pictures and make a bulletin board about the Chinese New Year.
   a. Have students sing the song in both Chinese and English.
   b. As students sing, have them keep the rhythm by clapping their hands together on beat 1 and waving their hands outward on beat 2. They should be able to feel and see the duple meter.
   c. Write in scale fashion the pitches used in the song. Sing and play the pentatonic scale, listening to its distinctive quality.

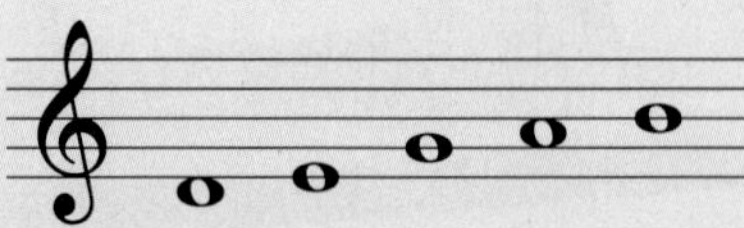

   d. As students sing the song, note that there is only *one* line of music (even though many people are singing it). This music is described as monophonic (mono = one; phonic = sound).

4. Download a recording of the piece "Winter Ravens Sporting over Water" played on the *zheng* (also spelled *cheng*; pronounced "zhung") and *xiao* (also spelled *hsiao;* pronounced "she-ao").
   a. Download and project pictures of the zheng and xiao. Briefly describe the instruments. The zheng is a plucked stringed instrument. It normally has sixteen strings, which are tuned to a pentatonic scale. Note how the performer plucks the strings with his or her right-hand thumb and fingers and how the left-hand fingers glide along the strings to produce different pitches. The xiao is a wind instrument made from bamboo. Point out the notch at the upper end of the instrument (across which the performer blows air to produce the sound), and that there are no keys on the instrument.
   b. Have students listen to the tone qualities of each instrument (clear, plucked-string sound of zheng and breathy, wind sound of xiao).
   c. Have students keep the beat and follow the duple meter by clapping lightly on beat 1 and waving on beat 2.
   d. Call attention to the nature theme in the title of the composition. This is programmatic music. Discuss how the music reflects this theme (sweeping melodic lines played on the zheng symbolize birds flying over water).

Listening Guide: "Winter Ravens Sporting over Water"

Circle the items as you listen to the music.

1. This music is from

a. China	*or*	b. Ghana

2. You are listening to

a. stringed and percussion instruments	*or*	b. stringed and wind instruments

3. In general the music

a. has soft to medium dynamic levels	*or*	b. is very loud

4. The meter of the music is

a. triple	*or*	b. duple

ASSESSMENT

1. Sing "Colorful Boats," with correct pitches and rhythms.
2. Have the class list some of the characteristics of Chinese music they have learned in this lesson.

LESSON PLAN

Traditional Chinese Instruments

Grades: 4–6

NATIONAL AND STATE MUSIC STANDARDS

1. Listening to, analyzing, and describing music

OBJECTIVES

Students will:

1. Identify the Chinese *sheng* (pronounced "shung) by sight and sound, and classify it as a wind instrument.
2. Compare the free reed structure of the sheng with the Western harmonica, its distant relative.
3. Listen to the distinctive tone color and harmony in the Chinese sheng composition "Old Monk Sweeping the Buddhist Temple."
4. Identify the *pipa* (pronounced "pee-pah") by sight and sound, and classify it as a stringed instrument.
5. Listen to the distinctive programmatic musical effects in the pipa composition "The Hero's Defeat."

MATERIALS

- Pictures of sheng and pipa (download from www.images.google.com)
- Recordings (download or stream [iTunes/Spotify]):
  "Old Monk Sweeping the Buddhist Temple" (sheng)
  "The Hero's Defeat" (pipa)
- Harmonica

PROCEDURES

1. Download and have students listen to the recording of "Old Monk Sweeping the Buddhist Temple" played on the sheng.
   a. Show a picture of the sheng and describe how the instrument is constructed. The sheng consists of a bowl-shaped base into which are inserted bamboo reed pipes, each designed to produce a different pitch. Within each pipe is a small reed, which vibrates to produce the sound as air moves through the pipe.
   b. Bring a harmonica to class. Show the reeds in the instrument. (They may be seen by looking carefully into the instrument; it may be possible to remove the upper or lower sections of the instrument to see the reeds clearly.)
   c. Play the harmonica. Notice that sound can be produced both by exhaling air into the instrument and by inhaling air from the instrument. Thus, one can produce *continuous* sound on the harmonica. The same is true for the sheng. Also, point out that one can produce several pitches at the same time on the harmonica, thus creating harmony. This is also true for the sheng.

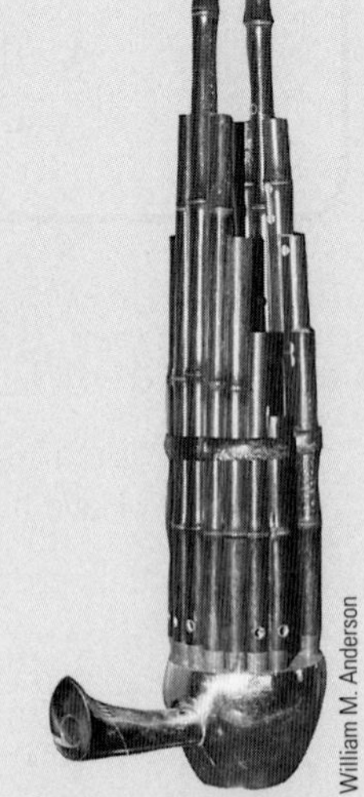

William M. Anderson

Chinese sheng

Listening Guide: "Old Monk Sweeping the Buddhist Temple"

Circle the items as you listen to the music.

1. This music is from
   a. the United States *or* b. China
2. You are listening to
   a. wind instrument *or* b. a stringed instrument
3. Music texture
   a. is one-line only (monophonic) *or* b. has harmony
4. The meter of the music is
   a. duple *or* b. triple

2. Download and have students listen to a recording of "The Hero's Defeat" played on the pipa.
   a. Show a picture of the pipa and describe how it is constructed and played. The pipa is a plucked stringed instrument somewhat similar in shape to the Western guitar. Point out the characteristic manner in which it is held upright as it is played. The strings are plucked with the fingernails of the right hand. Among the most characteristic sounds of the instrument are rapidly repeated notes in the melody executed by the quickly moving fingers of the right hand.
   b. This piece is programmatic, depicting a battle between the kingdoms of Han and Chu. Have students listen to the manner in which the music depicts soldiers marching back and forth and the battle sounds of clashing swords.
   c. Plan dramatic movement to accompany the music.

ASSESSMENT

Have the class list characteristics of Chinese music they have learned in this lesson.

- Instruments: sheng—wind instrument with reeds activated by air; pipa—plucked stringed instrument
- Rhythm: duple meter
- Texture: distinctive harmonic texture produced on the sheng
- Melody: rapidly repeating notes produced by the pipa
- Form: programmatic music

William M. Anderson

Chinese pipa

LESSON PLAN

Japanese Music

Grades: 3–4

Traditional Japanese Folk Song
Translated by
Joy E. Lawrence
Sakura
Key: E (Pentatonic)
Starting pitch: A
Meter: 2/4, begin on 1
SA - KU - RA SA - KU - RA YA - YO - I - NO SO - RA WA, MI - WA -
Sah - koo - rah sah - koo - rah yah - yoh - i - noh so - rah - wah mee wah
Sa - ku - ra Sa - ku - ra cher - ry blooms are eve - ry - where clouds of
TA - SU KA - GI RI, KA - SU - MI KA KU - MO KA NI - O - I - ZO
Tah - soo kah - gee - ree kah - soo - mi kah koo - moh kah ni - o - i - zoh
glo - ry fill the air. Mist of beau - ty in the sky Love - ly col - ors
I - ZU RU. I - ZA - YA, I - ZA - YA ME NI YU - KA - N.
i - zoo - roo i - zah - yah i - zah - yah me ni yoo - kah n.
float - ing by. Sa - ku - ra, Sa - ku - ra Let us come and see.

NATIONAL AND STATE MUSIC STANDARDS

1. Singing, alone and with others, a varied repertoire of music
2. Listening to, analyzing, and describing music
3. Understanding music in relation to history and culture

OBJECTIVES

Students will:

1. Be introduced to the geography and some cultural characteristics of Japan.
2. Sing the song "Sakura" (meaning cherry blossoms) in both Japanese and English, and identify the pentatonic scale and the duple meter.
3. Identify the koto by sight and sound and explain how it is played.
4. Listen to variations on "Sakura" played on the koto, and identify the theme-and-variation form.

MATERIALS

- Globe or map of the world
- Picture of koto (download from www.images.google.com)
- Melody bells
- Japanese props, such as kimono, fan, or parasol
- Recording of "Variations on Sakura" (*The Soul of the Koto* [iTunes/Spotify], Koto, Sakura)

PROCEDURES

1. Using a globe, map, or Google Earth, have students locate Japan. Compare its size with that of the United States. (Japan's total land area is approximately equal to that of the states of Iowa and Minnesota combined, yet it has approximately half the population of the United States.) Japan is an island country; have students find the four main islands: Hokkaido, Honshu, Shikoku, and Kyushu. Also have the class locate some of the major cities: Tokyo, Yokohama, Nagoya, Kyoto, and Osaka.
2. Have students sing the song "Sakura," one of the most popular folk songs in Japan. The song celebrates the national flower of Japan—the cherry blossom—which in springtime provides a profusion of pink-and-white blossoms throughout the country. Have students sing in both Japanese and English.
3. Call attention to the theme of nature. Ask students to identify the words (in English) that refer to nature (cherry blooms, clouds, air, mist, sky).
4. Have students write out, from low to high, the different pitches in the song:

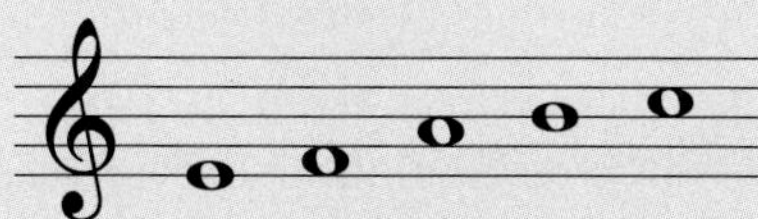

Because there are five notes, this is a pentatonic scale. Play the scale on melody bells; then sing it on the syllable "loo." Notice the particular sound quality of the pentatonic scale.

5. Dramatize "Sakura" by creating stylized movements that express ideas in the song and by adding a kimono, Japanese parasol, fan, and so on.
6. Show students a picture of the koto. The *koto* is one of the most important Japanese stringed instruments; it has a position in Japanese homes comparable to the piano in our own country. The instrument is approximately 6 feet long, 13 inches wide, and 2 inches thick. It has thirteen strings, which extend the length of the body and are tuned to the pentatonic scale by movable bridges inserted between the body of the instrument and the strings. The instrument is played with plectrums, which are attached to the right-hand thumb, index, and middle fingers. A variety of pitches and subtly executed ornamentation can be produced by the left hand pressing and pulling strings.

William M. Anderson

Japanese koto

7. Download the recording of "Variations on Sakura" played on the koto. Have students follow the outline of this form on the board:

- Short introduction
- *Theme*: "Sakura"
- *Variation 1:* "Sakura" theme played with added melodic figures; fast tempo
- *Variation 2:* "Sakura" theme played at a slow tempo
- *Variation 3:* "Sakura" theme played with many "running figures"; fast tempo

Plan dramatic movement to portray the changes in tempo.

ASSESSMENT

Summarize the lesson by having students make a list of "Characteristics of Japanese Music" on the board: pentatonic melody, duple meter, monophonic texture, theme-and-variation form, and nature theme.

LESSON PLAN

Traditional Japanese Instruments

Grades: 5-6

NATIONAL AND STATE MUSIC STANDARDS

1. Listening to, analyzing, and describing music
2. Understanding music in relation to history and culture

OBJECTIVES

Students will:

1. Listen to the composition "Shika no Tone" (Deer Calling to Each Other in the Distance) played on the shakuhachi and identify (a) the shakuhachi by sight and sound; (b) the programmatic theme of nature, in which two shakuhachi players imitate deer calling to each other; and (c) how the sense of understatement is created through the slow tempo, soft dynamic level, and monophonic texture.
2. Watch sections devoted to the koto and shakuhachi on the DVD/video *Discovering the Music of Japan* and note the following characteristics of Japanese traditional music: pentatonic scales, duple meter, tendency toward soft dynamic levels, programmatic nature of pieces, and sense of understatement (creation of maximum effect from minimal materials).

MATERIALS

- Picture of shakuhachi (download from www.images.google.com).
- Recording of "Shika no Tone" (Deer Calling to Each Other in the Distance) [iTunes/Spotify]
- DVD/video *Music of Japan* (available from Educational Video Network, www.edvidnet.com).
- Visit www.pbs.org/empires/japan/instruments.html for pictures, interactive instruments, and audio recordings.

William M. Anderson

Japanese shakuhachi

PROCEDURES

1. Download and project a picture of the *shakuhachi.* This instrument is made from bamboo and is approximately 18 inches in length. Sound is produced by blowing across a small notch at the upper end of the instrument.

2. Download and play the composition "Shika no Tone" (Deer Calling to Each Other in the Distance) as performed on the shakuhachi.
3. Download and project a picture of the shakuhachi.
4. Call attention to the nature theme in the title of the composition. Listen to the manner in which the two shakuhachi players imitate deer calling to each other.
5. Place the following statements on a chart or the writing board. As they listen to the composition, have students circle the appropriate items:

Special Learner Note

Present symbols or pictures with words (or instead of words) to include nonreaders in this "choice" process. This could be presented on a board for all to see and work with or as an individual handout for students to work with independently or in pairs.

Listening Guide: "Shika no Tone"

Music is loud	*or*	Music is soft
One line of music	*or*	Many lines of music
Strong beat in music	*or*	Weak beat in music
Tempo is slow	*or*	Tempo is fast

After students have completed this task, call attention to the manner in which understatement is created by each of the items.

6. Show the DVD/video *Music of Japan*. Three traditional musical instruments are played: the koto (plucked stringed instrument), the shakuhachi (wind instrument), and the *shamisen* (plucked stringed instrument). A short Japanese dance is also performed. Although you may wish to view the entire video, the first two segments, on the koto and shakuhachi, are suggested here. Before showing the video, review with the class some of the principal characteristics of Japanese music: pentatonic scales, duple meter, tendency toward soft dynamic levels, programmatic nature of pieces, and a sense of understatement–the creation of maximum effect from minimal materials.
7. Call attention to the cultural setting of the music on the video: beautiful color photography of a home and garden as well as a Japanese painting combine to create the proper setting (particularly the emphasis on nature) for the music.

ASSESSMENT

Conclude the lesson by having students summarize on the chalkboard or bulletin board some of the general characteristics of Japanese music: pentatonic melody, duple meter, monophonic texture, theme-and-variation form, and nature theme.

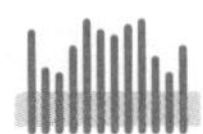

MUSIC OF EUROPEAN PEOPLES

Background Information for the Class

The European continent extends from the Mediterranean Sea in the south to the Arctic Ocean in the north, and from the Atlantic Ocean in the west to the Ural Mountains in Russia (see Figure 9.3). In total land area, Europe is actually the second-smallest continent (Australia is the smallest), having about one-fifteenth of the world's land area. Its more than 816 million people make up about 12 percent of the world's population.

Figure 9-3 Europe

A great variety of cultural backgrounds and languages are present on the European continent. Some indication of the great ethnic diversity is clearly evidenced in the more than thirty countries into which the continent is divided and the nearly fifty languages spoken.

Technology Enhancement

- Use Google Earth for students to gain geographical information on Europe and European countries: www.google.com/earth
- Interactive European map game: www.kidsgeo.com/geography-games/europe-map-game.php

Some General Characteristics of European Music

Because of the large number of cultural groups in Europe, there is considerable variety in the styles of music. Following is a list of general characteristics of European music. It should be understood, however, that not all of these characteristics will be present in music from every region. The attempt here is to provide general guidelines for presenting European music in the classroom.

- Melody is characterized by balanced phrases, particularly in western Europe; phrases of unequal length are sometimes present, particularly in eastern European music. Scales include major, minor, modal, pentatonic, and whole tone. Melodies from western Europe are not generally heavily ornamented; ornamentation is found in some music, however, particularly in eastern Europe.
- Rhythm is characterized by a moderately strong beat, with an even and constant tempo. Meter is mostly duple or triple; unequally divided meter (5/4, 7/8, etc.) is found in eastern Europe.
- Homophonic and polyphonic textures are common, along with much use of chordal harmony. "Drone" harmony is present in many areas.
- Timbre is characterized by a variety of vocal and instrumental tone colors. Open, relaxed singing quality predominates. Stringed- and wind-instrument tone qualities are most frequently found.
- There is much use of form in which a musical idea is stated and followed by contrasting material, which is in turn followed by a return to the first musical idea (ABA).

Teaching European Music: Sample Lessons

Following are some sample lessons on European music that are designed to introduce students to some of the traditional music of Europe in terms of rhythm, melody, tone color (timbre), texture, and form.

LESSON PLAN

Russian Music

Grades: 4-6

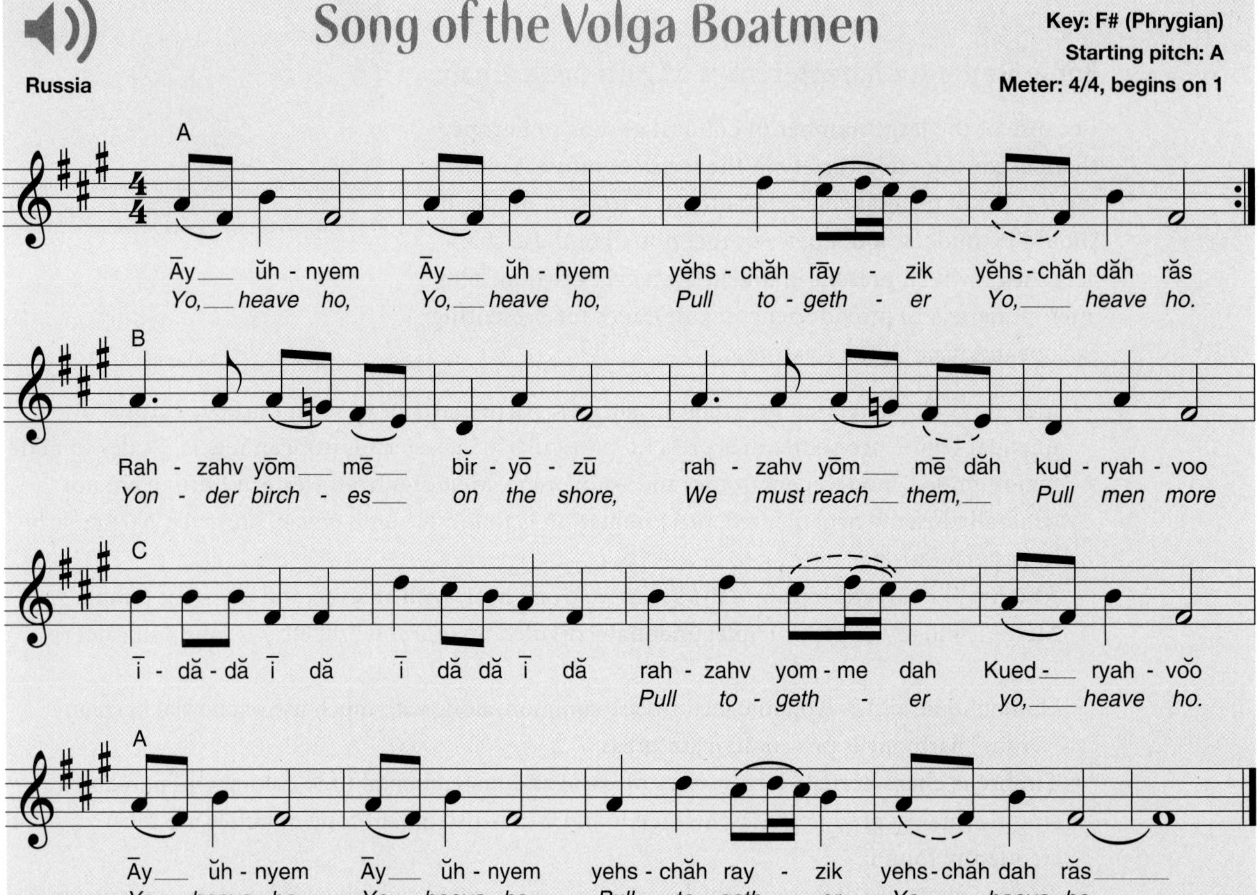
Song of the Volga Boatmen
Russia
Key: F# (Phrygian)
Starting pitch: A
Meter: 4/4, begins on 1
A
Āy___ ŭh - nyem Āy___ ŭh - nyem yĕhs - chăh rāy - zik yĕhs - chăh dăh răs
Yo,___ heave ho, Yo,___ heave ho, Pull to - geth - er Yo,___ heave ho.
B
Rah - zahv yōm___ mē___ bĭr - yō - zū rah - zahv yōm___ mē dăh kud - ryah - voo
Yon - der birch - es___ on the shore, We must reach___ them,___ Pull men more
C
ī - dă - dă ī dă ī dă dă ī dă rah - zahv yom - me dah Kued-___ ryah - vo͝o
Pull to - geth - er yo,___ heave ho.
A
Āy___ ŭh - nyem Āy___ ŭh - nyem yehs - chăh ray - zik yehs - chăh dah răs___
Yo,___ heave ho, Yo,___ heave ho, Pull to - geth - er Yo,___ heave ho___

NATIONAL AND STATE MUSIC STANDARDS

1. Singing, alone and with others, a varied repertoire of music
2. Listening to, analyzing, and describing music

OBJECTIVES

Students will:

1. Be introduced to the geography and cultures of Europe (with special attention to Russia).
2. Sing "Song of the Volga Boatmen" and identify the Phrygian scale (F#, G, A, B, C#, D, E), duple meter, and AABCA form.
3. Listen to a Russian balalaika orchestra and correctly identify musical events.

MATERIALS

- Globe or world map
- Pictures of balalaika (download from www.images.google.com)
- Recording of "Balalaika–Troika Bells Polka" (download or stream [iTunes/Spotify])
- Sleigh bells

PROCEDURES

Russian balalaika

William M. Anderson

1. Using a globe or map, have students find the European continent, individual countries, and some of the largest cities. Discuss with the class how closely many families in the United States are related to people from European countries. Undoubtedly, some students in the class will be from families that originally came from Europe.
2. Have the class sing "Song of the Volga Boatmen" in both Russian and English. Point out that this song is about the Volga River, one of the great waterways of Russia and the longest river in Europe. Have the students find the Volga River on the map.
3. While singing, have some students conduct the 4/4 meter. Point out the four-measure balanced phrases.
4. Write the Phrygian scale (F#, G, A, B, C#, D, E) on the board and have the students sing it or play it on instruments:

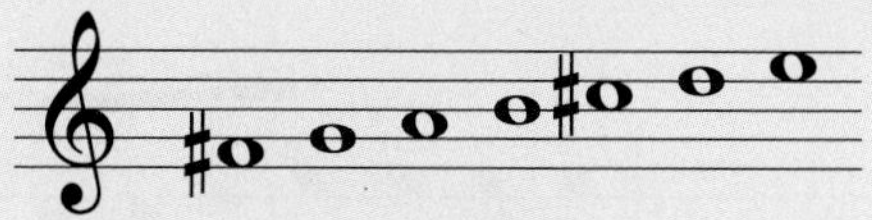

5. Diagram the form of the song:

A A B 

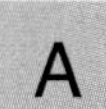

6. Download a recording of a *balalaika* orchestra playing a composition entitled "Balalaika–Troika Bells Polka." The orchestra is composed of many instruments; it includes balalaikas (stringed instruments) of various sizes and percussion instruments such as the bells heard in this composition.

Place the following listening guide (without the circled answers) on the board or on a transparency.
Have students circle the appropriate descriptions while listening to the music.
Students may also accompany the recording with sleigh bells.

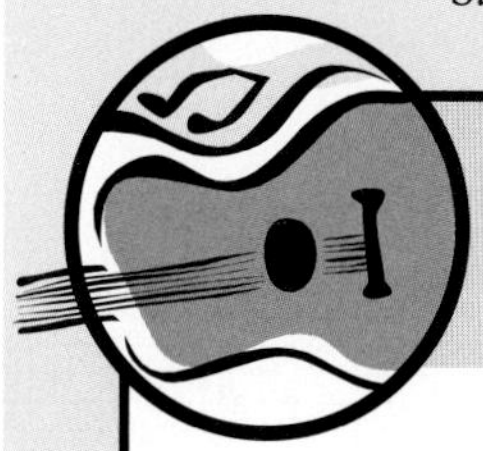

LISTENING GUIDE: "Balalaika—Troika Bells Polka"

[Mostly stringed instruments]	*or*	Mostly brass instruments
Slow tempo	*or*	[Fast tempo]
One line of music (monophonic)	*or*	[Many lines of music (polyphonic)]
[Duple meter]	*or*	Triple meter

ASSESSMENT

Have the class list characteristics of Russian music they have learned in this lesson.

Special Learner Note

Present symbols or pictures with words (or instead of words) to include nonreaders in this "choice" process. This could be presented on a board for all to see and work with or as an individual handout for students to work with independently or in pairs.

LESSON PLAN
Greek Music[4]
Grades: 4-6
English Version by Stella Phredopoulos
Music by D. A. Vergoni
Samiotissa
Key: G
Starting pitch: D
Meter: 7/8, begins on 6
Sa - mio - tis - sa, Sa - mio - tis - sa, You will re - turn to Sa - mos. Sa -
mio - tis - sa, Sa - mio - tis - sa, Is - land of beau - ty and de - light.
You will come home a - gain to me, Sa - mio - tis - sa, There's mu - sic in the sum - mer night.
You will come home a - gain to me, Sa - mio - tis - sa, There's mu - sic in the sum - mer night.

[4] Special thanks to Maria Foustalieraki for her assistance with this lesson.

NATIONAL AND STATE MUSIC STANDARDS

1. Listening to, analyzing, and describing music

OBJECTIVES

Students will:

1. Listen to the Greek music that accompanies the Kalamatianos dance. Identify the instruments of the ensemble (fiddle, clarinet, laouto [lute], and percussion), and the uneven quality of the 7/8 meter.
2. Perform the Kalamatianos dance.

MATERIALS

- Download or stream "Kalamatianos Dances: Kalamatiano (Dance of Kalamata)" [iTunes/Spotify]

PROCEDURES

1. Listen to Greek music in 7/8 meter performed by fiddle, clarinet, *laouto* (a Greek lute), and percussion, or sing the song "Samiotissa" (about the Greek island Samos).
2. Have students practice following the 7/8 meter:
   a. Without the music, count from 1 to 7, clapping on 1, 4, and 6; repeat.
   b. Add the music and count from 1 to 7, clapping on 1, 4, and 6; repeat.
   c. Again, without the music, count from 1 to 7, emphasizing 1, 4, and 6 by lightly stamping your feet on the floor; repeat.

Special Learner Note

You may want to create color-coded or "L" and "R" labels on streamers or cards to help students identify left and right.

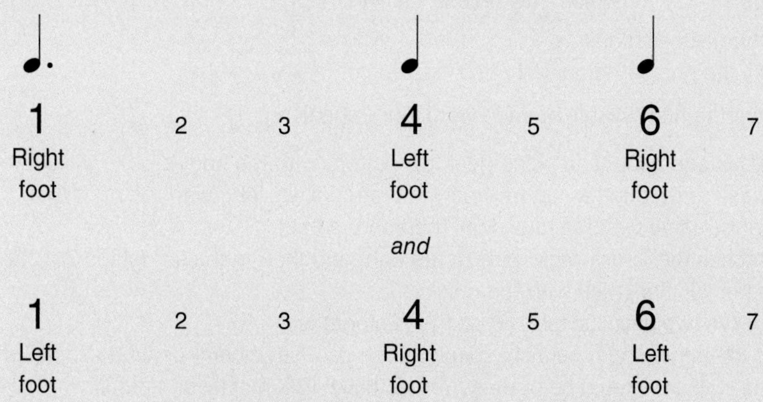

3. Repeat the foot movements in 2c, but this time with musical accompaniment.
4. Teach the dance Kalamatianos, which is done in 7/8 meter, with either recorded accompaniment or accompanied by the song "Samiotissa."
   a. Have students form an open circle, facing to the right:
   b. Circle to the right:

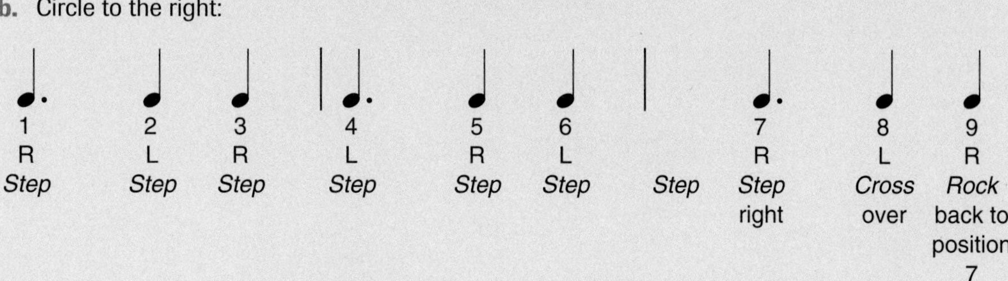

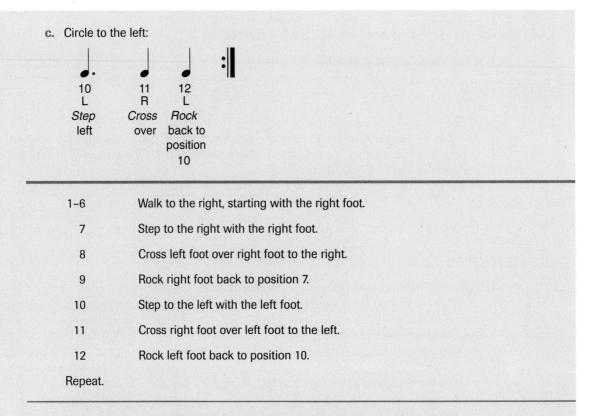

c. Circle to the left:

10	11	12
L	R	L
Step left	*Cross* over	*Rock* back to position 10

1–6	Walk to the right, starting with the right foot.
7	Step to the right with the right foot.
8	Cross left foot over right foot to the right.
9	Rock right foot back to position 7.
10	Step to the left with the left foot.
11	Cross right foot over left foot to the left.
12	Rock left foot back to position 10.

Repeat.

Note that the dancers face (body and head) to the right (direction of the line) for all measures except the last (numbers 10–12), for which they face to the left.

d. Teaching suggestions:

- Say the phrase "strawberry peaches apple": 
- Clap the first syllable of each word while speaking: 
- Speak and bounce in place (feel this pattern with the body): 
- Speak and walk the pattern freely in the room, starting with the right foot.
- Do the same with the music (all the above steps).
- Practice the "cross-rock" part to the right and then to the left (steps 7–12) a few times without the music first, then with the music.
- Put the two parts (steps 1–6 and 7–12) together.
- At the beginning it helps to speak the phrase "strawberry peaches apple" while dancing.
- The walking should be bouncy. You actually walk mainly on tiptoes.

ASSESSMENT

Have the class list the characteristics of Greek music that they have learned in this lesson.

LESSON PLAN
Spanish Music

Grades: 4–6

NATIONAL AND STATE MUSIC STANDARDS

1. Singing, alone and with others, a varied repertoire of music
2. Listening to, analyzing, and describing music

OBJECTIVES

Students will:

1. Sing the Spanish song "There's a Fiesta," perform the composition in harmony, and identify the triple meter and the AAB form.
2. Listen to a Spanish guitar composition entitled "Recuerdos de la Alhambra" (Recollections of the Alhambra), which depicts in music the ornamental quality of the Alhambra Palace in Granada, Spain. In particular, listen for (a) the triple meter, (b) the rapid, repetitive plucking producing the ornamental melody, and (c) the AABB (coda) form. While listening, view pictures of the Alhambra Palace.

MATERIALS

- Paper with letters A and B or two different geometric shapes
- Castanets and tambourines
- Recording: "Recuerdos de la Alhambra" (artist Narciso Yepes) (download or stream [iTunes/Spotify])
- Pictures of the Alhambra Palace in Granada, Spain (download from www.images.google.com)

PROCEDURES

1. Have students sing "There's a Fiesta." Ask the class what they think the Spanish term *fiesta* means (a celebration or festival).
2. Call attention to the Spanish instruments mentioned in the song (guitars, castanets). Also call attention to the word *dancers;* Spanish music is often accompanied by dance.
3. Have the class sing the song, first using just the top melodic line, until the words and tune are learned well. Then have the students with higher voices sing the top line and those with lower voices sing the lower line.
4. As the students sing, have them clap the triple meter.
5. Using letters or paper of different colors and geometric shapes, have students outline the form of the piece (AAB).
6. Add castanets or tambourines on the triplets (♩♩♩ with 3) to create a Spanish effect.
7. Download and play the Spanish guitar composition titled "Recuerdos de la Alhambra" (Reminiscences of the Alhambra), which depicts in music the Alhambra Palace in Granada (download and display pictures of the palace). In particular, listen for the following:
   - Rapid, repetitive plucking, which produces the ornamental melody (compare it with the ornamental motifs of the Alhambra Palace)
   - Triple meter (follow by conducting **1** 2 3 **1** 2 3, etc.)
   - Form: AABB coda (section A in minor; section B begins in major)
     Circle the letters as you listen to the piece:

     A A B B Coda

3
1 2

ASSESSMENT

Have the class briefly discuss some of the characteristics of Spanish music that they have learned in this lesson.

LESSON PLAN

Bagpipe Music

Grades: 4–6

NATIONAL AND STATE MUSIC STANDARDS

1. Singing, alone and with others, a varied repertoire of music
2. Listening to, analyzing, and describing music

OBJECTIVES

Students will:

1. Sing the Irish song "Galway Piper" and identify the following musical characteristics: balanced four-measure phrases, strong beat, duple meter, and AB form.
2. Listen to a medley of pieces played by a Scottish bagpipe band and identify the following musical characteristics: ornamental melody, drone harmony, loud dynamic level, strong beat, and duple meter.
3. Listen to the Irish bagpipe composition "Rakish Paddy" and identify the following musical characteristics: ornamental melody, duple meter, fast tempo, and drone and chordal harmony.

MATERIALS

Scottish bagpipe

William M. Anderson

- Red and blue paper
- Pictures of bagpipes (download from www.images.google.com)
- Recordings: *Bagpipe Marches and Music of Scotland* ("6/8 Marches") and *Festival of Irish Folk Music*, vol. 2 ("The Man of the House/Galway Rambler") [iTunes/Spotify]

PROCEDURES

1. Sing the song "Galway Piper." Point out that the song is about a bagpipe player–Piping Tim of Galway.
2. Using two pitches (D and A), have students sing a drone on the sound *Raa-*, making it very nasal. Half the class can be bagpipes while the other half sings.
3. Call attention to the repetition in the melodic line (measures 1 and 4 nearly alike; measure 2 like measure 1 except down one step; measures 5 and 6 nearly alike; measures 5 and 7 exactly alike).

Galway Piper

Traditional Irish Folk Song

Key: D
Starting pitch: D
Meter: 4/4, begins on 1

Lively

D | A7
Ev - 'ry per - son in the na - tion,__ Of a great or hum - ble sta - tion,__

D | A7 | D
Holds in high - est es - ti - ma - tion, Pip - ing__ Tim__ of__Gal - way. Loud - ly__ he can play or low.

A7 | D | A7 | D
He can__move you fast or slow, Touch your__hearts or stir your toe, Pip - ing__Tim of Gal - way.

4. Have students keep the beat and the duple meter in the song by clapping on the strong beats (1and 3) and waving outward on beats 2 and 4.
5. Ask students to diagram the overall form of the piece with letters and colored paper:

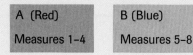

A (Red)	B (Blue)
Measures 1–4	Measures 5–8

6. Listen to Scottish bagpipe music.

7. Download (www.images.google.com) and show a picture of the Scottish bagpipe. Explain that the bagpipe is one of the oldest and most widespread instruments in Europe. The instrument consists of several distinct parts: (1) a *pipe* through which the player blows air; (2) the *bag*, a device that acts as a storage reservoir for the air, which makes possible the continuous sound produced on the instrument; (3) the *chanter*, a pipe with fingerholes on which the performer plays melodies; and (4) *drone pipes*, which, like the chanter, are activated by air from the bag (but unlike the chanter normally produce only a single pitch).
8. Give students copies of the following listening guide and, as they listen to Scottish bagpipe music, have them circle the appropriate musical events:

Listening Guide: Scottish Bagpipe Music

Brass and stringed instruments	*or*	Wind and percussion instruments
One line of music	*or*	Several lines of music
Loud	*or*	Soft
Rhythm: strongly felt beat	*or*	Rhythm: weakly felt beat
Triple meter	*or*	Duple meter

9. Play a recording of Irish bagpipe music. Irish bagpipes differ from Scottish bagpipes: Instead of blowing air through a pipe into the bag, a *bellows*, which is attached under the right elbow of the performer, is pumped to fill the bag with air. In addition, the Irish bagpipes have keys on both the chanter and the drones. Through these the performer can produce simple chords.
10. Give students the following listening guide and, as they listen to Irish bagpipe music, have them circle the appropriate musical events:

Special Learner Note

Present symbols or pictures with words (or instead of words) to include nonreaders in this "choice" process. This could be presented on a board for all to see and work with or as an individual handout for students to work with independently or in pairs.

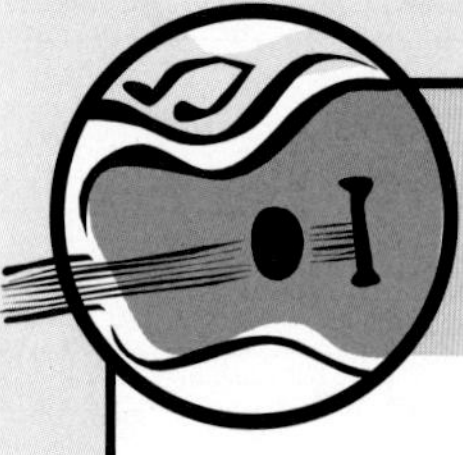

Listening Guide: Irish Bagpipe Music

Wind and stringed instruments	*or*	Brass instruments
One line of music	*or*	Many lines of music
The melody is plain	*or*	The melody is highly ornamented
Fast tempo	*or*	Slow tempo
Duple meter	*or*	Triple meter

ASSESSMENT

Have students summarize on the board some of the general characteristics of Scottish and Irish bagpipe music.

AMERICAN MUSIC

Background Information for the Class

America is a huge continental land mass extending almost 9,500 miles from north to south and about 3,000 miles at its widest east-west expanse (see Figure 9.4). The continent is generally divided into two principal areas, North and South America, with the narrow intervening strip referred to as Central America.

With more than twenty-five countries present on the American continents, there is considerable ethnic variety both among different countries and within countries. Much of the ethnic diversity of the United States results from numerous peoples who emigrated from other parts of the world. Some of the earliest inhabitants, those peoples commonly referred to today as Native Americans, are thought to have come across the Bering Strait from Asia beginning as early as 50,000 years ago. In more recent times (beginning around 1000 A.D.), people from a number of European countries traveled to the Americas. Shortly thereafter, numerous Africans were brought to both North and South America. In the past several hundred years, Asian peoples from a variety of countries have also immigrated to the Americas. It is clear that today many cultural groups now make up the United States, and each has its own distinctive music.

Figure 9-4 The Americas

Teaching American Music: Sample Lessons

Because of the enormous ethnic diversity resulting from the migration of peoples from all over the globe, it is impossible to describe "typical" American music. The following sections outline several sample lessons on some representative types of American music.

Native American Music[5]

LESSON PLAN

Used with permission of the National Association for Music Education.

NATIONAL AND STATE MUSIC STANDARDS

1. Singing, alone and with others, a varied repertoire of music
2. Understanding music in relation to history and culture

OBJECTIVES

Students will:

1. Be introduced to Native American cultures, and help prepare a bulletin board.
2. Learn the Hopi song "Mos', Mos'!" (a song about a cat) and the actions that go with it.
3. Discuss the text of "Mos', Mos'!" focusing on understanding the place of music in Native American life and some of the valuable aspects of Native American perspectives on the world.

MATERIALS

- Map and other bulletin-board materials showing where Native American peoples have traditionally lived, as well as aspects of their cultures (see www.google.com).

[5] Lessons derived from Edwin Schupman (ORBIS Associates, Washington, DC) and David P. McAllester, "Teaching the Music of the American Indian," in William M. Anderson, *Teaching Music with a Multicultural Approach* (Reston, VA: MENC, 1991), pp. 39–43.

PROCEDURES

1. Look for information and pictures to make a bulletin board about Native American cultures.
2. Invite Native Americans to speak to your class. Also, encourage students to attend Native American Pow Wow gatherings.
3. Locate on a map the home of the Hopi tribe of Arizona. (It can be found on several mesas extending east from Tuba City in western Arizona, east of the Grand Canyon.)
4. Have the students learn the song "Mos', Mos'!" by rote. Discuss some of the basic features of the song: paired phrases and three-tone scale.
5. Add animations: Have the children "sit like a cat," holding up their hands like a cat's paws. They should move their paws up and down on each beat of the song, and where the cat says "nya, ya," they should accelerate the tempo and pretend to scratch each other.
6. Discuss the role of animals in Native American cultures: Native Americans feel a close relationship to the animal world, believing that animals are creatures that think, feel, and even teach. Animals are our relatives, who share the world with us and with whom we should learn to live in harmony. (This is very different from the common Anglo-American attitude that animals exist for the benefit of humans.)

ASSESSMENT

1. Sing the song "Mos', Mos'!" with correct pitches and rhythm.
2. Discuss how the song relates to Native American beliefs about animals.

"Blessing Song" is found in Chesley Goseyun Wilson, Ruth Longcor Harnisch Wilson, and Bryan Burton, *When the Earth Was Like New: Western Apache Songs and Stories* (World Music Press © 1994/© 2009 Assigned to Plank Road Publishing, Inc.). Book and accompanying recording. World Music Press/Plank Road Publishing: Inc., P.O. Box 26627, Wauwatosa, WI 53226; www.musick8.com

NATIONAL AND STATE MUSIC STANDARDS

1. Singing, alone and with others, a varied repertoire of music
2. Performing on instruments, alone and with others, a varied repertoire of music

OBJECTIVES

Students will:

1. Learn about the Apache tribe of Arizona and New Mexico.
2. Sing the Apache "Blessing Song" (My Father's Son).
3. Accompany the song with a drum and rattle.
4. Learn several characteristics of Native American music:
    - Many songs, such as this one, are made up of nonsense syllables.
    - Songs often have a different number of pitches (here, four) than is generally found in European music (seven pitches).
    - Music is often a single line (monophonic texture).
    - Singing is often accompanied by a repetitive beat played on drum and rattle.

MATERIALS

- Map and other bulletin-board materials showing where Apache tribes have traditionally lived (see www.google.com)
- Drums and rattles[6]

PROCEDURES

1. Locate the traditional home of the Apache tribes in Arizona and New Mexico. Gather information for the bulletin board.
2. Have the students learn the "Blessing Song."
3. Add a repetitive, "pulsating" beat on a drum.
4. Add a rattle playing a pulsating beat.
5. Diagram the ABA form of the song.
6. Discuss some of the basic features of this Native American song:
    a. Many songs, such as this one, are made up of nonsense syllables.
    b. Music is often a single line (monophonic texture).
    c. Songs often have a different number of pitches (four, here) than is generally found in European music (seven pitches). Place the pitches on the board and listen to the distinctive sound as you sing them using a neutral syllable such as "loo."

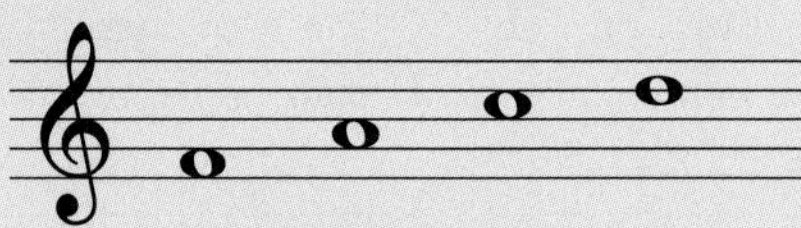

    d. Singing is often accompanied by a repetitive beat played on drum and/or rattle.

ASSESSMENT

1. Sing the Apache "Blessing Song" with correct pitches and rhythm.
2. Discuss some of the characteristics of the song.

---

[6] Native American drums can be purchased from West Music Company (www.westmusic.com) and House of Musical Traditions (www.hmtrad.com).

LESSON PLAN

Native America Music and Dance

Grades: 3–5

NATIONAL AND STATE MUSIC STANDARDS

1. Listening to, analyzing, and describing music
2. Understanding music in relation to history and culture

OBJECTIVES

Students will:

1. Learn about the close relationship between music and dance in Native American cultures.
2. Dance to listening examples from the Algonquin tribe of the northern Great Lakes region and Canada.
3. Learn several characteristics of Native American music:
   - Male voice sings a single line of music (monophonic texture).
   - Rhythm has a strong, pulsating drum beat that recurs throughout the piece.
   - Pulsating quality of rhythm also occurs in the voice.
4. View the DVD/video *Discovering American Indian Music.*

This lesson may need to extend over several periods.

MATERIALS

- Recording: Algonquin "Buffalo Head Dance" and "Grizzly Bear Dance" from *Songs and Dances of the Great Lakes Indians*, www.folkways.si.edu/ (American Indian)
- DVD/video: *Discovering American Indian Music* (available from http://store.discoveryeducation.com)

PROCEDURES

1. Explain that this music and dance are from the Algonquin tribe that resides throughout the northern Great Lakes region and Canada.
2. Explain that music and dance are closely intertwined and are often associated with animals. Discuss Native American emphasis on living in harmony with the natural world and with the animals who are our relatives.
3. For the Algonquin "Buffalo Head Dance":
   a. Have the students, alternating boys and girls, form a circle and face inward. Explain that the circle is an important symbol for Native American peoples, and that it signifies the cycle of the seasons and a sense of unity.
   b. Move counterclockwise in the circle, following the steady beat of the drum that accompanies the singing.
   c. When you hear a rapid roll-like effect on the drum, turn and face outward in the circle. Move sideways to the left in time to the music.
   d. When you hear the roll-like drum effect again, turn facing inward again and repeat b and c. Continue as long as the music lasts.
4. For the Algonquin "Grizzly Bear Dance":
   a. Form a straight line, alternating boys and girls.
   b. As the drummer plays a fast repetitive beat, move forward in time to the music—head facing downward and arms extended out in front of you.
   c. When you hear the drummer begin to play at a slower tempo, mark time in place to the music and "claw" the air over your head (imitating the bear).
   d. Repeat b and c.

5. After performing the dances, have the students identify some of the characteristics of the music:
   a. Male voice sings a single line of music (monophonic texture).
   b. Rhythm has a strong, pulsating drum beat that recurs throughout the piece.
   c. Pulsating quality of rhythm also occurs in the voice.
6. View the DVD/video *Discovering American Indian Music,* which includes the following songs, instruments, and dances of various North American peoples:
   a. Navajo (Plains) Corn Grinding Song
   b. Seneca (Southwest) Farewell Song
   c. Ute (Colorado) flute solo and Bear Dance accompanied by a serrated stick scraper
   d. Kiowa (Oklahoma) Plains War Dance
   e. Sioux (Plains) Love Song
   f. Pueblo (New Mexico) Eagle Dance
   g. Taos (New Mexico) Hoop Dance
   h. Pueblo (New Mexico) Bow and Arrow Dance
   i. Creek (Southeastern United States) Stomp Dance
   j. Tlingit (Northwest Coast) Chant (singing in harmony)
   k. Apache (Plains) Dance to Spirits of Mountain (includes a bull roarer)
   l. Composition by Native American composer Louis Ballard

ASSESSMENT

1. Perform the Native American dances learned in this lesson.
2. Discuss characteristics of Native American music learned in this lesson.

Folk and Country Music

LESSON PLAN
Mountain Dulcimer
Grades: 3-6
Old Joe Clark
Traditional
Key: C (Mixolydian)
Starting pitch: G
Meter: 2/4, begins on "and" of 2
C
Gm
I used to live on the moun - tain top. Now I live in town. I'm
Chorus
stay - ing at the big ho - tel, Court - ing Bet - sy Brown. Fare you well, Old Joe Clark,
Fare you well, I say. Fare you well, Old Joe Clark. I'm a - goin' a - way.
From Jean Ritchie, The Dulcimer Book, pg. 39, Old Oak Publications. (Originally published in 1918).

NATIONAL AND STATE MUSIC STANDARDS

1. Singing, alone and with others, a varied repertoire of music
2. Performing on instruments, alone and with others, a varied repertoire of music
3. Listening to, analyzing, and describing music

OBJECTIVES

Students will:

1. Sing the song "Old Joe Clark" and identify and perform the mixolydian scale (C, D, E, F, G, A, Bb,).
2. Accompany the song with a mountain dulcimer.
3. Listen to "Old Joe Clark" being accompanied by the mountain dulcimer.

MATERIALS

- Mountain dulcimer
- Recording: "Old Joe Clark" from Dulcimer Songs and Solos, http://www.folkways.si.edu/

PROCEDURES

1. Sing "Old Joe Clark."
2. Place the mixolydian scale on the board and have students sing and/or play it:

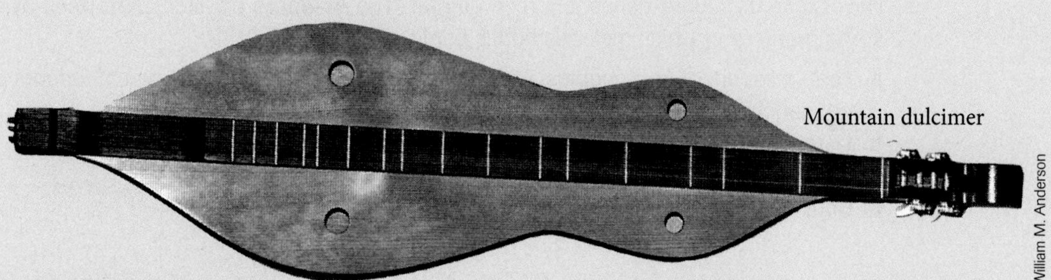

Mountain dulcimer

William M. Anderson

3. Accompany "Old Joe Clark" on the mountain dulcimer. Mountain dulcimers are sold throughout the United States.[7] The mountain dulcimer has four strings, two placed close together on which the melody is played, and a third and fourth designed to produce a drone sound. The strings are stroked with a plectrum held in the right hand. Different pitches are produced by a small piece of wood, which is held in the left hand and slid along the strings.
4. Practice playing the mixolydian mode. The rest of the class should quietly hum along. Notice the drone harmony produced by the instrument.
5. Slowly sing "Old Joe Clark," accompanying on the dulcimer. Gradually increase the tempo as you develop facility.
6. Play a recording of "Old Joe Clark" being sung and accompanied on the mountain dulcimer.

ASSESSMENT

1. Sing "Old Joe Clark" with correct pitches and rhythms.
2. Discuss how the mountain dulcimer is constructed and played, and the characteristic sound of the instrument.

[7] One source is House of Musical Traditions, 7010 Westmoreland Avenue, Takoma Park, MD 20912; (301) 270-9090; www.hmtrad.com.

LESSON PLAN

Bluegrass

Grades: 3–6

NATIONAL AND STATE MUSIC STANDARDS

1. Listening to, analyzing, and describing music

OBJECTIVES

Students will:

1. Perform a square dance to "The Arkansas Traveler" played on fiddle, banjo, and guitar.
2. Listen to "Foggy Mountain Breakdown" and "Orange Blossom Special" played by a bluegrass ensemble and follow the musical and programmatic events.

MATERIALS

- Recordings: "Arkansas Traveler," "Orange Blossom Special," and "Foggy Mountain Breakdown" [iTunes/Spotify]
- Pictures of various kinds of trains (www.images.google.com)

PROCEDURES

1. Have students square-dance to a recording of "The Arkansas Traveler" performed by a country string group (and which includes fiddle, banjo, and guitar).
   - **a.** Form a square of four couples, with the boys on the left side of the girls. Students clap beat when not dancing.
   - **b.** Listen for 4 counts.
   - **c.** Introduction: All clap 16 beats (two times).
   - **d.** Couples 1 and 3 take four steps to center, bow, and return.

   - **e.** Couples 2 and 4 take four steps to center, bow, and return.
   - **f.** Repeat steps d and e.
   - **g.** Each couple swings partner right (8 counts), then left (8 counts).
   - **h.** Repeat g.
   - **i.** Each couple passes shoulders with partner right (8 counts), then left (8 counts).
   - **j.** Repeat i.
   - **k.** Couples promenade counterclockwise and take new positions in square: couple 1 is now located in couple 2 position, couple 2 is now in couple 3 position, and so on.
   - **l.** Repeat steps c through k as often as needed.

2. Tell the class that they are going to hear bluegrass music. The name bluegrass came from a performing group organized in the 1940s by Bill Monroe in Kentucky, the "Bluegrass State." The bluegrass ensemble consists of guitar, fiddle, banjo, mandolin, string bass, and sometimes other instruments.
3. Download "Orange Blossom Special" and have students listen to it. This is a programmatic composition about a train. Listen to the manner in which this music imitates the sounds and movement of a train. You will hear the call to board the train, the train whistle, and the chugging, pulsating motion of the engine. The piece is characterized by virtuoso fiddle playing.
4. Download "Foggy Mountain Breakdown" and have students listen to it. The words "foggy mountain" refer to the often misty mountains of the Appalachian region. "Breakdown" refers to a piece that breaks down into a number of sections, each featuring a solo instrument. Follow the theme-and-variation form of the piece, using the following listening guide:

Listening Guide: "Foggy Mountain Breakdown"

1. Theme played by banjo with string bass accompaniment
2. Theme played by fiddle with banjo, guitar, and string bass accompaniment
3. Theme played by banjo with guitar accompaniment
4. Theme played by guitar with banjo and string bass accompaniment
5. Theme played by harmonica with guitar, banjo, and string bass accompaniment
6. Theme played by banjo with guitar and string bass accompaniment

ASSESSMENT

Have the students briefly discuss some of the characteristics of folk and country music they have learned in these lessons.

LESSON PLAN
Mexican Music
Grades: 3–5
La Raspa
Key: G
Starting pitch: D
Mexico
Meter: 4/4, begins on "and" of 4
A
G
D7
Now work of the day is done, And un - der the set - ting sun The
The band plays a live - ly beat, A - mi - gos, a - mi - gas meet, And
Castanets
Tambourine
mu - sic calls ev - 'ry one To come join in all the fun.
soon sou - ples fill the street With sounds of their danc - ing feet.
B
Their voic - es are lift - ed in hap - py song, No - bod - y has a care; And
Maracas
Cast.
Tamb.
Mar.
peo - ple re - joice that the night is long, Laugh - ter is ev - 'ry - where.
(Mar.)

NATIONAL AND STATE MUSIC STANDARDS

1. Singing, alone and with others, a varied repertoire of music
2. Listening to, analyzing, and describing music

OBJECTIVES

Students will:

1. Sing the song "La Raspa," add accompaniment by castanets, tambourines, and maracas, and add dance movements.
2. Sing the song "Cielito Lindo," in Spanish and in English, and add dance movements.
3. Listen to "Cielito Lindo" played by a mariachi ensemble. Learn about the various instruments of the ensemble and follow a listening chart.

MATERIALS

- Castanets
- Tambourines
- Maracas
- The mariachi composition entitled "Cielito Lindo"/mariachi [iTunes/Spotify]
- Pictures of a mariachi ensemble (download from www.images.google.com)

PROCEDURES

1. Have students sing the song "La Raspa."
2. Add the designated instrumental accompaniment of castanets, tambourines, and maracas.
3. Once students have learned the song well, have them form a circle, alternating boys and girls.

4. Have students place their hands on their hips and execute the following movements four times:
   a. Hop on left foot and at the same time extend right foot forward with heel down and toe up (beat 1).
   b. Hop on right foot and at the same time extend left foot forward with heel down and toe up (beat 2).
   c. Feet pause (beat 3); clap (beat 4).
5. Sing "Cielito Lindo" (p. 255), first in Spanish, and then in English. On the chorus, have students follow the triple meter by tapping against their legs on beat 1, clapping on beat 2, and waving outward on beat 3. Then add the dance (pp. 293–294).
6. Introduce the instruments of the mariachi ensemble: violins (several), guitar, vihuela (like a guitar, but somewhat smaller and higher pitched), guitarrón (larger guitar-like, bass instrument), and trumpets (several). View pictures of the mariachi ensemble obtained from Google Images.
7. Place the following listening guide (without the circled answers) on the board or on a transparency. Have students circle the appropriate descriptions while listening to the mariachi ensemble playing and singing the song "Cielito Lindo."

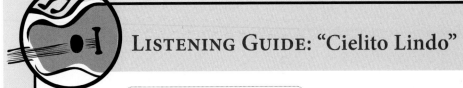

Listening Guide: "Cielito Lindo"

Stringed and brass instruments	*or*	Percussion instruments
Soft dynamic level	*or*	Loud dynamic level
Rhythm: weakly felt beat	*or*	Rhythm: strongly felt beat
Duple meter	*or*	Triple meter

ASSESSMENT

1. Perform the songs and dances with correct rhythms, pitches, and pronunciation.
2. Correctly identify the instruments in a Mexican mariachi ensemble. Successfully follow the listening guide while listening to the mariachi ensemble playing "Cielito Lindo."

African American Music

LESSON PLAN
Spiritual
Grades: 3-6
Swing Low, Sweet Chariot
Key: F
Starting pitch: A
Meter: 2/4, begins on 1
Spiritual
Solo
Chorus
Swing low, sweet char - i - ot,
Com - in' for to car - ry me home!
Swing low, sweet char - i - ot,
Com - in' for to car - ry me home.
Fine
I looked o - ver Jor - dan an' what did I see,
If you get there be - fore I do,
I'm some - time up an' some - times down,
Com - in' for to car - ry me home? Jes'
A
But
D.C. al fine
band of an - gels com - in' af - ter me,
tell my friends that I'm a - com - in' too,
still my soul feels heav - en - ly boun',
Com - in' for to car - ry me home.
An African American Spiritual written prior to 1862

NATIONAL AND STATE MUSIC STANDARDS

1. Singing, alone and with others, a varied repertoire of music
2. Listening to, analyzing, and describing music

OBJECTIVES

Students will:

1. Perform the spiritual "Swing Low, Sweet Chariot."
2. Identify some characteristics of the spiritual:.
   - Solo/chorus (call-and-response) style of performance
   - Pentatonic melody
   - Flexible rhythmic style
3. Listen to "Swing Low, Sweet Chariot" sung by Mavis Staples with piano accompaniment.

MATERIALS

- Recording: "Swing Low, Sweet Chariot" performed by Mavis Staples (download or stream [iTunes/Spotify])

PROCEDURES

1. Have students sing the spiritual "Swing Low, Sweet Chariot." Explain that spirituals are a very old form of African American music in the United States (although they actually contain aspects of both black and white musical styles). Spirituals were initially performed in churches but then moved out into the community, where they have traditionally been sung for a variety of social occasions.
   - Spirituals should be sung in a flexible rhythmic style that permits the full emotional impact of the song.
   - Pay particular attention to the alternating solo/chorus (call-and-response) style of performance, a very common African method of musical performance.
   - Call attention to the pentatonic (five-tone) scale of the song melody. Sing the scale on "loo" and/or play it on a xylophone, noticing the distinctive sound.

2. Listen to a recording of "Swing Low, Sweet Chariot" performed by Mavis Staples, following the overall ABA design of the piece.

Listening Guide: "Swing Low, Sweet Chariot"

1. Piano introduction
2. "Swing Low" sung in slow, drawn-out phrases; slides between pitches (A)
3. "Swing Low" sung in upbeat tempo in duple meter with rhythmic piano accompaniment (B)
4. Return to "Swing Low" sung in slow, drawn-out phrases (A)

ASSESSMENT

1. Perform "Swing Low, Sweet Chariot" using correct pitches and rhythms.
2. Discuss musical characteristics found in "Swing Low, Sweet Chariot."

Grades: 4–6

Key: D (Pentatonic
Starting pitch: D
Meter: 4/4, begins on 1
Lonesome Rider Blues
Traditional Folk Song
A
D
1. Ain't no - bod - y wants me, and they would - n't be in my shoes,
G7
A
D
Ain't no - bod - y wants me, and they would - n't be in my shoes,
B
A7
G7
D
I feel so bad, I got the lone - some rid - er blues.

1. If I had a-listened to what my mama said, (2 times)
   I'd be home sleepin' in my nice warm feather bed.
2. River is deep and the river sure is wide, (2 times)
   The woman (man) I love is on the other side.
3. Hey, baby, baby, I treated you so wrong, (2 times)
   Sweet lovin' baby, I'll be missin' you 'fore long.
4. If I mistreat you, I sure don't mean no harm, (2 times)
   'Cause I'm a motherless child, and I don't know right from wrong.
5. You used to be my sugar, but you ain't sweet no more. (2 times)
   You got another baby hangin' 'round your door.
6. I got the blues at midnight, and they don't leave till day, (2 times)
   Got to find another baby to drive those blues away.
7. I woke up this mornin,' the blues all in my head. (2 times)
   I rolled back the covers, the blues all in my bed.
8. Sun gonna shine on my back door someday, (2 times)
   Wind gonna rise up and blow my blues away.

NATIONAL AND STATE MUSIC STANDARDS

1. Singing, alone and with others, a varied repertoire of music
2. Listening to, analyzing, and describing music

OBJECTIVES

Students will:

1. Sing "Lonesome Rider Blues," identify the AAB form, and discuss the text.
2. Listen to "Lost Your Head Blues" sung by Bessie Smith. Identify the AAB form and the distinctive melodic characteristics, including "scoops," "slides," and descending melodic contours.

MATERIALS

- Recording: Bessie Smith, "Lost Your Head Blues" [iTunes/Spotify]

PROCEDURES

1. Sing "Lonesome Rider Blues." Identify the AAB blues form, and diagram on the board. As implied in the name, the blues were initially songs in which African Americans could talk about things that made them a melancholy, "blue" feeling. Briefly discuss the words of this piece and how they convey a "blues" feeling.
2. Listen to Bessie Smith's "Lost Your Head Blues," following the AAB form. The piece begins with a short instrumental introduction, followed by:
   - Section A: "I was with you, baby, when you did not have a dime."
   - Section A repeats: "I was with you, baby, when you did not have a dime."
   - Section B: "Now since you got plenty . . . money, you have throwed your good gal down." (AAB form continues with new segments of text.)

Particularly note the characteristic features of blues melodies: "scoops" and "slides" between notes and descending melodic contours.

3. Have students look for other recordings of the blues (home, library, record store, on-line) and bring them to class.

ASSESSMENT

Have students briefly discuss some of the characteristics of the blues learned in this lesson.

LESSON PLAN

Jazz

Grades: 4–6

NATIONAL AND STATE MUSIC STANDARDS

1. Listening to, analyzing, and describing music

OBJECTIVES

Students will:

1. Listen to the jazz composition "Hotter Than That" and identify the Dixieland ensemble, "scat" singing, and improvisatory form.
2. Listen to the jazz composition "Jumpin' at the Woodside" and identify the families of instruments (brass, woodwinds, percussion); harmonic texture; pulsating, driving beat; ostinato; and short phrases passed among instruments in call-and-response form.
3. Listen to the jazz composition "Take Five" and follow the steady, pulsating beat, the repeated melodic/rhythmic phrases (ostinato), syncopation, and the 5/4 meter.

MATERIALS

- Download or stream recordings [iTunes/Spotify]: "Hotter Than That," "Jumpin' at the Woodside," and "Take Five."

PROCEDURES

1. Play a recording of "Hotter Than That" performed by Louis Armstrong and His Hot Five. Explain that this type of jazz is called Dixieland. It is the earliest type of jazz. As its name implies, Dixieland began as a musical style of the southern United States before spreading throughout the United States and the world. The Dixieland ensemble in this selection features cornet, trombone, clarinet, piano, banjo, and guitar. The cornet player here is the famous Louis Armstrong, who also improvises with vocal syllables in a style called "scat" singing. One of the distinctive features of the Dixieland style is the emphasis on improvisation. Place the following on the board.

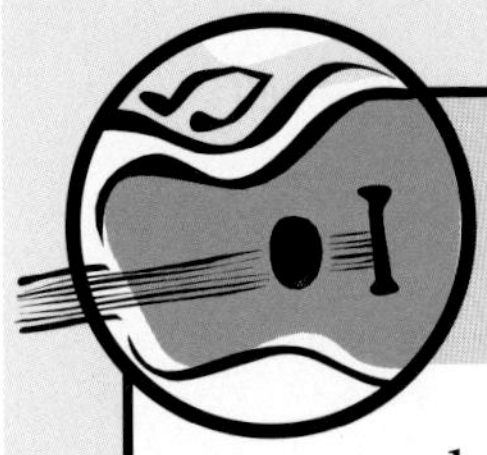

LISTENING GUIDE: "Hotter Than That"

1. Introduction: cornet and trombone
2. Cornet improvising: flat-four accompaniment (strongly felt four-beat measures)
3. Clarinet improvising: flat-four accompaniment
4. "Scat" vocal improvisation
5. Vocal and guitar interlude; flexible rhythm
6. Trombone improvising: flat-four accompaniment
7. Cornet and guitar improvising

2. Download and listen to "Jumpin' at the Woodside" performed by Count Basie. This type of jazz, known as swing, differs from Dixieland in its use of a larger ensemble consisting of families of instruments. Instead of just one of each instrument, there are multiple trumpets, trombones, saxophones, and percussion instruments. With the larger ensemble, it became necessary to have written arrangements in swing jazz. Swing often contains an interesting mixture of European and African traits. Large numbers of instruments playing together with written arrangements and a strongly harmonic musical style are European traits. Some prominent African traits in the music include the pulsating, driving beat; the use of ostinato; and the short phrases passed among instruments in call-and-response form. Place the following listening guide on the board.

Listening Guide: "Jumpin' at the Woodside"

1. Piano playing "up and down" scale figures—strong, pulsating beat
2. Full group playing with short melodic figures passed among instruments in call-and-response style
3. Short piano interlude to provide some variety in music
4. Full group playing again with short melodic figures passed among instruments in call-and-response style
5. Saxophone solo
6. Saxophone joined by piano
7. (to end) Full group with saxophone solo, along with brass instruments "calling out" to rest of group

3. Download and listen to "Take Five" by the Dave Brubeck Quartet. Place the following listening guide on the board.

Listening Guide: "Take Five"

1. Follow the strong, pulsating beat in the music.
2. Follow the uneven meter (5/4—group of 3 beats followed by a group of 2 beats) by counting the beats out loud and clapping on beats 1 and 4.

5
4

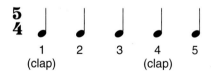

1 (clap) 2 3 4 (clap) 5

3. Listen to the saxophone as it improvises over the repeating 5/4 meter. Notice the "scoops" and "slides" in the melody.
4. Also notice the use of syncopation in the music.

ASSESSMENT

Have the class discuss some of the characteristics of jazz learned in this lesson.

Integrating Technology

The Music Education Premium Site contains chapter quizzing, Spotify playlists, and downloads of free MP3s of noted songs. Visit CengageBrain.com to purchase an access code or enter the code provided with your text materials.

Web Resources

- Search the Web (www.google.com) for information on world cultures including music (instruments, ensembles, etc.).

Video

- Access the YouTube playlist for videos referenced within the chapter.

Audio

- Download music discussed in this chapter from the Apple iTunes store.
- Spotify playlists allow students to stream music referenced within each chapter.
- Download free audio MP3s for the songs noted in the chapter.

CENGAGE**brain**.com

Questions for Discussion

1. Why is it important for teachers to present music from a number of different cultures?
2. What are some sources in the school and community that you might draw on for planning units of study (including music) on various cultures?
3. How would you go about planning a bulletin board around the theme of studying other cultures (including music)?
4. How might you as a classroom teacher collaborate with the art teacher, the music teacher, and the physical education teacher to study other cultures?
5. Give some examples of how you might combine music with social studies and language arts units in studying other cultures.
6. What are some characteristics of African, Asian, European, and American music that you could teach (using actual musical examples) to children in grades K–2, 3–4, and 5–6?.
7. How would you go about planning a multicultural or international festival for your school?

Assessment

Review ways the music standards listed at the beginning of the chapter have been met.

CHAPTER 10

Experiences with Music and Other Arts

© Ritchie Photography

Objectives

Students will learn to develop lessons:

- Using analogous concepts in relating music and the arts
  - Repetition and enlargement
  - Contrast
  - Unity
  - Balance
- Using a thematic approach in relating music and the arts
  - Nature
  - Stillness
  - Activity
- Using a historical approach in relating music and the arts
  - The age of the knights
  - The age of the American Revolution
- Using a cross-cultural approach in relating music and the arts
  - Arts of Japan

National and State Music Standards

This chapter provides experiences with the following national music standards and related state music standards:

- This chapter provides experiences with the following national music standards and related state music standards:
- Understanding relationships between music, the other arts, and disciplines outside the arts
- Understanding music in relation to history and culture
- Singing, alone and with others, a varied repertoire of music
- Performing on instruments, alone and with others, a varied repertoire of music
- Listening to, analyzing, and describing music
- Composing and arranging music within specified guidelines
- Improvising a short musical composition

This chapter is devoted to exploring ways of combining the study of music with that of other art forms, and integrating them into the elementary school curriculum. It is clear that the visual, literary, and musical arts each provide distinct ways for achieving aesthetic experiences. For example, in the visual arts of architecture, sculpture, and painting, ideas and feelings are expressed through such elements as color, line, texture, volume, perspective, and form. It is the skill with which artists manipulate these elements within their choice of media (such as marble, wood, steel, and plate glass in architecture and sculpture; watercolors, oils, fresco, mosaic, and egg tempera in painting) that determines the expressiveness and meaning in a work of art. In the literary arts, writers express ideas and feelings by using words, both for their meaning and for their sound. They use such elements of literature as grammar, figures of speech, rhyme, rhythm, and form. In music, composers express ideas and feelings by organizing sounds in terms of rhythm, melody, dynamics, tone color, texture, and form. In all of these arts, it is clear that a perception of basic elements is essential to understanding any single art medium.

William M. Anderson

Although it is evident that music, painting, sculpture, and poetry are separate and discrete art forms, it is possible to go beyond the perception of elements unique to a single art form and draw relationships among various art forms through understanding the characteristics that they share. For example, all art forms share the principles of enlargement through repetition, contrast, unity, and balance. Further, thematic, historical, and cultural ideas often inspire similar expressions in different art forms.

As a classroom teacher, you are in a unique position to help students interrelate their experiences in music with other areas of the school curriculum. Teachers can often enhance an experience with a particular musical artwork by showing students how some of its elements are shared by other art forms. Further, classroom teachers can help students understand how the arts are often closely allied with many other subject areas, such as history. In all experiences, the ultimate goal is to assist students in perceiving relationships among different modes of aesthetic experience and increasing their understanding of how and why the arts are so closely intertwined with people's lives.

There are many ways to organize a study of music and the arts. The sample lessons that follow center on four basic approaches: (1) an analogous-concepts approach, (2) a thematic approach, (3) a historical approach, and (4) a cross-cultural approach. The lessons are designed as a general guide and may need to be modified for use in various settings and with different interests and grade levels. Further, teachers are encouraged to develop other lessons based on the ideas presented here.

USING ANALOGOUS CONCEPTS IN RELATING MUSIC AND THE ARTS

The analogous-concepts approach is based on studying concepts held in common among different art forms. These include fundamental relationships such as repetition and enlargement, contrast, sense of unity, and balance.

LESSON PLAN

Repetition and Enlargement 1

Grades: 1–3

NATIONAL AND STATE STANDARDS

1. Singing, alone and with others, a varied repertoire of music
2. Performing on instruments, alone and with others, a varied repertoire of music
3. Understanding relationships between music, the other arts, and disciplines outside the arts

OBJECTIVES

Students will:

1. Create a visual picture that can be enlarged through repetition.
2. Examine poems that feature repetition and create a poem that shows enlargement through repetition.
3. Lengthen a song by repeating or adding verses or rhythm patterns.
4. Identify repetition as a means of enlargement in music and the visual and literary arts.

MATERIALS

- Construction-paper strips
- Reproduction of Warhol's painting *Campbell's Soup Cans* (download from www.images.google.com)
- Rhythm instruments
- Poems: "I Saw a Fish Pond" and "There Was a Crooked Man"

PROCEDURES

1. Create a paper chain by cutting out small strips of paper, forming loops, and linking and stapling them together. Students can make bracelets, necklaces, or even jump ropes by adding loops. Call attention to the use of repetition to enlarge or expand the chain.

2. Bring a Slinky to class and ask students to make a large shape by expanding the Slinky. (Be sure not to stretch it too much or it will not return to its original shape.) Ask students what is repeated to make the large shape (metal circles).
3. Select one student to be a leader. Have other students line up one at a time behind the leader. Notice how the line becomes longer (expands, enlarges).
4. Ask students to bring in soup cans and build a picture or shape based on repetition of these cans.
5. Download and project Andy Warhol's painting *Campbell's Soup Cans*. Discuss how one can build by repeating an idea.

6. Read the nursery rhyme "I Saw a Fishpond." Call attention to the repetition of the phrase *I saw.*

I Saw a Fishpond

I saw a fishpond all on fire
I saw a house bow to a squire
I saw a parson twelve feet high
I saw a cottage near the sky
I saw a balloon made of lead
I saw a coffin drop down dead
I saw two sparrows run a race
I saw two horses making lace
I saw a girl just like a cat
I saw a kitten wear a hat
I saw a man who saw these too
And said though strange they all were true.

7. Read the following nursery rhyme and identify the words that are repeated.

There was a crooked man, and he went a crooked mile;
He found a crooked sixpence against a crooked stile;
He bought a crooked cat, which caught a crooked mouse,
And all lived together in a little crooked house.

8. Perform "The People on the Bus" (p. 227). Notice that the song is lengthened by repeating the music and adding verses.
9. Play a simple ostinato pattern on a percussion instrument as students sing "The People on the Bus." Note the repetition of the rhythm pattern. You can use this rhythm as an introduction and ending (coda):

ASSESSMENT

1. Ask students to identify ways an artist repeats ideas in music, visual art, and poetry.
2. Ask students how repetition can make a work of art larger (or longer).

William M. Anderson

The Roman Colosseum

LESSON PLAN

Repetition and Enlargement 2

Grades: 4–6

NATIONAL AND STATE STANDARDS

1. Singing, alone and with others, a varied repertoire of music
2. Performing on instruments, alone and with others, a varied repertoire of music
3. Composing and arranging music within specified guidelines
4. Listening to, analyzing, and describing music
5. Understanding relationships between music, the other arts, and disciplines outside the arts

OBJECTIVES

Students will:

1. Identify repetition as a means of enlargement in music, visual art, and poetry.
2. Create artwork (visual art, poems, musical compositions) that show enlargement through repetition.

MATERIALS

1. Picture: Roman Colosseum (download from www.images.google.com)
2. Poem: Armour, "Money" [William]
3. Recording: Ravel, *Bolero* (download or stream from [iTunes/Spotify])

PROCEDURES

1. Look for examples of repetition in your classroom, such as windows and desks.
2. Download (www.images.google.com) and show students a side view of the Roman Colosseum. Ask them to look for repeated shapes (rounded arches). Also ask them to point out how the building is made larger by such repetition.
3. Have students create their own pictures by making use of enlargement through repeating lines, shapes, colors, and so on.
4. Read the following poem and identify the poet's use of repetition. Notice how the poem is enlarged through repetition.

Money[1]

Workers earn it,
Spendthrifts burn it,
Bankers lend it,
Women spend it,
Forgers fake it,
Taxes take it,
Dying leave it,
Heirs receive it,
Thrifty save it,
Misers crave it,
Robbers seize it,
Rich increase it,
Gamblers lose it . . .
I could use it.

5. Have students make up poems based on the principle of enlargement/expansion through repetition.
6. Have students sing "Row, Row, Row Your Boat" (pp. 46, 60) as a round—first as a two-part, then as a three-part, and finally as a four-part round.
   a. Put the following diagram on the board, illustrating the beginning of the singing of the four-part round:

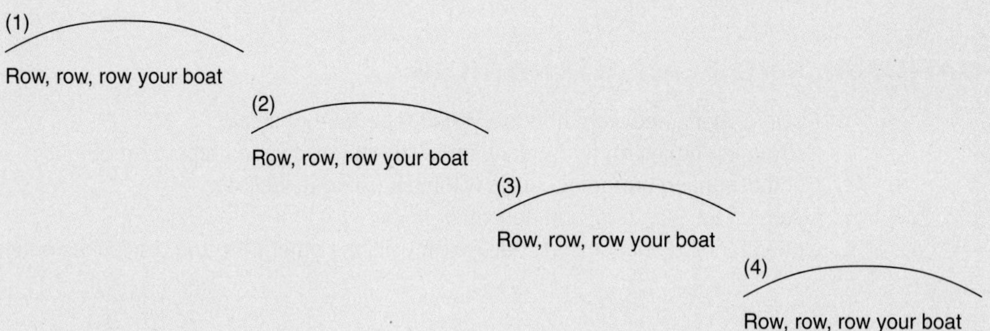
(1)
Row, row, row your boat
(2)
Row, row, row your boat
(3)
Row, row, row your boat
(4)
Row, row, row your boat

   b. Call attention to the organizational principle of enlargement/expansion through repetition.

[1] From Richard Armour, *An Armoury of Light Verse* (Boston: International Pocket Library, 1964). © Branden Publishing Company. Reprinted by permission of Branden Publishing Company. Permission courtesy of Branden Books, Boston.

7. Download and play Maurice Ravel's *Bolero*. During the first 2 minutes of the piece, have students softly play the following triple-meter pattern:

1	2	3
Drum	Tambourine shake	Tambourine shake

Have the rest of the class clap the underlying rhythmic motif that repeats throughout the piece:

8. Improvise a short piece of music by using repetition to create enlargement.

ASSESSMENT

Ask students to use specific examples to comment on how enlargement in artworks is created through repetition. Have them create artwork illustrating enlargement through repetition.

LESSON PLAN
Contrast 1

Grades: 1–3

NATIONAL AND STATE STANDARDS

1. Singing, alone and with others, a varied repertoire of music
2. Performing on instruments, alone and with others, a varied repertoire of music
3. Composing and arranging music within specified guidelines
4. Listening to, analyzing, and describing music
5. Understanding relationships between music, the other arts, and disciplines outside the arts

OBJECTIVES

Students will:

1. Identify characteristics of contrast in music, visual art, and poetry.
2. Create a sound composition in ABA form for each of the following: dynamics (loud/soft) and tempo (fast/slow).

MATERIALS

1. Pictures: Victor Vasarély, *Orion MC;* Miro, *The Moon*[2]; photographs of stained-glass windows in Chartres Cathedral (download from www.images.google.com)
2. Poem: Behn, "This Happy Day"

[2] See Gaston Diehl, *Miro* (New York: Crown, 1979, 1988), p. 71.

3. Percussion instruments, word cards, colored letters, writing board
4. Recording: Saint-Saëns, *Carnival of the Animals* (download or stream from [iTunes/Spotify])

PROCEDURES

1. Place the word "contrast" in different colors on a flannelboard. Emphasize that the word "contrast" refers to things that are different. Have letters cut in different colors, sizes, and shapes. Ask students to create various arrangements of the word on the board.
2. Explore contrast by having students print their names in at least six different ways (using different sizes, shapes, colors, and so on).
3. Inflate several balloons of varying sizes and colors and arrange them in highly contrasting ways.
4. Ask the students to look for contrast in paintings such as Victor Vasarély's *Orion MC*, Joan Miro's *The Moon,* or in stained-glass windows from the Cathedral of Notre Dame at Chartres, France. Students should find contrast in colors, sizes, and shapes.
5. Encourage students to create their own pictures, making use of contrast in colors, shapes, lines, sizes, and so on.
6. Read the poem "This Happy Day" by Harry Behn and discuss how the poet uses contrast to express his idea of morning and night. What is repeated, and what is different?

This Happy Day[3]

Every morning when the sun
Comes smiling up on everyone,
It's lots of fun
To say good morning to the sun.
  Good morning, Sun!

Every evening after play
When the sunshine goes away,
It's nice to say,
Thank you for this happy day,
  This happy day!

Technology Enhancement

Step 8 can also be accomplished by using electronic or software instruments. You can use any software available, such as "GarageBand" or "Mixcraft."

7. Perform the song "Tinga Layo" (p. 82). Use metal percussion instruments to accompany the verse and wooden percussion instruments to accompany the refrain. Discuss how these are "contrasting" sections.
8. Download and play selections from *Carnival of the Animals* by Saint-Saëns, and use cards with words to describe the sounds or expressiveness of various animals (for example, elephant–slow; birds–high and fast).
9. Create a short rhythm composition in ABA form (twelve measures), in which section B is different (contrasting). Using your composition, experiment with contrasting instruments, contrasting dynamics, and so on.

ASSESSMENT

Have students discuss how contrast is created in music, poetry, and visual art. Ask them to bring examples to class.

[3] From Harry Behn, *The Little Hill, Poems and Pictures* (New York: Harcourt Brace, 1949). © 1949 by Harry Behn. Copyright renewed 1977 by Alice L. Behn. Used by permission of Marian Reiner.

LESSON PLAN

Contrast 2

Grades: 4–6

NATIONAL AND STATE STANDARDS

1. Performing on instruments, alone and with others, a varied repertoire of music
2. Composing and arranging music within specified guidelines
3. Listening to, analyzing, and describing music
4. Understanding relationships between music, the other arts, and disciplines outside the arts

OBJECTIVES

Students will:

1. Identify characteristics of contrast in music, visual art, and poetry.
2. Create a sound composition in ABA form for each of the following: (a) dynamics (loud, soft); (b) tempo (fast/slow); (c) tessitura (high/low); and (d) texture (thick/thin).

MATERIALS

1. Different kinds of balls
2. The word *contrast* in different sizes, shapes, and colors
3. Rhythm instruments
4. Poem: Tippett, "Trucks"
5. Pictures (download from www.images. google.com): Victor Vasarély, *Orion MC*[4]*;* or Piet Mondrian, *Broadway Boogie Woogie*[5]
6. Recording: Ravel, *Bolero* (download or stream from [iTunes/Spotify])

PROCEDURES

1. Ask half the class to shout "School's out!" and the other half to whisper "School's out." Discuss the difference (include not only dynamics such as loud and soft but also the vocal mechanisms involved, such as shouting and whispering).
2. Explore types of balls, such as a football, basketball, tennis ball, and Ping-Pong ball. Discuss how they are different.
3. Place the word "contrast" in many shapes and colors on a board.
4. Play the following rhythm and ask individual students to respond with a contrasting rhythm in the same meter signature:

[4] See H. H. Arnason and Daniel Wheeler, *History of Modern Art*, 3rd ed. (New York: Harry N. Abrams, 1986), p. 384.

[5] See H. H. Arnason, Marla F. Prater, and Daniel Wheeler, *History of Modern Art,* 5th ed. (Upper Saddle River, NJ: Prentice Hall/Pearson, 2004), p. 362.

Response (contrast): 4/4 half note, two eighth notes, quarter note ||

Create several different rhythms that contrast with one another. Play these rhythms on contrasting rhythm instruments or sing them at different pitch levels.

5. Ask students to look for contrast in paintings such as Victor Vasarély's *Orion MC* or Piet Mondrian's *Broadway Boogie Woogie* (Download from www.images.google.com and project onto a screen.) Also, ask them to identify contrast in clothing, comic books, textbooks, and magazines.
6. Ask students to look for ways in which contrast is achieved in James Tippett's poem "Trucks" (for example, contrast in rhyme scheme—ABCB—and in word sounds: *big, rumbling, heavily, little, turning, rushing*).

Trucks[6]

Big trucks for steel beams
Big trucks for coal,
Rumbling down the broad streets,
Heavily they roll.

Little trucks for groceries
Little trucks for bread,
Turning into every street,
Rushing on ahead.

Big trucks, little trucks,
In never ending lines,
Rumble on and rush ahead
While I read their signs.

7. Download and play segments from Maurice Ravel's *Bolero*. Have the students discuss how the composer creates *contrast* by repeating the same melody—but each time with different tone colors and dynamics.
8. Create a composition in ABA form using different musical instruments. Discuss how contrast is achieved in the piece (different tone colors, dynamic levels, tempos, etc.).

ASSESSMENT

1. Lead a class discussion on how *contrast* is achieved in various artwork (music, painting, poetry, etc.).
2. Have the students bring to class and discuss examples of *contrast* in artwork.

[6] Edna Johnson et al., *Anthology of Children's Literature*, 5th ed. (Boston: Houghton Mifflin, 1977). © 1977. Reprinted by permission of Houghton Mifflin Co.

LESSON PLAN
Unity

Grades: 2–4

Unity refers to the process of tying an artwork together by systematically repeating certain elements.

NATIONAL AND STATE STANDARDS

1. Listening to, analyzing, and describing music
2. Understanding relationships between music, the other arts, and disciplines outside the arts

OBJECTIVES

Students will:

1. Identify how unity is created in music and in the visual and literary arts.
2. Create artwork that illustrates the concept of unity.

MATERIALS

1. Pictures: Roman Colosseum, Pisa Cathedral; Mondrian, *Broadway Boogie Woogie*; Vasarély, *Orion MC* (download from www.images.google.com)
2. Recording:"Spring" from Vivaldi's *The Four Seasons;* Rondo from Mozart's *Eine Kleine Nachtmusik* (download or stream from [iTunes/Spotify])

PROCEDURES

1. Reread the poem "Money" by Richard Armour (p. 340).
2. Ask students to notice how repetition of the word "it" helps tie the poem together and provide a sense of unity.
3. Also call attention to the use of the same number of syllables in the second and third words of each line.
4. Ask students to identify which words rhyme, and to notice the repetition of the rhyme pattern throughout the poem.
5. Have the class create a short poem in which a word or words are repeated to tie the work together, thus providing a sense of unity.
6. Download and project pictures of the Roman Colosseum, the Pisa Cathedral, Piet Mondrian's *Broadway Boogie Woogie,* and Victor Vasarély's *Orion MC.* Discuss how elements are repeated to provide a sense of unity in these structures and artwork.
7. Have students create their own examples of visual art by using repetition of items (shapes, colors, textures, and so on) to provide unity.
8. Download and listen to "Spring" from Vivaldi's *The Four Seasons.* This musical work is tied together by repetition of the opening section throughout the composition. Use the listening guide on the next page.
9. Ask students to create a listening guide by using different colors of construction paper to outline the form of the Rondo from Mozart's *Eine Kleine Nachtmusik:* A (red) B (blue) A (red)

Technology Enhancement

See Vivaldi and the Four Seasons Teacher Resource Kit for Classroom Teachers, Grades 4–6 (artsalive.ca/pdf/nusic/tour2004/vivaldi2004_en.pdf). Contains cross-curricular lessons and activities.

Listening Guide: Vivaldi's The Four Seasons, "Spring"

Section A: Vigorous, joyful melody—spring has arrived

Section B: Twittering of birds suggested by high trills on violins

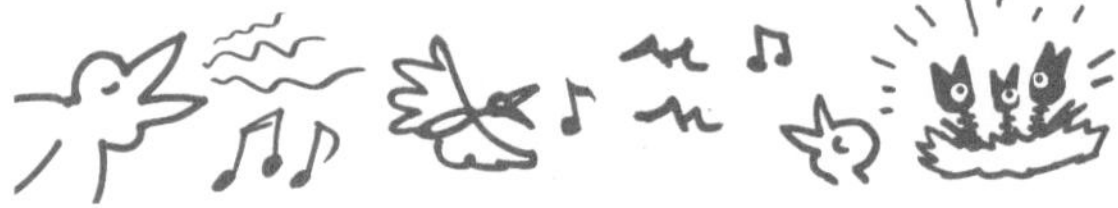

Section A: Return of a portion of the melody from beginning of piece

Section C: Gentle breezes and lazy streams of water portrayed by soft, lyrical music

Section A: Return of a portion of the melody from beginning of piece

Section D: The sky begins to turn black, and thunder and lightning signal an approaching storm; vividly portrayed by low quivering string sounds followed by passages that sweep upward

Section A: Return of a portion of the melody from beginning of piece

Section E: Storm is now over and birds begin to sing, again portrayed by trills and embellishments on violins

Section A: Return of melody from beginning of piece

C (green) A (red). Discuss how repetition of the main theme helps tie the piece together, thereby creating a sense of unity.

ASSESSMENT

1. Have students look at various artwork and identify how a sense of unity is created by repeating certain elements (shapes, colors, etc.)
2. Read poems of your choice and discuss how poets unify their works (repetition of words, rhyme scheme, etc.).
3. Ask students to identify techniques used by musicians to unify their works (repeating melodies, rhythms, etc.).

LESSON PLAN
Balance

Grades: 2–4

Balance is a state of equilibrium. In artwork it is created by "even proportion," as in the shapes and colors used in a painting, or in music ABA form, in which a musical idea is presented, followed by a contrasting musical section, and then there is a return to the early musical material.

NATIONAL AND STATE STANDARDS

1. Singing, alone and with others, a varied repertoire of music
2. Composing and arranging music within specified guidelines
3. Understanding relationships between music, the other arts, and disciplines outside the arts

OBJECTIVES

Students will:

1. Identify balance in music and in the visual and literary arts.
2. Create artwork that illustrates the concept of balance.

MATERIALS

- Geometric figures (square, circle)
- Red construction paper
- Rhythm pattern chart
- Nursery rhyme: "The Goblin"
- Pictures: Taj Mahal; da Vinci, *The Last Supper* (download from www.images. google.com)

PROCEDURES

1. Have students balance on one foot, as an ice skater might do, with arms extended in a "swan" position.
2. Have students cut out geometrical figures (square and circle, for example) and place them on a bulletin board so that the square represents a fulcrum and the two circles represent equal weights on each end:

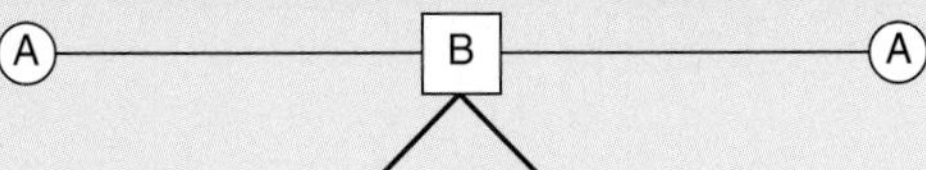

3. Place the following rhythm pattern on the board. Clap the pattern with the class. Ask students to discover balance in the rhythm pattern:

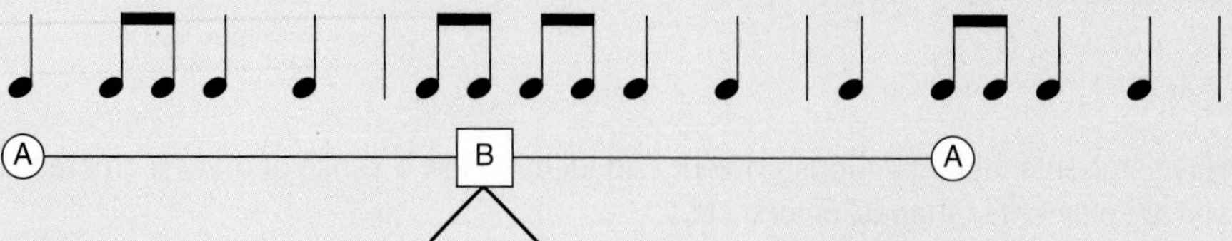

4. Have students read the nursery rhyme "The Goblin" and discover balance (opening words are repeated at end to make an ABA design); compare this structure to the ABA rhythm pattern.

The Goblin[7]

A goblin lives in *our* house, in *our* house, in *our* house,
A goblin lives in *our* house all the year round.
He bumps
And he jumps
And he thumps
And he stumps.
He knocks
And he rocks
And he rattles at the locks.
A goblin lives in *our* house, in *our* house, in *our* house,
A goblin lives in *our* house all the year round.

5. Download and display a picture of the Taj Mahal in Agra, India. Ask students to identify how balance is achieved in this structure.
   - Dome area in center has equal portions of the building on either side.
   - Two minarets are on either side of the building.
   - Large ogive-shaped doorway and window opening in the center are flanked by smaller ogive-shaped window openings on either side.

Taj Mahal (Agra, India)

[7] From *Sugar and Spice*, by Rose Fyleman.

6. Download and project *The Last Supper* by Leonardo da Vinci. Ask
students to identify how balance is achieved in this painting.
   - Jesus is in the center, with six apostles on either side.
   - Large window behind Jesus has two small windows, one on each side.
   - Wall area behind apostles has equal sides of wall on left and right.
   - Table in front of apostles has a center area with equally proportioned sections on either side.
7. Sing "We Wish You a Merry Christmas" (p. 61). Ask students if they hear the same melody in several places in the song (first eight measures and last eight measures). Cut out different geometrical shapes in several colors of construction paper. Place an *A* on two pieces of paper that have the same shape and color, and a *B* on a piece of paper that has a contrasting shape and color. Have students place the construction-paper diagrams on a board to indicate the form of the piece.

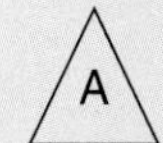

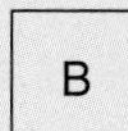

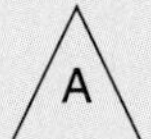

Technology Enhancement

Have students create a balanced composition in ABA form by using electronic or software instruments/programs. You can use any software available, such as "GarageBand" or "Mixcraft,"

You can also use these same programs to record your students' performances and save the recording as an MP3 file to be sent home to parents via e-mail or CD.

ASSESSMENT

1. Ask students to identify techniques used by poets, visual artists, and composers to balance their works of art. Find other songs that show balance.
2. Create a musical composition, poem, or work of visual art that shows balance.

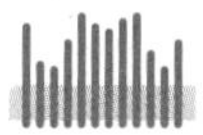

USING A THEMATIC APPROACH IN RELATING MUSIC AND THE ARTS

One of the most frequently used approaches to relating music and other arts is through a common theme. Visual artists, writers, and musicians use a large number of themes in their works, including religion, love, war, freedom, people, machines, nature, stillness, and activity. In organizing units of study through a thematic approach, the intent is to discover how musicians, painters, and poets have been able to express a particular theme by using materials that are unique to their art (sounds in music, words in poetry, paint in visual art).

The sample lessons in this section provide opportunities to explore (1) portrayals of nature, (2) portrayals of stillness, and (3) portrayals of activity.

LESSON PLAN

Nature

Grades: 4-6

Nature refers to the natural world that surrounds us, including plants, animals, the landscape, and so on. Nature is often a theme in artworks as they portray a river, clouds, or birds.

NATIONAL AND STATE STANDARDS

1. Singing, alone and with others, a varied repertoire of music
2. Composing and arranging music within specified guidelines
3. Understanding relationships between music, the other arts, and disciplines outside the arts

OBJECTIVES

Students will:

1. Identify phenomena of nature, such as storms, flowers, sunrise, sunset, and waterfalls.
2. Identify how nature themes are portrayed in selected examples of music, poetry, and visual arts.
3. Create original works of music, poetry, and visual art that focus on themes of nature.

MATERIALS

- Pictures: Durand, *Scene from Thanatopsis;* Hicks, *The Peaceable Kingdom* (download pictures from www.images.google.com for students to view)
- Poems: Wordsworth, "I Wandered Lonely as a Cloud"; Keats, "On the Grasshopper and Cricket"; Japanese haiku, "Snow Fell until Dawn"
- Rhythm instruments
- Recordings: Beethoven, "The Storm," Symphony no. 6 (fourth movement); Smetana, *The Moldau* (download or stream from [iTunes/Spotify])

Technology Enhancement

Website that includes outdoor activities along with other useful links: bblocks.samhsa.gov/educators/lesson_plans/nature_teaching.aspx

PROCEDURES

This lesson may need to extend over several days.

1. Lead a short discussion on ways we experience nature every day (walk past trees on the way to school, see and hear birds, watch fish swim in a pond, and so on).
2. Make a bulletin board titled "Nature." Look for pictures of landscapes, trees, birds, and animals.
3. Show students pictures of Asher Durand's *Scene from Thanatopsis* and Edward Hicks's *The Peaceable Kingdom* and ask them to find evidence of nature in the paintings (river, hills, trees, animals, and so on). Ask students to look for other examples of paintings that have a nature theme.

Asher B. Durand, *Scene from Thanatopsis* (formerly known as *Imaginary Landscape*)

4. Have students create pictures that reflect themes of nature, such as sunrise, sunset, and waterfall.
5. Read the following poems. Discuss how the writers portray nature (descriptive words).
    a. "I Wandered Lonely as a Cloud," by William Wordsworth (References to nature: cloud, vales and hills, golden daffodils, lake, trees, breeze, stars, milky way, bay, waves)

I Wandered Lonely as a Cloud

I wandered lonely as a cloud
  That floats on high o'er vales and hills,
When all at once I saw a crowd,
  A host, of golden daffodils.
Beside the lake, beneath the trees,
  Fluttering and dancing in the breeze.

Continuous as the stars that shine
  And twinkle on the milky way,
They stretched in never-ending line
  Along the margin of a bay:
Ten thousand saw I at a glance,
  Tossing their heads in sprightly dance.

The waves beside them danced, but they
  Outdid the sparkling waves in glee:
A poet could not but be gay,
  In such a jocund company.
I gazed—and gazed—but little thought
  What wealth the show to me had brought:

For oft, when on my couch I lie
  In vacant or in pensive mood,
They flash upon that inward eye
  Which is the bliss of solitude;
And then my heart with pleasure fills,
  And dances with the daffodils.

    b. "On the Grasshopper and Cricket," by John Keats (References to nature: birds, hot sun, cooling trees, hedge, mead, grasshopper, weed, frost, cricket, grassy hills)

On the Grasshopper and Cricket

The poetry of earth is never dead:
When all the birds are faint with the hot sun,
And hide in cooling trees, a voice will run
From hedge to hedge about the new-mown mead;
That is the Grasshopper's—he takes the lead
In summer luxury—he has never done
With his delights; for when tired out with fun
He rests at ease beneath some pleasant weed.

The poetry of earth is ceasing never:
On a lone winter evening, when the frost
Has wrought a silence, from the stove there shrills
The Cricket's song, in warmth increasing ever,
And seems to one in drowsiness half lost,
The Grasshopper's among some grassy hills.

c. "Snow Fell until Dawn," Japanese haiku[8] (References to nature: snow, twig, grove, sunlight)

Snow Fell until Dawn

Snow fell until dawn
now every twig in the grove
glitters in sunlight

6. Ask students to compose their own short poems based on themes of nature.
7. Ask students to create their own examples of music focusing on a theme or themes of nature. For example, using rhythm instruments, they might create a score that expresses the approach, arrival, and departure of a storm.
8. Download and have students listen to Beethoven's *Symphony no. 6,* fourth movement, "The Storm." Follow the listening guide below.
9. Download and have students listen to Smetana's *The Moldau*. This composition is a symphonic poem that tells the story of a famous river, the Moldau, which runs through Bohemia (now part of the Czech Republic). Follow the "musical trip" of the river, using the listening guide on the next page.

ASSESSMENT

1. Ask students to identify techniques used by artists to portray events in nature (e.g., storm, river).
2. Create a musical composition, poem, or work of visual art that focuses on some aspect of nature.

Listening Guide: "The Storm" from Beethoven's *Symphony no. 6*

1. As the piece begins, the low-pitched stringed instruments depict the rumbling of thunder in the distance.
2. The music gets louder and louder, leading to explosive fortissimo sounds portraying thunder and lightning, which are now close.
3. Timpani and brass instruments add to the musical depiction of the storm.
4. As the movement ends, the storm subsides and the music becomes soft and tranquil.

[8] From *Cricket Songs: Japanese Haiku,* translated by Harry Behn (New York: Harcourt, Brace & World, 1964). © 1949 by Harry Behn. Copyright renewed 1992 by Prescott Behn, Pamela Behn Adam, and Peter Behn. Used by permission of Marian Reiner.

Listening Guide: Smetana's *The Moldau*

1. In the shade of the Bohemian Forest, two springs bubble, their waves rippling over rocks to form a brook.	Active, rippling passages in the woodwinds depict the movement of the water.
2. As the brook winds through the Bohemian countryside, it gradually grows into a mighty river, the Moldau.	A long, smooth melody played by the stringed instruments portrays the Moldau.
3. The Moldau flows through dense forests.	The sounds of hunting horns, aptly portrayed by brass instruments, are heard.
4. The river flows through a meadow, where a peasant wedding is being celebrated.	The orchestra plays jubilant dance music in 3/4 meter.
5. As night falls, the river flows quietly in mysterious stillness as the moonlight sweeps over its surface. Fortresses and castles, projecting skyward on the surrounding slopes, remain as mute witnesses of the bygone glories and splendors of knighthood.	This section is portrayed by slow, soft, lyrical music.
6. Daybreak comes and the Moldau flows onward through a valley.	The river is again depicted by the long flowing melody in the stringed instruments.
7. The river now passes through a rough, rocky area.	This part of the river is depicted by loud, turbulent sounds in the orchestra.
8. As the rocky area is passed, the river again flows in majestic peace toward Prague (capital of the Czech Republic), where it passes another ancient fortress, afterward disappearing beyond the composer's sight.	This last part is once again portrayed by a flowing, lyrical melody.

LESSON PLAN
Stillness

Grades: 2–3

Stillness is a state of quietness and calm. The word has many synonyms: *subdued, hushed, peaceful, silent, tranquil, serene.* In artwork, a sense of stillness can be achieved in a number of ways, including muted colors, horizontal lines, descriptive words (*whisper, sleep*), soft dynamic levels, and slow tempos.

NATIONAL AND STATE STANDARDS

1. Listening to, analyzing, and describing music
2. Composing and arranging music within specified guidelines
3. Understanding relationships between music, the other arts, and disciplines outside the arts

OBJECTIVES

Students will:

1. Identify how stillness is achieved in selected examples of music, literature, and visual art.
2. Create artwork portraying stillness.

MATERIALS

- Pictures: Miro, *Blue III;* Tohaku, *Pine Trees in Snow* (download from www.images.google.com)
- Poems: Livingston, "Whispers"; Sandburg, "Fog"; de la Mare, "Silver"
- Handout: Listening guide for "Ave Maria"
- Recordings:
  - Gregorian chant, "Ave Maria" (download or stream from [iTunes/Spotify])
  - "Shika no Tone" (Deer Calling to Each Other in the Distance) (download or stream from [iTunes/Spotify])
  - Ives, "Serenity" from *Charles Ives Songs,* Vol. 2, Smithsonian Folkways Records (download from www.folkways.si.edu)
- Classroom instruments

PROCEDURES

This lesson may need to extend over several days.

1. Have students sit perfectly still for one minute and then describe how they feel. Ask for ideas about what causes stillness and quietness.
2. Find pictures of things that are still. Find words that describe things that are still, such as *sleep, quiet, slow, mist,* and *darkness.*
3. Read the following poems with the class, focusing on how the writer has achieved a sense of stillness.
   a. "Whispers" by Myra Cohn Livingston: Call attention to the word *whispers,* which is repeated several times.

      Whispers[9]

      Whispers
        tickle through your ear
        telling things you like to hear.

[9] From Myra Cohn Livingston, *Whispers and Other Poems* (New York: Harcourt Brace, 1958). © 1958 by Myra Cohn Livingston. Renewed 1986. Used by permission of Marian Reiner.

Whispers
  are as soft as skin
  letting little words curl in.
Whispers
  come so they can blow
    secrets others never know.

b. "Fog" by Carl Sandburg:

Fog[10]

The fog comes
on little cat feet.
It sits looking
over harbor and city
on silent haunches
and then moves on.

c. "Silver" by Walter de la Mare: Call attention to the use of the words *slowly, silently, sleeps,* and *moveless;* notice the use of alliteration for many words beginning with *s,* a sound that conveys tranquility.

Silver[11]

Slowly, silently, now the moon
Walks the night in her silver shoon;
This way, and that, she peers, and sees
Silver fruit upon silver trees;
One by one the casements catch
Her beams beneath the silvery thatch;
Couched in his kennel, like a log;
With paws of silver sleeps the dog;
From their shadowy cote the white breasts peep
Of doves in a silver-feathered sleep;
A harvest mouse goes scampering by,
With silver claws, and silver eye;
And moveless fish in the water gleam,
By silver reeds in a silver stream.

4. Ask students to write their own poems or phrases using words that create a sense of stillness.
5. Ask the class to draw pictures that convey a sense of stillness. Explore not only stillness as a theme for a picture but also ways of achieving the feeling of stillness or calmness (use of colors such as blue and green, which are more subdued than the active colors of red and orange; use of horizontal lines; etc.).
6. Download (www.images.google.com) and display pictures of paintings that portray stillness and tranquility.
   a. *Blue III* by Joan Miro[12]: Ask the class how the elements of line, shape, and color are used in the painting to create a sense of stillness, quiet, and inactivity (open, unobstructed space; the color blue; long, curvilinear line; round shapes).
   b. *Pine Trees in Snow* by Hasegawa Tohaku[13]: Ask students to point out how the sense of stillness is created through the delicate lines depicting this winter scene, by the areas left "open" in the painting, and by the use of subdued colors.
7. Listen to several selections of music that portray stillness and tranquility.
   a. Gregorian chant, "Ave Maria": Have students circle the elements in the listening guide below that help create the sense of stillness/calmness in the music.

   Discuss the setting of the music and why it needs to convey a sense of calm (performed as part of a religious service; quiet, serene atmosphere of a cathedral).

---

[10] From Carl Sandburg, *Chicago Poems* (New York: H. Holt and Company, 1916). © 1916 by Holt, Rinehart and Winston. Copyright renewed 1944 by Carl Sandburg.

[11] From *The Complete Poems of Walter De La Mare* (London: Faber, 1969; USA: 1970). Reprinted by permission of the Literary Trustees of Walter de la Mare and the Society of Authors as their representative.

[12] See Gaston Diehl, *Miro* (New York: Crown, 1979, 1988), p. 72.

[13] See Penelope Mason, *History of Japanese Art* (New York: Harry N. Abrams, 1993), p. 267.

b. "Serenity," by Charles Ives: Notice how the sense of stillness and calmness is created in the music to express the text "the silence of eternity" (soft dynamic level, weak feeling for the beat, slow tempo).
c. "Shika no Tone" (Deer Calling to Each Other in the Distance), as performed on the Japanese shakuhachi (wind instrument): Discuss how the soft dynamic level, the flexible rhythm, the slow tempo, the weak feeling for the beat, and the monophonic texture contribute to the sense of stillness, inactivity, and calm in the music.

8. Have students improvise with classroom instruments or their voices to convey a sense of stillness. Discuss how slow tempo, soft dynamic levels, smooth stepwise melodies, flexible rhythm, weak feeling for the beat, and so on help create a sense of stillness or calm.
9. Ask students to make up movements that express the stillness of the music.

ASSESSMENT

1. Ask students to identify techniques used by artists to express stillness in works of art.
2. Ask students to create a musical composition, poem, or work of visual art that shows stillness.

Listening Guide: "Ave Maria" (Gregorian Chant)

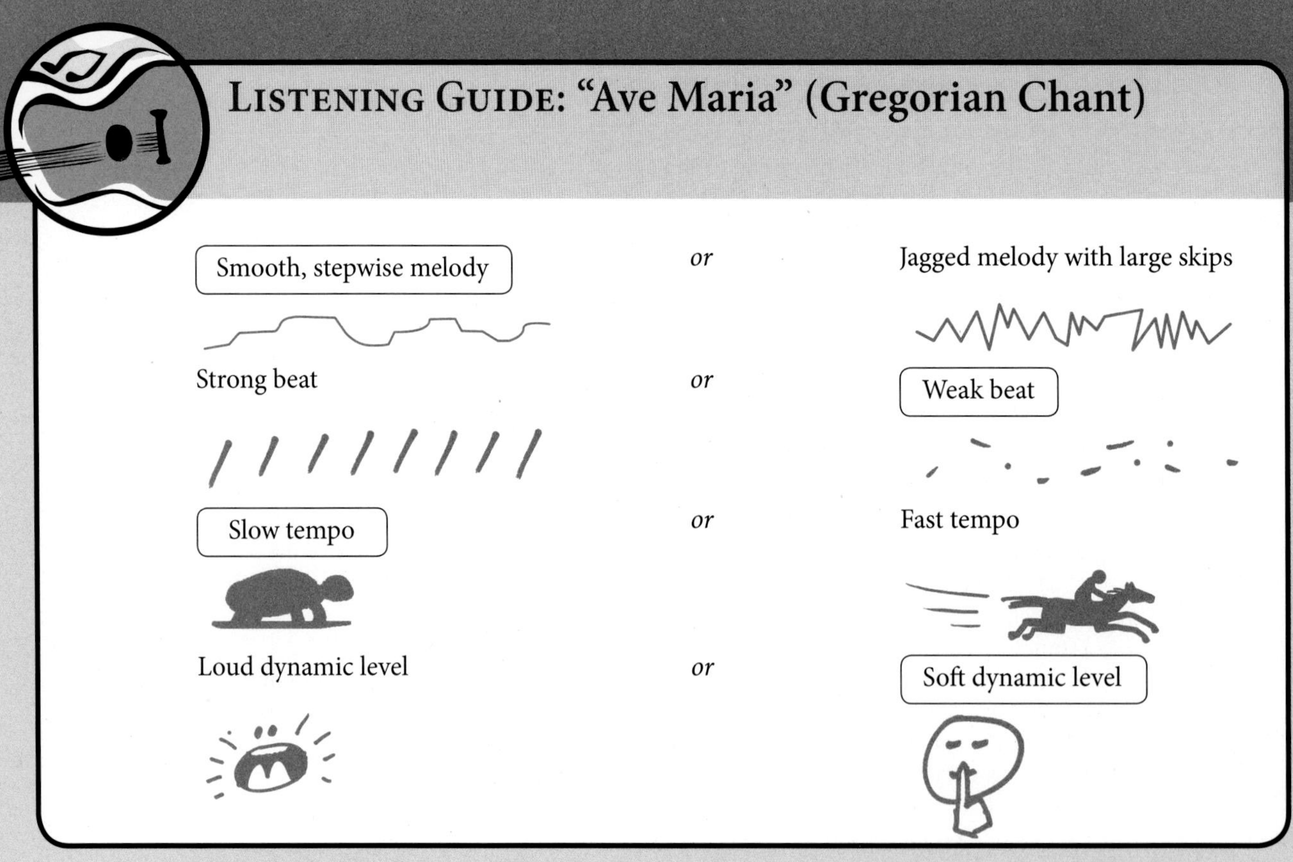

Smooth, stepwise melody
or
Jagged melody with large skips
Strong beat
or
Weak beat
Slow tempo
or
Fast tempo
Loud dynamic level
or
Soft dynamic level

LESSON PLAN
Activity

Grades: 5–6

Activity involves the state or condition of being energetic, lively, and vigorous.

NATIONAL AND STATE STANDARDS

1. Listening to, analyzing, and describing music
2. Composing and arranging music within specified guidelines
3. Performing on instruments, alone and with others, a varied repertoire of music
4. Understanding relationships between music, the other arts, and disciplines outside the arts

OBJECTIVES

Students will:

1. Describe how musicians, poets, and artists create a sense of activity in their works.
2. Create artwork that conveys a sense of activity.

MATERIALS

- Picture: Kandinsky, *Sketch I for Composition VII*[14] (download from www.images.google.com)
- Poem: Morrison, "The Sprinters"
- Recordings: Stravinsky, "Dance of the Adolescents" from *Rite of Spring;* Beethoven, "The Storm" from Symphony no. 6 (fourth movement) (download or stream from [iTunes/Spotify])
- Handout: Listening guide for "Dance of the Adolescents"
- Classroom instruments

PROCEDURES

This lesson may need to extend over several days.

1. Lead a class discussion about ways in which students see activity in everyday life.
2. Make a list on the board of words that convey a sense of action.
3. Read the poem "The Sprinters" by Lillian Morrison (www.google.com). Note the sense of action in words such as *explodes, pummeling, pistoning, fly, smash, outpace, runs, streaks, faster, shout, pound,* and *grace-driven stride.*
4. Ask students to compose their own poems or phrases using action themes and words.
5. Ask students to draw pictures that convey a sense of action. Explore not only action themes (running, playing ball, skating) but also ways of achieving the feeling of action in a painting (sharp, jagged lines; use of active colors, such as red; juxtaposition of strongly contrasting colors).
6. Look for ways in which the sense of action is created in Wassily Kandinsky's *Sketch I for Composition VII* (download from www.images.google.com). Ask students to discover what qualities in the painting create the feeling of vigor or activity (warm, active colors of red and orange; contrasts of colors; twisting, swirling lines; diagonal lines).

[14] See H. W. Janson, and Anthony F. Janson, *History of Art,* 4th ed. (New York: Harry N. Abrams, 1991), p. 715; 6th ed. (Upper Saddle River, NJ: Prentice Hall/Pearson, 2003), p. 808.

7. Download and play "Dance of the Adolescents" from Stravinsky's *Rite of Spring.*
   a. Using the following listening guide, have students listen for ways in which activity is created in the music and to circle the correct items:
   b. Ask students to make up a set of movements that express the activity of "Dance of the Adolescents."
8. Download and play "The Storm" from Beethoven's *Symphony no. 6.* Identify how activity is created by very loud dynamic levels, by dramatic contrasts between loud and soft dynamic levels, and by moderately fast tempo.
9. Have students improvise with classroom instruments or voices to convey a sense of activity. Discuss how loud dynamic levels, fast tempo, strong accentuation, syncopation, melodies with large skips, and so on, help create a sense of action in sound.

ASSESSMENT

1. Ask students to identify techniques used by artists to express activity in works of art.
2. Ask students to create a musical composition, poem, or work of visual art that shows activity.

Listening Guide: "Dance of the Adolescents" from Stravinsky's *Rite of Spring*

Weak beat	*or*	[Strong, pulsating beat]
[Strong accents]	*or*	No accents
[Loud dynamic level]	*or*	Soft dynamic level
Smooth, lyrical sounds	*or*	[Short, staccato sounds]
[Jagged, skipping melody]	*or*	Smooth, stepwise melody

Special Learner Note

Present symbols or pictures with words (or instead of words) to include nonreaders in this "choice" process. This could be presented on a board for all to see and work with or as an individual handout for students to work with independently or in pairs.

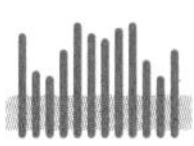

USING A HISTORICAL APPROACH IN RELATING MUSIC AND THE ARTS

An interesting approach to integrated learning experiences in the classroom involves art experiences that contribute to understanding our past. For example, students discover that events in a particular historical period, such as the American Revolution, are often reflected in sculpture, painting, and music. Through studying the arts in a historical context, students not only learn about aesthetic aspects of the arts, but also develop a broader perspective on the people and events of a particular era.

Teachers will find that interaction with examples of architecture, sculpture, painting, literature, and music greatly enhances students' understanding of the past. In effect, multi-art presentations help students go beyond the memorization of facts about the peoples and places of a particular time period and allow them to experience an era through actual examples of its finest artistic products.

The following two lessons are given as sample presentations only; you can use them as models for designing lessons on other historical periods.

Technology Enhancement

AGE OF THE AMERICAN REVOLUTION

Website with lesson plans and student activities:

http://americanhistory.mrdonn.org/revolution.html

Links to other websites with pertinent information:

http://free.ed.gov/subjects.cfm?subject_id=149&toplvl=0&res_feature_request=1

AGE OF THE KNIGHTS

This site includes lesson plans along with several student activities to do online:

http://medievaleurope.mrdonn.org/lessonplans.html

Discovery Education has an activity for students to do in class:

www.discoveryeducation.com/teachers/free-lesson-plans/the-middle-ages.cfm

LESSON PLAN

The Age of the Knights

Grades: 5–6

The age of the knights occurred during the European medieval period, which spanned the years from approximately 500 to 1400 A.D. During this time the Catholic Church was one of the most dominant institutions in Europe, greatly influencing all aspects of life. Many great cathedrals were built throughout Europe. In the latter part of the medieval period, many huge castles were constructed, where kings lived along with their knights. These men often dressed in metal armor to protect themselves in battle.

NATIONAL AND STATE STANDARDS

1. Listening to, analyzing, and describing music
2. Understanding relationships between music, the other arts, and disciplines outside the arts
3. Understanding music in relation to history and culture

OBJECTIVES

Students will:

1. Identify characteristics of music and the literary and visual arts of the European medieval period
2. Identify how, during the medieval period, music and the literary and visual arts were closely allied with the beliefs of Christianity.

MATERIALS

Eric Van Den Brulie/The Image Bank/Getty Images

- Download (www.images.google.com) and display images: Medieval cathedrals, such as Notre Dame in Paris, Notre Dame in Chartres, and Canterbury in England; stained-glass windows; diagram of a cathedral floor plan; medieval castles; suits of armor; tapestries; map of England
- Stories: Mockler, *King Arthur and His Knights*[15]; *King Arthur and His Knights Sound Recording*[16]; Chaucer, "The Friar," from The *Canterbury Tales*
- Recordings: Gregorian chant "Ave Maria" and a saltarello dance composition (download or stream from [iTunes/Spotify])
- Handout: Listening guide for Gregorian chant

PROCEDURES

This lesson will need to extend over several days.

1. Have students make a bulletin board titled "Life in a Castle." Download and display pictures of some of the great castles built during the medieval period in Europe. Discuss how these buildings were fortified to help protect their inhabitants against attack. Also download pictures of the armored suits worn by men to protect themselves in battle, and pictures of some of the large, multicolored tapestries that were hung on the walls of castles.
2. Read with the class stories about King Arthur and the Knights of the Round Table.
3. Download and project pictures of some of the cathedrals built during the medieval period: Notre Dame (Paris, France), Notre Dame (Chartres, France), and Canterbury (England).
   a. Call attention to the tall spires of the Chartres Cathedral. Ask students why people living during this period might have built such tall spires (to draw attention upward, toward heaven).
   b. Show a diagram of the cross: call attention to the three upper points of the cross that represent the Trinity ("three") of the medieval Christian church: God as (1) Father, (2) Son, and (3) Holy Ghost. Look at a diagram of the floor plans of the cathedrals, noticing that they are laid out in the form of a cross.
   c. Look at the windows and doorways of the Chartres Cathedral, noticing that they were also built in threes.

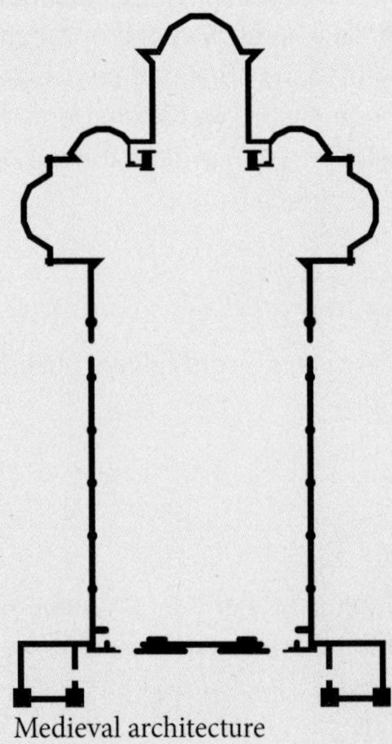

Pyma/Shutterstock.com

Medieval architecture

[15] Anthony Mockler, *King Arthur and His Knights* (New York: Oxford University Press, 1984).

[16] *King Arthur and His Knights Sound Recording,* narrated by Jim Weiss (Benicia, CA: Greathall Productions, 1990).

   d. Show pictures of the stained-glass windows in the very tall walls of the cathedrals. Note that these pictures depict religious subjects: people from the Bible; rose window with its groups of twelves, representing the twelve disciples.

4. In conjunction with showing pictures of the Canterbury Cathedral, have the class plan a hypothetical trip from London to Canterbury. Put a map of England on the bulletin board and highlight the travel route. Discuss the fact that during the medieval period a group of people traveled by foot to the town of Canterbury to see the cathedral and the archbishop. To pass the time on such a long trip, travelers often told stories. Read with the class several selections from *The Canterbury Tales* (for example, "The Friar," which is about a priest who enjoyed having a good time!). *The Canterbury Tales* was written by Geoffrey Chaucer, one of the most famous writers of the period.
5. Play recordings of some of the music performed in the church (Gregorian chant, "Ave Maria," see page 360). Take the students on a hypothetical trip to a large cathedral during medieval times. Discuss what the mood is as one enters the great building (calm, quietness, peacefulness, tranquility). Listen to the Gregorian chant. How does this music reflect the setting? Place the following listening guide on the board (or on a transparency), and have students circle the appropriate items as they listen to the music:
6. Play a saltarello, a popular piece of dance music from the medieval period. Follow the fast tempo and make up some dance movements to the music.
7. Discuss contributions that artists of the medieval period have made to the world today. Look for examples in your community of medieval-style architecture and stained-glass windows in churches.

ASSESSMENT

Have students briefly discuss the Middle Ages, commenting specifically on how the arts reflect this period in history.

LESSON PLAN

The Age of the American Revolution

Grades: 3–6

The age of the American Revolution occurred more than two hundred years ago. At that time the American colonies were seeking freedom from British control. Growing frustration with the British eventually led to the writing of the Declaration of Independence in 1776, which in turn set the stage for the Revolutionary War. In this conflict the thirteen colonies were pitted against the forces of the British Empire. Freedom became a major theme of the period.

During the eighteenth century, the people and arts of ancient Greece and Rome became sources of inspiration for the revolutionary spirit that was under way not only in the American colonies but also in Europe. Leaders such as Napoleon Bonaparte looked to the past for models and found them in men such as Alexander the Great and Julius Caesar. Napoleon, for example, used the eagles of the Roman legions for insignia in the French army and ultimately was crowned with the laurel wreath, an ancient symbol of fame. In the visual arts, Greek and Roman architectural and sculptural ideals greatly influenced innumerable pieces of art produced in the period.

NATIONAL AND STATE STANDARDS

1. Singing, alone and with others, a varied repertoire of music
2. Listening to, analyzing, and describing music
3. Understanding relationships between music, the other arts, and disciplines outside the arts
4. Understanding music in relation to history and culture

OBJECTIVES

Students will:

1. Design a bulletin board that will include examples of the arts and personalities of the eighteenth century.
2. Identify examples of visual arts from the eighteenth and early nineteenth centuries and demonstrate an understanding of how they reflect the period.
3. Sing songs that center around themes and personalities related to freedom and independence.
4. Identify the classical qualities of the music of eighteenth-century composers.

The Brooklyn Museum: Dick S. Ramsay and Museum Purchase Fund

Gilbert Stuart, *George Washington*

MATERIALS

- Download images (www.images.google.com) and display them: George Washington, Thomas Jefferson, Benjamin Franklin, Wolfgang Amadeus Mozart, Franz Joseph Haydn; colonial Williamsburg; the British flag; Monticello; Trumbull, *The Declaration of Independence;* Greenough's sculpture *George Washington;* Houdon's sculptures of Franklin and Jefferson; Wedgewood pottery
- Download or stream the following recordings [iTunes/Spotify]: Wolfgang Mozart, Variations for piano on "Ah! Vous dirai-je, Maman," K. 265; Leopold Mozart, *Toy Symphony,* first movement ("Marche").
- Handout: Listening guide for Variations on "Ah! Vous dirai-je, Maman" (grades 4–6, words; earlier grades, pictures)
- Melody bells

PROCEDURES

This lesson may need to extend over several days.

1. Make a bulletin board. Include pictures of some of the most outstanding personalities of the eighteenth century: George Washington, Thomas Jefferson, Benjamin Franklin, Wolfgang Amadeus Mozart, and Franz Joseph Haydn.
2. Project pictures of colonial Williamsburg, and ask students to describe how the buildings are different from those built today. Ask if anyone has seen buildings like these. Where? Are there any similar ones in your community? Show a picture of the British flag, which hung (and still hangs) over the capitol building in Williamsburg, and ask students why this flag would be flying there. (Britain ruled the American colonies until the American Revolution in the eighteenth century.)
3. Draw the students into a brief discussion about events that happened in this country around the year 1775 (Declaration of Independence, Revolutionary War).
4. Download and display a copy of the painting *The Declaration of Independence* by John Trumbull. Do the students recognize any of the figures? (Benjamin Franklin, Thomas Jefferson, John Hancock)
5. Read the first two paragraphs of the Declaration of Independence and identify the theme of the document (emphasis on freedom).

Yale University Art Gallery/Art Resource, NY

John Trumbull, *The Declaration of Independence*

6. The call for freedom in the Declaration of Independence rallied Americans in the thirteen colonies to go to war against the mighty British Empire. Have students sing the following song from the period to the tune of "America":

   God save the thirteen states,
   Long rule the United States
   God save our states,
   Make us victorious, happy and glorious,
   No tyrants over us
   God save our states.

7. Have students sing "Yankee Doodle," one of the most famous melodies of the period. Notice the reference to Washington, who would become commander of the Continental armies.
8. Download and project pictures of Monticello, Thomas Jefferson's home near Charlottesville, Virginia. Ask students to identify the influences of ancient Greek and Roman architecture: Greek columns (Doric), Roman dome over center of building, emphasis on symmetry and balance. Explain that the eighteenth century was called the classical period because of the attention to ideas drawn from classical Greece and Rome. Also download and project pictures of Greek and Roman architecture and place them along with pictures of Monticello.
9. Download and project a picture of Horatio Greenough's sculpture of George Washington. Note that Greenough's *George Washington* is patterned after an ancient Roman figure holding a toga, a one-piece cloth worn by Roman citizens in public. In addition, put on the bulletin board pictures of Houdon's sculptures of Franklin and Jefferson and of Wedgewood pottery, much of which was modeled after Greek artifacts (urns, for example).

Yankee Doodle

United States

Key: G
Starting pitch: D
Meter: 2/4, begins on "and" of 2

Broadly

1. O, fath - 'r and I went down to camp a - long with Cap - tain Good' - in, And
2. And there we saw a thou - sand men as rich as Squire___ Da - vid, And
3. And there was Cap - tain Wash - ing - ton up - on a slap - ping stal - lion, A -

there we saw the men and boys as thick as hast - y pud - ding!
what they wast - ed ev - 'ry day, I wish it could be sav - ed.
giv - ing or - ders to his men; I guess there were a mil - lion.

Yan - kee Doo - dle, keep it up, Yan - kee Doo - dle Dan - dy.

Mind the mu - sic, and the step, and with the girls be han - dy.

10. Download and display a picture of Wolfgang Amadeus Mozart, the famous European musician who lived from 1756 to 1791. Explain that Mozart was considered a child prodigy and that at a very early age he played both piano and violin. Compare the dress of Americans with that of Mozart. Note that the white powdered wigs, buckled shoes, and long dress were in style in both Europe and America. Discuss reasons for this. (Americans had come from Europe seeking freedom here and had brought their culture and traditions with them.)

David Muenker/Alamy Limited

Monticello, Thomas Jefferson's home near Charlottesville, Virginia

11. Download and listen to a recording of Mozart's piano composition, Variations on "Ah! Vous dirai-je, Maman," K. 265, better known as Variations on "Twinkle, Twinkle, Little Star."

a. Sing and play on melody bells the tune "Twinkle, Twinkle, Little Star."

Twinkle, Twinkle, Little Star

Key: C
Starting pitch: C
Meter: 2/4, begins on 1

Nursery Rhyme

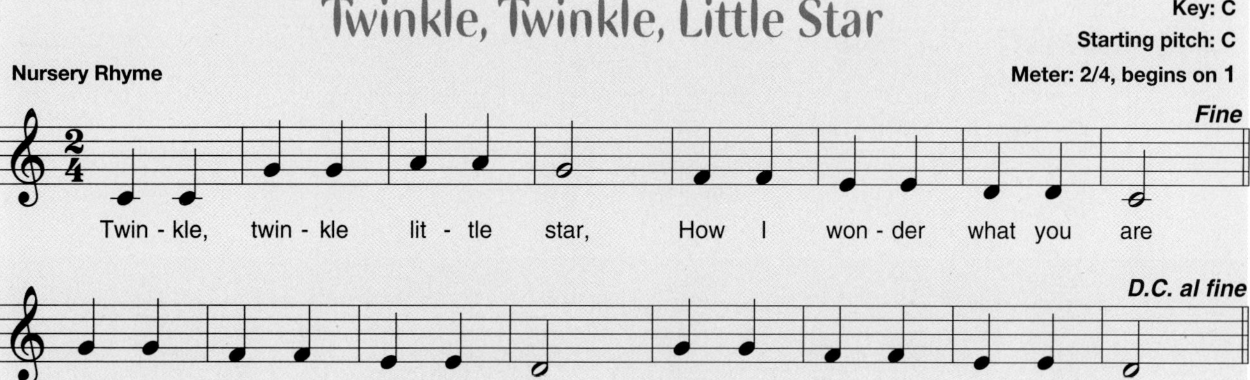
Fine
Twin - kle, twin - kle lit - tle star, How I won - der what you are
D.C. al fine
Up a - bove the world so high Like a dia - mond in the sky.

b. Hand out copies of the listening guide on the next page to each student (grades 4–6). Play the recording and have students follow the variations and circle each variation number. In each variation encourage students to listen first for the tune and then for ways in which the tune is varied. If time permits, discuss how repeating the "Twinkle, Twinkle" melody unifies the musical composition and how the variations provide contrast so that the piece will be more interesting. For earlier grades, have students make up movements for each variation.

Joy E. Lawrence

First-grade children dramatizing life during the eighteenth century

12. Download and play a recording of the first movement of the *Toy Symphony* by Leopold Mozart (Wolfgang Mozart's father). This is a three-movement work (Allegro, Minuet, Finale [Allegro]) featuring toy instruments, such as one-note trumpet, rattle, triangle, and drum. Call attention to the lighthearted quality of the music and the different bird calls executed by the instruments (twittering of the nightingale and the descending minor third [G, E] of the cuckoo).

13. Ask students to summarize by making a list of some of the things they have learned in this lesson. Put the items on a bulletin board under a general topic heading such as the "Age of the American Revolution." Group the items into categories (political events, people, dress, music, and so on).

ASSESSMENT

Have the class briefly discuss the period of the American Revolution, commenting specifically on how the arts reflect this period of history.

LISTENING GUIDE: Mozart's "Ah! Vous dirais-je, Maman"

Variation 1	Melody heard with running melodic line in right hand
Variation 2	Melody in right hand, running melodic line in left hand
Variation 3	Melody heard in triplet (3's) figure
Variation 4	Melody in right hand, triplets in left hand
Variation 5	Melody with off-beat patterns
Variation 6	Melody in right hand, running melodic line in left hand
Variation 7	Melody heard in running scale patterns in right hand
Variation 8	Melody heard in minor; use of imitation
Variation 9	Melody presented in clear, staccato fashion
Variation 10	Melody in right hand with accompaniment in left hand
Variation 11	Melody in slow, lyrical presentation
Variation 12	Melody in right hand with decoration
Variation 13	Melody with many fast running notes

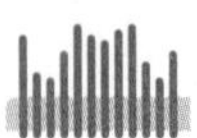

USING A CROSS-CULTURAL APPROACH IN RELATING MUSIC AND THE ARTS

In the elementary school curriculum, students learn about other people of the world and the multicultural diversity of American society. They study the geography, history, customs, and beliefs of many peoples. One significant way to help students better understand other cultures is through an examination of the arts. Often basic tenets of a cultural tradition are reflected in the aural, literary, and visual arts.

Following is a suggested sample lesson on the arts of Japan. The intent of this lesson is to illustrate some fundamental ideas that can help students better understand the Japanese culture. The lesson focuses on (1) the Japanese interest in being in harmony with nature and (2) their interest in understatement and the achievement of maximum effect with minimal materials.

LESSON PLAN

Arts of Japan

Grades: 4–6

NATIONAL AND STATE STANDARDS

1. Singing, alone and with others, a varied repertoire of music
2. Listening to, analyzing, and describing music
3. Understanding relationships between music, the other arts, and disciplines outside the arts
4. Understanding music in relation to history and culture

OBJECTIVES

Students will:

1. Identify how the Japanese interest in the surrounding natural world is reflected in music, literature, and visual art.
2. Identify how the Japanese interest in understatement and the achievement of maximum effect with minimal materials is reflected in music, literature, and visual art.

MATERIALS

- Download (www.images.google.com) and display images of Japanese countryside, gardens, traditional buildings, such as the *Kinkaka (Golden Pavilion) at Kyoto,* and paintings such as Hasegawa Tohaku's *Pine Trees*
- Download or stream [iTunes/Spotify] "Sakura" (Cherry Blossoms) and "Shika no Tone" (Deer Calling to Each Other in the Distance).
- DVD: *Music of Japan* (Educational Video Network, www.edvidnet.com)

PROCEDURES

This lesson may need to extend over several days.

1. Ask students to make a bulletin board about Japan, highlighting the scenic natural beauty of the countryside. Discuss how such surroundings might affect the lives of people, particularly the works of painters, writers, and musicians.
2. Download and display pictures of *traditional Japanese buildings,* calling attention to the emphasis on the natural settings of each. Notice that the outside surroundings of buildings are often developed into immaculately tailored gardens, which are artistically arranged with rocks, trees, flowers, and ponds to create a kind of microcosm of nature. Japanese buildings themselves often strongly reflect themes of nature. Many are constructed of wood, with the natural look preserved through the use of large numbers of unpainted surfaces. Within the buildings, some rooms have a *tokonoma,* a recessed area in the wall containing a print or scroll of a nature scene and with a flower arrangement placed in front of it.

3. Download and project pictures of "nature" in Japanese paintings: e.g., *Pine Trees in Snow* and *Kinkaku (Golden Pavilion) at Kyoto.* Ask students to look for ways in which nature is depicted (pine trees, snow, water surrounding building).
4. Read to the class the following haiku poems.[17] Ask students to identify references to nature (mountain, skylark, snow, twig, grove, sunlight).

High on a mountain
we heard a skylark singing
faintly, far below.

– *Basho*

Snow fell until dawn
Now every twig in the grove
glitters in sunlight.

– *Rokwa*

5. Sing the song "Sakura" (p. 302). Call attention to the references to nature in the words of the song: cherry blooms, flowering, wind, mist, clouds, air, cherry trees.
6. "Sakura" is a composition played on the koto, a popular Japanese stringed instrument (see pp. 303–304). Listen to it and follow the theme and variations form.
7. Show the painting *Pine Trees in Snow* again, calling attention to the manner in which Japanese artists seem to place emphasis on understatement and the achievement of maximum effect with minimal materials. Note the emphasis on simplicity and detail. The pictures are composed of a number of delicately drawn lines, which are subtly manipulated to indicate depth and volume. With their subdued, pastel shades, the colors in the pictures seem to complement this delicacy. Further, a large number of open-space areas contribute to a sense of understatement and simplicity.
8. Show pictures of Japanese building interiors, noting how they seem to be directed toward simplicity. Much of the Japanese house's interior is left open and uncluttered by a lot of furnishings. The feeling of openness is enhanced by doors that slide back to expose large areas of the house. The walls of rooms are often constructed of simple, unpainted surfaces that are tastefully accented with paintings.
9. Read the haiku poetry again with the students. Call attention to the sense of simplicity and directness. The poems are very short, being composed of just three short lines arranged in groups of five, seven, and five syllables.
10. Download and play the recording of "Shika no Tone" (Deer Calling to Each Other in the Distance), which is performed by two Japanese shakuhachi players. Notice how the sense of understatement is created by monophonic texture (just one line of music), slow tempo, flexible rhythm, and subtly executed ornaments.
11. Show the first two segments on koto and shakuhachi from the DVD *Music of Japan.* Direct particular attention to the emphasis on nature and the sense of simplicity and understatement.

ASSESSMENT

1. Have students discuss how the Japanese interest in nature is reflected in the arts of music, poetry, and painting. Encourage them to use specific examples.
2. Have students discuss, using artwork (music, painting, and poetry), the Japanese interest in understatement, and the principle of achieving maximum effect from minimal materials.

[17] From *Cricket Songs: Japanese Haiku,* translated by Harry Behn (New York: Harcourt, Brace & World, 1964). © 1949 by Harry Behn. Copyright renewed by Prescott Behn, Pamela Behn Adam, and Peter Behn. Used by permission of Marian Reiner.

Integrating Technology

CENGAGEbrain.com

The Music Education Premium Site contains chapter quizzing, Spotify playlists, and downloads of free MP3s of noted songs. Visit CengageBrain.com to purchase an access code or enter the code provided with your text materials.

Web Resource

- Download visuals related to the content of this chapter from www.images.google.com.

Audio

- Download music discussed in this chapter from the Apple iTunes store.
- Spotify playlists allow students to stream music referenced within each chapter.
- Download free audio MP3s for the songs noted in the chapter.

CENGAGEbrain.com

Questions for Discussion

1. Briefly describe several approaches to combining the study of music with that of other art forms.
2. Discuss some objectives for lessons that are based on the analogous concepts of *repetition, contrast, unity*, and *balance* in the arts.
3. Describe how you would use a "thematic" approach to organize lessons that incorporate music and other arts (for grades 1–3).
4. Describe how you would use a "historical" approach to organize a unit of study that incorporates music and other arts (for grades 4–6).
5. Briefly discuss how you would go about developing a lesson involving music and other arts that is based on a cross-cultural approach.

Assessment

Review ways the music standards listed at the beginning of the chapter have been met.

CHAPTER 11

Thematic and Content Pedagogy

Integrating Music with Other Subjects and Activitites

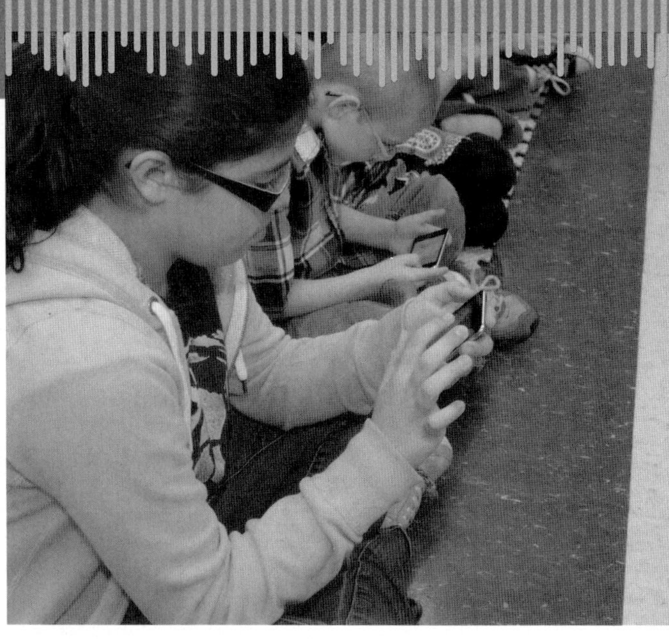

Objectives

Students will learn to develop lessons that integrate music with the following general thematic areas:

- Action
- Animals
- Circus
- Social studies
- Holidays
- Language arts
- Mathematics
- Science
- Seasons
- Transportation

Students will learn to plan and present a program. The following sample programs are discussed in the chapter:

- Program I: A Musical Horn of Plenty (Thanksgiving)
- Program II: Liberty
- Program III: A Musical Fiesta—South of the Border

National and State Music Standards

This chapter provides experiences with the following national music standards and related state music standards:

- Singing, alone and with others, a varied repertoire of music
- Performing on instruments, alone and with others, a varied repertoire of music
- Listening to, analyzing, and describing music
- Understanding music in relation to various cultures/geographical areas

Music should be an integral part of a child's daily life. One of the unique opportunities that the classroom teacher enjoys is introducing many musical experiences into the day's activities. Songs can be used to develop physical coordination; teach phonics; provide opportunities for creative dramatics; contribute to a greater understanding and appreciation of peoples, places, and cultures; and bring new meanings to the study of history. Holidays such as Halloween, Thanksgiving, Christmas, and Hanukkah have traditionally used songs to express feelings appropriate to the celebration. Other areas in the elementary curriculum that lend themselves to the use of music include the study of animals, learning about community helpers, and expressing ideas about nature (spring, summer, autumn, and winter).

The following integrative categories are of special interest to elementary-age children:

- Action
- Animals
- Circus
- Social studies
  - Geography
  - History
- Holidays
  - Ramadan (Muslim holiday)
  - Halloween
  - Thanksgiving, Sukkot, and Shavuot
  - Hanukkah
  - Christmas
  - Kwanzaa
  - New Year's Day
  - Martin Luther King Jr. Day
  - Chinese New Year
  - Valentine's Day
  - Presidents' Day—George Washington and Abraham Lincoln
- Patriotic songs of the United States of America
- Getting acquainted
- Human relationships and emotions
- Language arts
- Mathematics
- Science
- Seasons
  - Spring

Special Learner Notes

Integrating materials and presenting academic material through rhythm and song are essential in many special needs classrooms. This chapter contains some highly recommended music experiences that will help the teacher present academic tasks in a music-lesson context. Some general strategies to keep in mind when adapting the songs/activities include the following:

- Pictures will enhance lyric learning and recall, attention to task, and sequencing of material. Pictures should be easy to focus on (simple or no background), large enough to be seen by the student or students needing to see them, and presented individually or in small groups to avoid confusion. An additional activity for reinforcing the use of pictures might be to have the students color or cut out appropriate pictures to be used with the introduction of the songs.
- Emphasize clapping or playing rhythm instruments on the "macro" (larger) beats to keep group singing and playing together (e.g., "The Witch Rides," "Over the River and Through the Wood").
- Some lyrics may need to be omitted or changed for ease of singing and/or understanding ("orange pumpkins" instead of "yellow" in "Let's Make a Jack-O-Lantern"; omitting some words while maintaining basic meaning in "Over the River").
- Songs in foreign languages may cause confusion for some learners who are already struggling with language. Be observant of their frustration levels—learning new words and languages can also be fun!
- Songs with multiple verses may challenge attention spans, especially if the meaning of the lyrics/storyline is not engaging the students. In such situations, it may be useful to present the rest of the verses in subsequent classes.
- Sign language is always a good strategy for emphasizing the major objects, feelings, and actions of songs and may assist all students (even those with normal hearing) to "track" lyrics and learn and recall more accurately.
- Using motions and adding streamers or scarves to slower motions may enhance the learning of tempo and rhythm as well as form.

    - Summer
    - Autumn
    - Winter
- Transportation

Representative songs have been selected for many of these categories, and materials and suggestions for planning lessons are provided. You are encouraged to create your own lessons from the suggestions that follow each song. The authors recognize that additional holidays are celebrated by various groups, and we urge the classroom teacher to develop appropriate activities that highlight these special days.

You will find lists of additional songs, as well as CD-ROMs, DVDs, and videos, at the end of each integrative unit. These have been selected for a variety of grade levels and abilities. You are encouraged to teach these songs (which can be found in the basal music series of your school), add to the list of integrative categories, and devise other interesting ways to include songs in the classroom.

INTEGRATIVE CATEGORY: ACTION

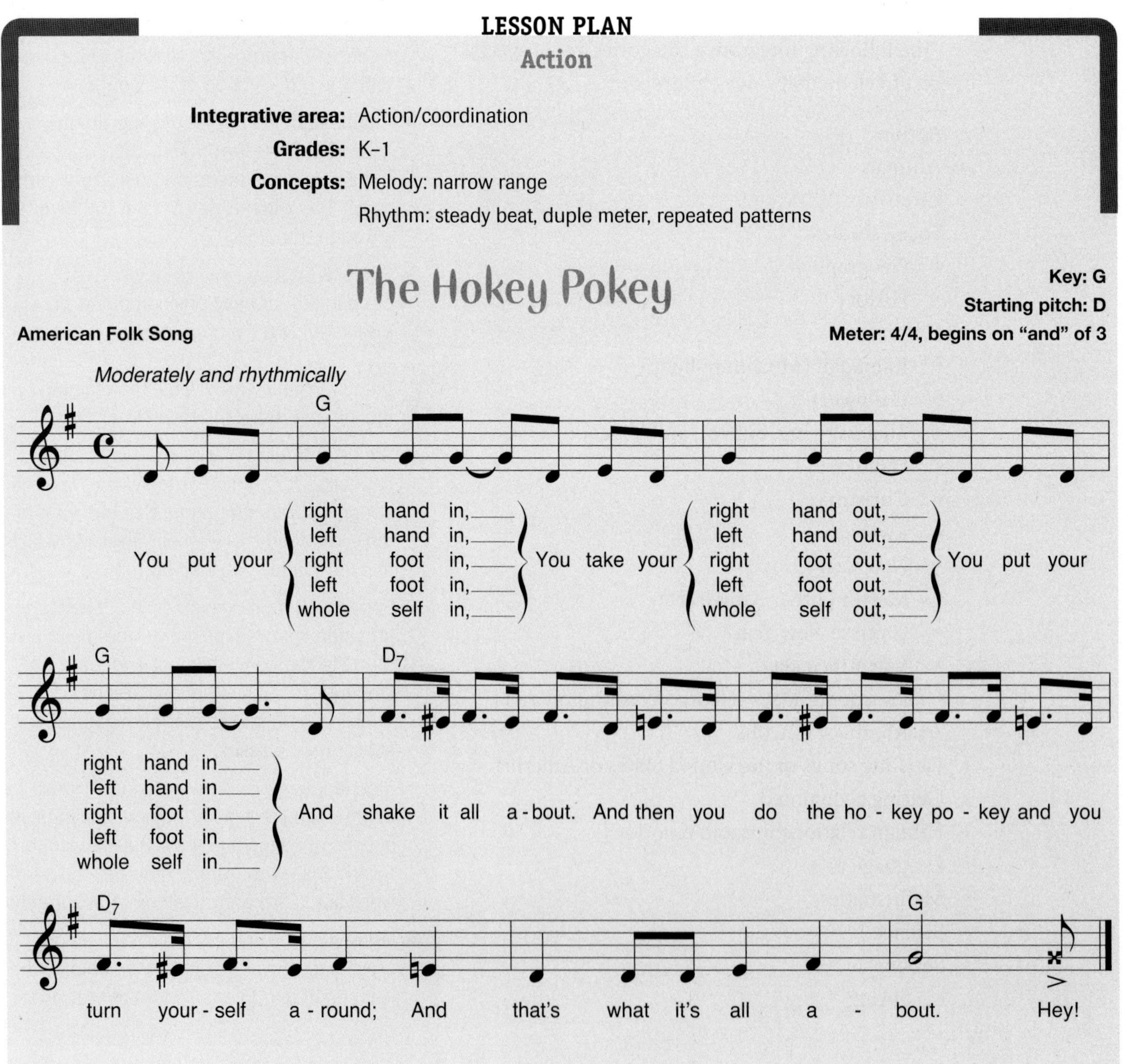

NATIONAL AND STATE MUSIC STANDARDS

1. Singing, alone and with others, a varied repertoire of music
2. Performing on instruments, alone and with others, a varied repertoire of music

OBJECTIVES

Students will:

1. Sing the song with good tone quality.
2. Indicate their knowledge of a narrow melodic range.
3. Clap the steady beat.
4. Clap in duple meter.
5. Perform repeated rhythmic and melodic patterns.
6. Perform appropriate movements.

MATERIALS

- Chart showing narrow and wide ranges
- Individual charts: D E F# G and sample keyboard (either a cardboard keyboard, a piano, or an electronic keyboard)
- Chart showing a steady beat
- Chart showing the following repeated rhythm pattern:

(2 times)

- Drum and tambourine

PROCEDURES

1. Warm up voices by using techniques for developing the head voice (see p. 73).
2. Sing the song or play a recording. Ask students to clap the steady beat as they listen.
3. Sing the song or play a recording and ask students what word they might say or sing for the highest note.
4. Show the chart that indicates a narrow range of sound. Match with the appropriate word.
5. Play D and G on the xylophone and show children that these pitches are close together, meaning that this music has a narrow range.
6. Select students to hold each letter and ask other students to count the number of letters in between. Use this visual to reinforce the sound of a narrow range.
7. Sing or play a recording of the song again. Ask students to clap the steady beat and accent the first and third beats. Be careful with the syncopation.
8. Perform the song again. Ask students how many times they can hear the following rhythm pattern:

    (10 times)

9. Ask students to sing the song, and select one student to play the repeated pattern on the tambourine.
10. Have students stand and imitate your motions as you sing the song or play a recording.
11. Closure: Ask students to form a circle and, as they sing the song, do the motions suggested by the words. Accompany on the drum (steady beat) and tambourine (repeated pattern).

ASSESSMENT

1. Review the concept of narrow range by asking students to define the term and point to it on the appropriate chart.
2. Ask a student to illustrate steady beat and duple meter by clapping.
3. Ask a student to play on the tambourine the rhythm pattern that was repeated.
4. Ask students what motions were referred to in the words of the song.
5. While still in the circle, ask children to sing the song and do the motions. Ask two children to accompany on drum and tambourine.

"If You're Happy"

Integrative areas: Action: movement, coordination

Grades: K–1

Concepts: Melody: steps and skips, repetition

Rhythm: duple

Tone color: rhythm sticks, drum

Rhythm sticks

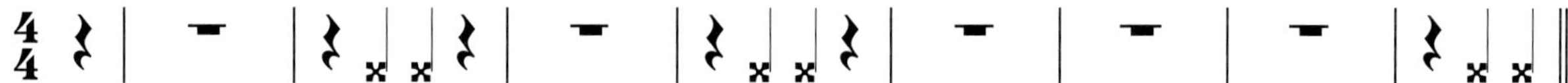

Drum (keep the beat)

SUGGESTIONS FOR LESSONS

1. Have children act out the directions in the song.
2. Discuss things we do when we're happy (smile, clap hands, and so on). Identify many words that describe happiness.
3. Play the game "Simon Says" to encourage the use of right and left ("Simon says, raise your right hand," and so forth).
4. Add rhythm instruments (rhythm sticks, drum) to accompany the song.

More Songs: Action

- "The Ants Go Marching" in Silver Burdett *Making Music 1,* p. S74
- "Bop 'til You Drop" in Macmillan/McGraw-Hill *Spotlight on Music 6,* p. T87
- "Bounce High, Bounce Low" in Silver Burdett *Making Music 1,* p. S47
- "Bouncing Balls" in Silver Burdett *Making Music 1,* p. T324
- "Busy Buzzy Bee" in Silver Burdett *Making Music K,* p. T77
- "Chase the Squirrel" in Macmillan/McGraw-Hill *Spotlight on Music 1,* p. T88
- "Che Che Koolay" in Silver Burdett *Music 3,* p. 34; Silver Burdett *Making Music 2,* p. 266
- "Circle 'Round the Zero" in Macmillan/McGraw-Hill *Spotlight on Music 3,* p. T267
- "Clap, Wiggle, and Stomp" in Silver Burdett *Making Music K,* p. T34
- "Dancing in the Street" in Macmillan/McGraw-Hill *Spotlight on Music 6,* p. T84
- "Happy Feet" in Silver Burdett *Making Music 2,* p. 252
- "How D'ye Do and Shake Hands" in Silver Burdett *Making Music 3,* p. 144; Holt, Rinehart and Winston *Music Book 1,* p. 4
- "Jump, Jim Joe" in Macmillan/McGraw-Hill *Spotlight on Music 1,* p. T89
- "Let's Go Dancing" " in Macmillan/McGraw-Hill *Spotlight on Music 3,* p. T196
- "Little Red Caboose" in Silver Burdett Ginn *World of Music K,* p. 72; Silver Burdett *Making Music K,* p. T229
- "Little Tommy Tinker" in Macmillan *Music and You 2,* p. 231
- "Loco-Motion" in Silver Burdett *Making Music 3,* p. T64; in MacMillan/McGraw-Hill *Spotlight on Music 4,* p. T312
- "Merrily, We Roll Along" in Macmillan/McGraw-Hill *Spotlight on Music K,* p. T110
- "One Finger, One Thumb" in Macmillan *Music and You K,* p. 109; Silver Burdett Ginn *World of Music K,* p. 120
- "Parade Came Marching" in Silver Burdett Making Music 1, p. 51
- "Propel, Propel, Propel" in Macmillan/McGraw-Hill *Spotlight on Music K,* p. T275
- "Rig a Jig Jig" in Macmillan/McGraw-Hill *Spotlight on Music 1,* p. T116
- "Rock Around the Clock" in Macmillan/McGraw-Hill *Spotlight on Music 6,* p. T234
- "Row, Row, Row Your Boat" in Macmillan/McGraw-Hill *Spotlight on Music K,* p. T274
- "Scrub-a-Dub" in Silver Burdett *Making Music 1,* p. 90
- "Shake My Sillies Out" in Silver Burdett Ginn *The Music Connection 1* (2000), p. 292
- "Step in Time" in Macmillan/McGraw-Hill *Spotlight on Music 1,* p. T6
- "Twist and Shout" in Macmillan/McGraw-Hill *Spotlight on Music 4,* p. T314
- "Wake Me, Shake Me" in Silver Burdett *Making Music 1,* p. T278

INTEGRATIVE CATEGORY: ANIMALS

LESSON PLAN

Integrative areas: Improvisation, creativity, movement, coordination, farm, chickens, dramatics, vocabulary

Grades: K–1

Concepts: Melody: steps and skips

Tempo: moderate

Rhythm: steady, mostly quarter and eighth notes

My Big Black Dog

English Play Song

Key: F
Starting pitch: F
Meter: 4/4, begins on 4

NATIONAL AND STATE MUSIC STANDARD

1. Singing, alone and with others, a varied repertoire of music

OBJECTIVES

Students will:

1. Identify melodic steps and skips.
2. Decide on an appropriate tempo.
3. Identify walking notes (quarter notes) and running notes (eighth notes).
4. Sing with energy and correct words, pitches, and rhythms.

MATERIALS

- Picture of dogs (download from www.images.google.com)
- Recording of song (optional)

PROCEDURES

1. Download and show pictures of various kinds of dogs, ending with a picture of a big black dog.
2. Ask whether anyone in the class has a big black dog.
3. Ask the class where they would find chicks.
4. Ask what the difference is between a "crack" and a "fence."
5. Sing the song or play a recording.
6. Teach the song by rote.
7. Ask students which words and music are the same. ("Whoever took my big black dog")
8. Have students sing the song with you or with the recording.
9. Guide students in creative motions for the following phrases:
   a. Big black dog
   b. Bring him back
   c. Big chicks over the fence
   d. Little chicks through the crack
10. Ask half the class to sing the song; ask the other half to do the motions. Then have them change roles.
11. Closure: When students know the song and motions very well, ask them to do both.

ASSESSMENT

1. Is the song mostly steps or skips?
2. What are some words that skip with the music? ("Whoever took my big black dog")
3. How would you decide how fast to sing the song?
4. Do you sing mostly quarter notes (walking) or eighth notes (running)?
5. What is the song about? Who is the main character?

"Six Little Ducks"

Integrative areas: Dramatics, movement, visual art, science, vocabulary

Grade: 2

Concepts: Rhythm: steady beat, duple meter

Melody: large skips

Six Little Ducks
Traditional American
Key: F
Starting pitch: A
Meter: 4/4, begins on 1
Moderately fast
F C7 C7
Six lit - tle ducks that I once knew, Fat ones, skin - ny ones,
Down to the riv - er they did go; Wib - ble wob - ble wib - ble wob - ble
F F C7
fuz - zy ones, too, But the one lit - tle duck with a feath - er in his back,
to and fro.
C7 F F
He ruled the oth - ers with a quack, quack, quack; quack, quack, quack.

SUGGESTIONS FOR LESSONS

1. Dramatize "Six Little Ducks" with movements.
2. Draw pictures of ducks in a pond or walking toward a pond. Show pictures of baby ducks and a mother duck.
3. Discuss characteristics of ducks, such as the fact that they swim, have wings, have webbed feet, and so on. Combine with a science unit on animals found around water, such as frogs and fish.
4. Create stick puppets to represent the ducks. Dramatize the song.

More Songs: Animals

- "All the Pretty Little Horses" in Silver Burdett *Making Music 3,* p. 48; Holt, Rinehart and Winston *Music Book 2,* p. 79
- "Animal Fair" in Macmillan/McGraw-Hill *Spotlight on Music 2,* p. T214
- "Animal Farm" in Macmillan *Music and You 3,* p. 144
- "Animals" in Spotlight on Music K, p. T192
- "Australia's on the Wallaby" in Spotlight on Music 2, p. 106
- "Baby Chicks" in Silver Burdett *Making Music K,* p. T166
- "Barnyard Song" in Macmillan *Music and You 2,* p. 52; Holt, Rinehart and Winston *Music Book 2,* p. 120
- "The Bear Went Over the Mountain" in Macmillan/McGraw-Hill *Spotlight on Music K,* p. T204
- "Bingo" in Macmillan/McGraw-Hill *Spotlight on Music K,* p. T64
- "Bow Wow Wow" in Macmillan/McGraw-Hill *Spotlight on Music 2,* p. T264
- "But the Cat Came Back" in Silver Burdett *Making Music 2,* p. T190
- "Caballito Blanco" (Little White Pony) in Silver Burdett *Making Music 2,* p. T193
- "Cat and Dog" in Macmillan/McGraw-Hill *Spotlight on Music 3,* p. T259
- "The Cat" in Holt, Rinehart and Winston *Music Book 2,* p. 36; Silver Burdett Ginn *World of Music 2,* p. 110
- "Der sad to katte" (Two Cats) in Silver Burdett *Making Music 2,* p. T300
- "Doggie Doggie" in Macmillan/McGraw-Hill *Share the Music 1* (2003), p. 134; Macmillan/McGraw-Hill *Spotlight on Music 2,* p. T59
- "Donkey, Donkey" in Macmillan/McGraw-Hill *Share the Music 2* (2003), p. 144; Spotlight on Music 2, p. 256
- "Ducklings" in Macmillan *Music and You 1,* p. 216, and *K,* p. 187
- "Elephant" in Silver Burdett *Making Music 1,* p. 48; Silver Burdett *Making Music 2,* p. 160; Macmillan/McGraw-Hill *Spotlight on Music 2,* p. T305
- "Five Fat Turkeys" in Macmillan/McGraw-Hill *Spotlight on Music Book 2,* p. T309
- "Four White Horses" in Silver Burdett *Making Music 3,* p. 304; *Spotlight on Music 2,* p. 301
- "Frog in the Bog" in Holt, Rinehart and Winston *Music Book 2,* p. 118
- "Frog in the Pond" in Silver Burdett Ginn *World of Music K,* p. 130
- "Grizzly Bear" in Silver Burdett Ginn *The Music Connection 1* (2000), p. 5; Silver Burdett *Making Music K,* p. T33; Macmillan/McGraw-Hill *Spotlight on Music K,* p. T252
- "I Bought Me a Cat" in Silver Burdett *Making Music 2,* p. 308; *Spotlight on Music 2,* p. 14
- "I Fed My Horse" in Silver Burdett Making Music 2, p. 94
- "I Have a Dog" in Silver Burdett *Making Music K,* p. T262
- "I'm in Love with a Dinosaur" in Silver Burdett Ginn *The Music Connection 1* (2000), p. 126
- "I Can't Spell Hippopotamus" in Silver Burdett *Music 1,* p. 79; *Spotlight on Music K,* p. T199
- "If a Tiger Calls" in Silver Burdett *Making Music 3,* p. 354
- *"The Kangaroo"* in Macmillan/McGraw-Hill *Spotlight on Music K,* p. T197
- "Kangaroo Song" in Silver Burdett *Making Music K,* p. T44
- "Kookaburra" in Silver Burdett *Making Music 4,* p. T186
- "Kou ri lengay" (The Strength of the Lion) in Silver Burdett Making Music 2, p. 217
- "The Lamb" in Silver Burdett *Making Music 4,* p. 242
- "The Lion Sleeps Tonight" in Silver Burdett *Making Music 4,* p. 131
- "Little Mouse" in Silver Burdett *Making Music 1,* p. 102
- "Little Spotted Puppy" in Macmillan/McGraw-Hill *Spotlight on Music K,* p. T146
- "Little White Pony" in Silver Burdett *Making Music 2,* p. 193; *Spotlight on Music 4,* p. 278
- "Mister Rabbit" in *Spotlight on Music 2,* p. 150
- "Mos', Mos'!" (song about a cat), p. 406; also in Macmillan *Share the Music 2* p. 325
- "My White Horse" in Macmillan/McGraw-Hill *Spotlight on Music 6,* p. T60
- "Naughty Tabby Cat" in Silver Burdett *Music 1,* p. 41
- "Old Grey Cat" in Macmillan/McGraw-Hill *Spotlight on Music K,* p. T43
- "Old MacDonald Had a Farm" in *Spotlight on Music K,* p. T211
- "One Little Elephant" in Macmillan *Music and You 1,* p. 230
- "Rabbit Footprints" in Silver Burdett *Making Music,* p. 304
- "Raccoon Dance Song" in Silver Burdett *Making Music 1,* p. T260
- "Rags" (dog) in Silver Burdett *Making Music 1,* p. T290
- "Riding on an Elephant" in *Spotlight on Music K,* p. 217
- "See the Pony Galloping" in *Spotlight on Music K,* p. T44
- "Three Little Pigs" in Silver Burdett *Making Music K,* p. 21
- "Three Little Kittens" in Macmillan/McGraw-Hill *Spotlight on Music K,* p. T146
- "Trot, Old Joe" in Macmillan/McGraw-Hill *Share the Music 2* p. 73
- "Two Bears" in Silver Burdett *Making Music K,* p. 268
- "We Have a Goat" in Silver Burdett *Making Music 1,* p. 57
- "A Whale of a Tale" in Silver Burdett Ginn *The Music Connection 2,* pp. 170–171

INTEGRATIVE CATEGORY: CIRCUS

LESSON PLAN

Circus

Integrative areas: Creative dramatics, visual art

Grade: 3

Concepts: Rhythm: duple meter; 4/4, steady beat
Melody: skips, contour, contrasting second melodic phrase, accidental (F#)
Form: two-part (AB)

Circus Parade

Key: C
Starting pitch: G
Meter: 4/4, begins on 3

Words and Music by Milton Kaye

> **Special Learner Note**
>
> Organize this melody in sections (A–B) using a vertical (marching) type of action for the "Oh, here comes the . . ." sections and a side-to-side swaying/swinging motion for the "Ta-ra-ra . . ." sections.

NATIONAL AND STATE MUSIC STANDARDS

1. Singing, alone and with others, a varied repertoire of music
2. Performing on instruments, alone and with others, a varied repertoire of music

OBJECTIVES

Students will:

1. Perform the song while clapping or tapping a steady beat.
2. Identify the use of an accidental (F#) throughout song, both visually and aurally.
3. Demonstrate an understanding of the contrasting second melodic phrase by singing or playing an instrument.
4. Use charts (AB) to identify the two sections of the song (verse and refrain).

MATERIALS

- Pictures of circuses
- Written score of song for each student or transparency of song for use with an overhead projector
- Xylophone, resonator bells, and drum
- Individual cards in two colors and marked *A* and *B*
- Charts showing steady beat and the word *duple*

PROCEDURES

1. Show pictures of a circus and a circus band.
2. Discuss the events, people, and animals found in a circus.
3. Sing or play a recording of "Circus Parade." Ask students to clap a steady beat, accenting the first beat as they listen.
4. Ask students to circle each F# on their copies, or ask a student to circle the F# on the transparency.
5. Point out that the F# is only a half step below G, and that is very close. Sing or play the distance from G to F#. Ask how many times this pattern occurs in the song (six times).
6. Have students read the words from their scores or from a chart or transparency.
7. Sing or play a recording of the song. Ask students to sing the verse and top melody of the chorus.

Read the verse of the song with Kodály rhythm syllables (ta-ah = 𝅗𝅥, ta = ♩, ti = ♪, ta-ah-ah-ah = 𝅝, ta-i = ♩.) Ask students to listen to the melody as you sing or play a recording. Sing the verse of the song and the refrain (top melody only), using rhythm syllables.

8. Ask the class to sing the entire song with words.
9. Ask a student to play on the xylophone or resonator bells the four pitches that make up the descending melodic phrase: F E D C. These are found in the refrain. The rest of the class should map the direction of these pitches with their hands.
10. Ask students to sing the top line and selected students to play the contrasting melody on instruments.
11. Use a drum for the last "Boom! Boom!" Sing the refrain again, using the xylophone and resonator bells for the descending melody and the drum for the final two notes.
12. Closure: Ask the class to sing the song with instruments used at appropriate places.

ASSESSMENT

1. Sing or play a recording of the song. Ask students which chart shows a steady beat and whether they tap two or four beats in each measure.
2. Show a chart of the interval G–F# and ask a student to demonstrate the sound of these two pitches by singing or playing an instrument.
3. Ask students to locate G–F# in their musical scores. Discuss how many times this pattern appears.
4. Sing or play a recording of the song and ask students which chart, AB or ABA, they might use to diagram the form (AB).

More Songs: Circus

- "Carousel" in Holt, Rinehart and Winston *Exploring Music 2,* p. 64
- "Circus" in Macmillan/McGraw-Hill *Share the Music 2* (2003), p. 54
- "Circus Band" in Holt, Rinehart and Winston *Exploring Music 7,* p. 134
- "Circus Parade" in Silver Burdett Ginn *World of Music 2,* p. 14
- "Greatest Show on Earth" in Macmillan/McGraw-Hill *Spotlight on Music 3,* p. T308
- "He's a Clown" in Silver Burdett Ginn *World of Music 3,* p. 172

INTEGRATIVE CATEGORY: SOCIAL STUDIES—GEOGRAPHY

"Catatumba"

Integrative areas: Culture, vocabulary, dramatics

Grades: 3–6

Concepts: Rhythm: steady beat, mostly eighth notes

Melody: narrow range, repeated phrases

Harmony: mostly thirds

Spanish Folk Song
Arranged by Francis Girard English
Version by Rosemary Jacques

Catatumba

Key: C
Starting pitch: G
Meter: 2/4, begins on 2

C
G7
Hur - ry, hur - ry, Ga - ta - tum - ba, Bring the tam - bour - ine and drum. Hur - ry,
Ga - ta - tum - ba, tum - ba, tum - ba, Con pan - de - ras y so najas, Ga - ta -
G7
C
hur - ry, Ga - ta - tum - ba, All is read - y, won't you come? Hur - ry,
tum - ba, tum - ba, tum - ba, No te me - tas en las pajas, Ga - ta -
C
F
hur - ry, Ga - ta - tum - ba, Strike the bell and let it ring. Hur - ry,
tum - ba, tum - ba, tum - ba, To - ca el pi - to y el ra - bel. Ga - ta -
F
C
G7
C
hur - ry, Ga - ta - tum - ba, Ev - 'ry - bod - y wants to sing!
tum - ba, tum - ba, tum - ba, Tam - bo - ril y cas - ca - bel.

The Spanish words of "Gatatumba" are pronounced as follows:

Ga-ta-tum-ba, tum-ba, tum-ba,	*Ga-ta-tum-ba, tum-ba, tum-ba,*
Gah-tah-toom-bah toom-bah toom-bah	Gah-tah-toom-bah toom-bah toom-bah
Con pan-de-ras y so na-jas,	*To-ca el pi-to y el ra-bel.*
Kohn pahn-deh-rahs ee soh-nah-hahs	Toh-kahl pee-toh yehl rah-behl
Ga-ta-tum-ba, tum-ba, tum-ba,	*Ga-ta-tum-ba, tum-ba, tum-ba,*
Gah-tah-toom-bah toom-bah toom-bah	Gah-tah-toom-bah toom-bah toom-bah
No te me-tas en las pa-jas,	*Tam-bo-ril y cas-ca-bel.*
Noh teh meh-tahs en lahs pah-hahs	Tahm-boh-reel ee kahs-kah-behl

Bass xylophone

Recorder (as a drone)

Drum (throughout)

SUGGESTIONS FOR LESSONS

1. Locate Spain on a world map. Note its relationship to surrounding areas (southern Europe, bounded by sea).
2. Discuss which Spanish instruments could be used to accompany the song (guitar, castanets).
3. View pictures of Spanish dress, cathedrals, and dances.
4. Discuss the use of the Spanish language in the United States (southern and southwestern states).

"Roll On, Columbia"

Integrative areas: Geography, science

Grades: 4–6

Concepts: Rhythm: steady beat, 3/4 meter, repeated patterns

Melody: moves mostly by steps, narrow range

Texture/harmony: descant on top provides harmony; harmony mostly in thirds or sixths; chords: F, B♭, C_7

Form: two sections, verse and refrain, AB

Words by Woody Guthrie
Music based on "Goodnight, Irene" by Huddie Ledbetter and John Lomax

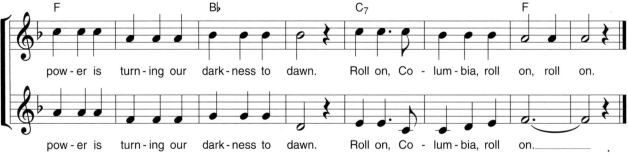

Roll On, Columbia

Key: F
Starting pitch: C
Meter: 3/4, begins on 1

F C7 F C7 F F
1. Green Doug - las fir where the wa - ters cut through, Down her wild moun - tains and can - yons she flew, Ca - na - di - an North - west to the o - cean so blue,
2. Oth - er big riv - ers add pow - er to you: Yak - i - ma, Snake, and the Klick - i - tat, too. San - dy, Wil - lam - ette, and the Hood Riv - er, too
(3.) Bon - ne - ville now there are ships in the locks. The wa - ter has ris - en and cov - ered the rocks. Ship - loads a - plen - ty are soon past the docks,
(4.) on up the riv - er is the Grand Cou - lee Dam: The big - gest thing built by the hand of a man To run the great fac - t'ries and wa - ter the land.
B♭ C7 F
Roll on, Co - lum - bia, roll on.
3. At
4. And
Refrain
Countermelody
F C7 F
Roll - ing a - long, roll - ing a - long, roll - ing a - long, Co - lum - bia, roll on. Your
Melody
Roll on, Co - lum - bia, roll on. Roll on, Co - lum - bia, roll on. Your
F B♭ C7 F
pow - er is turn - ing our dark - ness to dawn. Roll on, Co - lum - bia, roll on, roll on.
pow - er is turn - ing our dark - ness to dawn. Roll on, Co - lum - bia, roll on.

SUGGESTIONS FOR LESSONS

1. Review the location of the Columbia River and the function of the Grand Coulee Dam. (Look up information about the Columbia River and the Grand Coulee Dam on the Internet.)
2. Perform the rhythm of the song by clapping a steady beat and accenting the first beat of each measure (triple meter).
3. Play or sing the harmony (countermelody) found in the refrain.
4. Ask students to read pitches using solfège or rhythm syllables.

More Songs: Social Studies—Geography

- "Alabama Gal" in Silver Burdett *Making Music 3,* p. T106
- "Bluebonnets of Texas" in Silver Burdett *Making Music 3,* p. T332
- "The Coasts of High Barbary" in Macmillan/McGraw-Hill *Spotlight on Music 6,* p. T329
- "Crescent Moon" (China) in Silver Burdett Ginn *World of Music 5,* pp. 76–77
- "Cumberland Gap" in Macmillan/McGraw-Hill *Spotlight on Music 3,* p. T99
- "Deep in the Heart of Texas" in Silver Burdett Ginn *The Music Connection 3* (2000), p. 132; Silver Burdett *Making Music 4,* p. T22
- "Going to Boston" in Macmillan *Music and You 5,* p. 15
- "The Greenland Whale Fishery" in Macmillan/McGraw-Hill *Spotlight on Music 6,* p. T212
- "Hawaiian Rainbows" in Silver Burdett Ginn *World of Music 2,* p. 40
- "Just One Planet" in Macmillan/McGraw-Hill *Spotlight on Music 4,* p. T164
- "Land of the Silver Birch" (Canada) in Silver Burdett Ginn *World of Music 5,* pp. 80–81
- "Laredo" in Silver Burdett Ginn *World of Music 5,* pp. 72–73
- "Lone Star Trail" in Silver Burdett Ginn *World of Music 2,* p. 17
- "My Home's across the Blue Ridge Mountains" in Silver Burdett *Making Music 4,* p. T84
- "My Home's in Montana" in Macmillan *Music and You 3,* p. 48; Silver Burdett Ginn *World of Music 3,* p. 20; Silver Burdett Ginn *World of Music 6,* p. 88; Macmillan/McGraw-Hill *Spotlight on Music 4,* p. T274
- "On Top of Old Smokey" in Holt, Rinehart and Winston *Music Book 5,* p. 97
- "Rio Grande" in Silver Burdett Ginn *World of Music 5,* pp. 6–7
- "San Francisco" in Macmillan/McGraw-Hill *Share the Music 5,* pp. 182–183
- "Scotland's Burning" in Macmillan/McGraw-Hill *Spotlight on Music 3,* p. T257
- "This Land Is Your Land" in Macmillan/McGraw-Hill *Spotlight on Music 4,* p. T146

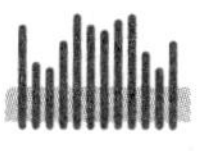

INTEGRATIVE CATEGORY: SOCIAL STUDIES—HISTORY

"Shenandoah"

Integrative areas: History, transportation, geography, social customs, visual art

Grades: 4–6

Concepts: Rhythm: 4/4 meter, syncopation

Melody: wide range

Dynamics: crescendo, decrescendo

Shenandoah

Traditional

Key: D
Starting pitch: A
Meter: 4/4, begins on 4

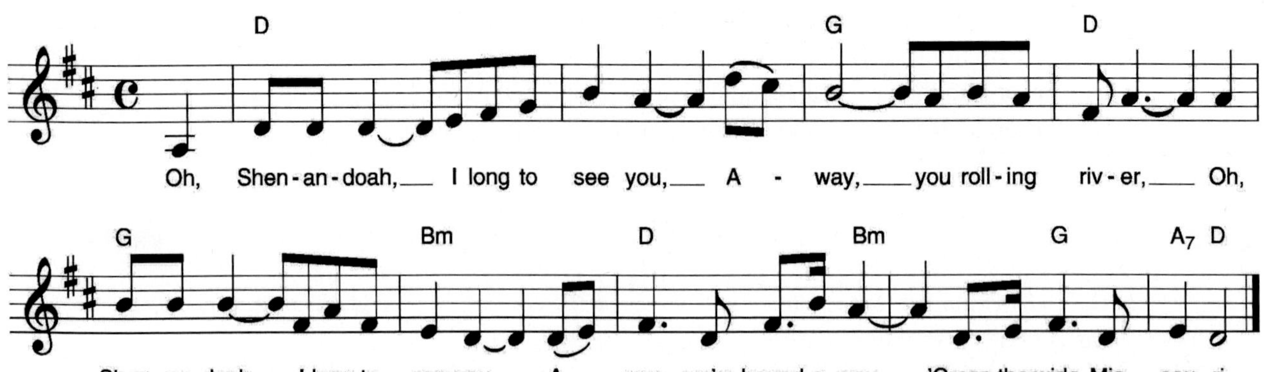
D
G
D
Oh, Shen-an-doah, I long to see you, A - way, you roll-ing riv-er, Oh,
G
Bm
D
Bm
G
A7 D
Shen-an-doah, I long to see you. A - way, we're bound a-way 'Cross the wide Mis - sou-ri.

1. The trader loved this Indian maiden,
   Away, you rolling river,
   With presents his canoe was laden.
   Refrain.
2. O Shenandoah, I'm bound to leave you,
   Away, you rolling river,
   O Shenandoah, I'll not deceive you.
   Refrain.
3. O Shenandoah, I long to hear you,
   Away, you rolling river,
   O Shenandoah, I long to hear you.
   Refrain.

Special Learner Note

The melody of this song and the text of a "rolling river" suggest the use of scarves or streamers to enhance the "flow" of the melody. This could also address large motor objectives/range of motion "exercise" for students with physical disabilities.

SUGGESTIONS FOR LESSONS

1. Background information: The song "Shenandoah" originated in the early 1800s and was very popular in the 1830s, during the presidency of Andrew Jackson. It speaks of a trader who fell in love with the daughter of the Indian chief Shenandoah, who lived near the Missouri River. As the song gained popularity, it was spread by sailors on the Missouri and Mississippi rivers. You may wish to study other historical events of the early 1800s. Find pictures of famous people who lived at that time and of the Missouri and Mississippi rivers, where the song originated.
2. Ask students where the highest note is (D) and where the lowest note is (A). Circle them on a transparency. Ask students whether this is a wide or a narrow range.
3. Perform the song or use a recording. Ask students to read the words.
4. Teach the song by rote, using the phrase method. Ask students to sing the entire song.
5. After the class has sung the song, ask on what words there is syncopation *(daugh-ter, ri-ver, wa-ter, Mis-sour-i).* Circle these words on the transparency.
6. Sing the song again with emphasis on syncopation.

More Songs: Social Studies—History

- "Ain't Gonna Let Nobody Turn Me 'Round" in Silver Burdett *Making Music 6,* p. T85
- "American Cowboys" in Silver Burdett *Making Music 5,* p. T69
- "America the Free" in Silver Burdett *Making Music 4,* p. T210
- "Ballad of the Underground Railroad" in Macmillan/McGraw-Hill *Spotlight on Music 5,* p. T145
- "Chester" in Holt, Rinehart and Winston *Music Book 5,* p. 67
- "Colors of the Wind" in Macmillan/McGraw-Hill *Spotlight on Music 3,* p. T84
- "Columbus Sailed with Three Ships" in Macmillan *Music and You K,* p. 44
- "The Cowboy" in Macmillan/McGraw-Hill *Spotlight on Music 6,* p. T278
- "Ellis Island" in Silver Burdett *Making Music 5,* p. T57
- "Follow the Drinkin' Gourd" in Silver Burdett *Music 4,* p. 266; *Spotlight on Music 5,* p. 142
- "George Washington" in Macmillan *Music and You K,* p. 156
- "Greatest American Hero" in Silver Burdett Ginn *World of Music 5,* p. 105
- "In My Merry Oldsmobile" in Silver Burdett Ginn *World of Music 5,* pp. 58–59
- "In the Good Old Colony Time" in Macmillan/McGraw-Hill *Spotlight on Music 3,* p. T326
- "Johnny Has Gone for a Soldier" in Silver Burdett Ginn *World of Music 5,* p. 26
- "Martin Luther King " in Silver Burdett *Making Music 5,* p. T484; *Spotlight on Music 2,* p. 364
- "The Navajo Nation" in Silver Burdett *Making Music 5,* p. T109
- "Route 66" in Silver Burdett *Making Music 4,* p. T276
- "St. Patrick's Day" in Macmillan/McGraw-Hill *Spotlight on Music 5,* p. T434
- "The Wells Fargo Wagon" in Macmillan/McGraw-Hill *Spotlight on Music 5,* p. T303
- "We Shall Not Be Moved" in Silver Burdett *Making Music 4,* p. T436
- "We Shall Overcome" in Silver Burdett Making Music 4, p. 326
- "When Johnny Comes Marching Home" in *Spotlight on Music 5,* p. 34
- "Yankee Doodle" in Silver Burdett *Making Music 2,* p. 405

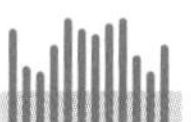

INTEGRATIVE CATEGORY: HOLIDAYS

Ramadan (Muslim Holiday)

Ramadan, the ninth month of the Muslim calendar, begins in October. At this time, Muslims observe the month-long Fast of Ramadan. During this period of contemplation and worship, Muslims fast (do not eat) during the daylight hours but in the evening eat small meals, often while visiting family and friends.

Technology Enhancement

As a complement to the lessons presented here, visit www.educationworld.com/holidays/ and search through their extensive list of holiday lessons plans and activities for all major holidays and events.

SUGGESTIONS FOR LESSONS

1. Search the Internet for information about Ramadan (e.g. www.kiddyhouse.com/Ramadan). Download information and pictures (www.images.google.com) and display them to guide a class discussion of Ramadan.
2. Go to the following website for a collection of *30 Children's Activities for Ramadan:* http://goodtreemontessori.wordpress.htm/Ramadan
3. Search the Internet for children's songs about Ramadan (e.g. www.nancymusic.com/Ramadan) and perform.

Halloween

Halloween is one of our oldest festive holidays. Its origin dates back to long before the Christian era. It was held on what is now the last day of October. Giant fires were lit in honor of the sun god, whose spirit, so it was believed, deserved recognition and honor for the important role it played in growing crops. The ceremony was a solemn, devout religious rite around the roaring flames of the fire.

It was not until the Middle Ages that ghosts and witches were introduced into the Halloween celebration, which by then took place on All Hallow's Eve, the night before the Christian festival called All Saints' Day. All sorts of pranks and mischievous antics were performed. The pranksters continued their mysterious ghostly deeds until midnight. When the midnight church bells rang, ushering in the holy day, the Halloween celebrations would cease. Over the years the customs of Halloween celebrations have changed from time to time and place to place. Today we celebrate with costumes and parties.

"The Witch Rides"

Integrative areas: Dramatics, movement

Grades: K–1

Concepts: Rhythm: duple meter

Melody: wide range, repeated pitches, ascending/descending

Music by Grace M. Meserve
Verses I and 3 by Grace M. Meserve
Verses 2 and 4 by Mary Joy

The Witch Rides

Key: D minor
Starting pitch: D
Meter: 6/8, begins on 6

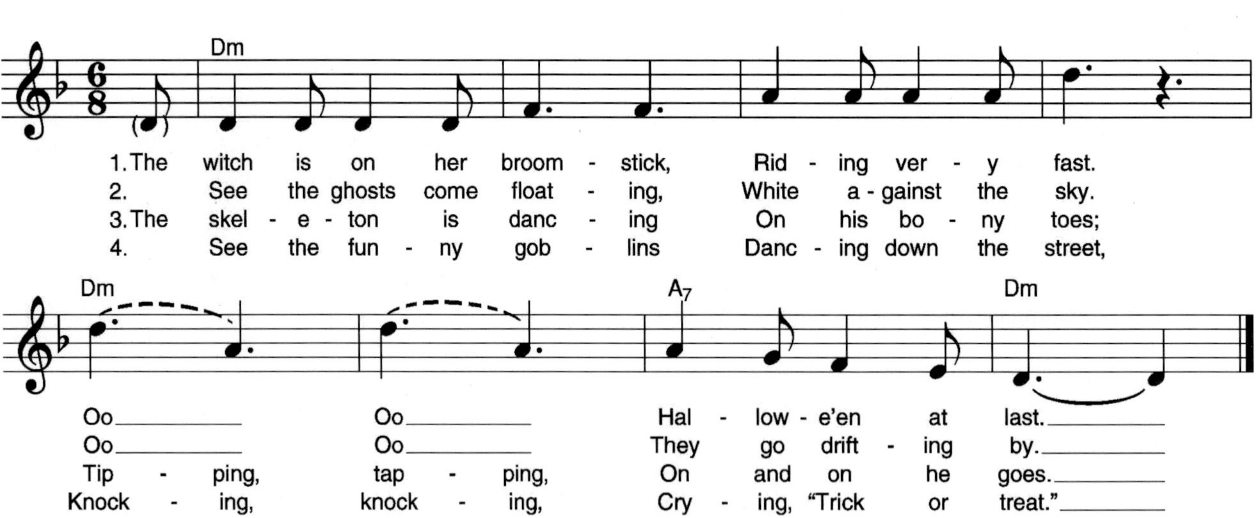

SUGGESTIONS FOR LESSONS

1. Dramatize "The Witch Rides" by galloping on phrases 1, 2, and 4. Stop on "Oo, Oo" and tip the imaginary broomstick down on the second beat of the measure.
2. Ask students to map the melody in the air as they hear it.

3. Play the steady beat (two beats to a measure) on rhythm sticks.
4. Add creative verses to the song.

"Let's Make a Jack-o'-Lantern"

Integrative areas: Visual art, candles, creative dramatics
Grades: 1–3
Concepts: Rhythm: repetition, steady beat

Words and Music by Daniel S. Hooley
Piano Accompaniment by
Kryste Andrews
Let's Make a Jack-o'-Lantern
Key: F
Starting pitch: C
Meter: 4/4, begins on "and" of 3
F C7 C7 F B♭ C7 F C7 F
1. Let's make a jack-, jack-, jack - o' lan - tern; I'll show you how, how, how it's done. You sim - ply scoop out a lit - tle yel - low pump - kin, And cut a pump - kin face for fun.
2. In - side we'll put, put, put a can - dle To make a shine, shine, shin - ing light. We'll make a fine jack - o' - lan - tern for our win - dow, To grin at peo - ple in the night.

SUGGESTIONS FOR LESSONS

1. Use pumpkins to make several jack-o'-lanterns.
2. Place candles in the jack-o'-lanterns. Turn out the lights so the jack-o'-lanterns glow.
3. Place the jack-o'-lanterns around the classroom.

Halloween Music and Abstract Drawings

1. Choose classical music selections that are connected with Halloween and appropriate for your students [iTunes/Spotify]:
   - Bach, J.S., *Toccata and Fugue in D minor,* BWV 565
   - Bartok, Bella, *Music for Strings, Percussion, and Celesta* (Movement 3, adagio)
   - Berlioz, Hector, *Symphonie Fantastique,* "March to the Scaffold"
   - Crumb, George, *Black Angels*
   - Grieg, Edvard, *In the Hall of the Mountain King*

More Songs: Halloween

- "Boo" in Macmillan/McGraw-Hill *Spotlight on Music 3,* p. T362
- "Dry Bones" in Silver Burdett Ginn *The Music Connection 4* (2000), pp. 78–79; Macmillan/McGraw-Hill *Spotlight on Music 5,* p T406
- "Halloween" in Macmillan/McGraw-Hill *Share the Music 1* (2003), p. 97; Macmillan/McGraw-Hill *Spotlight on Music 1,* p T340
- "Halloween Night" in Macmillan/McGraw-Hill *Share the Music 3* (2003), pp. 312–313
- "Halloween Is a Very Unusual Night" in Silver Burdett *Making Music 3,* p. 382
- "How Did You Know?" in Silver Burdett Ginn *World of Music 2,* pp. 200–201
- "Jack-o'-Lantern" in Macmillan/McGraw-Hill *Spotlight on Music K,* p. T307
- "On Halloween" in Silver Burdett Ginn *World of Music 2,* p. 198
- "Owl and the Pumpkin" in Silver Burdett *Making Music 2,* p. T377
- "Pick a Pumpkin" in Macmillan/McGraw-Hill *Share the Music 2,* p. 309; Macmillan/McGraw-Hill *Spotlight on Music 1,* p. T346
- "Pumpkin, Pumpkin" in Silver Burdett *Making Music 1,* p. T413
- "There Once Was a Witch" in Silver Burdett Ginn *World of Music 2,* p. 299
- "This Is Halloween" in Macmillan/McGraw-Hill *Spotlight on Music 2,* p. T346
- "Watch Out" in Silver Burdett Ginn *The Music Connection 4* (2000), p. 208
- "What Will You Be on Halloween?" in Macmillan/McGraw-Hill *Share the Music K* (2003), p. T266; Silver Burdett *Making Music K,* p. T308

    - Ives, Charles, *Robert Browning Overture*
    - Mozart, W.A., *Requiem,* "Dies Irae"
    - Mussorgsky, *A Night on Bald Mountain*
    - Orff, Carl, *Carmina Burana, O Fortuna*

2. Explain to students that while they listen to the song, they are to draw a picture of what they hear. (Students can either create abstract or realistic drawings for each selection they hear.)
3. Hand out blank paper and crayons, markers, or colored pencils.
4. Start the recording and let their imaginations be directed to drawing on the page.

Note: Using 3- to 5-minute samples of each selection works best. Also, try alternating between students creating abstract and realistic pictures of what they hear. You'll be amazed at how they visually represent different styles and articulations!

Thanksgiving, Sukkot, and Shavuot

There are many fall festivals that celebrate harvest time. Some of these are the American Thanksgiving and the Jewish Sukkot and Shavuot.

Thanksgiving is an American holiday on which people of all faiths give thanks in their own individual ways for freedom to work, play, and worship. It is usually associated with pumpkins, corn, and turkey, which were the chief foods used by the Native Americans in colonial times. It is also a time when the classroom teacher will want to impress on children the founding of our country, the trials and hardships that brought the first settlers to our shores, and the rugged individualism that has characterized American society ever since. A celebration of thanksgiving for the English settlers who survived their first winter in the American colonies, the holiday often focuses on the people known as Pilgrims.

The Jewish Sukkot is a celebration of a completed harvest. It is also known as the Feast of Tabernacles or the Feast of Booths. Many people build small structures out of leaves or branches in remembrance of their ancestors who wandered the desert. The Jewish Sukkot is a joyous celebration. Shavuot is another Jewish festival that celebrates the end of the harvest season and the beginning of the fruit season. It too is a joyful time of sharing.

"Mister Turkey"

Integrative areas: Creative dramatics, visual art
Grades: K–I
Concepts: Rhythm: steady beat
Melody: short phrases, repetition
Form: AA

Mister Turkey
Music by Robert W. Gibb
Words by L. E. Ashley
Key: G
Starting pitch: G
Meter: 4/4, begins on 1
G D7 G D7 G
See him strut - ting all a - round, Fat Mis - ter Tur - key!
G D7 G D7 G
Hear the gob - ble, gob - ble sound, Fat Mis - ter Tur - key.

SUGGESTIONS FOR LESSONS

1. Dramatize the song with appropriate actions—strutting, saying "gobble, gobble," and so on.
2. Draw pictures of turkeys.
3. Ask students to sing the song and to clap the duple meter.

"Five Fat Turkeys"

Integrative areas: Number sequences, creative dramatics
Grades: K–2
Concepts: Duple meter, steady beat, short phrases

Five Fat Turkeys

Traditional

Key: G
Starting pitch: G
Meter: 2/4, begins on 1

G D7 G7 G G D7 G D7
Five fat tur-keys are we. We slept all night in a tree. When the
G D7 G7 C G D7 G
cook came a - round, we could-n't be found, So that's why we're here, you see.

SUGGESTIONS FOR LESSONS

1. Dramatize the short story of the five fat turkeys.
2. Select a student to keep a steady beat with a drum.
3. Invite students to stand tall on the highest note (last line).

Special Learner Note

The lyrics to "Five Fat Turkeys" would be easily recalled with sign language emphasizing the major words.

"Over the River and Through the Wood"

Integrative areas: Social studies—history, geography
Weather
Visual art

Grades: 4–6

Concepts: Rhythm: repetition
Melody: range of one octave
Form: ABAC

Over the River and Through the Wood

Lydia Maria Child

Key: C
Starting pitch: G
Meter: 6/8, begins on 1

C F C
1. O - ver the riv - er and through the wood, To grand-fath - er's house we go. The
2. O - ver the riv - er and through the wood and straight to the barn - yard gate, We
3. O - ver the riv - er and through the wood, now soon we'll be on our way. There's
G7 C D7 G7
horse knows the way to car - ry the sleigh through the white and drift - ing snow.
seem to go so ver - y slow, and it's so hard to wait.
feast - ing and fun for ev - er - y - one, for this is Thanks - giv - ing day.

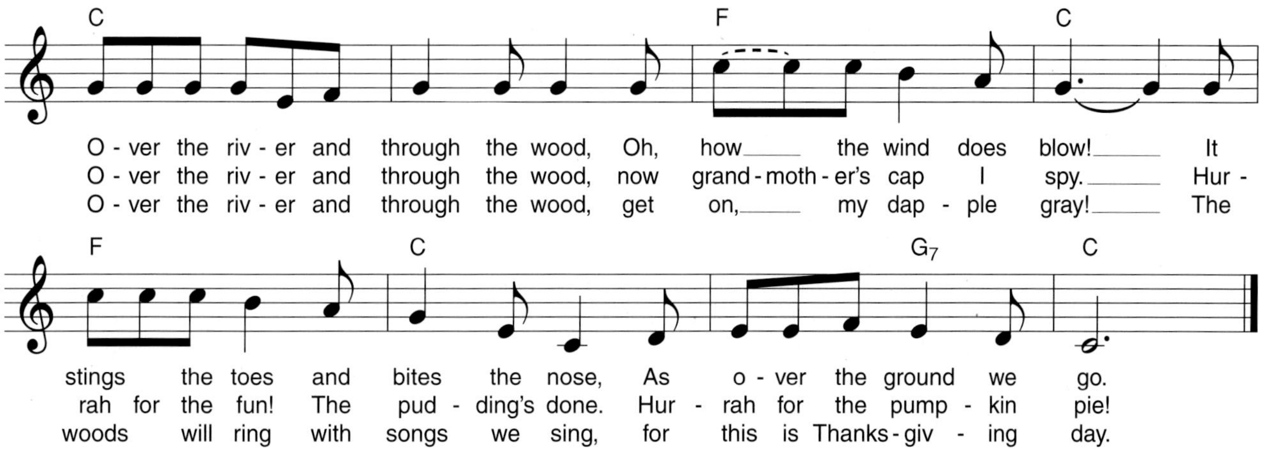
C F C
O - ver the riv - er and through the wood, Oh, how___ the wind does blow!___ It
O - ver the riv - er and through the wood, now grand - moth - er's cap I spy.___ Hur -
O - ver the riv - er and through the wood, get on,___ my dap - ple gray!___ The
F C G7 C
stings the toes and bites the nose, As o - ver the ground we go.
rah for the fun! The pud - ding's done. Hur - rah for the pump - kin pie!
woods will ring with songs we sing, for this is Thanks - giv - ing day.

SUGGESTIONS FOR LESSONS

1. Study pictures by Currier and Ives of early rural American scenes. Focus on pictures of sleighs and winter scenes. Discuss or dramatize what it might have been like to ride in a sleigh. Ask children to bring replicas of sleighs that they might have at home, such as those often used as Christmas decorations.
2. Create scenes in art class that express the verses of the song.
3. Play and clap the duple pulse: ♪♪♪ ♪♪♪
4. Identify the repeated pitches and rhythm patterns.

"We Gather Together"

Integrative areas: Social studies–history
Language arts–vocabulary

Grades: 4–6

Concepts: Rhythm: triple meter, repeated patterns ♩. ♪ ♩
Melody: wide range
Dynamics: < >

Holland
Translated by Theodore Baker
We Gather Together
Key: C
Starting pitch: G
Meter: 3/4, begins on 3
C G7 C G
We gath - er to - geth - er to ask the Lord's bless - ing; He chas - tens, and
C D7 G G7 C
has - tens, His will to make known. The wick - ed op - press - ing, cease
G7 C F C F G7 C
them___ from dis - tress - ing. Sing prais - es to His name. He for - gets not His own.

Source: Christian hymn of Dutch origin written in 1597

SUGGESTIONS FOR LESSONS

1. Read and study stories or pictures of the first Thanksgiving in America.
2. Discuss the role of Pilgrims, Native Americans, and traders.
3. Locate Plymouth, Massachusetts, on a map of the United States. Use an atlas to locate other cities in the United States that have the name *Plymouth.* Point out the coastal area of Plymouth, England, and discuss the use of English names for American regions or cities, such as "New" England, and "New" York.
4. Dramatize the first Thanksgiving. Sing "We Gather Together" as students reenact the Pilgrims gathering around the table to celebrate an abundant harvest. Teach the meaning of words such as *chasten, hasten, oppressing,* and *distressing.* Emphasize freedom from oppression and freedom of worship as reasons for coming to America.
5. Ask students to sing the song in its entirety.

More Songs: Thanksgiving, Sukkot, and Shavuot

Thanksgiving

- "Come, Ye Thankful People, Come" in Silver Burdett Ginn *World of Music 5,* p. 231; Macmillan/McGraw-Hill *Share the Music 5,* p. 328
- "For Thy Gracious Blessings" in Macmillan/McGraw-Hill *Share the Music 5,* p. 329
- "Gather 'Round" in Macmillan/McGraw-Hill *Share the Music 3,* pp. 314–315
- "Grandpa's Turkey" in Holt, Rinehart and Winston *Music Book 1,* p. 186
- "I'm a Very Fine Turkey" in Silver Burdett *Making Music K,* p. T310
- "I'm Thankful" in Silver Burdett *Making Music 1,* p. T414
- "Jack-o'-Lantern" in Macmillan/McGraw-Hill *Spotlight on Music K,* p. T307
- "Over the River and Through the Wood" in Silver Burdett *Making Music 3,* p. 384; in Macmillan/McGraw-Hill *Spotlight on Music 4,* p. T370
- "Perot" in Silver Burdett *Making Music 2,* p. T378
- "Song of Thanksgiving" in Macmillan/McGraw-Hill *Spotlight on Music 4,* p. T371
- "Tallis Canon" in Silver Burdett Ginn *World of Music 3,* p. 20
- "Thanksgiving" in Silver Burdett Ginn *World of Music 2,* pp. 202–203
- "Thanksgiving Is Near" in Silver Burdett *Making Music 2,* p. 380
- "The Turkey Game" in Silver Burdett Ginn *The Music Connection 1,* pp. 138–139

Sukkot

- "Hag Asif: Harvest Time" in Macmillan/McGraw-Hill *Share the Music 3,* pp. 316–317

Shavuot

- "Festival of First Fruits" in Macmillan *Share the Music 3,* p. 273

Hanukkah

Hanukkah, Christmas, and Kwanzaa celebrations occur in December. Children should experience the beautiful music of these holidays. The Jewish celebration is very old, and Kwanzaa is very new, but all three reflect joy.

Hanukkah is a Hebrew word meaning "dedication." Known as the Feast of Lights, it is an eight-day celebration commemorating the rededication of the Temple at Jerusalem (165 B.C.) after the Maccabees had defeated the Syrian Greek armies. During the festival a candle is lit for each day. Hanukkah is celebrated with parties and the exchange of gifts. The menorah, a candelabra that holds the eight candles, can be found in many Jewish homes.

"Hanukkah Is Here"

Integrative areas: Cultural heritage
Social studies—history

Grades: K–1

Concepts: Rhythm: duple meter, steady beat
Melody: narrow range, repeated phrases
Tonality: minor

Hanukkah Is Here
Words and Music by
Suzanne Clayton
Key: D Minor
Starting pitch: D
Meter: 4/4, begins on 1
Dm
A7
Dm
A7
Dm
1. Light the can - dles, light the can - dles, light the can - dles, Ha - nuk - kah is here.
2. Spin the drei - dl, spin the drei - dl, Spin the drei - dl, Ha - nuk - kah is here.
3. Dance the ho - ra, dance the ho - ra, Dance the ho - ra, Ha - nuk - kah is here.

SUGGESTIONS FOR LESSONS

1. Ask a Jewish student to bring a menorah to class and tell how his or her family celebrates Hanukkah.
2. Draw menorahs in art class.
3. Discuss the use of Hebrew in Jewish worship. Invite a Jewish student to sing a song in Hebrew for the class.

"O Hanukkah"

Integrative areas: Cultural heritage
Hanukkah
Social studies—history

Grades: 3–5

Concepts: Melody: repetition, steps and skips
Symbols: use of repeat sign; first and second endings
Harmony: in thirds
Rhythm: duple meter
Descant: melodic and rhythmic repetition

Jewish Folk Song
English words by
Judith Eisenstein

O Hanukkah

Key: D minor (Pentatonic)
Starting pitch: D
Meter: 4/4, begins on "and" of 4

Dm Dm

O Ha - nuk - kah, O Ha - nuk - kah, come light the me - no - rah.
Let's ___ have a par - ty, we'll all dance the ho - rah.

Dm A7 Dm

Gath - er round the ta - ble, we'll give you a treat.

Dm A7 Dm

Shin - ing tops to play with and pan - cakes to eat;

Dm Dm Gm Dm

And while we are play - ing, The can - dles are burn - ing ___ low,

Dm Gm Dm Gm

One for each night, they ___ shed a sweet light to re -

1. Dm A7 Dm

mind us of days long a - go,

2. Dm A7 Dm

mind us of days long a - go.

From *The Gateway to Jewish Song*, by Judith Eisenstein. Reprinted by permission of the estate of Judith Eisenstein.

Alto glockenspiel or alto xylophone

More Songs: Hanukkah (also spelled Chanukah)

- "Candles of Chanukah" in Silver Burdett Ginn *World of Music K*, p. 170
- "Chanukah Is Here" in Silver Burdett *Making Music 2*, p. 382
- "Chanukah Games" in Silver Burdett *Making Music 3*, p. 389
- "Driedel Spin" (S'vivon Sov) in Macmillan/McGraw-Hill *Spotlight on Music 1*, p. T374
- "Eight Days of Hanukkah" in Macmillan/McGraw-Hill *Spotlight on Music 3*, p. T370
- "Hanerot Halalu" in Macmillan/McGraw-Hill *Share the Music 5*, pp. 341–342
- "Hanukkah Chag Yafeh" in Macmillan/McGraw-Hill *Spotlight on Music 1*, p. T350
- "Hanuka, Hanuka" in Silver Burdett *Making Music 3*, p. 390
- "Hanukkah Is Here" in Macmillan/McGraw-Hill *Share the Music K*, p. T276; Silver Burdett Ginn *The Music Connection 1*, p. 220; *Spotlight on Music K*, p. T314
- "In the Window" in Silver Burdett Ginn *World of Music 2*, p. 206; Silver Burdett Ginn *The Music Connection 2*, p. 186
- "Joyous Chanukah" in Silver Burdett Ginn *World of Music 2*, p. 207; Silver Burdett Ginn *The Music Connection 2*, p. 187
- "Light the Candles" in Macmillan/McGraw-Hill *Share the Music 1*, p. 103
- "My Dreidel" in Macmillan/McGraw-Hill *Share the Music K*, p. T277; Macmillan/McGraw-Hill *Spotlight on Music 1*, p. T353
- "My Dreydl" in Silver Burdett *Making Music K*, p. T314
- "O Chanukah" in Silver Burdett *Making Music 5*, p. 464
- "O Hanukkah" in Macmillan/McGraw-Hill *Spotlight on Music 3*, p. T368
- "On This Night" in Silver Burdett Ginn *The Music Connection 1*, p. 221
- "Who Can Retell?" in Macmillan/McGraw-Hill *Share the Music 5*, p. 339

Christmas

Christmas is a time when Christians celebrate the birth of Jesus Christ. The scene often re-created is called the Nativity. Christmas Eve is a time of special music and pageantry in many Christian churches. Although there is much secular celebration, Christmas remains both a religious holiday featuring the giving of gifts and a time when thoughts turn to "peace on earth and goodwill toward men." Some of the most wonderful musical treasures we have found are in the Christmas carols from countries around the world.

"Jolly Old Saint Nicholas"

Integrative areas: Creative dramatics
Customs of Christmas

Grades: K–2

Concepts: Rhythm: duple meter, mostly eighth notes, steady beat
Melody: narrow range, repeated pitches, repeated phrases

Jolly Old Saint Nicholas

Key: G
Starting pitch: B
Meter: 2/4, begins on 1

Carol

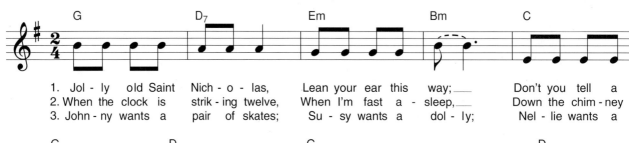

1. Jol - ly old Saint Nich - o - las, Lean your ear this way; Don't you tell a
2. When the clock is strik - ing twelve, When I'm fast a - sleep, Down the chim - ney
3. John - ny wants a pair of skates; Su - sy wants a dol - ly; Nel - lie wants a

sin - gle soul What I'm going to say; Christ - mas Eve is com - ing soon,
broad and black With your pack you'll creep; All the stock - ings you will find
sto - ry book; She thinks dolls are fol - ly. As for me, my lit - tle brain

Now you dear old man, Whis - per what you'll bring to me; Tell me, if you can.
Hang - ing in a row; Mine will be the short - est one; You'll be sure to know.
Is - n't ver - y bright; Choose for me, Dear San - ta Claus, What you think is right.

SUGGESTIONS FOR LESSONS

1. Read the following story of Saint Nicholas: According to an old legend, Saint Nicholas was the Bishop of Myra in the fourth century. Because of his great love for children, he was designated their patron saint. There were many tales of his kindness to the poor and the gifts he took to them. The custom of giving gifts is carried on in our exchange of Christmas presents.
2. Have a child act as Saint Nicholas, with other members of the class whispering to him something special they would like for Christmas.
3. Dramatize the text of the song. For example, on "lean your ear this way," cup your ear; on "don't you tell a single soul," shake your finger; on "when I'm fast asleep," hold hands to ears, and so on.

Special Learner Note

Present the song initially with the motions rather than introducing them after the song is sung. Some students may focus more on the visual presentation than the aural presentation. Actions may also provide a rhythmic structure for the students to follow.

"Las Posadas Songs"

Integrative areas: Creative dramatics
Customs of Christmas

Grades: 3–4

Concepts: Rhythm: steady beat, triple and duple meter
Melody: repeated phrases, narrow range
Form: AB

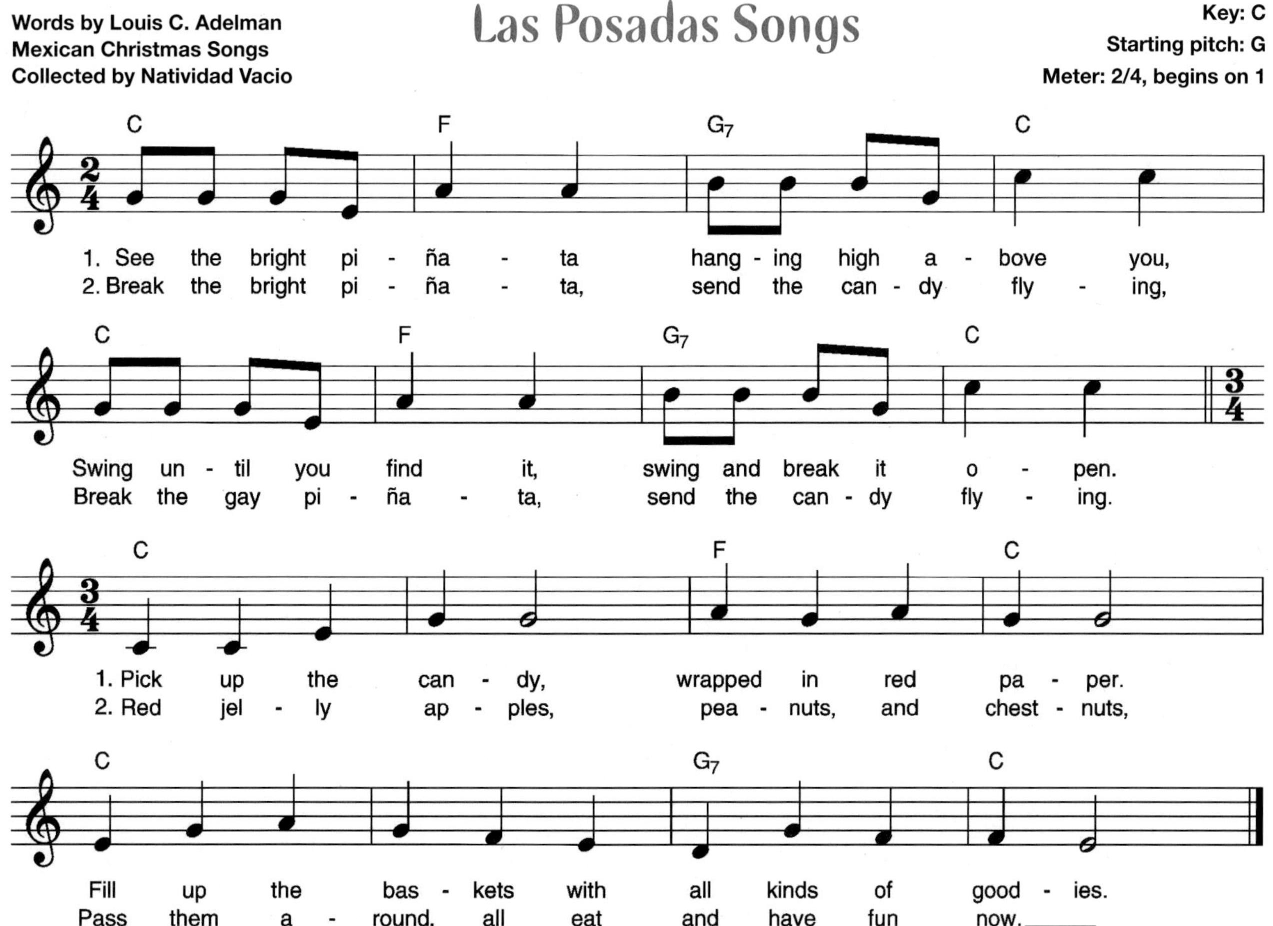

SUGGESTIONS FOR LESSONS

1. Describe Mexican customs of celebrating Christmas. Every night, during the weeks before Christmas, candlelit processions go from house to house, seeking lodging (posadas), as Mary and Joseph did in Bethlehem. Merrymaking follows the worship before the crèche (manger scene) and the breaking of the piñata, a decorated papier-mâché animal or object filled with candy and nuts. Someone is blindfolded and the piñata is dangled out of reach of the person's stick. After the person swings wildly, the piñata is placed so that it can be broken, and everyone scrambles for its contents.
2. Dramatize the breaking of the piñata.
3. Create a piñata in art class.
4. Compare the Mexican custom of celebrating Christmas with customs from other parts of the world.

"Deck the Halls"

Integrative areas: Visual arts and history

Grades: 3–6

Concepts: Rhythm: duple meter, steady beat, repeated patterns

Melody: repeated phrases, wide range, mostly steps

Tonality: major

Form: AABA

Key: D
Starting pitch: A
Meter: 4/4, begins on 1

Wales

D A7 D A7 D

1. Deck the halls with boughs of hol - ly, / 2. See the blaz - ing Yule be - fore us, / 3. Fast a - way the old year pass - es, — Fa la la la la la la la la.

D A7 D A7 D

'Tis the sea - son to be jol - ly, / Strike the harp and join the cho - rus, / Hail the new, ye lads and lass - es, — Fa la la la la la la la la.

A7 D A D A E7 A

Don we now our gay ap - par - rel, / Fol - low me in mer - ry mea - sure, / Sing we joy - ous all to - geth - er, — Fa la la la la la la la la.

D G D A7 D

Troll the an - cient Yule - tide car - ol, / While I tell of Yule - tide trea - sure, / Heed - less of the wind and weath - er, — Fa la la la la la la la la.

SUGGESTIONS FOR LESSONS

1. Study pictures from the time of Charles Dickens (1812–1870).
2. Create simple costumes and a "caroling" scene around a lamppost.
3. Discuss the use of *fa la la* as a refrain-type response in the song. Many joyful songs use nonsense syllables as a refrain.

Special Learner Note

Divide the group into two sections and have one group sing "Deck the halls . . . " and other group answer with "Fa-la-la . . . ." For those with limited speech, instruments could be played in place of "Fa-la-la . . . ."

"O Come, All Ye Faithful" (Adeste, Fideles)

Integrative areas: Language arts–Latin
Visual art

Grades: 5–6

Concepts: Rhythm: steady beat, duple meter
Melody: wide range, mostly steps, long phrases
Form: AB

SUGGESTIONS FOR LESSONS

1. Explain that during the Middle Ages, Latin was the only accepted language in the Christian Church. Introduce students to singing Latin with the verse found in "Adeste, Fideles" (O Come, All Ye Faithful).

   Pronunciation key for Latin words:

a = "ah"	ae = "ay"
i = "ee"	u = "oo"
e = "eh"	g = soft *g*

2. Dramatize the song with students taking the role of monks.
3. Create a stained-glass window and a cathedral atmosphere.
4. Perform the song phrase by phrase.
5. Teach the song phrase by phrase.
6. Ask students to sing the song.

More Songs: Christmas

- "A Holly Jolly Christmas" in Macmillan/McGraw-Hill *Share the Music 4*, pp. 324–325
- "Angeles We Have Heard on High" in *Spotlight on Music 6*, p. 406
- "Children, Go Where I Send Thee" in Silver Burdett Ginn *The Music Connection 3*, pp. 214–215
- "Christmas Is Coming" in Macmillan *Music and You 4*, p. 69; Holt, Rinehart and Winston *Exploring Music 2*, p. 73
- "Christmas, Don't Be Late" in Silver Burdett *Making Music 2*, p. 386
- "Christmas Eve" in *Spotlight on Music K*, p. T323
- "The Christmas Season" in Silver Burdett *Making Music 5*, p. 472
- "Deck the Hall" in *Spotlight on Music 3*, p. 374
- "Feliz Navidad" in Silver Burdett *Making Music 4*, p. T433; Macmillan/McGraw-Hill *Spotlight on Music 5*, p. T420
- "Frosty the Snowman" in Silver Burdett Ginn *World of Music 2*, pp. 208–209; Macmillan/McGraw-Hill *Spotlight on Music 3*, p. T366
- "Good King Wenceslas" in Silver Burdett *Making Music 4*, p. T431
- "Here Comes Santa Claus" in Silver Burdett Ginn *World of Music 1*, p. 197
- "The Huron Carol" in Silver Burdett Ginn *World of Music 5*, p. 243
- "I Saw Three Ships" in Silver Burdett *Making Music 1*, p. T426; Macmillan/McGraw-Hill *Spotlight on Music 1*, p. T359
- "It's Santa Again" in Silver Burdett *Making Music 2*, p. 385
- "It's Time to Get Ready for Christmas" in Macmillan/McGraw-Hill *Spotlight on Music 3*, p. T372
- "Jingle Bells" in Macmillan/McGraw-Hill *Spotlight on Music 1*, p. T354 and Silver Burdett *Making Music 2*, p. 388
- "Jolly Old St. Nicholas" in Silver Burdett *Making Music K*, p. T316; Macmillan/McGraw-Hill *Spotlight on Music 1*, p. 136; 4, p. 382
- "Joy to the World" in Silver Burdett *Making Music 3*, p. 22; Macmillan/McGraw-Hill *Spotlight on Music 1*, p. 383.
- "La Pinata" in Silver Burdett *Making Music 3, p. T399*
- "Little Drummer Boy" in Holt, *Rinehart and Winston Exploring Music 2*, p. 80
- "Merry Christm*as" in Spotlight on Music 6*, p. 410
- "Must Be Santa" in Silver Burdett *Making Music K*, p. 318; Macmillan/McGraw-Hill *Spotlight on Music K*, p. T316
- "Night of Stars/Silent Night" in Macmillan/McGraw-Hill *Spotlight on Music 6*, pp. T412–413
- "O Tannenbaum" (Oh, Christmas Tree) in Macmillan/McGraw-Hill *Spotlight on Music K*, p. T320
- "Rise Up Shepherd and Follow" in Silver Burdett Ginn *World of Music 5*, p. 238
- "Rockin' Around the Christmas Tree" in Silver Burdett *Making Music 5*, p. T466
- "Rudolph, the Red-Nosed Reindeer" in Silver Burdett Ginn *The Music Connection 3*, pp. 206–207; Silver Burdett *Making Music 1*, p. T428; Macmillan/McGraw-Hill *Spotlight on Music 1*, p. T354
- "Silent Night" in Silver Burdett *Making Music 3*, p. 394
- "Silver Bells" in Macmillan/McGraw-Hill *Share the Music 5*, pp. 348–349
- "Sleep Well, Little Children" in Silver Burdett Ginn *The Music Connection 3* (2000), p. 208
- "This Is Christmas Eve" in Spotlight on Music 2, p. 361
- "Twelve Days of Christmas" in Silver Burdett Making Music 4, p. 430
- "We Wish You a Merry Christmas" in Silver Burdett *Making Music 3*, p. 395; Macmillan/McGraw-Hill *Spotlight on Music 2*, p. T358

Kwanzaa

Kwanzaa is a holiday observed by many African Americans. It was created in 1966 by Dr. Maulana Karenga and is based on African harvest celebrations. Kwanzaa is a joyous occasion.

The word *Kwanzaa* means "first fruits" in the Swahili language, which is used in many parts of Africa. *Kwanzaa* has seven letters, signifying the seven principles of Kwanzaa: unity, self-determination, collective work and responsibility, cooperative economics, purpose, creativity, and faith. The celebration lasts from December 26 to January 1 and is similar to the Jewish celebration of Hanukkah, which lasts eight days but varies as to the day it starts.

Each evening a candle is lit and one of the seven principles is discussed. The candleholder is called the *kinara.* On the last day, there is feasting and dancing called the *karamu.*

The following song, suitable for grades 4–6, "Lift Every Voice and Sing," is frequently sung during Kwanzaa.

"Lift Every Voice and Sing"

Integrative areas: Cultural heritage
Social studies—history

Grades: 4–6

Concepts: Rhythm: ♫♩ ♩. ♩. ♩ ♪

Melody: 𝄐

Tonality: key of G

Lift Every Voice and Sing

Key: G
Starting pitch: F
Meter: 6/8 in duple (two groups of 3s), begins on 4 (if counting six counts to a measure) or on 2 (if in duple)

Music by Rosamond Johnson
Words by James Weldon Johnson

G
B
E
Am
B
C
Fac - ing the ris - ing sun of our new day be - gun,
G
D7
G
Let us march on till vic - to - ry is won.

From Macmillan/McGraw-Hill. *Share the Music 2* (2003), p. 331. Written as a poem in 1899 by James Weldon Johnson and set to music by his brother, John Rosamond Johnson, in 1900.

SUGGESTIONS FOR LESSONS

1. Discuss the meaning of Kwanzaa and why it is a celebration.
2. Discuss why we have an African celebration in America.
3. Have students select percussion instruments such as those found in Africa—drums, rattles, and bells—and create an ostinato that will go with the song.
4. Write the form of the song on a transparency or writing board: A B C C' (minor mode) B.
5. Sing the two B sections (lines 3 and 4, lines 7 and 8).
6. Sing or play the two C sections, one being slightly different.
7. Sing the first two lines, noticing the similarity of rhythms.
8. Sing the entire song through.
9. Discuss the meaning of the song. Why do students think this is called the African American national anthem?
10. What can students do to be American yet still value the African culture?
11. Have students identify a person in the African American community who they think embodies the spirit of Kwanzaa. Invite this person to share his or her experiences and goals with the class.

More Songs: Kwanzaa

- "Habari Gani" in Silver Burdett *Making Music 3,* p. T404
- "Happy Kwanzaa" in Silver Burdet *Making Music 5,* p. 476
- "Harambee" in Silver Burdett Ginn *The Music Connection 3,* p. 229; Silver Burdett *Making Music 4,* p. T434
- "The Joy of Kwanzaa" in Silver Burdett *Making Music 6,* p. T462
- "Kwanzaa Carol" in Silver Burdett *Making Music 2,* p. T392
- "Together in Unity" in Silver Burdett *Making Music K,* p. T320
- "Ujamaa" in Macmillan/McGraw-Hill *Spotlight on Music 3,* p. T380
- "Ujima" in Macmillan/McGraw-Hill *Spotlight on Music 5,* p. T427

New Year's Day

The Western New Year begins on January 1 with traditional festivities taking place on New Year's Eve. The Scots brought a tradition with them to the New World with the singing of "Auld Lang Syne."

"Auld Lang Syne"

Integrative areas: Cultural heritage
Social studies—history

Grades: 2-6

Concepts: Rhythm: ♩. ♪ ♩ ♩
Tonality: key of F
Form: AB

Auld Lang Syne
Scottish Air
Words by Robert Burns
Key: F
Starting pitch: C
Meter: 4/4, begins on 4
C F C7
1. Should auld ac - quain - tance be for - got, And
2. And here's a hand, my trust - y frien', And
F B♭ F
nev - er brought to mind? Should auld ac - quain - tance
gie's a hand o' thine; We'll tak' a cup o'
C7 B♭ C F
be for - got, And days of auld lang syne?
kind - ness yet, For auld lang syne.
Refrain
B♭ F C B♭ F B♭
For auld lang syne, my dear, For auld lang syne;
F C B♭ C7 F
We'll tak' a cup o' kind - ness yet, For auld lang syne.

SUGGESTIONS FOR LESSONS

1. Discuss the Scottish accent and its differences with regard to American usage. Example: *gie's* means "give us," *o* means "of," *auld* means "old," and so on.
2. Draw or show a map of Scotland.
3. Invite some natives of Scotland to come to class and share with students both their language and their experiences of childhood.

4. Ask students which measures are the same.
5. Teach students to sing the song.

Martin Luther King Jr. Day

"We Shall Overcome"

Integrative areas: Social studies—history, social problems, nonviolent protest

Grades: 3–6

Concepts: Melody: mostly steps, legato, repetition
Form: AB

We Shall Overcome

Civil Rights Song

Key: C
Starting pitch: G
Meter: 4/4, begins on 1

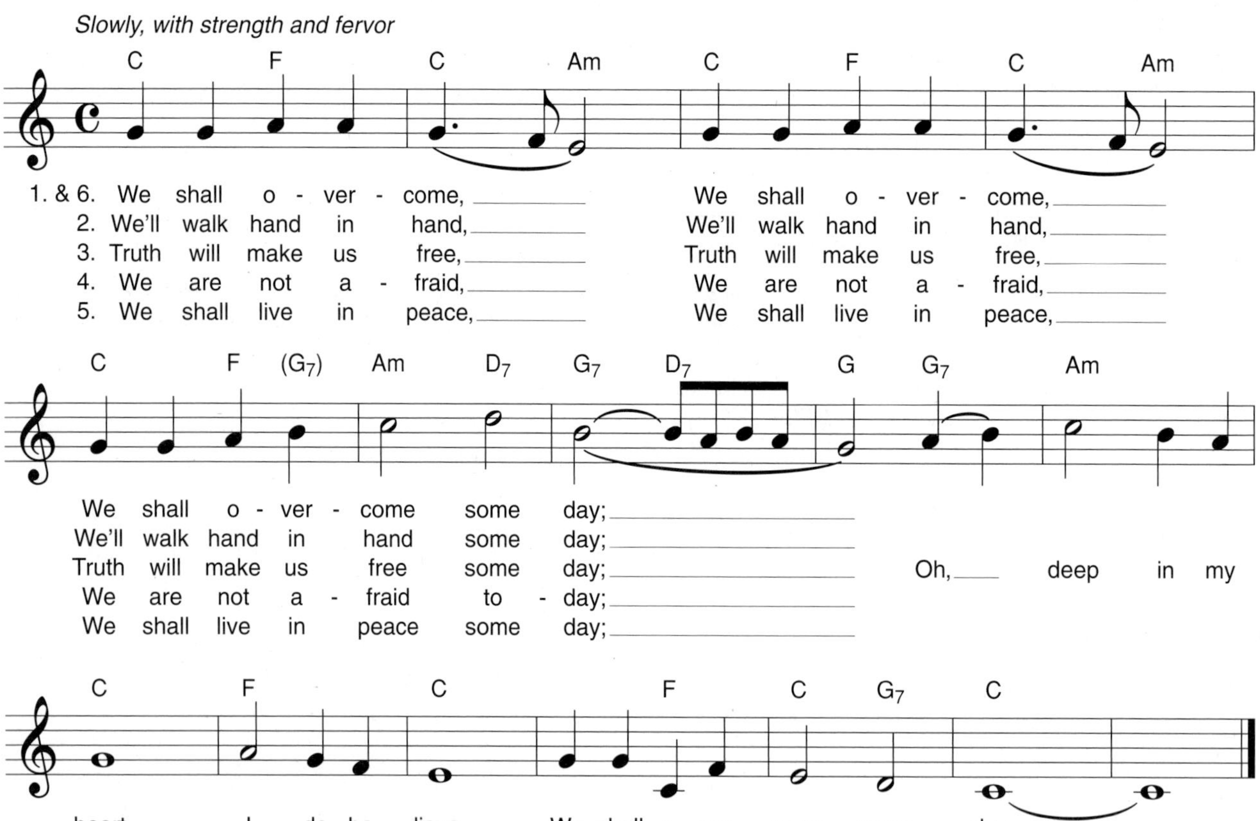

Slowly, with strength and fervor
C F C Am C F C Am
1. & 6. We shall o - ver - come, We shall o - ver - come,
2. We'll walk hand in hand, We'll walk hand in hand,
3. Truth will make us free, Truth will make us free,
4. We are not a - fraid, We are not a - fraid,
5. We shall live in peace, We shall live in peace,
C F (G7) Am D7 G7 D7 G G7 Am
We shall o - ver - come some day;
We'll walk hand in hand some day;
Truth will make us free some day;
We are not a - fraid to - day;
We shall live in peace some day;
Oh, deep in my
C F C F C G7 C
heart, I do be - lieve We shall o - ver - come some day.

Musical and Lyrical adaptation by Zilphia Horton, Frank Hamilton, Guy Carawan and Pete Seeger. Inspired by African American Gospel Singing, members of the Food & Tobacco Workers Union, Charleston, SC, and the southern Civil Rights Movement.

SUGGESTIONS FOR LESSONS

1. Review the events leading to the emergence of Dr. Martin Luther King Jr. as a civil rights leader. Look up information on, quotes from, and pictures of Martin Luther King Jr. on the Internet.
2. Read descriptions of the famous gathering at the Lincoln Memorial in 1963, and have students study the speech "I Have a Dream" given by Dr. King at this event (see www.usconstitution.net/dream.html).
3. Discuss the appropriateness of the setting—the Lincoln Memorial. Show pictures of this well-known national monument.

4. Play a recording of Dr. King delivering this speech ("I Have a Dream," www.youtube.com). Discuss with students the melodic flow of his vocal delivery and its roots in the gospel music of the African American church.
5. Dramatize the gathering of people from all over the United States and appoint a student to read the speech as the rest of the class hums and then sings "We Shall Overcome."

"Martin Luther King"

Integrative areas: Social studies–justice, history, protest, leadership

Grades: 2–4

Concepts: Rhythm: steady beat, 4/4 meter, repeated patterns

Melody: mostly steps, range within an octave

Form: ABCA

Martin Luther King

Key: D major
Starting pitch: D

Words and Music by Theresa Fulbright

Meter: 4/4, begins on "and" of 3

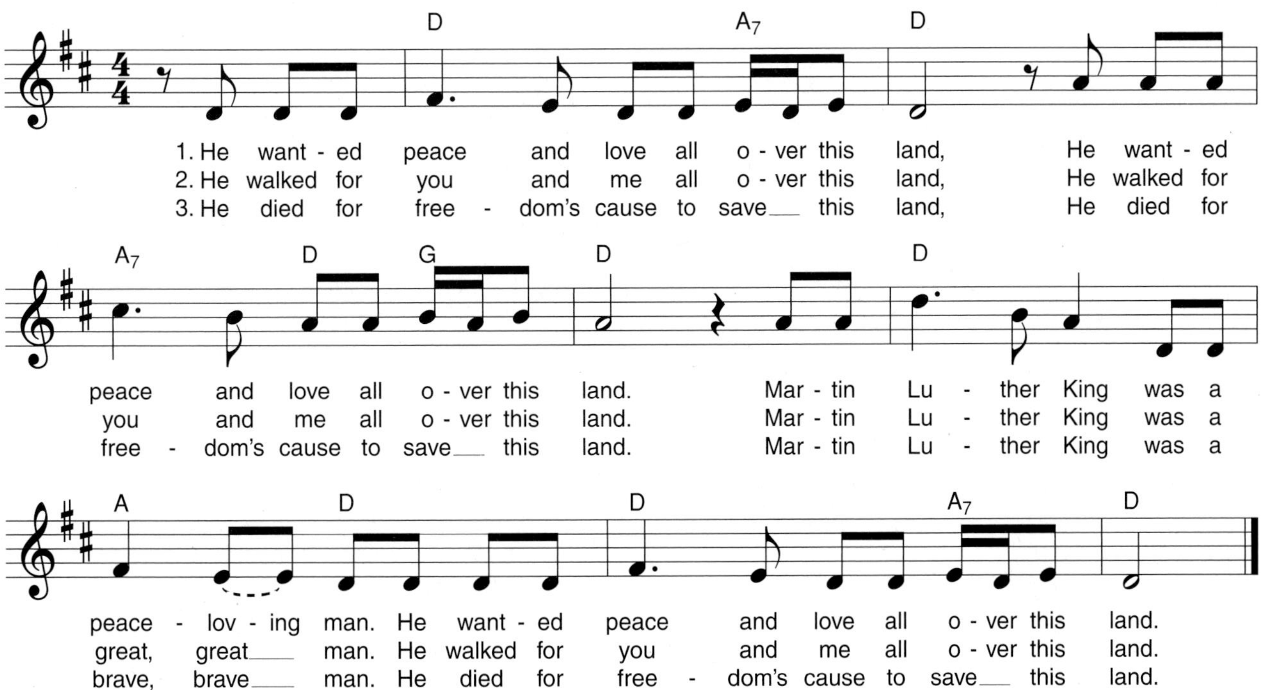

Words and Music by Theresa Fulbright. Macmillan Publishing Company's "Music and You", K, P. 258.

SUGGESTIONS FOR LESSONS

1. Ask students to discover the repeated words and rhythms as they view the song from a transparency or their books.
2. Discuss the meanings of such words as *peace, love,* and *freedom.* Place these words on cards.
3. Show pictures of Dr. Martin Luther King Jr. Discuss his role as a leader for freedom.

Special Learner Note

This song can be adapted as a way to learn about classmates after the initial verse about Dr. Martin Luther King Jr. Students' names and facts about them–interests, talents, and hobbies–may be added by students or by peers. This encourages socialization and enhances self-esteem and self-confidence.

4. Use green, yellow, and red strips of paper to diagram the song. Discuss the significance of these colors to African American culture.

Chinese New Year

The Chinese New Year occurs later than the Western celebration—it is in January or February. Each year of the Chinese calendar is named for an animal, such as a dog, rabbit, rat, or dragon. The Chinese calendar is 4,600 years old—the second-oldest known calendar. The Chinese New Year is a long holiday that ends with the Lantern Festival, which occurs with the first full moon of the New Year.

Sing the following two songs, which are representative of the Chinese New Year.

"Co A Tin"

Integrative areas: Cultural heritage
Social studies–history

Grades: 1–3

Concepts: Rhythm: quadruple: 

Taiwanese Folk Song
English version by
Macmillan/McGraw-Hill

Co A Tin

Starting pitch: A
Meter: 4/4, begins on 1

English: Lan - tern bright, lan - tern bright,
Taiwanese pronounciation: go a tin go a tin
(goh ah tĭn goh a tĭn

Light the way, my lan - tern bright.
aai ge iai gya go a tin
ah-ee gey e-aye gyah goh a tĭn)

From Macmillan/McGraw-Hill, *Share the Music 2* (2003), p. 331.

"Chinese New Year"

Integrative areas: Cultural heritage
Social studies–history

Grades: 1–3

Concepts: Rhythm: 
Melody: pentatonic (C, D, E, G, A)
Form: ABAC

Chinese New Year
Words and Music by Low Siew Poh
Starting pitch: C
Meter: 6/8, begins on 1
Chi - nese New Year is here a - gain,
Here a - gain, here a - gain,
Chi - nese New Year is here a - gain,
Let us all re - joice.

SUGGESTIONS FOR LESSONS

1. Use bells and drums for accompaniment.
2. Ask students to play the last two measures of line 4 as an interlude between verses.
3. Note that although the song is written in 6/8 meter, it is in duple with three eighth notes to a single beat.
4. Discuss the use of fireworks and parades in Chinese culture.
5. Create a dragon and have a parade. Children may sing or use recorded Chinese music.
6. If your school has a large and diverse Asian population, explore the many songs and activities associated with the variety of New Year celebrations.

Valentine's Day

"Somebody Loves Me"

Integrative areas: Friendship
Visual art

Grades: K–2

Concepts: Rhythm: syncopation, repetition, duple meter, rests (percussion only)
Melody: repetition, range

Somebody Loves Me

Key: C
Starting pitch: C
Meter: 4/4, begins on 1

Words and Music by Gaynor Jones

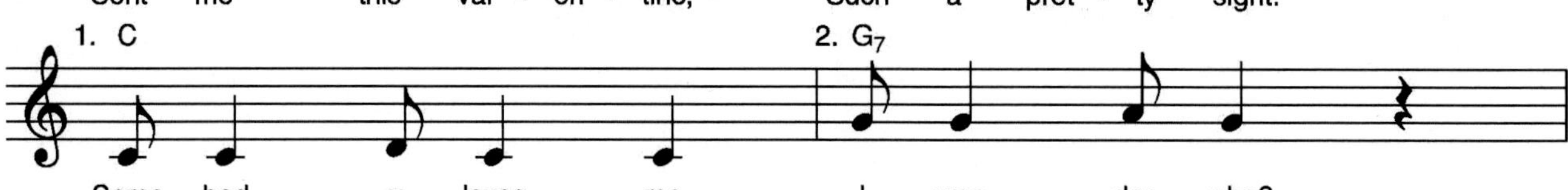

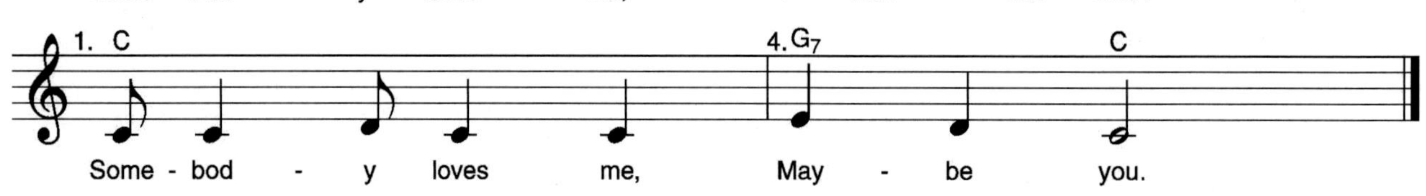

Recorded by Gaynor Jones Lowe.

Alto glockenspiel

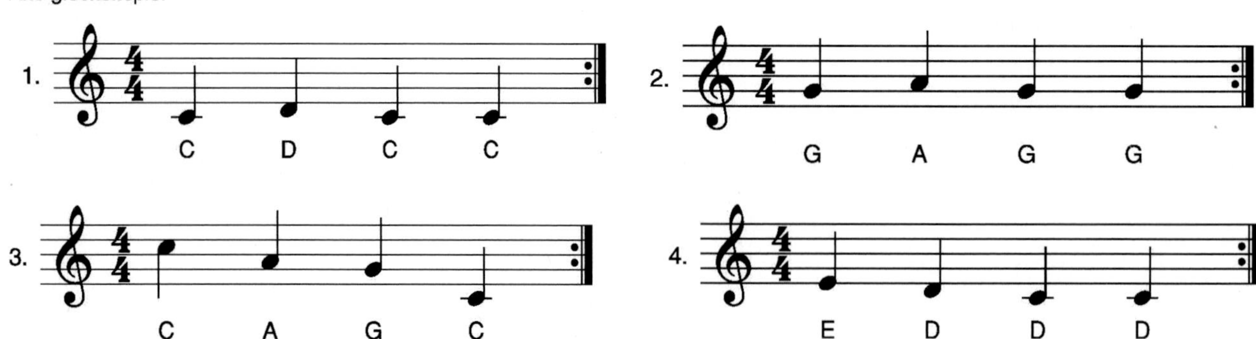

Percussion: drum or shaking instrument

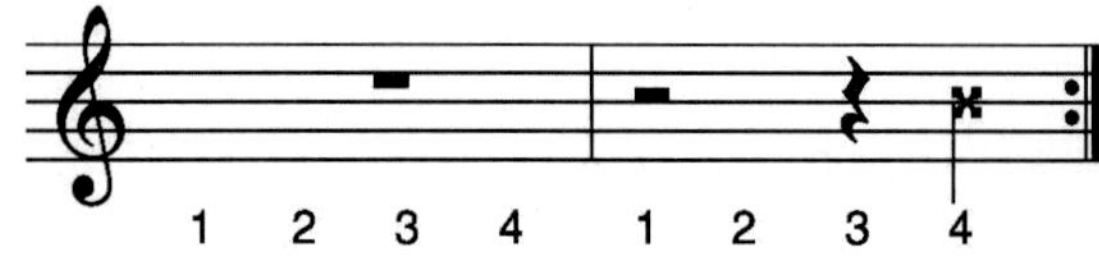

SUGGESTIONS FOR LESSONS

1. Read one of the many stories about the origin of Valentine's Day: Saint Valentine was a Roman priest who made friends with children. The Romans imprisoned him when he refused to worship their gods. Children missed their friend and tossed loving notes between the bars of his cell window. In 496 A.D. Pope Gelasius named February 14 Saint Valentine's Day, and the custom of sending messages of love and friendship spread throughout Europe and America.
2. Make valentines in art class to give to parents and friends.
3. Create short rhymes in language arts that focus on love and friendship.

More Songs: Valentine's Day

- "Be My Valentine" in Silver Burdett *Music 2,* p. 148
- "Best Friends" in Silver Burdett Ginn *World of Music 2,* p. 182
- "I Made a Valentine" in *Spotlight on Music K,* p. T333
- "Mail Myself to You" in Macmillan/McGraw-Hill *Share the Music 1,* p. T304
- "Making Valentines" in Silver Burdett *Making Music 1,* p. T437
- "My Valentine" in Silver Burdett *Making Music K,* p. 323
- "This-a Way and That-a Way" in Macmillan/McGraw-Hill *Spotlight on Music 3,* p. T386
- "Valentines" in Silver Burdett *Making Music 2,* 398
- "Valentine, Valentine" in Holt, Rinehart and Winston *Music Book 2,* p. 152
- "Viva Valentine" in Macmillan/McGraw-Hill *Spotlight on Music 1,* p. T365
- "You and Me" in Silver Burdett Ginn *World of Music 2,* p. 186
- "You Are My Sunshine" in Macmillan/McGraw-Hill *Spotlight on Music 1,* p. T369
- "When You Send a Valentine" in Macmillan/McGraw-Hill *Spotlight on Music K,* p. T332

Presidents' Day: George Washington

"Columbia, the Gem of the Ocean"

Integrative areas: Social studies–history, government, freedom/independence
Language arts–vocabulary
Visual art
Listening

Grades: 4–6

Concepts: Rhythm: 4/4 meter, repeated patterns:
Melody: octave skips, accidentals, descending scale melody

Columbia, the Gem of the Ocean
United States
Key: F
Starting pitch: C
Meter: 4/4, begins on 4
F C7 F B♭ F C7
O Co - lum - bia, the gem of the o - cean, The home of the brave and the free, The
G7 C G7 C
shrine of each pa - triot's de - vo - tion, A world of - fers hom - age to thee. Thy

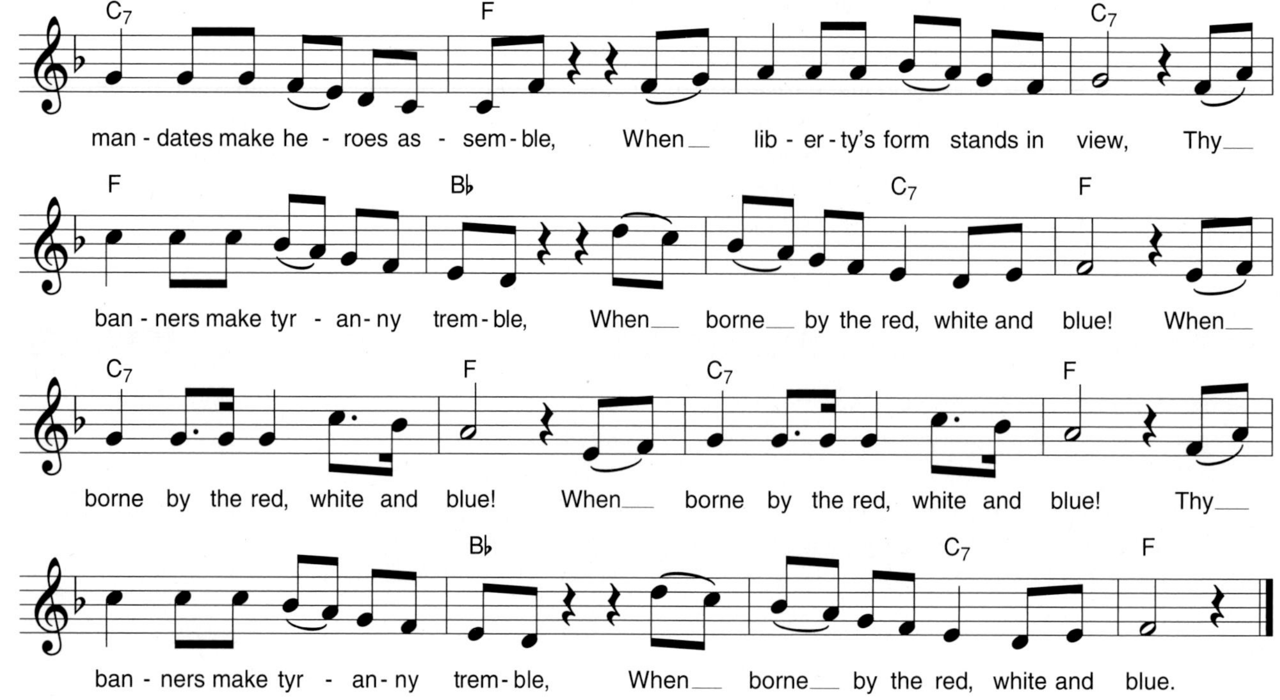
C7 F C7
man - dates make he - roes as - sem - ble, When__ lib - er - ty's form stands in view, Thy__
F B♭ C7 F
ban - ners make tyr - an - ny trem - ble, When__ borne__ by the red, white and blue! When__
C7 F C7 F
borne by the red, white and blue! When__ borne by the red, white and blue! Thy__
B♭ C7 F
ban - ners make tyr - an - ny trem - ble, When__ borne__ by the red, white and blue.

"Old Colony Times"

Integrative areas: Social studies—history, government, freedom/independence
Language arts—vocabulary
Visual art
Listening

Grades: 4–6

Concepts: Rhythm: fermata, duple meter

Melody: mostly steps, narrow range, repetition of phrases

Form: AB

Old Colony Times

American Song

Key: F
Starting pitch: C
Meter: 4/4, begins on 4

Allegro
f
F C7 F Gm C F
1. In__ good__ old Col - o - ny times__ When__ we__ were un - der the king,__ Three__
2. The__ first,__ he was a__ mil - ler, And the sec - ond,__ he was a weav - er, And the
3. Now the mil - ler,__ he stole__ corn,__ And the weav - er,__ he stole__ yarn,__ And the
4. The__ mil - ler got drown'd in his dam,__ The__ weav - er got hung in his yarn,__ And the

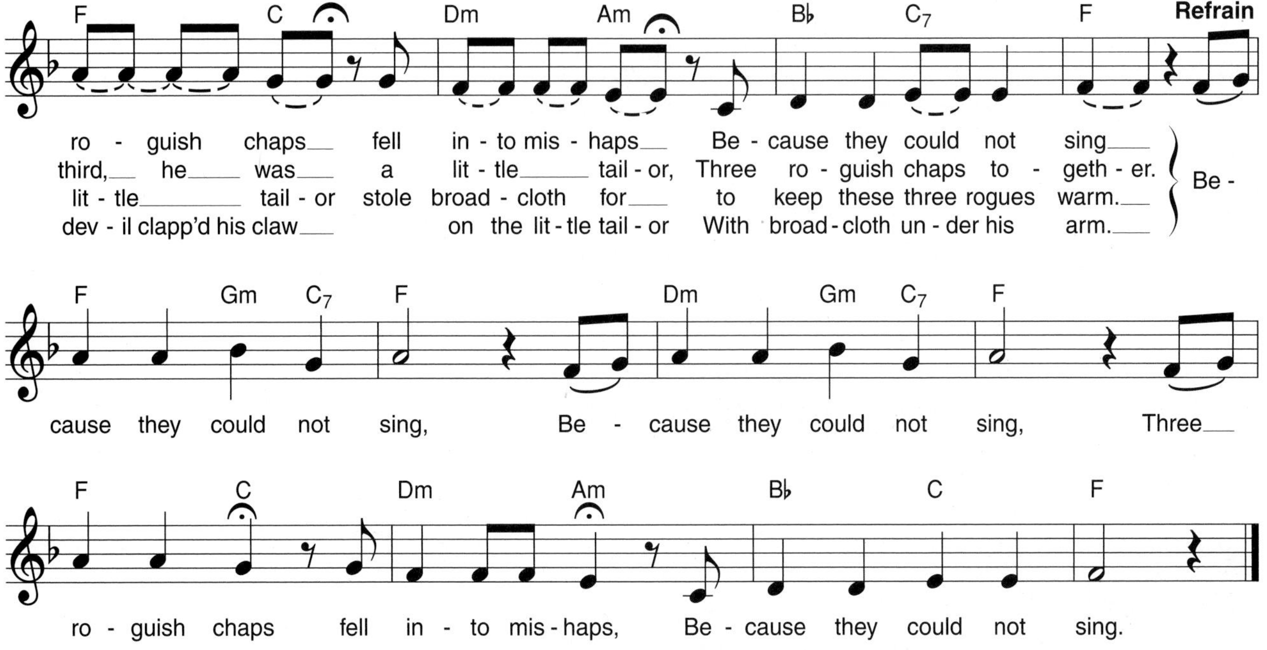
F C Dm Am B♭ C7 F
Refrain
ro - guish chaps fell in - to mis - haps Be - cause they could not sing
third, he was a lit - tle tail - or, Three ro - guish chaps to - geth - er.
lit - tle tail - or stole broad - cloth for to keep these three rogues warm.
dev - il clapp'd his claw on the lit - tle tail - or With broad - cloth un - der his arm.
Be -
F Gm C7 F Dm Gm C7 F
cause they could not sing, Be - cause they could not sing, Three
F C Dm Am B♭ C F
ro - guish chaps fell in - to mis - haps, Be - cause they could not sing.

SUGGESTIONS FOR LESSONS

1. Show pictures of Mount Vernon, home of George Washington. Explain that it is open to the public as a national monument.
2. Study the Revolutionary War period and the events that led to George Washington's election as the first president of the United States. Use the Internet to find information and pictures, such as Emanuel Gottlieb Leutze's *George Washington Crossing the Delaware*.
3. Show a picture of Horatio Greenough's sculpture *George Washington* (www.images.google.com). Note that the sculptor has portrayed him as a Roman statesman.
4. Read the words to "Columbia, the Gem of the Ocean." Discuss the meaning of such words as *Columbia, gem, shrine, patriot, homage, mandate,* and *tyranny.*
5. Discuss the relationship of the United States to England before the Revolutionary War. Dramatize the song "Old Colony Times."
6. Read stories about George Washington (available from www.amazon.com):
   - Ruth Ashby, *George & Martha Washington* (New York: Gareth Stevens Publishing, 2004).
   - Michael Burgan, *George Washington* (Mankato MN: Compass Point Books, 2002).
   - Rick Burke, *George Washington* (North Mankato, MN: Heinemann Library, 2003).
   - Sally Senzell Isaacs, *America in the Time of George Washington, 1747 to 1803* (North Mankato, MN : Heinemann Library, 1998).
7. Sing the section that has a fermata.
8. Note the repetition in the refrain.

Presidents' Day: Abraham Lincoln

"On Springfield Mountain"

Integrative areas: Social studies—history, geography, politics, Civil War
Poetry
Visual art

Grades: 4–6

Concepts: Rhythm: triple meter, rhythm patterns: ♩ ♩ ♫
Tempo: slow
Melody: melody centers around G and D (*do* and *sol*), many skips

On Springfield Mountain

American Folk Song

Key: G
Starting pitch: D
Meter: 3/4, begins on "and" of 2

G
D7
On Spring - field Moun - tain there did dwell A love - ly youth, I knew him

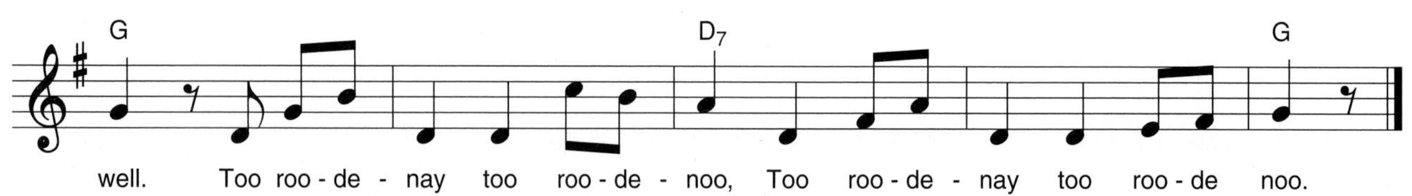

G
D7
G
well. Too roo - de - nay too roo - de - noo, Too roo - de - nay too roo - de noo.

"Battle Hymn of the Republic"

Integrative areas: Social studies—history, geography, politics, Civil War
Poetry
Visual art

Grades: 4–6

Concepts: Rhythm: duple meter, strong beat, repetition of rhythm patterns:
Melody: wide range, mostly steps, a few skips
Dynamics: loud
Form: AB

Battle Hymn of the Republic

Music by William Steffe
Words by Julia Ward Howe

Key: B♭
Starting pitch: F
Meter: 4/4, begins on 4

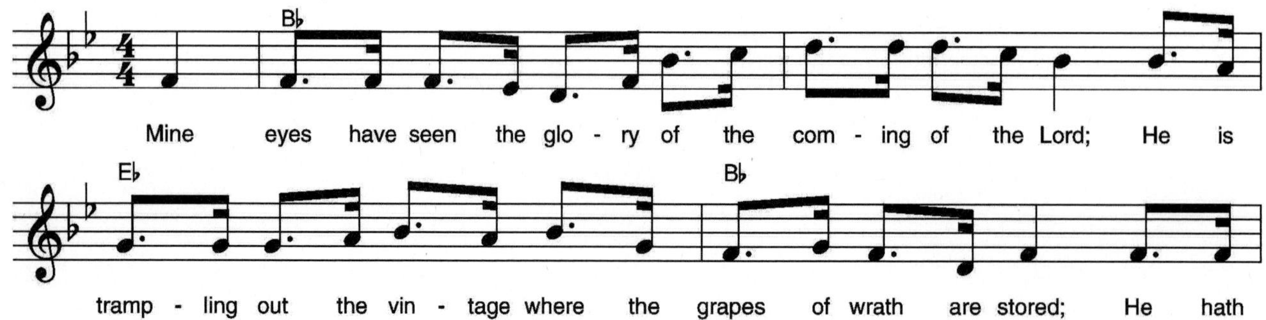

B♭
Mine eyes have seen the glo - ry of the com - ing of the Lord; He is
E♭
B♭
tramp - ling out the vin - tage where the grapes of wrath are stored; He hath

E♭
F7
B♭
loosed the fate - ful light - ning of His ter - ri - ble swift sword; His truth is march - ing on.
Chorus
E♭
B♭
Glo - ry, glo - ry hal - le - lu - jah! Glo - ry, glo - ry hal - le - lu - jah!
E♭
F7
B♭
Glo - ry, glo - ry hal - le - lu - jah! His truth is march - ing on.

SUGGESTIONS FOR LESSONS

1. Read the book *Abe Lincoln Grows Up* by Carl Sandburg.[1] Discuss how the writer portrays Abraham Lincoln as a boy and discuss the spirit and background of the man who became the sixteenth president of the United States.
2. Read the Gettysburg Address. Have students study the events that led to this occasion. Dramatize the event by asking a student to read the speech while the rest of the class sings "Battle Hymn of the Republic."
3. Show pictures of the Lincoln Memorial in Washington, D.C. Point out that this monument is modeled after the Parthenon in Athens, Greece. Discuss the power and stillness represented in the figure of Lincoln.
4. Download or stream and listen to *Lincoln Portrait* by Aaron Copland [iTunes/Spotify]. Identify the theme from "On Springfield Mountain." Sing the song in class.
5. Read stories about Abraham Lincoln:
   - Barbara Cary, *Meet Abraham Lincoln* (New York: Random House, 1994).
   - Russell Freedman, *Lincoln: A Photobiography* (New York: Clarion Books, 1987).
   - Carol Greene, *Abraham Lincoln: A President of a Divided Country* (Chicago: Children's Press, 1989).
   - Jim Hargrove, *Abraham Lincoln: The Freedom President* (New York: Ballantine, 1989).
   - Rebecca Stefoff, *Abraham Lincoln, 16th President of the United States* (Ada, OK: Garrett Educational Corporation, 1989).
6. Look up information on and pictures of Abraham Lincoln on the Internet.
7. Teach the song phrase by phrase.
8. Sing the song in its entirety.

Special Learner Note

Focus on major/macro beats for marching. Some students can sing the chorus while others sing the verse, creating a "two-part" presentation. Some students may be most successful learning just the chorus.

[1] New York: Harcourt Brace and Co., 1954 (available from www.amazon.com).

More Songs: Presidents' Day

- "Abraham Lincoln" in Silver Burdett Ginn *World of Music 4,* p. 119
- "George Washington" in Macmillan *Music and You K,* p. 156
- "George Washington" in Macmillan/McGraw-Hill *Share the Music K* (2003), p. T286; Macmillan/McGraw-Hill *Spotlight on Music 1,* p. T368
- "Out from the Wilderness" in Macmillan/McGraw-Hill *Spotlight on Music 3,* p. T388
- "Who Chopped the Cherry Tree Down" in Macmillan/McGraw-Hill *Spotlight on Music 2,* p. T371

INTEGRATIVE CATEGORY: LANGUAGE ARTS

"Old MacDonald Had a Farm"

Integrative areas: Linking sight and sound
Effect of accumulation in music and in poetry
Creativity
Word/phrase sequencing

Grades: K–2

Concepts: Rhythm: mostly half and quarter notes, repetition of patterns
Melody: short phrases, repetition of pitches, narrow range
Harmony: chords G, C, D_7

Old MacDonald Had a Farm

Key: G (Pentatonic)
Starting pitch: G
Meter: 4/4, begins on 1

United States

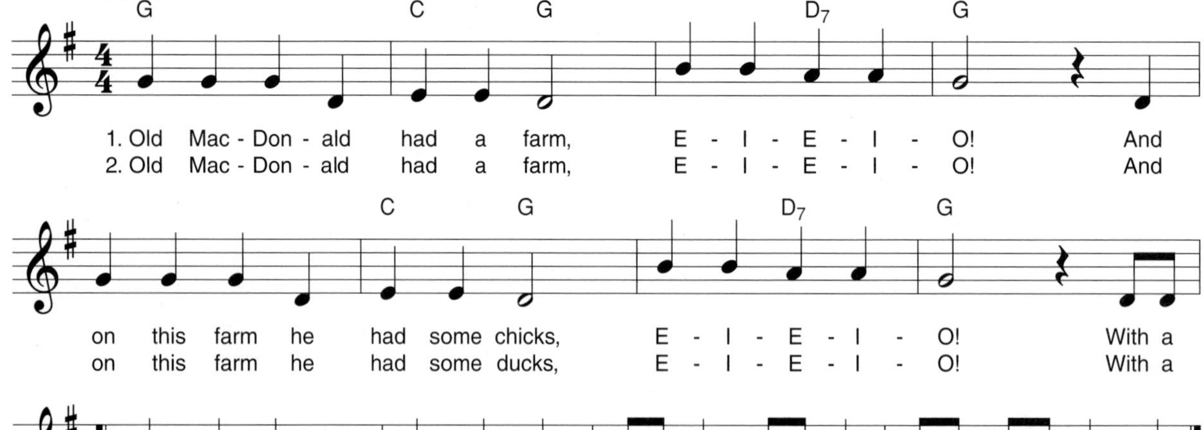

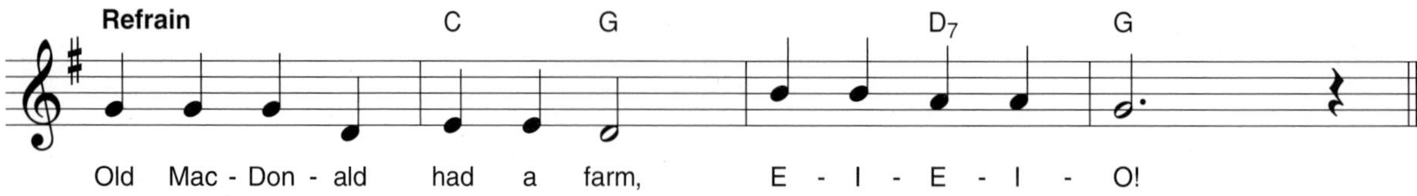

SUGGESTIONS FOR LESSONS

1. Have each child choose a particular animal or sound and remember where it is in the verse sequence.
2. Read poems that use the same type of sequencing, such as "The House That Jack Built" or "The Twelve Days of Christmas." Discuss the effect of such a technique. (It lengthens the poem or song, increases its complexity, and so on.)

More Songs: Language Arts

- "ABC Blues" in Silver Burdett *Making Music K,* p. T281
- "ABC Rock" in Silver Burdett *Making Music 1,* p. T262
- "Alphabet Song" in Macmillan/McGraw-Hill *Spotlight on Music K,* p. T54
- "America the Beautiful" in Silver Burdett *Making Music 4,* p. 158
- "Mister Frog Went A-Courtin' " in Silver Burdett Ginn *World of Music 2,* p. 18
- "Who Built the Ark?" in Silver Burdett Ginn *World of Music 2,* p. 52
- "Turn, Turn, Turn" in Silver Burdett Ginn *World of Music 5,* pp. 62–63

INTEGRATIVE CATEGORY: MATHEMATICS

"Five Green and Speckled Frogs"

Integrative areas: Nature
Numbers, number relationships

Grades: K–3

Concepts: Rhythm: duple meter, syncopation, repetition
Melody: direction of phrases

Five Green and Speckled Frogs

Words by Louise Binder Scott
Music by Virginia Pavelko

Key: C
Starting pitch: G
Meter: 4/4, begins on 1

C F

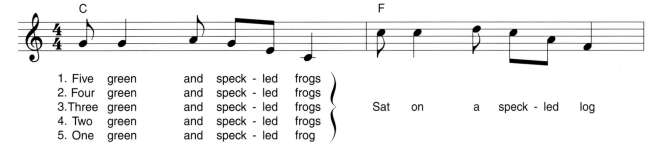

1. Five green and speck - led frogs
2. Four green and speck - led frogs
3. Three green and speck - led frogs
4. Two green and speck - led frogs
5. One green and speck - led frog

Sat on a speck - led log

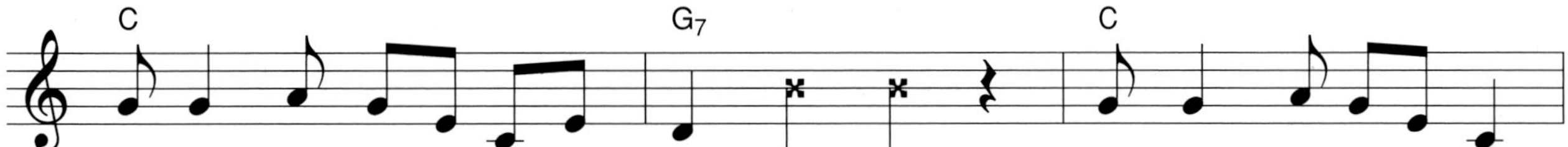

Eat - ing some most de - li - cious bugs. (Yum, yum!) 1.–4. One jumped in - to the pool,
5. He jumped in - to the pool,

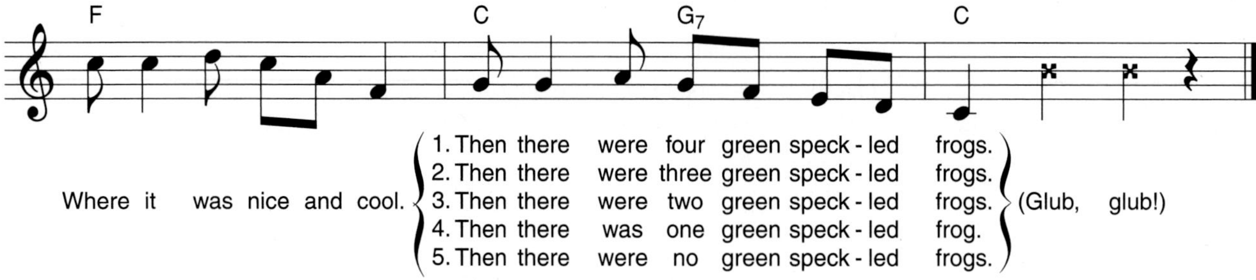
F
C
G7
C
Where it was nice and cool.
1. Then there were four green speck - led frogs.
2. Then there were three green speck - led frogs.
3. Then there were two green speck - led frogs.
4. Then there was one green speck - led frog.
5. Then there were no green speck - led frogs.
(Glub, glub!)

SUGGESTIONS FOR LESSONS

1. Dramatize the words of "Five Green and Speckled Frogs."
2. Chart repeating phrases with colors.
3. Map the direction of the melody.
4. Emphasize breath for octave skips.
5. Use fingers or charts showing *5, 4, 3, 2, 1* to indicate the number of frogs remaining.
6. Emphasize the subtraction of 1 from each set of frogs.

More Songs: Mathematics

- "The Ants Go Marching" in Silver Burdett *Making Music 1,* p. T250
- "Counting Song" in Macmillan *Music and You 1,* p. 213; Silver Burdett Ginn *World of Music 2,* p. 31; *Spotlight on Music K,* p. T92
- "How Many Miles to Babylon" in Silver Burdett *Making Music 2,* T128
- "One Potato, Two Potato" in Macmillan/McGraw-Hill *Spotlight on Music 3,* p. T267
- "Three Is a Magic Number" in Macmillan/McGraw-Hill *Spotlight on Music 3,* p. T296
- "The Twelve Days of Christmas" in Macmillan *Music and You 5,* p. 266; Silver Burdett *Making Music 4,* p. T430
- "Un, Deux, Trois" (One, Two, Three) in Silver Burdett *Making Music 2,* T198

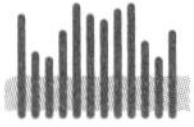

INTEGRATIVE CATEGORY: SCIENCE

"Follow the Drinkin' Gourd"

Integrative areas: Astronomy
Civil War (Underground Railroad)

Grades: 4–6

Concepts: Rhythm: duple meter, syncopation, triplets
Melody: repetition of phrases, narrow range
Form: AB

Follow the Drinkin' Gourd

Spiritual
Arranged by Paul Campbell

Key: E minor
Starting pitch: E
Meter: 2/2, begins on "and" of 2

Em
1. When the sun comes back and the first quail calls,
2. Now the river bank'll make a mighty good road; The
3. Now the riv - er ends be - tween two hills;
G Em
Fol - low the Drink - in' Gourd. Then the Old Man is a wait - in' for to
dead trees - 'll show you the way. And the left foot, peg - foot,
Fol - low the Drink - in' Gourd. And there's an - oth - er riv - er on the
3 Bm 3 Em
car - ry you to free - dom, Fol - low the Drink - in' Gourd.
trav - el - in' on, Just you fol - low the Drink - in' Gourd.
oth - er side, Just you fol - low the Drink - in' Gourd.
Refrain
Em Em
Fol - low the Drink - in' Gourd, Fol - low the Drink - in' Gourd, For the
G Am Em B Em Bm Em
Old Man is a wait - in' for to car - ry you to free - dom, Fol - low the Drink - in' Gourd.

SUGGESTIONS FOR LESSONS

1. Study the origins and locations of selected constellations in the galaxy, such as the Big Dipper and Orion.
2. Visit a local planetarium to learn more about astronomy.
3. Create charts showing some of the most common constellations and stories about them. Discover at what seasons of the year they are most readily visible.
4. Download and project pictures of the planets (www.images.google.com). Have the students look for the planets in the night sky. Listen to musical selections from Gustav Holst's *The Planets : Mars and Jupiter* [iTunes/Spotify]. Also listen/view performances of the planets found at www.youtube.com (e.g. "Mars Rover to Mars Holst the Planets").
5. Use a compass to demonstrate the magnetic pull to the north. Show students the location of the North Star and the Big Dipper. Discuss ways that a traveler could find his or her way home without a compass.

6. Have students read stories about the Civil War and the Underground Railroad. Be certain that they do not confuse this with a bona fide train. Explain that the North Star and the Big Dipper showed slaves the way to freedom.
7. Place the words on a chart. Have students read the words to each verse of the song. Explain what each means.
8. Listen to a recording of (or sing) "Follow the Drinkin' Gourd." Have students read the words as they listen.
9. Teach the song, starting with the chorus, followed by the verses. Pay particular attention to the repetition of the syncopated rhythmic pattern.
10. Sing the entire song through.

More Songs: Science

- "Apple Tree" in Silver Burdett *Making Music 1,* p. T228
- "Big Beautiful Planet" in Macmillan/McGraw-Hill *Spotlight on Music 2,* p. T376
- "Dry Bones" in Silver Burdett *Making Music 4,* p. T162
- "Frog Music" in Silver Burdett *Making Music 4,* p. T200
- "Here Is the Beehive" in Macmillan/McGraw-Hill *Spotlight on Music K,* p. T258
- "If a Tiger Calls" in Silver Burdett *Making Music 3,* p. T354
- "I Love the Mountains" in Silver Burdett *Making Music 5,* p. T35
- "It's Raining, It's Pouring" in Macmillan/McGraw-Hill *Spotlight on Music 2,* p. T233
- Just One Planet" in Macmillan/McGraw-Hill *Spotlight on Music 4,* p. T164
- "Never Smile at a Crocodile" in Silver Burdett *Making Music 3,* p. T100
- "Oh, Watch the Stars" in Silver Burdett *Making Music 2,* p. T144
- "The Planets Chant" in Silver Burdett *Making Music 4,* p. T376
- "Rabbit Footprints" in Silver Burdett *Making Music 3,* p. 304
- "The Rainbow" in Silver Burdett *Making Music 2,* p. 332
- "The Rainbow Connection" in Macmillan/McGraw-Hill *Spotlight on Music 3,* p. T310
- "The Rainbow Song" in Macmillan/McGraw-Hill *Spotlight on Music K,* p. T61
- "Rain, Rain" in Silver Burdett *Making Music 1,* p. T54
- "Shoo, Fly" in Silver Burdett *Making Music 2,* p. T200
- "Singin' in the Rain" in Silver Burdett *Making Music 4,* p. T372
- "Snowflakes" in Silver Burdett *Making Music 1,* p. T422
- "The Snowman" in Macmillan/McGraw-Hill *Spotlight on Music K,* p. T313
- "Twinkle, Twinkle, Little Star" in Macmillan/McGraw-Hill *Spotlight on Music K,* p. T90
- "The Wheel of the Water" in Silver Burdett *Making Music 4,* p. T362
- "Whirlwind" in Silver Burdett *Making Music 3,* p. T148

More Songs: Seasons

Spring

- "April Showers" in Silver Burdett Ginn *World of Music 6,* p. 251
- "At the Spring" in Silver Burdett Ginn *The Music Connection 4,* p. 86
- "Cherry Blossoms" in *Spotlight on Music 6,* p. 14
- "El Mes de Abril" in Silver Burdett *Making Music 3,* p. T328
- "Haru ga kita" in Silver Burdett *Making Music 2,* T401
- "Hop! Chirp! Moo! Oh, Happy Springtime Day!" in Macmillan/McGraw-Hill *Spotlight on Music 1,* p. T372
- "If All the Raindrops" in Silver Burdett Ginn *The Music Connection 2,* p. 75
- "May Day Carol" in Macmillan/McGraw-Hill *Spotlight on Music 3,* p. T393
- "Rain Song" in Silver Burdett Ginn *The Music Connection 4* (2000), p. 40
- "Sakura" in Silver Burdett *Making Music 4,* p. T308; Macmillan/McGraw-Hill *Spotlight on Music 6,* p. T14
- "Spring" in Macmillan/McGraw-Hill *Spotlight on Music 1,* p. T273
- "Spring Has Come" in Spotlight 3, p. 392
- "Springtime" in Macmillan/McGraw-Hill *Share the Music 2,* p. 340
- "Springtime Has Come" in Silver Burdett Ginn *the Music Connection 2,* p. 9; also Silver Burdett *Making Music 2,* p. 401

Summer

- "In the Good Old Summertime" in Macmillan/ McGraw-Hill *Share the Music 3* (2003), p. 351
- "Take Me Out to the Ballgame" in Macmillan/ McGraw-Hill *Share the Music 2,* p. 160; Silver Burdett Ginn *The Music Connection 3,* pp. 22–23

Fall

- "Autumn Leaves" in Macmillan/McGraw-Hill *Share the Music K,* p. T260; Macmillan/McGraw-Hill *Spotlight on Music 1,* p. T331
- "Autumn Leaves Now Are Falling" in Holt, Rinehart and Winston *Exploring Music 1,* p. 40
- "In the Pumpkin Patch" in Silver Burdett *Making Music 3,* p. T380
- "Gather 'Round" in Macmillan/McGraw-Hill *Share the Music 3,* p. 314

Winter

- "December Nights, December Lights" in Macmillan/ McGraw-Hill *Spotlight on Music 4,* p. T372
- "Frosty the Snowman" in Silver Burdett *Making Music 2,* p. T391; Macmillan/McGraw-Hill *Spotlight on Music 3,* p. T366
- "Jingle Bells" in Silver Burdett *Making Music 2,* p. T388
- "Let It Snow! Let It Snow! Let It Snow!" in Silver Burdett *Making Music 4,* pp. T426–427
- "Let's Play in the Snow" in Macmillan/McGraw-Hill *Share the Music 1,* p. T281
- "Mitten Song" in Macmillan/McGraw-Hill *Share the Music K* (2003), p. T275
- "North Winds Blow" in Macmillan/McGraw-Hill *Share the Music 1,* p. T280
- "Snowflakes" in Silver Burdett *Making Music 1,* p. T422
- "The Snowman" in Macmillan/McGraw-Hill *Spotlight on Music K,* p. T313
- "Winter Fantasy" in Silver Burdett Ginn *The Music Connection 4,* pp. 212–213
- "Winter Wonderland" in Silver Burdett Ginn *The Music Connection 3,* p. 202

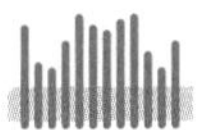

INTEGRATIVE CATEGORY: TRANSPORTATION

"Erie Canal"

Integrative areas: History, geography, visual art, poetry, vocabulary, science

Grades: 4–6

Concepts: Rhythm: duple meter, syncopation, repetition of patterns

Melody: repetition of phrases, many skips

Tonality: minor/major

Form: AB

Erie Canal
United States
Key: D minor, chorus in F major
Starting pitch: A
Meter: 2/2, begins on "and" of 2
I've got a mule, her name is Sal, Fif-teen miles on the E-rie Ca-nal. She's a
good old work-er and a good old pal, Fif-teen miles on the E-rie Ca-nal. We've
hauled some barg-es in our day. Filled with lum-ber coal and hay, And
we know ev-'ry inch of the way From Al-ban-y to Buf-fa-lo.
Chorus
Low bridge, ev-'ry-bo-dy down, Low bridge, 'cause we're
com-ing to a town; And you'll al-ways know your neigh-bor, You'll
al-ways know your pal, If you've ev-er nav-i-gat-ed on the E-rie Ca-nal.

SUGGESTIONS FOR LESSONS

1. Present the following background on the Erie Canal: The Erie Canal, authorized in 1817 and completed in 1825, connected Lake Erie (Buffalo) and the Hudson River (Albany). A 363-mile waterway, it was of immense significance in the development of commerce in the United States. This cheap, all-water route provided transportation for agricultural produce from the West to the East and manufactured products from the East to the West. The canal teemed with boats and barges as pioneers swarmed to find new lands. Songs of the muleskinners who drove the mules along the towpath as they hauled the flat-bottom boats echoed through the countryside both day and night. Because low bridges occurred at frequent intervals along the canal, the muleskinners

would shout a warning to the passengers on the boat so that they could duck. This song is about a muleskinner and his mule, Sal. It tells of the produce carried and the friendliness of the passengers.

2. Study the canal as a means of transportation. Use encyclopedias and the Internet as resources. Locate Albany and Buffalo on a map of New York and determine how long the canal was. Find Lake Erie and place it in relation to the other Great Lakes. When was the Erie Canal considered part of the "new" West? (1825) Discover when other cities in this area (Cleveland, Cincinnati, and Columbus) were founded. What was the Western Reserve? Have students learn about other canals, such as the Panama Canal, the Canal at Corinth (Greece), and the Suez Canal.
3. Use the dictionary to explore the meanings of such words as "barge," "muleskinner," and "navigation."
4. Listen to the two parts of the song: Part A is in the minor mode, and part B is in a major mode. Part B is also called the *chorus.*

Teach the song, starting with the chorus (part B). Note the repetition of the rhythm ♪. ♬, then teach the verses.

"I've Been Working on the Railroad (Dinah)"

Integrative areas: History, geography, social change, passenger/shipping, visual art, poetry

Grades: 2–5

Concepts: Rhythm: duple meter, steady beat, repetition patterns:

♪. ♬ ♪. ♬ 𝅗𝅥

♫ ♫ ♫ ♩ | 𝅗𝅥 𝅗𝅥

Melody: short phrases, repetition of phrases

Tonality: major

Form: AB

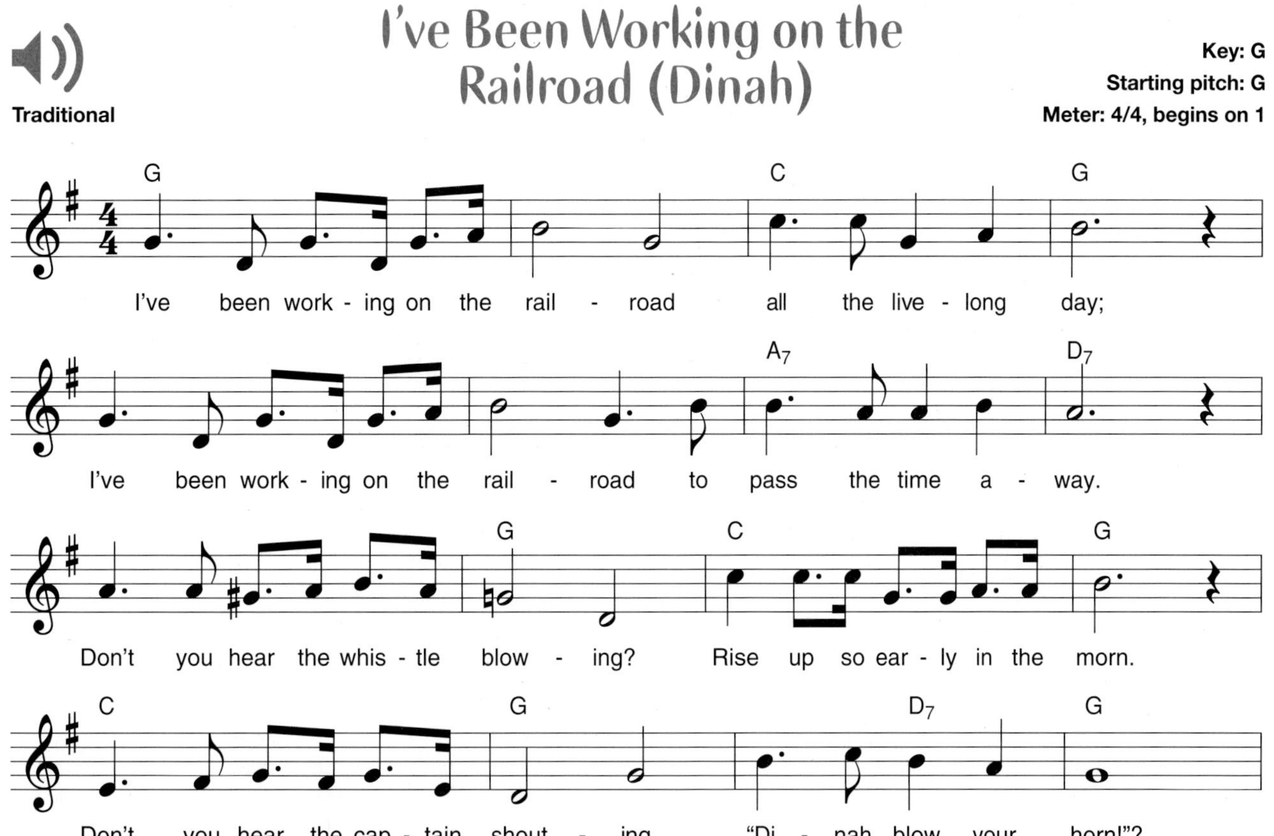
Traditional
I've Been Working on the Railroad (Dinah)
Key: G
Starting pitch: G
Meter: 4/4, begins on 1
G C G
I've been work - ing on the rail - road all the live - long day;
A7 D7
I've been work - ing on the rail - road to pass the time a - way.
G C G
Don't you hear the whis - tle blow - ing? Rise up so ear - ly in the morn.
C G D7 G
Don't you hear the cap - tain shout - ing, "Di - nah, blow your horn!"?

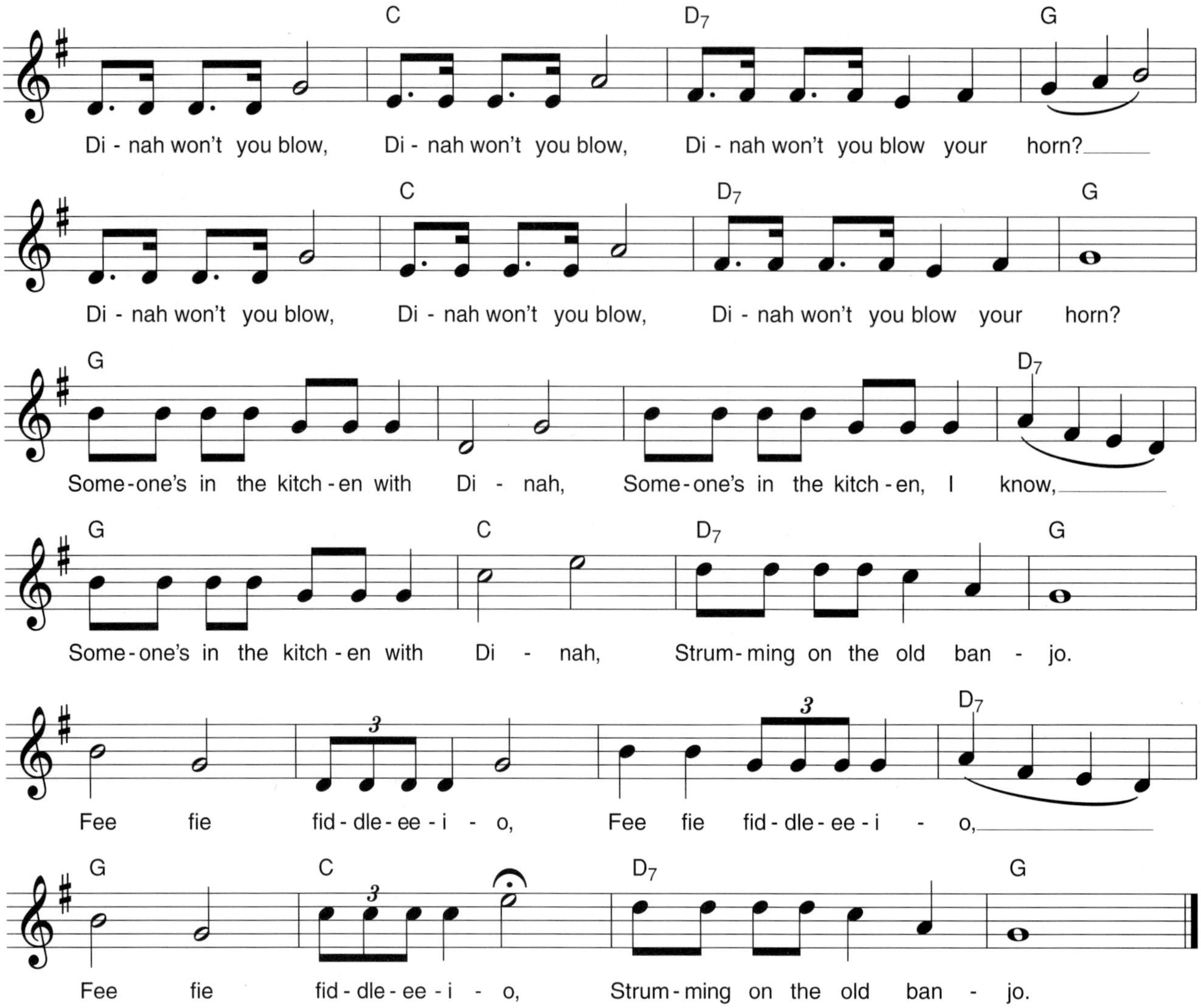

C D7 G
Di - nah won't you blow, Di - nah won't you blow, Di - nah won't you blow your horn?
C D7 G
Di - nah won't you blow, Di - nah won't you blow, Di - nah won't you blow your horn?
G D7
Some-one's in the kitch - en with Di - nah, Some-one's in the kitch - en, I know,
G C D7 G
Some-one's in the kitch - en with Di - nah, Strum-ming on the old ban - jo.
3 3 D7
Fee fie fid - dle - ee - i - o, Fee fie fid - dle - ee - i - o,
G C 3 D7 G
Fee fie fid - dle - ee - i - o, Strum-ming on the old ban - jo.

"Casey Jones"

Integrative areas: Trains, history

Grades: 4–6

Concepts: Rhythm: duple, steady beat, repetition of rhythm patterns, syncopation

Melody: repetition of phrases, range from B♭ to D

Form: verse and refrain, AB

Casey Jones

Words by T. Lawrence Seibert
Music by Eddie Newton

Key: B♭
Starting pitch: B♭
Meter: 4/4, begins on 1

B♭
1. Come, all you round - ers, if you want to hear A
2. Put in your wa - ter and shov - el your coal. Put your
3. Ca - sey pulled up at Re - no hill. He

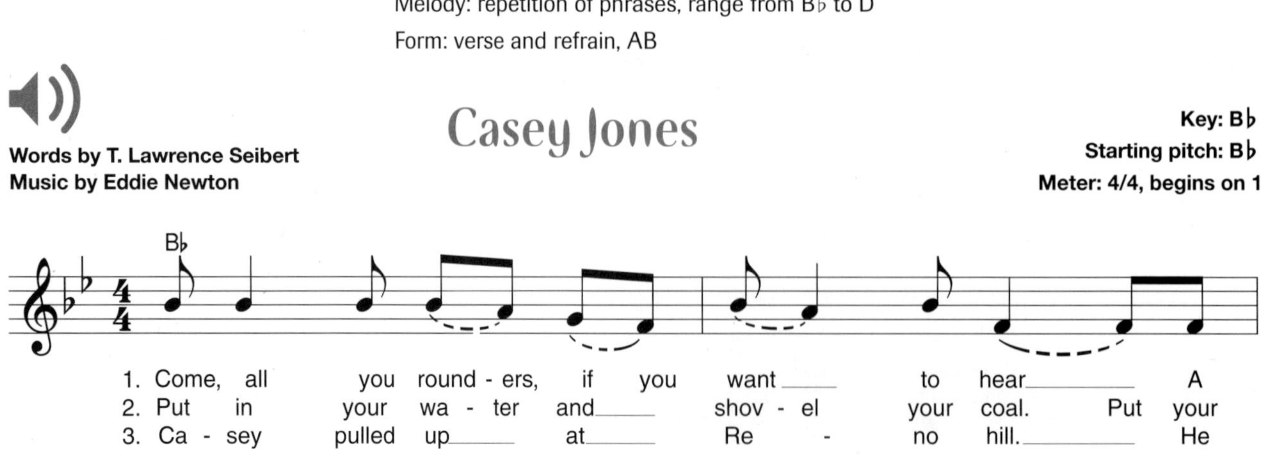

B♭ E♭ F B♭
sto - ry a - bout a brave en - gi - neer, And Ca - sey Jones was the
head out the win - dow, watch them driv - ers roll. I'll run her till she
toot - ed for the cross - ing with an aw - ful shrill. The switch - man knew by the
B♭ F7 B♭
round - er's name. On a six - eight wheel - er, boys, he won his fame. The
leaves the rail, 'Cause I'm eight hours late with the west - ern mail. He
en - gine's moans That the man at the throt - tle was Ca - sey Jones. He
B♭
call - er called Ca - sey at a half past four. Ca - sey
looked at his watch, and his watch was slow. He
pulled up with - in two miles of the place, And
B♭ E♭ F B♭
kissed his wife at the sta - tion door. He mount - ed to the cab - in with his
looked at the wa - ter, and the wa - ter was low. He turned to the fire - man, and
Num - ber Four stared him in the face. He turned to the fire - man, said,
B♭ F7 B♭
or - ders in his hand, And he took his fare - well trip to the Prom - ised Land.
then he said, "We're goin' to reach Fris - co, but we'll all be dead."
"Boy, you bet - ter jump, 'Cause there's two lo - co - mo - tives that's a - go - in' to bump."
Refrain
B♭ E♭
Ca - sey Jones mount - ed to the cab - in Ca - sey Jones, with his
Ca - sey Jones, Goin' to reach Fris - co. Ca - sey Jones, But we'll
Ca - sey Jones, Two lo - co - mo - tives, Ca - sey Jones, That's a -

B♭
F7
B♭
E♭
or - ders in his hand.
all___ be___ dead.
go - in' to bump,"
Ca - sey Jones___
Ca - sey Jones,___
Ca - sey Jones,___
Mount - ed to the cab - in, And he
Goin' to reach___ Fris - co, We're___
"Two___ lo - co - mo - tives that's a -
B♭
E♭
B♭
F
B♭
took his fare - well trip___ to the Prom - ised Land.
goin' to reach___ Fris - co, but we'll all___ be dead.
two___ lo - co - mo - tives that's a - go - in' to bump."

SUGGESTIONS FOR LESSONS

1. Review what is known about the character Casey Jones. He was known for the speed at which he could make a train travel and for the wonderful sound he could get out of the train whistle. Some stories tell us that the people who worked in the fields near the railroad tracks could tell when Casey was at the throttle by the sound of the whistle.
2. Review the difference between a diesel and a locomotive. Show pictures of each.
3. Discuss the meaning of a *ballad* (story song) and read the words of the song as a story.
4. Teach the syncopated patterns by playing and singing the rhythm patterns.
5. Use colored charts for repeating phrases.
6. Create an overlay for the overhead projector that shows the repeated melodic phrases in "Casey Jones."

7. Dramatize the story as students sing the song.
8. Invite students to bring in toy trains (steam locomotives, diesels). Discuss how train travel has changed over the past one hundred years.
9. View pictures of trains and train travel (www.images.google.com).
   - Claude Monet, *The Saint-Lazare Railroad Station*
   - Currier and Ives, *The "Lightning Express" Trains*[2]
10. Listen to musical compositions about trains—for example, Villa-Lobos, "Little Train of the Caipira" (available on the CD accompanying Macmillan/McGraw-Hill *Spotlight on Music K*, 2005); Honegger, "Pacific 231"; and Miller, "Chattanooga Choo-Choo" and "Orange Blossom Special."
11. Read the poem "Song of the Train" by David McCord (see www.google.com).

[2] Museum of New York, *100 Currier and Ives Favorites* (New York: Crown Publishers, 1978), p. 57.

More Songs: Transportation

Ships

- "A-Rovin'" in Macmillan/McGraw-Hill *Spotlight on Music 6,* p. 319
- "Away for Rio" in Macmillan/McGraw-Hill *Spotlight on Music 2,* p. 170
- "Bound for Southern Australia" in Silver Burdett *Making Music 5,* p. 22
- "Cape Cod Chantey" in Macmillan *Music and You 5,* p. 251; Silver Burdett Ginn *World of Music 4,* p. 29
- "Columbus Sailed with Three Ships" in *Spotlight on Music 2,* p. 344
- "Gallant Ship" in Holt, Rinehart and Winston *Exploring Music K,* p. 129
- "I Saw Three Ships" in *Spotlight on Music 2,* p. 359
- "Sail Away" in Silver Burdett *Making Music 5,* p. 404
- "Sailboat in the Sky" in Silver Burdett Ginn *The Music Connection 3* (2000), p. 176; Silver Burdett *Making Music 4,* p. 374
- "Sailing the Sea" in Silver Burdett *Music 1,* p. 98
- "Sailor, Sailor on the Sea" in Macmillan/McGraw-Hill *Spotlight on Music 2,* p. 262
- "Ship Ahoy" in Macmillan/McGraw-Hill *Spotlight on Music 3,* p. 314

Trains

- "Engine, Engine No. 9" in *Spotlight on Music 2,* p. 13
- "How Long the Train Been Gone" in *Spotlight on Music 4,* p. 264
- "I've Been Working on the Railroad" in Silver Burdett *Music 3,* p. 242
- "Orange Blossom Special" in *Spotlight on Music 6,* p. 32
- "O, The Train's Off the Track" in Macmillan/McGraw-Hill *Spotlight on Music 3,* p. T176
- "Paddy Works on the Railway" in Silver Burdett Ginn *The Music Connection 4,* p. 118
- "Page's Train" in *Spotlight on Music 4,* p. 246
- "Pat Works on the Railway" in Macmillan/McGraw-Hill *Spotlight on Music 4,* p. T86
- "Ride the Train" in Macmillan/McGraw-Hill *Spotlight on Music K,* p. T144
- "Rock Island Line" in Silver Burdett Ginn *The Music Connection 4,* p. 140
- "Same Train" in Silver Burdett *Making Music 2,* p. 164
- "This Train" in Silver Burdett *Making Music 5,* p. 27
- "The Train" in Silver Burdett *Making Music 2,* p. 260; Macmillan/McGraw-Hill *Spotlight on Music 2,* p. T326
- "Train Comes" in Macmillan/McGraw-Hill *Spotlight on Music K,* p. T152
- "Train is a Comin'" in Silver Burdett *Making Music 3,* p. 48
- "Wabash Cannonball" in Silver Burdett Ginn *World of Music 5,* pp. 14–15; Silver Burdett *Making Music 5,* p. 136; Macmillan/McGraw-Hill *Spotlight on Music 6,* p. T30
- "When the Train Comes Along" in Silver Burdett *Making Music 1,* p. T300

Airplanes

- "I'm Flying Home" in Silver Burdett Ginn *The Music Connection 2,* pp. 120–121

Automobiles

- "The Bus" in Macmillan/McGraw-Hill *Spotlight on Music K,* p. T137
- "Car Song" in Macmillan/McGraw-Hill *Share the Music K* (2003), p. T142; Silver Burdett *Music 1,* p. 34; Silver Burdett Ginn *World of Music 1,* p. 16
- "I Have a Car" in Macmillan/McGraw-Hill *Spotlight on Music 3,* p. T252
- "Let's Go Driving" in Macmillan/McGraw-Hill *Spotlight on Music 1,* p. T52
- "Little Blue Truck" in Macmillan/McGraw-Hill *Share the Music K,* p. T146; Macmillan/McGraw-Hill *Spotlight on Music K,* p. T136

PLANNING AND PRESENTING A PROGRAM

Purpose

A common expectation of classroom teachers is that they will plan and present programs that integrate many different classroom activities such as music, visual art, language arts, history, geography, and physical education. Of course, cognitive learning takes place during the preparation of such a program, but social learning also occurs. For example, students develop responsibility, exercise creativity, exert leadership, and work together. Careful planning by both teacher and students is essential. A primary purpose of such an activity is for students to share with parents, relatives, and friends in the community what they have learned.

Planning

The entire class should be involved in the selection of the overall theme so that many activities and ideas can be related to it in meaningful ways. After students have selected a theme, they should begin gathering resource materials for the program. These should include songs, pictures, poems, essays, ideas for dramatic presentation, and so on. As with all such activities, the opening number of the program should be performed especially well and enthusiastically; each subsequent event must be selected with emphasis on variety and interest; and the conclusion should be an upbeat activity that leaves the audience excited about the program and what the students are learning. The following sample programs are for a fifth-grade class, with resources included for each.

Rehearsals

Rehearsals must occur with enough care and frequency that *nothing* is left to chance. For a 30-minute program, fifth-grade students would need a minimum of six weeks' preparation (twice a week), with a few more props and special effects added each week. Because this is an integrated program, all students should be involved in the planning and performance, with each student contributing his or her best musical talent and skill.

Committees

Students should organize the following committees in the classroom:

1. Program committee
    a. Songs and accompaniments
    b. Instruments needed
    c. Welcome, poems, essays, "connecting" statements, closing
    d. Dramatics
    e. Order of events
2. Classroom decorations committee
    a. Put up decorations
    b. Take down decorations
3. Refreshments committee
4. Table decorations committee
5. Costumes committee
6. Audio/DVD/Video–recording committee

Additional Ideas for Festivals or Programs

- The Olympics (features song "The Power of a Dream" from Atlanta; movement: clasping hands and swaying)
- Humor in Music
- From Sea to Shining Sea
- America's Songbag
- The World through Music
- Celebrations
- Seasons
- Transportation
- Style in Music
- Immigrants (Past and Present)

"America the Beautiful"
Introduction: Words of Welcome
Thanksgiving Poem:

Now Thank We All Our God
Now thank we all our God
With hearts and hands and voices,
Who wondrous things has done,
In whom his world rejoices
Who, from our mothers' arms
Has blest us on our way
With countless gifts of love,
And still is ours today.
O may this bounteous God
Through all our life be near us,
With ever joyful hearts
And blessed peace to cheer us,
And keep us in his grace,
And guide us when perplexed,
And free us from all harm
In this world and the next.

(Rinkhart, tr. Winkworth)

Introduction to Rondo
Trumpet Concerto in E-flat Major, Rondo .... Wolfgang A. Mozart
Movement interpretation: ABACA

Introduction to Theme-and-Variation
Variations on "Simple Gifts" from *Appalachian Spring* .... Aaron Copland
Puppet interpretation

"Tinga Layo" (p. 82)
Ostinato accompaniment: claves, bongo drums, maracas

Thanksgiving Poem: Psalm 150
Praise Ye the Lord

Praise ye the Lord.
Praise God in his sanctuary;
Praise him in the firmament of his power.
Praise him for his mighty acts;
Praise him according to his excellent greatness.
Praise him with the sound of the trumpets;
Praise him with the psaltery and harp.

Praise him with the timbrel and dance;
Praise him with stringed instruments and organs.

Praise him upon the loud cymbals;
Praise him upon the high sounding cymbals.

Let every thing that hath breath
Praise the Lord.

Praise ye the Lord.

Over the River and Through the Wood (p. 392) (Guitar and/or Piano accompaniment)

Closing: Words of Thanks and Appreciation

Program II: Liberty

"The Yankee Doodle Boy"
Introduction: Words of Welcome
Short essay: The Meaning of Freedom

How can we define liberty? What is freedom? For people of the United States more than 200 years ago, it meant discussing how the thirteen American colonies could obtain liberty and freedom from Great Britain. Virginia's Patrick Henry stated emphatically, "Give me liberty or give me death," and another Virginian, Thomas Jefferson, penned the words of a Declaration of Independence signed on July 4, 1776:

> When in the Course of human events it becomes necessary for one people to dissolve the political bonds which have connected them with another and to assume among the powers of the earth, the separate and equal station to which the Laws of Nature and of Nature's God entitle them, a decent respect to the opinions of mankind requires that they should declare the causes which impel them to the separation.
>
> We hold these truths to be self-evident, that all men are created equal, that they are endowed by their Creator with certain unalienable Rights, that among these are Life, Liberty and the pursuit of Happiness . . . .

Ralph Waldo Emerson, an American poet, expressed the spirit of freedom when he wrote the Concord Hymn, first sung at the completion of the Battle Monument at Concord, Massachusetts, on July 4, 1837.

Concord Hymn
By the rude bridge that arched the flood,
Their flag to April's breeze unfurled,
Here once the embattled farmers stood,
And fired the shot heard round the world.

The foe long since in silence slept;
Alike the conqueror silent sleeps,
And Time the ruined bridge has swept,
Down the dark stream which seaward creeps.

On this great bank, by this soft stream,
We set today a votive stone;
That memory may their deed redeem,
When, like our sires, our sons are gone.

Spirit, that made those heroes dare
To die, and leave their children free,
Bid Time and Nature gently spare
The shaft we raise to them and thee.

Ralph Waldo Emerson

Yankee Doodle Boy
Words and Music by
George M. Cohan
Key: G
Starting pitch: B
Meter: 2/4, begins on 1
G A7
I'm a Yan - kee Doo - dle Dan - dy,
D7 G
A Yan - kee Doo - dle do, or die;
E7 Am E7 Am
A real live neph - ew of my Un - cle Sam,
A7 D7
Born on the Fourth of Ju - ly.
G A7
I've got a Yan - kee Doo - dle sweet - heart,
D7 G
She's my Yan - kee Doo - dle joy.
G D7 G
Yan - kee Doo - dle came to Lon - don, just to ride the po - nies,
A7 D7 G
I am the Yan - kee Doo - dle Boy.

Introduction to "There Are Many Flags"

The United States was founded on freedom from oppression—a nation composed of people from all cultures and religious beliefs who come together as Americans.

Tableau: four or five students with flags of several nations

There Are Many Flags
Traditional
Words by Mary H. Howliston
Key: A♭
Starting pitch: C
Meter: 4/4, begins on 3
Guitar: A♭
There are man - y flags in man - y lands,
There are flags of ev - 'ry hue;
But there is no flag, how - ev - er grand,
Like our own Red, White, and Blue.
Refrain
Then hur - rah for the flag, our coun - try's flag,
Its stripes and its white stars too,
For there is no flag in an - y land
Like our own Red, White, and Blue.

Words and Music by
George M. Cohan
You're a Grand Old Flag
Key: F
Starting pitch: C
Meter: 2/4, begins on 2
F C7 F
You're a grand old flag, you're a high - fly - ing flag;
F C7
And for - ev - er in peace may you wave;
C7 F
You're the em - blem of the land I love,
G7 C7
The home of the free and the brave.
F F
Ev - 'ry heart beats true un - der red, white, and blue,
D7 Gm C7
Where there's nev - er a boast or brag;
F C7
But should auld ac - quaint - ance be for - got,
B♭ C7 F
Keep your eye on the grand old flag.

Introduction to Revolutionary America
"Yankee Doodle" (p. 364)
Ostinato accompaniment: guitar, drums, rhythm sticks
Tableau: three minutemen

Introduction to War of 1812
"The Star-Spangled Banner" (p. 47)
Tableau: Francis Scott Key writing song

Introduction to Civil War
"Dixie"
Accompaniment: harmonica, guitar
Theme-and-Variation: *American Salute,* Morton Gould Movement interpretation

Introduction to World War I
"Over There"
Accompaniment: snare drum, bass drum; movement interpretation

Introduction to World War II
"Marine's Hymn"
Accompaniment: snare drum, bass drum
Tableau: raising of flag at Iwo Jima

Introduction to a Fanfare
Fanfare for the Common Man, Aaron Copland
Listening guide of tone colors: emphasis on brass and percussion

Introduction to Gettysburg Address
A Lincoln Portrait (III), Aaron Copland
Tableau: Lincoln giving speech at Gettysburg; people listening
"Battle Hymn of the Republic" (p. 414)
Audience is invited to join in singing the chorus

Finale: "You're a Grand Old Flag"
Introduction

There are many symbols of a country; ours is the American flag. It stands for everything that is special about being an American. "The Star-Spangled Banner" is played and the American flag is raised whenever an American wins a gold, silver, or bronze medal in the Olympics.

The American flag is composed of red and white stripes (representing the original thirteen states) and white stars on a field of blue (representing the fifty states that make up our country today). The American flag is presented to American families when a loved one is killed in battle, and we show our respect for the flag by taking off our hat or facing the flag when it goes by in a parade. In the United States, we honor the American flag on June 14, known as Flag Day.

Entire class sings song and joins in choreographed march

Closing: Words of Appreciation and Thanks

Introduction: Words of Welcome
Short essay: The Meaning of a Fiesta

The song "The First of January" (Uno de Enero) is a folk song from Mexico. It features counting from one to seven in Spanish: uno, dos, tres, cuatro, cinco, seis, siete. On the seventh of July, people of Spanish origin sing this song, which celebrates the fiesta in honor of the Spanish Saint Fermin. We will sing it in Spanish and then in English. Hand claps, tambourines, and triangles as well as chording instruments (keyboard, guitar or Q-chord) provide the accompaniment.

Hand claps:
Tambourines:
Triangle:

6
8

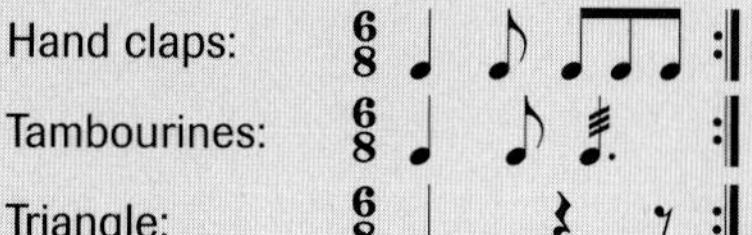

The First of January (Uno de Enero)

Folk Song from Mexico

Key: C
Starting pitch: G
Meter: 6/8, begins on 4

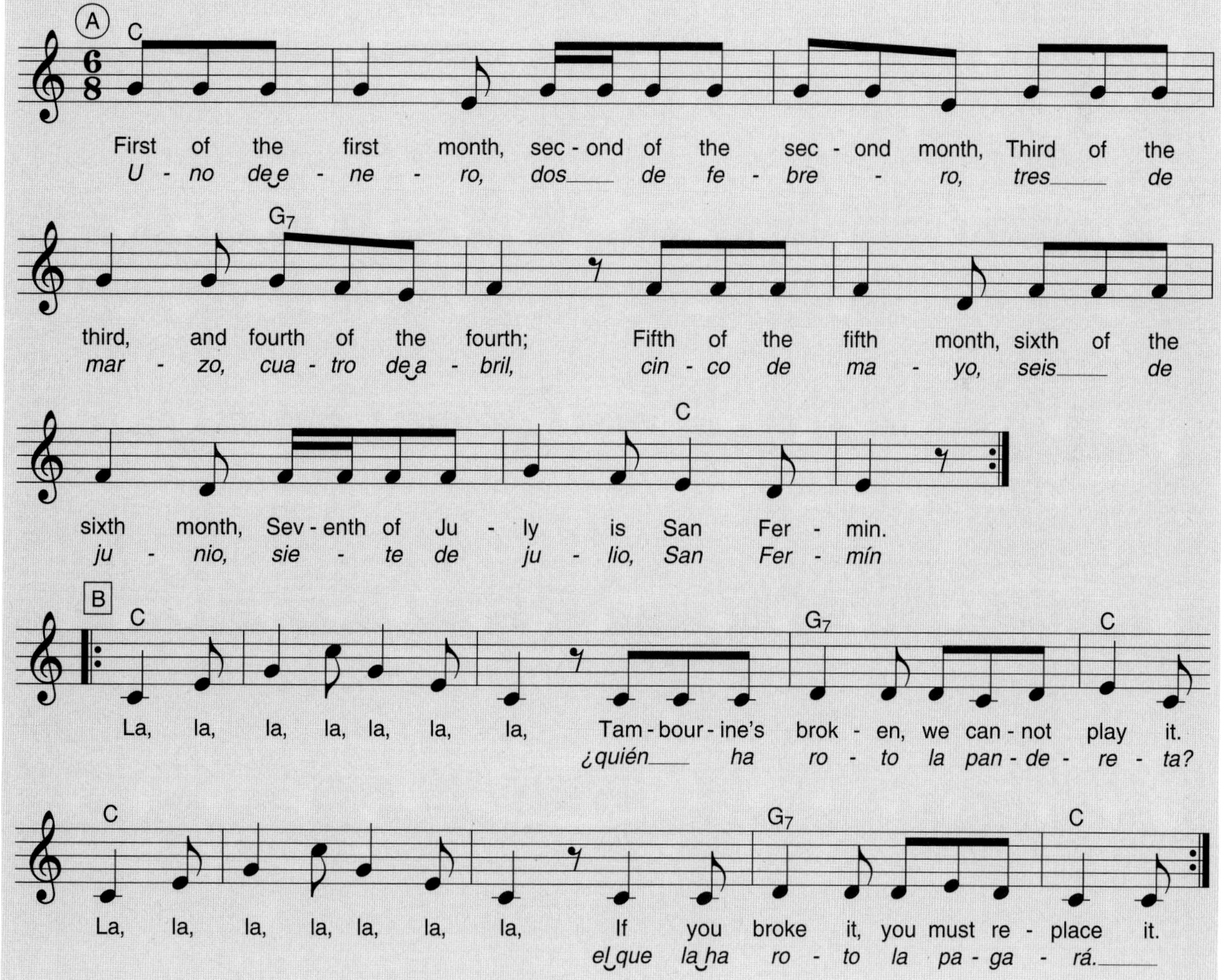

A
C
First of the first month, sec - ond of the sec - ond month, Third of the
U - no de e - ne - ro, dos de fe - bre - ro, tres de
G7
third, and fourth of the fourth; Fifth of the fifth month, sixth of the
mar - zo, cua - tro de a - bril, cin - co de ma - yo, seis de
C
sixth month, Sev - enth of Ju - ly is San Fer - min.
ju - nio, sie - te de ju - lio, San Fer - mín
B
C
G7
C
La, la, la, la, la, la, la, Tam - bour - ine's brok - en, we can - not play it.
¿quién ha ro - to la pan - de - re - ta?
C
G7
C
La, la, la, la, la, la, la, If you broke it, you must re - place it.
el que la ha ro - to la pa - ga - rá.

"La Raspa" (p. 326)

Song and dance

Dramatics: a short play with hand puppets or stick puppets featuring an aspect of Mexican life

De Colores

Traditional
English Words by Alice Pirgau

Key: C
Starting pitch: G
Meter: 3/4, begins on 1

C G7 C
When___ the mead-ows,___ when the mead-ows burst forth in the
De___ co - lo - res,___ De co - lo - res se vis - ten los

C G7
cool dew - y col - ors of spring-time;___
cam - pos en la pri - ma - ve - ra,___

G7
When___ the swal-lows,___ when the swal-lows come wing - ing in
De___ co - lo - res,___ De co - lo - res son los pa - ja -

G7 C
clouds of bright col - ors from far - off,___
ri - tos que vie - nen de‿a - fue - ra,___

C G7 C
When___ the rain - bow,___ when the rain - bow spreads rib - bons of
De___ co - lo - res,___ De co - lo - res es el ar - co

C7 F F
col - or all o - ver the sky:___ Then I know why the
i - ris que ve - mos lu - cir,___ y por e - so las

F C G7
splen - dors of true love are great and their col - ors, the
gran - des a - mo - res de mu - chas co - lo - res me

A traditional folk song that has been circulated throughout American since the 16th Century.

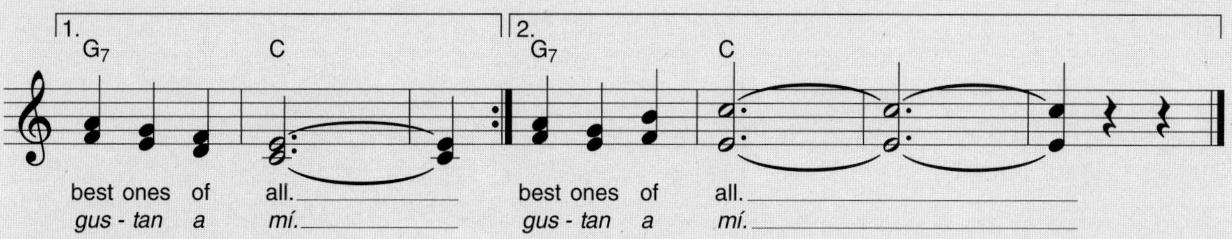
1.
G7
C
2.
G7
C
best ones of all.
gus - tan a mí.
best ones of all.
gus - tan a mí.

Chords

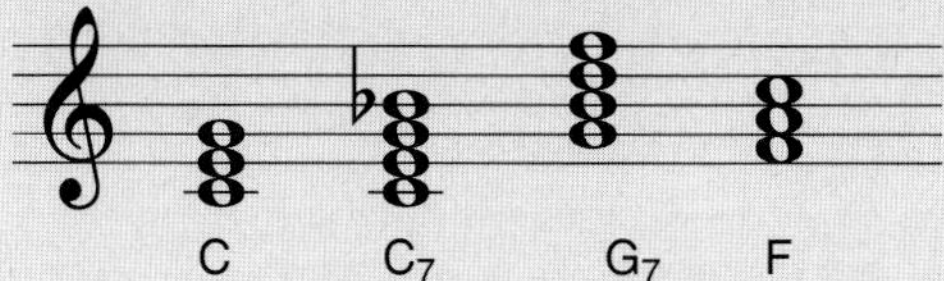
C
C7
G7
F

"De Colores"

[Each person is assigned a note; thus, three people play the C chord and four play the G_7 chord (on guitar or Q-chord, resonator bells, xylophone, handbells, or tone chimes).]

"La Cucaracha" (p. 251)

A song that is often sung in Mexico is "La Cucaracha." We will sing it today in both Spanish and in English, accompanied by maracas, claves, and chording instruments. The claves and chording instruments will keep a steady beat while the maracas improvise an appropriate rhythm.

"Cielito Lindo" (pp. 114, 254)
(recording: *World of Music* CD-4:2, 1991, book 4, p. 63)

A mariachi band or ensemble is composed of street musicians playing guitars, violins, and trumpets, who stroll into restaurants or open-air cafés during the long lunch hour. Sometimes the mariachi ensemble is hired to play for an entire evening. Raise your hands when you hear trumpets, violins, or guitars.

Piñata Ceremony

The piñata is a papier-mâché object filled with candy or nuts. The breaking of the piñata is accomplished at the close of the nine days of Christmas celebrations in Mexico. Each child is blindfolded and has a turn with a stick in hopes of breaking the piñata. After it is broken, children gather up their treats. We will sing "Piñata Song" first in Spanish and then in English.

Piñata Song (Al Quebrar la Piñata)

A Traditional Christmas Song, Mexico
English Words by Verne Muñoz

Key: C
Starting pitch: G
Meter: 3/4, begins on 2

A
C
F
In the hap - py days of Christ - mas,
En las no - ches de po - sa - das,
G7
C
Sounds of glad - ness fill the air;
La pi - ña - ta es lo me - jor;

C7 F
When it's time for the pi - ña - ta,
La ni - ña más re - mil - ga - da
G7 C
There's ex - cite - ment ev - 'ry - where.
Se͜ al - bo - ro - ta con ar - dor.
B F C G7 C
Take a stick and whack it. Be the one to crack it;
Da - le, da - le, da - le, no pier - das el ti - no,
C G7 C
Win pi - ña - ta's trea - sure, Can - dies for your plea - sure.
Que de la dis - tan - cia se pier - de͜ el ca - mi - no.

Closing

Thank you for coming, and we hope that you will join us for refreshments.

Integrating Technology

CENGAGEbrain.com

The Music Education Premium Site contains chapter quizzing, Spotify playlists, and downloads of free MP3s of noted songs. Visit CengageBrain.com to purchase an access code or enter the code provided with your text materials.

Web Resources

- Search the Web (www.google.com) for information on holidays and related songs and games, and for ways to integrate these into the classroom.

Videos

- Watch classroom videos that apply to chapter content and access the YouTube playlist for videos referenced within the chapter.

Audio

- Download music discussed in this chapter from the Apple iTunes store.
- Spotify playlists allow students to stream music referenced within each chapter.
- Download free audio MP3s for the songs noted in the chapter.

CENGAGEbrain.com

Questions for Discussion

1. Discuss some general ways in which music may be integrated into the classroom curriculum.
2. What can music share with the study of social studies?
3. What can music share with the study of mathematics?
4. What can music share with the study of science (e.g., physics)?
5. What can music share with the study of visual art?
6. What can music share with the study of language arts (including theatre)?
7. What can music share with the study of dance?
8. Discuss what integrative ideas you might have for teaching the following songs:
   - "The Witch Rides" (grades K–1), p. 388
   - "Six Little Ducks" (grades K–2), p. 378
   - "Somebody Loves Me" (grades K–2), p. 410
   - "Martin Luther King" (grades 2–4), p. 407
   - "Circus Parade" (grades 3–5), p. 380
   - "Gatatumba" (grades 3–6), p. 382

Assessment

Review ways the music standards listed at the beginning of this chapter have been met.

APPENDIX A

Selected Soprano Recorder Fingerings (Baroque System)

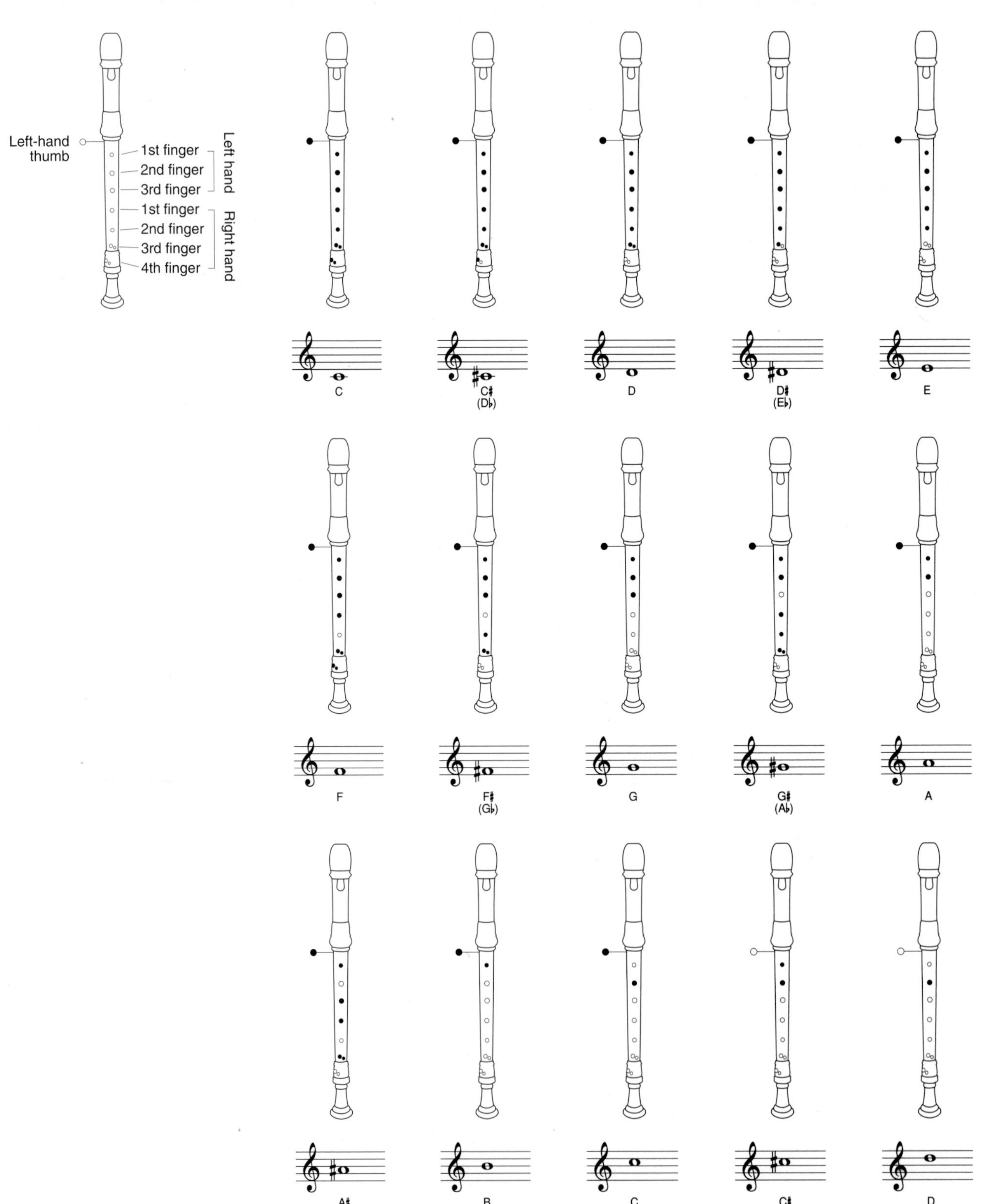

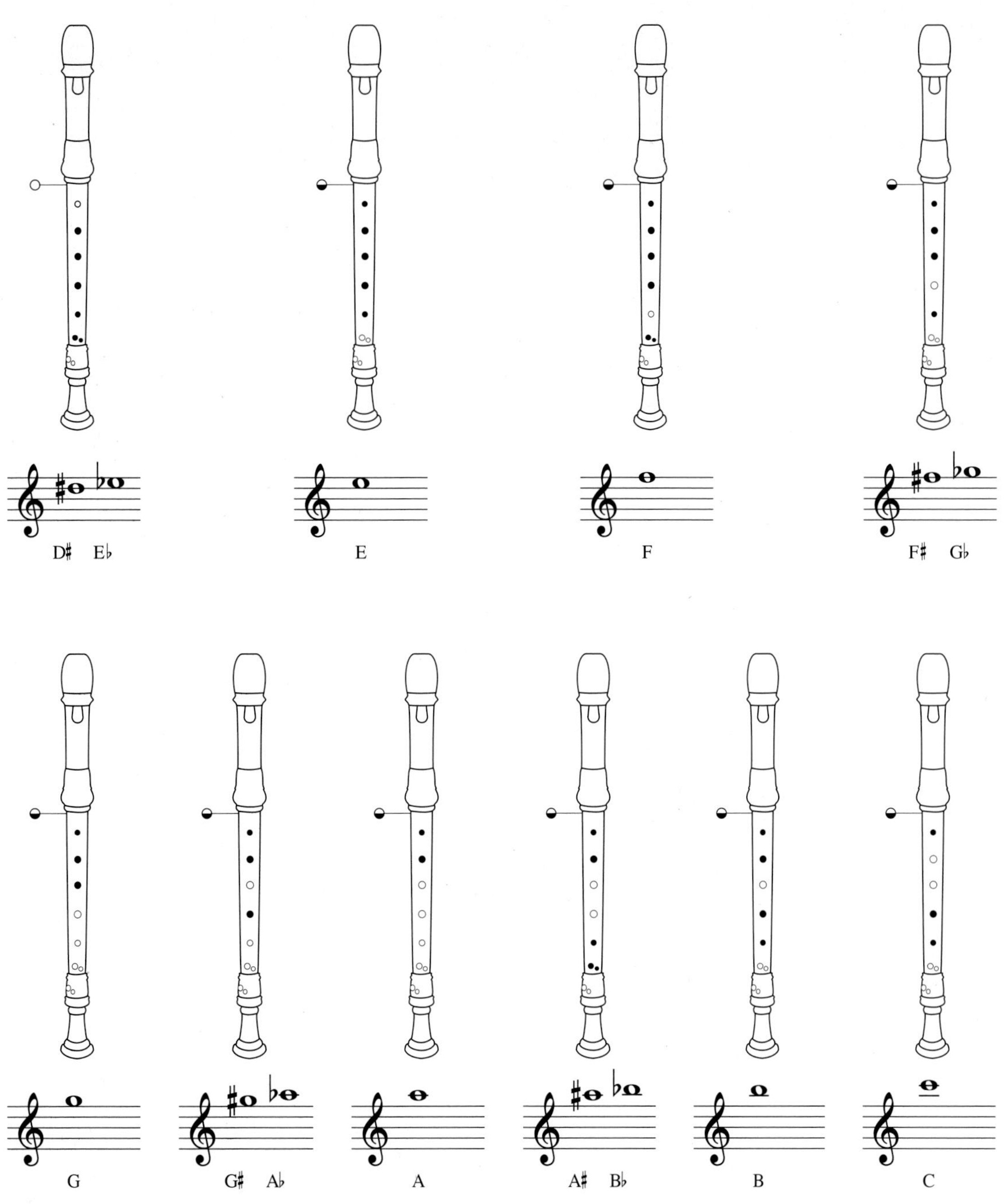

○ open hole ● closed hole ◒ slightly opened thumb hole

APPENDIX B

Common Chord Fingerings for the Guitar

Symbols:

X = String not played

0 = Open string

1 = Left index finger

2 = Left middle finger

3 = Left ring finger

4 = Left little finger

R = Root of chord

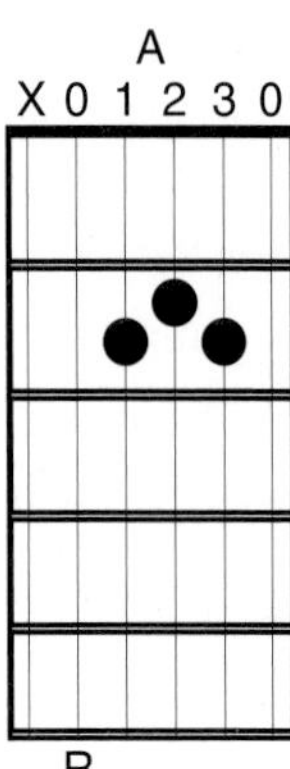

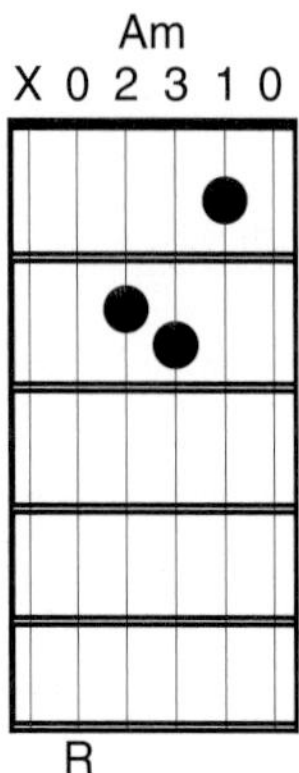

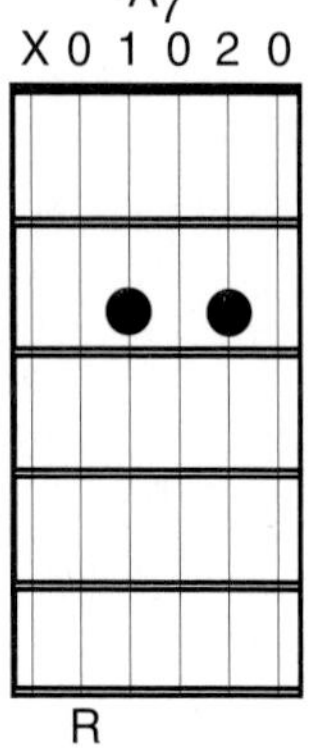

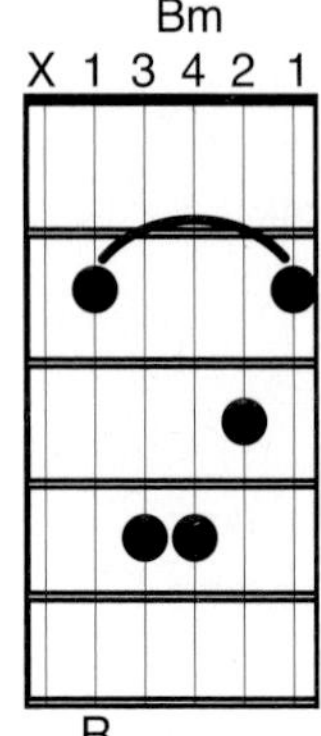

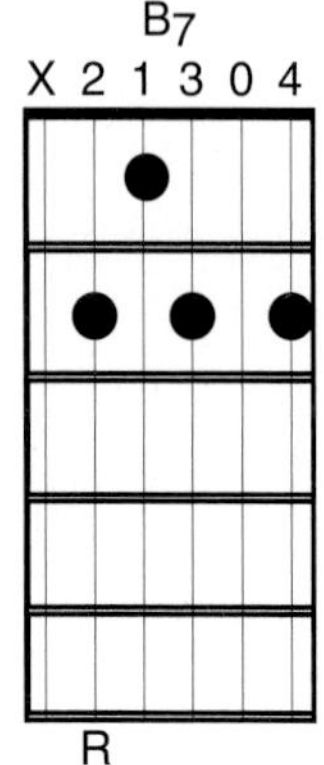

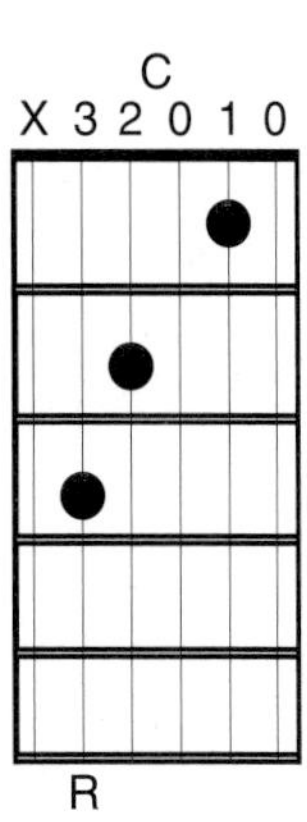

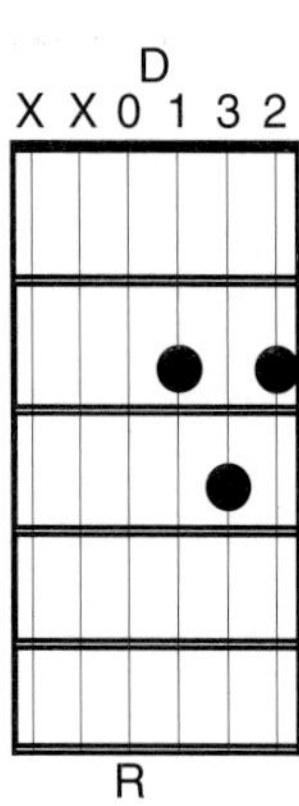

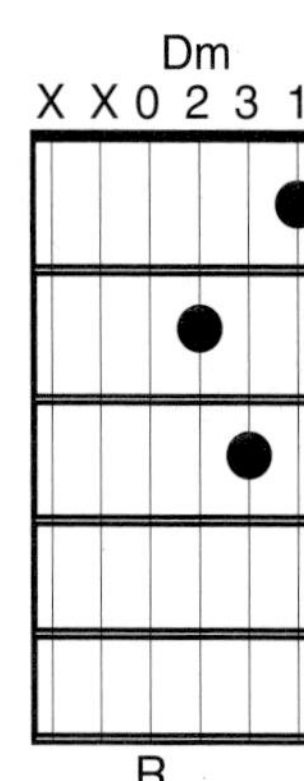

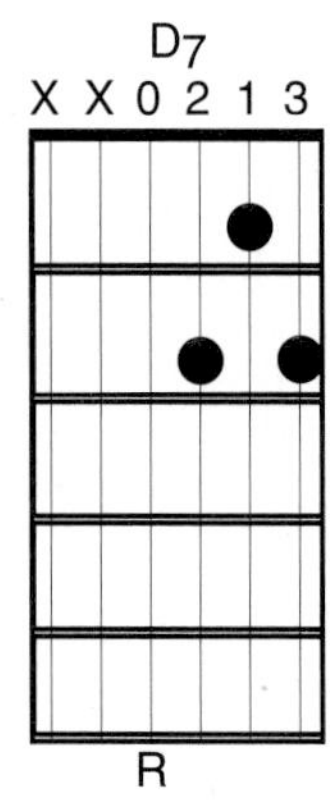

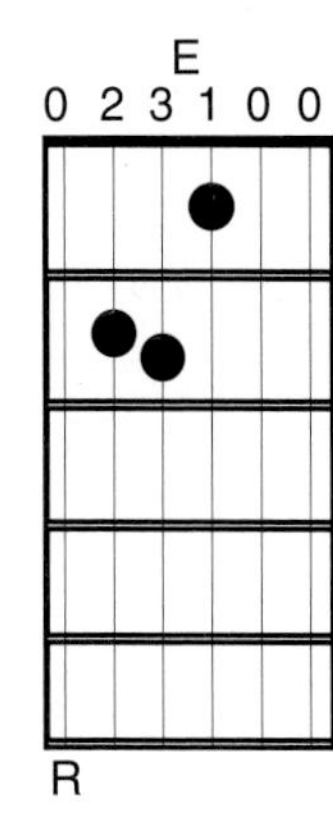

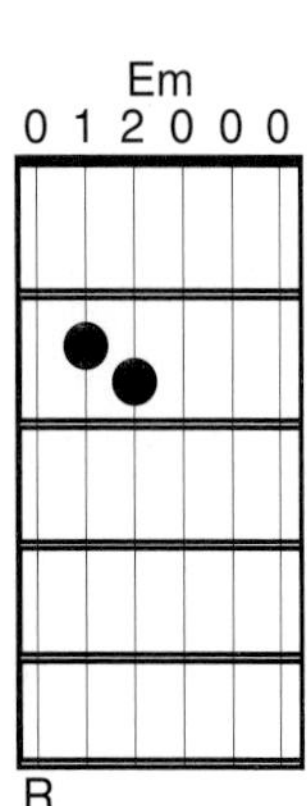

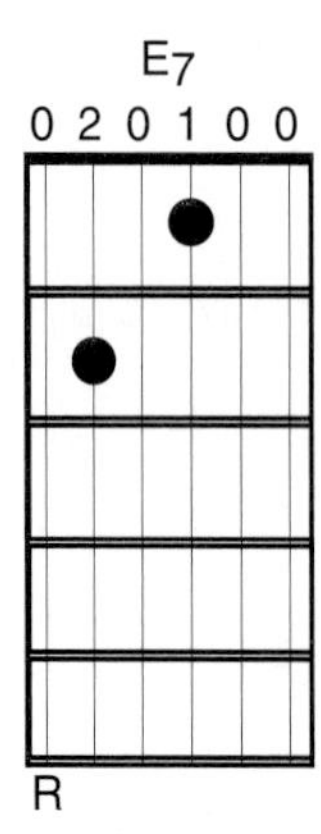

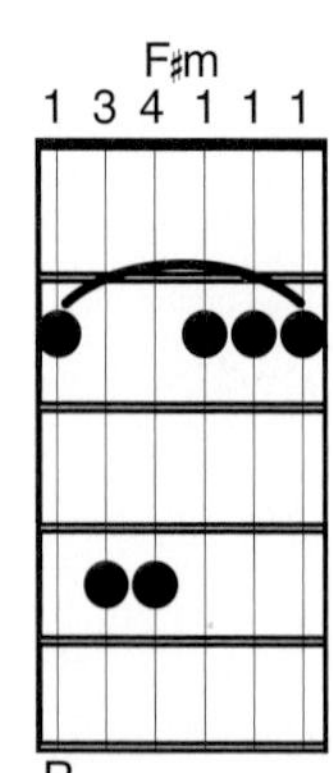

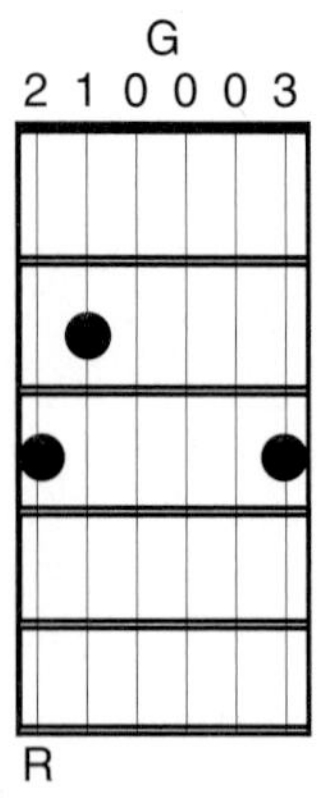

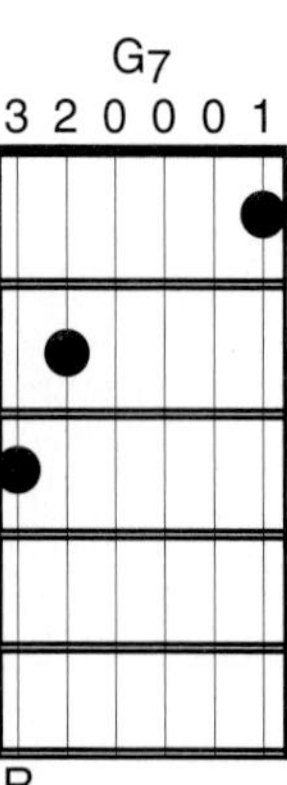

Glossary

a cappella Without instrumental accompaniment. The phrase is Italian for "in chapel style"—that is, in the style of a small place of worship.

accelerando, accel Gradually become faster.

accent Greater emphasis on note or chord. Often indicated by ^ or > placed above the note or chord.

accidental A sharp (♯), flat (♭), or natural (♮) that appears in the musical score but is not part of the key signature.

adagio Moderately slow tempo.

ad lib, ad libitum A direction indicating that the performer may vary the tempo in a musical composition.

affective Having to do with feeling.

agogo An African percussion instrument consisting of conical metal bells, each having a different pitch.

allargando Slowing of tempo.

alto The lowest female voice.

analogous concept A concept used in a similar same way across the arts, such as repetition or contrast.

aria An accompanied song for solo voice.

articulation The way in which musical tones are attacked. It is related to the clarity in vocal or instrumental performance. Legato and staccato are types of articulation.

a tempo A return to the previous tempo.

augmentation Presentation of a melody in longer notes.

balalaika A triangular-shaped Russian stringed instrument.

ballad A narrative song.

bar line A vertical line drawn on the staff to divide music into measures.

Baroque music European music from the period between 1600 and 1750.

bass The lowest male voice.

beat The ongoing pulse in music.

behavioral objective A statement that contains specific skills or behaviors that learners are expected to acquire.

binary form Music composed of two contrasting sections, A and B.

bongo drums Two connected drums of different pitches. The player holds them between the knees and strikes them with his or her hands.

cadence A melodic or harmonic formula that indicates the end of a section or piece.

canon A strict form of imitation in which a melody is stated in one part and is repeated in one or more other "voices."

cantata A sacred or secular choral composition of several movements.

capo (capotasto) A device that clamps over the strings of a guitar and holds them down tightly at a new pitch level, instantly providing transposition to a higher key.

changing meter Frequent changes of meter in a musical composition.

chant A single, unaccompanied melody.

child-centered approach An approach to teaching that focuses on having students actively involved in the learning process; rather than lecturing, the teacher presents students with a problem that needs to be solved and enlists the students' participation in solving it.

chord Three or more tones sounding simultaneously.

chorus A large group of singers. The term is also used to denote a refrain or a choral segment of an oratorio.

chromatic scale A scale entirely composed of half steps.

Classical period European music from the period between 1750 and 1825.

clef A sign placed at the beginning of the musical staff to designate the names of pitches.

coda A composed ending for a composition.

cognitive learning The process of mental learning.

concept A set of experiences or ideas that are grouped together based on some commonalities.

concerto A composition for solo instrument and orchestra.

concerto grosso A composition that contrasts more than one solo instrument with the orchestra.

conjunct A term used to describe melodies that move by stepwise intervals.

contour The shape of a melody.

cooperative learning Working together in a group to achieve learning.

countermelody A melody that is added above or below the main melody.

crescendo Gradually becoming louder.

cut time Dividing the meter by two; for example, 4/4 = 2/2 or ¢.

da capo (D.C.) Go back and repeat from the beginning.

dal segno al fine (D.S. al fine) Repeat from the sign, and perform until the word *fine*, which means "end."

decrescendo Gradually becoming softer.

descant A countermelody that is always above the main melody.

digital music player (DMP) A small, compact portable computer designed to hold large amounts of data in a music format for playing high-quality music.

diminution The presentation of a melody in shorter note values.

disjunct A melody in which the intervals are larger than a major second.

dominant The fifth degree of a scale.

double bar Two vertical lines that signify the end of a composition.

downbeat The first beat of a measure.

download To acquire data from a site (usually on the World Wide Web) by requesting the data to be transferred to your computer.

dulcimer A name given to several types of American traditional stringed instruments, including the plucked dulcimer and the hammered dulcimer.

duple meter Meter based on two beats or multiples of two.

dynamics Term indicating the degree of loudness or softness in a musical composition.

enharmonic Descriptive of notes that have the same sound but different names; for example, F# = G♭.

eurhythmics Term used by Carl Orff for the process of using rhythmic movement to teach music.

fermata To hold or pause.

fine The end.

flat (♭) A musical symbol that lowers the pitch a half step when placed before a note.

form How a work is designed; its structure.

forte Loud.

fortissimo Very loud.

fugue A musical composition based on imitation. It consists of an exposition, episodes, and the reappearance of the subject in different "voices."

grand staff The G and F clefs joined together.

guitarrón A Mexican guitarlike plucked stringed instrument that is larger and lower-pitched than a guitar.

half step The interval from one pitch to the next adjacent pitch, ascending or descending.

harmonic minor scale A minor scale with a raised 7th note.

harmonic texture Type of texture in which there are two or more different pitches sounding simultaneously.

harpsichord A stringed keyboard instrument shaped like a modern grand piano but whose strings are plucked rather than hammered to make the sound when the keys are depressed.

homophonic A musical texture in which a prominent melodic line is supported with an accompaniment.

interval The distance between two pitches.

key signature The sharps or flats placed at the beginning of a musical composition to affect the entire composition.

koto A Japanese stringed instrument that has thirteen strings and movable bridges.

laouto A Greek stringed instrument.

legato Connecting pitches smoothly.

listening guide A chart that uses graphics or words to depict various events as they occur in the music.

locomotor movement Moving the body.

major scale A seven-tone scale composed of W-W-H-W-W-W-H steps.

mbira An African instrument consisting of metal or wooden strips of different sizes attached to a resonator (gourd) and played with the thumbs. Also called *kalimba*.

measure A group of beats between the bar lines on the staff.

melismatic A melodic passage in which one syllable is sung on several different consecutive pitches.

melodic rhythm The rhythm of the melody in a musical composition.

melody A succession of musical sounds that are perceived as belonging together.

meter The recurring pattern of accented and unaccented beats in music.

meter signature The numbers placed at the beginning of a composition. The upper number indicates the number of beats per measure; the lower number tells what kind of a note will receive one beat.

metronome An instrument used to indicate a steady tempo.

MIDI (musical instrument digital interface) A method by which electronic musical instruments and software can communicate musical information to each other.

minor scale A seven-tone scale composed of W-H-W-W-H-W-W steps.

minuet A French country dance in triple meter.

mixed voices A combination of male and female voices.

mode Scalar arrangements of pitches with distinctive intervals. Common in medieval, Renaissance, and folk music.

modulation Changing from one key to another within a composition.

monophonic A type of musical texture in which there is a single line of music.

nonlocomotor movement Movement that occurs within a physically stationary position.

notation A system for writing music that indicates pitch and duration.

note A musical symbol that may indicate both pitch and duration.

obbligato A second melodic line that accompanies the main melody.

octave The interval of an eighth between the lowest pitch and the highest.

opera A musical drama in which all or most of the dialogue is sung.

operetta A musical drama in which the dialogue is generally spoken.

ostinato A repeated melodic or rhythmic pattern that recurs throughout a composition.

partner song Two songs that are in the same key and have the same length; can be sung together.

patschen Tapping thighs.

pentatonic scale A five-note scale.

phrase A division of a musical line, comparable to a line or sentence in poetry or prose.

pipa A pear-shaped Chinese stringed instrument that is held upright and plucked by the fingers of the right hand.

pitch The highness or lowness of a tone.

pizzicato Italian term that refers to the technique used for plucking the strings of a stringed instrument.

polyphonic Music in which there are two or more independent melodies.

polyrhythm Two or more contrasting rhythms sounding at the same time.

presto Very fast.

psychomotor learning Learning through movement.

range In melodies, the distance between the lowest and highest pitches.

recitative A declamatory style of singing.

recorder A small, vertical, flutelike instrument whose pitch is determined by the covering and uncovering of holes with the fingers.

refrain A relatively short section that is repeated at the end of each verse of a song.

relative major and minor The major and minor scales that have identical key signatures; for example, C major and A minor.

Renaissance The European historical period extending from approximately 1400 to 1600.

repeat sign Sign indicating that the section should be performed again.

rest The symbol used to denote silence in music.

rhythm The organization of musical sounds in time.

Romantic period The European historical period from approximately 1825 to 1900.

rondo A musical form diagrammed ABACA.

rote The process of learning a song by imitation.

rote-note The process of learning a song by imitation and notation.

round A song in which two or more groups perform the same melody but start at different times.

rubato Flexibility of tempo.

scale An arrangement of pitches from low to high.

sequence A melodic pattern that is repeated beginning on another pitch.

shakuhachi A notched, end-blown Japanese wind instrument.

sharp (#) A musical symbol that raises the pitch of a note a half step.

shekere An African percussion instrument.

sheng A Chinese wind instrument made of bamboo reed pipes placed into a bowl-shaped base.

slur A curved line above or below two or more notes, indicating that they should be performed legato.

solfège A system for identifying the pitches of the Western scale: *do, re, mi, fa, sol, la, ti, do.*

sonata form A European musical form that consists of thematic exposition, development, and recapitulation.

soprano The highest mature female voice.

staccato Short, detached tones.

staff A graph of five horizontal lines on which musical notes are placed.

stem The vertical line attached to a note head.

stepwise A melodic progression of pitches ascending or descending without skips.

syllabic Music in which each syllable is sung on one note (pitch).

symphony An orchestral composition in four movements: fast, slow, moderately fast, and fast.

syncopation Emphasis on a normally weak beat.

synthesizer A contemporary instrument that produces sounds electronically.

tablature Name given to specialized guitar notation that indicates which strings are to remain open and which strings are to be fretted.

teacher-centered approach An approach to teaching that features the teacher primarily as a lecturer who presents material to the class by defining and explaining.

tempo The speed of a musical composition.

tenor The highest mature male voice.

ternary form A musical form in three sections (ABA).

terraced dynamics Sudden contrasting dynamic levels.

text (word) painting Music that describes or enhances the words in the song.

texture Description of the number of lines of music and the relationships among the lines.

theme-and-variation form A musical form in which a theme is given and then followed by variations on the theme.

timbre (tone color) The unique quality of a sound.

tonal center The key center or home key of a piece.

tonality How melodic and harmonic elements are organized around a tonal center.

tone matching Physically singing a pitch that matches that being played or sung by another person.

treble Another name for the G clef.

triad A chord of three pitches, arranged in thirds.

triple meter Meter in threes.

upbeat One or more notes that occur before the first measure of a musical composition.

verse A stanza of a poem or song.

vihuela A Mexican guitarlike plucked stringed instrument that is somewhat smaller and higher-pitched than a guitar.

vocal techniques Ways of teaching children to sing.

whole step An interval formed by two half steps.

xiao A Chinese wind instrument made from bamboo.

zheng A plucked stringed instrument from China. The traditional form has sixteen strings; modern versions may have twenty-one strings.

Two-Chord Songs

TITLE	CHORDS	PAGE
Clementine	G, D7	150
Chinese New Year	G, C	409
Cuckoo, The	G, D7	111
Did You Ever See a Lassie?	F, C7	109
Down in the Valley	D, A7	150
Eency, Weency Spider	G, D7	228
Farmer in the Dell, The	G, D7; F, C7	152
First of January, The (Uno de Enero)	C, G7	435
Frère Jacques	G, D7	113
Good News	G, D7	126
Hanukkah Is Here	Dm, A7	395
Hello, There!	C, G7	76
He's Got the Whole World in His Hands	D, A7	110
Hokey Pokey, The	G, D7	372
Hot Cross Buns	G, D7	38
Jack-o'-Lantern	D, A,	81
La Cucaracha	G, D7	251
La Raspa	G, D7	325
Lightly Row	G, D7	126

TITLE	CHORDS	PAGE
Listen to the Wind	F, G7	76
Little Marionettes	G, D7	240
Little Tommy Tinker	D, A7	228
Looby Loo	F, C7	80
Mary Ann	C, G7	150
Merrily We Roll Along	C, G7	135
Michael Finnegan	F, C	89
Mister Turkey	G, D7	391
More We Get Together, The	D, A	57
Mulberry Bush, The	G, D7	244
My Hat	C, G7	59
On Springfield Mountain	G, D7	414
People on the Bus, The	G, D	227
Round and Round the Village	F, C7	247
Shoemaker's Dance, The	F, C7	247
Simple Gifts	F, C7	65
Six Little Ducks	F, C7	378
This Old Man	F, C7	142
Witch Rides, The	Dm, A7	388

Three-Chord Songs

TITLE	CHORDS	PAGE
America	G, C, D7	142
Battle Hymn of the Republic	B♭, E♭, F7	414
Cielito Lindo	Bb, Eb, F7	114
Circus Parade	C, G7, F	380
De Colores	C, G7, F	436
Five Fat Turkeys	G, D7, C	392
Five Green and Speckled Frogs	C, F, G7	43
Gatatumba	C, G7, F	382
Go, Tell It on the Mountain	F, C7, B♭	107
Hickory Dickory Dock	F, B♭, C	46
If You're Happy	F, C7, B♭	374
I'm Gonna Sing When the Spirit Says Sing	G, D7, C	240
Keeper, The	D, G, A7	108
Las Posadas Songs	C, F, G7	399
Let's Make a Jack-o'-Lantern	F, C7, B♭	389
Little Shoemaker, The	F, C7, B♭	230

TITLE	CHORDS	PAGE
Lullaby	C, G7, F	36
Martin Luther King	D, A7, G	407
Michael, Row the Boat Ashore	C, F, G7	126
Muffin Man	G, A7, D	137
My Big Black Dog	F, B♭, C7	376
O Hanukkah	Dm, A7, Gm	396
O Susanna	F, C7, B♭	49
Old MacDonald Had a Farm	G, C, D7	416
Peddler, The (Korobushka)	A7, Dm, Gm	141
Piñata Song (Al Quebrar la Piñata)	C, F, G7	437
Roll On, Columbia	F, C7, B♭	384
Somebody Loves Me	C, G7, F	410
Sweet Betsy from Pike	C, G7, F	50
Swing Low, Sweet Chariot	F, C7, B♭	264
Tideo	D, G, A7	98
Tinga Layo	F, C, G7	82
Yankee Doodle	G, D7, C	135

Index of Listening Examples

General Index

D

Q

R

S

T

U

V

W

X

Y

Z